Smoking
Concerns
SOURCEBOOK

Health Reference Series

First Edition

Smoking Concerns SOURCEBOOK

Basic Consumer Health Information about Nicotine Addiction and Smoking Cessation, Featuring Facts about the Health Effects of Tobacco Use, Including Lung and Other Cancers, Heart Disease, Stroke, and Respiratory Disorders, Such as Emphysema and Chronic Bronchitis

Along with Information about Smoking Prevention Programs, Suggestions for Achieving and Maintaining a Smoke-Free Lifestyle, Statistics about Tobacco Use, Reports on Current Research Initiatives, a Glossary of Related Terms, and Directories of Resources for Additional Help and Information

Edited by
Karen Bellenir

Omnigraphics

615 Griswold Street • Detroit, MI 48226

Bibliographic Note

Because this page cannot legibly accommodate all the copyright notices, the Bibliographic Note portion of the Preface constitutes an extension of the copyright notice.

Edited by Karen Bellenir

Health Reference Series

Karen Bellenir, *Managing Editor*
David A. Cooke, M.D., *Medical Consultant*
Elizabeth Barbour, *Permissions Associate*
Dawn Matthews, *Verification Assistant*
Laura Pleva Nielsen, *Index Editor*
EdIndex, Services for Publishers, *Indexers*

* * *

Omnigraphics, Inc.

Matthew P. Barbour, *Senior Vice President*
Kay Gill, *Vice President—Directories*
Kevin Hayes, *Operations Manager*
Leif Gruenberg, *Development Manager*
David P. Bianco, *Marketing Director*

* * *

Peter E. Ruffner, *Publisher*

Frederick G. Ruffner, Jr., *Chairman*

Copyright © 2004 Omnigraphics, Inc.

ISBN 0-7808-0323-X

Library of Congress Cataloging-in-Publication Data

Smoking concerns sourcebook : basic consumer health information about nicotine addiction and smoking cessation, featuring facts about the health effects of tobacco use, including lung and other cancers, heart disease, stroke, and respiratory disorders, such as emphysema and chronic bronchitis; along with information about smoking prevention programs, suggestions for achieving and maintaining a smoke-free lifestyle, statistics about tobacco use, reports on current research initiatives, a glossary of related terms, and directories of resources for additional help and information / edited by Karen Bellenir.-- 1st ed.
    p. cm. -- (Health reference series)
Includes bibliographical references and index.
ISBN 0-7808-0323-X (hardcover : alk. paper)
1. Smoking--Health aspects. 2. Smoking cessation programs. 3. Nicotine--Physiological effect. I. Bellenir, Karen. II. Series.
RA1242.T6S589 2004
616.86'5--dc22

2004015382

∞

Table of Contents

Visit www.healthreferenceseries.com to view *A Contents Guide to the Health Reference Series*, a listing of more than 10,000 topics and the volumes in which they are covered.

Part II: Tobacco-Related Health Hazards

Part III: Smoking Cessation

Part IV: Tobacco-Related Research

Preface

About This Book

According to the Centers for Disease Control and Prevention, 8.6 million people in the United States have at least one serious illness caused by smoking, and 440,000 die annually from diseases attributed to smoking. Worldwide, the annual death toll related to smoking is four million. Cancer, heart disease, stroke, and emphysema are among the most well-known and feared effects of smoking. Other associated problems include chronic bronchitis, musculoskeletal disorders, diabetes, digestive disorders, erectile dysfunction, reproductive disorders, complications of pregnancy, and depression. Because of the health hazards associated with tobacco use and other concerns, nearly three-quarters of current smokers want to quit. Breaking free from nicotine addiction, however, is not easy. According to various studies, former smokers often make three, four, or many more attempts before they finally succeed in achieving smoking cessation goals.

Smoking Concerns Sourcebook provides basic facts about tobacco use, including how nicotine affects the body and how addiction develops. It offers facts about the health effects of smoking or using smokeless tobacco. A section on smoking cessation offers tips on preparing for, achieving, and sustaining a smoke-free lifestyle. Statistics about tobacco use, reports on current research initiatives, and information about public health policies regarding tobacco control and use prevention are also included. Readers seeking additional help will find a glossary of related terms and directories of resources.

How to Use This Book

This book is divided into parts and chapters. Parts focus on broad areas of interest. Chapters are devoted to single topics within a part.

Part I: Smoking and Tobacco Products: An Overview includes facts about cigarettes, cigars, pipes, and smokeless tobacco products. It explains how nicotine addiction develops and describes the different types of chemicals commonly found in tobacco products. Statistical information about trends in tobacco use is also included.

Part II: Tobacco-Related Health Hazards discusses diseases and disorders that can be caused by or worsen as a result of tobacco use. These include various types of cancer, respiratory disorders, and cardiovascular diseases. Hazards associated with smoking during pregnancy and the effects of smoking on the digestive system, musculoskeletal health, and sexual functioning are also explained.

Part III: Smoking Cessation provides information about how to quit smoking. It outlines the recommended steps for preparing to quit, explains what to expect during the first few days of a cessation program, and offers tips for coping with commonly experienced problems. Nicotine replacement therapy and other medications that can help people achieve smoking cessation goals are also described.

Part IV: Tobacco-Related Research reports on areas of current investigation into how nicotine addiction develops, the health-risks associated with tobacco products, and strategies to lessen the impact of tobacco-related damage on body organs and systems.

Part V: Tobacco Control and Use Prevention explains various public health policies used to reduce tobacco consumption, including programs to restrict minors' access to tobacco, clean indoor air regulations, taxation policies, counter advertising campaigns, and tobacco labeling requirements.

Part VI: Additional Help and Information includes a glossary of terms related to tobacco use and smoking cessation, a directory of resources for tobacco-related information, and a list of resources for help with smoking cessation.

Bibliographic Note

This volume contains documents and excerpts from publications issued by the following U.S. government agencies: Centers for Disease

Control and Prevention (CDC); National Cancer Institute (NCI); National Center for Chronic Disease Prevention and Health Promotion; National Heart, Lung, and Blood Institute (NHLBI); National Institute of Diabetes and Digestive and Kidney Diseases (NIDDK); National Institute of Mental Health (NIMH); National Institute of Standards and Technology, Building and Fire Research Laboratory; National Institute on Drug Abuse (NIDA); Substance Abuse and Mental Health Services Administration (SAMHSA); Task Force on Community Preventive Services; U.S. Department of Health and Human Services (DHHS); and the U.S. Public Health Service, Office of the Surgeon General.

In addition, this volume contains copyrighted documents from the following organizations: American Academy of Family Physicians; American Academy of Orthopaedic Surgeons; American Academy of Otolaryngology–Head and Neck Surgery; American Academy of Periodontology; American Burn Association; American College of Physicians; American Council on Science and Health, Inc.; American Heart Association; American Lung Association; American Medical Student Association; Arizona Department of Health Services, Tobacco Education and Prevention Program (TEPP), State of Arizona; California Thoracic Society; Center for Social Gerontology, Inc.; Cleveland Clinic Foundation; Cornell University Program on Breast Cancer and Environmental Risk Factors in New York State (BCERF); Healthcommunities.com, Inc.; March of Dimes Birth Defects Foundation; Massachusetts Department of Public Health; H. Lee Moffitt Cancer Center and Research Institute; Nemours Center for Children's Health Media, a division of The Nemours Foundation; New York State Office for the Aging; Trustees of Indiana University; University of Buffalo (State University of New York); University of Pittsburgh Medical Center; and the University of Southern California.

Full citation information is provided on the first page of each chapter. Every effort has been made to secure all necessary rights to reprint the copyrighted material. If any omissions have been made, please contact Omnigraphics to make corrections for future editions.

Acknowledgements

In addition to the organizations, agencies, and individuals listed above, special thanks go to many others who have worked hard to help bring this book to fruition, especially editorial assistants Elizabeth Bellenir and Dawn Matthews, permissions associate Liz Barbour, and indexer Edward J. Prucha.

About the Health Reference Series

The *Health Reference Series* is designed to provide basic medical information for patients, families, caregivers, and the general public. Each volume takes a particular topic and provides comprehensive coverage. This is especially important for people who may be dealing with a newly diagnosed disease or a chronic disorder in themselves or in a family member. People looking for preventive guidance, information about disease warning signs, medical statistics, and risk factors for health problems will also find answers to their questions in the *Health Reference Series*. The *Series*, however, is not intended to serve as a tool for diagnosing illness, in prescribing treatments, or as a substitute for the physician/patient relationship. All people concerned about medical symptoms or the possibility of disease are encouraged to seek professional care from an appropriate health care provider.

Locating Information within the Health Reference Series

The *Health Reference Series* contains a wealth of information about a wide variety of medical topics. Ensuring easy access to all the fact sheets, research reports, in-depth discussions, and other material contained within the individual books of the series remains one of our highest priorities. As the *Series* continues to grow in size and scope, however, locating the precise information needed by a reader may become more challenging.

A Contents Guide to the Health Reference Series was developed to direct readers to the specific volumes that address their concerns. It presents an extensive list of diseases, treatments, and other topics of general interest compiled from the Tables of Contents and major index headings. To access *A Contents Guide to the Health Reference Series*, visit www.healthreferenceseries.com.

Medical Consultant

Medical consultation services are provided to the *Health Reference Series* editors by David A. Cooke, M.D. Dr. Cooke is a graduate of Brandeis University, and he received his M.D. degree from the University of Michigan. He completed residency training at the University of Wisconsin Hospital and Clinics. He is board-certified in Internal Medicine. Dr. Cooke currently works as part of the University of Michigan Health System and practices in Brighton, MI. In his free time, he enjoys writing, science fiction, and spending time with his family.

Our Advisory Board

We would like to thank the following board members for providing guidance to the development of this series:

Health Reference Series *Update Policy*

The inaugural book in the *Health Reference Series* was the first edition of *Cancer Sourcebook* published in 1989. Since then, the *Series* has been enthusiastically received by librarians and in the medical community. In order to maintain the standard of providing high-quality health information for the layperson the editorial staff at Omnigraphics felt it was necessary to implement a policy of updating volumes when warranted.

Medical researchers have been making tremendous strides, and it is the purpose of the *Health Reference Series* to stay current with the most recent advances. Each decision to update a volume will be made on an individual basis. Some of the considerations will include how much new information is available and the feedback we receive from people who use the books. If there is a topic you would like to see added to the update list, or an area of medical concern you feel has not been adequately addressed, please write to:

Editor
Health Reference Series
Omnigraphics, Inc.
615 Griswold Street
Detroit, MI 48226
E-mail: editorial@omnigraphics.com

Part One

Smoking and Tobacco Products: An Overview

Chapter 1

Cigarettes and Other Nicotine Products: The Facts

Historical Facts

- Cigarettes were first introduced in the United States in the early 19th century. Before this, tobacco was used primarily in pipes and cigars, by chewing, and in snuff.[1]

- By the time of the Civil War, cigarette use had become more popular. Federal tax was first imposed on cigarettes in 1864. Shortly afterwards, the development of the cigarette manufacturing industry led to their quickly becoming a major U.S. tobacco product.[1]

- At the same time, the populist health reform movement led to early anti-smoking activity. From 1880–1920, this activity was largely motivated by moral and hygienic concerns rather than health issues.[1]

This chapter begins with "Historical Facts," from the National Center for Chronic Disease Prevention and Health Promotion, Centers for Disease Control and Prevention, reviewed March 2003. "American Lung Association® Fact Sheet: Smoking," is reprinted with permission. © 2004 American Lung Association. For more information on how you can support the fight against lung disease, the third leading cause of death in the U.S., please contact The American Lung Association at 1-800-LUNG-USA (1-800-586-4872) or visit the website at www.lungusa.org. Text under the heading "Facts about Cigarettes and Other Nicotine Products" is from *NIDA InfoFacts*, National Institute on Drug Abuse (NIDA), revised March 2004.

- The milder flue-cured tobacco blends used in cigarettes during the early 20th century made the smoke easier to inhale and increased nicotine absorption into the bloodstream.[1]

- During World War I, Army surgeons praised cigarettes for helping the wounded relax and easing their pain.[1]

- Smoking was first linked to lung cancer and other diseases in the late 1940s and early 1950s.[1]

- In 1956, a Surgeon General's scientific study group determined that there was a causal relationship between excessive cigarette smoking and lung cancer.[1]

- In England, the 1962 Royal College of Physicians report emphasized smoking's causative role in lung cancer.[1]

- On January 11, 1964, the first-ever *Surgeon General's Report on Smoking and Health* concluded that cigarette smoking is a cause of lung cancer in men.[2]

- In 1965 Congress passed the Federal Cigarette Labeling and Advertising Act requiring health warnings on all cigarette packages.[3]

- In 1967 the Federal Communications Commission ruled that the Fairness Doctrine applies to cigarette advertising and that radio and television stations broadcasting cigarette commercials must donate equal air time to anti-smoking messages.[3]

- Anti-smoking messages had a significant impact on cigarette sales; however, when cigarette advertising on television and radio was banned in 1969, anti-smoking messages were discontinued.[1]

- The 1972 Surgeon General's report became the first of a series of science-based reports to identify environmental tobacco smoke (ETS) as a health risk to nonsmokers.[1]

- In 1973 Arizona became the first state to restrict smoking in a number of public places explicitly because ETS exposure is a public hazard.[1]

- By the mid-1970s, the federal government began administratively regulating smoking within government domains. In 1975, the Army and Navy stopped including cigarettes in rations for service members. Smoking was restricted in all federal government facilities in 1979 and was banned in the White House in 1993.[1]

- In 1988 Congress prohibited smoking on domestic commercial airline flights scheduled for two hours or less. By 1990, the ban was extended to all commercial U.S. flights.[1]

- In 1992 the Environmental Protection Agency (EPA) classified ETS as a "Group A" carcinogen, the most dangerous class of carcinogen.[1]

- In 1994 six major U.S. cigarette manufacturers testified before Congress that nicotine is not addictive and that they do not manipulate nicotine in cigarettes.[4]

- Food and Drug Administration (FDA) Commissioner David A. Kessler, M.D., testified before a congressional subcommittee in 1994 that cigarettes may qualify as drug-delivery systems, bringing them within the jurisdiction of the FDA. The following year, Dr. Kessler declared tobacco use a "pediatric disease." [4]

- In 1994 Mississippi became the first state to sue the tobacco industry to recover Medicaid costs for tobacco-related illnesses, settling its suit in 1997. A total of 46 states eventually filed similar suits. Three other states settled individually with the tobacco industry—Florida (1997), Texas (1998), and Minnesota (1998).[1,4]

- In 1995 the Department of Justice reached an agreement with Philip Morris to remove tobacco advertisements from the line of sight of television cameras in sports stadiums to ensure compliance with the federal ban on tobacco ads on television.[4]

- On August 23, 1996, President Clinton announced the release of the FDA's rule regulating tobacco sales and marketing aimed at minors.[4]

- In 1996 the Liggett Group, the smallest of the nation's five major tobacco companies, offered to settle a class action suit by taking financial responsibility for tobacco-related diseases and death for the first time.[4]

- In 1996 the FDA approved nicotine gum and two nicotine patches for over-the-counter sale to increase their availability to smokers who want to quit. The U.S. Public Health Service released its *Smoking Cessation Clinical Practice Guidelines for Clinicians.*[4]

- On June 20, 1997, all major U.S. tobacco companies signed an agreement that would have restricted tobacco advertising, put cigarettes and chewing tobacco behind retail counters, restricted smoking in public places, and created a national education campaign. This settlement would have required the tobacco industry to expend $360 billion over 25 years. The June 1997 settlement required Congressional approval; however, this was never approved.[6,7]

- On April 1, 1998, the Senate Commerce Committee voted in favor of the McCain bill, which gave complete authority to the FDA to regulate nicotine as a drug. It also raised the cigarette tax by $1.10 per pack and mandated penalties for the industry if specific targets for reducing youth smoking levels were not met. The bill was defeated by the full Senate in June 1998.[5]

- On November 23, 1998, the tobacco industry approved a 46-state Master Settlement Agreement, the largest settlement in history, totaling nearly $206 billion to be paid through the year 2025. The settlement agreement contained a number of important public health provisions.[1]

- In April 1999, as part of the Master Settlement Agreement, the major U.S. tobacco companies agreed to remove all advertising from outdoor and transit billboards across the nation. The remaining time on at least 3,000 billboard leases, valued at $100 million, was turned over to the states for posting anti-tobacco messages.[1]

- On March 21, 2000, the U.S. Supreme Court narrowly affirmed a 1998 decision of the U.S. Court of Appeals for the 4th Circuit and ruled that the FDA lacks jurisdiction under the Federal Food, Drug, and Cosmetic Act to regulate tobacco products. As a result, the FDA's proposed rule to reduce access and appeal of tobacco products for young people became invalid.[1]

- In July 2000 a Florida jury ordered the tobacco industry to pay $145 billion in punitive damages to sick Florida smokers. The tobacco industry is appealing verdict.

References

1. U.S. Department of Health and Human Services. *Reducing Tobacco Use: A Report of the Surgeon General.* Atlanta: U.S. Department of Health and Human Services, Centers for Disease Control and Prevention, 2000.

2. U.S. Department of Health, Education, and Welfare. *Smoking and Health: Report of the Advisory Committee to the Surgeon*

   to the Surgeon General of the Public Health Service. Washington: U.S. Department of Health, Education, and Welfare, Public Health Service, 1964. PHS Publication No. 1103.

3. U.S. Department of Health and Human Services. *Reducing the Health Consequences of Smoking: 25 Years of Progress. A Report of the Surgeon General.* Atlanta: U.S. Department of Health and Human Services, Centers for Disease Control and Prevention, 1989. U.S. Department of Health and Human Services, Centers for Disease Control and Prevention, Office on Smoking and Health. Significant Developments Related to Smoking and Health.

4. Campaign for Tobacco-Free Kids. *Special Reports Year in Review 1998.*

5. *USA Today.* Tobacco Settlement: Tobacco Chronology, http://www.usatoday.com/news/smoke/smoke26.htm.

6. Campaign for Tobacco-Free Kids. *Special Reports Year in Review 1997.*

7. U.S. Department of Health and Human Services, HHS News, Tobacco Billboards Replaced with Pro-Health Messages, 1999.

American Lung Association® Fact Sheet Smoking

Smoking-related diseases claim an estimated 440,000 American lives each year, including those affected indirectly, such as babies born prematurely due to prenatal maternal smoking and some of the victims of "secondhand" exposure to tobacco's carcinogens. Smoking costs the United States approximately $150 billion each year in health-care costs and lost productivity.

- Cigarettes contain at least 43 distinct cancer-causing chemicals. Smoking is directly responsible for 87 percent of lung cancer cases and causes most cases of emphysema and chronic bronchitis. Smoking is also a major factor in coronary heart disease and stroke; may be causally related to malignancies in other parts of the body; and has been linked to a variety of other conditions and disorders, including slowed healing of wounds, infertility, and peptic ulcer disease.

- Smoking in pregnancy accounts for an estimated 20 to 30 percent of low-birth weight babies, up to 14 percent of preterm deliveries, and some 10 percent of all infant deaths. Even apparently healthy, full-term babies of smokers have been found to be born with narrowed airways and curtailed lung function. Only about 30 percent of women who smoke stop smoking when they find they are pregnant; the proportion of quitters is highest among married women and women with higher levels of educational attainment. In 1999, 12.3 percent of women who gave birth smoked during pregnancy.

- Smoking by parents is also associated with a wide range of adverse effects in their children, including exacerbation of asthma, increased frequency of colds and ear infections, and sudden infant death syndrome. An estimated 150,000 to 300,000 cases of lower respiratory tract infections in children less than 18 months of age, resulting in 7,500 to 15,000 annual hospitalizations, are caused by secondhand smoke.

- Secondhand smoke involuntarily inhaled by nonsmokers from other people's cigarettes is classified by the U.S. Environmental Protection Agency as a known human (Group A) carcinogen, responsible for approximately 3,000 lung cancer deaths annually in U.S. nonsmokers.

- Approximately 22.2 million American women are smokers. Current female smokers aged 35 years or older are 12 times more likely to die prematurely from lung cancer than nonsmoking females. More American women die annually from lung cancer than any other type of cancer; for example, lung cancer will cause an estimated 65,700 female deaths in 2002, compared with 39,600 estimated female deaths caused by breast cancer.

- As smoking has declined among the White non-Hispanic population, tobacco companies have targeted both African Americans and Hispanics with intensive merchandising, which includes billboards, advertising in media targeted to those communities, and sponsorship of civic groups and athletic, cultural, and entertainment events.

- The prevalence of smoking is highest among Native Americans/Alaskan Natives (40.89 percent), next highest among African Americans and whites (24.3 percent), followed by Hispanics (18.1 percent) and Asians and Pacific Islanders (15.1 percent).

- Tobacco advertising plays an important role in encouraging young people to begin a lifelong addiction to smoking before they are old enough to fully understand its long-term health risk. It is estimated that 4.5 million U.S. teenagers are cigarette smokers; 22.4 percent of high school seniors smoke on a daily basis. Approximately 90 percent of smokers begin smoking before the age of 21.

- Workplaces nationwide are going smoke-free to provide clean indoor air and protect employees from the life-threatening effects of secondhand smoke. Nearly 70 percent of the U.S. workforce worked under a smoke-free policy in 1999 but the percentage of workers protected varies by state, ranging from a high of 89.3 percent in Utah to 48.7 percent in Nevada.

- Employers have a legal right to restrict smoking in the workplace, or implement a totally smoke-free workplace policy. Exceptions may arise in the case of collective bargaining agreements with unions.

- Nicotine is an addictive drug, which when inhaled in cigarette smoke reaches the brain faster than drugs that enter the body intravenously. Smokers become not only physically addicted to nicotine; they also link smoking with many social activities, making smoking a difficult habit to break.

- In 1999, an estimated 45.7 million adults were former smokers. Of the current 46.5 million smokers, more than 32 million persons reported they wanted to quit smoking completely. Currently, both nicotine patches and nicotine gum are available over-the-counter, and a nicotine nasal spray and inhaler, as well as a non-nicotine pill, Zyban®, are currently available by prescription; all help relieve withdrawal symptoms people experience when they quit smoking. Nicotine replacement therapies are helpful in quitting when combined with a behavior change program such as the American Lung Association's Freedom From Smoking® (FFS), which addresses psychological and behavioral addictions to smoking and strategies for coping with urges to smoke.

Facts about Cigarettes and Other Nicotine Products

Nicotine is one of the most heavily used addictive drugs in the United States. In 2002, 30 percent of the U.S. population 12 and older—71.5 million people—used tobacco at least once in the month prior to being interviewed. This figure includes 3.8 million young people age 12 to 17; 14 million people age 18 to 25; and 53.7 million age 26 and older.[1] Most of them smoked cigarettes.

Cigarette smoking has been the most popular method of taking nicotine since the beginning of the 20th century. In 1989, the U.S. Surgeon General issued a report that concluded that cigarettes and other forms of tobacco, such as cigars, pipe tobacco, and chewing tobacco, are addictive and that nicotine is the drug in tobacco that causes addiction. The report also determined that smoking was a major cause of stroke and the third leading cause of death in the United States. Statistics from the Centers for Disease Control and Prevention indicate that tobacco use remains the leading preventable cause of death in the United States, causing more than 440,000 deaths each year and resulting in an annual cost of more than $75 billion in direct medical costs (see www.cdc.gov/tobacco/issue.htm).

Health Hazards

Nicotine is highly addictive. Nicotine provides an almost immediate "kick" because it causes a discharge of epinephrine from the adrenal cortex. This stimulates the central nervous system, and other endocrine glands, which causes a sudden release of glucose. Stimulation is then followed by depression and fatigue, leading the abuser to seek more nicotine.

Nicotine is absorbed readily from tobacco smoke in the lungs, and it does not matter whether the tobacco smoke is from cigarettes, cigars, or pipes. Nicotine also is absorbed readily when tobacco is chewed. With regular use of tobacco, levels of nicotine accumulate in the body during the day and persist overnight. Thus, daily smokers or chewers are exposed to the effects of nicotine for 24 hours each day.

Addiction to nicotine results in withdrawal symptoms when a person tries to stop smoking. For example, a study found that when chronic smokers were deprived of cigarettes for 24 hours, they had increased anger, hostility, and aggression, and loss of social cooperation. Persons suffering from withdrawal also take longer to regain emotional equilibrium following stress. During periods of abstinence and/or craving, smokers have shown impairment across a wide range of psychomotor and cognitive functions, such as language comprehension.

Women who smoke generally have earlier menopause. If women smoke cigarettes and also take oral contraceptives, they are more prone to cardiovascular and cerebrovascular diseases than are other smokers; this is especially true for women older than 30.

Pregnant women who smoke cigarettes run an increased risk of having stillborn or premature infants or infants with low birth weight. Children of women who smoked while pregnant have an increased risk for developing conduct disorders. National studies of mothers and daughters have also found that maternal smoking during pregnancy increased the probability that female children would smoke and would persist in smoking.

Adolescent smokeless tobacco users are more likely than nonusers to become cigarette smokers. Behavioral research is beginning to explain how social influences, such as observing adults or other peers smoking, affect whether adolescents begin to smoke cigarettes. Research has shown that teens are generally resistant to anti-smoking messages.

In addition to nicotine, cigarette smoke is primarily composed of a dozen gases (mainly carbon monoxide) and tar. The tar in a cigarette, which varies from about 15 mg for a regular cigarette to 7 mg in a low-tar cigarette, exposes the user to an increased risk of lung cancer, emphysema, and bronchial disorders.

The carbon monoxide in the smoke increases the chance of cardiovascular diseases. The Environmental Protection Agency has concluded that secondhand smoke causes lung cancer in adults and greatly increases the risk of respiratory illnesses in children and sudden infant death.

Promising Research

Research has shown that nicotine, like cocaine, heroin, and marijuana, increases the level of the neurotransmitter dopamine, which affects the brain pathways that control reward and pleasure. Scientists now have pinpointed a particular molecule (the beta 2 (b2) subunit of the nicotine cholinergic receptor) as a critical component in nicotine addiction. Mice that lack this subunit fail to self-administer nicotine, implying that without the b2 subunit, the mice do not experience the positive reinforcing properties of nicotine. This new finding identifies a potential site for targeting the development of nicotine addiction medications.

Other new research found that individuals have greater resistance to nicotine addiction if they have a genetic variant that decreases the function of the enzyme CYP2A6. The decrease in CYP2A6 slows the breakdown of nicotine and protects individuals against nicotine addiction. Understanding the role of this enzyme in nicotine addiction gives a new target for developing more effective medications to help people stop smoking. Medications might be developed that can inhibit the function of CYP2A6, thus providing a new approach to preventing and treating nicotine addiction.

Another study found dramatic changes in the brain's pleasure circuits during withdrawal from chronic nicotine use. These changes are comparable in magnitude and duration to similar changes observed during the withdrawal from other abused drugs such as cocaine, opiates, amphetamines, and alcohol. Scientists found significant decreases in the sensitivity of the brains of laboratory rats to pleasurable stimulation after nicotine administration was abruptly stopped. These changes lasted several days and may correspond to the anxiety and depression experienced by humans for several days after quitting smoking "cold turkey." The results of this research may help in the development of better treatments for the withdrawal symptoms that may interfere with individuals' attempts to quit smoking.

Treatment

Studies have shown that pharmacological treatment combined with behavioral treatment, including psychological support and skills training to overcome high-risk situations, results in some of the highest long-term abstinence rates. Generally, rates of relapse for smoking cessation are highest in the first few weeks and months and diminish considerably after about three months.

Behavioral economic studies find that alternative rewards and reinforcers can reduce cigarette use. One study found that the greatest reductions in cigarette use were achieved when smoking cost was increased in combination with the presence of alternative recreational activities.

Nicotine chewing gum is one medication approved by the Food and Drug Administration (FDA) for the treatment of nicotine dependence. Nicotine in this form acts as a nicotine replacement to help smokers quit smoking.

The success rates for smoking cessation treatment with nicotine chewing gum vary considerably across studies, but evidence suggests that it is a safe means of facilitating smoking cessation if chewed according to instructions and restricted to patients who are under medical supervision.

Another approach to smoking cessation is the nicotine transdermal patch, a skin patch that delivers a relatively constant amount of nicotine to the person wearing it. A research team at the National Institute on Drug Abuse (NIDA)'s Intramural Research Program studied the safety, mechanism of action, and abuse liability of the patch that was consequently approved by FDA. Both nicotine gum and the nicotine patch, as well as other nicotine replacements such as sprays and inhalers, are used to help people fully quit smoking by reducing withdrawal symptoms and preventing relapse while undergoing behavioral treatment.

Another tool in treating nicotine addiction is a medication that goes by the trade name Zyban. This is not a nicotine replacement, as are the gum and patch. Rather, this works on other areas of the brain, and its effectiveness is in helping to make controllable nicotine craving or thoughts about cigarette use in people trying to quit.

Extent of Use

Despite the demonstrated health risk associated with smoking, young Americans continue to smoke. However, past-month smoking rates among high school students are declining from peaks reached in 1996 for 8th-graders (21.0 percent) and 10th-graders (30.4 percent) and in 1997 for seniors (36.5 percent). In 2003, rates reached the lowest levels ever reported by MTF (Monitoring the Future Study); 10.2 percent of 8th-graders, 16.7 percent of 10th-graders, and 24.4 percent of high school seniors reported smoking during the month preceding their responses to the survey.[2]

The decrease in smoking rates among young Americans corresponds to several years in which increased proportions of teens said they believe there is a "great" health risk associated with cigarette smoking and expressed disapproval of "pack-a-day" smokers. Students' personal disapproval of smoking had risen for some years, but showed no further increase in 2003 among 8th-graders and only small increases among 10th- and 12th-graders. In 2003, 84.6 percent of 8th-graders, 81.4 percent of 10th-graders, and 74.8 percent of 12th-graders stated that they "disapprove" or "strongly disapprove" of people smoking one or more packs of cigarettes per day.[2]

Notes

1. These findings are from the 2002 National Survey on Drug Use and Health, produced by HHS's Substance Abuse and Mental Health Services Administration. The survey is based on interviews with 68,126 respondents who were interviewed in their homes. The interviews represent 98 percent of the U.S. population age 12 and older. Not included in the survey

are persons in the active military, in prisons, or other institutionalized populations, or who are homeless. Findings from the 2002 National Survey on Drug Use and Health are available online at www.DrugAbuseStatistics.samhsa.gov.

2. These data are from the 2003 Monitoring the Future Survey, funded by the National Institute on Drug Abuse, National Institutes of Health, DHHS, and conducted by the University of Michigan's Institute for Social Research. The survey has tracked 12th-graders' illicit drug use and related attitudes since 1975; in 1991, 8th- and 10th-graders were added to the study. The latest data are online at www.drugabuse.gov.

Chapter 2

Understanding
Nicotine Addiction

What is nicotine?

Nicotine, one of more than 4,000 chemicals found in the smoke from tobacco products such as cigarettes, cigars, and pipes, is the primary component in tobacco that acts on the brain. Smokeless tobacco products such as snuff and chewing tobacco also contain many toxins as well as high levels of nicotine. Nicotine, recognized as one of the most frequently used addictive drugs, is a naturally occurring colorless liquid that turns brown when burned and acquires the odor of tobacco when exposed to air. There are many species of tobacco plants; the tabacum species serves as the major source of tobacco products today. Since nicotine was first identified in the early 1800s, it has been studied extensively and shown to have a number of complex and sometimes unpredictable effects on the brain and the body.

Cigarette smoking is the most prevalent form of nicotine addiction in the United States. Most cigarettes in the U.S. market today contain 10 milligrams (mg) or more of nicotine. Through inhaling smoke, the average smoker takes in 1 to 2 mg nicotine per cigarette. There have been substantial increases in the sale and consumption of smokeless tobacco products also, and more recently, in cigar sales.

Nicotine is absorbed through the skin and mucosal lining of the mouth and nose or by inhalation in the lungs. Depending on how tobacco is

This chapter includes excerpts from "Research Report Series—Nicotine Addiction," National Institute on Drug Abuse (NIDA), November 2002. The entire text can be found online at www.nida.nih.gov/ResearchReports/Nicotine.

15

taken, nicotine can reach peak levels in the bloodstream and brain rapidly. Cigarette smoking, for example, results in rapid distribution of nicotine throughout the body, reaching the brain within 10 seconds of inhalation. Cigar and pipe smokers, on the other hand, typically do not inhale the smoke, so nicotine is absorbed more slowly through the mucosal membranes of their mouths. Nicotine from smokeless tobacco also is absorbed through the mucosal membranes.

Is nicotine addictive?

Yes, nicotine is addictive. Most smokers use tobacco regularly because they are addicted to nicotine. Addiction is characterized by compulsive drug-seeking and use, even in the face of negative health consequences, and tobacco use certainly fits the description. It is well documented that most smokers identify tobacco as harmful and express a desire to reduce or stop using it, and nearly 35 million of them make a serious attempt to quit each year. Unfortunately, less than 7 percent of those who try to quit on their own achieve more than one year of abstinence; most relapse within a few days of attempting to quit.

Other factors to consider besides nicotine's addictive properties include its high level of availability, the small number of legal and social consequences of tobacco use, and the sophisticated marketing and advertising methods used by tobacco companies. These factors, combined with nicotine's addictive properties, often serve as determinants for first use and, ultimately, addiction.

Recent research has shown in fine detail how nicotine acts on the brain to produce a number of behavioral effects. Of primary importance to its addictive nature are findings that nicotine activates the brain circuitry that regulates feelings of pleasure, the so-called reward pathways. A key brain chemical involved in mediating the desire to consume drugs is the neurotransmitter dopamine, and research has shown that nicotine increases the levels of dopamine in the reward circuits. Nicotine's pharmacokinetic properties have been found also to enhance its abuse potential. Cigarette smoking produces a rapid distribution of nicotine to the brain, with drug levels peaking within 10 seconds of inhalation. The acute effects of nicotine dissipate in a few minutes, causing the smoker to continue dosing frequently throughout the day to maintain the drug's pleasurable effects and prevent withdrawal.

What people frequently do not realize is that the cigarette is a very efficient and highly engineered drug-delivery system. By inhaling, the smoker can get nicotine to the brain very rapidly with every puff. A typical smoker will take 10 puffs on a cigarette over a period of 5 minutes that the cigarette is lit. Thus, a person who smokes about 1½ packs (30 cigarettes) daily, gets 300 "hits" of nicotine to the brain each day. These factors contribute considerably to nicotine's highly addictive nature.

Scientific research is also beginning to show that nicotine may not be the only psychoactive ingredient in tobacco. Using advanced neuroimaging technology, scientists can see the dramatic effect of cigarette smoking on the brain and are finding a marked decrease in the levels of monoamine oxidase (MAO), an important enzyme that is responsible for breaking down dopamine. The change in MAO must be caused by some tobacco smoke ingredient other than nicotine, since we know that nicotine itself does not dramatically alter MAO levels. The decrease in two forms of MAO, A and B, then results in higher dopamine levels and may be another reason that smokers continue to smoke—to sustain the high dopamine levels that result in the desire for repeated drug use.

How does nicotine deliver its effect?

Nicotine can act as both a stimulant and a sedative. Immediately after exposure to nicotine, there is a "kick" caused in part by the drug's stimulation of the adrenal glands and resulting discharge of epinephrine (adrenaline). The rush of adrenaline stimulates the body and causes a sudden release of glucose as well as an increase in blood pressure, respiration, and heart rate. Nicotine also suppresses insulin output from the pancreas, which means that smokers are always slightly hyperglycemic. In addition, nicotine indirectly causes a release of dopamine in the brain regions that control pleasure and motivation. This reaction is similar to that seen with other drugs of abuse—such as cocaine and heroin—and it is thought to underlie the pleasurable sensations experienced by many smokers. In contrast, nicotine can also exert a sedative effect, depending on the level of the smoker's nervous system arousal and the dose of nicotine taken.

What happens when nicotine is taken for long periods of time?

Chronic exposure to nicotine results in addiction. Research is just beginning to document all of the neurological changes that accompany the development and maintenance of nicotine addiction. The behavioral consequences of these changes are well documented, however. Greater than 90 percent of those smokers who try to quit without seeking treatment fail, with most relapsing within a week.

Repeated exposure to nicotine results in the development of tolerance, the condition in which higher doses of a drug are required to produce the same initial stimulation. Nicotine is metabolized fairly rapidly, disappearing from the body in a few hours. Therefore some tolerance is lost overnight, and smokers often report that the first cigarettes of the day are the strongest and/or the "best." As the day progresses, acute tolerance develops, and later cigarettes have less effect.

Cessation of nicotine use is followed by a withdrawal syndrome that may last a month or more; it includes symptoms that can quickly drive people back to tobacco use. Nicotine withdrawal symptoms include irritability, craving, cognitive and attentional deficits, sleep disturbances, and increased appetite and may begin within a few hours after the last cigarette. Symptoms peak within the first few days and may subside within a few weeks. For some people, however, symptoms may persist for months or longer.

An important but poorly understood component of the nicotine withdrawal syndrome is craving, an urge for nicotine that has been described as a major obstacle to successful abstinence. High levels of craving for tobacco may persist for six months or longer. While the withdrawal syndrome is related to the pharmacological effects of nicotine, many behavioral factors also can affect the severity of withdrawal symptoms. For some people, the feel, smell, and sight of a cigarette and the ritual of obtaining, handling, lighting, and smoking the cigarette are all associated with the pleasurable effects of smoking and can make withdrawal or craving worse. While nicotine gum and patches may alleviate the pharmacological aspects of withdrawal, cravings often persist.

Chapter 3

What's in Tobacco Products?

Tobacco Products

- More than 4,000 chemical compounds have been identified in tobacco smoke. Of these, at least 43 are known to cause cancer.[1]

- Current tobacco product regulation requires cigarette manufacturers to disclose levels of tar and nicotine. Smokers receive very little information regarding chemical constituents in tobacco smoke, and the use of terms such as "light" and "ultra light" on packaging and in advertising may be misleading.[1]

- Cigarettes with low tar and nicotine contents are not substantially less hazardous than higher-yield brands. Consumers may be misled by the implied promise of reduced toxicity underlying the marketing of such brands.[1]

- Vents are used in cigarette filters to lower tar and nicotine yields in smoke, but they may be difficult to see. To examine the vents in some brands, the smoker would have to take off the filter wrapping, hold the filter up to a bright light, and look through magnifying glass.[2]

This chapter includes "Tobacco Products: Fact Sheet," reviewed April 2001, and excerpts from "Toxic Chemicals in Tobacco Products," reviewed September 2003, National Center for Chronic Disease Prevention and Health Promotion, Centers for Disease Control and Prevention (CDC). A table with information from the Arizona Smokers' Helpline is cited separately within the chapter.

- The potential health benefit of low tar cigarettes has been challenged. Smokers who switch to lower-tar and lower-nicotine cigarettes frequently change their smoking habits. They may block the vents in the filter portion of a cigarette, puff more frequently, inhale more deeply, or smoke more cigarettes per day, thus negating any risk reduction from low-tar and low-nicotine cigarettes.[2]

- Early data showed a lower cancer risk from low-tar cigarettes; however, more recent data suggest otherwise. Lower-yield cigarettes may be somewhat better than very high-yield cigarettes; but, when comparing full-flavor cigarettes and current light cigarettes, there is no evidence to suggest a lower cancer risk from the low-tar cigarettes.[1]

Cigarette Additives

- Federal law (the Comprehensive Smoking Education Act of 1984 and the Comprehensive Smokeless Tobacco Health Education Act of 1986) requires cigarette and smokeless tobacco manufacturers to submit a list of ingredients added to tobacco to the Secretary of Health and Human Services.[1]

- Hundreds of ingredients are used in the manufacture of tobacco products. Additives make cigarettes more acceptable to the consumer—they make cigarettes milder and easier to inhale, improve taste, and prolong burning and shelf life.[1]

- In 1994 six major cigarette manufacturers reported 599 ingredients that were added to the tobacco of manufacture cigarettes. Although, these ingredients are regarded as safe when ingested in foods, some may form carcinogens when heated or burned.[1]

- Knowledge about the impact of additives in tobacco products is negligible and will remain so as long as brand-specific information on the identity and quantity of additives is unavailable.[1]

Smokeless Additives

- In 1994 ten manufacturers of smokeless tobacco products released a list of additives used in their products. The additives list contained 562 ingredients approved for foods by the FDA.[1]

- The list of additives to smokeless tobacco includes sodium carbonate and ammonium carbonate, which increase the level of

"free" nicotine in moist snuff by raising the pH level. Unpro-
tonated (free) nicotine is the chemical form of nicotine that is
most readily absorbed through the mouth into the blood-stream.
Therefore, increases in pH can increase the snuff user's nicotine
absorption rate. Studies with nicotine and other addictive drugs
suggest that the absorption rate of drugs into the body is an important determinant of their addiction potential.[3]

- Moist snuff products with low nicotine content and pH levels
  have a smaller proportion of free nicotine. In contrast, moist
  snuff products with high nicotine content and pH levels have a
  higher proportion of free nicotine.[1]

- The epidemiology of moist snuff use among teenagers and
  young adults indicates that most novices start with brands having low levels of free nicotine and then "graduate" to brands
  with higher levels.[1]

- Sweeteners and flavorings, such as cherry juice concentrate,
  apple juice, chocolate liqueur, or honey are used in various
  smokeless tobacco products. As with manufactured cigarettes,
  these additives increase palatability and may increase the use
  of smokeless tobacco, at least among novices.[1]

References

1. U.S. Department of Health and Human Services. *Reducing To-
    bacco Use: A Report of the Surgeon General*. Atlanta: U.S. De-
    partment of Health and Human Services, Centers for Disease
    Control and Prevention, 2000.

2. Centers for Disease Control and Prevention. Filter ventilation
    levels in selected U.S. cigarettes, 1997. *MMWR* 1997; 46:1043-47.

3. Centers for Disease Control and Prevention. Determination of
    nicotine, pH, and moisture content of six U.S. commercial
    moist snuff products—Florida, January–February 1999.
    MMWR 1999; 48:398-401.

Toxic Chemicals in Tobacco Products

Relevance

Cigarette smoking is a major cause of lung cancer, the leading cause
of cancer death in both men and women in the United States. Worldwide,

Table 3.1. What's in Cigarette Smoke? (*continued on next page*)

There are over 4,000 identified chemicals in cigarette smoke. Listed here are 109 of the more toxic chemicals. Those proven to cause **cancer** are in **boldface** type. Those proven to cause *birth defects* are in *italic* type.

A
Acetaldehyde
Acetic Acid
Acetone
Acetylene
Acrolein
Acrylonitrile
Aluminum
Aminobiphenyl
Ammonia
Anabasine
Anatabine
Aniline
Anthracenes
Argon
Arsenic

B
Benz(a)anthracene
Benzene
Benzo(a)pyrene
Benzo(b)fluoranthene
Benzo(j)fluoranthene
Butadiene
Butane

C
Cadmium
Campesterol
Carbon Monoxide
Carbon Sulfide
Catechol
Chromium
Chrysene
Copper

Crotonaldehyde
Cyclotenes

D
DDT/Dieldrin
Dibenz(a,h)acridine
Dibenz(a,h)anthracene
Dibenz(a,j)acridine
Dibenzo(a,l)pyrene
Dibenzo(c,g)carbazole
Dimenthylhydrazine

E
Ethanol
Ethylcarbamate

F
Fluoranthenes
Fluorenes
Formaldehyde
Formic Acid
Furan

G
Glycerol

H
Hexamine
Hydrazine
Hydrogen cyanide
Hydrogen sulfide

I
Indeno(1,2,3-c,d)pyrene
Indole
Isoprene

Table 3.1. What's in Cigarette Smoke? (*continued*)

L

Lead
Limonine
Linoleic Acid
Linolenic Acid

M

Magnesium
Mercury
Methane
Methanol
Methyl formate
Methylamineethylchrysene
Methylamine
Methylnitrosamino
Methylpyrrolidine

N

n-Nitrosoanabasine
n-Nitrosodiethanolamine
n-Nitrosodiethylamine
n-nitrosodimethylamine
n-Nitrosoethyl methylamine
n-Nitrosomorpholine
n-Nitrosopyrrolidine
Naphthalene
Naphthylamine
Neophytadienes
Nickel
Nicotine
Nitric Oxide
Nitrobenzene
Nitropropane
Nitrosamines
Nitrosonomicotine
Nitrous oxide phenols
Nomicotine

P

Palmitic acid
Phenanthrenes
Phenol
Picolines
Polonium-210
Propionic acid
Pyrenes
Pyrrolidine

Q

Quinoline
Quinones

S

Scopoletin
Sitosterol
Skatole
Solanesol
Stearic acid
Stigmasterol
Styrene

T

Titanium
Toluene
Toluidine

U

Urethane

V

Vinyl Chloride
Vinylpyridine

lung cancer kills over one million people each year. Tobacco smoke contains more than 60 cancer-causing chemicals (carcinogens). These chemicals represent approximately seven chemical classes (polycyclic aromatic hydrocarbons, arenes, N-nitrosamines, aromatic and hetero-cyclic aromatic amines, aldehydes, organic compounds, and inorganic compounds). Twenty of the carcinogens cause cancer in the respiratory tract. In an exposed individual, numerous irritants, inflammatory agents, and reactive species work in concert with the carcinogens to induce replication of initiated or precancerous cells. Because of the chemical complexity of tobacco smoke it is unlikely that there is a single measurable mechanism of tobacco carcinogenesis.

Tobacco-specific nitrosamines (TSNAs) are a class of known carcinogens that are formed during the curing, processing, fermentation, and combustion of tobacco. They have been identified in cigarette tobacco, tobacco smoke, environmental tobacco smoke, smokeless tobacco and other tobacco products such as cigars and bidi cigarettes.

There are seven known TSNAs. N'-nitrosonornicotine (NNN), (4-methylnitrosamino)-1-(3-pyridyl)-1-butanone (NNK), and N-nitrosoanatabine (NAT) generally occur in greater quantities in tobacco products than the others and NNN, NNK and N-oxide, 4-(methylnitrosamino)-1-(3-pyridyl N-oxide)-1-butanol (NNAL), a metabolic product of NNK, are clearly the most carcinogenic. The TSNAs, NNN, and NNK are categorized as "reasonably anticipated to be human carcinogens" by the National Toxicology Program. The International Agency for Research on Cancer has classified NNN and NNK as "possibly carcinogenic to humans" (Group 2B).)

Levels in Tobacco and Exposure

The TSNAs show the highest concentration of any group of strong carcinogens in mainstream cigarette smoke. TSNAs are also considered the carcinogen class of concern in smokeless tobacco. NNN is measured at 0.3 to 89 µg/g (microgram per gram) in processed tobacco, at 0.12 to 3.7 µg per cigarette in mainstream smoke and at 0.15 to 1.7 µg per cigarette in sidestream smoke. NNK is measured at 0.2 to 7 µg/g in processed tobacco, at 0.08 to 0.77 µg per cigarette in mainstream smoke and at 0.2 to 1.4 µg per cigarette in sidestream smoke. Information on levels of TSNAs in cigarette tobacco filler is relevant to levels of TSNAs in tobacco smoke. An average of 9% (6.9 to 11%) of NNK transfers from tobacco to smoke when the tobacco is burned and this represents, on average, 32% (26 to 37%) of the NNK in smoke.

Exposure to TSNAs from tobacco products is confirmed by their detection in a variety of biological samples. TSNAs have been measured in saliva, urine, and cervical mucus of people exposed to tobacco or tobacco smoke, and in fetal tissue and the urine of infants born to smoking mothers.

An extensive body of scientific evidence spanning about three decades provides clear evidence that TSNAs are an important group of potent carcinogens in tobacco and tobacco smoke. People are exposed to TSNAs by using tobacco (smoking or oral) and by exposure to other people's smoke (that is, environmental tobacco smoke, ETS, or second hand smoke). Evidence is sufficient that the lung is a target of TSNA-induced cancer and that NNK is one carcinogen likely to play a role in human tobacco-induced lung cancer. NNN occurs in greater concentrations in cigarette smoke than any other esophageal carcinogen. Smoking is also a cause of esophageal cancer and is responsible for 70–80% of esophageal cancer deaths in the United States.

Analyzing the Carcinogens in Cigarettes

Cigarettes analyzed represent the top brands of the major U.S. cigarette manufacturers. The cigarettes were purchased in various locations in the United States in the first half of 2001. Several varieties of each brand were tested. [A discussion of the methodology used in this study, along with additional statistical information within the tables, and references for the text can be found online in the full-text version of the original document at http://www.cdc.gov/tobacco/research_data/product/objective21-20.htm. Results are shown in Tables 3.2, 3.3, and 3.4 beginning on page 26.]

Table 3.2. NNK levels in 14 brands of commercial cigarettes

	Number of cigarettes tested (N)*	Median (µg/g)
Brown & Williamson Tobacco Corporation Brands		
Carlton: Full Flavor King, Regular Soft Pack, Full Flavor Hard Pack	22	0.39
GPC: Full Flavor 100s, Full Flavor Hard Pack, Full Flavor Soft Pack, Mediums Hard Pack, Full Flavor Kings Soft Pack	22	0.34
Kool (menthol): Filter Kings, Classic Menthol Filter Kings	22	0.41
Lorillard Tobacco Company Brands		
Kent: King Soft Pack, Full Flavor Soft Pack	24	0.26
Newport (menthol): Menthol Kings, Full Flavor Box	19	0.39
True: King Size, Full Flavor Soft Pack	18	0.32
Altria Group, Inc. (Philip Morris) Brands		
Basic: Full Flavor, Full Flavor Soft Pack	24	0.28
Benson & Hedges: Full Flavor Hard Box 100s, Full Flavor Soft Pack 100s	22	0.38
Marlboro: Full Flavor Hard Box, Full Flavor Box King Size, Full Flavor Hard Pack	22	0.44
Virginia Slims: Full Flavor, Full Flavor Soft Pack	22	0.34
R.J. Reynolds Tobacco Company Brands		
Camel: Full Flavor Filters, Full Flavor Soft Pack, Full Flavor Box	22	0.31
Doral: Full Flavor, Full Flavor Box King Size, Full Flavor Soft Pack	22	0.30
Salem (menthol): Full Flavor, Full Flavor Soft Pack	16	0.31
Winston: Full Flavor, Full Flavor Box, Full Flavor Hard Pack	24	0.28

*At least one cigarette from 15 different packs of each brand was analyzed.

Table 3.3. NNN levels in 14 brands of commercial cigarettes

	Number of cigarettes analyzed (N)*	Median (µg/g)
Brown & Williamson Tobacco Corporation Brands		
Carlton: Full Flavor King, Regular Soft Pack, Full Flavor Hard Pack	19	1.4
GPC: Full Flavor 100s, Full Flavor Hard Pack, Full Flavor Soft Pack, Mediums Hard Pack, Full Flavor Kings Soft Pack	20	1.5
Kool (menthol): Filter Kings, Classic Menthol Filter Kings	16	1.6
Lorillard Tobacco Company Brands		
Kent: King Soft Pack, Full Flavor Soft Pack	16	1.0
Newport (menthol): Menthol Kings, Full Flavor Box	23	1.5
True: King Size, Full Flavor Soft Pack	18	1.4
Altria Group, Inc. (Philip Morris) Brands		
Basic: Full Flavor, Full Flavor Soft Pack	18	1.3
Benson & Hedges: Full Flavor Hard Box 100s, Full Flavor Soft Pack 100s	20	1.6
Marlboro: Full Flavor Hard Box, Full Flavor Box King Size, Full Flavor Hard Pack	19	1.6
Virginia Slims: Full Flavor, Full Flavor Soft Pack	18	1.7
R.J. Reynolds Tobacco Company Brands		
Camel: Full Flavor Filters, Full Flavor Soft Pack, Full Flavor Box	20	1.8
Doral: Full Flavor, Full Flavor Box King Size, Full Flavor Soft Pack	19	1.9
Salem (menthol): Full Flavor, Full Flavor Soft Pack	19	1.6
Winston: Full Flavor, Full Flavor Box, Full Flavor Hard Pack	19	1.2

*At least one cigarette from 15 different packs of each brand was analyzed.

Table 3.4. Total TSNA (NNK + NNN) levels in 14 brands of commercial cigarettes

	Number of cigarettes analyzed (N)*	Median (µg/g)
Brown & Williamson Tobacco Corporation Brands		
Carlton: Full Flavor King, Regular Soft Pack, Full Flavor Hard Pack	18	1.78
GPC: Full Flavor 100s, Full Flavor Hard Pack, Full Flavor Soft Pack, Mediums Hard Pack, Full Flavor Kings Soft Pack	20	1.79
Kool (menthol): Filter Kings, Classic Menthol Filter Kings	16	1.97
Lorillard Tobacco Company Brands		
Kent: King Soft Pack, Full Flavor Soft Pack	16	1.29
Newport (menthol): Menthol Kings, Full Flavor Box	18	1.83
True: King Size, Full Flavor Soft Pack	16	1.68
Altria Group, Inc. (Philip Morris) Brands		
Basic: Full Flavor, Full Flavor Soft Pack	16	1.59
Benson & Hedges: Full Flavor Hard Box 100s, Full Flavor Soft Pack 100s	19	1.97
Marlboro: Full Flavor Hard Box, Full Flavor Box King Size, Full Flavor Hard Pack	16	2.06
Virginia Slims: Full Flavor, Full Flavor Soft Pack	18	1.98
R.J. Reynolds Tobacco Company Brands		
Camel: Full Flavor Filters, Full Flavor Soft Pack, Full Flavor Box	17	2.14
Doral: Full Flavor, Full Flavor Box King Size, Full Flavor Soft Pack	18	2.31
Salem (menthol): Full Flavor, Full Flavor Soft Pack	15	1.86
Winston: Full Flavor, Full Flavor Box, Full Flavor Hard Pack	18	1.49

*At least one cigarette from 15 different packs of each brand was analyzed.

Chapter 4

Cigarette Brand Preferences

In Brief

- In 2001, Marlboro was the cigarette brand used most often by past month cigarette smokers, followed by Newport, Camel, Basic, and Doral.

- Approximately 85 percent of cigarette smokers aged 12 to 25 smoked one of the three most used brands, whereas smokers aged 26 or older reported more diversity in cigarette brand selection.

- White and Hispanic smokers were most likely to use Marlboro, while black smokers were most likely to use Newport.

The National Household Survey on Drug Abuse (NHSDA) asks respondents to report whether they smoked part or all of a cigarette during the 30 days prior to the survey interview. Respondents who reported smoking part or all of a cigarette in the past 30 days were also asked to report which cigarette brand they smoked most often during that time.[1] Responses were analyzed by age, gender, race/ethnicity, and geographic region for comparative purposes.[2]

"Cigarette Brand Preferences," from *The NHSDA Report*, National Household Survey on Drug Abuse, Substance Abuse and Mental Health Services Administration (SAMHSA), July 11, 2003.

Cigarette Prevalence

According to the 2001 NHSDA, an estimated 56 million persons aged 12 or older (25 percent) smoked part or all of a cigarette during the past month. Thirteen percent of youths aged 12 to 17, 39 percent of young adults aged 18 to 25, and 24 percent of adults 26 or older reported past month smoking, as did about one fourth of males (27 percent) and females (23 percent). Twenty-six percent of whites were past month smokers, as were 24 percent of blacks and 21 percent of Hispanics. Past month smoking was reported by 27 percent of persons living in the Midwest, 24 percent in the Northeast, 26 percent in the South, and 22 percent in the West.

Cigarette Brands Used Most Often

In 2001, Marlboro was the brand used most often by past month cigarette smokers, followed by Newport, Camel, Basic, and Doral (Table 4.1.). Other brands reported by at least 2 percent of past month smokers were Winston, Kool, GPC, Salem, and Virginia Slims.

Demographic Differences in Cigarette Brand Use

Prior research has shown that cigarette brand use varies by age, gender, and race.[3,4,5] Among past month smokers, Marlboro was the brand used most often in the past month by youths aged 12 to 17 (55 percent), young adults aged 18 to 25 (54 percent), and older adults aged 26 or older (38 percent) (Table 4.2.). Older adults aged 26 or older reported a greater diversity of brand preference compared with youths and young adults. Among past month smokers, the 5 brands used most often by youths and young adults accounted for 91 percent of youth smokers and 89 percent of young adult smokers, whereas the 5 brands used most among smokers aged 26 or older accounted for only 62 percent of smokers in this age group.

Among white smokers, Marlboro was the brand used most often in the past month followed by Camel (Table 4.3.). Marlboro also was the brand used most often by Hispanics, followed by Newport. Among blacks, Newport was the brand used most often, followed by Kool.

Among past month smokers aged 12 or older, males (44 percent) and females (39 percent) were more likely to smoke Marlboro than any other brand (data not shown in any table). Newport was the second most used brand among males (10 percent) and females (11 percent). Camel was the third most used brand among males (9 percent), while Basic was the third most used brand among females (5 percent).

Geographic Differences in Cigarette Brand Use

Marlboro was the cigarette brand used most often by past month smokers in the Northeast, Midwest, South, and West (Table 4.4.). Newport was the second most smoked brand in the Northeast, Midwest,

Table 4.1. Percentages of Past Month Cigarette Smokers Aged 12 or Older Reporting Cigarette Brands Used Most Often During the Past Month: 2001.

Cigarette brand	Percentage of smokers (%)
Marlboro	41.9
Newport	10.2
Camel	6.8
Basic	5.4
Doral	4.2
Winston	3.4
Kool	2.9
GPC	2.7
Salem	2.5
Virginia Slims	2.1

Table 4.2. Percentages of Past Month Cigarette Smokers Aged 12 or Older Reporting Cigarette Brands Used Most Often During the Past Month, by Age Group: 2001.

	Age group (years old)		
Cigarette brand	12–17	18–25	26 and older
Marlboro	55.2%	53.9%	37.6%
Camel	22.8%	17.2%	7.4%
Newport	9.4%	13.6%	4.7%
Basic	2.2%	1.7%	6.7%
Doral			5.4%
Parliment	1.6%	3.0%	

and South, while Camel was the second most smoked brand in the West. Among white smokers, Marlboro was used more often than any other brand in all four geographic regions, Newport was ranked second in the Northeast, and Camel was ranked second in the West. Among black smokers, Newport was used more than any other brand in all four geographic regions and Kool was the second most smoked brand in the Midwest and South. In the Northeast, Marlboro was the second most smoked brand while Basic was ranked second in the West. Among Hispanic smokers, Marlboro was used more often than any other brand in the Midwest, South, and West. In the Northeast, Marlboro and Newport were used by similar percentages of Hispanic smokers.

End Notes

1. Respondents who reported smoking part or all of a cigarette during the 30 days prior to the survey interview were asked, "During the past 30 days, what brand of cigarettes did you smoke most often?" Respondents were given 60 brands of cigarettes to choose from, and could write in the brand used most often if it was not included on the list.

2. Regions consist of the following groups of States: Northeast Region: Maine, New Hampshire, Vermont, Massachusetts, Rhode Island, Connecticut, New York, New Jersey, Pennsylvania. Midwest Region: Wisconsin, Illinois, Michigan, Indiana,

Table 4.3. Percentages of Past Month Cigarette Smokers Aged 12 or Older Reporting Cigarette Brands Used Most Often During the Past Month, by Race/Ethnicity*: 2001.

	Race		
Cigarette brand	White	Black	Hispanic
Marlboro	44.5%		59.5%
Camel	7.8%		5.3%
Newport	5.0%	45.2%	12.1%
Basic	5.8%	6.1%	
Doral	4.5%	6.1%	
Kool		10.7%	
Benson and Hedges			2.9%
Salem		5.8%	
Winston			2.5%

Table 4.4. Percentages and Standard Errors of Past Month Cigarette Smokers Aged 12 or Older Reporting Cigarette Brands Used Most Often During the Past Month, by Race/Ethnicity** and Geographic Division: 2001.

	Geographic Division							
Cigarette Brand	Northeast		Midwest		South		West	
	%	SE	%	SE	%	SE	%	SE
Total								
Marlboro	41.4	1.29	40.2	0.98	40.4	1.20	47.4	1.51
Camel	4.7	0.60	7.2	0.40	5.1	0.45	11.4	0.93
Basic	3.3	0.51	7.3	0.62	5.5	0.57	4.7	0.77
Newport	17.4	0.98	9.3	0.62	10.3	0.62	4.5	0.73
Doral	1.6	0.37	4.1	0.54	7.2	0.69	1.2	0.34
Kool	2.1	0.51	3.3	0.35	3.5	0.48	2.0	0.46
White								
Marlboro	44.9	1.43	44.3	1.03	44.6	1.44	44.4	1.76
Camel	5.6	0.74	8.1	0.46	6.3	0.60	13.0	1.13
Basic	3.5	0.49	7.6	0.68	5.7	0.64	5.7	1.13
Newport	11.0	0.80	4.1	0.33	4.2	0.35	1.1	0.24
Doral	1.8	0.44	4.6	0.63	7.2	0.84	1.7	0.50
Kool	1.5	0.38	2.3	0.32	2.1	0.44	2.2	0.71
Black								
Marlboro	7.5	2.58	3.0	0.95	4.8	1.06	*	*
Camel	0.3	0.23	0.5	0.29	0.3	0.23	*	*
Basic	*	*	7.3	2.50	7.1	1.77	5.2	2.60
Newport	60.6	5.48	49.1	3.54	39.8	2.34	43.8	5.85
Doral	*	*	0.7	0.52	10.3	1.96	*	*
Kool	*	*	11.7	2.08	12.1	2.18	2.4	1.53
Hispanic								
Marlboro	40.3	5.90	38.4	4.94	67.8	3.18	65.9	3.31
Camel	1.1	0.46	*	*	3.5	1.09	8.4	2.16
Basic	*	*	*	*	1.8	1.03	1.9	0.96
Newport	35.3	4.26	22.1	4.45	7.1	1.12	4.3	1.07
Doral	*	*	0.1	0.09	2.8	1.00	*	*
Kool	0.1	0.05	*	*	0.8	0.59	0.7	0.50

* Low precision; no estimate reported.

** Estimates for American Indian or Alaska Native, Native Hawaiian or Other Pacific Islander, or Asian respondents are not shown due to low precision.

33

Ohio, North Dakota, South Dakota, Nebraska, Kansas, Minnesota, Iowa, Missouri. South Region: West Virginia, Virginia, Maryland, Delaware, District of Columbia, North Carolina, South Carolina, Georgia, Florida, Mississippi, Tennessee, Kentucky, Alabama. West Region: Idaho, Nevada, Arizona, New Mexico, Utah, Colorado, Wyoming, Montana, California, Oregon, Washington, Hawaii, Alaska.

3. Kopstein, A. (2001). Tobacco use in America: Findings from the 1999 National Household Survey on Drug Abuse (DHHS Publication No. SMA 02–3622, Analytic Series A–15). Rockville, MD: Substance Abuse and Mental Health Services Administration, Office of Applied Studies.

4. Johnston, L. D., O'Malley, P. M., Bachman, J. G., & Schulenberg, J. E. (1999). Cigarette brands smoked by American teens: One brand predominates; three account for nearly all of teen smoking [press release]. University of Michigan News and Information Services: Ann Arbor, MI.

5. Centers for Disease Control and Prevention. (1990, September 28). Cigarette brand use among adult smokers—United States, 1986. *Morbidity and Mortality Weekly Report*, 39(38), 665, 671–673. [Also available at http://www.cdc.gov/mmwr/ preview/mmwrhtml/00001783.htm]

The National Household Survey on Drug Abuse (NHSDA) is an annual survey sponsored by the Substance Abuse and Mental Health Services Administration (SAMHSA). The 2001 data are based on information obtained from 69,000 persons aged 12 or older. The survey collects data by administering questionnaires to a representative sample of the population through face-to-face interviews at their place of residence.

The *NHSDA Report* is prepared by the Office of Applied Studies (OAS), SAMHSA, and by RTI in Research Triangle Park, North Carolina. Information and data for this issue are based on the following publication:

Office of Applied Studies. (2002). Results from the 2001 National Household Survey on Drug Abuse: Volume I. Summary of national findings (DHHS Publication No. SMA 02-3758, NHSDA Series H–17). Rockville, MD: Substance Abuse and Mental Health Services Administration. Also available on-line: http://www.drugabusestatistics.samhsa .gov. Additional tables available upon request.

Chapter 5

The Truth About "Light" Cigarettes

Key Points

- The lower tar and nicotine numbers on light cigarette packs and in ads are misleading.

- Light cigarettes trick the smoking machines so that they record artificially low tar and nicotine levels.

- Light cigarettes provide no benefit to smokers' health.

- Resources are available for people who want to quit smoking.

Many smokers choose "low-tar," "mild," or "light" cigarettes because they think that light cigarettes may be less harmful to their health than "regular" or "full-flavor" cigarettes.

After all, the smoke from light cigarettes feels smoother and lighter on the throat and chest—so lights must be healthier than regulars, right? Wrong.

The truth is that light cigarettes do not reduce the health risks of smoking. The only way to reduce your risk, and the risk to others around you, is to stop smoking completely.

"The Truth about 'Light' Cigarettes: Questions and Answers," National Cancer Institute (NCI), reviewed January 3, 2003.

What about the lower tar and nicotine numbers on light cigarette packs and in ads for lights?

- These numbers come from smoking machines that "smoke" every brand of cigarettes exactly the same way.

- These numbers do not really tell how much tar and nicotine a particular smoker may get because people do not smoke cigarettes the same way the machines do. And no two people smoke the same way.

How do light cigarettes trick the smoking machines?

- Tobacco companies designed light cigarettes with tiny pinholes on the filters. These "filter vents" dilute cigarette smoke with air when light cigarettes are "puffed" on by smoking machines, causing the machines to measure artificially low tar and nicotine levels.

- Many smokers do not know that their cigarette filters have vent holes. The filter vents are uncovered when cigarettes are smoked on smoking machines. However, without realizing it and because they cannot avoid it, many smokers block the tiny vent holes with their fingers or lips—which basically turns the light cigarette into a regular cigarette.

- Because people, unlike machines, crave nicotine, they may inhale more deeply; take larger, more rapid, or more frequent puffs; or smoke a few extra cigarettes each day to get enough nicotine to satisfy their craving. This is called "compensating," and it means that smokers end up inhaling more tar, nicotine, and other harmful chemicals than the machine-based numbers suggest.

- Cigarette makers can also make the paper wrapped around the tobacco of light cigarettes burn faster so that the smoking machines get in fewer puffs before the cigarettes burn down. The result is that the machine measures less tar and nicotine in the smoke of the cigarette.

What is the scientific evidence about the health effects of light cigarettes?

- The Federal Government's National Cancer Institute (NCI) recently concluded that light cigarettes provide no benefit to smokers' health. (National Cancer Institute. *Risks Associated with Smoking Cigarettes with Low Machine-Measured Yields of Tar and Nicotine.* Smoking and Tobacco Control Monograph 13, Bethesda, MD: NCI, 2001.)

- According to the NCI report, people who switch to light cigarettes from regular cigarettes are likely to inhale the same amount of hazardous chemicals, and they remain at high risk for developing smoking-related cancers and other diseases.

- There is also no evidence that switching to light or ultra-light cigarettes actually helps smokers quit.

What do tobacco companies say about the health effects of light cigarettes?

- The tobacco industry's own documents show that companies were well aware that smokers of light cigarettes compensate by taking bigger puffs.

- Industry documents also show that the companies were aware early on of the difference between machine-measured yields of tar and nicotine and what the smoker actually inhales.

- The NCI report concluded that strategies used by the tobacco industry to advertise and promote light cigarettes were intended to reassure smokers and to prevent them from quitting, and to lead consumers to perceive filtered and light cigarettes as safer alternatives to regular cigarettes.

What is the bottom line for smokers who want to protect their health?

- There is no such thing as a safe cigarette. The only proven way to reduce your risk of smoking-related disease is to quit smoking completely.

- Here's good news: Smokers who quit before age 50 cut their risk of dying in half over the next 15 years compared with people who keep smoking.

- Quitting also decreases your risk of lung cancer, heart attacks, stroke, and chronic lung disease.

How can you quit smoking for your health—and for the ones you love?

For more information about smoking and advice on quitting, contact:

Centers for Disease Control and Prevention
Phone: 800-CDC-1311 (800-232-1311)
Website: http://www.cdc.gov/tobacco

National Cancer Institute
Phone: Smoking Quitline 877-44U-QUIT (877-448-7848)
Website: http://www.smokefree.gov

Chapter 6

Cigar and Pipe Use

Facts about Cigar and Pipe Smoking

A century ago, "Robber Barons" of the Gilded Age adopted the cigar as a symbol of conspicuous consumption and masculine power. In recent times, manufacturers of cigars and related paraphernalia have sought to recreate this image of privilege, exclusivity, and wealth. Encouraged by advertising efforts of the cigar and pipe tobacco industry, men and women are urged to attend "smokers" or "cigar seminars" to learn arcane information about cigars, but not to learn the most important fact of all: cigars kill. Cigars and pipe tobacco are dangerous to one's health as is tobacco in any other form.

Pipe tobacco and cigars are made from the dried leaves and stems of the tobacco plant, *Nicotiana tabacum*. Originally native to North America, the plant is now cultivated and grown around the world. One of the chemicals contained in tobacco is nicotine, a powerful and toxic nerve stimulant. Two or three drops of nicotine, if taken all at once, could kill an average person.

This chapter begins with text excerpted with permission from "FactLine on Cigar and Pipe Smoking," by the Indiana Prevention Resource Center at Indiana University. © Copyright 1998 The Trustees of Indiana University. All rights reserved. "Cigar and Pipe Smoking Are as Dangerous as Cigarettes to Periodontal Health," is reprinted with permission from the American Academy of Periodontology, © 2001. All rights reserved. "Trends in Pipe and Cigar Use" is from "Cigar Use," *NHSDA Report*, National Household Survey on Drug Abuse (NHSDA), Substance Abuse and Mental Health Services Administration (SAMHSA), December 21, 2001.

Pipe tobacco is shredded tobacco leaf in loose form, it may be aged, it may also be sprayed with chemicals or flavorings. Cigar construction differs from that of cigarettes in that the wrappers are made from whole tobacco leaf, rather than paper, and are filled with shredded tobacco, or, as is said of cheaper "stogies," "sweepings off the floor." Some cigars have filter tips or plastic holders built in, some are long and narrow. A large cigar may have as much tobacco in volume as an entire pack of cigarettes.

Health Issues

Cigars and pipes are not a safe alternative to cigarettes. Like other forms of tobacco, use of cigars and pipes brings risks of lung, breast, pancreatic, prostate, colorectal, liver, and oral cancer, lung disease, stroke, and heart attack. Tobacco smoking is the principal cause of death from chronic obstructive pulmonary disease (COPD) and lung cancer. Smoke from cigars and pipes also causes respiratory infections, headaches, and burning eyes.

Cigars come in many different sizes, so comparisons are difficult, but cigars can contain 7 times more tar and 4 times more nicotine than cigarettes. Particle emissions from one cigar may be more than those of three cigarettes, and the amount of carbon monoxide produced by one cigar can be 30 times higher than cigarettes.

Cardiovascular Health: Nicotine can cause irregular or skipped heart beats, an increase in blood pressure, a decreased tolerance for exercise or exertion, a tendency for clotting, and vasoconstriction. One study showed that pipe smokers had almost the same coronary heart disease risk as cigarette smokers. Another study demonstrated that pipe smokers had a higher mortality rate from coronary heart disease, and 40% more deaths from all causes.

Chronic Cough and Phlegm, Lung Function and Emphysema: Cigar and pipe smokers have increased rates of chronic cough and phlegm. Cigar smokers have up to twice the rate of cough and phlegm as nonsmokers. Use of tobacco can cause or worsen the effects of chronic obstructive pulmonary disease (COPD), asthma, emphysema, and decrease lung function.

Oral and Dental Health: Tobacco secretions stain teeth and cause sores in the mouth and gums. These lesions can be precancerous, including leukoplakia also called "smoker's white patch," and erythroplakia, a red, velvety lesion. Cigar and pipe smoking may also cause "hairy tongue."

Cancer: The National Cancer Institute says that were it not for tobacco use, oral cancer would be almost nonexistent as a cause of death. Oral cancer, the sixth most common cancer in the world, can develop in any part of the mouth, most commonly on the lips, tongue, roof, or floor of the mouth, pharynx or esophagus. Pipe smokers are particularly prone to cancer of the lip.

Cigars and pipes use black (air-cured) tobacco, which carries a higher risk of causing esophageal cancer than the tobacco used for cigarettes. Even for pipe and cigar smokers who say they "don't inhale," the risk of lung cancer is still four times greater than that of nonsmokers.

One study showed a significant increase in colon and rectal cancer, not only in cigarette, but in pipe and cigar smokers. The study suggests that tobacco is responsible for 16% of colon cancer and 22% of rectal cancer deaths.

Cigar and Pipe Smoking Are as Dangerous as Cigarettes to Periodontal Health

Pierce Brosnan and Demi Moore have appeared on covers of cigar magazines sending the message that cigar smoking, a growing habit among the young and affluent, is sophisticated. What the covers don't show is models with missing teeth. Yet, according to a study published in the newly released *Journal of Periodontology*, cigar and pipe smoking may have nearly the same adverse effects on periodontal health and tooth loss as cigarette smoking.

Researchers analyzed 705 individuals ranging in age from 21 to 92 years old, and found that 17.6 percent of current or former cigar or pipe smokers had moderate to severe periodontitis—nearly three times the percent of nonsmokers. In addition, they averaged four missing teeth. For each given tobacco product, current smokers were defined as individuals who smoke daily. Former heavy smokers were defined as individuals who had smoked daily for 10 or more years, but had quit smoking. The nonsmokers group included individuals who had quit smoking cigarettes after smoking for less than 10 years and those with no history of smoking.

"Cigarette, cigar, and pipe smokers all had a much higher prevalence of moderate and severe periodontitis compared to former smokers and nonsmokers," explained Jasim Albandar, D.D.S., Ph.D., professor of periodontology at Temple University School of Dentistry and lead researcher of the study. "Research also indicated that there was a correlation with the number of missing teeth with the current, former and nonsmokers having 5.1, 3.9 and 2.8 missing teeth, respectively."

Cigar smokers are at a higher risk of alveolar bone loss than non-smokers. "This increase in risk is similar in magnitude to that of cigarette smokers," explained Albandar.

"Smoking cessation efforts should be considered a way of improving periodontal health and protecting against tooth loss in cigarette, cigar and pipe smokers," said Michael McGuire, D.D.S., president of the American Academy of Periodontology (AAP). "My patients who smoke understand the health consequences, so I like to remind them of another possible outcome—a toothless smile."

For More Information

For additional information about tobacco's effects on periodontal health, or a referral to a periodontologist, visit the American Academy of Periodontology website at www.perio.org, or call 1-800 FLOSS EM (1-800-356-7736). The American Academy of Periodontology is an association of dental professionals specializing in the prevention, diagnosis and treatment of diseases affecting the gums and supporting structures of the teeth and in the placement and maintenance of dental implants. Periodontics is one of nine dental specialties recognized by the American Dental Association.

Trends in Pipe and Cigar Use

Since the 1950's, epidemiological studies have found an increased risk of esophageal, lung, oral, and laryngeal cancer among cigar smokers.[1] According to the 2000 National Household Survey on Drug Abuse (NHSDA), 4.8 percent of persons aged 12 or older (more than 10 million individuals) were current cigar users (that is, they smoked cigars in the past month). The 2000 NHSDA collected data on the number of new cigar users each year, as well as on the current use of cigars.

From 1990 to 1998, the annual number of new cigar users climbed steadily, but decreased 22 percent between 1998 and 1999. In 2000, current cigar use was higher among young adults than among those from other age groups. More than half of current cigar users also smoked cigarettes during the past month.

Trends in New Cigar Use

The annual number of new cigar users rose dramatically in the 1990s despite widespread tobacco prevention initiatives. From 1990 to 1998,[2] the number of new cigar users increased by 208 percent, climbing from almost 2 million in 1990 to nearly 5 million in 1998.

However, between 1998 and 1999, the number of persons who took up cigar smoking declined nearly 22 percent. In 1999, over 400,000 fewer youths aged 12 to 17 and 400,000 fewer young adults aged 18 to 25 were new cigar smokers than in 1998.

Table 6.1. Cigar and Pipe Use Statistics

	Cigar Use	Pipe Use
All Ages		
Population (in thousands) reporting lifetime use, 2000	76,377	36,726
Population (in thousands) reporting lifetime use, 2001	79,932	38,373
Population (in thousands) reporting current use, 2000	10,712	2,131
Population (in thousands) reporting current use, 2001	12,103	2,349
All Ages		
Percentage reporting lifetime use, 2000	34.2%	16.4%
Percentage reporting lifetime use, 2001	35.4%	17.0%
Percentage reporting current use, 2000	4.8%	1.0%
Percentage reporting current use, 2001	5.4%	1.0%
Youths Aged 12 to 17		
Percentage reporting lifetime use, 2000	17.1%	2.9%
Percentage reporting lifetime use, 2001	16.4%	2.9%
Percentage reporting current use, 2000	4.5%	0.8%
Percentage reporting current use, 2001	4.3%	0.7%
Persons Aged 18 to 25		
Percentage reporting lifetime use, 2000	42.3%	8.2%
Percentage reporting lifetime use, 2001	43.8%	8.6%
Percentage reporting current use, 2000	10.4%	1.2%
Percentage reporting current use, 2001	10.4%	1.3%
Persons Aged 26 or Older		
Percentage reporting lifetime use, 2000	35.2%	19.7%
Percentage reporting lifetime use, 2001	36.6%	20.4%
Percentage reporting current use, 2000	3.9%	0.9%
Percentage reporting current use, 2001	4.7%	1.0%

Source: Excerpted and compiled from "Alcohol or Tobacco Use Tables–Tables H.21 to H.25," from the 2001 National Household Survey on Drug Abuse, (NHSDA), Office of Applied Studies, Substance Abuse and Mental Health Services Administration (SAMHSA).

Prevalence of Cigar Use

Young adults aged 18 to 25 (10.4 percent) were more likely to report past month cigar use compared with youths aged 12 to 17 (4.5 percent) and adults aged 26 or older (3.9 percent). Among young adults, 18 to 20 year olds (12.9 percent) were significantly more likely to have smoked cigars in the past month than those aged 21 to 25 (8.7 percent). Males (8.4 percent) were more likely than females (1.5 percent) to report past month cigar use. This gender difference was less pronounced for 12 to 17 year olds (6.4 percent males, 2.5 percent females) than it was for those aged 18 to 25 (16.5 percent males, 4.4 percent females) or those aged 26 or older (7.3 percent males, 0.8 percent females). The rate of past month cigar use was higher among whites (5.0 percent) and blacks (5.1 percent) than it was for Hispanics (3.9 percent). Among youths aged 12 to 17, the rate was higher for whites (5.3 percent) than for blacks (2.8 percent) and Hispanics (3.1 percent). For young adults aged 18 to 25, the rate was higher for blacks (13.1 percent) than it was for whites (11.3 percent) and Hispanics (6.0 percent).

Cigarette, Smokeless Tobacco, and Pipe Use Among Current Cigar Users

According to the NHSDA, current cigar users were more likely to smoke cigarettes (56.1 percent) than use smokeless tobacco (11.9 percent) or smoke pipes (5.6 percent). Younger cigar users were more likely to use other tobacco products than older cigar users. For example, current cigar users aged 12 to 17 (71.8 percent) and aged 18 to 25 (71.4 percent) were more likely than those aged 26 or older (46.7 percent) to smoke cigarettes during the past month. Current cigar users aged 12 to 17 (15.2 percent) and aged 18 to 25 (13.9 percent) were also more likely than those aged 26 or older (10.4 percent) to use smokeless tobacco during the past month. Current cigar users aged 12 to 17 (8.4 percent) were more likely than those aged 18 to 25 (6.1 percent) or those aged 26 or older (4.9 percent) to smoke pipes during the past month.

Notes

1. Baker, F., Ainsworth, S.R., Dye, J.T., Crammer, C., Thun, M.J., Hoffman, D., Repace, J.L., Henningfield, J.E., Slade, J., Pinney, J., Shanks, T., Burns, D.M., Connolly, G.N., and Shopland, D.R. (2000). Health risks associated with cigar smoking. *Journal of the American Medical Association*, 284, 735-740.

2. Because estimates of new use are based on retrospective reports, the most recent year available for 2000 data is 1999.

Information and data are based on the following publication and statistics:

Substance Abuse and Mental Health Services Administration. (2001). *Summary of findings from the 2000 National Household Survey on Drug Abuse* (National Household Survey on Drug Abuse Series: H-13, DHHS Publication No. SMA 01-3549). Rockville, MD: Author. Also available on-line: http://www.drugabusestatistics.samhsa.gov. Additional tables 2.1B; 2.2B; 2.3B; 2.4B; 2.8B; 2.9B; 2.40B; 2.41B; 2.42B; 2.43B from http://www.samhsa.gov/oas/nhsda/2kdetailedtabs/Vol_1 _Part_2/V1P2.htm and 4.18A from http://www.samhsa.gov/oas/nhsda/ 2kdetailedtabs/Vol_1_Part_3/V1P3a.htm.

Chapter 7

Smokeless Tobacco

Spit Tobacco—It's No Game

Sean Marsee of Ada, Oklahoma, lifted weights and ran the 400 meter relay. By the time he was 18 years of age, he had won 28 medals. To keep his body strong, he did not smoke or drink. But he did use smokeless tobacco, because he thought it wasn't harmful to his health.

When oral cancer was discovered, part of Sean's tongue was removed. But the cancer spread. More surgeries followed, including removal of his jaw bone. In his last hours, Sean wrote—he could no longer speak—a plea to his peers: "Don't dip snuff". He died at age 19.

What Is Spit Tobacco?

There are two forms of spit tobacco: chewing tobacco and snuff. Chewing tobacco is usually sold as leaf tobacco (packaged in a pouch) or plug tobacco (in brick form) and both are put between the cheek and gum. Users keep chewing tobacco in their mouths for several hours to get a continuous high from the nicotine in the tobacco.

Snuff is a powdered tobacco (usually sold in cans) that is put between the lower lip and the gum. Just a pinch is all that's needed to

This chapter begins with text reprinted from "Spit Tobacco—It's No Game" with permission of the American Academy of Otolaryngology–Head and Neck Surgery Foundation. Copyright © 2002. All rights reserved. "Women and Smokeless Tobacco Use" is from *NIDA Notes*, National Institute on Drug Abuse (NIDA), Vol. 16, No. 1, March 2001.

release the nicotine, which is then swiftly absorbed into the bloodstream, resulting in a quick high. Sounds OK, right? Not exactly, keep reading.

What's in Spit Tobacco?

Chemicals. Keep in mind that the spit tobacco you or your friends are putting into your mouths contains many chemicals that can have a harmful effect on your health. Here are a few of the ingredients found in spit tobacco:

- Polonium 210 (nuclear waste)
- N-Nitrosamines (cancer-causing)
- Formaldehyde (embalming fluid)
- Nicotine (addictive drug)
- Cadmium (used in car batteries)
- Cyanide
- Arsenic
- Benzene
- Lead (nerve poison)

The chemicals contained in chew or snuff are what make you high. They also make it very hard to quit. Why? Every time you use smokeless tobacco your body adjusts to the amount of tobacco needed to get that high. Then you need a little more tobacco to get the same feeling. You see, your body gets used to the chemicals you give it. Pretty soon you'll need more smokeless tobacco, more often or you'll need stronger spit tobacco to reach the same level. This process is called addiction.

Some people say spit tobacco is OK because there's no smoke, like a cigarette has. Don't believe them. It's not a safe alternative to smoking. You just move health problems from your lungs to your mouth.

Physical and Mental Effects

If you use spit tobacco, here's what you might have to look forward to:

- **Cancer.** Cancer of the mouth (including the lip, tongue, and cheek) and throat. Cancers most frequently occur at the site where tobacco is held in the mouth.

48

- **Leukoplakia.** Whoa, what's this? When you hold tobacco in one place in your mouth, your mouth becomes irritated by the tobacco juice. This causes a white, leathery like patch to form, and this is called leukoplakia. These patches can be different in size, shape, and appearance. They are also considered pre-cancerous. If you find one in your mouth, see your doctor immediately!

- **Heart disease.** The constant flow of nicotine into your body causes many side effects including: increased heart rate, increased blood pressure, and sometimes irregular heart beats (this leads to a greater risk of heart attacks and strokes). Nicotine in the body also causes constricted blood vessels which can slow down reaction time and cause dizziness, not a good move if you play sports.

- **Gum and tooth disease.** Spit tobacco permanently discolors teeth. Chewing tobacco causes halitosis (bad breath). Its direct and repeated contact with the gums causes them to recede, which can cause your teeth to fall out. Spit tobacco contains a lot of sugar which, when mixed with the plaque on your teeth, forms acid that eats away at tooth enamel, causes cavities, and chronic painful sores.

- **Social effects.** The really bad breath, discolored teeth, gunk stuck in your teeth, and constant spitting can have a very negative effect on your social and love life. An even more serious effect of spit tobacco is oral cancer, and the surgery for this could lead to removal of parts of your face, tongue, cheek or lip.

Early Warning Signs

Check your mouth often, looking closely at the places where you hold the tobacco. See your doctor right away if you have any of the following:

- a sore that bleeds easily and doesn't heal
- a lump or thickening anywhere in your mouth or neck
- soreness or swelling that doesn't go away
- a red or white patch that doesn't go away
- trouble chewing, swallowing, or moving your tongue or jaw
- even if you don't find a problem today, see your doctor or dentist every three months to have your mouth checked. Your chances for a cure are higher if oral cancer is found early.

Tips to Quit

You've just read the bad news, but there is good news. Even though it is very difficult to quit using spit tobacco, it can be done. Read the following tips to quit for some helpful ideas to kick the habit. Remember, most people don't start chewing on their own, so don't try quitting on your own. Ask for help and positive reinforcement from your support groups (friends, parents, coaches, teachers, whomever...)

1. Think of reasons why you want to quit. You may want to quit because:

    • You don't want to risk getting cancer.

    • The people around you find it offensive.

    • You don't like having bad breath after chewing and dipping.

    • You don't want stained teeth or no teeth.

    • You don't like being addicted to nicotine.

    • You want to start leading a healthier life.

2. Pick a quit date and throw out all your chewing tobacco and snuff. Tell yourself out loud every day that you're going to quit.

3. Ask your friends, family, teachers, and coaches to help you kick the habit by giving you support and encouragement. Tell friends not to offer you smokeless tobacco. You may want to ask a friend to quit with you.

4. Ask your doctor about a nicotine chewing gum tobacco cessation program.

5. Find alternatives to spit tobacco. A few good examples are sugarless gum, pumpkin or sunflower seeds, apple slices, raisins, or dried fruit.

6. Find activities to keep your mind off of spit tobacco. You could ride a bike, talk or write a letter to a friend, work on a hobby, or listen to music. Exercise can help relieve tension caused by quitting.

7. Remember that everyone is different, so develop a personalized plan that works best for you. Set realistic goals and achieve them.

8. Reward yourself. You could save the money that would have been spent on spit tobacco products and buy something nice for yourself.

Women and Smokeless Tobacco Use

Although more than 90 percent of smokeless tobacco users in the United States are male, a substantial number of women also use smokeless tobacco products. In 1998, 0.5 percent of females over the age of 12, about 573,000, were current users of smokeless tobacco products, according to the National Household Survey on Drug Abuse.

The comparatively small percentage of women who use smokeless tobacco accounts in part for the lack of research on the patterns of smokeless tobacco use among women, says Dr. Dorothy Hatsukami of the University of Minnesota School of Medicine. In addition, "women rarely respond to our advertisements to participate in smokeless tobacco treatment studies," she says. For example, Dr. Hatsukami recently reported that 99.8 percent of 402 people who responded to advertisements for participation in a smokeless tobacco treatment study with the nicotine patch were male.

"Women may be embarrassed about admitting smokeless tobacco use because the general perception is that smokeless tobacco use is socially undesirable, and women don't use it," Dr. Hatsukami speculates. Among the unattractive features of smokeless tobacco use is the need to spit tobacco juice from time to time and dislodge particles of loose tobacco that get trapped between the teeth. This disadvantage of smokeless tobacco use was the one most frequently cited by women who participated in a study of female smokeless tobacco users who weren't seeking treatment, conducted by Dr. Hatsukami and her colleagues.

In the study, 20 female smokeless tobacco users from the upper Midwest completed a questionnaire and brief interview. The study revealed some similarities between females' smokeless tobacco use and what research has shown about males' smokeless tobacco use. For example, on average, both sexes began using smokeless tobacco between 16 and 18, and friends played a major role in their initiating use. About 25 percent of men and women also indicated they used smokeless tobacco to help them stop smoking.

The study also revealed some differences in patterns of smokeless tobacco use by females and the patterns of use reported in a previous study that assessed features of smokeless tobacco use among males who weren't seeking treatment. For example, on average, the women said they used 3.6 dips of moist snuff daily, compared to the 6.3 dips reported by males, and women held the tobacco in their mouths about 22.5 minutes, compared to 39.9 minutes for men. A tin of snuff lasted women anywhere from 2 days to 3 months with a median duration of 6 days per tin. In contrast, men used approximately 2.8 tins per week.

The women in this study may have used less smokeless tobacco than men because they had used smokeless tobacco for less than 4 years, Dr. Hatsukami says. This contrasts with the men, who averaged more than 5 years of smokeless tobacco use. Perceived social disapproval of women using smokeless tobacco also may contribute to lower patterns of use in women. In fact, 38 percent of the women in Dr. Hatsukami's study said they could not use smokeless tobacco in the presence of certain people, and another 25 percent cited social disapproval as a drawback to smokeless tobacco use. These social concerns may reduce opportunities for women to use smokeless tobacco and lead to lower levels of use, Dr. Hatsukami says. In spite of these drawbacks, a significant percentage of women in the study said the relaxing and calming effects and pleasure they associate with smokeless tobacco use are advantages of using these products.

Identifying factors associated with smokeless tobacco use by women and their current patterns of use could generate ways to prevent and treat smokeless tobacco use among women, Dr. Hatsukami says. "The data from this research could help target some of the educational and prevention messages that we should be giving to women," she says. "However, first we have to make women smokeless tobacco users aware that other women use smokeless tobacco products and that they are not abnormal, so they are willing to seek help," she says.

Sources

Boyle, R.G.; Gerend, M.A.; Peterson, C.B.; and Hatsukami, D.K. Use of smokeless tobacco by young adult females. *Journal of Substance Abuse* 10:19-25, 1998. [Abstract]

Hatsukami, D.K.; Keenan, R.M.; and Anton, D.J. Topographical features of smokeless tobacco use. *Psychopharmacology* 96:428-429, 1988.

Chapter 8

Marijuana: Are Hazards Similar to Those for Tobacco?

Marijuana

Marijuana is a green, brown, or gray mixture of dried, shredded leaves, stems, seeds, and flowers of the hemp plant *Cannabis sativa*. Cannabis is a term that refers to marijuana and other drugs made from the same plant. Strong forms of cannabis include sinsemilla (sin-seh-me-yah), hashish ("hash" for short), and hash oil. All forms of cannabis are mind-altering (psychoactive) drugs. They all contain THC (delta-9-tetrahydrocannabinol), the main active chemical in marijuana. They also contain more than 400 other chemicals.

Marijuana's effect on the user depends on the strength or potency of the THC it contains. Most ordinary marijuana has an average of three percent THC. Sinsemilla (made from just the buds and flowering tops of female plants) has an average of 7.5 percent THC, with a range as high as 24 percent. Hashish (the sticky resin from the female plant flowers) has an average of 3.6 percent, with a range as high as 28 percent. Hash oil, a tar-like liquid distilled from hashish, has an average of 16 percent, with a range as high as 43 percent.

"Marijuana" by Melisse Leung, Premedical Student, University of California, Berkeley, is reprinted with permission from the American Medical Student Association, www.amsa.org. Copyright © 1998 American Medical Student Association; reviewed and revised by David A. Cooke, M.D., on May 9, 2004. This chapter also includes "Study Finds Marijuana Ingredient Promotes Tumor Growth, Impairs Anti-Tumor Defenses," a NIDA News Release, National Institute on Drug Abuse (NIDA), June 20, 2000.

Route of Administration

Marijuana is usually smoked as a cigarette. Most users roll loose marijuana into a cigarette (called a joint or a nail) or smoke it in a pipe. One well-known type of water pipe is the bong. Some users mix marijuana into foods or use it to brew a tea. Another method is to slice open a cigar and replace the tobacco with marijuana, making what is called a blunt. When the blunt is smoked with a 40 oz. bottle of malt liquor, it is called a "B-40." Lately, marijuana cigarettes or blunts often include crack cocaine, a combination known by various street names, such as "primos" or "woolies." Joints and blunts often are dipped in PCP and are called "happy sticks," "wicky sticks," "love boat," or "tical."

Effect on Body (Pathology, Pathophysiology)

Marijuana cigarettes contain four to five times as much of certain cancer-causing substances as tobacco cigarettes. Marijuana has more than 400 different chemicals, many of which are dangerous. It is a dangerous, addictive drug that acts like both a stimulant and a depressant. It makes the heart beat faster, lowers body temperature, increases hunger, slows down the ability to react, and interferes with the proper working of muscles. Marijuana is very harmful, poisoning the structures that trigger cells to grow and replace themselves. Marijuana smokers also seem more likely to get sick than are people who stay away from the drug, so it seems that the drug weakens the body's ability to fight germs. Users have personality problems that include loss of mental energy, lack of interest in everyday things, loss of concentration, and difficulty in recalling events and actions.

The effects of marijuana on each person depend on the type of cannabis, how much THC it contains, the way the drug is taken (by smoking or eating), the experience and expectations of the user, the setting where the drug is used and whether drinking or other drug use is also going on. Some people feel nothing at all when they first try marijuana while others may feel high (intoxicated and/or euphoric). Usually within a few minutes of inhaling marijuana smoke, the user will feel its effects. Along with intoxication, the user will experience a dry mouth, rapid heartbeat, increased appetite, some loss of coordination and poor sense of balance, and slower reaction time. Blood vessels in the eye expand, so the user's eyes look red. For some people, marijuana raises blood pressure slightly and can double the normal heart rate. This effect can be greater when other drugs are mixed with marijuana; but users do not always know when that happens. As the immediate effects fade, usually after two to three hours, the user may become sleepy.

It is common for marijuana users to feel happy and calm, although depression sometimes occurs. Users become engrossed with ordinary sights, sounds, or tastes, and trivial events may seem extremely interesting or funny. Time seems to pass very slowly, so minutes feel like hours. Sights and sounds become more vivid, imagination increases and random connections between things seem more relevant. Sometimes the drug causes the users to feel thirsty and very hungry— an effect called "the munchies."

A user can also have a bad reaction to marijuana. Some users, especially someone new to the drug or in a strange setting, may suffer acute anxiety, have paranoid thoughts and illusions. This is more likely to happen with high doses of THC. In some cases, true psychosis (loss of contact with reality) occurs, producing paranoid delusions, confusion, and other symptoms. These scary feelings usually disappear within several days as the effects of the drug wear off. In rare cases, a user who has taken a very high dose of the drug can have severe psychotic symptoms and need emergency medical treatment. Other kinds of bad reactions can occur when marijuana is mixed with other drugs, such as PCP or cocaine.

THC in marijuana is readily absorbed by the fatty tissues in various organs. The drug does not dissolve in water, so it can stay in the body for as long as three weeks. Generally, traces (metabolites) of THC can be detected by standard urine testing methods several days after a smoking session. However, in heavy, chronic users, traces can sometimes be detected for weeks after they have stopped using marijuana.

Marijuana can be harmful in a number of ways, through both immediate effects and damage to health over time. Marijuana hinders the user's short-term memory (memory for recent events), concentration, learning abilities, and he or she may have trouble handling complex tasks. In 1982, the Georgetown University School of Medicine found that memory loss can stay with teens for up to six weeks after they stop smoking the drug. The drug has also been found to affect speaking and concentration and to slow reaction time. It also leads to a drop in motivation, and this creates poor grades, loss of self-esteem, and loss of career goals. With the use of more potent varieties of marijuana, even performing simple tasks can be difficult. Marijuana also impairs reaction time, perception, judgment, and the coordination and motor skills necessary to drive a car, so users could be involved in auto crashes. The user may experience distorted perception (sights, sounds, time, touch) and have trouble with thinking and problem-solving. There can be loss of coordination and increased heart rate and anxiety. Drug users also may become involved in risky sexual behavior. There is a strong link between drug use and unsafe sex and the spread of HIV, the virus that causes AIDS. Under the influence of marijuana, students may find it hard to study and learn. Young athletes could find their performance is off; timing, movements, and coordination are all affected by THC. Another damaging effect of regular marijuana use by teens is that it can slow down the body's rate of development by lowering the level of hormones the body produces.

Organ Systems Most Affected by This Substance

As marijuana is inhaled and held in the lungs, repeated use can damage the lungs and heart. Marijuana users may have many of the same respiratory problems that tobacco smokers have, such as chronic bronchitis and inflamed sinuses. While all of the long-term effects of marijuana use are not yet known, there are studies showing serious health concerns. For example, a group of scientists in California examined the health status of 450 daily smokers of marijuana but not tobacco. They found that the marijuana smokers had more sick days and more doctor visits for respiratory problems and other types of illness than did a similar group who did not smoke either substance. As to long-term effects of marijuana use, findings so far show that the regular use of marijuana or THC may play a role in cancer and problems in the respiratory, immune, and nervous systems.

It is hard to find out whether marijuana alone causes cancer because many people who smoke marijuana also smoke cigarettes and use other drugs. Marijuana smoke contains some of the same cancer-causing compounds as tobacco, sometimes in higher concentrations. Studies show that someone who smokes five joints per week may be taking in as many cancer-causing chemicals as someone who smokes a full pack of cigarettes every day. Tobacco smoke and marijuana smoke may work together to change the tissues lining the respiratory tract. Marijuana smoking could contribute to early development of head and neck cancer in some people.

Our immune system protects the body from many agents that cause disease. It is not certain whether marijuana damages the immune system of people. But both animal and human studies have shown that marijuana impairs the ability of T-cells in the lungs' immune defense system to fight off some infections. People with HIV and others whose immune system is impaired should avoid marijuana use.

People who smoke marijuana often develop the same kinds of breathing problems that cigarette smokers have. They have symptoms of daily cough and phlegm (chronic bronchitis) and more frequent chest colds. They are also at greater risk of getting lung infections such as pneumonia. Continued marijuana smoking can lead to abnormal function of the lungs and airways. Scientists have found signs of lung tissue that was injured or destroyed by marijuana smoke.

Marijuana smoking also affects the brain and leads to impaired short-term memory, perception, judgment, attention, learning, and motor skills. THC affects the nerve cells in the part of the brain where memories are formed. This makes it hard for the user to recall recent events (such as what happened a few minutes ago). It is hard to learn while high—a working short-term memory is required for learning and performing tasks that call for more than one or two steps. Among a group of long-time heavy marijuana users in Costa Rica, researchers found that the people had great trouble when asked to recall a short list of words (a standard test of memory). People in that study group also found it very hard to focus their attention on the tests given to them.

Smoking marijuana causes some changes in the brain that are like those caused by cocaine, heroin, and alcohol. Some researchers believe that these changes may put a person more at risk of becoming addicted to other drugs, such as cocaine or heroin. Long-term studies of high school students and their patterns of drug use show that very few young people use other illegal drugs without first trying marijuana. For example, the risk of using cocaine is 104 times greater for those who have tried marijuana than for those who have never tried it. Using marijuana puts children and teens in contact with people who are users and sellers of other drugs. So there is more of a risk that a marijuana user will be exposed to and urged to try more drugs.

Many researchers fear that marijuana damages brain cells, and the long-term effects are still being researched. In laboratory research, scientists found that high doses of THC given to young rats caused a loss of brain cells such as that seen with aging. At 11 or 12 months of age (about half their normal life span), the rats' brains looked like those of animals in old age. It is not known whether a similar effect occurs in humans. Researchers are still learning about the many ways that marijuana could affect the brain.

Scientists do not yet know how the use of marijuana relates to mental illness. It is known that rates of mental illness are higher among marijuana users. Mental illness is also more likely to appear for the first time in heavy marijuana users. However, it remains unclear whether marijuana use increases risk of mental illness, or if people predisposed to mental illness are more likely to use marijuana. Some researchers in Sweden report that regular, long-term intake of THC (from cannabis) can increase the risk of developing certain mental diseases, such as schizophrenia. Others maintain that regular marijuana use can lead to chronic anxiety, personality disturbances, and depression. Some frequent, long-term marijuana users show signs of a lack of motivation (amotivational syndrome). Their problems include not caring about what happens in their lives, no desire to work regularly, fatigue, and a lack of concern about how they look. As a result of these symptoms, some users tend to perform poorly in school or at work.

Secondary Effects of Marijuana Use

Marijuana has adverse effects on many of the skills for driving a car. Driving while high can lead to car accidents. This is because marijuana affects many skills required for safe driving: alertness, the ability to concentrate, coordination, and reaction time. These effects can last up to 24 hours after smoking marijuana. Marijuana use can make it difficult to judge distances and react to signals and sounds on the road. There is data showing that marijuana can play an important role in crashes. When users combine marijuana with alcohol, as they often do, the hazards of driving can be more severe than with either drug alone.

A study of patients in a shock-trauma unit who had been in traffic accidents revealed that 15 percent of those who had been driving a car or motorcycle had been smoking marijuana, and another 17 percent had both THC and alcohol in their blood. In one study conducted in Memphis, Tennessee, researchers found that of 150 reckless drivers who were tested for drugs at the arrest scene, 33 percent tested positive for marijuana, and 12 percent tested positive for both marijuana and cocaine. Data also show that while smoking marijuana, people show the same lack of coordination on standard "drunk driver" tests as do people who have had too much to drink.

Doctors advise pregnant women not to use any drugs because they might harm the growing fetus. One animal study has linked marijuana use to loss of the fetus very early in pregnancy. Some scientific studies have found that babies born to marijuana users were shorter, weighed less, and had smaller head sizes than those born to mothers who did not use the drug. Smaller babies are more likely to develop health problems. Other scientists have found effects of marijuana that resemble the features of fetal alcohol syndrome. There are also research findings that show nervous system problems in children of mothers who smoked marijuana.

Researchers are not certain whether a newborn baby's health problems, if they are caused by marijuana, will continue as the child grows. Preliminary research shows that children born to mothers who used marijuana regularly during pregnancy may have trouble concentrating. When a nursing mother uses marijuana, some of the THC is passed to the baby in her breast milk. This is a matter for concern, since the THC in the mother's milk is much more concentrated than that in the mother's blood. One study has shown that the use of marijuana by a mother during the first month of breastfeeding can impair the infant's motor development (control of muscle movement).

> —*Information by Melisse Leung, Premedical Student*
> *at University of California, Berkeley*

Study Finds Marijuana Ingredient Promotes Tumor Growth, Impairs Anti-Tumor Defenses

Researchers report in the July 2000 issue of the *Journal of Immunology* that tetrahydrocannabinol (THC), the major psychoactive component of marijuana, can promote tumor growth by impairing the body's anti-tumor immunity system. While previous research has shown that THC can lower resistance to both bacterial and viral infections, this is the first time that its possible tumor-promoting activity has been reported.

A team of researchers at UCLA's Jonsson Comprehensive Cancer Center found in experiments in mice that THC limits immune response by increasing the availability of two forms (IL-10 and TGF-ß) of cytokine, a potent, tumor-specific, immunity suppresser.

The authors also suggest that smoking marijuana may be more of a cancer risk than smoking tobacco. The tar portion of marijuana smoke, compared to that of tobacco, contains higher concentrations of carcinogenic hydrocarbons, including benzopyrene, a key factor in promoting human lung cancer. And marijuana smoke deposits four times as much tar in the respiratory tract as does a comparable amount of tobacco, thus increasing exposure to carcinogens.

Dr. Steven M. Dubinett, head of the research team that conducted the study, says, "What we already know about marijuana smoke, coupled with our new finding that THC may encourage tumor growth, suggests that regular use of marijuana may increase the risk of respiratory tract cancer and further studies will be needed to evaluate this possibility."

The UCLA researchers examined the effects of THC on the immune response to lung cancer in mice. Over a two-week period, the animals were injected four times per week with either THC or a saline solution. Fourteen days after the injections were started, murine Lewis lung cancer and line 1 alveolar cell cancer cells were implanted in the mice. The mice continued to receive THC or saline injections after the tumor cells were implanted, and tumor growth was assessed three times each week. To test the hypothesis that THC impairs tumor-specific immune system response, a group of mice with compromised immune systems was also studied.

The researchers found that in the mice with normal immune systems there was significant enhancement of tumor growth, but THC had no effect on tumor growth in the immunodeficient mice. The study also showed that when lymphocytes from the THC-treated mice were injected into untreated mice, the immune deficit was transferred and tumor growth was accelerated in the normal controls.

Additionally, the UCLA research team demonstrated that when anti-IL-10 and anti-TGF-ß were administered, there was no acceleration of tumor growth in THC-treated mice. These results suggest that enhanced tumor growth is prompted by THC's ability to stimulate production of IL-10 and TGF-ß, which inhibits anti-tumor immune response.

Chapter 9

Tobacco Use Statistics

Cigarette Smoking Among U.S. Adults

One of the national health objectives for the United States for 2010 is to reduce the prevalence of cigarette smoking among adults to 12% or less.[1] To assess progress toward this objective, the Centers for Disease Control and Prevention (CDC) analyzed self-reported data from the 2001 National Health Interview Survey (NHIS). The findings of this analysis indicate that, in 2001, approximately 22.8% of U.S. adults were current smokers compared with 25.0% in 1993. During 1965–2001, smoking prevalence declined faster among non-Hispanic blacks aged 18 years and older than among non-Hispanic whites the same age. Preliminary data for January–March 2002 indicate a continuing decline in current smoking prevalence among adults overall.[2] However,

This chapter includes excerpts from "Cigarette Smoking Among Adults— United States, 2001," *Morbidity and Mortality Weekly Report (MMWR)*, Centers for Disease Control and Prevention (CDC), 52(40);953–956, October 10, 2003. The complete document, including information about statistical calculations, can be found online at www.cdc.gov/mmwr/preview/mmwrhtml/mm5240a1.htm. Additional information is also included from "Smoking Prevalence among U.S. Adults," National Center for Chronic Disease Prevention and Health Promotion, CDC, reviewed October 2003; "Tobacco Use, Income, and Educational Level," *The NHSDA Report*, National Household Survey on Drug Abuse (NHSDA, Substance Abuse and Mental Health Services Administration (SAMHSA), updated May 2003; and excerpts from *Results from the 2002 National Survey on Drug Use and Health: National Findings*, Office of Applied Studies, NHSDA Series H-22, DHHS Publication No. SMA 03-3836. Rockville, MD: SAMHSA.

the overall decline in smoking is not occurring at a rate that will meet the national health objective by 2010. Increased emphasis on a comprehensive approach to cessation that comprises educational, economic, clinical, and regulatory strategies is required to further reduce the prevalence of smoking in the United States.

The 2001 NHIS adult core questionnaire was administered by personal interview to a nationally representative sample of the U.S. civilian, noninstitutionalized population aged 18 years and older; the overall survey response rate was 73.8%. Respondents were asked, "Have you smoked 100 or more cigarettes in your entire life?" and those who answered "yes" were asked, "Do you now smoke cigarettes every day, some days, or not at all?" Ever smokers were those who reported having smoked 100 or more cigarettes during their lifetime. Current smokers were persons who reported both having smoked 100 or more cigarettes during their lifetime and currently smoking every day or some days. Former smokers were ever smokers who currently did not smoke. Data were adjusted for nonresponses and weighted to provide national estimates of cigarette smoking prevalence.

In 2001, an estimated 46.2 million adults (22.8%) were current smokers; of these an estimated 37.8 million (81.8%) smoked every day, and 8.4 million (18.2%) smoked some days. Of current smokers who smoked every day, an estimated 15.3 million (40.6%) had stopped smoking for one or more days during the preceding 12 months because they were trying to quit. In 2001, an estimated 44.7 million adults were former smokers, representing 49.2% of persons who had ever smoked.

The prevalence of cigarette smoking was higher among men (25.2%) than women (20.7%. Among racial/ethnic populations, Asians, excluding native Hawaiians and other Pacific islanders (12.4%) and Hispanics (16.7%) had the lowest prevalence of current smoking; American Indians/Alaska Natives (AI/ANs) had the highest prevalence (32.7%. By education level, adults who had earned a General Educational Development diploma (47.8%) and those with a grade 9–11 education (34.3%) had the highest prevalence of smoking; persons with master's, professional, and doctoral degrees had the lowest prevalence (9.5%). Current smoking prevalence was highest among persons aged 18–24 years (26.9%) and among those aged 25–44 years (25.8%) and lowest among those aged 65 years and older (10.1%). The prevalence of current smoking was higher among adults living below the poverty level (31.4%) than those at or above the poverty level (23.0%).

Comparing current smoking prevalence data from 1965–1966 and 2000–2001 indicates a slow but steady decrease among non-Hispanic blacks and whites. Since 1970–1974, prevalence has declined more rapidly among non-Hispanic black men than among non-Hispanic white men. During 2000–2001, for the first time, current smoking prevalence among non-Hispanic black men was similar to that among non-Hispanic white men. Smoking prevalence also declined more rapidly among non-Hispanic black women than non-Hispanic white

Table 9.1. Percentage of current smokers (persons who reported having smoked 100 or more cigarettes during their lifetime and who reported currently smoking every day or some days during the previous 30 days) aged 18 and older, by selected characteristics.

Characteristic	Men	Women	Total
Race/Ethnicity			
White, non-Hispanic	25.4	22.8	24.0
Black, non-Hispanic	27.7	17.2	22.3
Hispanic	21.6	11.9	16.7
American Indian/Alaska Native	33.5	31.7	32.7
Asian*	18.5	6.3	12.4
Education**			
0–12 years (no diploma)	32.2	23.3	28.4
General Education Development (diploma)	47.9	47.7	47.8
12 years (diploma)	29.3	23.4	26.1
Associate degree	23.7	19.8	21.6
Some college (no degree)	26.6	22.1	24.2
Undergraduate degree	13.3	11.2	12.3
Graduate degree	9.0	10.0	9.5
Age Group (years)			
18–24	30.4	23.4	26.9
25–44	27.3	24.5	25.8
45–64	26.4	21.4	23.8
65 and older	11.5	9.2	10.1
Poverty Level			
At or above	25.1	21.0	23.0
Below	36.2	28.1	31.4
Unknown	22.0	17.1	19.3
Total	25.2	20.7	22.8

* Excludes native Hawaiians and other Pacific islanders.

** Persons aged 25 and older, excluding those with an unknown number of years of education women. Before 1993–1995, current smoking prevalences among non-Hispanic black and white women generally were comparable, except during 1970–1974, when prevalence among non-Hispanic white women was lower. Since 1993–1995, prevalence among non-Hispanic black women has been lower, except during 1997–1999, when no difference was observed.

—*Reported by: T Woollery, PhD, A Trosclair, MS, C Husten, MD, RC Caraballo, PhD, J Kahende, PhD, Office on Smoking and Health, National Center for Chronic Disease Prevention and Health Promotion, CDC.*

Comments

The findings in this report indicate that smoking prevalence has declined among adults since 1965. Although selected population groups have met the national health objective for 2010, slow or no progress has been observed in other sections of the U.S. population.[3] For this reason, the overall decline in cigarette smoking prevalence in the adult U.S. population is not occurring at a rate that will meet the 2010 national health objective.

The findings in this report are subject to at least three limitations. First, questionnaire wording and NHIS data collection procedures have changed since 1993. Because of these changes, trend analyses or comparisons with data from years preceding 1993 should be interpreted with caution. Second, in 1997, the Office of Management and Budget changed its data collection guidelines to require that data on Asians and Native Hawaiians and Other Pacific Islanders be collected separately. For this reason, trend data on smoking prevalence for the combined category of Asians/Pacific Islanders cannot be estimated by using publicly available data. Finally, because NHIS data for some subpopulations (for example, AI/ANs) are small, data for a single year might be unstable. Combining data from several years would produce more reliable estimates for these subpopulations.

Comprehensive tobacco-control programs at the state level have helped to reduce tobacco use.[4] In 2000, the U.S. Surgeon General concluded that the 2010 objective could be attained only if comprehensive approaches to tobacco control were implemented.[5] In 2002, six states were funding comprehensive programs at the minimum levels recommended by CDC.[6] In 2002 and 2003, state budget cuts reduced state support for tobacco-prevention and -cessation programs by $86.2 million (11.2%).[7] To attain the 2010 national health objective, comprehensive tobacco-control programs that meet CDC's recommended funding levels are needed.[5,8–10] Within these comprehensive programs, a focus on reducing tobacco use among persons in different socioeconomic strata, racial/ethnic populations, and education levels could help reduce cigarette smoking and tobacco use and reduce the substantial morbidity and mortality and economic costs associated with tobacco use.

References

1. U.S. Department of Health and Human Services. *Healthy people 2010, 2nd ed. With understanding and improving health and objectives for improving health (2 vols.).* Washington, DC: U.S. Department of Health and Human Services, 2000.

2. CDC. Early release of selected estimates from the National Health Interview Survey (NHIS). Available at http://www.cdc.gov/nchs/about/major/nhis/released200207/about.htm.

3. CDC. Surveillance for selected tobacco-use behaviors—United States, 1900–1994. In: CDC Surveillance Summaries (November 18). *MMWR* 1994;43(No. SS-3).

4. Farrelly MC, Pechacek TF, Chaloupka FJ. The impact of tobacco control program expenditures on aggregate cigarette sales: 1981–2000. *Health Econ* 2003;22:843–59.

5. U.S. Department of Health and Human Services. *Reducing tobacco use: a report of the Surgeon General.* Atlanta, Georgia: U.S. Department of Health and Human Services, CDC, National Center for Chronic Disease Prevention and Health Promotion, Office on Smoking and Health, 2000.

6. CDC. *Tobacco control state highlights 2002: impact and opportunity.* Atlanta, Georgia: U.S. Department of Health and Human Services, CDC, National Center for Chronic Disease Prevention and Health Promotion, Office on Smoking and Health, 2002.

7. Campaign for Tobacco-Free Kids. Show us the money: a report on the states' allocation of the tobacco settlement dollars. Available at http://tobaccofreekids.org/reports/settlements/2003/fullreport.pdf.

8. CDC. *Best practices for comprehensive tobacco control programs—August 1999.* Atlanta, Georgia: U.S. Department of Health and Human Services, CDC, National Center for

Chronic Disease Prevention and Health Promotion, Office on Smoking and Health, 1999.

9. Fiore MC, Bailey WC, Cohen SJ, et al. *Treating tobacco use and dependence: clinical practice guideline.* Rockville, Maryland: U.S. Department of Health and Human Services, Public Health Service, 2000.

10. Task Force on Community Preventive Services. Recommendations regarding interventions to reduce tobacco use and exposure to environmental tobacco smoke. *Am J Prev Med* 2001;20:10–5.

Trends in Smoking Prevalence among U.S. Adults

In 2001, an estimated 46.2 million adults 18 years of age and older were current smokers in the United States. Overall prevalence of current smoking represents a modest and statistically significant reduction from 1993 (25.0%) to 2001 (22.8%). During this period of time, smoking among the adult male population declined from 27.7 to 25.2%; adult female smoking declined from 22.5 to 20.7%.

Overall, the decline in cigarette smoking prevalence in the adult U.S. population is not occurring at a rate that will meet the 2010 national health objective of 12 percent. Sustaining or increasing implementation of comprehensive tobacco control programs to meet the CDC recommended funding levels are necessary to attain the 2010 national objective.

Tobacco Use, Income, and Educational Level

• In 1999 and 2000, past month use of most tobacco products was more common among persons from families with lower incomes than among persons from families with higher incomes.

• Rates of past month use of most tobacco products were higher among persons with lower levels of education than among those with higher levels of education.

• Past month cigarette use was lowest at all income levels among persons who had completed college.

The National Household Survey on Drug Abuse (NHSDA) asks respondents to report their use of tobacco products during the month before the survey interview. Tobacco products include cigarettes, cigars, smokeless tobacco (chewing tobacco or snuff), and pipe tobacco.

Respondents are also asked for their total combined family income for the previous calendar year and for the highest grade or year of school they had completed. This report focuses on responses of persons aged 18 or older to estimate the prevalence of tobacco use across different levels of income and education. Analyses of the relationships between tobacco use and income and educational level are based on data combined from the 1999 and 2000 surveys.

Table 9.2. Percentage of Smoking Prevalence Among U.S. Adults, 18 Years of Age and Older, 1955–2001.

Year	Overall Population	Males	Females	Whites	Blacks
1955	——	56.9	28.4	——	——
1965	42.4	51.9	33.9	42.1	45.8
1966	42.6	52.5	33.9	42.4	45.9
1970	37.4	44.1	31.5	37.0	41.4
1974	37.1	43.1	32.1	36.4	44.0
1978	34.1	38.1	30.7	33.9	37.7
1979	33.5	37.5	29.9	33.3	36.9
1980	33.2	37.6	29.3	32.9	36.9
1983	32.1	35.1	29.5	31.8	35.9
1985	30.1	32.6	27.9	29.6	34.9
1987	28.8	31.2	26.5	28.5	32.9
1988	28.1	30.8	25.7	27.8	31.7
1990	25.5	28.4	22.8	25.6	26.2
1991	25.7	28.1	23.5	25.5	29.1
1992*	26.5	28.6	24.6	26.6	27.8
1993	25.0	27.7	22.5	24.9	26.1
1994	25.5	28.2	23.1	26.3	27.2
1995	24.7	27.0	22.6	25.6	25.8
1997	24.7	27.6	22.1	25.3	26.7
1998	24.1	26.4	22.0	25.0	24.7
1999	23.5	25.7	21.5	24.3	24.3
2000	23.3	25.7	21.0	24.1	23.2
2001	22.8	25.2	20.7	24.0	22.3

*Estimates since 1992 incorporate some-day smokers (people who do not smoke every day).

Prevalence of Tobacco Use

According to the 2000 NHSDA, an estimated 62 million persons aged 18 or older (31 percent) had used one or more tobacco products during the past month. Approximately 53 million (26 percent) smoked cigarettes, 10 million (5 percent) smoked cigars, 7 million (4 percent) used smokeless tobacco, and 2 million (1 percent) smoked pipes.

Tobacco Use and Income

Persons aged 18 or older from lower-income families were more likely than persons from families with higher incomes to use most tobacco products in the past month. For example, 35 percent of persons with total combined family incomes of less than $9,000 reported smoking cigarettes during the past month compared with 29 percent of those from families with incomes between $20,000 and $39,999 and 19 percent of those from families with incomes of $75,000 or more. Persons with total combined family incomes of less than $75,000 were more likely than those with incomes of $75,000 or more to use smokeless tobacco during the past month. Similarly, persons with total combined family incomes of less than $20,000 were more likely than those with total incomes of more than $20,000 to smoke pipes during the past month. In contrast, persons with total combined family incomes of $75,000 or more were more likely than those with incomes between $9,000 and $74,999 to smoke cigars during the past month.

Tobacco Use and Educational Level

Persons aged 18 or older with lower levels of completed education were more likely than those with higher levels of education to use most tobacco products during the past month. For example, 33 percent of persons who did not complete high school reported past month cigarette use compared with 28 percent of those who completed between one and three years of college and 14 percent of those who completed four years of college. (According to the combined 1999 and 2000 NHSDA data, approximately 18 percent of persons aged 18 or older who reported that they completed less than four years of college were current college students when the survey interview was administered.) Almost 5 percent of persons who did not complete 12th grade reported past month smokeless tobacco use compared with 2 percent of those who completed four years of college. In contrast, persons who completed between one and three years of college were more likely to report past month cigar use than persons at any other educational level. The prevalence of past month pipe use was low for all educational levels, but persons without a high school education were more likely to report past month pipe use than persons who had completed at least high school.

Cigarette Use, Income, and Educational Level

Because persons with higher levels of education generally have higher incomes, the relationship between income, educational level, and tobacco use was examined. Among persons who had completed at least some college, past month cigarette use was generally higher among persons from families with lower incomes than among those from families with higher incomes. Among persons who had completed a high school education or less, past month cigarette use was not consistently related to income level. Past month cigarette use was lowest at all income levels among college graduates.

About NHSDA

The National Household Survey on Drug Abuse (NHSDA) is an annual survey sponsored by the Substance Abuse and Mental Health Services Administration (SAMHSA). The 1999 and 2000 data are based on information obtained from nearly 142,000 persons aged 12 or older (about 70,000 each year). The survey collects data by administering questionnaires to a representative sample of the population through face-to-face interviews at their place of residence.

Information and data for this report are based on the following publications and statistics:

Substance Abuse and Mental Health Services Administration. (2000) *Summary of findings from the 1999 National Household Survey on Drug Abuse* (National Household Survey on Drug Abuse Series: H-12, DHHS Publication No. SMA 00-3466). Rockville, MD: Author.

Substance Abuse and Mental Health Services Administration (2001). *Summary of findings from the 2000 National Household Survey on Drug Abuse* (National Household Survey on Drug Abuse Series: H-13, DHHS Publication No. SMA 01-3549). Rockville, MD: Author. Also available on-line at http://www.drugabusestatistics.samhsa.gov.

Kopstein, A. (2001). *Tobacco use in America: Findings from the 1999 National Household Survey on Drug Abuse* (Analytic Series: A-15, DHHS Publication No. SMA 02-3622). Rockville, MD: Substance Abuse and Mental Health Services Administration, Office of Applied Studies. Also available on-line at http://www.samhsa.gov/oas/NHSDA/tobacco.pdf.

Additional tables are available online at http://www.samhsa.gov/oas/nhsda/2kdetailedtabs/Vol_1_Part_2/V1P2.htm.

This report may be downloaded from http://www.samhsa.gov/oas/nhsda.htm. Other reports from the Office of Applied Studies are also available on-line at http://www.drugabusestatistics.samhsa.gov.

National Survey on Drug Use and Health

The National Survey on Drug Use and Health (NSDUH) includes a series of questions asking about the use of several tobacco products, including cigarettes, chewing tobacco, snuff, cigars, and pipe tobacco. For analysis purposes, data for chewing tobacco and snuff are combined and referred to as "smokeless tobacco." Cigarette use is defined as smoking "part or all of a cigarette." Findings from the 2002 NSDUH are summarized below.

- An estimated 71.5 million Americans reported current use (past month use) of a tobacco product in 2002, a prevalence rate of 30.4 percent for the population aged 12 or older.

- Among that same population, 61.1 million (26.0 percent of the total population aged 12 or older) smoked cigarettes, 12.8 million (5.4 percent) smoked cigars, 7.8 million (3.3 percent) used smokeless tobacco, and 1.8 million (0.8 percent) smoked tobacco in pipes.

Age and Gender

- Young adults aged 18 to 25 continued to report the highest rate (45.3 percent) of use of tobacco products. Past month rates of use for this age group were 40.8 percent for cigarettes, 11.0 percent for cigars, 4.8 percent for smokeless tobacco, and 1.1 percent for pipes.

- Current cigarette smoking rates increased steadily by year of age up to age 21, from 1.7 percent at age 12 to 4.7 percent at age 13, 8.5 percent at age 14, 14.1 percent at age 15, 21.9 percent at age 16, and 28.1 percent at age 17. The rate peaked at 46.2 percent at age 21. After age 21, rates generally declined, reaching 19.9 percent for persons aged 60 to 64 years and 10.3 percent for persons aged 65 or older. By age group, the prevalence of cigarette use was 13.0 percent among 12 to 17 year olds, 40.8

Table 9.3. Past Month Tobacco Use among Persons Aged 12 or Older: 2002

Product	Percent Using in Past Month
Any Tobacco	30.4
Cigarettes	26.0
Smokeless Tobacco	3.3
Cigars	5.4
Pipes	0.8

Table 9.4. Past Month Tobacco Use among Persons Aged 12 or Older, by Age Group: 2002

Age and Gender	Percent Using in Past Month
12–17 years, Male	12.3
12–17 years, Female	13.6
18–25 years, Male	44.4
18–25 years, Female	37.1
26+ years, Male	28.3
26+ years, Female	22.5

percent among young adults aged 18 to 25 years, and 25.2 percent among adults aged 26 or older.

• As was found in prior surveys, males were more likely than females to report past month use of any tobacco product. In 2002, 37.0 percent of males aged 12 or older were current users of any tobacco product, a significantly higher proportion than among females (24.3 percent).

• A higher proportion of males than females aged 12 or older smoked cigarettes in 2002 (28.7 vs. 23.4 percent). However, among youths aged 12 to 17, girls were slightly more likely than boys to smoke (13.6 vs. 12.3 percent).

• Males were much more likely than their female counterparts to report current use of smokeless tobacco (6.4 percent of males aged 12 or older vs. 0.4 percent of females).

71

- As seen for smokeless tobacco, males were more likely than females to report past month cigar use. Specifically, males aged 12 or older were more than 5 times as likely as females to report past month use of cigars (9.4 vs. 1.7 percent).

- In 2002, 17.3 percent of pregnant women aged 15 to 44 smoked cigarettes in the past month compared with 31.1 percent of non-pregnant women of the same age group.

- Young adults aged 18 to 22 enrolled full time in college in 2002 were less likely to report current cigarette use than their peers not enrolled full time (this category includes part-time college students and persons not enrolled in college). Past month cigarette use was reported by 32.6 percent of full-time college students compared with 45.8 percent of their peers who were not enrolled full time.

Employment Status

- Rates of current cigarette smoking were 49.8 percent for unemployed adults aged 18 or older in 2002 compared with 27.2 percent of adults working part time and 29.6 percent of full-time employed adults.

- Rates of smokeless tobacco use by employment status in 2002 displayed a somewhat different pattern from the rates of cigarette use. The rates of past month smokeless tobacco use among persons aged 18 or older were 4.1 percent among unemployed persons, 2.2 percent among part-time workers, and 4.5 percent for those employed full time.

Geographic Area

- Cigarette use rates among persons aged 12 or older varied by region of the country. Past month cigarette use ranged from a low of 21.0 percent for persons living in the Pacific division to 28.7 percent of persons living in the East South Central part of the country.

- Rates of current cigarette use among persons aged 12 or older were higher in less densely populated areas. In large metropolitan areas, 24.6 percent smoked in the past month compared with 27.1 percent in small metropolitan areas and 27.9 percent in nonmetropolitan areas. The rate of smoking was 30.6 percent in completely rural nonmetropolitan areas. For youths aged 12 to

17 in large metropolitan areas, 11.0 percent smoked in the past month compared with 20.7 percent of youths in completely rural nonmetropolitan areas.

Frequency of Cigarette Use

- Of the 61.1 million past month cigarette smokers, 63.4 percent (38.7 million) reported smoking every day in the past 30 days. Among youths aged 12 to 17 who smoked in the past month, 31.8 percent (1 million) were daily smokers. The percentage of smokers who were daily smokers increased with age to 51.8 percent for 18–25-year-old smokers and to 68.8 percent for smokers aged 26 or older.

- Although 52.9 percent of all daily smokers aged 12 or older smoked a pack or more of cigarettes a day, 21.6 percent of daily smokers aged 12 to 17 reported doing so.

Association with Illicit Drug and Alcohol Use

- Current (past month) cigarette smokers were more likely to use other tobacco products, alcohol, and illicit drugs than current nonsmokers. Comparing current smokers with current nonsmokers, rates of binge alcohol use were 43.1 versus 15.8 percent, rates of heavy alcohol use were 15.9 versus 3.5 percent, and rates of current (past month) illicit drug use were 19.5 versus 4.4 percent. Rates of use of other tobacco products were 1.7 times higher for

Table 9.5. Past Month Any Illicit Drug, Binge Alcohol, and Heavy Alcohol Use among Smokers and Nonsmokers Aged 12 or Older: 2002

Substance Use Status	Percent Using in Past Month
Any Illicit Drug	
Smokers	19.5
Nonsmokers	4.4
Binge Alcohol Use	
Smokers	43.1
Nonsmokers	15.8
Heavy Alcohol Use	
Smokers	15.9
Nonsmokers	3.5

73

smokeless tobacco and 3.9 times higher for cigars among current smokers compared with current nonsmokers.

Usual Brand of Cigarettes Smoked

- There were notable racial/ethnic differences with regard to brand of cigarettes smoked most often in the past month. In 2002, almost half of white smokers aged 12 or older (43.6 percent) and more than half of Hispanic smokers (56.9 percent) reported smoking Marlboro cigarettes. Among black smokers, only 6.0 percent smoked Marlboro cigarettes, while 49.4 percent smoked Newport cigarettes.

- Three brands accounted for most of the youth cigarette smoking in 2002. Among current smokers who were 12 to 17 years of age, 49.8 percent reported Marlboro as their usual brand, 25.1 percent reported Newport, and 10.5 percent reported Camel. No other individual cigarette brand was reported by more than 2.2 percent of these youths.

- Racial/ethnic differences in usual cigarette brand used also were evident among youth smokers aged 12 to 17. Marlboro was the most frequently cited brand among white and Hispanic youth smokers (55.1 and 44.1 percent, respectively). Newport was the usual brand reported by 32.4 percent of Hispanic youth smokers. Among black youth smokers, Newport was the most frequently cited brand (73.4 percent).

Chapter 10

Tobacco-Related Morbidity and Mortality

Understanding the Health Consequences of Smoking

Four Major Conclusions of the 2004 Surgeon General's Report

- Smoking harms nearly every organ of the body, causing many diseases and reducing the health of smokers in general.

- Quitting smoking has immediate as well as long-term benefits, reducing risks for diseases caused by smoking and improving health in general.

- Smoking cigarettes with lower machine-measured yields of tar and nicotine provides no clear benefit to health.

"Understanding the Health Consequences of Smoking," comprises two fact sheets from *The Health Consequences of Smoking: A Report of the Surgeon General.* U.S. Department of Health and Human Services, Centers for Disease Control and Prevention, National Center for Chronic Disease Prevention and Health Promotion, Office on Smoking and Health, 2004. This chapter also includes text excerpted from "Cigarette Smoking-Attributable Morbidity–United States, 2000," *Morbidity and Mortality Weekly Report (MMWR),* 52(35);842–844, September 5, 2003. The complete text, including formulas used for calculations and statistical data, can be found online at www.cdc.gov/mmwr/preview/mmwrhtml/mm5235a4 .htm. Additional information is from "Cigarette Smoking-Related Mortality," reviewed April 2003, and "Targeting Tobacco Use: The Nation's Leading Cause of Death," July 2003, National Center for Chronic Disease Prevention and Health Promotion, Centers for Disease Control and Prevention (CDC).

- The list of diseases caused by smoking has been expanded to include abdominal aortic aneurysm, acute myeloid leukemia, cataract, cervical cancer, kidney cancer, pancreatic cancer, pneumonia, periodontitis, and stomach cancer. These are in addition to diseases previously known to be caused by smoking, including bladder, esophageal, laryngeal, lung, oral, and throat cancers, chronic lung diseases, coronary heart and cardiovascular diseases, as well as reproductive effects and sudden infant death syndrome.

Smoking remains the leading cause of preventable death and has negative impacts on people at all stages of life. It harms unborn babies, infants, children, adolescents, adults, and seniors.

How Smoking Harms People of All Ages

- Toxic ingredients in cigarette smoke travel throughout the body, causing damage in several different ways.

- Nicotine reaches the brain within 10 seconds after smoke is inhaled. It has been found in every part of the body and in breast milk.

- Carbon monoxide binds to hemoglobin in red blood cells, preventing affected cells from carrying a full load of oxygen.

- Cancer-causing agents (carcinogens) in tobacco smoke damage important genes that control the growth of cells, causing them to grow abnormally or to reproduce too rapidly.

- The carcinogen benzo[a]pyrene binds to cells in the airways and major organs of smokers.

- Smoking affects the function of the immune system and may increase the risk for respiratory and other infections.

- There are several likely ways that cigarette smoke does its damage. One is oxidative stress that mutates DNA, promotes atherosclerosis, and leads to chronic lung injury. Oxidative stress is thought to be the general mechanism behind the aging process, contributing to the development of cancer, cardiovascular disease, and COPD (chronic obstructive pulmonary disease).

- The body produces antioxidants to help repair damaged cells. Smokers have lower levels of antioxidants in their blood than do nonsmokers.

• Smoking is associated with higher levels of chronic inflammation, another damaging process that may result from oxidative stress.

Cigarette Smoking-Attributable Morbidity

Each year in the United States, approximately 440,000 persons die of a cigarette smoking-attributable illness, resulting in 5.6 million years of potential life lost, $75 billion in direct medical costs, and $82 billion in lost productivity[1]. To assess smoking-attributable morbidity, the Roswell Park Cancer Institute, Research Triangle Institute, and CDC analyzed data from three sources: the Behavioral Risk Factor Surveillance System (BRFSS), the National Health and Nutrition Examination Survey III (NHANES III), and the U.S. Census. This report summarizes the results of that analysis, which indicate that an estimated 8.6 million persons in the United States have serious illnesses attributed to smoking; chronic bronchitis and emphysema account for 59% of all smoking-attributable diseases. These findings underscore the need to expand surveillance of the disease burden caused by smoking and to establish comprehensive tobacco-use prevention and cessation efforts to reduce the adverse health impact of smoking.

Data on the number of persons by sex, age group (18–34 years, 35–49 years, 50–64 years, and less than or equal to 65 years), and race (white or other race) for each state and the District of Columbia were obtained from the 2000 U.S. Census. National estimates of the prevalence of current, former, and never smokers were derived from the combined data from the 1999, 2000, and 2001 BRFSS surveys. (Current smokers were defined as persons who reported smoking 100 or more cigarettes during their lifetime and who now smoke some days or every day. Former smokers were defined as persons who reported having smoked 100 or more cigarettes during their lifetime but did not smoke at the time of interview. Never smokers were defined as persons who reported having smoked less than 100 cigarettes during their lifetime.)

Estimates of the prevalence of smoking-related conditions were obtained from the NHANES III survey for 1988–1994 for current, former, and never smokers for each demographic group to estimate the smoking-attributable fractions of morbid conditions. The smoking-related conditions for which data were collected are those categorized by the U.S. Surgeon General as caused by smoking[2] and addressed in NHANES III. Respondents reported whether a "doctor ever told" them if they had any of the following conditions: stroke, heart attack, emphysema, chronic bronchitis, and specific cancer types, including lung, bladder, mouth/pharynx, esophagus, cervix, kidney, larynx, or pancreas. Smoking-attributable morbidity estimates were obtained in two ways. For one estimate, each person was considered as the unit of analysis, and persons with at least one smoking-related condition were counted as having a condition. For the second estimate, the condition was treated as the unit of analysis, so persons with multiple conditions were counted more than once. Estimates were derived separately for each condition, and the total of all conditions was summed.

The number of persons with a smoking-attributable morbid condition was estimated by state and demographic subpopulations from the following five steps:

1. BRFSS smoking status estimates by demographic group were applied to census data to estimate the number of current, former, and never smokers in each demographic group in each state

2. NHANES III smoking-related disease frequency data were applied to the numbers from the first step to estimate the number of adults with a smoking-related condition

3. Attributable fractions for current and former smokers in each demographic group were multiplied by the number of persons with a smoking-related disease to yield an estimate of the number of persons with a disease that is attributable to smoking.

4. The numbers obtained from the third step were summed across all demographic categories in each state to yield an estimate of persons with smoking-attributable conditions in each state

5. The numbers of smoking-attributable morbid conditions obtained in each state from step four were summed to yield an overall U.S. estimate.

In 2000, an estimated 8.6 million persons in the United States had an estimated 12.7 million smoking-attributable conditions. For current smokers, chronic bronchitis was the most prevalent (49%) condition, followed by emphysema (24%). For former smokers, the three most prevalent conditions were chronic bronchitis (26%), emphysema (24%), and previous heart attack (24%). Lung cancer accounted for 1% of all cigarette smoking-attributable illnesses.

Reported by: A Hyland, PhD, C Vena, J Bauer, PhD, Q Li, MS, GA Giovino, PhD, J Yang, PhD, KM Cummings, PhD, Dept of Cancer Prevention, Epidemiology, and Biostatistics, Roswell Park Cancer Institute, Buffalo, New York. P Mowery, MS, Research Triangle Institute, Research Triangle Park, North Carolina. J Fellows, PhD, T Pechacek, PhD, L Pederson, PhD, Office on Smoking and Health, CDC.

Editorial Note: [in original document]

This report provides the first national estimates of the number of persons with serious chronic illnesses caused by smoking and the total number of their smoking-attributable conditions. The findings

Table 10.1. Number and percentage of cigarette smoking-attributable conditions* among current and former smokers[+], by condition— United States, 2000[§]

Condition	Current Smokers No.	(%)	Former Smokers No.	(%)	Overall No.	(%)
Chronic Bronchitis	2,633,000	(49)	1,872,000	(26)	4,505,000	(35)
Emphysema	1,273,000	(24)	1,743,000	(24)	3,016,000	(24)
Heart attack	719,000	(13)	1,755,000	(24)	2,474,000	(19)
All cancer except lung cancer	358,000	(7)	1,154,000	(16)	1,512,000	(12)
Stroke	384,000	(7)	637,000	(9)	1,021,000	(8)
Lung cancer	46,000	(1)	138,000	(2)	184,000	(1)
Total[¶]	5,412,000	(100)	7,299,000	(100)	12,711,000	(100)

* Cigarette smoking-attributable conditions considered are stroke, heart attack, emphysema, chronic bronchitis, and cancer of the lung, bladder, mouth/pharynx, esophagus, cervix, kidney, larynx, and pancreas.

+ Current smokers were defined as persons who reported smoking 100 or more cigarettes during their lifetime and who now smoke some days or every day. Former smokers were defined as persons who reported having smoked 100 or more cigarettes during their lifetime but did not smoke at the time of interview.

§ Results are adjusted for age, race, sex and state/area of residence and rounded to the nearest 1,000.

¶ Numbers might not add to total because of rounding.

indicate that more persons are harmed by tobacco use than is indicated by mortality estimates. Examining trends in tobacco-attributable morbidity provides another way to monitor the progress of tobacco-control efforts.

Smoking-attributable mortality estimates published in 2002[1] differ from the estimates described in this report. Mortality data indicate the number of persons who die of a disease each year, and morbidity data from this study are used to estimate the prevalence of persons living with diseases caused by smoking at a point in time. In addition, mortality estimates are based on official cause of death data and smoking-attributable fractions derived from data from the Cancer Prevention Study II, and the smoking-attributable morbidity fractions in this study are based solely on self-reported survey data on diseases addressed in NHANES III.

The findings in this report are subject to at least three limitations. First, the estimates do not adjust for potential confounders (for example, diet, exercise, or geography) other than age, sex, and race/ethnicity. The impact of confounding was examined in a prospective cohort study of approximately one million persons; findings indicated that adjusting for several demographic, behavioral, medical, and occupational factors reduced the smoking attributable mortality estimate by only 2.5%. However, no analyses have been performed that examine smoking-attributable morbidity or that use a broader range of potential confounders[5]. Second, disease data are self-reported and might not represent the true rate or type of disease. A Canadian study found that the rate of underreporting of the chronic conditions cancer, stroke, and hypertension was approximately two times greater than the rate of over reporting[6]. In addition, 63% of NHANES III respondents with documented low-lung function (forced expiratory volume in 1 second was less than 80% of the predicted value) did not self-report any diagnosis of obstructive lung disease[7]. Therefore, these self-reported data are probably substantial underestimates of a true disease burden. Finally, the scope of diseases considered in this report was limited to those diseases for which survey data were available and those the U.S. Surgeon General implicated smoking as the cause. Various additional chronic and acute conditions affect quality of life and are caused by cigarette smoking. Inclusion of additional diseases would increase the amount of morbidity attributable to smoking.

The findings in this report complement CDC mortality data and estimates of the number of adults with chronic diseases caused by smoking. Approximately 10% of all current and former adult smokers have a smoking-attributable chronic disease. Many of these persons are already experiencing decreased quality of life, and society will likely bear substantial direct and indirect economic costs from these diseases[1]. More persons will experience serious chronic diseases attributable to smoking if they continue to smoke[8]. This report underscores the need to expand the implementation of proven strategies to reduce tobacco use such as increasing the cost of cigarettes, increasing clean indoor air regulations, and implementing comprehensive tobacco-use—prevention and cessation programs.

References

1. CDC. Annual smoking-attributable mortality, years of potential life lost, and economic costs—United States, 1995–1999. *MMWR* 2002;51: 300–3.

2. CDC. *Reducing the health consequences of smoking: 25 years of progress—a report of the Surgeon General*. Rockville, Maryland: U.S. Department of Health and Human Services, CDC, 1989; DHHS publication no. (CDC) 89-8411.

3. Walter SD. Calculation of attributable risks from epidemiologic data. *Int J Epidemiol* 1978;7:175–82.

4. Winer BJ, Brown DR, Michels KM. *Statistical principles in experimental design, 3rd ed.* New York, New York: McGraw-Hill, 1991.

5. Thun MJ, Apicella LF, Henley SJ. Smoking vs other risk factors as the cause of smoking-attributable deaths. *JAMA* 2000; 284:706–12.

6. Baker M, Stabile M, Deri C. What do self-reported, objective, measures of health measure? Cambridge, Massachusetts: National Bureau of Economic Research, 2001; NBER working paper no. 8419.

7. Mannino DM, Gagnon RC, Petty TL, Lydick E. Obstructive lung disease and low lung function in adults in the United States: data from the National Health and Nutrition Examination Survey, 1988–1994. *Arch Intern Med* 2000;160:1683–9.

8. Peto R, Lopez AD, Boreham J, Thun M, Heath C. *Mortality from smoking in developed countries 1950–2000. Indirect estimates from national vital statistics.* Oxford, United Kingdom: Oxford University Press, 1994.

Cigarette Smoking-Related Mortality

Cigarette smoking is the single most preventable cause of premature death in the United States. Each year, more than 400,000 Americans die from cigarette smoking. In fact, one in every five deaths in the United States is smoking related. Every year, smoking kills more than 276,000 men and 142,000 women.[1]

- Between 1960 and 1990, deaths from lung cancer among women have increased by more than 400%—exceeding breast cancer deaths in the mid-1980s.[2] The American Cancer Society estimated that in 1994, 64,300 women died from lung cancer and 44,300 died from breast cancer.[3]

- Men who smoke increase their risk of death from lung cancer by more than 22 times and from bronchitis and emphysema by

Table 10.2. Cigarette Smoking-Related Mortality

Disease	Men	Women	Overall
Cancers			
Lung	81,179	35,741	116,920
Lung from ETS	1,055	1,945	3,000
Other	21,659	9,743	31,402
Total	103,893	47,429	151,322
Cardiovascular Diseases			
Hypertension	3,233	2,151	5,450
Heart Disease	88,644	45,591	134,235
Stroke	14,978	8,303	23,281
Other	11,682	5,172	16,854
Total	118,603	61,117	179,820
Respiratory Diseases			
Pneumonia	11,292	7,881	19,173
Bronchitis/Emphysema	9,234	5,541	14,865
Chronic Airway Obstruction	30,385	18,579	48,982
Other	787	668	1,455
Total	51,788	32,689	84,475
Other			
Diseases Among Infants	1,006	705	1,711
Burn Deaths	863	499	1,362
All Causes	**276,153**	**142,537**	**418,690**

nearly 10 times. Women who smoke increase their risk of dying from lung cancer by nearly 12 times and the risk of dying from bronchitis and emphysema by more than 10 times. Smoking triples the risk of dying from heart disease among middle-aged men and women.[1]

- Every year in the United States, premature deaths from smoking rob more than five million years from the potential lifespan of those who have died.[1]

- Annually, exposure to secondhand smoke (or environmental tobacco smoke) causes an estimated 3,000 deaths from lung cancer among American adults.[4] Scientific studies also link secondhand smoke with heart disease.

References

1. Centers for Disease Control and Prevention. Smoking-attributable mortality and years of potential life lost—United States, 1990. *Morbidity and Mortality Weekly Report* 1993; 42(33):645-8.

2. Centers for Disease Control and Prevention. Mortality trends for selected smoking-related and breast cancer—United States, 1950–1990. *Morbidity and Mortality Weekly Report* 1993;42(44):857, 863–6.

3. American Cancer Society. *Cancer Facts & Figures—1996*. Atlanta (GA): American Cancer Society, 1996.

4. U.S. Environmental Protection Agency. *Respiratory Health Effects of Passive Smoking: Lung Cancer and Other Disorders.* Washington (DC): U.S. Environmental Protection Agency, Office of Health and Environmental Assessment, Office of Research and Development. EPA/600/6-90/006F. December 1992.

Targeting Tobacco Use: The Nation's Leading Cause of Death

The Burden of Tobacco Use

Smoking-related illnesses cost the nation more than $150 billion each year. An estimated 46.5 million adults in the United States smoke cigarettes even though this single behavior will result in death or disability for half of all regular users. Cigarette smoking is responsible for more than 440,000 deaths each year, or one in every five deaths. Additionally, if current patterns of smoking persist, 6.4 million people currently younger than 18 will die prematurely from a tobacco-related disease. Paralleling this enormous health toll is the economic burden of tobacco use: more than $75 billion in medical expenditures and another $80 billion in indirect costs resulting from lost productivity.

Since the release in 1964 of the first Surgeon General's report on smoking and health, scientific knowledge about the health consequences of tobacco use has greatly increased. Smoking is known to cause chronic lung disease, heart disease, and stroke, as well as cancer of the lungs, larynx, esophagus, mouth, and bladder. In addition, smoking contributes to cancer of the cervix, pancreas, and kidneys. Researchers have identified more than 250 chemicals in tobacco smoke that are toxic or cause cancer in humans and animals. Smokeless tobacco and cigars also have deadly consequences, including lung, larynx, esophageal, and mouth cancer. Moreover, novel tobacco products such as bidis and clove cigarettes should not be considered safe alternatives to conventional cigarettes or smokeless tobacco.

The harmful effects of smoking do not end with the smoker. Women who smoke during pregnancy are more likely to have babies who have an increased risk of death from sudden infant death syndrome and respiratory distress. These babies are also more likely to have low birth weight and a variety of infant health disorders. In addition, secondhand smoke has harmful effects on nonsmokers. Each year, an estimated 3,000 nonsmoking Americans die of lung cancer, and more than 35,000 die of heart disease. Moreover, up to 300,000 children suffer from respiratory tract infections because of exposure to secondhand smoke.

CDC's Tobacco Control Framework

With fiscal year 2003 funding of approximately $100 million, the Centers for Disease Control and Prevention (CDC) provides national leadership for a comprehensive, broad-based approach to reducing tobacco use. A variety of federal, state, and local government agencies; professional and voluntary organizations; and academic institutions have joined together to advance this comprehensive approach, which involves:

- Preventing young people from starting to smoke.

- Eliminating exposure to secondhand smoke.

- Promoting quitting.

- Identifying and eliminating disparities in tobacco use among different population groups.

Essential elements of this approach include state- and community-based interventions, counter marketing, policy development, surveillance, and evaluation. These activities target groups—such as young people, racial and ethnic minority groups, people with low incomes or low levels of education, and women—at highest risk for tobacco-related health problems.

Future Directions

CDC will continue to broaden support for comprehensive tobacco control programs by expanding the science base and by increasing technical assistance, training, and funding to states. As part of this effort, CDC will help state and local programs develop media campaigns to reach high-risk populations.

For more information or a copy of the complete text of this document, please contact:

Centers for Disease Control and Prevention
National Center for Chronic Disease Prevention and Health Promotion
Mail Stop K–50
4770 Buford Highway, NE
Atlanta, GA 30341-3717
800-CDC-1311
ccdinfo@cdc.gov
http://www.cdc.gov/tobacco

Chapter 11

Minors' Access to Tobacco

Facts on Youth Smoking, Health, and Performance

Among young people, the short-term health effects of smoking include damage to the respiratory system, addiction to nicotine, and the associated risk of other drug use. Long-term health consequences of youth smoking are reinforced by the fact that most young people who smoke regularly continue to smoke throughout adulthood.

- Smoking hurts young people's physical fitness in terms of both performance and endurance—even among young people trained in competitive running.

- Smoking among youth can hamper the rate of lung growth and the level of maximum lung function.

- The resting heart rates of young adult smokers are two to three beats per minute faster than those of nonsmokers.

- Among young people, regular smoking is responsible for cough and increased frequency and severity of respiratory illnesses.

This chapter contains "Facts on Youth Smoking, Health, and Performance," November 2, 2000, "Minors' Access to Tobacco," April 10, 2001, and "Education Fact Sheet," April 3, 2003, Tobacco Information and Prevention Source (TIPS), National Center for Chronic Disease Prevention and Health Promotion, Centers for Disease Control and Prevention (CDC). "Research News: Understanding Some Factors that Affect Teen Smoking Decisions," is excerpted from "Research News," *NewsScan*, National Institute on Drug Abuse (NIDA), March 17, 2004.

- The younger people start smoking cigarettes, the more likely they are to become strongly addicted to nicotine.

- Teens who smoke are three times more likely than nonsmokers to use alcohol, eight times more likely to use marijuana, and 22 times more likely to use cocaine. Smoking is associated with a host of other risky behaviors, such as fighting and engaging in unprotected sex.

- Smoking is associated with poor overall health and a variety of short-term adverse health effects in young people and may also be a marker for underlying mental health problems, such as depression, among adolescents. High school seniors who are regular smokers and began smoking by grade nine are

  - 2.4 times more likely than their nonsmoking peers to report poorer overall health

  - 2.4 to 2.7 times more likely to report cough with phlegm or blood, shortness of breath when not exercising, and wheezing or gasping

  - 3.0 times more likely to have seen a doctor or other health professional for an emotional or psychological complaint.

Minors' Access to Tobacco

- It is illegal in all states to sell cigarettes to persons under age 18. Progress has been made in the past several years in reducing the percentage of retailers willing to sell tobacco to minors.[1]

- In 1991 an estimated 225 million packs of cigarettes were sold illegally to minors, and in 1997 daily smokers aged 12 to 17 years smoked approximately 924 million packs of cigarettes.[1]

- An estimated 20% to 70% of teenagers who smoke report purchasing their own tobacco; the proportion varies by age, social class, amount smoked, and factors related to availability.[1]

- The CDC's 1999 Youth Risk Behavior Surveillance (YRBS) survey found that among grade 9–12 students who smoked, 23.5% purchased their tobacco products from a store or gas station. However, there is growing evidence that many of the cigarettes these students obtain from other students were originally illegally sold to minors.[2]

- According to the 1999 YRBS survey, about two-thirds of students (69.6%) who purchased or tried to purchase cigarettes during the past month in a store or gas station were not asked to show proof of age. African American male students (19.8%) were significantly less likely to be asked to show proof of age than white (36.6%) and Hispanic (53.5%) male students.[2]

- The 1999 Monitoring the Future Survey found that about 72% of 8th-grade students and 88% of 10th-grade students believe they can get cigarettes "fairly easily" or "very easily" if they wanted to purchase them.[3]

- Since 1996, the accessibility of cigarettes among 8th-grade students has been falling, which may be an indicator that federal and state government tobacco prevention efforts are starting to have an effect.[3]

- More than two-thirds of states restrict cigarette vending machines, but many of these restrictions are weak. Only two states (Idaho and Vermont) have total bans on vending machines.[1]

- Results from nine published studies found illegal vending machine sales to minors ranged from 82% to 100% between 1989 and 1992.[1]

- More than 290 local jurisdictions, including New York City, successfully adopted and enforced outright bans on cigarette vending machines or restricted them to locations such as taverns and adult clubs where minors often are denied entry.[1]

- Almost two-thirds of the states and many local jurisdictions require retailers to display signs that state the minimum age for purchase of tobacco products. Some regulations specify the size, wording, and location of these signs.[1]

- All states have a specific restriction on the distribution of free tobacco samples to minors, and a few states or local jurisdictions prohibit free distribution altogether because of the difficulty of controlling who receives free samples.[1]

- Several studies have found that single or loose cigarettes are sold in some locations. Such sales often are prohibited by state or local law, given single cigarettes do not display the required state tax stamp or federal health warning.[1]

- Other regulations specify a minimum age for salespersons. These regulations recognize the difficulty young salespersons may have in refusing to sell cigarettes to their peers.[1]

- Many state or local laws specify penalties only for the sales-person. However, applying penalties to business owners, who generally set hiring, training, supervising, and selling policies, is considered essential to preventing the sale of tobacco to minors.[1]

- License suspensions or revocations imposed as penalties for repeated violation of youth access laws would communicate a clear message that illegal tobacco sales to minors should never be accepted or tolerated. Revenues from fines could be used for enforcement and retailer education programs.[1]

- Numerous studies have shown that comprehensive merchant education and training programs help reduce illegal sales to minors.[1]

- Growing number of states and local jurisdictions are imposing sanctions against minors who purchase, attempt to purchase, or possess tobacco products. Although these laws are a potential deterrent, some tobacco control advocates believe such laws deflect responsibility from retailers to underage youth.[1]

- In 1992 the Synar Amendment (Public Law 102-321), was passed to curb the illegal sale of tobacco products to minors. An amended Synar Regulation, was issued by the Substance Abuse and Mental Health Services Administration in January 1996, and requires each state receiving federal grant money to conduct annual random, unannounced inspections of retail tobacco outlets to assess the extent of sales to minors. In 1999, seven states and the District of Columbia failed to attain their Synar Amendment targets. Failure to comply with the law puts states at risk of forfeiting federal block grant funds for substance abuse prevention and treatment services.[1]

- In 1996, the Food and Drug Administration issued a regulation prohibiting the sale of tobacco products to persons under the age of 18 years and requiring that all persons under the age of 27 years show a photograph identification to purchase cigarettes or smokeless tobacco. The regulation also banned cigarette vending machines and self-service displays, except in certain venues for adults only (e.g., bars and nightclubs).

- On March 21, 2000, the United States Supreme Court ruled that the FDA lacked jurisdiction to regulate tobacco products and to enforce rules to reduce the access and appeal of tobacco products for children and adolescents. The loss of the FDA's education and enforcement program eliminates vital federal support for state tobacco control programs.[1]

- The 2010 national health objectives call for reducing the percentage of retailers willing to sell tobacco products to minors to 5% or less through enforcement of existing laws. To date, no state has met this objective.[4]

References

1. U.S. Department of Health and Human Services. *Reducing Tobacco Use: A Report of the Surgeon General*. Atlanta: U.S. Department of Health and Human Services, Centers for Disease Control and Prevention, 2000.

2. Centers for Disease Control and Prevention. "Youth Risk Behavior Surveillance, United States, 1999," *MMWR,* 2000, 49:SS-5.

3. The University of Michigan. "Cigarette Smoking Among American Teens Continues Gradual Decline" (press release). December 17, 1999.

4. U.S. Department of Health and Human Services. *Healthy People 2010* (Conference edition, in Two Volumes) Washington, DC: January 2000.

Education

- The high rate of cigarette, smokeless tobacco, and cigar use among youth, along with the emergence of novel tobacco products such as bidis (or beedies) and kreteks (also known as clove cigarettes), suggests that a major proportion of U.S. youth already exhibit or are at risk for nicotine addiction and the subsequent health problems caused by tobacco use.[1]

- More than 4 million adolescents under the age of 18 in the United States smoke cigarettes.[2] Each day, more than 6,000 young people try a cigarette and nearly 3,000 become regular smokers—that adds up to more than one million new smokers each year.[3]

- In 1999 more than one-third (34.8%) of U.S. high school students in grades 9 through 12 reported smoking cigarettes in the past month. Data from 1995 (34.8%) and 1997 (36.4%) show that current smoking prevalence rates among high school students remain high but appear to have plateaued.[4]

- Many factors interact to encourage tobacco use among youth, including tobacco advertising and promotion, tobacco use by peers and family members, and easy access to tobacco products.[6]

- Early adolescence (age 11–15 years, or sixth through tenth grade) is the period when young people are most likely to try smoking for the first time.[6]

- Tobacco-free policies involving the school's faculty, staff, and students have a critical role in reducing tobacco use among young people, especially when these policies apply to all school facilities, property, vehicles, and school-sponsored events. While two-thirds of schools (62.8%) had smoke-free building policies in 1994, significantly fewer (36.5%) reported having policies that included the entire school environment.[6]

- Adopting strong tobacco-free policies are only the first step. Schools should rigorously enforce these policies to protect children from the hazards of tobacco smoke at school, to model a tobacco-free environment, and to reduce opportunities for young people to experiment with tobacco on school grounds.

- Implementing effective educational programs for preventing tobacco use could postpone or prevent smoking onset in 20% to 40% of U.S. adolescents.[6]

- Programs with the most educational contacts during the critical years for smoking adoption (age 11–15 years) are more likely to be effective, as are programs that address a broad range of educational needs.[6]

- Educational strategies to prevent tobacco use must become more consistent and effective. This will require continuing efforts to build strong, multiyear prevention units into school health education curricula. It will also require expanded efforts to make use of the influence of parents, the mass media, and community resources.[6]

- Existing data suggest that evidence-based curricula and national guidelines have not been widely adopted. Less than 5% of schools nationwide are implementing the major components of CDC's *Guidelines for School Health Programs to Prevent Tobacco Use and Addiction*, which recommends schools should:[6]

  - Develop and enforce a school policy on tobacco use.

  - Provide instruction about the short- and long-term effects of tobacco use, social influences on tobacco use, peer norms regarding tobacco use, and refusal skills.

- Provide tobacco-use prevention education in kindergarten through 12th grade, with especially intensive instruction in junior high or middle school.

- Provide program-specific training for teachers.

- Involve parents and families in support of school-based programs to prevent tobacco use.

- Support cessation efforts among students and school staff who use tobacco.

- Assess the tobacco-use prevention program at regular intervals.

- Educational curricula that address social influences (of friends, family, and media) that encourage tobacco use among youth, have shown consistently more effectiveness than programs based on other models.[6]

- Two middle school programs that have demonstrated effectiveness in reducing tobacco use behaviors in youth have been identified by the Centers for Disease Control and Prevention as programs that work, and they are Life Skills Training Program, and Project Toward No Tobacco (TNT).[6]

- Schools can not bear the sole responsibility for preventing tobacco use. School-based programs are more effective when combined with mass media programs and with community-based efforts involving parents and other community resources.[6]

References

1. Centers for Disease Control and Prevention. "Tobacco use among middle and high school students—United States," *MMWR*, 1999, 49:49–53.

2. Substance Abuse and Mental Health Services Administration. "Annual national drug survey results from the 1998 National Household Survey on Drug Abuse," Office of Applied Studies, August 1999.

3. Centers for Disease Control and Prevention. "Incidence of Initiation of Cigarette Smoking—United States, 1965–1996," *MMWR* 1997, 47:837–840.

4. Centers for Disease Control and Prevention. "Youth risk behavior surveillance—United States, 1999," *MMWR*, 2000, 49 (SS-5).

5. Centers for Disease Control and Prevention. *Preventing Tobacco Use Among Young People: A Report of the Surgeon General*. Atlanta: U.S. Department of Health and Human Services, 1994, pages 129–131, 166, and 248–249.

6. U.S. Department of Health and Human Services. *Reducing Tobacco Use: A Report of the Surgeon General*. Atlanta: U.S. Department of Health and Human Services, Centers for Disease Control and Prevention, 2000.

Research News: Understanding Some Factors that Affect Teen Smoking Decisions

Novelty-Seeking Teens May Be More Easily Influenced by Tobacco Advertisements

Teens with higher levels of a personality trait known as novelty-seeking have been shown to be more receptive to tobacco industry promotional campaigns than teens with low levels of the trait. Novelty-seeking is a heritable trait characterized by a tendency toward excitement in response to new experiences; engagement in sensation-seeking, impulsive, and risk-taking behavior; and sensitivity to reward. Scientific data indicate that teens' receptivity to tobacco marketing campaigns may play an important role in the choice to start smoking. Building on this research, scientists at the University of Pennsylvania and Georgetown University found that teens with high levels of the novelty-seeking trait may be more than twice as likely as those low in the trait to be moderately to highly receptive to tobacco promotional campaigns.

The research team, led by Dr. Janet Audrain-McGovern, collected survey data from 1,071 9th-graders at five Northern Virginia high schools. Surveys included questions about smoking habits, peer and family smoking exposure, novelty-seeking personality traits, and demographics. Researchers used a standardized scale to measure the teens' receptivity to tobacco advertising and marketing campaigns.

Overall, 33 percent of the teens reported high levels of receptivity to the advertising campaigns and 20 percent reported minimal levels of receptivity. Almost one-half of the highly receptive teens also scored high for novelty-seeking compared with one-quarter of the teens who were minimally receptive to tobacco advertising.

Of the teens who had never smoked, 37 percent of those highly receptive to tobacco promotions scored high for novelty-seeking compared with 19 percent of the teens who were minimally receptive.

However, this relationship was not significant among teens who had ever smoked.

In a separate study, Drs. Kenneth Tercyak and Janet Audrain-McGovern administered standardized questionnaires to 1,136 10th-graders enrolled in Mid-Atlantic high schools to evaluate their tendencies for novelty-seeking, symptoms of attention deficit hyperactivity disorder (ADHD), lifetime cigarette smoking, and age of first cigarette. They found that teens with high degrees of symptoms for ADHD who had smoked cigarettes during their lifetimes also rated highest for novelty-seeking compared with other teens. The researchers say that teens with ADHD and novelty-seeking traits may be at a higher risk for smoking cigarettes than teens without these traits. This is likely because novelty-seeking and ADHD symptoms have common, basic behavioral elements such as poor self-control, attention dysfunction, and risk-taking behavior, which may contribute to tobacco use.

What It Means: Novelty-seeking teens may be more vulnerable to cigarette smoking. Therefore, anti-tobacco campaigns that take this trait into consideration may be the most effective in preventing these teens from smoking.

Dr. Audrain-McGovern, Dr. Tercyak, and colleagues published the studies in the October 2003 issue of *Health Communication* and the December 2003 issue of *Substance Use and Misuse*. The studies were funded in part by the National Institute on Drug Abuse.

Behavioral Symptoms May Indicate Increased Smoking Risk Among Adolescents

Adolescents who show a high level of aggression and hyperactivity may be at greater risk for smoking cigarettes than those who do not present these behavioral symptoms, according to a study by researchers at the National Institute on Drug Abuse (NIDA)'s Intramural Research Program, the University of California, Los Angeles, and the National Institute of Mental Health.

The researchers recruited 59 adolescents ages 12 to 14 in the Baltimore-Washington, DC area, with no history of substance use, to participate in the study. At the beginning of the study, the adolescents and their parents completed standardized questionnaires to assess the adolescents' aggression, hyperactivity, conduct problems, inattention, impulsivity, anxiety/depression, and social problems. Follow-up interviews were conducted at 4-month intervals for the next two years, and researchers recorded if and when the adolescents began smoking as well as how often they smoked. Family, school, social functioning, and substance use status also were updated.

The researchers found that more than 30 percent of the adolescents began smoking an average of 19 months after the study began. Adolescents who started smoking were more aggressive, more hyperactive, and tended to have more conduct problems upon entering the study than the adolescents who did not smoke.

What It Means: These findings indicate that the severity of certain behavioral symptoms, such as aggression and hyperactivity, may help identify adolescents who are at higher risk of smoking at a young age. Determining risk factors for smoking among adolescents may aid in the development and implementation of more effective prevention programs.

Lead investigators Drs. Monique Ernst and Michelle K. Leff published this study in the September 2003 issue of the *Journal of Child and Adolescent Substance Abuse*. It was funded by NIDA and the American Psychiatric Association's Drug Abuse Research Scholars Program in Psychiatry.

Chapter 12

Women and Smoking

The Burden

This year alone, lung cancer will kill nearly 68,000 U.S. women. That's one in every four cancer deaths among women, and about 27,000 more deaths than from breast cancer (41,000). In 1999, approximately 165,000 women died prematurely from smoking-related diseases, like cancer and heart disease. Women also face unique health effects from smoking such as problems related to pregnancy.

In the 1990s, the decline in smoking rates among adult women stalled and, at the same time, rates were rising steeply among teen-aged girls, blunting earlier progress. Smoking rates among women with less than a high school education are three times higher than for college graduates. Nearly all women who smoke started as teen-agers—and 30 percent of high school senior girls are still current smokers.

This chapter contains text from "At A Glance," "Pattern of Tobacco Use Among Women and Girls," "Health Consequence of Tobacco Use Among Women," and "Marketing Cigarettes to Women," fact sheets from the Tobacco Information and Prevention Source (TIPS), National Center for Chronic Disease Prevention and Health Promotion, Centers for Disease Control and Prevention (CDC), reviewed September 11, 2003. The text under the heading "Reproductive Health," is from *The Health Consequences of Smoking: A Report of the Surgeon General*. U.S. Department of Health and Human Services, Centers for Disease Control and Prevention, National Center for Chronic Disease Prevention and Health Promotion, Office on Smoking and Health, 2004.

Major Conclusions of the Surgeon General's Report on Women and Smoking

- In 2000, 29.7 percent of high school senior girls reported having smoked within the past 30 days. Smoking prevalence among white girls declined from the mid-1970s to the early 1980s, followed by a decade of little change. Smoking prevalence then increased markedly in the early 1990s, and declined somewhat in the late 1990s. The increase dampened much of the earlier progress. Among black girls, smoking prevalence declined substantially from the mid-1970s to the early 1990s, followed by some increases until the mid-1990s. Data on long-term trends in smoking prevalence among high school seniors of other racial or ethnic groups are not available.

- Since 1980, approximately 3 million U.S. women have died prematurely from smoking related neoplastic, cardiovascular, respiratory, and pediatric diseases, as well as cigarette-caused burns. Each year during the 1990s, U.S. women lost an estimated 2.1 million years of life due to these smoking attributable premature deaths. Additionally, women who smoke experience gender-specific health consequences, including increased risk of various adverse reproductive outcomes.

- Lung cancer is now the leading cause of cancer death among U.S. women; it surpassed breast cancer in 1987. About 90 percent of all lung cancer deaths among women who continue to smoke are attributable to smoking.

- Exposure to environmental tobacco smoke is a cause of lung cancer and coronary heart disease among women who are lifetime nonsmokers. Infants born to women exposed to environmental tobacco smoke during pregnancy have a small decrement in birth weight and a slightly increased risk of intrauterine growth retardation compared to infants of non-exposed women.

- Women who stop smoking greatly reduce their risk of dying prematurely, and quitting smoking is beneficial at all ages. Although some clinical intervention studies suggest that women may have more difficulty quitting smoking than men, national survey data show that women are quitting at rates similar to or even higher than those for men. Prevention and cessation interventions are generally of similar effectiveness for women and men and, to date, few gender differences in factors related to smoking initiation and successful quitting have been identified.

- Smoking during pregnancy remains a major public health problem despite increased knowledge of the adverse health effects of smoking during pregnancy. Although the prevalence of smoking during pregnancy has declined steadily in recent years, substantial numbers of pregnant women continue to smoke, and only about one-third of women who stop smoking during pregnancy are still abstinent one year after the delivery.

- Tobacco industry marketing is a factor influencing susceptibility to and initiation of smoking among girls in the United States and overseas. Myriad examples of tobacco ads and promotions targeted to women indicate that such marketing is dominated by themes of social desirability and independence. These themes are conveyed through ads featuring slim, attractive, athletic models, images very much at odds with the serious health consequences experienced by so many women who smoke.

Cigarette Smoking Prevalence among Women

- Cigarette smoking was rare among women in the early 20th century. Cigarette smoking became prevalent among women after it did among men, and smoking prevalence has always been lower among women than among men. However, the gender-specific difference in smoking prevalence narrowed between 1965 and 1985. Since 1985, the decline in prevalence among men and women has been comparable.

- Smoking prevalence decreased among women from 33.9% in 1965 to 22.0% in 1998. Most of this decline occurred from 1974 through 1990; prevalence declined very little from 1992 through 1998.

- The prevalence of current smoking is three times higher among women with 9–11 years of education (32.9%) than among women with 16 or more years of education (11.2%).

- Smoking prevalence is higher among women living below the poverty level (29.6%) than among those living at or above the poverty level (21.6%).

Cigarette Smoking among Racial/Ethnic Populations of Women

- In 1997–1998, 34.5% of American Indian or Alaska Native, 23.5% of white, 21.9% of African American, 13.8% of Hispanic, and 11.2% Asian/Pacific Islander women were current smokers.

- Among white women and African American women, smoking prevalence decreased from 1965 through 1998. The prevalence of current smoking was generally comparable, but from 1970 through 1985 it was higher—some years significantly so— among African American women. In 1990, it was higher among white women in 1990.

- From 1965 through 1998, the decline in smoking prevalence among Hispanic women was significantly less than among white and African American women.

- Among Asian American or Pacific Islander women, smoking prevalence decreased from 1979 through 1992, but then increased from 1995 through 1998. Prevalence changed little from 1979 through 1998 among American Indian or Alaska Native women.

Cigarette Smoking Among Girls and Young Women

- Among high school senior girls, past-month current smoking rates decreased from 39.9% in 1977 to 25.8% in 1992, but increased to 35.3% during 1997. In 2000, smoking prevalence declined again to 29.7%.

- Much of the progress in reducing smoking prevalence among girls in the 1970s and 1980s was lost with the increase in prevalence in the 1990s. Current smoking rates among high school senior girls were the same in 2000 as in 1988.

- In the late 1970s and early 1980s, the prevalence of smoking among high school seniors was higher among girls than among boys, but the decline in smoking prevalence from 1976 through 1992 was more rapid among girls than among boys. Since the mid 1980s, smoking prevalence among girls and boys has been similar.

- From 1991 to 1996, current smoking prevalence in the past 30 days increased from 13.1% to 21.1% among 8th grade girls but decreased to 14.7% in 2000. Among 10th grade girls, current smoking prevalence in the past 30 days increased from 20.7% in 1991 to 31.1% in 1997 but decreased to 23.6% in 2000.

- Aggregated data from 1976–1977 through 1991–1992 showed a dramatic decline in past-month cigarette smoking among African American high school senior girls (from 37.5% to 7.0%) compared with the decline among white girls (from 39.9% to 31.2%). From 1991–1992 through 1997–1998, past-month smoking prevalence increased among white girls (from 31.2% to 41.0%) and African American girls (from 7.0% to 12.0%)—but the increase was statistically significant only among white girls.

- In 1990–1994, smoking prevalence for high school senior girls was highest among American Indians or Alaska Natives (39.4%) and whites (33.1%) and lowest among Hispanics (19.2%), Asian Americans or Pacific Islanders (13.8%), and African Americans (8.6%).

- Smoking among young women (aged 18 through 24 years) declined from 37.3% in 1965–1966 to 25.1% in 1997–1998. However, recent trends show that smoking rates in this population may be rising.

- In 1998, nearly 14 million women of reproductive age were smokers, and smoking prevalence in this group was higher (25.3%) than in the overall population of women aged 18 years or older (22.0%).

Cigarette Smoking among Pregnant Women

- Despite increased knowledge of the adverse health effects of smoking during pregnancy, survey data suggest that a substantial number of pregnant women and girls smoke. Cigarette smoking during pregnancy declined from 19.5% in 1989 to 12.9% in 1998.

- Smoking prevalence during pregnancy differs by age and by race and ethnicity. In 1998, smoking prevalence during pregnancy was consistently highest among young adult women aged 18 through 24 (17.1%) and lowest among women aged 25 through 49 (10.5%).

- Smoking during pregnancy declined among women of all racial/ethnic populations. From 1989 to 1998, smoking among American

Indian or Alaska Native pregnant women decreased from 23.0%
to 20.2%; among pregnant white women from 21.7% to 16.2%;
African American pregnant women from 17.2% to 9.6%; Hispanic pregnant women from 8.0% to 4.0%; and Asian American
or Pacific Islander pregnant women from 5.7% to 3.1%.

Nicotine Dependence

- The level of nicotine dependence is strongly associated with the
  quantity of cigarettes smoked per day.

- When results are stratified by the number of cigarettes smoked
  per day, girls and women who smoke appear to be equally dependent on nicotine, as measured by first cigarette after waking, smoking for a calming and relaxing effect, withdrawal
  symptoms, or other measures of nicotine dependence.

- Of the women who smoke, more than three-fourths report one
  or more indicators of nicotine dependence, and nearly three-
  fourths report feeling dependent on cigarettes.

Quitting Smoke and Attempts to Quit

- More than three-fourths (75.2%) of women want to quit smoking
  completely, and nearly half (46.6%) report having tried to quit
  during the previous year.

- In 1998, the percentage of people who had ever smoked and who
  had quit was lower among women (46.2%) than among men
  (50.9%). This finding may be because men began to stop smoking earlier in the 20th century than did women and because
  these data do not take into account that men are more likely
  than women to switch to, or to continue to use, other tobacco
  products when they stop smoking.

- Since the late 1970s or early 1980s, the probability of attempting to quit smoking and succeeding has been equal among
  women and men.

Other Tobacco Use

- The use of cigars, pipes, and smokeless tobacco among women is
  generally low, but recent data suggest that cigar smoking
  among women and girls is increasing.

- A California study found that current cigar smoking among women increased five-fold from 1990 through 1996.

- The prevalence of cigar use appears to be higher among adolescent girls than among women. In 1999, past-month cigar use among high school girls younger than 18 was 9.8%.

- The prevalence of pipe smoking among women is low, and women are much less likely than men to smoke a pipe.

- The prevalence of smokeless tobacco use among girls and women is low and remains considerably lower than that among boys and men.

- For tobacco use other than cigarettes among high school girls, cigar use is the most common, bidi and kretek use are intermediate, and pipe and smokeless tobacco use are the least common.

Health Consequence of Tobacco Use Among Women

Mortality

- Cigarette smoking plays a major role in the mortality of U.S. women. Since 1980, when the Surgeon General's *Report on Women and Smoking* was released, about three million women have died prematurely of smoking-related diseases.

- Each year throughout the 1990s, about 2.1 million years of the potential life of U.S. women were lost prematurely because of smoking-attributable diseases. Women smokers who die of a smoking-related disease lose on average 14 years of potential life.

- Women who stop smoking greatly reduce their risk of dying prematurely. The relative benefits of smoking cessation are greater when women stop smoking at younger ages, but smoking cessation is beneficial at all ages.

Lung Cancer

- Cigarette smoking is the major cause of lung cancer among women. About 90% of all lung cancer deaths among U.S. women smokers are attributable to smoking.

- In 1950, lung cancer accounted for only 3% of all cancer deaths among women; however, by 2000, it accounted for an estimated 25% of cancer deaths.

- Since 1950, lung cancer mortality rates for U.S. women have increased an estimated 600%. In 1987, lung cancer surpassed breast cancer to become the leading cause of cancer death among U.S. women. In 2000, about 27,000 more women died of lung cancer (67,600) than breast cancer (40,800).

Other Cancers

- Smoking is a major cause of cancer of the oropharynx and bladder among women. Evidence is also strong that women who smoke have increased risk for cancer of the pancreas and kidney. For cancer of the larynx and esophagus, evidence that smoking increases the risk among women is more limited but consistent with large increases in risk.

- Women who smoke may have a higher risk for liver cancer and colorectal cancer than women who do not smoke.

- Smoking is consistently associated with an increased risk for cervical cancer. The extent to which this association is independent of human papillomavirus (tumor caused by virus) infection is uncertain.

- Several studies suggest that exposure to environmental tobacco smoke is associated with an increased risk for breast cancer; however, this association remains uncertain.

Cardiovascular Disease

- Smoking is a major cause of coronary heart disease among women. Risk increases with the number of cigarettes smoked and the duration of smoking.

- Women who smoke have an increase risk for ischemic stroke (blood clot in one of the arteries supplying the brain) and subarachnoid hemorrhage (bleeding in the area surrounding the brain).

- Women who smoke have an increased risk for peripheral vascular atherosclerosis.

- Smoking cessation reduces the excess risk of coronary heart disease, no matter at what age women stop smoking. The risk is substantially reduced within 1 or 2 years after they stop smoking.

- The increased risk for stroke associated with smoking begins to reverse after women stop smoking. About 10 to 15 years after stopping, the risk for stroke approaches that of a women who never smoked.

Chronic Obstructive Pulmonary Disease (COPD) and Lung Function

- Cigarette smoking is the primary cause of COPD in women, and the risk increases with the amount and duration of cigarette use.

- Mortality rates for COPD have increased among women for the past 20 to 30 years. About, 90% of mortality from COPD among U.S. women is attributed to smoking.

- Exposure to maternal smoking is associated with reduced lung function among infants, and exposure to environmental tobacco smoke during childhood and adolescence may be associated with impaired lung function among girls.

- Smoking by girls can reduce their rate of lung growth and the level of maximum lung function. Women who smoke may experience a premature decline of lung function.

Menstrual Function

- Some studies suggest that cigarette smoking may alter menstrual function by increasing the risks for painful menstruation, secondary amenorrhea (abnormal absence of menstrual), and menstrual irregularity.

- Women smokers have natural menopause at a younger age than do nonsmokers, and they may experience more severe menopausal symptoms.

Reproductive Health

- Smoking harms many aspects and every phase of reproduction. Despite having greater increased knowledge of the adverse health effects of smoking during pregnancy, many pregnant women and girls continue to smoke (estimates range from 12% to 22%). It is estimated that only 18% to 25% quit smoking once they become pregnant.

- Women who smoke are at an increased risk for infertility. Studies have shown that smoking makes it more difficult for women to become pregnant.

- Research also has shown that smoking during pregnancy causes health problems for both mothers and babies, such as pregnancy complications, premature birth, low-birth-weight infants, stillbirth, and infant death. Low birth weight is a leading cause of infant deaths, resulting in more than 300,000 deaths annually in the United States.

- Once pregnant, women who smoke are about twice as likely to experience complications such as placenta previa, a condition where the placenta grows too close to the opening of the uterus. This condition frequently leads to delivery by a Caesarean section.

- Pregnant women who smoke also are more likely to have placental abruption, where the placenta prematurely separates from the wall of the uterus. This can lead to preterm delivery, stillbirth, or early infant death. Estimates for risk of placental abruption among smokers range from 1.4 to 2.4 times that of nonsmokers.

- Pregnant smokers also are at a higher risk for premature rupture of membranes before labor begins. This makes it more likely that a smoker will carry her baby for a shorter than normal gestation period.

- Risk for having a baby in the smallest 5% to 10% of birth weights is as high as 2.5 times greater for pregnant smokers.

- For reasons that are currently unknown, smokers are less likely to have preeclampsia, a condition that results in high blood pressure and an excess of protein in the urine.

Bone Density and Fracture Risk

- Postmenopausal women who smoke have lower bone density than women who never smoked.

- Women who smoke have an increased risk for hip fracture than women who never smoked.

Other Conditions

- Women who smoke may have a modestly elevated risk for rheumatoid arthritis.

- Women smokers have an increased risk for cataract, and may have an increased risk for age-related macular degeneration.

- The prevalence of smoking generally is higher for women with anxiety disorders, bulimia, depression, attention deficit disorder, and alcoholism; it is particularly high among patients with diagnosed schizophrenia. The connection between smoking and these disorders requires additional research.

Health Consequences of Environmental Tobacco Smoke (ETS)

- Exposure to ETS is a cause of lung cancer among women non-smokers.

- Studies support a causal relationship between exposure to ETS and coronary heart disease mortality among women non-smokers.

- Infants born to women who are exposed to ETS during pregnancy may have a small decrement in birth weight and a slightly increased risk for intrauterine growth retardation.

Factors Influencing Tobacco Use among Women

- Girls who initiate smoking are more likely than those who do not smoke to have parents or friends who smoke. They also tend to have weaker attachments to parents and family and stronger attachments to peers and friends. They perceive smoking prevalence to be higher than it actually is, are inclined to risk taking and rebelliousness, have a weaker commitment to school or religion, have less knowledge of the adverse consequences of smoking and the addictiveness of nicotine, believe that smoking can control weight and negative moods, and have a positive image of smokers.

- Women who continue to smoke and those who fail at attempts to stop smoking tend to have lower education and employment levels than do women who quit smoking. They also tend to be more addicted to cigarettes, as evidenced by the smoking of a higher number of cigarettes per day, to be cognitively less ready to stop smoking, to have less social support for stopping, and to be less confident in resisting temptations to smoke.

- Women have been extensively targeted in tobacco marketing, and tobacco companies have produced brands specifically for women, both in the United States and overseas. Myriad examples of tobacco ads and promotions targeted to women indicated that such marketing is dominated by themes of both social desirability and independence, which are conveyed through ads featuring slim, attractive, athletic models.

- The dependence of the media on revenues from tobacco advertising oriented to women, coupled with tobacco company sponsorship of women's fashions and of artistic, athletic, political, and other events, has tended to stifle media coverage of the health consequences of smoking among women and to mute criticism of the tobacco industry by women public figures.

Marketing Cigarettes to Women

History of Advertising Strategies

- Tobacco advertising geared toward women began in the 1920s. By the mid-1930s, cigarette advertisements targeting women were becoming so commonplace that one advertisement for the mentholated Spud brand had the caption "To read the advertisements these days, a fellow'd think the pretty girls do all the smoking."

- As early as the 1920s, tobacco advertising geared toward women included messages such as "Reach for a Lucky instead of a sweet" to establish an association between smoking and slimness. The positioning of Lucky Strike as an aid to weight control led to a greater than 300% increase in sales for this brand in the first year of the advertising campaign.

- Through World War II, Chesterfield advertisements regularly featured glamour photographs of a Chesterfield girl of the month, usually a fashion model or a Hollywood star such as Rita Hayworth, Rosalind Russell, or Betty Grable.

- The number of women aged 18 through 25 years who began smoking increased significantly in the mid-1920s, the same time that the tobacco industry mounted the Chesterfield and Lucky Strike campaigns directed at women. The trend was most striking among women aged 18 though 21. The number of women in this age group who began smoking tripled between 1911 and 1925 and had more than tripled again by 1939.

- In 1968, Philip Morris marketed Virginia Slims cigarettes to women with an advertising strategy showing canny insight into the importance of the emerging women's movement. The slogan "You've come a long way, Baby" later gave way to "It's a woman thing" in the mid-1990s, and more recently the "Find your voice" campaign featuring women of diverse racial and ethnic backgrounds. The underlying message of these campaigns has been that smoking is related to women's freedom, emancipation, and empowerment.

- Initiation rates among girls aged 14 though 17 years rapidly increased in parallel with the combined sales of the leading women's-niche brands (Virginia Slims, Silva Thins, and Eve) during this period.

- In 1960, about 10% of all cigarette advertisements appeared in popular women's magazines, and by 1985, cigarette advertisements increased by 34%.

Current Advertising Strategies

- Women have been extensively targeted in tobacco marketing. Such marketing is dominated by themes of an association between social desirability, independence, and smoking messages conveyed through advertisements featuring slim, attractive, and athletic models. In 1999, expenditures for domestic cigarette advertising and promotion was $8.24 billion—increasing 22.3% from the $6.73 billion spent in 1998.

- Advertising is used in part to reduce women's fear of the health risks from smoking by presenting information on nicotine and tar content or by using positive images (e.g., models engaged in exercise or pictures of white capped mountains against a background of clear blue skies).

- Because cigarette brands developed exclusively for women (e.g., Virginia Slims, Eve, Misty, and Capri) account for only 5% to 10% of the cigarette market. Many women are also attracted to brands that appear gender neutral or overtly targeted to males.

- Research has shown that women's magazines that accept tobacco advertising are significantly less likely to publish articles critical of smoking than are magazines that do not accept such advertising.

Sponsorship/Promotions

- The tobacco industry has targeted women through innovative promotional campaigns offering discounts on common household items unrelated to tobacco. For example, Philip Morris has offered discounts on turkeys, milk, soft drinks, and laundry detergent with the purchase of tobacco products.

- Cigarette brand clothing and other giveaway accessories have been use to promote cigarettes products to women and girls.

- Virginia Slims offered a yearly engagement calendar and the V-Wear catalog featuring clothing, jewelry, and accessories coordinated with the themes and colors of the print advertising and product packaging.

- Capri Superslims used point-of-sale displays and value-added gifts featuring items such as mugs and caps bearing the Capri label in colors coordinated with the advertisement and package.

- Misty Slims offered color-coordinated items in multiple-pack containers. The manufacturer also offered an address book, cigarette lighter, T-shirt, and fashion booklet.

Global Advertising Strategies

- Evidence suggests a pattern of international tobacco advertising that associates smoking with success, similar to that seen in the United States. This development emphasizes the enormous potential of advertising to change social norms.

- As western-styled marketing has increased, campaigns commonly have focused on women. For example, in 1989, the brand Yves Saint Laurent introduced a new elegant package designed to appeal to women in Malaysia and other Asian countries. National tobacco monopolies and companies, such as those in Indonesia and Japan, began to copy this promotional targeting of women.

- One of the most popular media for reaching women—particularly in places where tobacco advertising is banned on television—is women's magazines. Magazines can lend an air of social acceptability or stylish image to smoking. This may be particularly important in countries where smoking rates are low among women and where tobacco companies are attempting to associate smoking with Western values.

- One of the most common advertisement themes in developed countries is that smoking is both a passport to and a symbol of the independence and success of the modern women.

- Events and activities popular among young people are often sponsored by tobacco companies. Free tickets to films and to pop and rock concerts have been given in exchange for empty cigarette packets in Hong Kong and Taiwan. Popular U.S. female stars have allowed their names to be associated with cigarettes in other countries.

- Many countries have banned tobacco advertising and promotion. In 1998, the European Union adopted a directive to ban most tobacco advertising and sponsorship by July 30, 2006. Other countries have banned direct advertising, and still others have instituted partial restraints. Such bans are often circumvented by tobacco companies through various promotional venues such as the creation of retail stores named after cigarette brands or corporate sponsorship of sporting and other events. Moreover, national bans on tobacco advertisements may be rendered ineffective by tobacco promotion on satellite television, by cable broadcasting, or via the internet.

Efforts to Reduce Tobacco Use among Women

- Using evidence from studies that vary in design, sample characteristics, and intensity of the interventions studied, researchers to date have not found consistent gender-specific differences in the effectiveness of intervention programs for tobacco use.

- A higher percentage of women stop smoking during pregnancy, both spontaneously and with assistance, than at other times in

111

their lives. Using pregnancy-specific programs can increase smoking cessation rates, which benefits infant health and is cost effective. Only about one-third of women who stop smoking during pregnancy are still abstinent one year after the delivery.

• Successful interventions have been developed to prevent smoking among young people, but little systematic effort has been focused on developing and evaluating prevention interventions specifically for girls.

For More Information

To obtain a copy of *Women and Smoking: A Report of the Surgeon General*, full report or executive summary, call CDC's Office on Smoking and Health at (770) 488-5705 and press 3 to speak with an information specialist. The report, along with supporting documents, is also available on-line at the Office on Smoking and Health Website at www.cdc.gov/tobacco.

Chapter 13

Smoking among Older Adults

Facts about Tobacco and Older Persons

- Of the over 430,000 smoking-related deaths annually in the U.S., over 94% are to persons aged 50 and over; over 70% are to persons aged 65 and over.

- One in three smokers die prematurely in the U.S., losing an average of 12 to 15 years of life versus normal life expectancy—thereby eliminating retirement years for most of these people. We refer to smoker's continuing to smoke in spite of these odds as "Smoker's Russian Roulette."

- Nationally about 10.6% of persons aged 65 and over are smokers—over 3.7 million persons nationally. Nationally about 23.3% of persons aged 50 to 64 are smokers—about nine million persons nationally. Thus, nationally almost 13 million Americans

"Fact Sheet on Tobacco and Older Persons" is reprinted with permission from The Center for Social Gerontology, Inc., Ann Arbor, Michigan. © 2001. For additional information visit The Center for Social Gerontology website at http://www.tcsg.org. "The U.S. Surgeon General Reports Additional Health Risks Associated with Smoking Among Seniors" is from *The Health Consequences of Smoking: A Report of the Surgeon General*, U.S. Department of Health and Human Services, Centers for Disease Control and Prevention, National Center for Chronic Disease Prevention and Health Promotion, Office on Smoking and Health, 2004.

aged 50 and over are currently smokers. The almost 13 million smokers aged 50 and over account for over 27% of all adult smokers in the U.S.

• Today's generation of older Americans—those persons born between 1900 and 1948—had smoking rates among the highest of any U.S. generation. In the mid-1960s, about 54% of adult males smoked and another 21% were former smokers; over 34% of adult females were smokers and another 8% were former smokers. Today's epidemic of smoking-related deaths is the result of these high smoking rates.

• Of the approximately three million pipe smokers in the U.S., over half are over the age of 46.

• All the major causes of death among the elderly are associated with smoking or secondhand smoke—cancer, heart disease, and stroke. And, each of these diseases generally is associated with months and years of disabling pain and suffering.

• Tobacco-related fires claimed almost 1,400 deaths in 1995; of these over 700 occurred to persons aged 50 and over (over 50%) and almost 440 of these deaths were to persons aged 65 and over (over 30%). Smoking is the number one cause of fires that kill older persons.

• Of cases of oral and throat cancer in the U.S., 95% occur in persons aged 40 and over; the average age at diagnosis is 60 years. Smoking, particularly when combined with heavy alcohol consumption, is the primary risk factor for approximately 75% of oral cancers in the U.S. In 1998, about 30,000 Americans will be diagnosed with oral and throat cancer; about 8,000 deaths will result, of which 5,200 will be men and 2,800 women.

• Recent research has indicated that smoking use is related to a number of other health problems/diseases that are generally associated with aging, including hearing loss, vision loss, oral health problems, impotence, wrinkles, dementia and Alzheimer's.

• Research has shown that stopping smoking results in improvement in health status at any age, including in those persons aged 65 and over. Some health benefits are almost immediate, and the longer people refrain from smoking, the more their health improves.

The U.S. Surgeon General Reports Additional Health Risks Associated with Smoking Among Seniors

- Smoking reduces bone density among postmenopausal women.

- Smoking is causally related to an increased risk for hip fractures in men and women.

- Of the 850,000 fractures among those over age 65 in the United States each year, 300,000 are hip fractures. Persons with a hip fracture are 12% to 20% more likely to die than those without a hip fracture. Estimated costs related to hip fractures range from $7 billion to $10 billion each year.

- Smoking is related to nuclear cataracts of the lens of the eye, the most common type of cataract in the United States. Cataracts are the leading cause of blindness worldwide and a leading cause of visual loss in the United States. Smokers have two to three times the risk of developing cataracts as nonsmokers.

- Chronic obstructive pulmonary disease (COPD) is consistently among the top 10 most common chronic health conditions and among the top 10 conditions that limit daily activities. Prevalence of COPD is highest in men and women 65 years of age and older (16.7% among men and 12.6% among women).

Chapter 14

African Americans and Tobacco Use

African Americans continue to suffer disproportionately from chronic and preventable disease compared with white Americans.[1] Of the three leading causes of death in African Americans—heart disease, cancer, and stroke—smoking and other tobacco use are major contributors.[2]

Health Effects

- Each year, approximately 45,000 African Americans die from a preventable smoking-related disease.[3]

- If current trends continue, an estimated 1.6 million African Americans who are now under the age of 18 years will become regular smokers. About 500,000 of those smokers will die of a smoking-related disease.[4]

- Smoking is responsible for 87% of lung cancers. African American men are at least 50% more likely to develop lung cancer than white men.[1] African American men have a higher mortality rate of cancer of the lung and bronchus (100.8 per 100,000) than do white men (70.1 per 100,000).[5]

"African Americans and Tobacco," Tobacco Information and Prevention Source (TIPS), National Center for Chronic Disease Prevention and Health Promotion, Centers for Disease Control and Prevention (CDC), reviewed September 5, 2003.

- Stroke is associated with cerebrovascular disease and is a major cause of death in the United States. Smoking significantly elevates the risk of stroke. Cerebrovascular disease is twice as high among African American men (53.1 per 100,000) as among white men (26.3 per 100,000) and twice as high among African American women (40.6 per 100,000) as among white women (22.6 per 100,000).[1]

- Levels of serum cotinine (metabolized nicotine) are higher among African American smokers than among white or Mexican American smokers for the same number of cigarettes.[6]

Cigarette Smoking Prevalence

- In 1997, smoking prevalence rates were similar among African American adults (26.7%) and white adults (25.3%) in the United States.[7]

- In 1997, African American men (32.1%) smoked at a higher rate than white men (27.4%); African American women (22.4%) and white women (23.3%), however, smoked at a similar rate.[7]

- The decline of smoking among African American young people during the 1970s and 1980s was widely viewed as a great public health success. Unfortunately, subsequent national surveys have shown that smoking rates among African American high school students are starting to increase, although those rates are still lower than those for other students.[8]

- The 1999 National Youth Tobacco Survey (NYTS) estimates that cigarette smoking prevalence during the past month was higher among white high school students (32.8%) and lower among African American (15.8%) students. However, the rate of smoking among middle school students was similar; about 1 in 10 African American (9.0%) and white (8.8%) middle school students reported having smoked cigarettes in the past month.[8]

- The Centers for Disease Control and Prevention's 1999 Youth Risk Behavior Surveillance System (YRBSS) report estimates that cigarette smoking prevalence during the past month was higher among white (38.6%) and Hispanic (32.7%) high school students than among African American (19.7%) students.[9]

- According to 1999 the Monitoring the Future Survey data, past month smoking prevalence was lower among African American high school seniors (14.9%) than among white (40.1%) high school seniors.[10]

Cigarette Smoking Behavior

- Approximately three of every four African American smokers prefer menthol cigarettes. Among whites, approximately a quarter of smokers prefer menthol cigarettes. Menthol may facilitate absorption of harmful cigarette smoke constituents.[1]

- Among adult African American smokers the most popular brands are Newport, Kool, and Salem. Similar brand preference was found among African American teens with 61.3% preferred Newport, 10.9% preferred Kool, and 9.7% preferred Salem.[1]

Prevalence of Other Forms of Tobacco Use

- Aggregated National Health Interview Survey data from 1987 and 1991 show that more white men (4.8%) smoked cigars than did African American men (3.9%).[1]

- African American men (3.1%) use chewing tobacco or snuff less than white men (6.8%).[1]

- The 1999 NYTS study found that cigar use was nearly similar among white (16.0%) and African American (14.8%) high school students; African American middle school students (8.8%) were significantly more likely to smoke cigars than were white students (4.9%).[8]

- In 1999, the prevalence of smokeless tobacco use was lower among African American high school (2.4%) and middle school (1.9%) male students than among white high school (8.7%) and middle school (3.0%), and among Hispanic high school (3.6%) and middle school (2.2%) male students.[8]

African Americans and Quitting

- Of current African American adult smokers, more than 70% indicated that they want to quit smoking completely.[11] African American smokers are more likely than white smokers to have quit for at least one day during the previous year (29.7% compared with 26.0%).[1]

- Prevalence of cessation (the percentage of persons who have smoked at least 100 cigarettes and quit) is higher among whites (50.5%) than among African Americans (35.4%).[1]

Tobacco Industry Economic Influence

- A one-year study found that three major African American publications—*Ebony*, *Jet*, and *Essence*—received proportionately higher profits from cigarette advertisements than did other magazines.[1]

- The tobacco industry attempts to maintain a positive image and public support among African Americans by supporting cultural events and making contributions to minority higher education institutions, elected officials, civic and community organizations, and scholarship programs.[1]

References

1. U.S. Department of Health and Human Services. *Tobacco Use Among U.S. Racial/Ethnic Minority Groups—African Americans, American Indians and Alaska Natives, Asian Americans and Pacific Islanders, and Hispanics: A Report of the Surgeon General.* Atlanta: U.S. Department of Health and Human Services, Centers for Disease Control and Prevention, 1998.

2. Centers for Disease Control and Prevention, *Chronic Disease in Minority Populations.* Atlanta: CDC, 1994: 2–16.

3. Centers for Disease Control and Prevention, Office on Smoking and Health, Unpublished data, 1995.

4. Centers for Disease Control and Prevention. At-A-Glance. *Tobacco Use Among U.S. Racial/Ethnic Minority Groups—African Americans, American Indians and Alaska Natives, Asian Americans and Pacific Islanders, and Hispanics*, Atlanta: CDC, 1998.

5. American Cancer Society, Inc. *Cancer Facts and Figures 2000.* Atlanta: ACS, 2000.

6. Caraballo R. "Racial and ethnic differences in serum cotinine levels of cigarette smokers, Third National Health and Nutrition Examination Survey, 1988–1991." *JAMA* 1998; 280(2): 135–9.

7. Centers for Disease Control and Prevention. Cigarette smoking among adults—United States, 1997. *MMWR* 1999; 48: 993–6.

8. Centers for Disease Control and Prevention. Tobacco use among middle and high school students—United States, 1999. *MMWR* 2000; 49: 49–53.

9. Centers for Disease Control and Prevention. Youth risk behavior surveillance—United States, 1999. *MMWR* 2000; 49, No. SS-5.

10. The University of Michigan. Cigarette Smoking Among American Teens Continues Gradual Decline (press release). December 17, 1999.

11. Centers for Disease Control and Prevention. Cigarette smoking among adults—United States, 1993. *MMWR* 1994 43: 925–29.

Chapter 15

Hispanics and Tobacco Use

Approximately 31.3 million (11.2%) Americans are of Latin American or other Spanish descent. By 2005, Hispanics are expected to surpass African Americans as the nation's second largest racial/ethnic group, behind non-Hispanic whites.[1] Most Hispanic Americans are of Mexican, Puerto Rican, Cuban, or South/Central American ancestry. Although cultural differences exist among subgroups, most Hispanics speak Spanish and are Roman Catholic. Hispanic Americans have settled across the United States; however, 84% reside in Arizona, California, Colorado, Florida, Illinois, New Jersey, New Mexico, New York, and Texas.[2] Population survey data results vary, depending on the location and the language used in the surveys.

Health Effects

- Smoking is responsible for 87% of the lung cancer deaths in the United States. Overall, lung cancer is the leading cause of cancer deaths among Hispanics.[3]

- Lung cancer deaths are about three times higher for Hispanic men (23.1 per 100,000) than for Hispanic women (7.7 per 100,000). The rate of lung cancer deaths per 100,000 were

"Hispanics and Tobacco," Tobacco Information and Prevention Source (TIPS), National Center for Chronic Disease Prevention and Health Promotion, Centers for Disease Control and Prevention (CDC), reviewed September 5, 2003.

higher among Cuban American men (33.7) than among Puerto Rican (28.3) and Mexican American (21.9) men.[3]

- Coronary heart disease is the leading cause of death for Hispanics living in the United States. Among Hispanic subgroups in 1992–1994, death rates for coronary heart disease were 82 per 100,000 for Mexican American men and 44.2 per 100,000 for Mexican American women, 118.6 per 100,000 for Puerto Rican men and 67.3 per 100,000 for Puerto Rican women, and 95.2 per 100,000 for Cuban men and 42.4 per 100,000 for Cuban women.[3]

Cigarette Smoking Prevalence

- The 1997 National Health Interview Survey data show that overall smoking prevalence among Hispanic adults was 20.4%, compared with 16.9% for Asian Americans and Pacific Islanders, 25.3% for whites, 26.7% for African Americans, and 34.1% for American Indians and Alaska Natives.[4]

- In 1997, 26.2% of Hispanic men smoked compared with 27.4% of white men. The smoking rate among Hispanic women was 14.3 %, compared with 23.3% among white women.[4]

- The Monitoring the Future Study shows that cigarette smoking among Hispanic high school seniors declined from 35.7% in 1977 to 20.6% in 1989; however, smoking prevalence has been increasing in the 1990s—from 21.7% in 1990 to 27.3% in 1999.[5]

- The Centers for Disease Control and Prevention's 1999 Youth Risk Behavior Surveillance System (YRBSS) found that about one-third of Hispanic high school students in grades 9 through 12 were current cigarette smokers. Smoking prevalence increased by one-third among Hispanic students from 1991 (25.3%) to 1997 (34.0%). Recent YRBSS data shows that current smoking trends among Hispanic students remain high, but appeared to have plateaued with no statistically significant difference between 1997 and 1999—34.0% and 32.7%, respectively.[6]

- The 1999 National Youth Tobacco Survey (NYTS) estimates that current cigarette smoking prevalence use by racial/ethnic groups was higher among white high school students (32.8%) than among Hispanic (25.8%) and African American (15.8%) students. However, the rate of smoking among middle school students by racial/ethnic groups was relatively similar; about 1 in 10 Hispanic (11.0%), African American (9.0%), and white

(8.8%) middle school students reported smoking cigarettes in the past 30 days.[7]

Prevalence of Other Forms of Tobacco Use

- Aggregated National Health Interview Survey data from 1987 and 1991 show that more Cuban American men (2.5%) smoked cigars than Mexican American (1.5%) and Puerto Rican (1.3%) men.[3]

- The 1999 YRBSS study found that 21.9% of Hispanic male high school students reported smoking a cigar on one or more days during the past month compared with about 28.3% of white male and 16.0% of African American male students.[6]

- The 1999 NYTS shows that among high school students, 13.4% of Hispanics, 14.8% of African Americans, and 16.0% of whites smoked cigars, and that among middle school students, 7.6% of Hispanics, 8.8% of African Americans, and 4.9% of whites smoked cigars in the past 30 days.[7]

- The 1999 NYTS found that smokeless tobacco use among middle and high school for white male students was 3.0% and 8.7%, respectively, for Hispanic male students 2.2% and 3.6%, respectively, and for African American students 1.9% and 2.4%, respectively.[7]

Tobacco Industry Influence

- Tobacco products are advertised and promoted disproportionately to racial/ethnic minority communities. Examples of target promotions include the introduction of a cigarette product with the brand name "Rio" and an earlier cigarette product named "Dorado," which was advertised and marketed to the Hispanic American community.[3]

- To increase its credibility in the Hispanic community, the tobacco industry has contributed to programs that aim to enhance the primary and secondary education of children, has funded universities and colleges, and has supported scholarship programs targeting Hispanics. Tobacco companies have also placed advertising in many Hispanic publications. The industry also contribute to cultural Hispanic events and provide significant support to the Hispanic art community.[3,8]

References

1. United States Department of Commerce, Bureau of the Census. U.S. Census Facts for Hispanic Americans, http://www .census.gov/population/estimates/nation/intfiles3-1.txt.

2. United States Department of Commerce, Bureau of the Census. U.S. Census Facts for Hispanic Americans, http://www .census.gov/population/estimates/state/srh/srhus96.txt.

3. U.S. Department of Health and Human Services. *Tobacco Use Among U.S. Racial/Ethnic Minority Groups—African Americans, American Indians and Alaska Natives, Asian Americans and Pacific Islanders, and Hispanics: A Report of the Surgeon General*. Atlanta: U.S. Department of Health and Human Services, Centers for Disease Control and Prevention, 1998.

4. Centers for Disease Control and Prevention. Cigarette smoking among adults–United States, 1997. *MMWR* 1999; 48: 993–6.

5. The University of Michigan. Cigarette Smoking Among American Teens Continues Gradual Decline (press release). December 17, 1999.

6. Centers for Disease Control and Prevention. Youth risk behavior surveillance—United States, 1999. *MMWR* 2000; 49, No. SS-5.

7. Centers for Disease Control and Prevention. Tobacco use among middle and high school students—United States, 1999. *MMWR* 2000; 49: 49–53.

8. Glode WF. RJR puts on the Ritz, PM goes to Rio. *Advertising Age* 1985 (56.2):1, 78; Leviten P. Manufacturers send changing smoking signals. *Supermarket Business* 1985 (40.12):39–43; and Walters DKH. Cigarettes: Makers Aim at Special Niches to Boost Sales. *Los Angeles Times* 1985 Sept 15; Business Section:1 (col 3).

Chapter 16

Asian Americans and Pacific Islanders and Tobacco Use

Asian Americans and Pacific Islanders are persons of Asian or Pacific Islander ancestry whose origins are from China and Mongolia to the north, Indonesia to the south, the Indian subcontinent to the west, and the U.S.-related Pacific Islands to the east.[1] The six largest subgroups of Asian Americans are from China, the Philippines, Japan, Asian India, Korea, and Vietnam. Hawaiians, Samoans, and Guamanians are the three largest Pacific Islander subgroups. Although Asian Americans reside across the country, approximately 66% live in California, Hawaii, Illinois, New York, and Texas. Approximately 75% of the Pacific Islanders population live in just two states—California and Hawaii. Asian American population nearly doubled in size from an estimated 3.5 million in 1980 to almost 7 million in 1990, while Pacific Islanders population grew by 41% between 1980 (259,566) and 1990 (365,024).[2]

Health Effects

- Smoking is responsible for 87% of the lung cancer deaths in the United States. In 1993, lung cancer was the leading cause of cancer death (22.3%) among Asian Americans and Pacific Islanders.[3]

"Asian Americans and Pacific Islanders and Tobacco," Tobacco Information and Prevention Source (TIPS), National Center for Chronic Disease Prevention and health Promotion, Centers for Disease Control and Prevention (CDC), reviewed September 5, 2003.

- The death rate for lung cancer was 27.9 per 100,000 for Asian American and Pacific Islander men and 11.4 per 100,000 for women. Among subgroups, both Hawaiian men (88.9 per 100,000) and women (44.1 per 100,000) had the highest rate of lung cancer deaths, and Filipino men (29.8 per 100,000) and women (10.0 per 100,000) had the lowest.[3]

- Asian Americans and Pacific Islanders had the lowest rates of death from coronary heart disease among the primary racial/ ethnic groups in the United States. Among Asian Americans and Pacific Islanders subgroups, Koreans (82 per 100,000) had the lowest death rates for cardiovascular diseases and Japanese (162 per 100,000) had the highest rate.[3]

Cigarette Smoking Prevalence

- The 1997 National Health Interview Survey data show that overall adult smoking prevalence was lower among Asian Americans and Pacific Islanders (16.9%) than among Hispanics (20.4%), whites (25.3%), African Americans (26.7%), and American Indians and Alaska Natives (34.1%).[4]

- In 1997, 21.6% of Asian American and Pacific Islander men smoked, compared with 27.4% of white men. However, Asian American and Pacific Islander women (12.4%) were significantly less likely to smoke than white women (23.3%).[4] Smoking rates are much higher among Asian American and Pacific Islander men than among Asian American and Pacific Islander women, regardless of country of origin.[3]

- A 1990–1991 California survey estimated that smoking rates for men were 35.8% for Korean Americans, 24% for Filipino Americans, 20.1% for Japanese Americans, and 19.1% for Chinese Americans. Among women, smoking prevalence was 14.9% for Japanese Americans, 13.6% for Korean Americans, 8.9% for Filipino Americans, and 4.7% for Chinese Americans.[3]

- Among high school seniors, aggregated 1990–1994 Monitoring the Future Survey data show that for racial/ethnic groups, smoking prevalence was highest among American Indians and Alaska Natives (males, 41.1 percent; females, 39.4 percent) followed by whites (males, 33.4%; females, 33.1%), Hispanics (males, 28.5%; females, 19.2%), Asian Americans and Pacific

Islanders (males, 20.6%; females, 13.8%), and African Americans (males, 11.6%; females, 8.6%).[3]

- Among Asian American and Pacific Islander high school seniors 4.4% of male students and 4.5% of females students reported smoking one-half pack or more per day.[3]

Cigarette Smoking Behavior

- Research shows an association between cigarette smoking and acculturation among Asian American and Pacific Islander adults from Southeast Asia. Those who had a higher English-language proficiency and those living in the United States longer were less likely to be smokers.[3]

- Among Chinese men, the average number of cigarettes smoked per day increased with the percentage of their lifetime spent in the United States.[3]

- Among Vietnamese, the prevalence of smoking was higher among men who immigrated to the United States in 1981 or later and who were not fluent in English.[3]

Asian Americans and Pacific Islanders and Quitting

- Among current smokers, Asian Americans and Pacific Islanders were slightly more likely than white smokers to have quit for at least one day during the previous year (32.0%, compared with 26.0%). Asian Americans and Pacific Islanders (2.5%), however, are less likely than whites (3.4%) to remain abstinent for one to 90 days.[3]

- According to aggregated 1994–1995 National Health Interview Survey data, the prevalence of cessation among Asian Americans and Pacific Islanders aged 55 years and older was higher than among younger Asian Americans and Pacific Islanders.[3]

- A community intervention trial for Vietnamese men conducted in San Francisco significantly increased the likelihood of quitting smoking. This program included a long-running anti-tobacco media campaign and school- and family-based components.[3]

Tobacco Industry

- Studies have found a higher density of tobacco billboards in racial/ethnic minority communities. For example, a 1993 study in San

Diego, California, found the highest proportion of tobacco bill-boards were posted in Asian American communities and the lowest proportion were in white communities.[3]

- Among racial/ethnic minority communities in San Diego, the highest average number of tobacco displays was found in Asian American stores (6.4), compared with Hispanic (4.6) and African American (3.7) stores.[3]

References

1. Chen MS, Jr. Cancer prevention and control among Asian and Pacific Islander Americans: findings and recommendations. *Cancer* (suppl. 8) 1998; 83: 1856–1862.

2. United States Department of Commerce. Bureau of the Census. Economic and Statistics Administration. We the Americans: Asians and Pacific Islanders. http://www.census.gov/apsd/www/wepeople.html, September 1993.

3. U.S. Department of Health and Human Services. *Tobacco Use Among U.S. Racial/Ethnic Minority Groups—African Americans, American Indians and Alaska Natives, Asian Americans and Pacific Islanders, and Hispanics: A Report of the Surgeon General.* Atlanta: U.S. Department of Health and Human Services, Centers for Disease Control and Prevention, 1998.

4. Centers for Disease Control and Prevention. Cigarette smoking among adults—United States, 1997." *MMWR* 1999; 48: 993–6.

Chapter 17

American Indians and Alaska Natives and Tobacco Use

Surveys of Tobacco Use among American Indians and Alaska Natives

Approximately 2 million American Indians and Alaska Natives live in the United States. Since July 1, 1990, the U.S. population of American Indians and Alaska Natives has increased by 10.4%. The number of American Indians and Alaska Natives is expected to increase steadily to 2.4 million in 2000, 3.1 million in 2020, and 4.4 million in 2050. Major subgroups in this population are American Indians, Eskimos, and Aleuts. Most American Indians and Alaska Natives have settled across the country; the largest percentage resides in Oklahoma (13%).[1] Although many tribes consider tobacco a sacred gift and use it during religious ceremonies and as traditional medicine, the tobacco-related health problems they suffer are caused by chronic cigarette smoking and spit tobacco use. Because of the cultural and geographic diversity of American Indians and Alaska Natives, tobacco use often varies widely by region or subgroup.[2]

"American Indians and Alaska Natives and Tobacco," Tobacco Information and Prevention Source (TIPS), National Center for Chronic Disease Prevention and Health Promotion, Centers for Disease Control and Prevention (CDC), reviewed September 5, 2003; and "Cigarette Use Among American Indian/Alaska Native Youths," National Household Survey on Drug Abuse (NHSDA), U.S. Department of Health and Human Services, January 25, 2002.

Health Effects

- Nationally, lung cancer is the leading cause of cancer death among American Indians and Alaska Natives.[2]

- Smoking-attributable deaths from cancers of the lung, trachea, and bronchus were slightly higher among American Indian and Alaska Native men (33.5 per 100,000) and women (18.4 per 100,000) than those among Asian American and Pacific Islander men (27.9 per 100,000) and women (11.4 per 100,000) and Hispanic men (23.1 per 100,000) and women (7.7 per 100,000), but lower than rates among African American men (81.6 per 100,000) and women (27.2 per 100,000) and white men (54.9 per 100,000) and women (27.9 per 100,000).[2]

- Cardiovascular disease is the leading cause of death among American Indians and Alaska Natives, and tobacco use is an important risk factor for this disease.[2]

Cigarette Smoking Prevalence

- Data from the 1997 National Health Interview Survey show that among the five major racial and ethnic populations adult smoking prevalence was highest among American Indians and Alaska Natives (34.1%) followed by African Americans (26.7%), whites (25.3%), Hispanics (20.4%), and Asian Americans and Pacific Islanders (16.9%).[3]

- In 1997, 37.9% of American Indian and Alaska Native men smoked, compared with 27.4% of white men. The smoking rate among American Indian and Alaska Native women was 31.3% compared with 23.3% among white women.[3]

- Smoking rates and consumption among American Indians and Alaska Natives vary by region and state. Smoking rates are highest in Alaska (45.1%) and the North Plains (44.2%) and lowest in the Southwest (17.0%). The prevalence of heavy smoking (25 or more cigarettes per day) is also highest in the North Plains (13.5%).[2]

- Since 1978, the prevalence of cigarette smoking has declined for African American, Asian American and Pacific Islander, Hispanic, and white women of reproductive age (18–44 years), but not for American Indian and Alaska Native women. In 1994–1995, the rate of smoking among American Indian and

Alaska Native women of reproductive age was 44.3%, compared with white (29.4%), African American (23.4%), Hispanic (16.4%), and Asian American and Pacific Islander (5.7%) women of reproductive age.[2]

- Aggregated 1990–1994 Monitoring the Future Survey data show that racial/ethnic smoking prevalence is highest among American Indian and Alaska Native high school seniors (males, 41.1%; females, 39.4%) followed by white high school seniors (males, 33.4%; females, 33.1%), Hispanics (males, 28.5%; females, 19.2%), Asian Americans and Pacific Islanders (males, 20.6%; females, 13.8%), and African Americans (males, 11.6%; females, 8.6 %).[2]

Cigarette Smoking Behavior

- Compared with whites, American Indians and Alaska Natives smoke fewer cigarettes each day. In 1994–1995, the percentage of American Indians and Alaska Natives who reported that they were light smokers (smoking fewer than 15 cigarettes per day) was 49.9%, compared with 35.3% for whites.[2]

- American Indian and Alaska Native lands are sovereign nations and are not subject to state laws prohibiting the sale and promotion of tobacco products to minors. As a result, American Indian and Alaska Native young people have access to tobacco products at a very young age.[4]

Prevalence of Other Forms of Tobacco Use

- Aggregated National Health Interview Survey data from 1987 and 1991 show that 5.3% of American Indian and Alaska Native men smoked cigars, compared with 4.8% of white men and 3.9% of African American men.[2]

- Pipe smoking prevalence was higher among American Indians and Alaska Natives (6.9%), compared with whites (2.9%), African American (2.4%), and Asian Americans and Pacific Islanders (2.3%), who smoked pipes at nearly similar rates.[2]

- Among men and women combined, the use of chewing tobacco or snuff was 4.5% among American Indians and Alaska Natives, compared with 3.4% for whites, 3.0% for African Americans, 0.8% for Hispanics, and 0.6% for Asian Americans and Pacific Islanders.[2]

• The use of smokeless tobacco among American Indian and Alaska Native men varies by state and region. The prevalence among men is highest in the Northern Plains (24.6%) and lowest in the Pacific Northwest (1.8%).[2]

Tobacco Industry Influence

• To build its image and credibility in the community, the tobacco industry targets American Indians and Alaska Natives by funding cultural events such as powwows and rodeos.[2]

• The tobacco industry commonly uses cultural symbols and designs to target racial/ethnic populations that include American Indians and Alaska Natives. American Spirit cigarettes were promoted as "natural" cigarettes; the package featured an American Indian smoking a pipe. In addition, certain tobacco product advertisements have used visual images, such as American Indian warriors, to target their product.[2]

References

1. United States Department of Commerce, Bureau of the Census. U.S. Census Facts for Native Americans http://www.census .gov./population/estimates/nation/intfile3-1.txt, October 1997.

2. U.S. Department of Health and Human Services. *Tobacco Use Among U.S. Racial / Ethnic Minority Groups—African Americans, American Indians and Alaska Natives, Asian Americans and Pacific Islanders, and Hispanics: A Report of the Surgeon General*. Atlanta: U.S. Department of Health and Human Services, Centers for Disease Control and Prevention, 1998.

3. Centers for Disease Control and Prevention. Cigarette smoking among adults—United States, 1997. *MMWR* 1999; 48: 993-6.

Cigarette Use among American Indian/Alaska Native Youths

In Brief

• American Indian/Alaska Native youths aged 12 to 17 were more likely than youths from other racial/ethnic groups to smoke cigarettes during the past month

- American Indian/Alaska Native youths were less likely than youths from other racial/ethnic groups to believe that their parents would strongly disapprove of their smoking one or more packs of cigarettes per day

- American Indian/Alaska Native youths were also less likely than youths from other racial/ethnic groups to strongly or somewhat disapprove of their peers' smoking one or more packs of cigarettes per day

The 1999 and 2000 National Household Surveys on Drug Abuse (NHSDAs) asked respondents aged 12 or older to report cigarette use during the month prior to the survey (that is, current use). Respondents were analyzed by race and ethnic subgroups and by geographic regions for comparative purposes. Youths aged 12 to 17 were also asked to report how they thought their parents would feel about their smoking one or more packs of cigarettes per day and how they felt about someone their own age smoking one or more packs of cigarettes per day. The three response categories were (a) strongly disapprove, (b) somewhat disapprove, and (c) neither approve nor disapprove.

Prevalence of Cigarette Use

According to the 2000 NHSDA, approximately 144,000 youths aged 12 to 17 in the United States were American Indians/Alaska Natives. Among youths, 28 percent of American Indians/Alaska Natives were current smokers compared with 16 percent of whites, 10 percent of Hispanics, 8 percent of Asians, and 6 percent of blacks.

Combined data from the 1999 and 2000 surveys indicated no significant differences between males and females in rates of current smoking among American Indian/Alaska Native youths. However, among youths from other racial ethnic groups, smoking rates were higher among females (15 percent) than males (14 percent). Furthermore, rates of current cigarette use were similar among American Indian/Alaska Native youths who lived in the South and West but youths from other racial/ethnic groups who lived in the South (15 percent) were more likely to be current cigarette smokers compared with those who resided in the West (11 percent). Likewise, rates of current cigarette use were similar among American Indians/Alaska Native youths who lived in small and non-metropolitan counties, but among youths from other racial/ethnic groups, those who lived in non-metropolitan counties

(16 percent) were more likely to be current cigarette smokers than youths who lived in small metropolitan counties (15 percent).

Perceptions of Parental Attitudes Regarding Cigarette Use

American Indian/Alaska Native youths (80 percent) were significantly less likely to report that they thought their parents would strongly disapprove of their smoking one or more packs of cigarettes per day compared with youths from other racial/ethnic groups (80 vs. 88 percent). Previous research has shown that rates of substance use are lower among youths whose parents disapproved of such use than among youths whose parents did not disapprove. The 2000 NHSDA showed that 9 percent of youths who felt their parents would strongly disapprove of their smoking one or more packs of cigarettes per day reported past month cigarette use compared with 46 percent of youths who felt their parents would somewhat disapprove or neither approve nor disapprove.

Youths' Attitudes Regarding Peer Cigarette Use

American Indian/Alaska Native youths (77 percent) were less likely to report that they strongly or somewhat disapproved of someone their own age smoking one or more packs of cigarettes per day than youths from other racial/ethnic groups (85 percent). Prior research has demonstrated that youths who disapproved of their peers' cigarette use are less likely to use cigarettes themselves than youths who did not disapprove of such use. Results from the 2000 NHSDA indicated that 9 percent of youths who strongly or somewhat disapproved of someone their own age smoking one or more packs of cigarettes per day reported current cigarette use compared with 38 percent of youths who neither approved nor disapproved.

Part Two

Tobacco-Related Health Hazards

Chapter 18

The Health Consequences of Smoking

The Surgeon General is appointed by the President of the United States to help promote and protect the health of citizens. As the nation's highest-ranking public health officer, the Surgeon General can direct studies on health risks—such as smoking. The 2004 *Surgeon General's Report on the Health Consequences of Smoking* was prepared by 19 of the country's top scientists, doctors, and public health experts. The full report is nearly 1,000 pages long and is written for a scientific audience. The text in this chapter explains what the report says and what it means to you. The full report can be accessed online at www.surgeongeneral.gov.

After reviewing scientific evidence, the Surgeon General of the United States, working with a team of leading experts on smoking and health, reached these important conclusions:

- Smoking harms nearly every organ of your body. It causes diseases and worsens your health.

- Quitting smoking has many benefits. It lowers your risk for diseases and death caused by smoking and improves your health.

Excerpted from "The Health Consequences of Smoking: What It Means to You," prepared by the Centers for Disease Control and Prevention (CDC) based on U.S. Department of Health and Human Services. *The Health Consequences of Smoking: A Report of the Surgeon General.* U.S. Department of Health and Human Services, Centers for Disease Control and Prevention, National Center for Chronic Disease Prevention and Health Promotion, Office on Smoking and Health, 2004.

- Low-tar and low-nicotine cigarettes are not safer to smoke.

- The list of diseases that we know are caused by smoking has grown even longer. The list now includes cancers of the cervix, pancreas, kidneys, and stomach, aortic aneurysms, leukemia, cataracts, pneumonia, and gum disease.

The 2004 Surgeon General's report has new information about how smoking harms your health. A new database of more than 1,600 articles cited in the report is available on the internet. By going to the Centers for Disease Control and Prevention (CDC) website at www.cdc.gov/tobacco/sgr/sgr_2004/ you can search many of the studies cited. Topics include cancer, cardiovascular diseases, respiratory diseases, reproductive effects, and other harmful health effects.

Smoking Causes Cancer

Cancer is the second leading cause of death in the United States. One out of every four people in this country dies because of cancer. In 2003, researchers estimated that more than half a million Americans—that's over 1,500 people a day—would die of cancer. The cost of treating cancer in the United States is overwhelming. In 2002, cancer cost our nation over $170 billion. This included more than $110 billion in lost work by people who were disabled or who died, and at least $60 billion for medical treatments.

Cancer was among the first diseases found to be caused by smoking. The earliest major studies, carried out in the 1950s and 1960s, focused on lung cancer. The number of lung cancer cases among smokers reached very high levels during that time.

Since the first Surgeon General's report on smoking in 1964 concluded that smoking causes lung cancer, the list of diseases linked to smoking has grown to include cancers in organs throughout the body. Your risk for these cancers increases with the number of cigarettes you smoke and the number of years you smoke. Your risk decreases after quitting completely.

Facts You Should Know

- Smoking causes cancers of the mouth, throat, larynx (voice box), lung, esophagus, pancreas, kidney, and bladder.

- Smoking causes cancers of the stomach, cervix, and acute myeloid leukemia, which is a cancer of the blood.

- Cigarette smoking causes most cases of lung cancer. Smokers are about 20 times more likely to develop lung cancer than non-smokers. Smoking causes about 90 percent of lung cancer deaths in men and almost 80 percent in women.

- Using both cigarettes and alcohol causes most cases of larynx cancer.

- Certain agents in tobacco smoke can damage important genes that control the growth of cells and lead to cancer.

- Smoking low-tar cigarettes does not reduce your risk for lung cancer.

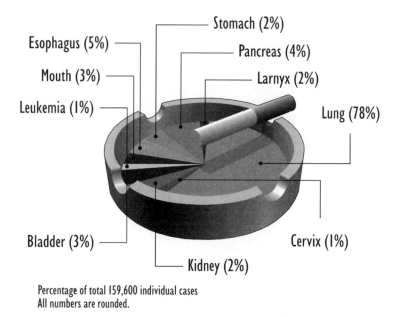

Percentage of total 159,600 individual cases
All numbers are rounded.

Figure 18.1. *Cancers You Get from Smoking.*

Smoking Causes Cardiovascular Diseases

Heart disease and stroke are cardiovascular (heart and blood vessel) diseases caused by smoking. Heart disease and stroke are also the first and third leading causes of death in the United States.

More than 61 million people in the United States suffer from some form of heart and blood vessel disease. This includes high blood pressure, coronary heart disease, stroke, and congestive heart failure. Nearly 2,600 Americans die every day as a result of cardiovascular diseases. This is about one death every 33 seconds. You are up to four times more likely to die from heart disease if you smoke. In 2003, heart disease and stroke cost the United States an estimated $351 billion in health care costs and lost productivity from death and disability.

The link between smoking and heart disease was noted in the first Surgeon General's report in 1964. Later reports revealed a much stronger connection. Researchers found that smoking is a major cause of diseases of blood vessels inside and outside the heart.

Most cases of these diseases are caused by atherosclerosis, a hardening and narrowing of the arteries. Damage to your arteries and blood clots that block blood flow can cause heart attacks or strokes.

Cigarette smoking speeds up this process even in smokers in their 20s. Cigarette smoke damages the cells lining the blood vessels and heart. The damaged tissue swells. This makes it hard for blood vessels to get enough oxygen to cells and tissues. Your heart and all parts of your body must have oxygen. Perhaps most important, cigarette smoking can increase your risk of dangerous blood clots, both because of swelling and redness and by causing blood platelets to clump together.

Cigarettes aren't the only dangerous kind of tobacco. Even smokeless tobacco can lead to heart and blood vessel disease.

Facts You Should Know

- Coronary heart disease is the leading cause of death in the United States.

- You are up to four times more likely to die from coronary heart disease if you smoke.

- In 2000, about 1.1 million Americans had heart attacks.

- Even with treatment, 25 percent of men and 38 percent of women die within one year of a heart attack.

- Smoking causes atherosclerosis, or hardening and narrowing of your arteries.

- Smoking causes coronary heart disease.

- Smoking low-tar or low-nicotine cigarettes rather than regular cigarettes does not reduce the risk of coronary heart disease.

- Smoking causes strokes.

- Smoking causes abdominal aortic aneurysm, a dangerous weakening and ballooning of the major artery near your stomach.

Smoking Causes Respiratory Diseases

Smoking harms your lungs. If you smoke, your lungs can't fight infection well and this causes injuries to lung tissues. Tissue injury leads to chronic obstructive pulmonary disease (COPD), sometimes called emphysema, and other respiratory diseases. People with COPD slowly start to die from lack of air.

COPD is the fourth leading cause of death in the United States. It is responsible for more than 100,000 deaths per year. Smoking causes more than 90 percent of these deaths.

Most sudden respiratory illnesses, such as bronchitis or pneumonia, are caused by viral or bacterial infections. They are usually diagnosed as upper respiratory tract infections (nose, throat, and larynx) or lower respiratory tract infections (below the larynx). Smokers have more upper and lower respiratory tract infections than nonsmokers. This happens because smoking damages your body's defenses against infections.

Normally, your body helps keep dangerous viruses and bacteria out by clearing your nose with mucus. But this defense takes almost twice as long in smokers as in nonsmokers. Once viruses and bacteria are inside your body, cells in your immune system usually kill them and prevent infection. But in smokers, some of the cells that destroy germs are decreased while others are increased. This imbalance makes a smoker's immune system weaker.

Chronic lung diseases are long lasting. They usually affect your airways and the tiny sacs where oxygen is absorbed into your lungs. Lung injury in smokers begins when smoke causes lung tissues to become red and swollen. This releases unwanted oxygen molecules that damage the lung. It also causes enzymes to be released that can eat delicate lung tissue.

Normally, your body fights damaging oxygen molecules with antioxidants. It fights the destructive enzymes with defensive enzymes. Smoking makes antioxidants and defensive enzymes less effective. Over time, redness and swelling cause scarring and destroy your lungs, causing COPD.

Smoking harms people of all ages.

- **Infants:** Effects of smoking on lung development can begin before birth. When mothers smoke during pregnancy, it hurts their babies' lungs.

- **Children:** Children and teens who smoke are less physically fit and have more breathing problems. Smoking at this age can slow lung growth. If you smoke as a teenager, your lung function begins to decline years earlier than nonsmokers. This hurts you when you want to be active.

- **All Ages:** At any age, smoking damages your lungs. The more cigarettes you smoke, the faster this happens. Air pollution, being overweight, and not eating enough fresh fruit increase your risk of lung disease even more if you smoke. However, if you quit smoking, your lungs can gradually return to normal for your age.

Facts You Should Know

- Smoking causes injury to the airways and lungs, leading to a deadly lung condition.

- Smokers are more likely than nonsmokers to have upper and lower breathing tract infections.

- Mothers who smoke during pregnancy hurt the lungs of their babies.

- If you smoke during childhood and teenage years, it slows your lung growth and causes your lungs to decline at a younger age.

- Smoking is related to chronic coughing, wheezing, and asthma among children and teens.

- Smoking is related to chronic coughing and wheezing among adults.

- After stopping smoking, former smokers eventually return to normal age-related lung function.

Smoking Harms Reproduction

Smoking harms every phase of reproduction. Women who smoke have more difficulty becoming pregnant and have a higher risk of never becoming pregnant. Women who smoke during pregnancy have a greater chance of complications, premature birth, low birth weight infants, stillbirth, and infant mortality.

Low birth weight is a leading cause of infant deaths. More than 300,000 babies die each year in the United States because of low birth weight. Many of these deaths are linked to smoking. Even though we now know the danger of smoking during pregnancy, fewer than one out of four women quit smoking once they become pregnant.

High Risk Pregnancy: Smoking makes it more difficult for women to become pregnant. Once they are pregnant, women who smoke have more complications. One complication is *placenta previa*, a condition where the placenta (the organ that nourishes the baby) grows too close to the opening of the womb. This condition frequently requires delivery by caesarean section. Pregnant women who smoke are also more likely to have *placental abruption.* In this condition, the placenta separates from the wall of the womb earlier than it should. This can lead to preterm delivery, stillbirth, and early infant death. If you smoke while you are pregnant, you are also at a higher risk that your water will break before labor begins. All these conditions make it more likely that, if you smoke, your baby will be born too early.

Low Birth Weight Babies: Babies of mothers who smoked during pregnancy have lower birth weights, often weighing less than 5.5 pounds. Low birth weight babies are at greater risk for childhood and adult illnesses and even death. Babies of smokers have less muscle mass and more fat than babies of nonsmokers. Nicotine causes the blood vessels to constrict in the umbilical cord and womb. This decreases the amount of oxygen to the unborn baby. This can lead to low birth weight. It also reduces the amount of blood in the baby's system. Pregnant smokers actually eat more than pregnant nonsmokers, yet their babies weigh less. If you quit smoking before your third trimester (the last 3 months), your baby is more likely to be close to normal weight.

Sudden Infant Death Syndrome: The death rate from sudden infant death syndrome (SIDS) has fallen by more than half since the "Back to Sleep" campaign began in the 1990s. This campaign reminds parents that babies should lie on their backs while sleeping. Yet more can be done. Babies exposed to secondhand smoke after birth have double the risk of SIDS. Babies whose mothers smoke before and after birth are three to four times more likely to die from SIDS.

Facts You Should Know

- Smoking causes lower fertility in women.

- Babies of women who smoke are more likely to be born too early.

- Smoking during pregnancy causes *placenta previa* and *placental abruption.* These conditions can cause a baby to be born too early and then be sick.

- The nicotine in cigarette smoke reduces the amount of oxygen reaching the fetus.

- Smoking causes reduced fetal growth and low birth weight.

- Smoking by the mother can cause SIDS.

Other Effects of Smoking

Smoking damages your health in many other ways. Smokers are less healthy overall than nonsmokers. Smoking harms your immune system and increases your risk of infections. The toxic ingredients in

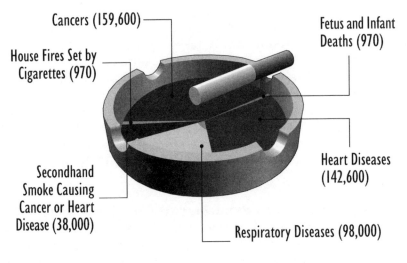

Cancers (159,600)

House Fires Set by Cigarettes (970)

Fetus and Infant Deaths (970)

Secondhand Smoke Causing Cancer or Heart Disease (38,000)

Heart Diseases (142,600)

Respiratory Diseases (98,000)

All numbers are rounded.

Figure 18.2. 440,000 Deaths Each Year Caused by Smoking.

cigarette smoke travel throughout your body. For example, nicotine reaches your brain within 10 seconds after you inhale smoke. It has been found in every organ of the body, as well as in breast milk. If you smoke, your cells will not get the amount of oxygen needed to work properly. This is because carbon monoxide keeps red blood cells from carrying a full load of oxygen. Carcinogens, or cancer-causing poisons, in tobacco smoke bind to cells in your airways and throughout your body.

Smoking harms your whole body. It increases your risk of fractures, dental diseases, sexual problems, eye diseases, and peptic ulcers. If you smoke, your illnesses last longer and you are more likely to be absent from work. In a study of U.S. military personnel, those who smoked were hospitalized 28 percent to 55 percent longer than nonsmokers. And the more cigarettes they smoked, the longer their hospitalization. Smokers also use more medical services than nonsmokers. Among people younger than 65 enrolled in a health maintenance organization, or HMO, health care costs for smokers were 25 percent higher than for nonsmokers.

Facts You Should Know

- Smokers are less healthy than nonsmokers.

- Smokers are more likely to be absent from work than nonsmokers.

- Smokers use medical care services more often than nonsmokers.

- After surgery, smokers have more problems with wound healing and more respiratory complications.

- For women, smoking causes your bones to lose density after menopause.

- Smoking increases your risk of hip fractures.

- Smoking causes half of all cases of adult periodontitis, a serious gum infection that can cause pain and tooth loss.

- For men, smoking may cause sexual problems.

- Smoking increases your risk for cataracts, a leading cause of blindness in the United States and worldwide. Smokers are two to three times more likely to develop cataracts than nonsmokers.

- Smoking causes peptic ulcers in smokers with *Helicobacter pylori* infections. Compared with nonsmokers, smokers with this infection are more likely to develop ulcers and to have complications of an ulcer. In severe cases, this condition can lead to death.

Chapter 19

Risks Associated with Short-Term and Low-Level Smoking

Though most people now understand that smoking can be a very harmful habit over the long run, some folks believe they are protected from harm if they smoke "just a few" cigarettes each day. Unfortunately, there really is no low level of smoking that can be said to be completely safe for any given person. In fact, in some circumstances, just one cigarette can be harmful.

Dose-Response

First, let's talk about a concept called the "dose-response" relationship. Basically, this means that if a small dose of a medication has a small amount of benefit, then a larger dose of that medication will have a larger benefit. This is true for the majority of prescription as well as over-the-counter medications. You probably already know that two aspirin will have a greater effect on your headache than just one. In the case of medications, there is usually a maximum dose that gives maximum benefit, and going to an even higher dose only produces side effects. For example, a dose of three aspirin won't work any better for your headache than two aspirin and is much more likely to upset your stomach. When we use the "dose-response" relationship to talk about the risks of smoking, we use cigarettes per day as the measure of dose, and we measure the adverse effects rather than benefit. For the majority of

"The Risks of Smoking 'Just a Few'," by Trudy Manchester, M.D. Reprinted with permission from www.trytostop.org, © 2001 Massachusetts Department of Public Health. All rights reserved.

medical problems that are caused by smoking, researchers have been able to identify that there is a definite relationship between the "dose" (in this case, cigarettes per day) and the adverse effects; the higher the "dose," the greater the negative effects.

Let's talk about lung function as an example. All individuals will have a decrease in lung capacity as they get older. However, heavy smokers lose their lung capacity more quickly than moderate smokers and moderate smokers lose their lung capacity more quickly than light smokers. It's important to note, however, that even light smokers lose lung capacity more rapidly than nonsmokers do. In this example, it is clear that someone who smokes "just a few" is better protected from loss of lung function than a heavy smoker, but there is no specific low level of cigarettes per day that can be said to be as safe as not smoking at all.

Lung cancer is another example where researchers have identified a clear dose response relationship between cigarettes per day and risk for developing cancer. Heavy smokers are at the highest risk, moderate smokers are at moderate risk, and light smokers are at lowest risk. But all active smokers are at greater risk for lung cancer than nonsmokers. Even passive smokers (people who have secondhand exposure to tobacco smoke) are at higher risk than people who have no exposure at all. In the example of lung cancer, a person who smokes "just a few" will be at lower risk than a moderate or heavy smoker, but that person will still have more risk for developing lung cancer than a nonsmoker. And there is no such thing as "just a little" lung cancer. Once you have cancer, you have cancer, being a light smoker does not necessarily mean that you will have a greater chance for cure than any other person who has lung cancer.

The Effects of a Single Cigarette

Now, let's talk about the situation where even one cigarette can be harmful. In this case, we are talking about the acute effects of smoking, rather than the long-term effects that build up over time. Smoking just a single cigarette causes platelets in your blood to become sticky and they are thus more likely to block tiny blood vessels. Many other measurable changes occur with each single cigarette: the heart rate increases a bit, blood pressure increases a bit, blood vessels which supply the heart muscle constrict a bit, and carbon monoxide levels in the blood increase a bit. All of these changes together can significantly increase the stress to the heart muscle. Even more importantly, these changes and the additional stress can cause an acute heart attack in a person who may already have some blockages in his/her coronary arteries. Once the heart attack has occurred, the damage is done. It doesn't really matter if it was just one out of only five cigarettes per day or one out of forty cigarettes per day that led to the specific heart attack. The good news here is that research has shown that a person who already has blockages can significantly reduce his/her risk for heart attack by quitting smoking. Quitting doesn't make the heart disease or the blockages go away, but it does remove the acute stresses imposed by each and every cigarette.

Any Amount of Smoking Is Not Safe

Researchers who have studied the effects of secondhand smoking have made the strongest arguments against the idea that smoking "just a few" cigarettes is safe. When compared to nonsmokers, passive smokers have been shown to have more lung cancers, more heart disease, and more heart attacks. Even young, otherwise healthy adults with passive smoke exposure have been shown to have early signs of damage to the lining of their arteries that are not seen in people who have no exposure to tobacco smoke at all. Since even passive smokers have been shown to have arterial damage and higher risk for several smoking-related problems, then active smokers who smoke "just a few" cigarettes must certainly be at risk as well. When it comes to smoking, there just is no level that can be considered safe.

Chapter 20

Tobacco and Cancer

Questions and Answers about Cigarette Smoking and Cancer

Tobacco use, particularly cigarette smoking, is the single most preventable cause of death in the United States. Cigarette smoking alone is directly responsible for at least one-third of all cancer deaths annually in the United States, and contributes to the development of low birth weight babies and cardiovascular disease. Quitting smoking can significantly reduce a person's risk of developing heart disease and diseases of the lung, and can limit adverse health effects on unborn children.

What are the effects of cigarette smoking on cancer rates?

Cigarette smoking is the most significant cause of lung cancer and the leading cause of lung cancer death in both men and women. Smoking is also responsible for most cancers of the larynx, oral cavity, and esophagus. In addition, it is highly associated with the development of, and deaths from, bladder, kidney, pancreatic, and cervical cancers.

This chapter contains "Questions and Answers about Cigarette Smoking and Cancer," Reviewed December 2003, "Questions and Answers about Cigar Smoking and Cancer," March 2000, and "Smokeless Tobacco and Cancer: Questions and Answers," May 2003. All three documents are *Cancer Facts* Fact Sheets produced by the National Cancer Institute.

Are there any health risks for nonsmokers?

The health risks with cigarette smoking are not limited to smokers—exposure to environmental tobacco smoke (ETS) significantly increases a nonsmoker's risk of developing lung cancer. (ETS is the smoke that nonsmokers are exposed to when they share air space with someone who is smoking.) The U.S. Environmental Protection Agency (EPA) released a risk assessment report in December 1992 in which ETS was classified as a Group A (known human) carcinogen—a category reserved for only the most dangerous cancer-causing agents. The EPA report estimates that ETS is responsible for lung cancers in several thousand nonsmokers each year, and ETS exposure is also linked to severe respiratory problems in infants and young children. More recently, the California Environmental Protection Agency issued a comprehensive report on the health effects of ETS and concluded that ETS is directly related to coronary heart disease.

What harmful chemicals are found in cigarettes?

Tobacco smoke contains thousands of chemical agents, including 60 substances that are known to cause cancer (carcinogens). During smoking, nicotine is absorbed quickly into the bloodstream and travels to the brain, causing an addictive effect. The Surgeon General Reports noted the following conclusions about nicotine: cigarettes and other forms of tobacco are addicting, and the aspects that determine tobacco addiction are similar to those that determine heroin and cocaine addiction.

How does exposure affect the cigarette smoker?

The risk of developing lung and other smoking-associated cancers, as well as non-cancerous diseases, is related to total lifetime exposure to cigarette smoke. This includes the number of cigarettes a person smokes each day, the age at which smoking began, the number of years a person has smoked, and ETS exposure.

Questions and Answers about Cigar Smoking and Cancer

What are the health risks associated with cigar smoking?

Scientific evidence has shown that cancers of the oral cavity (lip, tongue, mouth, and throat), larynx, lung, and esophagus are associated with cigar smoking. Furthermore, evidence strongly suggests a link between cigar smoking and cancer of the pancreas. In addition, daily cigar smokers, particularly those who inhale, are at increased risk for developing heart and lung disease.

Like cigarette smoking, the risks from cigar smoking increase with increased exposure. For example, compared with someone who has never smoked, smoking only one to two cigars per day doubles the risk for oral and esophageal cancers. Smoking three to four cigars daily can increase the risk of oral cancers to more than eight times the risk for a nonsmoker, while the chance of esophageal cancer is increased to four times the risk for someone who has never smoked. Both cigar and cigarette smokers have similar levels of risk for oral, throat, and esophageal cancers.

The health risks associated with occasional cigar smoking (less than daily) are not known. About three-quarters of cigar smokers are occasional smokers.

What is the effect of inhalation on disease risk?

One of the major differences between cigar and cigarette smoking is the degree of inhalation. Almost all cigarette smokers report inhaling while the majority of cigar smokers do not because cigar smoke is generally more irritating. However, cigar smokers who have a history of cigarette smoking are more likely to inhale cigar smoke. Cigar smokers experience higher rates of lung cancer, coronary heart disease, and chronic obstructive lung disease than nonsmokers, but not as high as the rates for cigarette smokers. These lower rates for cigar smokers are probably related to reduced inhalation.

How are cigars and cigarettes different?

Cigars and cigarettes differ in both size and the type of tobacco used. Cigarettes are generally more uniform in size and contain less than one gram of tobacco each. Cigars, on the other hand, can vary in size and shape and can measure more than seven inches in length. Large cigars typically contain between 5 and 17 grams of tobacco. It is not unusual for some premium cigars to contain the tobacco equivalent of an entire pack of cigarettes. U.S. cigarettes are made from different blends of tobaccos, whereas most cigars are composed primarily of a single type of tobacco (air-cured or dried burley tobacco). Large cigars can take between one and two hours to smoke, whereas most cigarettes on the U.S. market take less than ten minutes to smoke.

How are the health risks associated with cigar smoking different from those associated with smoking cigarettes?

Health risks associated with both cigars and cigarettes are strongly linked to the degree of smoke exposure. Since smoke from cigars and cigarettes are composed of many of the same toxic and carcinogenic (cancer causing) compounds, the differences in health risks appear to be related to differences in daily use and level of inhalation.

Most cigarette smokers smoke every day and inhale. In contrast, as many as three-quarters of cigar smokers smoke only occasionally, and the majority do not inhale.

All cigar and cigarette smokers, whether or not they inhale, directly expose the lips, mouth, tongue, throat, and larynx to smoke and its carcinogens. Holding an unlit cigar between the lips also exposes these areas to carcinogens. In addition, when saliva containing smoke constituents is swallowed, the esophagus is exposed to carcinogens. These exposures probably account for the fact that oral and esophageal cancer risks are similar among cigar smokers and cigarette smokers.

Cancer of the larynx occurs at lower rates among cigar smokers who do not inhale than among cigarette smokers. Lung cancer risk among daily cigar smokers who do not inhale is double that of nonsmokers, but significantly less than the risk for cigarette smokers. However, the lung cancer risk from moderately inhaling smoke from five cigars a day is comparable to the risk from smoking up to one pack of cigarettes a day.

What are the hazards for nonsmokers exposed to cigar smoke?

Environmental tobacco smoke (ETS), also known as secondhand or passive smoke, is the smoke released from a lit cigar or cigarette. The ETS from cigars and cigarettes contains many of the same toxins and irritants (such as carbon monoxide, nicotine, hydrogen cyanide, and ammonia), as well as a number of known carcinogens (such as benzene, nitrosamines, vinyl chloride, arsenic, and hydrocarbons). Because cigars contain greater amounts of tobacco than cigarettes, they produce greater amounts of ETS.

There are, however, some differences between cigar and cigarette smoke due to the different ways cigars and cigarettes are made. Cigars go through a long aging and fermentation process. During the fermentation process, high concentrations of carcinogenic compounds are produced. These compounds are released when a cigar is smoked.

Also, cigar wrappers are less porous than cigarette wrappers. The nonporous cigar wrapper makes the burning of cigar tobacco less complete than cigarette tobacco. As a result, compared with cigarette smoke, the concentrations of toxins and irritants are higher in cigar smoke.

In addition, the larger size of most cigars (more tobacco) and longer smoking time produces higher exposures to nonsmokers of many toxic compounds (including carbon monoxide, hydrocarbons, ammonia, cadmium, and other substances) than a cigarette. For example, measurements of the carbon monoxide (CO) concentration at a cigar party and a cigar banquet in a restaurant showed indoor CO levels comparable to those measured on a crowded California freeway. Such exposures could place nonsmoking workers attending such events at significantly increased risk for cancer as well as heart and lung diseases.

Are cigars addictive?

Nicotine is the agent in tobacco that is capable of causing addiction or dependence. Cigarettes have an average total nicotine content of about 8.4 milligrams, while many popular brands of cigars will contain between 100 and 200 milligrams, or as many as 444 milligrams of nicotine.

As with cigarette smoking, when cigar smokers inhale, nicotine is absorbed rapidly. However, because of the composition of cigar smoke and the tendency of cigar smokers not to inhale, the nicotine is absorbed predominantly through the lining of the mouth rather than in the lung. It is important to note that nicotine absorbed through the lining of the mouth is capable of forming a powerful addiction, as demonstrated by the large number of people addicted to smokeless tobacco. Both inhaled and non-inhaled nicotine can be addictive. The infrequent use by the average cigar smoker, low number of cigars smoked per day, and lower rates of inhalation compared with cigarette smokers have led some to suggest that cigar smokers may be less likely to be dependent than cigarette smokers.

Addiction studies of cigarettes and spit tobacco show that addiction to nicotine occurs almost exclusively during adolescence and young adulthood when young people begin using these tobacco products. Also, several studies raise the concern that use of cigars may predispose individuals to the use of cigarettes. A recent survey showed that the relapse rate of former cigarette smokers who smoked cigars was twice as great as the relapse rate of former cigarette smokers who did not smoke cigars. The study also observed that cigar smokers were more than twice as likely to take up cigarette smoking for the first time than people who never smoked cigars.

What are the benefits of quitting?

There are many health benefits to quitting cigar smoking. The likelihood of developing cancer decreases. Also, when someone quits, an improvement in health is seen almost immediately. For example, blood pressure, pulse rate, and breathing patterns start returning to normal soon after quitting. People who quit will also see an improvement in their overall quality of life. People who decide to quit have many options available to them. Some people choose to quit all at once. Other options gaining popularity in this country are nicotine replacement products, such as patches, gum, and nasal sprays. If considering quitting, ask your doctor to recommend a plan that could best suit you and your lifestyle.

What are the current trends in cigar smoking?

Although cigar smoking occurs primarily among males between the ages of 35 and 64 who have higher educational backgrounds and incomes, recent studies suggest new trends. Most new cigar users today are teenagers and young adult males (ages 18 to 24) who smoke occasionally (less than daily). According to two large statewide studies conducted among California adults in 1990 and 1996, cigar use has increased nearly five times among women and appears to be increasing among adolescent females as well. Furthermore, a number of studies have reported high rates of use among not only teens but preteens. Cigar use among older males (age 65 and older), however, has continued to decline since 1992.

How are current trends in cigar smoking different from past decades?

Total cigar consumption declined by about 66 percent from 1973 until 1993. Cigar use has increased more than 50 percent since 1993. The increase in cigar use in the early 1990s coincided with an increase in promotional media activities for cigars.

What additional information is available about the effects of cigar smoking?

The 1998 NCI monograph *Cigars: Health Effects and Trends* can be ordered from the Cancer Information Service (see end of chapter).

U.S. residents can order the monograph online at https://cissecure
.nci.nih.gov/ncipubs on the internet. (The monograph can also be
viewed and downloaded from this website.)

Additional information on the health effects of tobacco is available
from the Centers for Disease Control and Prevention (CDC)'s Tobacco
Information and Prevention Source (TIPS) at http://www.cdc.gov/
tobacco on the internet. This program collects and distributes reports
and news about tobacco, lists services available for people trying to
quit using tobacco products, and produces publications about tobacco
and the dangers of its use.

Smokeless Tobacco and Cancer: Questions and Answers

Key Points

- Snuff is a finely ground or shredded tobacco that is either sniffed
  through the nose or placed between the cheek and gum. Chewing tobacco is used by putting a wad of tobacco inside the cheek.

- Chewing tobacco and snuff contain 28 cancer-causing agents.

- Smokeless tobacco users have an increased risk of developing
  cancer of the oral cavity.

- Several national organizations offer information about the
  health risks of smokeless tobacco and how to quit.

What is smokeless tobacco?

There are two types of smokeless tobacco—snuff and chewing tobacco. Snuff, a finely ground or shredded tobacco, is packaged as dry,
moist, or in sachets (tea bag-like pouches). Typically, the user places
a pinch or dip between the cheek and gum. Chewing tobacco is available in loose leaf, plug (plug-firm and plug-moist), or twist forms, with
the user putting a wad of tobacco inside the cheek. Smokeless tobacco
is sometimes called "spit" or "spitting" tobacco because people spit out
the tobacco juices and saliva that build up in the mouth.

What harmful chemicals are found in smokeless tobacco?

Chewing tobacco and snuff contain 28 carcinogens (cancer-causing
agents). The most harmful carcinogens in smokeless tobacco are the
tobacco-specific nitrosamines (TSNAs). They are formed during the
growing, curing, fermenting, and aging of tobacco. TSNAs have been

159

detected in some smokeless tobacco products at levels many times higher than levels of other types of nitrosamines that are allowed in foods, such as bacon and beer.

- Other cancer-causing substances in smokeless tobacco include N-nitrosamino acids, volatile N-nitrosamines, benzo(a)pyrene, volatile aldehydes, formaldehyde, acetaldehyde, crotonaldehyde, hydrazine, arsenic, nickel, cadmium, benzopyrene, and polonium-210.

- All tobacco, including smokeless tobacco, contains nicotine, which is addictive. The amount of nicotine absorbed from smokeless tobacco is three to four times the amount delivered by a cigarette. Nicotine is absorbed more slowly from smokeless tobacco than from cigarettes, but more nicotine per dose is absorbed from smokeless tobacco than from cigarettes. Also, the nicotine stays in the bloodstream for a longer time.

What cancers are caused by or associated with smokeless tobacco use?

- Smokeless tobacco users increase their risk for cancer of the oral cavity. Oral cancer can include cancer of the lip, tongue, cheeks, gums, and the floor and roof of the mouth.

- People who use oral snuff for a long time have a much greater risk for cancer of the cheek and gum than people who do not use smokeless tobacco.

- The possible increased risk for other types of cancer from smokeless tobacco is being studied.

What are some of the other ways smokeless tobacco can harm users' health?

Some of the other effects of smokeless tobacco use include addiction to nicotine, oral leukoplakia (white mouth lesions that can become cancerous), gum disease, and gum recession (when the gum pulls away from the teeth). Possible increased risks for heart disease, diabetes, and reproductive problems are being studied.

Is smokeless tobacco a good substitute for cigarettes?

In 1986, the Surgeon General concluded that the use of smokeless tobacco "is not a safe substitute for smoking cigarettes. It can cause cancer and a number of non-cancerous conditions and can lead to nicotine addiction and dependence." Since 1991, NCI has officially recommended that the public avoid and discontinue the use of all tobacco products, including smokeless tobacco. NCI also recognizes that nitrosamines, found in tobacco products, are not safe at any level. The accumulated scientific evidence does not support changing this position.

What about using smokeless tobacco to quit cigarettes?

Because all tobacco use causes disease and addiction, NCI recommends that tobacco use be avoided and discontinued. Several non-tobacco methods have been shown to be effective for quitting cigarettes. These methods include pharmacotherapies such as nicotine replacement therapy and bupropion SR, individual and group counseling, and telephone quitlines.

Who uses smokeless tobacco?

In the United States, the 2000 National Household Survey on Drug Abuse, which was conducted by the Substance Abuse and Mental Health Services Administration, reported the following statistics:

- An estimated 7.6 million Americans age 12 and older (3.4 percent) had used smokeless tobacco in the past month.

- Smokeless tobacco use was most common among young adults ages 18 to 25.

- Men were ten times more likely than women to report using smokeless tobacco (6.5 percent of men age 12 and older compared with 0.5 percent of women).

People in many other countries and regions, including India, parts of Africa, and some Central Asian countries, have a long history of using smokeless tobacco products.

Where can people find help to quit using smokeless tobacco?

Several national organizations provide information about the health risks of smokeless tobacco and how to quit:

The *National Institute of Dental and Craniofacial Research's National Oral Health Information Clearinghouse* offers educational booklets that discuss spit tobacco use in a colorful and graphic format. These booklets are designed specifically for young men who have decided to quit or are thinking about it.

National Oral Health Information Clearinghouse
National Institute of Dental and Craniofacial Research
One NOHIC Way
Bethesda, MD 20892-3500
Phone: 301-402-7364
Website: http://www.nohic.nidcr.nih.gov
E-mail: nohic@nidcr.nih.gov

The *Centers for Disease Control and Prevention's Office on Smoking and Health* distributes a brochure for teens who are trying to quit cigarettes or smokeless tobacco. The Office also maintains a database of smoking and health-related materials.

Office on Smoking and Health
Centers for Disease Control and Prevention
Mail Stop K-50
4770 Buford Highway, NE
Atlanta, GA 30341-3724
Phone: 1-800-232-1311 (1-800-CDC-1311)
Website: http://www.cdc.gov/tobacco/how2quit.htm
E-mail: tobaccoinfo@cdc.gov

The mission of the *National Spit Tobacco Education Program* (NSTEP) is to prevent people, especially young people, from starting to use tobacco, and to help users to quit. NSTEP offers information and materials on spit tobacco use, prevention, and cessation.

National Spit Tobacco Education Program
Oral Health America
Suite 352
410 North Michigan Avenue
Chicago, IL 60611
Phone: 312-836-9900
Website: http://www.nstep.org

The *American Cancer Society* publishes a series of pamphlets with helpful tips and techniques for smokeless tobacco users who want to quit.

American Cancer Society
1599 Clifton Road, NE
Atlanta, GA 30329

Phone: 1-800-227-2345 (1-800-ACS-2345)
Website: http://www.cancer.org

The American Academy of Family Physicians has a fact sheet with information on how to quit using smokeless tobacco. The fact sheet is available at http://familydoctor.org/handouts/177.html on the internet.

American Academy of Family Physicians
11400 Tomahawk Creek Parkway
Leawood, KS 66211-2672
Website: http://familydoctor.org
E-mail: email@familydoctor.org

A number of other organizations provide information about where to find help to stop using smokeless tobacco. State and local health agencies often have information about community tobacco cessation programs. The local or county government section in the phone book (blue pages) has phone numbers for health agencies. Information to help smokers who want to quit is also available through community hospitals, the yellow pages (under "drug abuse and addiction"), public libraries, health maintenance organizations, health fairs, and community helplines.

What other resources are available?

A person's dentist or doctor can be a good source of information about the health risks of smokeless tobacco and about quitting. Friends, family members, teachers, and coaches can help a person quit smokeless tobacco use by giving them support and encouragement.

More Information from the National Cancer Institute

National Cancer Institute (NCI)
Office of Cancer Communications
31 Center Drive, MSC-2580
Building 31, Room 10A24
Toll-free: 1-800-4-CANCER (1-800-422-6237)
TTY (for deaf and hard of hearing callers): 1-800-332-8615
Smoking Quitline: 877-44U-QUIT
TTY: 800-332-8615
Website: http://cancer.gov

Chapter 21

What You Need to Know about Lung Cancer

Understanding the Cancer Process

All types of cancer develop in our cells, the body's basic unit of life. To understand cancer, it is helpful to know how normal cells become cancerous.

The body is made up of many types of cells. Normally, cells grow, divide, and produce more cells as needed to keep the body healthy and functioning properly. Sometimes, however, the process goes astray—cells keep dividing when new cells are not needed. The mass of extra cells forms a growth or tumor. Tumors can be benign or malignant.

Benign tumors are not cancer. They often can be removed and, in most cases, they do not come back. Cells in benign tumors do not spread to other parts of the body. Most important, benign tumors are rarely a threat to life.

Malignant tumors are cancer. Cells in malignant tumors are abnormal and divide without control or order. These cancer cells can invade and destroy the tissue around them. Cancer cells can also break away from a malignant tumor and enter the bloodstream or lymphatic system (the tissues and organs that produce, store, and carry white blood cells that fight infection and other diseases). This process, called metastasis, is how cancer spreads from the original

This chapter includes excerpts from "What You Need To Know About™ Lung Cancer," National Cancer Institute (NCI), NIH Pub. No. 99-1553, updated September 2002. The complete text of this document, including references, can be accessed through the NCI's website at http://www.cancer.gov.

(primary) tumor to form new (secondary) tumors in other parts of the body.

The Lungs

The lungs, a pair of sponge-like, cone-shaped organs, are part of the respiratory system. The right lung has three sections, called lobes; it is a little larger than the left lung, which has two lobes. When we breathe in, the lungs take in oxygen, which our cells need to live and carry out their normal functions. When we breathe out, the lungs get rid of carbon dioxide, which is a waste product of the body's cells.

Understanding Lung Cancer

Cancers that begin in the lungs are divided into two major types, non-small cell lung cancer and small cell lung cancer, depending on how the cells look under a microscope. Each type of lung cancer grows and spreads in different ways and is treated differently.

Non-small cell lung cancer is more common than small cell lung cancer, and it generally grows and spreads more slowly. There are three main types of non-small cell lung cancer. They are named for the type of cells in which the cancer develops: squamous cell carcinoma (also called epidermoid carcinoma), adenocarcinoma, and large cell carcinoma.

Small cell lung cancer, sometimes called oat cell cancer, is less common than non-small cell lung cancer. This type of lung cancer grows more quickly and is more likely to spread to other organs in the body.

Lung Cancer: Who's at Risk?

Researchers have discovered several causes of lung cancer—most are related to the use of tobacco.

- **Cigarettes:** Smoking cigarettes causes lung cancer. Harmful substances, called carcinogens, in tobacco damage the cells in the lungs. Over time, the damaged cells may become cancerous. The likelihood that a smoker will develop lung cancer is affected by the age at which smoking began, how long the person has smoked, the number of cigarettes smoked per day, and how deeply the smoker inhales. Stopping smoking greatly reduces a person's risk for developing lung cancer.

- **Cigars and Pipes:** Cigar and pipe smokers have a higher risk of lung cancer than nonsmokers. The number of years a person smokes, the number of pipes or cigars smoked per day, and how deeply the person inhales all affect the risk of developing lung cancer. Even cigar and pipe smokers who do not inhale are at increased risk for lung, mouth, and other types of cancer.

- **Environmental Tobacco Smoke:** The chance of developing lung cancer is increased by exposure to environmental tobacco smoke (ETS)—the smoke in the air when someone else smokes. Exposure to ETS, or secondhand smoke, is called involuntary or passive smoking.

Other causes of lung cancer include:

- **Radon:** Radon is an invisible, odorless, and tasteless radioactive gas that occurs naturally in soil and rocks. It can cause damage to the lungs that may lead to lung cancer. People who work in mines may be exposed to radon and, in some parts of the country, radon is found in houses. Smoking increases the risk of lung cancer even more for those already at risk because of exposure to radon. A kit available at most hardware stores allows homeowners to measure radon levels in their homes. The home radon test is relatively easy to use and inexpensive. Once a radon problem is corrected, the hazard is gone for good.

- **Asbestos:** Asbestos is the name of a group of minerals that occur naturally as fibers and are used in certain industries. Asbestos fibers tend to break easily into particles that can float in the air and stick to clothes. When the particles are inhaled, they can lodge in the lungs, damaging cells and increasing the risk for lung cancer. Studies have shown that workers who have been exposed to large amounts of asbestos have a risk of developing lung cancer that is 3 to 4 times greater than that for workers who have not been exposed to asbestos. This exposure has been observed in such industries as shipbuilding, asbestos mining and manufacturing, insulation work, and brake repair. The risk of lung cancer is even higher among asbestos workers who also smoke. Asbestos workers should use the protective equipment provided by their employers and follow recommended work practices and safety procedures.

- **Pollution:** Researchers have found a link between lung cancer and exposure to certain air pollutants, such as by-products of the combustion of diesel and other fossil fuels. However, this relationship has not been clearly defined, and more research is being done.

- **Lung Diseases:** Certain lung diseases, such as tuberculosis (TB), increase a person's chance of developing lung cancer. Lung cancer tends to develop in areas of the lung that are scarred from TB.

- **Personal History:** A person who has had lung cancer once is more likely to develop a second lung cancer compared with a person who has never had lung cancer. Quitting smoking after lung cancer is diagnosed may prevent the development of a second lung cancer.

Researchers continue to study the causes of lung cancer and to search for ways to prevent it. We already know that the best way to prevent lung cancer is to quit (or never start) smoking. The sooner a person quits smoking the better. Even if you have been smoking for many years, it's never too late to benefit from quitting.

Recognizing Symptoms

Common signs and symptoms of lung cancer include:

- A cough that doesn't go away and gets worse over time
- Constant chest pain
- Coughing up blood
- Shortness of breath, wheezing, or hoarseness
- Repeated problems with pneumonia or bronchitis
- Swelling of the neck and face
- Loss of appetite or weight loss
- Fatigue

These symptoms may be caused by lung cancer or by other conditions. It is important to check with a doctor.

Diagnosing Lung Cancer

To help find the cause of symptoms, the doctor evaluates a person's medical history, smoking history, exposure to environmental and occupational substances, and family history of cancer. The doctor also performs a physical exam and may order a chest x-ray and other tests. If lung cancer is suspected, sputum cytology (the microscopic examination of cells obtained from a deep-cough sample of mucus in the lungs) is a simple test that may be useful in detecting lung cancer. To confirm the presence of lung cancer, the doctor must examine tissue from the lung. A biopsy—the removal of a small sample of tissue for examination under a microscope by a pathologist—can show whether a person has cancer. A number of procedures may be used to obtain this tissue:

- **Bronchoscopy:** The doctor puts a bronchoscope (a thin, lighted tube) into the mouth or nose and down through the windpipe to look into the breathing passages. Through this tube, the doctor can collect cells or small samples of tissue.

- **Needle aspiration:** A needle is inserted through the chest into the tumor to remove a sample of tissue.

- **Thoracentesis:** Using a needle, the doctor removes a sample of the fluid that surrounds the lungs to check for cancer cells.

- **Thoracotomy:** Surgery to open the chest is sometimes needed to diagnose lung cancer. This procedure is a major operation performed in a hospital.

Staging the Disease

If the diagnosis is cancer, the doctor will want to learn the stage (or extent) of the disease. Staging is done to find out whether the cancer has spread and, if so, to what parts of the body. Lung cancer often spreads to the brain or bones. Knowing the stage of the disease helps the doctor plan treatment. Some tests used to determine whether the cancer has spread include:

- **CAT (or CT) scan** (computed tomography): A computer linked to an x-ray machine creates a series of detailed pictures of areas inside the body.

- **MRI** (magnetic resonance imaging): A powerful magnet linked to a computer makes detailed pictures of areas inside the body.

- **Radionuclide scanning:** Scanning can show whether cancer has spread to other organs, such as the liver. The patient swallows or receives an injection of a mildly radioactive substance. A machine (scanner) measures and records the level of radioactivity in certain organs to reveal abnormal areas.

- **Bone scan:** A bone scan, one type of radionuclide scanning, can show whether cancer has spread to the bones. A small amount of radioactive substance is injected into a vein. It travels through the bloodstream and collects in areas of abnormal bone growth.

An instrument called a scanner measures the radioactivity levels in these areas and records them on x-ray film.

- **Mediastinoscopy/Mediastinotomy:** A mediastinoscopy can help show whether the cancer has spread to the lymph nodes in the chest. Using a lighted viewing instrument, called a scope, the doctor examines the center of the chest (mediastinum) and nearby lymph nodes. In mediastinoscopy, the scope is inserted through a small incision in the neck; in mediastinotomy, the incision is made in the chest. In either procedure, the scope is also used to remove a tissue sample. The patient receives a general anesthetic.

Treatment for Lung Cancer

Treatment depends on a number of factors, including the type of lung cancer (non-small or small cell lung cancer), the size, location, and extent of the tumor, and the general health of the patient. Many different treatments and combinations of treatments may be used to control lung cancer, and/or to improve quality of life by reducing symptoms.

- Surgery is an operation to remove the cancer. The type of surgery a doctor performs depends on the location of the tumor in the lung. An operation to remove only a small part of the lung is called a segmental or wedge resection. When the surgeon removes an entire lobe of the lung, the procedure is called a lobectomy. Pneumonectomy is the removal of an entire lung. Some tumors are inoperable (cannot be removed by surgery) because of the size or location, and some patients cannot have surgery for other medical reasons.

- Chemotherapy is the use of anticancer drugs to kill cancer cells throughout the body. Even after cancer has been removed from the lung, cancer cells may still be present in nearby tissue or elsewhere in the body. Chemotherapy may be used to control cancer growth or to relieve symptoms. Most anticancer drugs are given by injection directly into a vein (IV) or by means of a catheter, a thin tube that is placed into a large vein and remains there as long as it is needed. Some anticancer drugs are given in the form of a pill.

- Radiation therapy, also called radiotherapy, involves the use of high-energy rays to kill cancer cells. Radiation therapy is directed to a limited area and affects the cancer cells only in that area. Radiation therapy may be used before surgery to shrink a tumor, or after surgery to destroy any cancer cells that remain in the treated area. Doctors also use radiation therapy, often combined with chemotherapy, as primary treatment instead of surgery. Radiation therapy may also be used to relieve symptoms such as shortness of breath. Radiation for the treatment of lung cancer most often comes from a machine (external radiation). The radiation can also come from an implant (a small container of radioactive material) placed directly into or near the tumor (internal radiation).

- Photodynamic therapy (PDT), a type of laser therapy, involves the use of a special chemical that is injected into the bloodstream and absorbed by cells all over the body. The chemical rapidly leaves normal cells but remains in cancer cells for a longer time. A laser light aimed at the cancer activates the chemical, which then kills the cancer cells that have absorbed it. Photodynamic therapy may be used to reduce symptoms of lung cancer—for example, to control bleeding or to relieve breathing problems due to blocked airways when the cancer cannot be removed through surgery. Photodynamic therapy may also be used to treat very small tumors in patients for whom the usual treatments for lung cancer are not appropriate.

- Clinical trials (research studies) to evaluate new ways to treat cancer are an option for many lung cancer patients. In some studies, all patients receive the new treatment. In others, doctors compare different therapies by giving the new treatment to one group of patients and the usual (standard) therapy to another group. Through research, doctors are exploring new and possibly more effective ways to treat lung cancer. More information about treatment studies can be found in the NCI publication *Taking Part in Clinical Trials: What Cancer Patients Need To Know.*[1] PDQ®, NCI's cancer information database, contains detailed information about ongoing studies for lung cancer. NCI's Website includes a section on clinical trials at http://www.cancer.gov/clinical_trials. This section provides detailed information about ongoing studies for lung cancer for patients, health professionals, and the public.

Treating Non-Small Cell Lung Cancer

Patients with non-small cell lung cancer may be treated in several ways. The choice of treatment depends mainly on the size, location, and extent of the tumor. Surgery is the most common way to treat this type of lung cancer. Cryosurgery, a treatment that freezes and destroys cancer tissue, may be used to control symptoms in the later stages of non-small cell lung cancer. Radiation therapy and chemotherapy may also be used to slow the progress of the disease and to manage symptoms.

Treating Small Cell Lung Cancer

Small cell lung cancer spreads quickly. In many cases, cancer cells have already spread to other parts of the body when the disease is diagnosed. In order to reach cancer cells throughout the body, doctors almost always use chemotherapy. Treatment may also include radiation therapy aimed at the tumor in the lung or tumors in other parts of the body (such as in the brain). Some patients have radiation therapy to the brain even though no cancer is found there. This treatment, called prophylactic cranial irradiation (PCI), is given to prevent tumors from forming in the brain. Surgery is part of the treatment plan for a small number of patients with small cell lung cancer.

Side Effects

The side effects of cancer treatment depend on the type of treatment and may be different for each person. Side effects are often only temporary. Doctors and nurses can explain the possible side effects of treatment, and they can suggest ways to help relieve symptoms that may occur during and after treatment.

- Surgery for lung cancer is a major operation. After lung surgery, air and fluid tend to collect in the chest. Patients often need help turning over, coughing, and breathing deeply. These activities are important for recovery because they help expand the remaining lung tissue and get rid of excess air and fluid. Pain or weakness in the chest and the arm and shortness of breath are common side effects of lung cancer surgery. Patients may need several weeks or months to regain their energy and strength.

- Chemotherapy affects normal as well as cancerous cells. Side effects depend largely on the specific drugs and the dose (amount of drug given). Common side effects of chemotherapy include nausea and vomiting, hair loss, mouth sores, and fatigue.

- Radiation therapy, like chemotherapy, affects normal as well as cancerous cells. Side effects of radiation therapy depend mainly on the part of the body that is treated and the treatment dose. Common side effects of radiation therapy are a dry, sore throat; difficulty swallowing; fatigue; skin changes at the site of treatment; and loss of appetite. Patients receiving radiation to the brain may have headaches, skin changes, fatigue, nausea and vomiting, hair loss, or problems with memory and thought processes.

• Photodynamic therapy makes the skin and eyes sensitive to light for six weeks or more after treatment. Patients are advised to avoid direct sunlight and bright indoor light for at least six weeks. If patients must go outdoors, they need to wear protective clothing, including sunglasses. Other temporary side effects of PDT may include coughing, trouble swallowing, and painful breathing or shortness of breath. Patients should talk with their doctor about what to do if the skin becomes blistered, red, or swollen.

Today, because of what has been learned in clinical trials, doctors are able to control, lessen, or avoid many of the side effects of treatment. Several useful NCI booklets, including *Chemotherapy and You*, *Radiation Therapy and You*, and *Eating Hints for Cancer Patients*, suggest ways to cope with the side effects of cancer treatment.[1]

Doctors and nurses can explain the possible side effects of treatment, and they can suggest ways to help relieve symptoms that may occur during and after treatment.

The Importance of Follow-up Care

Follow-up care after treatment for lung cancer is very important. Regular checkups ensure that changes in health are noticed, and if the cancer returns or a new cancer develops, it can be treated as soon as possible. Checkups may include physical exams, chest x-rays, or lab tests. Between scheduled appointments, people who have had lung cancer should report any health problems to their doctor as soon as they appear.

Providing Emotional Support

Living with a serious disease, such as cancer, is challenging. Apart from having to cope with the physical and medical challenges, people with cancer face many worries, feelings, and concerns that can make life difficult. They may find they need help coping with the emotional as well as the practical aspects of their disease. In fact, attention to the emotional and psychological burden of having cancer is often part of a patient's treatment plan. The support of the health care team (doctors, nurses, social workers, and others), support groups, and patient-to-patient networks can help people feel less alone and upset, and improve the quality of their lives. Cancer support groups provide a safe environment where cancer patients can talk about living with cancer with others who may be having similar experiences. Patients may want to speak to a member of their health care team about finding a support group. Many also find useful information in NCI fact sheets and booklets, including *Taking Time* and *Facing Forward*.[1]

Questions for Your Doctor

This information is designed to help you get the facts you need from your doctor, so that you can make informed decisions about your health care. In addition, asking your doctor the following questions will help you further understand your condition. To help you remember what the doctor says, you may take notes or ask whether you may use a tape recorder. Some people also want to have a family member or friend with them when they talk to the doctor—to take part in the discussion, to take notes, or just to listen.

Diagnosis

- What tests can diagnose lung cancer? Are they painful?
- How soon after the tests will I learn the results?
- What type of lung cancer do I have?

Treatment

- What treatments are recommended for me?
- What clinical trials are appropriate for my type of cancer?
- Will I need to be in the hospital to receive my treatment? For how long?
- How might my normal activities change during my treatment?

Side Effects

- What side effects should I expect? How long will they last?
- What side effects should I report? Whom should I call?

Follow-up

- After treatment, how often do I need to be checked? What type of follow-up care should I have?

- Will I eventually be able to resume my normal activities?

The Health Care Team

- Who will be involved with my treatment and rehabilitation? What is the role of each member of the health care team in my care?

- What has been your experience in caring for patients with lung cancer?

Resources

- Are there support groups in the area with people I can talk to? Are there organizations where I can get more information about cancer, specifically lung cancer?

Note

1. NCI booklets mentioned in this chapter are available free of charge by calling the Cancer Information Service at 1-800-4-CANCER or by visiting NCI's website at www.cancer.gov.

Chapter 22

What You Need to Know about Oral Cancer

The Oral Cavity

This chapter deals with cancer of the oral cavity (mouth) and the oropharynx (the part of the throat at the back of the mouth). The oral cavity includes many parts: the lips; the lining inside the lips and cheeks, called the buccal mucosa; the teeth; the bottom (floor) of the mouth under the tongue; the front two-thirds of the tongue; the bony top of the mouth (hard palate); the gums; and the small area behind the wisdom teeth. The oropharynx includes the back one-third of the tongue, the soft palate, the tonsils, and the part of the throat behind the mouth. Salivary glands throughout the oral cavity make saliva, which keeps the mouth moist and helps digest food.

What Is Cancer?

Cancer is a group of diseases. It occurs when cells become abnormal and divide without control or order. More than 100 different types of cancer are known.

Like all organs of the body, the mouth and throat are made up of many kinds of cells. Cells normally divide in an orderly way to produce more cells only when the body needs them. This process helps keep the body healthy.

This chapter contains excerpts from "What You Need To Know About™ Oral Cancer," National Cancer Institute (NCI), NIH Pub. No. 97-1574, updated September 2002. The complete text of this document, including references, can be accessed through the NCI's website at http://www.cancer.gov.

Cells that divide when new cells are not needed form too much tissue. The mass of extra tissue, called a tumor, can be benign or malignant.

- Benign tumors are not cancer. They can usually be removed, and in most cases, they don't grow back. Most important, the cells in benign tumors do not invade other tissues and do not spread to other parts of the body. Benign tumors usually are not a threat to life.

- Malignant tumors are cancer. They can invade and damage nearby tissues and organs. Also, cancer cells can break away from a malignant tumor and enter the bloodstream or the lymphatic system. This is how cancer spreads and forms secondary tumors in other parts of the body. The spread of cancer is called metastasis.

When oral cancer spreads, it usually travels through the lymphatic system. Cancer cells that enter the lymphatic system are carried along by lymph, an almost colorless, watery fluid containing cells that help the body fight infection and disease. Along the lymphatic channels are groups of small, bean-shaped organs called lymph nodes (sometimes called lymph glands). Oral cancer that spreads usually travels to the lymph nodes in the neck. It can also spread to other parts of the body. Cancer that spreads is the same disease and has the same name as the original (primary) cancer.

Early Detection

Regular checkups that include an examination of the entire mouth can detect precancerous conditions or the early stages of oral cancer. Your doctor and dentist should check the tissues in your mouth as part of your routine exams.

Symptoms

Oral cancer usually occurs in people over the age of 45 but can develop at any age. These are some symptoms to watch for:

- A sore on the lip or in the mouth that does not heal
- A lump on the lip or in the mouth or throat
- A white or red patch on the gums, tongue, or lining of the mouth
- Unusual bleeding, pain, or numbness in the mouth

- A sore throat that does not go away, or a feeling that something is caught in the throat

- Difficulty or pain with chewing or swallowing

- Swelling of the jaw that causes dentures to fit poorly or become uncomfortable

- A change in the voice

- Pain in the ear

These symptoms may be caused by cancer or by other, less serious problems. It is important to see a dentist or doctor about any symptoms like these, so that the problem can be diagnosed and treated as early as possible.

Diagnosis and Staging

If an abnormal area has been found in the oral cavity, a biopsy is the only way to know whether it is cancer. Usually, the patient is referred to an oral surgeon or an ear, nose, and throat surgeon, who removes part or all of the lump or abnormal-looking area. A pathologist examines the tissue under a microscope to check for cancer cells.

Almost all oral cancers are squamous cell carcinomas. Squamous cells line the oral cavity.

If the pathologist finds oral cancer, the patient's doctor needs to know the stage, or extent, of the disease in order to plan the best treatment. Staging tests and exams help the doctor find out whether the cancer has spread and what parts of the body are affected.

A patient who needs a biopsy may want to ask the doctor these questions:

- How much tissue will be removed for the biopsy?

- How long will the biopsy take? Will I be awake? Will it hurt?

- How should I care for the biopsy site afterward?

- How soon will I know the results?

- If I do have cancer, who will talk with me about treatment? When?

Staging generally includes dental x-rays and x-rays of the head and chest. The doctor may also want the patient to have a CT (or CAT) scan. A CT scan is a series of x-rays put together by a computer to form detailed pictures of areas inside the body. Ultrasonography is another way to produce pictures of areas in the body. High-frequency sound waves (ultrasound), which cannot be heard by humans, are bounced off organs and tissue. The pattern of echoes produced by these waves creates a picture called a sonogram. Sometimes the doctor asks for MRI (magnetic resonance imaging), a procedure in which pictures are created using a magnet linked to a computer. The doctor also feels the lymph nodes in the neck to check for swelling or other changes. In most cases, the patient will have a complete physical examination before treatment begins.

Treatment

After diagnosis and staging, the doctor develops a treatment plan to fit each patient's needs. Treatment for oral cancer depends on a number of factors. Among these are the location, size, type, and extent of the tumor and the stage of the disease. The doctor also considers the patient's age and general health. Treatment involves surgery, radiation therapy, or, in many cases, a combination of the two. Some patients receive chemotherapy, treatment with anticancer drugs.

For most patients, it is important to have a complete dental exam before cancer treatment begins. Because cancer treatment may make the mouth sensitive and more easily infected, doctors often advise patients to have any needed dental work done before treatment begins.

Most people with cancer want to learn all they can about their disease and their treatment choices so they can take an active part in decisions about their medical and dental care. The doctor is the best person to answer their questions. Also, the patient may want to talk with the doctor about taking part in a research study of new treatment methods. Such studies, called clinical trials, are designed to improve cancer treatment.

Many patients find it useful to make a list of questions before seeing the doctor. Taking notes can make it easier to remember what the doctor says. Some patients also find that it helps to have a family member or friend with them—to take part in the discussion, to take notes, or just to listen.

Before treatment begins, the patient may want to ask the doctor these questions:

- What are my treatment choices? Which do you recommend for me? Why?

- What are the risks and possible side effects of each treatment?

- What are the expected benefits of each kind of treatment?

- What can be done about side effects?

- Would a clinical trial be appropriate for me?

There is a lot to learn about cancer and its treatment. Patients do not need to ask all their questions or understand all the answers at once. They will have many chances to ask the doctor to explain things that are not clear and to ask for more information.

Planning Treatment

Treatment decisions can be complex. Before starting treatment, the patient may want to have another doctor review the diagnosis and treatment plan. A short delay will not reduce the chance that treatment will be successful. There are a number of ways to find a doctor for a second opinion:

- The patient's doctor or dentist may suggest a specialist who treats oral cancer.

- The Cancer Information Service, at 1-800-4-CANCER, can tell callers about cancer centers and other NCI-supported programs in their area.

- Patients can get the names of specialists from their local medical or dental society, a nearby hospital, or a medical or dental school.

- The American Board of Medical Specialties (ABMS) has a list of doctors who have met certain education and training requirements and have passed specialty examinations. The Official ABMS Directory of Board Certified Medical Specialists lists doctors' names along with their specialty and their educational background. The directory is available in most public libraries. Also, ABMS offers this information on the Internet at http://www.abms.org. (Click on "Who's Certified.")

Methods of Treatment

Patients with oral cancer may be treated by a team of specialists. The medical team may include an oral surgeon; an ear, nose, and throat surgeon; a medical oncologist; a radiation oncologist; a prosthodontist; a general dentist; a plastic surgeon; a dietitian; a social worker; a nurse; and a speech therapist.

Surgery to remove the tumor in the mouth is the usual treatment for patients with oral cancer. If there is evidence that the cancer has spread, the surgeon may also remove lymph nodes in the neck. If the disease has spread to muscles and other tissues in the neck, the operation may be more extensive.

Before surgery, the patient may want to ask the doctor these questions:

- What kind of operation will it be?

- How will I feel after the operation? If I have pain, how will you help me?

- Will I have trouble eating?

- Where will the scars be? What will they look like?

- Do you expect that there will be long-term effects from the surgery?

- Will there be permanent changes in my appearance?

- Will I lose my teeth? Can they be replaced? How soon?

- If I need to have plastic surgery, when can that be done?

- Will I need to see a specialist for help with my speech?

- When can I get back to my normal activities?

Radiation therapy (also called radiotherapy) is the use of high-energy rays to damage cancer cells and stop them from growing. Like surgery, radiation therapy is local therapy; it affects only the cells in the treated area. The energy may come from a large machine (external radiation). It can also come from radioactive materials placed directly into or near the tumor (internal radiation). Radiation therapy is sometimes used instead of surgery for small tumors in the mouth. Patients with large tumors may need both surgery and radiation therapy.

Radiation therapy may be given before or after surgery. Before surgery, radiation can shrink the tumor so that it can be removed. Radiation after surgery is used to destroy cancer cells that may remain.

For external radiation therapy, the patient goes to the hospital or clinic each day for treatments. Usually, treatment is given five days a week for 5 to 6 weeks. This schedule helps protect healthy tissues by dividing the total amount of radiation into small doses.

Implant radiation therapy puts tiny "seeds" containing radioactive material directly into the tumor or in tissue near it. Generally, an implant is left in place for several days, and the patient will stay in the hospital in a private room. The length of time nurses and other caregivers, as well as visitors, can spend with the patient will be limited. The implant is removed before the patient goes home.

Before radiation therapy, a patient may want to ask the doctor these questions:

- When will the treatments begin? When will they end?
- How will I feel during therapy?
- What can I do to take care of myself during therapy?
- Can I continue my normal activities?
- How will my mouth and face look afterward?
- Will I need a special diet? For how long?
- If my mouth becomes dry, what can I do about it?

Chemotherapy is the use of drugs to kill cancer cells. Researchers are looking for effective drugs or drug combinations to treat oral cancer. They are also exploring ways to combine chemotherapy with other forms of cancer treatment to help destroy the tumor and prevent the disease from spreading.

Clinical Trials

Researchers are developing treatment methods that are more effective against oral cancer, and they are also finding ways to reduce side effects of treatment. When laboratory research shows that a new method has promise, doctors use it to treat cancer patients in clinical trials. These trials are designed to answer scientific questions about the new approach and to find out whether it is both safe and effective. Patients who take part in clinical trials make an important contribution to medical science and may have the first chance to benefit from improved treatment methods.

Clinical trials to study new treatments for oral cancer are under way in hospitals throughout the country. Some trials involve ways to shrink or destroy the primary tumor. In others, scientists are testing ways to prevent the cancer from coming back in the mouth or spreading to other parts of the body. Still others involve treatments to slow or stop cancer that has already spread.

Researchers are studying the timing of treatments and new ways to combine various types of treatment. For example, they are trying to increase the effectiveness of radiation therapy by giving treatments twice a day instead of once a day. They are also working with hyperthermia (heat) and with drugs called radiosensitizers to try to make cancer cells more sensitive to radiation. Researchers are also using drugs to help protect normal cells from radiation damage. In addition, they are exploring various new anticancer drugs and drug combinations.

People who have had oral cancer have an increased risk of getting a new cancer of the mouth or another part of the head or neck. Doctors are trying to find ways to prevent these new cancers. Some research has shown that a substance related to vitamin A may prevent a new cancer from developing in someone who has already been successfully treated for oral cancer.

Oral cancer patients who are interested in taking part in a trial should talk with their doctor. They may want to read *Taking Part in Clinical Trials: What Cancer Patients Need To Know*[1], a booklet that explains what treatment studies are and outlines some of their possible benefits and risks.

One way to learn about clinical trials is through PDQ®, a computerized resource developed by the National Cancer Institute. PDQ® contains information about cancer treatment and an up-to-date list of trials all over the country. The Cancer Information Service, at 1-800-4-CANCER, can provide PDQ information to patients and the public.

Side Effects of Treatment

It is hard to limit the effects of cancer treatment so that only cancer cells are removed or destroyed. Because healthy cells and tissues may also be damaged, treatment often causes side effects.

The side effects of cancer treatment vary. They depend mainly on the type and extent of the treatment and the specific area being treated. Also, each person reacts differently. Some side effects are temporary; others are permanent. Doctors try to plan the patient's therapy to keep side effects to a minimum. They also watch patients very carefully so they can help with any problems that occur.

Surgery to remove a small tumor in the mouth usually does not cause any lasting problems. For a larger tumor, however, the surgeon may need to remove part of the palate, tongue, or jaw. Such surgery is likely to change the patient's ability to chew, swallow, or talk. The patient may also look different.

After surgery, the patient's face may be swollen. This swelling usually goes away within a few weeks. However, removing lymph nodes can slow the flow of lymph, which may collect in the tissues; this swelling may last for a long time.

Before starting radiation therapy, a patient should see a dentist who is familiar with the changes this therapy can cause in the mouth. Radiation therapy can make the mouth sore. It can also cause changes in the saliva and may reduce the amount of saliva, making it hard to chew and swallow. Because saliva normally protects the teeth, mouth dryness can promote tooth decay. Good mouth care can help keep the teeth and gums healthy and can make the patient feel more comfortable. The health care team may suggest the use of a special kind of toothbrush or mouthwash. The dentist usually suggests a special fluoride program to keep the teeth healthy. To help relieve mouth dryness, the health care team may suggest the use of artificial saliva and other methods to keep the mouth moist. Mouth dryness from radiation therapy goes away in some patients, but it can be permanent.

Weight loss can be a serious problem for patients being treated for oral cancer because a sore mouth may make eating difficult. Your doctor may suggest ways to maintain a healthy diet. In many cases, it helps to have food and beverages in very small amounts. Many patients find that eating several small meals and snacks during the day works better than trying to have three large meals. Often, it is easier to eat soft, bland foods that have been moistened with sauces or gravies; thick soups, puddings, and high protein milkshakes are nourishing and easy to swallow. It may be helpful to prepare other foods in a blender. The doctor may also suggest special liquid dietary supplements for patients who have trouble chewing. Drinking lots of fluids helps keep the mouth moist and makes it easier to eat.

Some patients are able to wear their dentures during radiation therapy. Many, however, will not be able to wear dentures for up to a year after treatment. Because the tissues in the mouth that support the denture may change during or after treatment, dentures may no longer fit properly. After treatment is over, a patient may need to have dentures refitted or replaced.

Radiation therapy can also cause sores in the mouth and cracked and peeling lips. These usually heal in the weeks after treatment is completed. Often, good mouth care can help prevent these sores. Dentures should not be worn until the sores have healed.

During radiation therapy, patients may become very tired, especially in the later weeks of treatment. Resting is important, but doctors usually advise their patients to try to stay reasonably active. Patients should match their activities to their energy level. It's common for radiation to cause the skin in the treated area to become red and dry, tender, and itchy. Toward the end of treatment, the skin may become moist and "weepy." There may be permanent darkening or "bronzing" of the skin in the treated area. This area should be exposed to the air as much as possible but should also be protected from the sun. Good skin care is important at this time, but patients should not use any lotions or creams without the doctor's advice. Men may lose all or part of their beard, but facial hair generally grows back after treatment is done. Usually, men shave with an electric razor during treatment to prevent cuts that may lead to infection. Most effects of radiation therapy on the skin are temporary. The area will heal when the treatment is over.

The side effects of chemotherapy depend on the drugs that are given. In general, anticancer drugs affect rapidly growing cells, such as blood cells that fight infection, cells that line the mouth and the digestive tract, and cells in hair follicles. As a result, patients may have side effects such as lower resistance to infection, loss of appetite, nausea, vomiting, or mouth sores. They also may have less energy and may lose their hair.

The side effects of cancer treatment are different for each person, and they may even be different from one treatment to the next. Doctors, nurses, and dietitians can explain the side effects of cancer treatment and can suggest ways to deal with them. The booklets *Radiation Therapy and You* and *Eating Hints for Cancer Patients* contain helpful information about cancer treatment and coping with side effects. Patients receiving anticancer drugs will find useful information in *Chemotherapy and You.*[1]

Rehabilitation

Rehabilitation is a very important part of treatment for patients with oral cancer. The goals of rehabilitation depend on the extent of the disease and the treatment a patient has received. The health care team makes every effort to help the patient return to normal activities as soon as possible. Rehabilitation may include dietary counseling, surgery, a dental prosthesis, speech therapy, and other services.

Sometimes, a patient needs reconstructive and plastic surgery to rebuild the bones or tissues of the mouth. If this is not possible, a prosthodontist may be able to make an artificial dental and/or facial part (prosthesis). Patients may need special training to use the device.

Speech therapy generally begins as soon as possible for a patient who has trouble speaking after treatment. Often, a speech therapist visits the patient in the hospital to plan therapy and teach speech exercises. Speech therapy usually continues after the patient returns home.

Follow-up Care

Regular follow-up exams are very important for anyone who has been treated for oral cancer. The physician and the dentist watch the patient closely to check the healing process and to look for signs that the cancer may have returned. Patients with mouth dryness from radiation therapy should have dental exams three times a year.

The patient may need to see a dietitian if weight loss or eating problems continue. Most doctors urge their oral cancer patients to stop using tobacco and alcohol to reduce the risk of developing a new cancer.

Support for Cancer Patients

Living with a serious disease isn't easy. Cancer patients and those who care about them face many problems and challenges. Finding the strength to cope with these difficulties is easier when people have helpful information and support services. Several useful booklets, including *Taking Time: Support for People With Cancer and the People Who Care About Them*[1], are available from the Cancer Information Service.

Cancer patients may worry about holding a job, caring for their family, or starting new relationships. Worries about tests, treatments, hospital stays, and medical bills are common. Doctors, nurses, and other members of the health care team can help calm fears and ease confusion about treatment, working, or daily activities. Also, meeting with a nurse, social worker, counselor, or member of the clergy can be helpful for patients who want to talk about their feelings or discuss their concerns.

Friends and relatives, especially those who have had personal experience with cancer, can be very supportive. Also, many patients find it helpful to discuss their concerns with others who are facing similar problems. Cancer patients often get together in support groups, where they can share what they have learned about cancer and its treatment and about coping with the disease. It is important to keep in mind, however, that each patient is different. Treatments and ways of dealing with cancer that work for one person may not be right for another—even if they both have the same kind of cancer. It is always a good idea to discuss the advice of friends and family members with the doctor.

Often, a social worker at the hospital or clinic can suggest groups that can help with rehabilitation, emotional support, financial aid, transportation, or home care.

What the Future Holds

Patients and their families are naturally concerned about what the future holds. Sometimes they use statistics to try to figure out whether the patient will be cured or how long he or she will live. It is important to remember, however, that statistics are averages based on large numbers of patients. They cannot be used to predict what will happen to a certain patient because no two cancer patients are alike. The doctor who takes care of the patient knows his or her medical history and is in the best position to discuss the person's outlook (prognosis).

People should feel free to ask the doctor about their chance of recovery, but not even the doctor knows for sure what will happen. When doctors talk about surviving cancer, they may use the term remission rather than cure. Even though many patients with oral cancer recover completely, doctors use this term because oral cancer can recur.

Causes and Prevention

Scientists at hospitals and medical centers all across the country are studying this disease to learn more about what causes it and how to prevent it. Doctors do know that no one can "catch" cancer from another person: it is not contagious. Two known causes of oral cancer are tobacco and alcohol use.

Tobacco use—smoking cigarettes, cigars, or pipes; chewing tobacco; or dipping snuff—accounts for 80 to 90 percent of oral cancers. A number of studies have shown that cigar and pipe smokers have the same risk as cigarette smokers. Studies indicate that smokeless tobacco users are at particular risk of developing oral cancer. For long-time users, the risk is much greater, making the use of snuff or chewing tobacco among young people a special concern.

People who stop using tobacco—even after many years of use—can greatly reduce their risk of oral cancer. Special counseling or self-help groups may be useful for those who are trying to give up tobacco. Some hospitals have groups for people who want to quit. Also, the Cancer Information Service and the American Cancer Society may have information about groups in local areas to help people quit using tobacco.

Chronic and/or heavy use of alcohol also increases the risk of oral cancer, even for people who do not use tobacco. However, people who use both alcohol and tobacco have an especially high risk of oral cancer. Scientists believe that these substances increase each other's harmful effects.

Cancer of the lip can be caused by exposure to the sun. The risk can be avoided with the use of a lotion or lip balm containing a sunscreen. Wearing a hat with a brim can also block the sun's harmful rays. Pipe smokers are especially prone to cancer of the lip.

Some studies have shown that many people who develop oral cancer have a history of leukoplakia, a whitish patch inside the mouth. The causes of leukoplakia are not well understood, but it is commonly associated with heavy use of tobacco and alcohol. The condition often occurs in irritated areas, such as the gums and mouth lining of smokeless tobacco users and the lower lip of pipe smokers.

Another condition, erythroplakia, appears as a red patch in the mouth. Erythroplakia occurs most often in people 60 to 70 years of age. Early diagnosis and treatment of leukoplakia and erythroplakia are important because cancer may develop in these patches.

People who think they might be at risk for developing oral cancer should discuss this concern with their doctor or dentist, who may be able to suggest ways to reduce the risk and plan an appropriate schedule for checkups.

Note

1.   NCI booklets mentioned in this chapter are available free of charge by calling the Cancer Information Service at 1-800-4-CANCER or by visiting NCI's website at www.cancer.gov.

Chapter 23

Head and Neck Cancer

More than 55,000 Americans will develop cancer of the head and neck (most of which is preventable) this year; nearly 13,000 of them will die from it.

Find It Early and Be Cured

Tobacco is the most preventable cause of these deaths. In the United States, up to 200,000 people die each year from smoking-related illnesses. The good news is that this figure has decreased due to the increasing number of Americans who have quit smoking. The bad news is that some of these smokers switched to smokeless or spit tobacco, assuming it is a safe alternative. This is untrue—they are merely changing the site of the cancer risk from their lungs to their mouth. While lung cancer cases are down, cancers in the head and neck appear to be increasing. Cancer of the head and neck is curable if caught early. Fortunately, most head and neck cancers produce early symptoms. You should know the possible warning signs so you can alert your doctor to your symptoms as soon as possible. Remember—successful treatment of head and neck cancer can depend on early detection. Knowing and recognizing the signs of head and neck cancer can save your life.

Reprinted from "Head and Neck Cancer" with permission of the American Academy of Otolaryngology–Head and Neck Surgery Foundation. Copyright © 2002. All rights reserved.

Here's What You Should Watch for

A lump in the neck: Cancers that begin in the head or neck usually spread to lymph nodes in the neck before they spread elsewhere. A lump in the neck that lasts more than two weeks should be seen by a physician as soon as possible. Of course, not all lumps are cancer. But a lump (or lumps) in the neck can be the first sign of cancer of the mouth, throat, voicebox (larynx), thyroid gland, or of certain lymphomas or blood cancers. Such lumps are generally painless and continue to enlarge steadily.

Change in the voice: Most cancers in the larynx cause some change in voice. Any hoarseness or other voice change lasting more than two weeks should alert you to see your physician. An otolaryngologist is a head and neck specialist who can examine your vocal cords easily and painlessly. While most voice changes are not caused by cancer, you shouldn't take chances. If you are hoarse more than two weeks, make sure you don't have cancer of the larynx. See your doctor.

A growth in the mouth: Most cancers of the mouth or tongue cause a sore or swelling that doesn't go away. These sores and swellings may be painless unless they become infected. Bleeding may occur, but often not until late in the disease. If an ulcer or swelling is accompanied by lumps in the neck, be very concerned. Your dentist or doctor can determine if a biopsy (tissue sample test) is needed and can refer you to a head and neck surgeon to perform this procedure.

Bringing up blood: This is often caused by something other than cancer. However, tumors in the nose, mouth, throat, or lungs can cause bleeding. If blood appears in your saliva or phlegm for more than a few days, you should see your physician.

Swallowing problems: Cancer of the throat or esophagus (swallowing tube) may make swallowing solid foods difficult. Sometimes liquids can also be troublesome. The food may "stick" at a certain point and then either go through to the stomach or come back up. If you have trouble almost every time you try to swallow something, you should be examined by a physician. Usually a barium swallow x-ray or an esophagoscopy (direct examination of the swallowing tube with a telescope) will be performed to find the cause.

Changes in the skin: The most common head and neck cancer is basal cell cancer of the skin. Fortunately, this is rarely a major problem if treated early. Basal cell cancers appear most often on sun-exposed areas like the forehead, face, and ears, although they can occur almost anywhere on the skin. Basal cell cancer often begins as a small, pale patch that enlarges slowly, producing a central "dimple" and eventually an ulcer. Parts of the ulcer may heal, but the major portion remains ulcerated. Some basal cell cancers show color changes. Other kinds of cancer, including squamous cell cancer and malignant melanoma, also occur on the skin of the head and neck. Most squamous cell cancers occur on the lower lip and ear. They may look like basal cell cancers and, if caught early and properly treated, usually are not much more dangerous. If there is a sore on the lip, lower face, or ear that does not heal, consult a physician. Malignant melanoma classically produces dense blue-black or black discolorations of the skin. However, any mole that changes size, color, or begins to bleed may be trouble. A black or blue-black spot on the face or neck, particularly if it changes size or shape, should be seen as soon as possible by a dermatologist or other physician.

Persistent Earache: Constant pain in or around the ear when you swallow can be a sign of infection or tumor growth in the throat. This is particularly serious if it is associated with difficulty in swallowing, hoarseness, or a lump in the neck. These symptoms are best evaluated by an otolaryngologist.

Identifying High Risk of Head and Neck Cancer

As many as 90 percent of head and neck cancers arise after prolonged exposure to specific factors. Use of tobacco (cigarettes, cigars, chewing tobacco, or snuff) and alcoholic beverages are closely linked with cancers of the mouth, throat, voice box, and tongue. (In adults who neither smoke nor drink, cancer of the mouth and throat are nearly nonexistent.) Prolonged exposure to sunlight is linked with cancer of the lip and is also an established major cause of skin cancer.

What you should do: All of the symptoms and signs described here can occur with no cancer present. In fact, many times complaints of this type will be due to some other condition. But you can't tell without an examination. So, if they do occur, see your doctor—and be sure.

Remember: When found early, most cancers in the head and neck can be cured with relatively little difficulty. Cure rates for these cancers could be greatly improved if people would seek medical advice as soon as possible. So play it safe. If you think you have one of the warning signs of head and neck cancer, see your doctor right away.

Be safe: See your doctor early! And practice health habits which will make these diseases unlikely to occur.

Find an otolaryngologist: To locate an otolaryngologist in your area, please visit www.entnet.org/ent_otolaryngologist.cfm. "Find an Otolaryngologist" is an online service of the American Academy of Otolaryngology–Head and Neck Surgery and provides listings of member otolaryngologists practicing in the United States and abroad.

Chapter 24

Smoking and Breast Cancer Risk

Tobacco smoke is highly addictive and has been linked to 20 percent of all deaths in the United States. It contains many cancer-causing chemicals, and almost one third of all cancer deaths are related to tobacco use. Tobacco smoking has generally been considered to have little or no association with breast cancer risk. Newer studies have challenged this conclusion and suggested a connection between smoking and an increased risk of breast cancer, but more investigation is needed to resolve this issue. Passive smoking has been linked with an increased risk of lung cancer and heart disease. Studies have also indicated a possible linkage between passive smoking and breast cancer risk, but settling this concern will require more study. Understanding the potential association of active and passive smoking with breast cancer risk is important because women have some control over their exposure to tobacco smoke, unlike many other breast cancer risk factors.

Is smoking related to breast cancer risk?

The relationship between cigarette smoking and breast cancer risk is uncertain. Many studies have examined this relationship, and cigarette smoking has been considered to have little or no association with

"Smoking and Breast Cancer Risk," by Barbour Warren, Ph.D., Research Associate, and Carol Devine, Ph.D., R.D., Division of Nutritional Sciences and Education Project Leader, Program on Breast Cancer and Environmental Risk Factors in New York State (BCERF), Fact Sheet #46, November 2002, © 2002 Cornell University, reprinted with permission.

breast cancer risk. But recent studies of women who did not smoke but who lived or worked in environments where other people smoked (they were exposed to passive or second-hand smoke) have questioned the design and results of these earlier studies. Four studies have compared women who smoked to women who had no exposure to tobacco smoke (they had neither smoked nor had ever been passively exposed to tobacco smoke). In contrast, earlier studies had compared smokers to women who had never smoked or did not currently smoke but whose passive smoke exposure was unknown. All four of the newer studies reported increased breast cancer risk among the women who smoked cigarettes. They were all small case-control studies, and only one reported an increase in risk among women who smoked longer. Nonetheless, three of the studies reported that smokers had a statistically significant increased breast cancer risk of two to four times that of women who neither smoked nor were ever passively exposed to tobacco smoke. This is an area of research with considerable disagreement. Recent review of this area of research by the International Agency for Research on Cancer (IARC) dismissed a linkage between smoking and breast cancer risk. A large number of women smoke or have smoked and resolution of this issue is important.

Is passive smoking related to breast cancer risk?

Although passive exposure to tobacco smoke has been linked to a number of health problems, it is unresolved whether it alters breast cancer risk. Most, but not all, studies that compared women who were passively exposed to tobacco smoke to women with no exposure to tobacco smoke reported an association of passive smoking with an increased risk of breast cancer. Only two of these studies showed a "dose-relationship", where an increase in breast cancer risk was related to more tobacco smoke exposure. Other studies, which compared the risk of breast cancer of women exposed to passive smoke to women with less clearly defined passive smoke exposure (nonsmokers or those who have never smoked), have reported conflicting associations with breast cancer risk; some studies reported increases in risk, some reported decreases in risk and some reported no association with risk. All of these studies were also recently reviewed by the IARC. They found that it was unlikely that passive smoking increased breast cancer risk.

Several studies have found similar increases in breast cancer risk for both active and passive smoke exposures. These results have been criticized by some researchers. These researchers argue that this is an unlikely result as smokers have much greater exposure since they are exposed to smoke both actively and passively, but further investigation will be required to resolve this issue. Possible reasons for the differences in the results of these studies are discussed below.

Is the smoke inhaled during active smoking different from the smoke inhaled during passive smoking?

The tobacco smoke a smoker inhales is different from the smoke inhaled by those nearby. The major source of passive smoke is from the burning of the cigarette rather than what is exhaled by smokers. Both types of smoke contain thousands of chemicals. The chemicals present in both these types of smoke are similar, but the concentrations of the chemicals are different. Many of the toxic chemicals in tobacco smoke are found in higher concentrations in the tobacco smoke as it leaves the cigarette compared to inhaled smoke; in some cases, the concentrations are far higher. This smoke is largely produced from the lower temperature burning of cigarettes between inhalations and the chemicals are less degraded than in the smokers' inhalations. However many factors, such room size and air flow, can affect the dilution of the smoke and the resulting exposure can differ greatly.

Why are there differences in the results of the human epidemiological studies examining breast cancer risk and passive exposure to tobacco smoke?

The inconsistencies in the results of these studies arise from differences in their methodologies, the way they were carried out. The first difference is in the choice of women who served as the reference group, the women whose breast cancer risk was used as the level for risk comparison. Ideally, the women in the reference group and the women under study would differ only in their active or passive exposure to tobacco smoke. This ideal is seldom reached, and some of the differences in the results come from the extent to which these groups of women differ from this ideal.

Recent studies have used as a reference group women who had no exposure to tobacco smoke—that is, they have never actively or passively smoked. These studies in most cases have reported increases in breast cancer risk for women who smoked or were passively exposed to tobacco smoke compared to reference women who were never exposed. Critics of this approach cite studies that indicate the reference women who have never been exposed to tobacco smoke are healthier, in general. They argue that the difference in risk is due to the better health of these women used as references for risk. Older studies used as a reference group women who had never actively smoked or who were not current smokers but whose exposure to environmental smoke was unknown. These studies have largely reported no link between any exposure to tobacco smoke and breast cancer risk. Critics of this approach cite the potential for passive smoking and previous smoking to increase risk in control women and mask effects on the women under study.

A second potential source of the discrepancies may come from how the exposure or lack of exposure to environmental tobacco smoke is determined. Studies have shown that people can recall recent exposure very well but that remembering the duration and degree of distant exposure (such as whether their grandparents or baby-sitter smoked) is difficult. Yet one study examined this issue and found that women tended to underestimate their exposure, an effect which would decrease the observed risk. Thus, the information used in these studies may be inaccurate which could influence the reported breast cancer risk association. More work is needed to resolve these issues.

How might smoking increase the risk of cancer in the breast, an organ that is not exposed to smoke?

It is biologically possible for active cigarette smoking or passive exposure to tobacco smoke to affect a woman's breast cancer risk. There is direct documentation that breasts are exposed to chemicals within tobacco smoke in active smokers. Study of the fluid in the ducts of the breast of smoking women has shown the presence of tobacco chemicals at higher concentrations than were found in blood. Women passively exposed to tobacco smoke have tobacco chemicals in their blood too, but examinations of their breast fluid have not been carried out.

Both active and passive tobacco smoke exposure have been linked to non-respiratory cancers. Active cigarette smoking has been associated with cancer of the bladder, cervix, stomach, pancreas, and kidney. The effects of passive exposure to tobacco smoke have been studied much less, but associations with cervical cancer in adult women, as well as leukemia and brain cancer in children, have been reported.

Does smoking at a young age or being passively exposed to tobacco smoke at a young age affect a woman's breast cancer risk?

Exposure to tobacco smoke at a young age either by smoking or by being around people who smoke may be related to an increased breast cancer risk. Sixteen studies have examined smoking at a young age. These studies compared women who smoked at a young age to women who had never smoked or who were not currently smokers. Most studies reported a small increase in breast cancer risk associated with starting smoking under age 17. Two studies used women who were never passively exposed to tobacco smoke as the comparison group and found about a doubling of breast cancer risk among young smokers; one of the studies reported this effect only for premenopausal breast cancer.

The association of exposure to passive smoke at a young age with breast cancer risk has been examined in five studies. These studies typically looked at exposure up to age 19. Four of these studies used women with no exposure to tobacco smoke as controls and reported approximately a doubling of breast cancer risk among women who were exposed to passive smoke. The remaining study used women who never smoked as the comparison and found no association between tobacco smoke exposure and breast cancer risk.

The breast undergoes a major period of development during adolescence, and studies in animals have demonstrated that this is a period of great susceptibility to cancer-causing agents. More study is needed in this area.

Does the number of years a woman has been smoking or the amount she smokes affect her breast cancer risk?

Increases in breast cancer risk, relative to how long a woman has smoked or the number of cigarettes she smoked a day, have been found in several studies. However, the relationship between breast cancer and the level of smoking exposure is not as clear as it is for lung cancer. For example, people who smoke the least (or for the shortest time) have the lowest risk of lung cancer, while people who smoke the most (or for the longest time) have the highest risk. People who smoke amounts between these two extremes, have risks that fall between the two extremes. This is called a "dose-relationship" between lung cancer risk and smoking; the risk of lung cancer increases with the dose or amount a person smokes. Most breast cancer studies have not seen a dose-relationship between smoking and breast cancer risk. A possible explanation would be that there is an exposure level that must be exceeded for risk to increase; such a level is called a threshold. A threshold effect is possible but has not been described for other smoking-related diseases.

Why did some earlier studies report an association of active smoking and decreased breast cancer risk?

Most of the epidemiological studies which compared breast cancer risk of active smokers to women who were not smokers (regardless of their passive smoke exposure) have found no association of smoking and breast cancer risk. But several studies found that women who smoked had a decreased breast cancer risk. It is not uncommon for epidemiological studies to come to different assessments of health risk, especially when, as in these studies, the associated risk is not large. Epidemiological studies differ in many ways, such as the groups of women being studied, how information is obtained and what other exposures and risk factors are taken into consideration. These differences can affect the study's outcome. For this reason, many epidemiological studies must be conducted and evaluated before there is an agreement on the relationship between a potential risk factor and a disease.

The clarity of these studies' results is also affected by the very complicated relationship between tobacco smoke exposure and breast cancer risk—which could support associations with either increased or decreased risk. Smoking has effects that can both increase and decrease breast cancer risk. On one hand, tobacco smoke contains chemicals that can cause breast cancer in animals and could thus be associated with an increase in breast cancer risk. On the other hand, smoking has been shown to have many effects which suggest an opposition of the effects of estrogen and could decrease breast cancer risk. The interplay between the effects of the cancer-causing chemicals and the apparent opposition of estrogen is critical to breast cancer risk. The nature of this interplay is poorly understood.

Does quitting smoking affect breast cancer risk?

Quitting smoking may lead to a temporary increase in breast cancer risk. Most of the studies that have examined the breast cancer risk of women who have quit smoking have reported an increase in breast cancer risk. In many of these studies, breast cancer risk was highest shortly after the women stopped smoking and gradually decreased over 5 years to 20 years depending on the study.

It is possible that the interplay between the effects of toxic tobacco chemicals and the effects that may oppose estrogen matter here. Opposition of estrogen's effects is lost in women who quit smoking and this may allow the expression of the accumulated toxic effects of cigarette smoke.

The increase in breast cancer risk associated with quitting smoking should be considered in the context of overall health. After quitting smoking, a woman's risk of breast cancer temporarily increases between 25 and 450 percent (depending on the study examined). This is in sharp contrast to the high risks for other health problems associated with continued smoking. For example, there is a well established 1,000 to 2,000 percent increase in lung cancer risk associated with smoking. Without question, the effects of quitting smoking on overall health are beneficial.

Does smoking marijuana affect breast cancer risk?

The relationship between smoking marijuana and breast cancer risk has not been studied. Marijuana smoke has been shown to contain many of the toxic substances found in tobacco smoke. Unfortunately, there has not been enough study to evaluate a possible link of marijuana smoking with breast or even lung cancer.

Are some women more susceptible to tobacco smoke?

Studies have shown that people differ in how their bodies process different chemicals, including the toxic chemicals in tobacco. Examinations of the connection between breast cancer risk and differences in the processing of these toxic tobacco chemicals have produced conflicting results. This is an active area of research that may allow the identification of women who are more susceptible to the cancer-causing chemicals in tobacco smoke.

Does smoking affect the survival of women with breast cancer?

The effect of smoking on the survival of women with breast cancer is unclear. Some studies have reported an association between smoking and an increase in the risk of death, while others found no association with the risk of death from breast cancer. Smokers may be at increased risk for metastasis (the spread of cancer). Two studies have reported an increase in the spread of tumors from the breast to the lungs in women who smoked. The survival of women with breast cancer who stopped smoking has been examined in one study. Their survival was found to be similar to that of women with breast cancer who never smoked.

What can women do now?

Quitting smoking and avoiding passive exposure to tobacco smoke makes good sense. Although it is unclear if smoking and passive exposure to tobacco smoke are associated with breast cancer risk, women can control their exposure to these potential risk factors. There are also many other health benefits to be gained by decreasing or eliminating either of these exposures.

Quitting smoking is difficult, but a number of drug and behavioral programs have been shown to increase the likelihood of success. Quitting smoking will not only make one ultimately feel better, but will decrease the risk of many diseases including heart disease, stroke, many respiratory diseases, and cancer of the lung, mouth, larynx, kidney, pancreas, stomach, and some types of leukemia.

The effects of passive exposure to tobacco smoke are just beginning to be understood. Until more is known, decreasing exposure is desirable. Minimizing tobacco smoke exposure is particularly important for children, who appear to be more sensitive to its toxic effects.

Additional Information

Program on Breast Cancer and Environmental Risk Factors
Sprecher Institute for Comparative Cancer Research
Cornell University
Box 31
Ithaca, NY 14853
Phone: 607-254-2893
Website: http://envirocancer.cornell.edu
E-mail: breastcancer@cornell.edu

Chapter 25

Bladder Cancer

Overview

The bladder is an organ located in the pelvic cavity that stores and discharges urine. Urine is produced by the kidneys, carried to the bladder by the ureters, and discharged from the bladder through the urethra. Bladder cancer accounts for approximately 90% of cancers of the urinary tract (renal pelvis, ureters, bladder, urethra).

Types

Bladder cancer usually originates in the bladder lining, which consists of a mucous layer of transitional epithelial cells (surface cells that expand and deflate), smooth muscle, and a fibrous layer. The tumor is categorized as low stage (superficial) or high stage (muscle invasive).

In industrialized countries (for example, United States, Canada, France), more than 90% of cases originate in the transitional epithelial cells (called transitional cell carcinoma; TCC). In developing countries, 75% of cases are squamous cell carcinomas caused

---

This chapter begins with excerpts from "Bladder Cancer," reprinted with permission. © Healthcommunities.com, Inc., 2004. All rights reserved. "Female Smokers Appear More Susceptible to Bladder Cancer than Male Smokers," by Alicia DiRado, *HSC Weekly*, April 6, 2001, is reprinted with permission from the University of Southern California Health Sciences Center Office of Public Relations. © 2001 University of Southern California.

by *Schistosoma haematobium* (parasitic organism) infection. Rare types of bladder cancer include small cell carcinoma, carcinosarcoma, primary lymphoma, and sarcoma.

Incidence and Prevalence

According to the National Cancer Institute, the highest incidence of bladder cancer occurs in industrialized countries such as the United States, Canada, and France. Incidence is lowest in Asia and South America, where it is about 70% lower than in the United States.

Incidence of bladder cancer increases with age. People over the age of 70 develop the disease 2 to 3 times more often than those aged 55–69 and 15 to 20 times more often than those aged 30–54.

Bladder cancer is 2 to 3 times more common in men. In the United States, approximately 38,000 men and 15,000 women are diagnosed with the disease each year. Bladder cancer is the fourth most common type of cancer in men and the eighth most common type in women. The disease is more prevalent in Caucasians than in African Americans and Hispanics.

Causes and Risk Factors

Cancer-causing agents (carcinogens) in the urine may lead to the development of bladder cancer. Cigarette smoking contributes to more than 50% of cases, and smoking cigars or pipes also increases the risk. Other risk factors include the following:

- Age
- Chronic bladder inflammation (recurrent urinary tract infections, urinary stones)
- Consumption of *Aristolochia fangchi* (herb used in some weight-loss formulas)
- Diet high in saturated fat
- Exposure to second-hand smoke
- External beam radiation
- Family history of bladder cancer (several genetic risk factors identified)
- Gender (male)
- Infection with *Schistosoma haematobium* (parasite found in many developing countries)

- Personal history of bladder cancer
- Race (Caucasian)
- Treatment with certain drugs (for example, cyclophosphamide—used to treat cancer)

Exposure to carcinogens in the workplace also increases the risk for bladder cancer. Medical workers exposed during the preparation, storage, administration, or disposal of antineoplastic drugs (used in chemotherapy) are at increased risk. Occupational risk factors include recurrent and early exposure to hair dye, and exposure to dye containing aniline, a chemical used in medical and industrial dyes. Workers at increased risk include the following:

- Hairdressers
- Machinists
- Printers
- Painters
- Truck drivers
- Workers in rubber, chemical, textile, metal, and leather industries

Signs and Symptoms

The primary symptom of bladder cancer is blood in the urine (hematuria). Hematuria may be gross (visible to the naked eye) or microscopic (visible only under a microscope) and is usually painless. Other symptoms include frequent urination and pain upon urination (dysuria).

Diagnosis

Diagnosis of bladder cancer includes urological tests and imaging tests. A complete medical history is used to identify potential risk factors (for example, smoking, exposure to dyes). Laboratory tests may include the following:

- Urinalysis (to detect microscopic hematuria)
- Urine cytology (to detect cancer cells by examining cells flushed from the bladder during urination)
- Urine culture (to rule out urinary tract infection)

Various imaging tests may also be performed. Intravenous pyelogram (IVP) is the standard imaging test for bladder cancer. In this procedure, a contrast agent (radiopaque dye) is administered intravenously and x-rays are taken as the dye moves through the urinary tract. IVP provides information about the structure and function of the kidneys, ureters, and bladder. Other imaging tests include CT scan, MRI scan, bone scan, and ultrasound.

If bladder cancer is suspected, cystoscopy and biopsy are performed. Local anesthesia is administered and a cystoscope (thin, telescope-like tube with a tiny camera attached) is inserted into the bladder through the urethra to allow the physician to detect abnormalities. In biopsy, tissue samples are taken from the lesion(s) and examined for cancer cells. If the sample is positive, the cancer is staged using the tumor, node, metastases (TNM) system.

Female Smokers Appear More Susceptible to Bladder Cancer Than Male Smokers

Cigarette for cigarette, smoking appears to pack a bigger punch for women than men when it comes to bladder cancer risk, according to a new study led by USC (University of Southern California) preventive medicine researchers.

As a whole, cigarette smokers were found to run 2.5 times the risk of contracting bladder cancer than nonsmokers; but within this increased risk due to smoking, women appear to face an even greater risk than men, according to the report in the April 4, 2001 issue of the *Journal of the National Cancer Institute*.

"Our large, case-control study provides the first evidence, to our knowledge, that when comparable numbers of cigarettes are smoked, the risk of bladder cancer is higher in women than in men," said J. Esteban Castelao, researcher in preventive medicine and lead author of the study.

Castelao and colleagues at USC and the Massachusetts Institute of Technology conducted the epidemiological study among 1,514 patients with bladder cancer and 1,514 other comparable study participants in the Los Angeles area. Researchers asked about general smoking habits, how many cigarettes participants smoked and how often, as well as which types of cigarettes they smoked and how they inhaled (deeply, moderately or lightly).

For both genders, the risk of bladder cancer appeared to rise both with the number of cigarettes smoked each day and with the number of years that participants had smoked regularly. In nearly every category of smoking, however, the risks to women were greater than those to men.

Women who smoked 40 or more cigarettes a day for 40 years or more, for example, faced more than twice the risk of contracting bladder cancer as men with the same smoking habit. These women incurred more than 11 times the risk of bladder cancer than a nonsmoker, while men ran approximately five times the risk of a nonsmoker.

The researchers also analyzed blood samples from 1,363 study participants, looking for evidence of exposure to arylamines, chemicals in cigarette smoke known to cause bladder cancer. They found that among men and women who smoked at the same level, concentrations of 3- and 4-aminobiphenyl hemoglobin adducts in the blood— markers of arylamine exposure and indices of their carcinogenic potential—were higher in women than in men.

"It suggests that women somehow either activate or detoxify these (chemicals) differently than men do," says Ron Ross, study co-author and the Flora Thronton Chair of preventive medicine.

"The question for us now is: Why does that occur?" he asked.

When comparing types of cigarettes, researchers found no difference in bladder cancer risk associated with filtered versus unfiltered cigarettes or low-tar versus high-tar cigarettes—nor any difference in risk tied to whether smokers reported deep or shallow inhalations.

Bladder cancer currently accounts for 6 percent of all new cancer cases in men and 2 percent of all new cancer cases in women.

The American Cancer Society estimates that 53,200 Americans were diagnosed with the cancer and 12,200 Americans died from it in 2000. About half of all cases are believed to be caused by smoking.

The authors also noted that growing evidence indicates that when smoking levels are equal, women incur a higher risk of lung cancer than men, as well.

Co-authors of the study included preventive medicine researchers Jian-Min Yuan, Manuela Gago-Dominguez, J. Slade Crowder, Ronald K. Ross and Mimi C. Yu of the USC/Norris Comprehensive Cancer Center and the Keck School of Medicine of USC, as well as Paul L. Skipper and Steven R. Tannenbaum of the Department of Chemistry and Division of Toxicology at MIT.

Chapter 26

Smoking and Your Lungs

What Cigarettes Do

When you smoke cigarettes, many chemicals enter your body through your lungs. Burning tobacco produces more than 4,000 chemicals. Nicotine, carbon monoxide, and tars are some of these substances. Smoking greatly affects your lungs and airways. Smokers get a variety of problems related to breathing. Problems range from an annoying cough to grave illness like emphysema and cancer.

How Your Lungs and Airways Change

Smoking cigarettes causes many changes in your lungs and airways. Some changes are sudden, last a short time, and then go away. These changes are acute. Colds and pneumonia are acute changes. Other changes happen slowly and last a long time. These are chronic changes. Some chronic changes may last the rest of your life. Emphysema is an example of a chronic change.

"Smoking and Your Lungs" is a patient information brochure from the University of Pittsburgh Medical Center. © 2003 University of Pittsburgh Medical Center. Reprinted with permission. For additional information, visit www .upmc.com, or for help in finding a doctor or health service that suits your needs, call the UPMC Referral Service at 800-533-UPMC (8762). This information is not intended to be used as a substitute for professional medical advice, diagnosis, or treatment. You should not rely entirely on this information for your health care needs. Ask your own doctor or health care provider any specific medical questions that you have.

Here is a list of the changes that happen in your lungs and airways when you smoke:

- The cells that produce mucus in your lungs and airways grow in size and number. As a result, the amount of mucus increases. The mucus is also thicker.

- The cleaning system in your lungs does not work well. The lungs have broom-like hairs, called cilia. The cilia clean your lungs. A few seconds after you start smoking a cigarette, the cilia slow down. Smoking one cigarette can slow the action of your cilia for several hours. Smoking also reduces the number of cilia, so there are fewer cilia to clean your lungs.

- Your lungs and airways have more mucus, and the mucus is not cleaned out well. So the mucus stays in your airways, clogs them, and makes you cough. This extra mucus can easily get infected.

- Your lungs and airways get irritated and inflamed. They become narrow and reduce the air flow. Even one or two cigarettes cause irritation and coughing.

- As you age, it's normal for your lungs not to work as well. When you smoke, your lungs age faster.

- Your lungs can be destroyed. When lung tissue is destroyed, the number of air spaces and blood vessels in the lungs decreases. Less oxygen is carried to your body.

- You are less protected from infection. When you smoke, the natural defenses your lungs have against infection do not work well.

- Cigarette smoke has chemicals that can make normal cells change into cancer cells.

Weigh the Benefits of Quitting Smoking

When you smoke, you have a much greater chance of getting health problems. In this chapter, you will learn about the kinds of problems you can get from smoking. You will also learn how you benefit when you quit smoking.

Breathing-Related Symptoms

When you smoke:

- chronic cough
- more mucus

- shortness of breath
- wheezing

When you quit:

- fast decrease in breathing-related symptoms no matter how much or how long you smoked
- easier breathing within 72 hours
- marked decrease in cough, mucus, shortness of breath, and wheezing within one month
- less irritated and inflamed airways
- cilia growth in one to nine months
- lungs more able to handle mucus, self-clean, and fight infection

Colds and Lung Infections

When you smoke:

- more colds and lung infections
- worse colds and lung infections

When you quit:

- fewer colds and lung infections
- milder colds and lung infections

Flu and Pneumonia

Smoking increases the number of deaths from flu and pneumonia. As fewer people smoke, the death rate from flu and pneumonia drops rapidly.

When you smoke:

- more and worse bouts of the flu
- more chance of pneumonia
- poor response to flu vaccine

When you quit:

- 50 percent less risk of pneumonia within five years

- fewer and milder bouts of the flu
- better response to flu vaccine

Chronic Obstructive Pulmonary Disease (COPD)

Cigarette smoking is a major cause of COPD. COPD stands for chronic obstructive pulmonary disease. COPD blocks the flow of air into and out of your lungs. It is a leading cause of death in the United States. More than 80 percent of COPD deaths are related to smoking. When you smoke, your risk of death from COPD is ten times greater than if you did not smoke.

COPD includes two diseases: chronic bronchitis and emphysema.

When you have chronic bronchitis:

- you get a long-lasting cough every year
- your cough produces a lot of mucus that blocks air flow

When you quit smoking:

- symptoms of chronic bronchitis decrease
- symptoms of chronic bronchitis may disappear over time

When you have emphysema:

- your lung tissue is destroyed over time
- your lungs are less able to take in fresh air and let out stale air
- your lungs and airways produce a lot of mucus that blocks air flow

When you quit smoking:

- you get a small improvement right away
- the disease slows down
- you have a better chance of living longer

Asthma

Asthma is a chronic airway disease. People with asthma have periods of shortness of breath, wheezing, chest tightness, and cough.

When you smoke:

- symptoms of asthma are harder to control

When you quit:

- symptoms of asthma decrease

Cancer

Lung cancer is the leading cause of cancer death in the United States. Smoking causes 85 percent of lung cancer. Smokers have a higher number of pre-cancer changes in their airways than nonsmokers.

When you smoke:

- pre-cancer tissue can change to cancer
- your risk of lung cancer and death is 20 times greater than a nonsmoker's
- your risk increases the more you smoke and the longer you smoke

When you quit:

- pre-cancer tissue may return to normal
- your risk of lung cancer decreases within five years
- your risk of lung cancer keeps decreasing over time

How Second-Hand Smoke Affects You

When people are smoking, the air around them is polluted with tobacco smoke. This is called second-hand smoke. Second-hand smoke comes from two sources. The burning end of the cigarette produces smoke, and the smoker exhales smoke.

When near a person smoking, nonsmokers breathe second-hand smoke. Other names for breathing second-hand smoke are "passive smoking" and "involuntary smoking." Passive smoking has bad effects on the lungs and airways in both adults and children.

Researchers have studied adult nonsmokers who breathe cigarette smoke in the work place. Results show these adults have impaired lungs. Second-hand smoke is a carcinogen. A carcinogen is a substance known to cause cancer. When you breathe second-hand smoke, your risk of lung cancer increases. In the United States each year, an estimated 3,000 people die from lung cancer caused by second-hand smoke.

When you breathe second-hand smoke, you can get:

- wheezing
- chronic cough
- increased mucus
- shortness of breath
- trouble controlling asthma
- more lung infections and pneumonia
- lung cancer

Stay away from second-hand smoke.

Chapter 27

Emphysema

What Is Emphysema?

Emphysema is a condition in which there is over-inflation of structures in the lungs known as alveoli or air sacs. This over-inflation results from a breakdown of the walls of the alveoli, which causes a decrease in respiratory function (the way the lungs work) and often, breathlessness.

Early symptoms of emphysema include shortness of breath and cough. Emphysema and chronic bronchitis together comprise chronic obstructive pulmonary disease (COPD).

How Serious Is Emphysema?

Emphysema is a widespread disease of the lungs. Close to three million Americans have been diagnosed with emphysema.

Emphysema ranks 15th among chronic conditions that contribute to activity limitations: almost 44 percent of individuals with emphysema report that their daily activities have been limited by the disease.

Men tend to have higher rates of emphysema. In 2001, the emphysema prevalence rate was 40% higher in males compared to females.

Causes of Emphysema

It is known from scientific research that the normal lung has a remarkable balance between two classes of chemicals with opposing action. The elastic fibers in the lung allow the lungs to expand and contract. When the chemical balance is altered, the lungs lose the ability to protect themselves against the destruction of these elastic fibers. This is what happens in emphysema.

There are a number of reasons this chemical imbalance occurs. Smoking is responsible for the majority (80%–90%) of COPD (chronic obstructive pulmonary disease) cases, including emphysema.

In addition, it is estimated that 50,000 to 100,000 Americans living today were born with a deficiency of a protein known as alpha 1-antitrypsin (AAT) which can lead to an inherited form of emphysema called alpha 1-antitrypsin (AAT) deficiency-related emphysema.

How Does Emphysema Develop?

Emphysema begins with the destruction of air sacs (alveoli) in the lungs where oxygen from the air is exchanged for carbon dioxide in the blood. The walls of the air sacs are thin and fragile. Damage to the air sacs is irreversible and results in permanent "holes" in the tissues of the lower lungs.

As air sacs are destroyed, the lungs are able to transfer less and less oxygen to the bloodstream, causing shortness of breath. The lungs also lose their elasticity, which is important to keep airways open. The patient experiences great difficulty exhaling.

Emphysema doesn't develop suddenly, it comes on very gradually. Years of exposure to the irritation of cigarette smoke usually precede the development of emphysema.

A person may initially visit the doctor because he or she has begun to feel short of breath during activity or exercise. As the disease progresses, a brief walk can be enough to bring on difficulty in breathing. Some people may have had chronic bronchitis before developing emphysema.

Treatment for Emphysema

Doctors can help persons with emphysema live more comfortably with their disease. The goal of treatment is to provide relief of symptoms and prevent progression of the disease with a minimum of side effects. The doctor's advice and treatment may include:

- *Quitting smoking:* The single most important factor for maintaining healthy lungs.

- *Bronchodilator drugs* (prescription drugs that relax and open air passages in the lungs): May be prescribed to treat emphysema if there is a tendency toward airway constriction or tightening. These drugs may be inhaled as aerosol sprays or taken orally.

- *Antibiotics:* If you have a bacterial infection, such as pneumococcal pneumonia.

- *Exercise:* Including breathing exercises to strengthen the muscles used in breathing as part of a pulmonary* rehabilitation program to condition the rest of the body. (*The term "pulmonary" refers to the lungs.)

- *Treatment:* With alpha 1-proteinase inhibitor (A1PI) only if a person has AAT deficiency-related emphysema. A1PI is not recommended for those who develop emphysema as a result of cigarette smoking or other environmental factors.

- *Lung transplantation:* This is a major procedure, which can be effective.

- *Lung volume reduction surgery (LVRS):* Is a surgical procedure in which the most severely diseases portions of the lung are removed to allow the remaining lung and breathing muscles to work better. The short term results are promising but those with severe forms are at higher risk of death. Recently, the Centers for Medicare and Medicaid Services (CMS) announced that they intend to cover LVRS for people with non-high risk severe emphysema, who meet the criteria stated in the National Emphysema Treatment Trial (NETT). In addition, CMS has decided that LVRS is "reasonable and necessary" only for qualified patients that undergo pulmonary rehabilitation therapy before and after the surgery. CMS is currently composing accreditation standards for LVRS facilities and will use these standards to determine where the surgery will be covered.

Prevention of Emphysema

Continuing research is being done to find answers to many questions about emphysema, especially about the best ways to prevent the disease.

Researchers know that quitting smoking can prevent the occurrence and decrease the progression of emphysema. Other environmental controls can also help prevent the disease.

If an individual has emphysema, the doctor will work hard to prevent the disease from getting worse by keeping the patient healthy and clear of any infection. The patient can participate in this prevention effort by following these general health guidelines:

Emphysema is a serious disease. It damages your lungs, and it can damage your heart. See your doctor at the first sign of symptoms.

DON'T SMOKE. The majority of those who get emphysema are smokers. Continued smoking makes emphysema worse, especially for those who have AAT deficiency, the inherited form of emphysema.

Maintain overall good health habits, which include proper nutrition, adequate sleep, and regular exercise to build up your stamina and resistance to infections.

Reduce your exposure to air pollution, which may aggravate symptoms of emphysema. Refer to radio or television weather reports or your local newspaper for information about air quality. On days when the ozone (smog) level is unhealthy, restrict your activity to early morning or evening. When pollution levels are dangerous, remain indoors and stay as comfortable as possible.

Consult your doctor at the start of any cold or respiratory infection because infection can make your emphysema symptoms worse. Ask about getting vaccinated against influenza and pneumococcal pneumonia.

Chapter 28

Chronic Bronchitis: Smoking Is the Most Common Cause

What Is Chronic Bronchitis?

Bronchitis is an inflammation of the lining of the bronchial tubes. These tubes connect the windpipe with the lungs. When the bronchi are inflamed and/or infected, less air is able to flow to and from the lungs and a heavy mucus or phlegm is coughed up. This is bronchitis. Many people suffer a brief attack of acute bronchitis with cough and mucus production when they have severe colds. Acute bronchitis is usually not associated with fever.

Chronic bronchitis is defined by the presence of a mucus-producing cough most days of the month, three months of a year for two successive years without other underlying disease to explain the cough. It may precede or accompany pulmonary emphysema.

What Causes Chronic Bronchitis?

Cigarette smoking is by far the most common cause of chronic bronchitis. The bronchial tubes of people with chronic bronchitis may also have been irritated initially by bacterial or viral infections. Air pollution and industrial dusts and fumes are also causes.

"Chronic Bronchitis," is reprinted with permission. © 2004 American Lung Association. For more information on how you can support the fight against lung disease, the third leading cause of death in the U.S., please contact The American Lung Association at 1-800-LUNG-USA (1-800-586-4872) or visit the website at www.lungusa.org.

Once the bronchial tubes have been irritated over a long period of time, excessive mucus is produced constantly, the lining of the bronchial tubes becomes thickened, an irritating cough develops, air flow may be hampered, and the lungs are endangered. The bronchial tubes then make an ideal breeding place for infections.

Who Gets Chronic Bronchitis?

Over 11 million Americans are diagnosed with chronic bronchitis annually. The prevalence rate of chronic bronchitis has been consistently higher in females than in males. Chronic bronchitis affects people of all ages, but is higher in those over 45 years old.

No matter what their occupation or lifestyle, people who smoke cigarettes are those most likely to develop chronic bronchitis. But workers with certain jobs, especially those involving high concentrations of dust and irritating fumes, are also at high risk of developing this disease.

Higher rates of chronic bronchitis are found among coal miners, grain handlers, metal molders, and other workers exposed to dust.

Chronic bronchitis symptoms worsen when atmospheric concentrations of sulfur dioxide and other air pollutants increase. These symptoms are intensified when individuals also smoke.

How Serious Is Chronic Bronchitis?

In 2000, aver 11 million Americans were diagnosed with chronic bronchitis.

During that same year over 1,100 American died as a result of chronic bronchitis. This is an underestimate of the number of deaths actually attributed to this disease.

Together with emphysema and other chronic lower respiratory disease, excluding asthma, COPD is the fourth leading cause of death in the US.

Chronic bronchitis is often neglected by individuals until it is in an advanced state, because people mistakenly believe that the disease is not life-threatening. By the time a patient goes to his or her doctor the lungs have frequently been seriously injured. Then the patient may be in danger of developing serious respiratory problems or heart failure.

How Chronic Bronchitis Attacks

Chronic bronchitis doesn't strike suddenly. After a winter cold seems cured, an individual may continue to cough and produce large amounts of mucus for several weeks. Since people who get chronic bronchitis are often smokers, the cough is usually dismissed as only "smoker's cough."

As time goes on, colds become more damaging. Coughing and bringing up phlegm last longer after each cold.

Without realizing it, one begins to take this coughing and mucus production as a matter of course. Soon they are present all the time, before colds, during colds, after colds, all year round. Generally, the cough is worse in the morning and in damp, cold weather. An ounce or more of yellow mucus may be coughed up each day.

Treatment for Chronic Bronchitis

The treatment of chronic bronchitis is primarily aimed at reducing irritation in the bronchial tubes. The discovery of antibiotic drugs has been helpful in treating acute bacterial infection associated with chronic bronchitis. However people with chronic bronchitis do not need to take antibiotics continually.

Bronchodilator drugs may be prescribed to help relax and open up air passages in the lungs, if there is a tendency for these to close up. These drugs may be inhaled as aerosol sprays or taken as pills.

To effectively control chronic bronchitis, it is necessary to eliminate sources of irritation and infection in the nose, throat, mouth, sinuses, and bronchial tubes. This means an individual must avoid polluted air and dusty working conditions and give up smoking. Your local American Lung Association can suggest methods to help you quit smoking.

If the person with chronic bronchitis is exposed to dust and fumes at work, the doctor may suggest changing the work environment. All persons with chronic bronchitis must develop and follow a plan for a healthy lifestyle. Improving one's general health also increases the body's resistance to infections.

What Should You Do If You Have Chronic Bronchitis?

A good health plan for any person with chronic bronchitis should include these rules:

- See your doctor or follow your doctor's instructions at the beginning of any cold or respiratory infection.

- Don't smoke! Contact your local American Lung Association at 1-800-LUNG-USA (1-800-586-4872) for information on how to quit smoking.

- Follow a nutritious, well-balanced diet, and maintain your ideal body weight.

- Get regular exercise daily, without tiring yourself too much.

- Ask your doctor about getting vaccinated against influenza and pneumococcal pneumonia.

- Avoid exposure to colds and influenza at home or in public, and avoid respiratory irritants such as secondhand smoke, dust, and other air pollutants.

Chapter 29

Asthma and Smoking

What is the link between smoking and asthma?

Smoke from cigars, cigarettes, and pipes harms your body in many ways, but it is especially harmful to the respiratory system. Asthma is a disease of the bronchial tubes, the airways that branch into the lungs. When a person has asthma, there are three main changes in the airways that make breathing difficult:

- The band of muscles that surround the airways tighten and make the airways narrow.

- The lining of the airways becomes swollen and inflamed.

- The cells that line the airways produce more and thicker mucus than normal.

It's not fully known why these changes occur. The airways in a person with asthma are very sensitive and can react to many things, or "triggers." Coming into contact with these triggers often produces asthma symptoms. Tobacco smoke is a powerful asthma trigger.

"Smoking and Asthma," is reprinted with permission. © 2003 The Cleveland Clinic Foundation, 9500 Euclid Avenue, Cleveland, OH 44195, 800-223-2273 ext. 48950, www.clevelandclinic.org. Additional information is available from the Cleveland Clinic Health Information Center, 216-444-3771, or www.clevelandclinic.org/health.

Why is tobacco smoke so harmful?

When a person inhales tobacco smoke, irritating substances settle in the moist lining of the airways and can set off asthma episodes. Often, people with asthma who smoke keep their lungs in a constant state of poor asthma control and have ongoing asthma symptoms.

Tobacco smoke also damages tiny hair-like projections in the airways called "cilia." Normally, cilia sweep dust and mucus out of the airways. Cigarette smoke damages cilia so they are unable to work. Cigarette smoke also causes the lungs to make more mucus than normal. As a result, when cilia don't work, mucus and other irritating substances build up in the airways.

Tobacco smoke also contains many cancer-causing substances ("carcinogens," such as tar). These substances deposit in the lungs and can cause lung diseases such as lung cancer and emphysema.

What is second-hand smoke and is it harmful?

Second-hand smoke is the combination of smoke from a burning cigarette and smoke exhaled by a smoker. Inhaling second-hand smoke (also called passive smoke or environmental tobacco smoke) from another person's smoking may be even more harmful than smoking yourself. The smoke that burns off the end of a cigar or cigarette contains more harmful substances (tar, carbon monoxide, nicotine, and others) than the smoke inhaled by the smoker.

Adults and children who live with a smoker are more likely to develop respiratory illnesses. Children are especially at risk because their lungs are still developing. Exposure to second-hand smoke can lead to decreased lung function and symptoms of airway inflammation such as cough, wheeze, and increased mucus production, especially in children.

How does second-hand smoke harm a person with asthma?

When a person with asthma is exposed to second-hand smoke, he or she is more likely to have asthma symptoms. Children with asthma are especially sensitive to second-hand smoke.

How can smoking harm my child?

Second-hand smoke harms children with asthma even more than adults. When a child is exposed to tobacco smoke, his or her lungs also become irritated and produce more mucus than normal. But the child's lungs are smaller, so smoke can cover them quickly.

Children of parents who smoke are also more likely to develop lung and sinus infections. These infections can make asthma symptoms worse and more difficult to control.

How can I protect my child from second-hand tobacco smoke?

If you are the parent of a child with asthma, there are a number of steps you can take to protect your child from second-hand tobacco smoke:

- If you smoke, quit for yourself and your children. If your spouse or other family members smoke, help them understand the dangers of smoking and encourage them to quit. Quitting is not easy. There are many programs and methods to help you quit. Ask your health care provider to help you find the method that is best for you.
- Do not allow smoking in your home or your car.
- Do not permit your child's caregiver to smoke.
- Avoid restaurants and public places that permit smoking.

Can smoking harm my unborn child?

Smoking harms the mother and her unborn child in many ways. Nicotine, the addictive substance in tobacco products, is carried through the bloodstream of the mother and goes directly to the baby. Children of mothers who smoked during pregnancy are more likely to have respiratory problems and are ten times more likely to develop asthma. Smoking during pregnancy has also been linked with low-weight newborns, premature births, and sudden infant death syndrome (SIDS).

How can I quit smoking?

- Hide your matches, lighters, and ashtrays.
- Whenever you get the urge to smoke, take a deep breath and hold it for five to ten seconds.
- Don't let others smoke in your home.
- Keep finger foods (like carrot sticks) handy or chew gum when you get the urge to smoke.

- Stay active to keep your mind off smoking. Go for walks or read a book.

- Join a support group or smoking cessation class.

Chapter 30

Smoking and Cardiovascular Diseases

AHA Scientific Position

Cigarette smoking is the most important preventable cause of premature death in the United States. It accounts for more than 440,000 of the more than 2.4 million annual deaths. Cigarette smokers have a higher risk of developing a number of chronic disorders. These include fatty buildups in arteries, several types of cancer and chronic obstructive pulmonary disease (lung problems). Atherosclerosis (clogged arteries) is the chief contributor to the high number of deaths from smoking. Many studies detail the evidence that cigarette smoking is a major cause of coronary heart disease, which leads to heart attack.

How does smoking affect coronary heart disease risk?

Cigarette and tobacco smoke, high blood cholesterol, high blood pressure, physical inactivity, obesity and diabetes are the six major independent risk factors for coronary heart disease that you can modify or control. Cigarette smoking is so widespread and significant as a risk factor that the Surgeon General has called it "the most important of the known modifiable risk factors for coronary heart disease in the United States."

"Cigarette Smoking and Cardiovascular Diseases," reproduced with permission from the American Heart Association World Wide Web Site, www.americanheart.org. © 2004, Copyright American Heart Association.

Cigarette smoking increases the risk of coronary heart disease by itself. When it acts with other factors, it greatly increases risk. Smoking increases blood pressure, decreases exercise tolerance and increases the tendency for blood to clot.

Cigarette smoking is the most important risk factor for young men and women. It produces a greater relative risk in persons under age 50 than in those over 50.

Women who smoke and use oral contraceptives greatly increase their risk of coronary heart disease and stroke compared with non-smoking women who use oral contraceptives.

Smoking increases LDL (bad) cholesterol and decreases HDL (good) cholesterol. Cigarette smoking combined with a family history of heart disease also seems to greatly increase the risk.

What about cigarette smoking and stroke?

Studies show that cigarette smoking is an important risk factor for stroke. Inhaling cigarette smoke produces several effects that damage the cardiovascular system. Women who take oral contraceptives and smoke increase their risk of stroke many times.

What about cigar and pipe smoking?

People who smoke cigars or pipes seem to have a higher risk of death from coronary heart disease (and possibly stroke), but their risk isn't as great as that of cigarette smokers. This is probably because they're less likely to inhale the smoke. Currently, there's very little scientific information on cigar and pipe smoking and cardiovascular disease.

What about passive or secondhand smoking?

The American Heart Association believes more research is needed on the effects of passive smoking (also called secondhand smoke or environmental tobacco smoke) on heart and blood vessel disease in nonsmokers. Several studies document the health hazards posed by passive smoking. About 37,000 to 40,000 people die from heart and blood vessel disease caused by other people's smoke each year. Of these, about 35,000 nonsmokers die from coronary heart disease, which includes heart attack.

Chapter 31

Cigarette Smoke Chokes the Heart

Cigarette smoking contributes to heart disease by choking off the heart's blood supply, according to a study in today's [09/12/2000] *Circulation: Journal of the American Heart Association*.

Cigarette smoking is a major risk factor for coronary heart disease. The by-products of smoking damage the linings of arteries and promote the build-up of blood vessel-clogging plaque.

This is the first study to demonstrate that the harmful effects of smoking extend beyond the heart's large arteries into the network of tiny blood vessels that supply blood to most of the heart muscle. These small vessels are not visible during angiography, a standard x-ray procedure that detects blood flow abnormalities.

Researchers in London and Zurich used positron emission tomography (PET) to measure blood flow through coronary arteries in 11 smokers and 8 nonsmokers. They found that the additional blood supply that should be available to the heart during stress was reduced by 21 percent in smokers compared with the nonsmokers.

"Smokers had less blood supply to their hearts, which is an indicator of future heart attacks or strokes," says the study's lead author Philipp A. Kaufmann, M.D., an assistant professor at University Hospital in Zurich Switzerland.

Individuals in the study did not have symptoms of heart disease.

"Our study shows that PET can be used to investigate damage at a stage before heart disease is present and is possibly still reversible," says Paolo Camici, M.D., senior author of the study.

The mechanisms by which smoking damages the coronary system is not fully understood but the researchers say their findings support the hypothesis that free radicals, or unstable oxygen molecules, in cigarette smoke may be responsible.

"We provide evidence that the free radicals present in cigarette smoking are responsible for the initial damage to the circulatory system," says Camici, a professor at Imperial College in London. "The proof is that when individuals were given an antioxidant like vitamin C, the blood flow was restored."

In the study, researchers administered vitamin C intravenously to normalize blood flow in smokers. Smoking cigarettes is known to deplete levels of vitamin C and other antioxidants.

"Vitamin C had an immediate effect on blood flow, but long-term use of vitamin C has not been studied yet," says Kaufmann.

The authors suggest that it might be worth testing whether daily oral vitamin C supplementation would have protective effects on the development of heart disease in smokers in a long-term, large-scale trial. They note that the greater amount of vitamin C in the Mediterranean diet could be one reason why there is not more heart disease in the Mediterranean region despite a higher prevalence of smoking there.

—American Heart Association / Co-authors:
Tomaso Gnecchi-Ruscone, M.D.; Marco di Terlizzi, M.D.;
Klaus P. Schafers, MSc; and Thomas F. Luscher, M.D.

Chapter 32

Smoking Increases Stroke Risk

Are You at Risk of Stroke?

Stroke ranks as the third leading killer in the United States. A stroke can be devastating to individuals and their families, robbing them of their independence. It is the most common cause of serious, long-term adult disability.

What is a stroke?

A stroke occurs when blood flow to the brain is interrupted. When a stroke occurs, brain cells in the immediate area begin to die because they no longer receive the oxygen and nutrients they need to function.

What are the risk factors for stroke?

Stroke occurs in all age groups, in both sexes, and in all races in every country. It can even occur before birth, when the fetus is still in the womb. In African Americans, the death rate from stroke is almost twice that of the white population.

High blood pressure increases your risk of stroke four to six times. Heart disease can double your risk of stroke. Your risk also increases

---

This chapter begins with "Are You At Risk Of Stroke?" Copyright © 2003 New York State Office for the Aging. Reprinted with permission. For additional information, visit http://www.agingwell.state.ny.us. Additional information from the American Heart Association is cited separately within the chapter.

if you smoke, have diabetes, sickle cell disease, high cholesterol, transient ischemic attacks (TIAs), or a family history of stroke.

Having a risk factor for stroke doesn't mean you'll have a stroke. On the other hand, not having a risk factor doesn't mean you'll avoid a stroke. But your risk of stroke grows as the number and severity of risk factors increases.

What are the signs of stroke?

What makes stroke symptoms distinct is their sudden onset:

- Sudden numbness or weakness of face, arm, or leg—especially on one side of the body.

- Sudden confusion or trouble speaking or understanding.

- Sudden trouble seeing in one or both eyes.

- Sudden trouble walking, dizziness, loss of balance, or coordination.

- Sudden severe headache with no known cause.

What can I do to reduce my risk of stroke?

To reduce your risk of stroke monitor your blood pressure, track your cholesterol level, stop smoking, exercise regularly, know stroke's warning signs, and find out if you should be taking a drug to reduce blood clotting.

Some of the most important risk factors for stroke can be determined during a physical exam at your doctor's office, especially if you are over 55 years old.

Blood Pressure Control, Smoking Cessation at Heart of Stroke Prevention

Reproduced with permission from the American Heart Association World Wide Web Site, www.americanheart.org. © 2004, Copyright American Heart Association.

Saying no to cigarettes and yes to blood pressure screenings is the bedrock of stroke prevention, according to an expert scientific panel of the American Stroke Association, a division of the American Heart Association, which has issued a statement to physicians on strategies to prevent stroke.

The scientific statement "Primary Prevention of Ischemic Stroke" is published in the January [2001] issue of *Stroke: Journal of the American Heart Association* and the combined January 2/9 [2001] issue of *Circulation: Journal of the American Heart Association.*

Hypertension (high blood pressure) increases the risk of stroke up to four-fold. Proper treatment can diminish that risk by 38 percent. Cigarette smoking nearly doubles stroke risk, but quitting can slash the risk in half within one year and decrease it to a level similar to nonsmokers after five years, according to the statement.

Stroke is currently the third leading cause of death in the United States and a leading cause of serious, long-term disability. According to the association's *2001 Heart and Stroke Statistical Update,* about 600,000 strokes occur annually, and the economic burden of stroke is more than $45 billion in direct and indirect expenses.

Despite new approaches to stroke treatment such as using the clot-dissolving drug tissue plasminogen activator (TPA) to treat stroke, prevention remains the primary goal, according to the expert writing group chaired by Larry B. Goldstein, M.D., executive committee member of the association's Stroke Council and director of the Center for Cerebrovascular Disease and Stroke Policy Program at Duke University Medical Center, Durham, N.C.

"For all the promise TPA has heralded in stroke treatment, it is only being given to about 2 percent of people who suffer a stroke because of its limited time window—which is within hours after stroke onset. The treatment has a great potential benefit to those who qualify, but from a public health standpoint effective prevention is the best way to fight stroke," says Goldstein.

The association formed a panel of stroke experts to review evidence on established and potential risk factors for stroke. The compilation succinctly catalogs the best scientific evidence to date and identifies where there are gaps in knowledge.

Some risk factors for stroke cannot be controlled, but help identify those at high risk—increasing age, family history, and being black. The risk of stroke more than doubles for each decade of life after age 55. African Americans have a much higher risk of death and disability from a stroke than whites, in part because blacks have a greater incidence of high blood pressure and diabetes. But many risk factors can be controlled, treated or modified by changes in lifestyle habits, medication, or surgical intervention.

A significant portion of the population has undiagnosed or inadequately treated hypertension. The panel recommends all adults have their blood pressure checked at least once every two years and urges health care providers to encourage people with high blood pressure to follow a healthy lifestyle and take their medication.

"Hypertension is very prevalent and it can be treated, so its identification is an important component of stroke prevention," notes Goldstein. "Unless it's checked, you don't know you have high blood pressure. That's why it's called the silent killer."

Among other risk factors for stroke cited in the statement:

- Atrial fibrillation, a disorder in which the upper heart chambers improperly contract, potentially leading to blood clots that can travel to the brain and cause stroke. This increases the stroke risk approximately three- to five-fold in those age 65 or older or with additional risk factors. Treating the condition can cut the risk of stroke by as much as 68 percent.

- Clogged neck arteries, which double the risk. Surgery to unblock it (endarterectomy) performed by a highly skilled surgeon can halve the risk.

- Sickle cell disease in children, which magnifies the stroke risk 200 to 400 times compared to children without it. Blood transfusions for high risk children can slash risk 91 percent.

- High cholesterol levels, which increase the risk in men 1.8 to 2.6-fold. Medication can ease risk 20 percent to 30 percent in those who also have coronary heart disease.

The panel had less clear evidence on the risk reduction offered by other factors but made these lifestyle suggestions for limiting stroke risk:

- avoid illicit drug use;

- weight reductions in overweight persons;

- a minimum of 30 minutes of moderate intensity activity daily;

- a healthy diet with five servings of fruits and vegetables daily;

- avoid secondhand tobacco smoke; and

- limit alcoholic drinks to no more two per day for men and one per day for women.

Also, the panel suggests that physicians encourage tight control of diabetes; avoid prescribing oral contraceptives for women with risk factors such as smoking; and consider folic acid and B vitamins for patients with elevated homocysteine, pending results of ongoing studies.

—American Heart Association:
Other authors are Robert Adams, M.D.; Kyra Becker, M.D.,
Curt D. Furberg, M.D.; Philip Gorelick, M.D.; George Hademenos,
Ph.D.; Martha Hill, Ph.D., R.N.; George Howard, Ph.D.; Virginia J.
Howard, MSPH; Bradley Jacobs, M.D.; Steven R. Levine, M.D.; Lori
Mosca, M.D.; Ralph L. Sacco, M.D.; David G. Sherman, M.D.; Philip
A. Wolf, M.D.; and Gregory J. del Zoppo, M.D.

Chapter 33

Smoking Increases Risk for Brain Aneurysms

Cigarette smoking appears to increase the risk for developing large brain aneurysms in patients who are predisposed to these life-threatening, blood-vessel malformations, a study headed by researchers in the University at Buffalo (UB)'s Department of Neurosurgery has shown.

Results published in the journal *Neurosurgery* show that, in their multi-center study, 92 percent of patients with the aneurysms larger than 24 mm, and 78 percent with aneurysms ranging in size from 13 mm to 24 mm were smokers. Sixty-six percent of patients with aneurysms smaller than 13 mm were smokers.

"It is clear from our study that smoking leads to growth of larger aneurysms," said Lee R. Guterman, assistant professor of neurosurgery and lead author on the study. "This may be due to direct effects of the nicotine on the blood vessel wall or indirect effects like hypertension."

A brain aneurysm is a blood-filled, balloon-like structure that forms at a weak spot in the vessel caused by damage to the vessel lining. A ruptured aneurysm can kill instantaneously, and at the very least it is a medical emergency. The larger the aneurysm, the greater the risk of rupture and the poorer the outcome.

Because aneurysm size is critical to survival and disability, and because little definitive information exists on what causes an aneurysm to be large or small, researchers set out to assess the relationship between aneurysm size and factors known to damage the brain's blood vessels.

The study group was composed of 298 patients in the placebo-treated group taking part in a trial of a drug thought to decrease brain-cell damage in persons with bleeding aneurysms. The trial was conducted at UB and the University of Colorado in Denver.

Demographic, health, and lifestyle data were collected from participants when they were admitted to the hospital. Of the 298 participants, 218 were women and 63 had large aneurysms.

Analysis of patient data with aneurysm size showed that smoking at any time was independently associated with large aneurysms. However, other known risk factors for cerebrovascular disease, including hypertension, diabetes, and use of alcohol or illicit drugs, showed no relationship to aneurysm size.

In addition, patients with large aneurysms were:

- More likely to die within three months than those with small aneurysms
- More likely to have multiple aneurysms
- Lower functioning at admission

Guterman said cigarette smoking may contribute to large aneurysm size by promoting degradation of elastin in blood vessel walls. Elastin helps blood vessels retain their shape. If elastin has deteriorated, the vessel wall may be susceptible to expanding or ballooning at sites where blood flow is especially turbulent, such as the middle cerebral artery. Large aneurysms were found to be more prevalent at this location.

"These findings on the effect of cigarette smoking on aneurysm size, coupled with our earlier findings, suggest smoking predisposes individuals to multiple intracranial aneurysms. The only way people may be able to prevent formation of large or giant aneurysms is to stop smoking. Patients with known unruptured small aneurysms should definitely stop smoking," Guterman said.

Also participating in the study from the UB Department of Neurosurgery were postdoctoral fellows Adan I. Quershi and M. Fareed K. Suri, and L. Nelson Hopkins, department chair. University of Colorado researchers were Gene Y. Sung and Robert Straw. The initial drug trial from which the study group was drawn was funded by Pharmacia & Upjohn.

—by Lois Baker

Chapter 34

Smoking and Eye Disease

Diseases of the visual system, and possible subsequent visual loss, represent substantial social and economic concerns to the U.S. public. In the last three decades, Gallup polls have consistently indicated that blindness is second only to mental incapacity as the disability Americans fear most. There is ample reason for concern. An estimated 3.4 million Americans aged 40 years and older have visual impairment and 1 million of these people are legally blind. Because most vision loss results from eye disease associated with advancing age, and the "baby boom" population in the United

States is aging, the public health impact of this problem is projected to double by 2030.

Substantial contributions to the social and economic welfare of the public are possible by finding and controlling the causes of these eye diseases, particularly the factors that present the opportunity to prevent disease or loss of sight.

Epidemiologic investigation into risk factors for eye disease did not begin in earnest until the 1970s, bolstered by the establishment of the National Eye Institute (NEI) in 1968. Reports of the Surgeon General on smoking and health published before 2001 did not include

Excerpted from U.S. Department of Health and Human Services. "Chapter 6: Other Effects," *The Health Consequences of Smoking: A Report of the Surgeon General*. U.S. Department of Health and Human Services, Centers for Disease Control and Prevention, National Center for Chronic Disease Prevention and Health Promotion, Office on Smoking and Health, 2004. The complete text, including references, is available online at www.surgeongeneral.gov.

eye disease as a topic simply because there were scant data indicating that smoking was related to eye disease, although a compelling biologic basis did exist for considering theories for such associations. At least two of the three leading causes of visual loss worldwide, cataract and age-related macular degeneration (AMD), probably are due, at least in part, to smoking.

Cataract

Cataract is the leading cause of blindness worldwide and a leading cause of visual loss in the United States. Currently, the most common and effective means of restoring vision is through surgical removal of the opacified lens and insertion of an artificial lens into the eye. If risk factors that either delay the onset or slow the progression of cataracts could be identified, major socioeconomic gains would be realized. The research findings that link cigarette smoking to cataract, specifically nuclear cataract, have identified one of the few modifiable risk factors for cataract.

The ocular lens is a normally transparent organ. The lens itself is composed of a central core, or nucleus, of inert, protein-filled, former epithelial cells. The interior proteins are highly structured to ensure transparency.

The loss of lens transparency is termed lens opacity, and lens opacification becomes increasingly common with advancing age. When the opacity becomes sufficiently dense or extensive or both so as to interfere with vision, the lens opacity is called a cataract.

There are three main types of lens opacity or cataract, which are distinct in terms of risk factors, location in the lens, and epidemiologic pattern: nuclear, cortical, and posterior subcapsular lens opacity. The different types of opacities also can occur together in the lens, resulting in a "mixed" opacity. The frequency of each type of lens opacity in the population increases with age and varies by racial or ethnic group.

Theories about Smoking and Cataract Formation

Several hypotheses have been advanced to explain a possible association of smoking and cataract. Given the plethora of aromatic compounds and trace metals in cigarette smoke that are capable of damaging lens proteins, it is difficult to know which mechanism is likely to be the most important. One researcher has postulated that cadmium, lead, thiocyanate, and aldehydes from cigarette smoke lead to lens damage. Others suggest that smoking may cause cataract through an indirect route, by lowering antioxidants; however, the role of antioxidants in protecting against the formation of cataracts still is controversial.

Research Evidence

Substantial evidence has accrued linking nuclear, and possibly posterior subcapsular, cataract to cigarette smoking. There is a dose-response relationship and evidence that former smokers have a lower risk of cataract and of progression of cataract compared with current smokers. On the basis of the epidemiologic studies, researchers now are investigating the mechanisms by which smoking may damage the lens, by using animal and lens cell culture models. The laboratory data are not yet sufficiently mature to inform the discussion of smoking and cataract, in part because there are few animal models of age-related cataract. However, smokers are exposed to a number of agents that may cumulatively damage the lens, which lacks the ability to repair itself.

Conclusions and Implications

- The evidence is sufficient to infer a causal relationship between smoking and nuclear cataract.

- The evidence is suggestive but not sufficient to infer that smoking cessation reduces the risk of nuclear opacity.

There is moderate evidence to suggest that smoking also may be associated with an increased risk of posterior subcapsular opacities as well, but more research is needed before a causal association can be inferred for this cataract type.

The difficulty the lens has in repairing damage suggests that opacification at the time of smoking cessation is likely to be irreversible. Studies of cataract in clinical trials of smoking cessation would provide more definitive evidence for any protective effect, although feasibility would be constrained by the need for large populations.

Age-Related Macular Degeneration

Age-related macular degeneration (AMD) is the leading cause of blindness in whites aged 65 years and older in the United States. There currently is no well accepted treatment to prevent or halt the progression of the most common form of AMD (atrophic AMD). Treatment to halt vision loss from a less common, severe form of AMD, often is short lived. A recent large-scale clinical trial has provided evidence that antioxidant supplements plus zinc may delay the progression of some signs of AMD. Otherwise, no preventive therapy for AMD is available, so considerable attention has focused on identifying risk factors for this disease.

The macula is a component of the retina at the center of the optical axis; it contains the fovea, a highly specialized area of the retina responsible for high-resolution vision. The retina consists of neural tissues, including the photoreceptors that convert energy from visible light into electrical signals sent on to the brain for processing. The photoreceptors—rods and cones—have high metabolic requirements and replace their outer segments daily. This high rate of activity is made possible by the exchange of nutrients (and removal of waste) through the retinal blood supply. Changes in each of the tissues in this complex have been hypothesized to result in AMD. However, the beginning of the AMD disease process—and even being able to tell the difference between changes in early AMD and those of normal aging—is uncertain.

AMD is an umbrella designation for a variety of degenerative changes in the macula. It is likely that multiple pathways are responsible for the degenerative changes in the macula with age, and a reasonable basis exists for presuming that smoking may operate through one or more of these pathways.

Research Evidence

The data provide evidence that current smoking is associated with exudative AMD and possibly atrophic AMD. Dose-response relationships with the amount of smoking have been described. Maintaining smoking cessation at least 20 years decreased the risk of severe AMD and exudative AMD. The possibility that smoking is associated with the neovascular form of AMD is further bolstered by the findings from a study of ocular histoplasmosis, where neovascularization can result from the infection. In that study, smokers were twice as likely as nonsmokers to develop disciform scars. Moreover, in a clinical trial of photocoagulation to halt progression of neovascularization, smokers were more likely than nonsmokers to have recurrent neovascularization over time. However, smoking did not predict development of neovascularization in the previously unaffected companion eyes of the eyes with neovascularization.

Conclusions and Implications

- The evidence is suggestive but not sufficient to infer a causal relationship between current and past smoking, especially heavy smoking, with risk of exudative (neovascular) age-related macular degeneration.

- The evidence is suggestive but not sufficient to infer a causal relationship between smoking and atrophic age-related macular degeneration.

There is a need for more research into gender differences, dose-response relationships, and a possible threshold effect. Further research is also needed to determine the effect of smoking cessation on the risk of neovascular AMD.

Diabetic Retinopathy

Diabetic retinopathy is a serious ocular complication of diabetes associated primarily with long-term duration of diabetes and poor control in both type 1 and type 2 diseases. The retinopathy is likely the result of vascular changes occurring in the retinal circulation that feeds the inner layers of the retina.

Several researchers have theorized that smoking may contribute to the onset of diabetic retinopathy and/or drive progression of existing retinopathy through its effect on the retinal circulation. Although there is a reasonable biologic basis to the hypothesis that smoking is related to diabetic retinopathy, the data suggest otherwise.

Research Evidence

Although smoking might plausibly worsen diabetic retinopathy, the evidence is inconsistent. The strongest studies do not show an association. The level of diabetes control is a potential major confounder that has not been considered in a number of the studies.

Conclusion and Implication

- The evidence is suggestive of no causal relationship between smoking and the onset or progression of retinopathy in persons with diabetes.

As research on diabetes continues, possible effects of smoking should be reassessed.

Glaucoma

Glaucoma is the third leading cause of blindness worldwide. In the United States,

African Americans and Hispanics are more affected than other groups. Glaucoma is a disease characterized by loss of retinal ganglion cells, probably through a variety of mechanisms. The two main types of primary glaucoma are primary open-angle glaucoma and angle closure glaucoma. There are distinct differences between the two types of glaucoma, and their distribution differs in populations. In the United States, primary open-angle glaucoma is the more common type.

There is no evident basis for proposing that smoking might predispose a person to either developing glaucoma or having more severe glaucoma. Investigators have proposed that factors that diminish perfusion of the optic nerve head with blood may be associated with glaucoma. Because smoking affects the retinal circulation (although any direct effect of smoking on the optic nerve head is unknown), several investigators have examined the association of glaucoma with smoking. However, the effects of smoking on blood flow in ocular circulation are difficult to measure, in part because studies often do not consider separating acute effects in smokers and nonsmokers from the chronic effects that result from repeated exposures. The role of smoking in altering intraocular pressure also is variable. In one study, smoking (including cumulative consumption) was not associated with intraocular pressure differences.

Research Evidence

The few studies conducted do not indicate any relationship between smoking and glaucoma.

Conclusion and Implication

- The evidence is inadequate to infer the presence or absence of a causal relationship between smoking and glaucoma.

As further studies of glaucoma are undertaken, the role of smoking should remain under investigation.

Graves Ophthalmopathy

Graves' ophthalmopathy, an ocular complication of Graves' disease, is an uncommon condition. Graves' disease is thought to be an autoimmune disease of the thyroid. It is likely that both genetic and environmental factors are related to the risk of the disease. Among its clinical manifestations, the ophthalmologic complications appear to be related to smoking. Graves' ophthalmopathy is characterized by proptosis (protrusion of the eyeball), diplopia (double vision), optic neuropathy, and conjunctival and periorbital inflammation. The process that starts the development of Graves' ophthalmopathy is not completely understood, and the mechanism by which smoking may cause or aggravate Graves' ophthalmopathy is unknown.

Research Evidence

Although there are suggestive epidemiologic (studying how much something occurs within a population) findings, the biologic basis for a role of smoking in Graves' ophthalmopathy is unclear. The data are still limited, although consistent in indicating an increased risk in smokers. Dose-response is not well documented.

Conclusion and Implication

- The evidence is suggestive but not sufficient to infer a causal relationship between ophthalmopathy associated with Graves' disease and smoking.

Data on the role of smoking cessation in preventing or lessening the severity of the ophthalmopathy would be important to understanding the relationship between Graves' disease and smoking.

Chapter 35

Smoking and Diabetes Risk

Smoking Increases Your Risk of Getting Type 2 Diabetes

The more you smoke, the more chance you have of getting diabetes. If you smoke 16 to 25 cigarettes a day, your risk for Type 2 diabetes is three times greater than a nonsmoker's risk. When you quit smoking, your risk decreases during the years that follow.

Smoking Affects the Way Insulin Works in Your Body

In Type 2 diabetes, the body does not respond to the insulin made by the pancreas. Insulin helps blood sugar, or glucose, enter the body's cells for fuel. When you smoke, your body is less able to respond to insulin. When your body resists insulin, your glucose levels increase. Resistance does not start to reverse until you do not smoke for 10 to 12 hours.

"Smoking and Diabetes" is a patient information brochure from the University of Pittsburgh Medical Center. © 2003 University of Pittsburgh Medical Center. Reprinted with permission. For additional information, visit www .upmc.com, or for help in finding a doctor or health service that suits your needs, call the UPMC Referral Service at 800-533-UPMC (8762). This information is not intended to be used as a substitute for professional medical advice, diagnosis, or treatment. You should not rely entirely on this information for your health care needs. Ask your own doctor or health care provider any specific medical questions that you have.

Smoking Makes It Harder to Control Your Diabetes

Studies show that smokers have poorer glucose control than non-smokers do. Ex-smokers have the same blood glucose control as non-smokers. When you have Type 1 or Type 2 diabetes, glucose control is very important.

The A1c (read "A-one-C") test checks how well you control your glucose level over three months. The goal is to keep your A1c at seven percent or less. When you have diabetes and you smoke, your A1c level increases. If you quit smoking, your A1c level may decrease to the same level as a nonsmoker's.

Smoking Increases Your Risk for Getting Other Problems from Diabetes

When you have diabetes and smoke, your chances are greater for getting other health problems from diabetes. These other health problems are called complications. You can get serious eye problems, kidney problems, and nerve problems. You can get heart and blood vessel disease, such as heart attack, stroke, and hardening of the arteries, especially in the legs.

Even for people who do not have diabetes but smoke, the risk of getting other health problems is greater. The more and the longer you smoke, the more your risk increases. Smoking and diabetes together greatly increase the danger of getting complications. To lower your risk, you must control your glucose levels and quit smoking.

You Benefit in Important Ways when You Have Diabetes and Quit Smoking

When you quit smoking, you have:

- less resistance to insulin
- less chance of eye damage
- less chance of kidney damage and kidney failure
- less chance of nerve damage

Results of Your Blood Tests May Improve when You Quit Smoking

Possible effects on your blood test results are:

- lower A1c levels
- lower glucose levels
- lower cholesterol levels
- lower LDL (bad) cholesterol levels
- lower triglycerides (fats) levels
- higher HDL (good) cholesterol levels

You Get Other Benefits when You Quit Smoking

You benefit in many ways when you quit smoking. You may have:

- a longer life
- more energy

You will have:

- less chance of a heart attack or stroke
- less chance of lung cancer and other cancers
- less chance of chronic bronchitis and emphysema
- fewer colds and respiratory infections
- less shortness of breath and coughing
- better blood flow to arms and legs
- warmer hands, legs, and feet
- better healing of wounds
- better ability to smell and taste
- less risk of gum disease
- money you saved from not buying cigarettes
- no odor of stale smoke about you
- better hygiene
- freedom from addiction

Chapter 36

Smoking and Your Digestive System

Cigarette smoking causes a variety of life-threatening diseases, including lung cancer, emphysema, and heart disease. An estimated 430,000 deaths each year are directly caused by cigarette smoking. Smoking is responsible for changes in all parts of the body, including the digestive system. This fact can have serious consequences because it is the digestive system that converts foods into the nutrients the body needs to live.

Current estimates indicate that about one-third of all adults smoke. And, while adult men seem to be smoking less, women and teenagers of both sexes seem to be smoking more. How does smoking affect the digestive system of all these people?

Harmful Effects

Smoking has been shown to have harmful effects on all parts of the digestive system, contributing to such common disorders as heartburn and peptic ulcers. It also increases the risk of Crohn's disease and possibly gallstones. Smoking seems to affect the liver, too, by changing the way it handles drugs and alcohol. In fact, there seems to be enough evidence to stop smoking solely on the basis of digestive distress.

"Smoking and Your Digestive System," National Digestive Diseases Information Clearinghouse, National Institute on Diabetes, Digestive, and Kidney Diseases (NIDDK), March 2002.

Heartburn

Heartburn is common among Americans. More than 60 million Americans have heartburn at least once a month, and about 15 million have it daily.

Heartburn happens when acidic juices from the stomach splash into the esophagus. Normally, a muscular valve at the lower end of the esophagus, the lower esophageal sphincter (LES), keeps the acid solution in the stomach and out of the esophagus. Smoking decreases the strength of the esophageal valve, thereby allowing stomach acids to reflux, or flow backward into the esophagus.

Smoking also seems to promote the movement of bile salts from the intestine to the stomach, which makes the stomach acids more harmful. Finally, smoking may directly injure the esophagus, making it less able to resist further damage from refluxed fluids.

Peptic Ulcer

A peptic ulcer is an open sore in the lining of the stomach or duodenum, the first part of the small intestine. The exact cause of ulcers is not known. A relationship between smoking cigarettes and ulcers, especially duodenal ulcers, does exist. The 1989 Surgeon General's report stated that ulcers are more likely to occur, less likely to heal, and more likely to cause death in smokers than in nonsmokers.

Why is this so? Doctors are not really sure, but smoking does seem to be one of several factors that work together to promote the formation of ulcers.

For example, some research suggests that smoking might increase a person's risk of infection with the bacterium *Helicobacter pylori (H. pylori)*. Most peptic ulcers are caused by this bacterium.

Stomach acid is also important in producing ulcers. Normally, most of this acid is buffered by the food we eat. Most of the unbuffered acid that enters the duodenum is quickly neutralized by sodium bicarbonate, a naturally occurring alkali produced by the pancreas. Some studies show that smoking reduces the bicarbonate produced by the pancreas, interfering with the neutralization of acid in the duodenum. Other studies suggest that chronic cigarette smoking may increase the amount of acid secreted by the stomach.

Whatever causes the link between smoking and ulcers, two points have been repeatedly demonstrated: People who smoke are more likely to develop an ulcer, especially a duodenal ulcer, and ulcers in smokers are less likely to heal quickly in response to otherwise effective treatment. This research tracing the relationship between smoking and ulcers strongly suggests that a person with an ulcer should stop smoking.

Liver Disease

The liver is an important organ that has many tasks. Among other things, the liver is responsible for processing drugs, alcohol, and other toxins to remove them from the body. There is evidence that smoking alters the ability of the liver to handle such substances. In some cases, this may influence the dose of medication necessary to treat an illness. Some research also suggests that smoking can aggravate the course of liver disease caused by excessive alcohol intake.

Crohn's Disease

Crohn's disease causes inflammation deep in the lining of the intestine. The disease, which causes pain and diarrhea, usually affects the small intestine, but it can occur anywhere in the digestive tract. Research shows that current and former smokers have a higher risk of developing Crohn's disease than nonsmokers do. Among people with the disease, smoking is associated with a higher rate of relapse, repeat surgery, and immunosuppressive treatment. In all areas, the risk for women, whether current or former smokers, is slightly higher than for men. Why smoking increases the risk of Crohn's disease is unknown, but some theories suggest that smoking might lower the intestine's defenses, decrease blood flow to the intestines, or cause immune system changes that result in inflammation.

Gallstones

Several studies suggest that smoking may increase the risk of developing gallstones and that the risk may be higher for women. However, research results on this topic are not consistent, and more study is needed.

Can the Damage Be Reversed?

Some of the effects of smoking on the digestive system appear to be of short duration. For example, the effect of smoking on bicarbonate production by the pancreas does not appear to last. Within a half-hour after smoking, the production of bicarbonate returns to normal.

The effects of smoking on how the liver handles drugs also disappear when a person stops smoking. However, people who no longer smoke still remain at risk for Crohn's disease. Clearly, this question needs more study.

For More Information

Information about smoking and health is available from:

Office on Smoking and Health
National Center for Chronic Disease Prevention and Health Promotion
Mail Stop K-50
4770 Buford Highway NE
Atlanta, GA 30341-3717
Phone: 800-CDC-1311 (232-1311)
Fax: 888-CDC-FAXX (888-232-3299)
Website: http://www.cdc.gov/tobacco
E-mail: tobaccoinfo@cdc.gov

National Digestive Diseases Information Clearinghouse
2 Information Way
Bethesda, MD 20892-3570
E-mail: http://digestive.niddk.nih.gov/about/contact.htm

The National Digestive Diseases Information Clearinghouse (NDDIC) is a service of the National Institute of Diabetes and Digestive and Kidney Diseases (NIDDK). The NIDDK is part of the National Institutes of Health under the U.S. Department of Health and Human Services. Established in 1980, the clearinghouse provides information about digestive diseases to people with digestive disorders and to their families, health care professionals, and the public. NDDIC answers inquiries, develops and distributes publications, and works closely with professional and patient organizations and Government agencies to coordinate resources about digestive diseases.

Chapter 37

Smoking and Musculoskeletal Health

Smoking remains the number one cause of preventable death. Each year more than 400,000 people in the United States alone die from tobacco-related diseases. In fact, smokers can expect to live 7 to 10 years less than nonsmokers. Smoking is linked to heart and respiratory diseases and to several cancers. In addition, smoking has a significant impact on your bones and joints. Here's what scientists have found about the relationship between smoking and musculoskeletal health.

Smoking increases your risk of developing osteoporosis. Smoking has a detrimental effect on bone density. Studies have shown that smoking reduces the blood supply to bones and that nicotine slows the production of bone-forming cells (osteoblasts) and impairs the absorption of calcium. With less bone mineral, smokers develop fragile bones (osteoporosis). Smoking also reduces the protective effect of estrogen replacement therapy.

Smoking increases your risk of a hip fracture as you age. Osteoporosis is often a risk factor in hip fractures. Elderly smokers have a 41 percent increase in the rate of hip fracture.

Smoking increases your risk of developing exercise-related injuries. Rotator cuff (shoulder) tears in smokers are nearly twice as large as those in nonsmokers. Additionally, a study of young army recruits showed that smokers were 1.5 times more likely to suffer overuse injuries such as bursitis or tendinitis than nonsmokers. Smokers were also more likely to suffer traumatic injuries, such as sprains or fractures.

Smoking has a detrimental effect on fracture and wound healing. Fractures take longer to heal in smokers because of the harmful effects of nicotine on the production of bone-forming cells. Smokers also have a higher rate of complications after surgery than nonsmokers, and outcomes are less satisfactory.

Smoking has a detrimental effect on athletic performance. Because smoking slows lung growth and impairs lung function, there is less oxygen available for muscles used in sports. Smokers suffer from shortness of breath almost three times more often than nonsmokers. Smokers cannot run or walk as fast or as far as nonsmokers.

Smoking is associated with low back pain and rheumatoid arthritis. Every tissue in the human body is affected by smoking, but many effects are reversible. By avoiding or quitting smoking, you can reduce your risk for incurring many conditions. Quitting smoking can also help your body regain some of its normal healthy functioning. If you are a smoker, talk to your physician about stop-smoking techniques.

Chapter 38

Smoking and Sexual Health

Cigarette Smoking and Sexual Health

While the majority of Americans recognize that cigarette smoking is a health hazard, many are unaware of how varied its adverse health consequences are—despite the vastness of the scientific evidence of such consequences and of their remarkable diversity. Among the least publicized risks of cigarette smoking are its possible effects on reproductive processes and human sexual behavior.

Approximately 30 percent of Americans of reproductive age smoke cigarettes. Cigarette smoking affects reproductive processes in both males and females. In women, it can adversely affect the menstrual cycle, the function of the fallopian tubes (ducts through which ova [eggs] pass from the ovaries to the uterus), and the viability of ova. As for men, cigarette smoking can decrease both the quality and quantity of spermatozoa and can cause erectile dysfunction (a consistent inability to sustain a penile erection sufficient for sexual intercourse).

Effects of Smoking on Fertility in Women

Cigarette smoking can diminish the ability to become pregnant and to bear a full-term child. Women who smoke cigarettes are three times

"Cigarette Smoking and Sexual Health," by Panayiotis M. Zavos is reprinted with permission of the American Council on Science and Health (ACSH). © 2000 American Council on Science and Health, Inc. For additional information about ACSH, visit www.acsh.org.

likelier than nonsmoking women to have difficulty conceiving; and the higher the average number of cigarettes a woman of reproductive age smokes, the smaller her chances are of becoming pregnant. Such smokers are also less likely to benefit from treatments for infertility than are their nonsmoking peers. Although there is no definite consensus on whether cigarette smoking is a direct cause of infertility, research has consistently shown that cigarette smokers have a higher risk of being unable to conceive than do nonsmokers. Perhaps lifestyle factors among cigarette smokers other than smoking account for this elevated risk. For example, the number of sexual partners of adolescent and/or unwed smokers may exceed those of corresponding nonsmokers, and having many sexual partners increases one's risk of contracting sexually transmitted diseases, which in most instances can cause infertility.

Menstruation

Cigarette smoking alters bodily concentrations of several hormones, including estrogen. Such changes can disrupt ovulation and, consequently, menstruation; and menstrual irregularity reduces the chances of becoming pregnant. Women who smoke cigarettes tend to have amenorrhea (abnormal stoppage of menses) more often than do nonsmoking women. They are also likelier to have menstrual irregularity in middle age. Menopause tends to begin earlier in smokers. Thus, the reproductive window is longer in nonsmoking women. Clinical reports and evidence from animal experiments suggest that nicotine may be principally responsible for menstrual effects of smoking.

Fallopian Tubes

Abnormalities in the function of the fallopian tubes—where conception normally occurs—have been found in cigarette smokers. Cigarette smoking increases concentrations of the hormones epinephrine and vasopressin. Such an increase can accelerate the passage of ova through the fallopian tubes, and early entrance of a fertilized ovum (embryo) into the uterus can increase the probability of a miscarriage.

In one large study, researchers found that ectopic pregnancy—extrauterine implantation and development of a fertilized ovum—is 2–4 times likelier among women who smoke cigarettes than among those who do not smoke. The fallopian tubes are the most common sites of ectopic pregnancy. If it is not detected early, ectopic pregnancy can result in fallopian-tube rupture and even death.

Evidence from numerous studies suggests that cigarette smoking adversely affects the immune system. Some scientists have speculated that such changes may result in infertility through an increase in the frequency of fallopian-tube infection.

Ova

Evidence from research on rats and mice suggests that cigarette smoking can affect the quality and functionality of ova. Some of this evidence suggests that nicotine can prevent formation of cortical granules. These are specialized vesicles near the surface of an ovum that fuse and, upon fertilization of the ovum, release their contents and thus prevent passage into the ovum of more than one sperm cell. Such passage, termed "poly-spermy," renders the embryo incapable of becoming a fetus. The incidence of poly-spermy is larger among cigarette smokers than among nonsmokers.

Scientists hypothesize, largely on the basis of animal studies, that cigarette smoking diminishes the number and/or viability of ova. Such an effect may result in premature menopause.

Spontaneous Abortion

A spontaneous abortion, or miscarriage, is a spontaneous, unintentional, and usually early termination of pregnancy, with expulsion from the uterus of a nonviable or lifeless fetus. Women who smoke cigarettes have a greater risk of spontaneous abortion than women who do not smoke.

Of the approximately 140,000 cases of miscarriage per year in the United States, approximately 19,000 have been attributed to cigarette smoking. The fetuses of nonsmokers who miscarry are likelier to have abnormalities—a common cause of spontaneous abortion—than are those of cigarette smokers who miscarry. This finding suggests that cigarette smoking can account for spontaneous abortion independently of fetal abnormalities. Smoking can, nonetheless, cause birth defects and neonatal underweight.

Effects of Smoking on Fertility in Men

While research on the reproductive effects of smoking has focused on women, evidence has increasingly suggested that cigarette smoking adversely affects the male reproductive system as well. Cigarette smoking damages sperm, affects hormone concentrations in men, and reduces blood flow to the penis. This reduction in blood flow can result in erectile dysfunction, or impotence. Recent experimental findings have also linked cigarette smoking in men with low sex drive and low sexual satisfaction.

Sperm

Several chemicals found in the semen of cigarette smokers are components of cigarette smoke or are metabolic by-products of such components. Some of these chemicals—nicotine, for instance—are found at higher concentrations in semen than in blood. This suggests that some components of cigarette smoke tend to build up in the semen of cigarette smokers.

The ejaculate of cigarette smokers is less than that of their non-smoking counter-parts. This difference is more pronounced with heavy smokers. Scientists hypothesize that the effects of nicotine on the nervous system, or possibly the low testosterone concentrations that characterize cigarette smokers, account for the low volume of ejaculate. Although low ejaculate volume does not alone impede reproduction, it may be a sign of other reproductive irregularities.

Smokers' sperm density (the concentration of spermatozoa in semen) has been estimated at 22–57 percent less than that of nonsmokers. Such decreases in sperm density can cause infertility in men.

Sperm motility—the ability of spermatozoa to propel themselves through the female reproductive tract—is critical to conception. Smokers' sperm cells, on average, are 20 percent less motile than nonsmokers' sperm cells.

Some evidence suggests that men who smoke cigarettes are likelier to generate sperm of abnormal shape than are men who do not smoke. Sperm malformation may contribute to the occurrence of spontaneous abortion and birth defects.

Cigarette smoking raises the concentration in semen of white blood cells—whose function is to counteract infection—without infection. This increase tends to diminish the ability of the smoker's sperm to enter and unite with the ovum.

Research findings suggest that cigarette smoking may result in damage to the seminiferous tubules. These tubules, which make up the bulk of the testes, are the sites of sperm production. Damage to them can cause diminishment of the production and quality of sperm.

Establishing the apparent relationship of smoking to decreases in the quantity and quality of sperm would require much more research.

Hormones

Cigarette smoking significantly alters concentrations of the sex hormone testosterone, growth hormone, and other hormones in men. Male cigarette smokers have less testosterone than do male nonsmokers. Men with low testosterone concentrations have a lower sex drive and lower sperm counts than do those with normal or high concentrations of the hormone.

Erectile Dysfunction

In numerous studies cigarette smoking has been linked to a doubling of the incidence of erectile dysfunction. Smoking diminishes blood flow both in the heart and in the penis. This decrease can result in a type of erectile dysfunction termed "vascular impotence." In one study, 97 percent of those patients diagnosed with vascular impotence were cigarette smokers. In another study, 87 percent of those patients with this condition smoked cigarettes. Heavy smoking has been connected to a high risk of impotence.

Frequency of Sex and Sexual Satisfaction

How cigarette smoking affects sex drive and sexual satisfaction was investigated in a 1999 study of 290 couples undergoing treatment for infertility. None of the female subjects smoked. On average the cigarette-smoking subjects stated that they had sex about six times a month, while on average the nonsmokers said that their lovemaking was about twice as frequent. Moreover, nonsmoking couples described their sexual satisfaction more approvingly than did those couples in which the male smoked.

The Bottom Line

Specialists who treat infertility often omit that cigarette smoking can significantly impair both male and female fertility in varied ways, but scientific evidence has clearly implicated cigarette smoking with infertility. Further research should better define their relationship.

—by Panayiotis M. Zavos

ACSH scientific advisor Panayiotis M. Zavos, Ed.S., Ph.D., is Professor of Reproductive Physiology and Andrology at the University of

Kentucky and Director of the Andrology Institute of America (www
.aia-zavos.com), in Lexington, Kentucky.

Chapter 39

Hazards Related to Smoking during Pregnancy

Today, about 12 percent of women worldwide smoke cigarettes. In developed countries, about 15 percent of women smoke, and in developing countries, about 8 percent smoke, according to the World Health Organization. In the United States, about 15 to 30 percent of women smoke, many of them while they are pregnant. This is a major public health problem because not only can smoking harm a woman's health, but smoking during pregnancy can lead to serious health problems in newborns.

Statistics from the United States are compelling. If all pregnant women in the United States stopped smoking, there would be an estimated 10 percent reduction in infant deaths, according to the U.S. Public Health Service. Currently, about 12 percent of women in the United States smoke during pregnancy.

Cigarette smoke contains more than 2,500 chemicals. It is not known for certain which of these chemicals are harmful to a developing baby. However, both nicotine and carbon monoxide are believed to play a role in causing adverse pregnancy outcomes.

How can smoking harm the newborn?

Smoking nearly doubles a woman's risk of having a low-birthweight baby. In 2001, 11.9 percent of babies born to smokers in the United

States were of low birthweight, compared to 7.3 percent of babies of non-smokers. Low-birthweight babies, who weigh less than 5 1/2 pounds at birth, face an increased risk of serious health problems during the newborn period, chronic disabilities (such as cerebral palsy, mental retardation, and learning problems) and even death. These health consequences can be devastating, inflicting major emotional and economic costs on families and on communities.

Low birthweight can result from poor intrauterine growth, preterm delivery or a combination of both. Smoking has long been known to slow fetal growth. Studies also suggest that smoking increases the risk of preterm delivery (before 37 weeks of gestation) by at least 20 percent. However, if a woman stops smoking by the end of her first trimester of pregnancy, she is no more likely to have a low-birthweight baby than a woman who never smoked. Even if a woman has not been able to stop smoking in her first or second trimester, stopping during the third trimester can still improve her baby's growth. According to the American College of Obstetricians and Gynecologists, women who stop smoking at any time up to the 30th week of pregnancy have babies with higher birthweights than women who smoke throughout pregnancy.

Pregnant women who do not smoke should avoid exposure to other people's smoke. Studies suggest that regular exposure to secondhand smoke may reduce fetal growth and, therefore, increase a woman's chances of having a low-birthweight baby.

Although it has long been known that smoking can increase the risk of preterm delivery and low birthweight, more recent studies suggest that smoking also may contribute to certain birth defects, especially when certain gene-environment interactions are present. One study found that women who smoked in the early months of pregnancy were 34 percent more likely than nonsmoking mothers to have a baby with a foot deformity called club foot. While nonsmoking women with a family history of club foot were about six times as likely as women without a family history of this disorder to have an affected baby, women who both smoked and had a family history of club foot had a 20-fold increased risk. Similarly, another study found that babies with a predisposing gene were at increased risk of developing cleft lip and/or cleft palate (an opening in the roof of the mouth or the soft tissue in the back of the mouth) if their mothers smoked during the first three months of pregnancy.

Can smoking cause pregnancy complications?

Smoking has been associated with a number of pregnancy complications. Smoking early in pregnancy appears to increase a woman's risk of having an ectopic pregnancy. In an ectopic pregnancy, the embryo becomes implanted in a fallopian tube or other abnormal site instead of the uterus. With the rarest of exceptions, these pregnancies do not result in the birth of a baby, and the embryo must be removed surgically or with drug treatment to protect a woman's life. Smoking also may increase a woman's risk of miscarriage.

Cigarette smoking also appears to double a woman's risk of developing placental complications (which occur in about 1 percent of pregnancies). These include placenta previa, a condition in which the placenta is attached too low in the uterus and covers part or all of the cervix, and placental abruption, in which the placenta separates from the uterine wall before delivery. Both can result in a delivery that jeopardizes the life of mother and baby, although a cesarean delivery can prevent most deaths. Placental problems contribute to the slightly increased risk of stillbirth that is associated with smoking.

Does smoking affect fertility?

Cigarette smoking can cause reproductive problems before a woman even becomes pregnant. Studies show that women who smoke may have more trouble conceiving than nonsmokers. A 2000 British study reported that women who smoked were about 50 percent less likely to conceive within 12 months than nonsmokers. This study also found that heavy smoking by the father was associated with delayed conception.

Does parents' smoking cause other problems in babies or young children?

Babies whose mothers smoked during pregnancy are three times as likely to die from sudden infant death syndrome (SIDS) as babies of nonsmokers. Babies who are exposed to their parents' cigarette smoke after birth also may face an increased risk of SIDS; however, recent studies suggest that exposure to smoke while still in the womb poses a bigger risk.

Children who are exposed to cigarette smoke before birth also may be at increased risk of lasting problems, including asthma and autism. A recent Swedish study found that babies of mothers who smoked in early pregnancy were 40 percent more likely than babies of nonsmokers to have autism (a serious developmental disorder characterized by difficulties communicating with others and mental retardation). Children of mothers who smoked during pregnancy also may be at increased risk of learning and behavioral problems, including impulsive behavior, conduct disorders and attention problems. Studies also suggest that children whose mothers were regularly exposed to other people's smoke during pregnancy may be at increased risk of learning and behavioral problems.

How can a woman protect her baby from the risks associated with smoking?

The March of Dimes recommends that women stop smoking before they become pregnant and remain smoke-free throughout pregnancy and after the baby is born. A woman's health care provider can refer her to a smoking cessation program that is right for her, or suggest other ways to help her quit. Even later in pregnancy, a woman can reduce the risks to her baby by stopping smoking. The fewer cigarettes a woman smokes, the less likely her baby will be born with smoking-related problems.

Studies suggest that certain factors make it more likely that a woman will be successful in her efforts to quit smoking during pregnancy. These include: attempting to quit in the past, having a partner who doesn't smoke, getting support from family or other important people in her life, and understanding the harmful effects of smoking.

It is important to stay smoke-free after the baby is born. Both mother and father should refrain from smoking in the home and should ask visitors to do the same. Babies who are exposed to smoke suffer from more respiratory illnesses and ear infections than other babies. For example, infants whose mothers smoke are 38 percent more likely to be hospitalized for pneumonia during their first year of life than babies of nonsmoking mothers. A child exposed to smoking at home during the first few years of life also is at increased risk of developing asthma.

Of course, cigarette smoking harms a woman's own health: smokers have an increased risk of lung and other cancers, heart disease, stroke, and emphysema (a potentially disabling and, sometimes, deadly lung condition). Quitting smoking will make parents healthier—and better role models for their children.

Does the March of Dimes fund research on the risks of smoking during pregnancy?

The March of Dimes has long supported research on the risks of smoking during pregnancy. In the 1970s, March of Dimes-supported research suggested that nicotine and carbon monoxide reduce the supply of oxygen to the baby, perhaps explaining how these chemicals in cigarette smoke reduce fetal growth. A March of Dimes grantee recently published a study that may shed light on why some women who smoke cigarettes during pregnancy have low-birthweight babies and others do not. The researcher reported that pregnant women who smoke are more likely to have a premature or low-birthweight baby if two genes that normally control the body's chemical modification of components of cigarette smoke are missing or inactive. These findings could lead to better ways to identify and treat those women at high risk of having a low-birthweight baby.

References

American College of Obstetricians and Gynecologists (ACOG). "Smoking Cessation During Pregnancy." *ACOG Educational Bulletin*, number 260, September 2000.

Centers for Disease Control and Prevention (CDC). *Women and Smoking: A Report of the Surgeon General—2001*. CDC Office on Smoking and Health, Atlanta, GA.

Honein, M. Family History, Maternal Smoking, and Clubfoot: An Indication of a Gene-environment Interaction. *American Journal of Epidemiology*, volume 152, number 7, October 2000, pages 658–665.

Hull, M.G., *et al*. Delayed Conception and Active and Passive Smoking. *Fertility and Sterility*, volume 72, number 4, October 2000, pages 725–733.

Hwang, Shih-Jen, *et al*. Association Study of Transforming Growth Factor Alpha Taq1 Polymorphism and Oral Clefts: Indication of Gene-environment Interaction in a Population-based Sample of Infants with Birth Defects. *American Journal of Epidemiology*, volume 141, number 7, 1995, pages 629–636.

Samet, J.M. and Yoon, S.Y. *Women and The Tobacco Epidemic: Challenges for the 21st Century*. World Health Organization in Collaboration with the Institute for Global Tobacco Control, Johns Hopkins School of Public Health, 2001.

Wang, X., et al. Maternal Cigarette Smoking, Metabolic Gene Polymorphism, and Infant Birth Weight. *Journal of the American Medical Association*, volume 287, number 2, January 9, 2002, pages 195–202.

Chapter 40

The Link Between Smoking and Depression

By now, you are quite aware that smoking is not in your best interests. Well, here's just one more reason to strongly consider stopping. To no one's great surprise, there are some rather strong connections between smoking cigarettes and depression. You may have noticed that many smokers, perhaps even you, are more likely to show signs of depression than people who don't smoke. So what do we know about this connection?

First of all, we know that people who are at risk in their lives for developing depression are much more likely to become dependent on tobacco. Many of you may have had the experience of being depressed, and know that the tendency is to smoke more when this happens. For people with a history of depression, a greater dependence on smoking seems to happen even when they are not actually experiencing a depression. This means that there is probably some biological connection between depression and tobacco use.

The other part of the connection is that people who smoke are more likely to develop depression. Nicotine has an effect on the brain. Initially, that effect may help decrease depression. A lot of people talk about how smoking a cigarette helps them feel less stressed out. However, when smoking continues for more than a few weeks, it has an opposite effect on the brain and depression may develop or get worse. This may be one of the ways that tobacco exerts its "addictive" effect.

Withdrawal from nicotine, which happens when people quit smoking, can actually cause or worsen depression. Because of this, people who are depressed are more likely to fail in their attempts to quit smoking. Failing feels lousy, and may add to the depression.

Now, it is important to know what we mean by depression. Depression is not simply feeling blue. Everybody has bad days here and there, especially if something is not going well in their life. No, serious depression is more than that. It is actually an illness, which doctors call major depressive disorder. In this condition, people have depressed mood for weeks to months, virtually some part of every day. They lose interest in activities, have changes in their appetite, sleeping, and energy, may isolate themselves from others, have problems with concentration, and may feel quite hopeless about life. Occasionally, these feelings may include thoughts of suicide, and people with major depression are at much greater risk for committing suicide than people who are not depressed. Major depression is familial, and people with depressed family members are more likely to develop it themselves.

So, what do you do if you are depressed, or have a history of depression, and want to quit smoking? First of all, remember that wanting to quit is always the first important step, and feel good about making that choice. It is important to tell your doctor about your depressive symptoms and history. In most cases, you should have your depression treated first; some doctors may even treat with medication to prevent depression from starting. Once the depression has been treated, then a good program of quitting smoking can be developed. Luckily, some of the medications for the treatment of depression can also be used to assist in smoking cessation. Addition of nicotine patches or gum may also be important, as nicotine replacement therapy will help to blunt or lessen withdrawal symptoms. Lastly, support groups and/or counseling may be useful in helping to prevent depression from recurring.

Stopping smoking is not easy for anyone. For people prone to depression, quitting can feel impossible. A failed attempt to quit may leave us feeling inadequate, which may make depression worse. On the other hand, a successful effort at stopping can really boost our morale and self-esteem, which may help keep depression away. What is most important is to realize that depression won't prevent your attempt to stop if you follow the right path to quitting.

Part Three

Smoking Cessation

Chapter 41

Questions and Answers about Smoking Cessation

How important is it to stop smoking?

It is very important. Tobacco use remains the single most preventable cause of death in the United States. Cigarette smoking accounts for nearly one-third of all cancer deaths in this country each year.

Smoking is the most common risk factor for the development of lung cancer, which is the leading cause of cancer death. It is also associated with many other types of cancer, including cancers of the esophagus, larynx, kidney, pancreas, and cervix. Smoking also increases the risk of other health problems, such as chronic lung disease and heart disease. Smoking during pregnancy can have adverse effects on the unborn child, such as premature delivery and low birth weight.

What are the immediate benefits of stopping smoking?

The health benefits of smoking cessation (quitting) are immediate and substantial. Almost immediately, a person's circulation begins to improve and the carbon monoxide (chemical carcinogen found in cigarettes) level in the blood begins to decline. A person's pulse rate and blood pressure, which are abnormally high while smoking, begin to return to normal. Within a few days of quitting, a person's sense of taste and smell return, and breathing becomes increasingly easier.

Excerpted from "Questions and Answers about Smoking Cessation" Cancer Facts, National Cancer Institute, reviewed December 2000.

What are the long-term benefits of stopping smoking?

People who quit smoking live longer than those who continue to smoke. After 10 to 15 years, a previous tobacco user's risk of premature death approaches that of a person who has never smoked. About ten years after quitting, an ex-smoker's risk of dying from lung cancer is 30 percent to 50 percent less than the risk for those who continue to smoke. Women who stop smoking before becoming pregnant or who quit in the first three months of pregnancy can reverse the risk of low birth weight for the baby and reduce other pregnancy-associated risks. Quitting also reduces the risk of other smoking-related diseases, including heart disease and chronic lung disease.

There are also many benefits to smoking cessation for people who are sick or who have already developed cancer. Smoking cessation reduces the risk for developing infections, such as pneumonia, which often causes death in patients with other existing diseases.

Does cancer risk change after quitting smoking?

Quitting smoking reduces the risk for developing cancer, and this benefit increases the longer a person remains "smoke free." People who quit smoking reduce their risk of developing and dying from lung cancer. They also reduce their risk of other types of cancer. The risk of premature death and the chance of developing cancer due to cigarettes depends on the number of years of smoking, the number of cigarettes smoked per day, the age at which smoking began, and the presence or absence of illness at the time of quitting. For people who have already developed cancer, quitting smoking reduces the risk of developing another primary cancer.

At what age is smoking cessation the most beneficial?

Smoking cessation benefits men and women at any age. Some older adults may not perceive the benefits of quitting smoking; however, smokers who quit before age 50 have half the risk of dying in the next 16 years compared with people who continue to smoke. By age 64, their overall chance of dying is similar to that of people the same age who have never smoked. Older adults who quit smoking also have a reduced risk of dying from coronary heart disease and lung cancer. Additional, immediate benefits (such as improved circulation, and increased energy and breathing capacity) are other good reasons for older adults to become smoke free.

What are some of the difficulties associated with quitting smoking?

Quitting smoking may cause short-term after-effects, especially for those who have smoked a large number of cigarettes for a long period of time. People who quit smoking are likely to feel anxious, irritable, hungry, more tired, and have difficulty sleeping. They may also have difficulty concentrating. Many tobacco users gain weight when they quit, but usually less than ten pounds. These changes do subside. People who kick the habit have the opportunity for a healthier future.

How can health care providers help their patients to stop smoking?

Doctors and dentists can be good sources of information about the health risks of smoking and about quitting. They can tell their patients about the proper use and potential side effects of nicotine replacement therapy, and help them find local smoking cessation programs.

Doctors and dentists can also play an important role by asking patients about smoking at every office visit advising patients to stop; assisting patients by setting a quit date, providing self-help materials, and suggesting nicotine replacement therapies (when appropriate); and arranging for follow-up visits.

What is nicotine replacement therapy?

Nicotine is the drug in cigarettes and other forms of tobacco that causes addiction. Nicotine replacement products deliver small, steady doses of nicotine into the body, which helps to relieve the withdrawal symptoms often felt by people trying to quit smoking. These products, which are available in four forms (patches, gum, nasal spray, and inhaler), appear to be equally effective. There is evidence that combining the nicotine patch with nicotine gum or nicotine nasal spray increases long-term quit rates compared with using a single type of nicotine replacement therapy. Nicotine gum, in combination with nicotine patch therapy, may also reduce withdrawal symptoms better than either medication alone. Researchers recommend combining nicotine replacement therapy with advice or counseling from a doctor, dentist, pharmacist, or other health provider.

- The nicotine patch, which is available over the counter (without a prescription), supplies a steady amount of nicotine to the body through the skin. The nicotine patch is sold in varying strengths as an eight-week smoking cessation treatment. Nicotine doses are gradually lowered as the treatment progresses. The nicotine patch may not be a good choice for people with skin problems or allergies to adhesive tape.

- Nicotine gum is available over the counter in 2- and 4-mg strengths. Chewing nicotine gum releases nicotine into the bloodstream through the lining of the mouth. Nicotine gum might not be appropriate for people with temporomandibular joint disease (TMJ) or for those with dentures or other dental work such as bridges.

- Nicotine nasal spray was approved by the U.S. Food and Drug Administration (FDA) in 1996 for use by prescription only. The spray comes in a pump bottle containing nicotine that tobacco users can inhale when they have an urge to smoke. This product is not recommended for people with nasal or sinus conditions, allergies, or asthma, nor is it recommended for young tobacco users.

- A nicotine inhaler, also available only by prescription, was approved by the FDA in 1997. This device delivers a vaporized form of nicotine to the mouth through a mouthpiece attached to a plastic cartridge. Even though it is called an inhaler, the device does not deliver nicotine to the lungs the way a cigarette does. Most of the nicotine only travels to the mouth and throat, where it is absorbed through the mucous membranes. Common side effects include throat and mouth irritation and coughing. Anyone with a bronchial problem such as asthma should use it with caution.

Are there smoking cessation aids that do not contain nicotine?

Bupropion, a prescription antidepressant marketed as Zyban®, was approved by the FDA in 1997 to treat nicotine addiction. This drug can help to reduce nicotine withdrawal symptoms and the urge to smoke. Some common side effects of bupropion are dry mouth, difficulty sleeping, dizziness, and skin rash. People should not use this drug if they have a seizure condition such as epilepsy or an eating disorder such as anorexia nervosa or bulimia, or if they are taking other medicines that contain bupropion hydrochloride.

What if efforts to quit result in relapse?

Many smokers find it difficult to quit smoking, and it may take two or three attempts before they are finally able to quit. Although relapse rates are most common in the first few weeks or months after quitting, people who stop smoking for three months are often able to remain cigarette-free for the rest of their lives.

What agencies and organizations are available to help people stop smoking?

A number of organizations provide information and materials about where to find help to stop smoking. State and local health agencies often have information about community smoking cessation programs. The local or county government section in the phone book (blue book) has current phone numbers for health agencies. Information to help people quit smoking is also available through community hospitals, the yellow pages (under "drug abuse and addiction"), public libraries, health maintenance organizations, health fairs, bookstores, and community helplines.

A directory of state and national resources can be found in Chapter 86—Smoking Cessation: Hotlines, Helplines, and Internet Resources.

Chapter 42

Are There Effective Treatments for Nicotine Addiction?

Extensive research has shown that behavioral and pharmacological treatments for nicotine addiction do work. For those individuals motivated to quit smoking, a combination of behavioral and pharmacological treatments can increase the success rate approximately twofold over placebo treatments. Furthermore, smoking cessation can have an immediate positive impact on an individual's health; for example, a 35-year-old man who quits smoking will, on the average, increase his life expectancy by 5.1 years.

Nicotine Replacement Treatments

Nicotine was the first pharmacological agent approved by the Food and Drug Administration (FDA) for use in smoking cessation therapy. Nicotine replacement therapies, such as nicotine gum, the transdermal patch, nasal spray, and inhaler, have been approved for use in the United States. They are used to relieve withdrawal symptoms, because they produce less severe physiological alterations than tobacco-based

Excerpted from "Research Report Series—Nicotine Addiction," National Institute on Drug Abuse (NIDA), October 2002. The complete text can be accessed online at www.nida.nih.gov/ResearchReports/Nicotine. Information on hypnosis and acupuncture is excerpted from *Reducing Tobacco Use: A Report of the Surgeon General*. Atlanta, Georgia: U.S. Department of Health and Human Services, Centers for Disease Control and Prevention, National Center for Chronic Disease Prevention and Health Promotion, Office on Smoking and Health, 2000.

systems, and generally provide users with lower overall nicotine levels than they receive with tobacco. An added benefit is that these forms of nicotine have little abuse potential since they do not produce the pleasurable effects of tobacco products. Nor do they contain the carcinogens and gases associated with tobacco smoke.

The FDA's approval of nicotine gum in 1984 marked the availability (by prescription) of the first nicotine replacement therapy on the U.S. market. In 1996, the FDA approved gum (Nicorette®) for over-the-counter sales. Whereas nicotine gum provides some smokers with the desired control over dose and ability to relieve cravings, others are unable to tolerate the taste and chewing demands. In 1991–1992, FDA approved four transdermal nicotine patches, two of which became over-the-counter products in 1996, thus meeting the needs of many additional tobacco users.

Since the introduction of nicotine gum and the transdermal patch, estimates based on FDA and pharmaceutical industry data indicate that more than one million individuals have been successfully treated for nicotine addiction. In 1996 a nicotine nasal spray, and in 1998 a nicotine inhaler, became available by prescription. All the nicotine replacement products—gum, patch, spray, and inhaler—appear to be equally effective. In fact, the over-the-counter availability of many of these medications, combined with increased messages to quit smoking in the media, has produced about a 20 percent increase in successful quitting each year.

Non-Nicotine Therapies

Although the major focus of pharmacological treatments of nicotine addiction has been nicotine replacement, other treatments are being developed for relief of nicotine withdrawal symptoms. For example, the first non-nicotine prescription drug, bupropion, an antidepressant marketed as Zyban®, has been approved for use as a pharmacological treatment for nicotine addiction. In December 1996, a Federal advisory committee recommended that the FDA approve bupropion to become the first drug to help people quit smoking that could be taken in pill form, and the first to contain no nicotine.

Behavioral Treatments

Behavioral interventions can play an integral role in nicotine addiction treatment. Over the past decade, this approach has spread from primarily clinic-based, formal smoking-cessation programs to application in numerous community and public health settings, and now to telephone and written formats as well. In general, behavioral methods are employed to discover high-risk relapse situations; create an aversion to smoking; develop self-monitoring of smoking behavior, and establish competing coping responses.

Other key factors in successful treatment include avoiding smokers and smoking environments and receiving support from family and friends. The single most important factor, however, may be the learning and use of coping skills for both short- and long-term prevention of relapse. Smokers must not only learn behavioral and cognitive tools for relapse prevention but must also be ready to apply those skills in a crisis.

Although behavioral and pharmacological treatments can be extremely successful when employed alone, science has taught us that integrating both types of treatments will ultimately be the most effective approach. More than 90 percent of the people who try to quit smoking relapse or return to smoking within one year, with the majority relapsing within a week. There are, however, an estimated 2.5 to 5 percent who do in fact succeed on their own. It has been shown that pharmacological treatments can double the odds of their success. However, a combination of pharmacological and behavioral treatments further improves their chances. For example, when use of the nicotine patch is combined with a behavioral approach, such as group therapy or social support networks, the efficacy of treatment is significantly enhanced.

Hypnosis

Some smokers try hypnosis therapy to help them quit. Strategies for hypnosis interventions include direct hypnotic suggestions to quit, suggestions intended to produce aversion to smoking, and training in self-hypnosis to reinforce formal treatment.

Efficacy: The methodological shortcomings of hypnosis research make it difficult to estimate the value of this therapy for smoking cessation. Reviewers have noted that, in general, hypnosis is not very effective when used alone, but it may be useful as part of a multicomponent intervention in which subjects see a therapist many times. In methodologically sound studies, hypnosis often fails to outperform comparison techniques, such as self-help strategies. Hypnosis techniques may work best for the relatively small proportion of people highly susceptible to hypnosis. Since the late 1980s, there have been only two trials of hypnosis in smoking cessation, with inconclusive results.

Relevant Process Measures: Appropriate process measures for studies of hypnosis are those that assess the various means of hypnotic induction and the motivational changes that are presumed to accrue from them. Because measures have rarely been collected, little is known about the mechanisms of hypnotic treatments for smoking cessation.

Acupuncture

The typical acupuncture treatment for smoking cessation involves the insertion of needles or staples into the outer ear, but a number of other techniques have been investigated. The most commonly cited rationale for using acupuncture is that it relieves the discomfort of nicotine withdrawal.

Efficacy: The available evidence suggests that acupuncture is no more effective in smoking cessation than placebo treatments. For example, one evaluation (conducted in 1988) reviewed eight studies in which acupuncture at a theoretically appropriate site was contrasted with acupuncture at a placebo site. Only one of these studies found greater success among participants undergoing the procedure with theoretically appropriate sites. A meta-analysis of five studies (conducted in 2000) found that acupuncture was no more effective than placebo.

Relevant Process Measures: Acupuncture is commonly presumed to exert its effects by easing tobacco withdrawal. At present there is no evidence that acupuncture is capable of relieving withdrawal symptoms associated with smoking cessation.

Gender Differences in Tobacco Smoking

Several avenues of research now indicate that men and women differ in their smoking behavior and that differences in nicotine sensitivity may be the root cause. Studies of smoking behavior seem to indicate that women smoke fewer cigarettes per day, tend to use cigarettes with lower nicotine content, and do not inhale as deeply as men. Whether this is because of differences in sensitivity to nicotine is an important research question. Some researchers are finding that women may be more affected by factors other than nicotine, such as the sensory aspects of the smoke or social factors, than they are by nicotine itself.

The number of smokers in the United States declined in the 1970s and 1980s, but has been relatively stable throughout the 1990s. Because this decline of smoking was greater among men than women, the prevalence of smoking is only slightly higher for men today than it is for women. Several factors appear to be contributing to this trend, including increased initiation of smoking among female teens and, more critically, women being less likely than men to quit smoking.

Large-scale smoking-cessation trials show that women are less likely to initiate quitting and may be more likely to relapse if they do quit. In cessation programs using nicotine replacement methods, such as the patch or gum, the nicotine does not seem to reduce craving as effectively for women as for men. Other factors that may contribute to women's difficulty with quitting are that the withdrawal syndrome may be more intense for women and that they appear more likely than men to gain weight upon quitting. It is important for women entering smoking cessation programs to be aware that standard treatment regimens may have to be adjusted to compensate for gender differences in nicotine sensitivity.

Chapter 43

Nicotine Replacement Therapy

Using the Nicotine Patch, Nicotine Gum, Nicotine Nasal Spray, or Nicotine Inhaler

When you are ready to quit smoking, you may want to use nicotine replacement therapy to help you give up cigarettes. The cost of nicotine replacement therapy is about the same or less than the cost of cigarettes.

The nicotine patch, gum, nasal spray, and inhaler are all forms of nicotine replacement therapy. All forms of nicotine replacement can help lessen your urge to smoke. This means you have less craving for nicotine when you stop smoking. You may still feel a craving to smoke, but don't smoke while using the patch, gum, nasal spray, or inhaler.

Who should use nicotine replacement therapy?

Almost every smoker can benefit from using nicotine replacement therapy. If you are pregnant or if you have heart or blood vessel problems, your doctor will be careful about giving you the nicotine patch or gum.

How do I know what strength is right for me?

Patch: Most smokers should start using a full-strength patch (15 to 22 mg of nicotine) every day for four weeks and then a weaker patch (5 to 14 mg of nicotine) for another four weeks.

Gum: Many smokers should start using the 2-mg dose. However, you may want to start with 4-mg gum if you:

- Smoke more than 20 cigarettes a day.
- Smoke as soon as you wake up in the morning.
- Have severe withdrawal symptoms when you don't smoke.
- Have tried to quit on a lower dose and failed.

If you are a very light smoker (less than 10 to 15 cigarettes a day) or have health problems, your doctor can help you select the right dose.

Should I use the nicotine patch, gum, nasal spray, or inhaler?

Any of these treatments can help once you are ready to quit. The choice is up to you. Some people don't like the taste of the gum or don't like chewing in public. They prefer the patch. Other people have been unable to quit on the patch and want to try the gum. Some people prefer to use a nasal spray and some prefer the inhaler. Using the nicotine patch, gum, nasal spray, or inhaler almost doubles your chances of quitting. Here is some information to help you decide which one is right for you.

Nicotine Patch

- *Directions for use:* At the start of each day, place a new patch on a part of your body between the neck and the waist. Put the patch on a new spot each day to lessen skin irritation.
- *Treatment period:* The patch is usually used for up to eight weeks.
- *Side effects:* Some people who use the patch get a rash on their body where the patch is placed. Skin rashes are usually mild and easily treated. Moving the patch to another area of the body helps.
- If you have any side effects from the patch, be sure to tell your doctor right away.

- *How to get the patch:* You can buy the patch without a doctor's prescription. To be safe, carefully read and follow the directions inside the package. You can talk to your doctor about how to use it and how long to use it.

Nicotine Gum

- *Directions for use:* The gum must be chewed in a special way to make it work. Chew it slowly until you notice a "peppery" taste. Then stop chewing and move the nicotine gum between your cheek and your gum. Each piece of nicotine gum should be kept in your mouth for about 30 minutes.

- *Treatment period:* A regular schedule (at least one piece of nicotine gum every one to two hours for one to three months) may give the best results. Some people don't chew enough pieces of gum a day and/or they don't chew the gum for eight weeks. They might not get the most benefit from nicotine gum.

- *Side effects:* Some people have mild side effects such as hiccups, upset stomach, or sore jaws. Most of these side effects go away if the gum is used correctly. If you have any side effects from the gum, be sure to tell your doctor right away.

- *How to get nicotine gum:* You can buy the gum without a doctor's prescription. To be safe, carefully read and follow the directions inside the package. Also, you can talk to your doctor about how to use it and how long to use it.

Nicotine Nasal (Nose) Spray

- *Directions for use:* Apply one spray in each nostril. Use the spray one to two times each hour while you are awake. Use the spray at least eight times a day. Don't use it more than 40 times a day.

- *Side Effects:* The nasal spray may cause nasal irritation, diarrhea, and a fast heart rate. If you have hay fever or sinus infection, ask your doctor about using one of the other forms of nicotine replacement therapy. If you have any side effects from the nasal spray, be sure to tell your doctor right away.

- *How to get the nasal spray:* You can only get the nasal spray with a doctor's prescription. To be safe, carefully read and follow the directions inside the package.

Nicotine Inhaler

- *Directions for use:* Inhale from a cartridge when you have a desire for a cigarette. Use no more than 16 cartridges a day for up to 12 weeks.

- *Side Effects:* You might have irritation of throat and mouth when you first start to use the inhaler. It might make you cough. You should get over this after a while. If you have any side effects from the inhaler, be sure to tell your doctor right away.

- *How to get the inhaler:* You can only get the inhaler with a doctor's prescription. To be safe, carefully read and follow directions inside the package.

Chapter 44

Non-Nicotine Medications for Smoking Cessation

Several options are now available to aid smokers who wish to quit, including medications available both "over-the-counter" and by prescription. This chapter reviews the efficacy of the most widely available non-nicotine medications and describes how they may be used.

Non-Nicotine Agents

Bupropion (Zyban®) Sustained-Release Tablets

Introduction: Bupropion is a non-nicotine aid to smoking cessation which was initially developed and marketed as an antidepressant, Wellbutrin®. The active ingredient in Zyban® and Wellbutrin® is identical. The efficacy of bupropion as an aid to smoking cessation has been demonstrated in three placebo-controlled, double-blind trials with abstinence rates similar to nicotine-containing therapies. The mechanism by which bupropion enhances the ability of patients to abstain from smoking is unknown, although the drug is known to be a relatively weak inhibitor of the neuronal uptake of substances associated with addiction, including norepinephrine, serotonin, and dopamine.

The information in this chapter is excerpted with permission from *Methods to Enhance Smoking Cessation*, an official statement of the California Thoracic Society Medical Section of the American Lung Association of California. © 1998 California Thoracic Society, Reviewed 2002. The complete text of this statement, including references, is available at http://www.thoracic.org/chapters/california.

How to use: Patients should be started on a lower dose (150 mg a day for the first 3 to 7 days) while they are still smoking. The dosage is then increased to 150 mg b.i.d. [twice a day] for 7 to 12 weeks. Patients should be on the higher dose two weeks prior to their smoking quit date. If the patient has not stopped or significantly reduced smoking by week seven, the drug should be stopped. Dose tapering is not required.

Adverse effects: The most commonly observed adverse events are dry mouth, dizziness (10% at 300 mg/day) and insomnia (40% at 300 mg/day). These are dose-dependent adverse events. Avoiding bedtime doses may minimize insomnia. Bupropion is contraindicated in patients with a seizure disorder, those taking Wellbutrin® or a monoamine oxidase (MAO) inhibitor, and persons with a current or prior diagnosis of bulimia or anorexia nervosa.

Clonidine

Introduction: Clonidine has been used with some success in treating symptoms associated with opiate and alcohol withdrawal. Both oral and transdermal preparations have been used for treating nicotine withdrawal. Results of clinical trials of clonidine to improve smoking cessation rates are mixed. Many studies show a short-term reduction in craving and anxiety, but few demonstrate an increase in cessation rates at one year.

Clonidine may be useful for heavily addicted patients whose previous attempts to quit are characterized by severe anxiety and craving symptoms. Most studies find that withdrawal symptoms are most severe during the first two weeks, so clonidine should be limited to short-term therapy and combined with nicotine replacement.

How to use: Oral clonidine is generally given at least twice daily to provide benefit throughout the waking hours. Regular administration tends to produce smoother plasma levels, which reduces adverse effects. Transdermal patches are sometimes better tolerated than oral clonidine. Regardless of the route chosen, treatment should begin one week before quitting smoking rather than waiting for symptoms to appear.

Adverse effects: Adverse effects are dose-dependent and occur in up to 70% of patients, with self-discontinuation rates approaching 20%. Sedation, dizziness, and dry mouth are common. Orthostasis occurs in approximately 10% of normotensive patients using clonidine, with a mean drop of 8/6 mm Hg in blood pressure. Transdermal clonidine in equivalent doses produces less severe adverse effects, probably due to its consistent blood levels for up to one week. Transdermal clonidine is associated with a high frequency of skin reactions, most commonly rash or pruritus. Clonidine should be used with caution in patients with cardiovascular disease, chronic renal failure, a history of depression, and in lactating women.

Other Treatment Options

Nortriptyline has been tried as an adjunct to smoking cessation with some success. In two studies, nortriptyline significantly reduced withdrawal symptoms and increased abstinence rates over the course of the studies (6 months). However, adverse anticholinergic effects were significantly higher in the active treatment group causing a high dropout rate. Nortriptyline should be reserved for those patients who are refractory to the better-tolerated treatments.

Trials of buspirone in smoking cessation produced conflicting results. Possible benefits of this anxiolytic include mild adverse effects and lack of addiction potential. Preliminary data suggest some effectiveness in high-anxiety patients, but the studies are too small and too short to draw any conclusions.

One trial and several case reports of naltrexone as a cessation aid have been published. In the trial, naltrexone trended towards a modest advantage over placebo, but only one subgroup of patients reached statistical significance, women with a past history of major depression (usually a refractory subgroup). The dropout rate from intolerance to naltrexone was high (25%). Two case reports regarding naltrexone involved patients who spontaneously and rapidly reduced their tobacco intake while on naltrexone due to an inability to taste the tobacco. Both patients resumed smoking upon discontinuation of naltrexone.

Chapter 45

Is Zyban Right for You?

Smokers who try to quit on their own are successful about 10% to 12% of the time. Thus, the development of nicotine replacement treatments (patch, gum, inhaler, and nasal spray) was a very important step forward for smokers. Individuals who use any of these treatments are two to three times more likely to be successful. Zyban® is the first non-nicotine prescription medication available to help smokers to quit smoking. The generic name for Zyban is bupropion SR. It is also available under the name Wellbutrin®.

We don't know exactly how Zyban works but we believe that it has a direct effect on the part of the brain that is addicted to nicotine. It seems to reduce the cravings for cigarettes that smokers experience when they try to quit. It also seems to reduce many of the nicotine withdrawal symptoms that people experience when they quit. Specifically, people who used Zyban to help them quit had less irritability, less frustration, and less anger than people who quit on their own without medication. They also had less difficulty with concentration, less restlessness, and less depression. These same things are true for people who use the nicotine patch or the gum, but Zyban has a different way of working. The patch and the gum provide the nicotine that you would get from smoking whereas Zyban seems to change the way your brain deals with not having nicotine.

"Is Zyban Right for You?" by Trudy Manchester, M.D. Reprinted with permission from www.trytostop.org, © 2001 Massachusetts Department of Public Health. All rights reserved. Reviewed by David A. Cooke, M.D., on May 9, 2004.

Is Zyban better than nicotine replacement therapy?

In most studies, it appears that Zyban works as well as the nicotine replacement therapies. It works differently, however, and research is continuing to try to identify which types of smokers would do better with Zyban and which might do better with nicotine replacement. It is very clear from all of the studies on quitting, however, that your chances of being successful depend a great deal on your motivation and commitment to quitting. This is true, no matter what therapy you may choose.

Can anyone use Zyban?

No, patients with seizure disorders or eating disorders should not use Zyban, nor should women who are pregnant or breastfeeding. Individuals with allergic reactions to bupropion as well as patients who are treated with monoamine oxidase inhibitor medication (a specific type of antidepressant) should not receive Zyban. In addition to these conditions, caution is advised in many other medical conditions, such as liver disease, kidney disease, hypertension, and any history of brain injury or brain surgery.

How do I take Zyban?

It is best to begin Zyban one to two weeks before your actual quit date. You will begin with one tablet per day for the first three days and then increase to one tablet two times per day on the fourth day. These two doses must be at least eight hours apart. [Note: While there is now a once-daily form of Wellbutrin, a corresponding once daily form of Zyban has not yet been produced.] It takes about one week for the Zyban to reach the right levels in your system, so you should plan a specific quit date at some point in the second week of therapy. If you realize that you have missed a dose, you should not take an extra dose.

How long do I need to take Zyban?

If all goes well and you are successful in quitting, you should plan to stay on the Zyban for 7 to 12 weeks. Your primary care provider may recommend a longer course of treatment, however, depending on your unique circumstances. If you continue to have difficulty in giving up cigarettes after about 7 weeks of Zyban treatment, it is best simply to stop the Zyban and then try again at another time. You should discuss this with your physician, so that you can determine what might have gone wrong and make better plans for the next quit attempt.

What about side effects?

As with all prescription medications, there are many possible side effects from Zyban. The most common ones are dry mouth and difficulty with sleep. Drinking water, using throat lozenges, and chewing gum may all help with the dry mouth. If you have trouble with sleep, you can try taking your second Zyban dose earlier in the day. (Remember that you must allow at least 8 hours between the first and the second dose, however.) You should also reduce your caffeine intake if sleeping is difficult. Don't let these possible side effects scare you. Most people do not have side effects. If side effects do occur, they can usually be minimized by simple means. And side effects are temporary— they last only as long as you are on a medication and not for the rest of your life. Putting up with mild side effects for a short while is a small price to pay if you ultimately can free yourself from smoking.

Is Zyban right for me?

The best way to determine this is to visit your primary care provider to review all of your options for treatment. Together you can select the best therapy for you and monitor your progress. If you are committed to quitting, work closely with your primary care provider, and use any form of medication, then you will be well on your way to becoming a nonsmoker.

Chapter 46

You Can Quit Smoking

Nicotine: A Powerful Addiction

If you have tried to quit smoking, you know how hard it can be. It is hard because nicotine is a very addictive drug. For some people, it can be as addictive as heroin or cocaine.

Quitting is hard. Usually people make two or three tries, or more, before finally being able to quit. Each time you try to quit, you can learn about what helps and what hurts.

Quitting takes hard work and a lot of effort, but you can quit smoking.

Good Reasons for Quitting

Quitting smoking is one of the most important things you will ever do:

- You will live longer and live better.

- Quitting will lower your chance of having a heart attack, stroke, or cancer.

- If you are pregnant, quitting smoking will improve your chances of having a healthy baby.

From "You Can Quit Smoking," Office of the Surgeon General, U.S. Public Health Service, June 2000. The complete text of this document, including additional resources, can be found online at www.surgeongereral.gov/tobacco/consquits.htm.

- The people you live with, especially your children, will be healthier.

- You will have extra money to spend on things other than cigarettes.

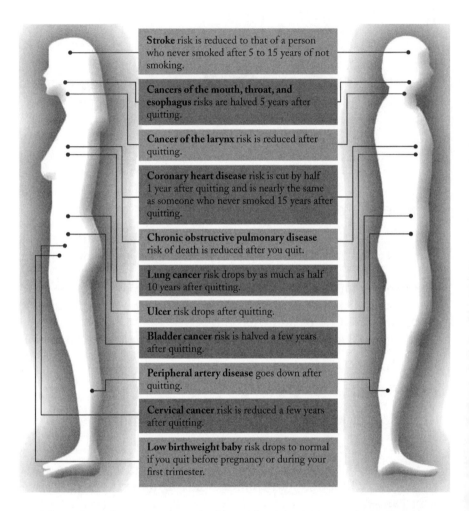

Figure 46.1. *The Benefits of Quitting. (Source: "The Health Consequences of Smoking: What It Means to You," prepared by the Centers for Disease Control and Prevention (CDC) based on U.S. Department of Health and Human Services.* The Health Consequences of Smoking: A Report of the Surgeon General. *U.S. Department of Health and Human Services, Centers for Disease Control and Prevention, National Center for Chronic Disease Prevention and Health Promotion, Office on Smoking and Health, 2004.)*

Five Keys for Quitting

Studies have shown that these five steps will help you quit and quit for good. You have the best chances of quitting if you use them together:

1. Get ready.

2. Get support.

3. Learn new skills and behaviors.

4. Get medication and use it correctly.

5. Be prepared for relapse or difficult situations.

Get Ready

- Set a quit date.

- Change your environment.

- Get rid of all cigarettes and ashtrays in your home, car, and place of work.

- Don't let people smoke in your home.

- Review your past attempts to quit. Think about what worked and what did not.

- Once you quit, don't smoke—not even a puff.

Get Support and Encouragement

Studies have shown that you have a better chance of being successful if you have help. You can get support in many ways:

- Tell your family, friends, and coworkers that you are going to quit and want their support. Ask them not to smoke around you or leave cigarettes out.

- Talk to your health care provider (for example, doctor, dentist, nurse, pharmacist, psychologist, or smoking counselor).

- Get individual, group, or telephone counseling. The more counseling you have, the better your chances are of quitting. Programs are given at local hospitals and health centers. Call your local health department for information about programs in your area.

Learn New Skills and Behaviors

- Try to distract yourself from urges to smoke. Talk to someone, go for a walk, or get busy with a task.

- When you first try to quit, change your routine. Use a different route to work. Drink tea instead of coffee. Eat breakfast in a different place.

- Do something to reduce your stress. Take a hot bath, exercise, or read a book.

- Plan something enjoyable to do every day.

- Drink a lot of water and other fluids.

Get Medication and Use It Correctly

Medications can help you stop smoking and lessen the urge to smoke.

- The U.S. Food and Drug Administration (FDA) has approved five medications to help you quit smoking:

  1. Bupropion SR—Available by prescription.

  2. Nicotine gum—Available over-the-counter.

  3. Nicotine inhaler—Available by prescription.

  4. Nicotine nasal spray—Available by prescription.

  5. Nicotine patch—Available by prescription and over-the-counter.

- Ask your health care provider for advice and carefully read the information on the package.

- All of these medications will more or less double your chances of quitting and quitting for good.

- Everyone who is trying to quit may benefit from using a medication. If you are pregnant or trying to become pregnant, nursing, under age 18, smoking fewer than ten cigarettes per day, or have a medical condition, talk to your doctor or other health care provider before taking medications.

Be Prepared for Relapse or Difficult Situations

Most relapses occur within the first three months after quitting. Don't be discouraged if you start smoking again. Remember, most people try several times before they finally quit. Here are some difficult situations to watch for:

- **Alcohol:** Avoid drinking alcohol. Drinking lowers your chances of success.

- **Other smokers:** Being around smoking can make you want to smoke.

- **Weight gain:** Many smokers will gain weight when they quit, usually less than ten pounds. Eat a healthy diet and stay active. Don't let weight gain distract you from your main goal—quitting smoking. Some quit-smoking medications may help delay weight gain.

- **Bad mood or depression:** There are a lot of ways to improve your mood other than smoking [see Chapter 55—Smoking, Stress, and Mood for some specific suggestions].

If you are having problems with any of these situations, talk to your doctor or other health care provider.

Special Situations or Conditions

Studies suggest that everyone can quit smoking. Your situation or condition can give you a special reason to quit.

- **Pregnant women/new mothers:** By quitting, you protect your baby's health and your own.

- **Hospitalized patients:** By quitting, you reduce health problems and help healing.

- **Heart attack patients:** By quitting, you reduce your risk of a second heart attack.

- **Lung, head, and neck cancer patients:** By quitting, you reduce your chance of a second cancer.

- **Parents of children and adolescents:** By quitting, you protect your children and adolescents from illnesses caused by second-hand smoke.

Questions to Think About

Think about the following questions before you try to stop smoking. You may want to talk about your answers with your health care provider.

- Why do you want to quit?

- When you tried to quit in the past, what helped and what didn't?

- What will be the most difficult situations for you after you quit? How will you plan to handle them?

- Who can help you through the tough times? Your family? Friends? Health care provider?

- What pleasures do you get from smoking? What ways can you still get pleasure if you quit?

Here are some questions to ask your health care provider.

- How can you help me to be successful at quitting?

- What medication do you think would be best for me and how should I take it?

- What should I do if I need more help?

- What is smoking withdrawal like? How can I get information on withdrawal?

Quitting takes hard work and a lot of effort, but you can quit smoking.

Chapter 47

What You Should Know before You Start a Smoke-Free Life

Why Is Quitting So Hard?

Many ex-smokers say quitting was the hardest thing they ever did. Do you feel hooked? You're probably addicted to nicotine. Nicotine is in all tobacco products. It makes you feel calm and satisfied. At the same time, you feel more alert and focused. The more you smoke, the more nicotine you need to feel good. Soon, you don't feel "normal" without nicotine. It takes time to break free from nicotine addiction. It may take more than one try to quit for good. So don't give up too soon. You will feel good again. Quitting is also hard because smoking is a big part of your life. You enjoy holding cigarettes and puffing on them. You may smoke when you are stressed, bored, or angry. After months and years of lighting up, smoking becomes part of your daily routine. You may light up without even thinking about it.

Smoking goes with other things, too. You may light up when you feel a certain way or do certain things. For example:

- Drinking coffee, wine, or beer
- Talking on the phone
- Driving
- Being with other smokers

Excerpted from "Clearing the Air: Quit Smoking Today," National Cancer Institute (NCI), NIH Pub. No. 03-1647, April 2003; available online at http://smokefree.gov/pubs/clearing_the_air.pdf.

You may even feel uncomfortable not smoking at times or in places where you usually have a cigarette. These times and places are called "triggers." That's because they trigger, or turn on, cigarette cravings. Breaking these habits is the hardest part of quitting for some smokers.

Quitting isn't easy. Just reading this book won't do it. It may take several tries. But you learn something each time you try. It takes will power and strength to beat your addiction to nicotine. Remember that millions of people have quit smoking for good. You can be one of them.

Just thinking about quitting may make you anxious. But your chances will be better if you get ready first. Quitting works best when you're prepared. Before you quit, START by taking these five important steps:

S = **Set** a quit date.

T = **Tell** family, friends, and co-workers that you plan to quit.

A = **Anticipate** and plan for the challenges you'll face while quitting.

R = **Remove** cigarettes and other tobacco products from your home, car, and work.

T = **Talk** to your doctor about getting help to quit.

Some Things to Think about before you START

Think about why you want to quit. Decide for sure that you want to quit. Promise yourself that you'll do it. It's OK to have mixed feelings. Don't let that stop you. There will be times every day that you don't feel like quitting. You will have to stick with it anyway.

Find reasons to quit that are important to you. Think of more than just health reasons. For example, think of:

- How much money you'll save by not buying cigarettes
- The time you'll have for yourself instead of taking cigarette breaks, rushing out to buy a pack, or searching for a light
- Not being short of breath or coughing as much
- Setting a better example for your children

Write down all the reasons why you want to quit. List ways to fight the urge to smoke, too. Keep your list where you'll see it often. Good places are:

- Where you keep your cigarettes
- In your wallet or purse
- In the kitchen
- In your car

When you reach for a cigarette you'll find your list. It will remind you why you want to stop.

Here are some examples of reasons to quit:

- I will feel healthier right away. I will have more energy and better focus. My senses of smell and taste will be better. I will have whiter teeth and fresher breath. I will cough less and breathe better.

- I will be healthier the rest of my life. I will lower my risk for cancer, heart attacks, strokes, early death, cataracts, and skin wrinkling.

- I will make my partner, friends, family, kids, grandchildren, and co-workers proud of me.

- I will be proud of myself. I will feel more in control of my life. I will be a better role model for others.

- I will no longer expose others to my second-hand smoke.

- I will have a healthier baby. (If you're pregnant)

- I will have more money to spend.

- I won't have to worry: "When will I get to smoke next?" or "What do I do when I'm in a smoke-free place?"

Nicotine Addiction Test

The quiz in this section is modified from Fagerstrom KO, Schneider NG. Measuring nicotine dependence: A review of the Fagerstrom Tolerance Questionnaire. Journal of Behavioral Medicine *1989; 12 (2): 159–182.*

Find Out How Much You Depend on Nicotine

Knowing how addicted you are to nicotine can help you quit. It can help you decide if you need extra help, such as medicine or support from a program. Take this test to find out how hooked you are. Count how many times you answer "Yes" to the following questions:

- Do you usually smoke your first cigarette within a half hour after you wake up?
- Do you find it hard not to smoke where smoking isn't allowed? (At the library, movie theater, or doctor's office?)
- Do you smoke 10 or more cigarettes a day?
- Do you smoke 25 or more cigarettes a day?
- Do you smoke more during the morning than during the rest of the day?
- Do you smoke even when you're sick?

How many "Yes" answers did you accumulate? The more "Yes" answers, the more addicted you are. Remember, no matter how hooked you are, you can stop smoking. The key is staying strong and sticking with it.

Keep Track of When and Why You Smoke

Think about when you smoke and why you smoke. Do this for the next few weeks. Keep a record of every cigarette you smoke. Make a "Craving Journal" to record the time, where you were, what you were doing, and who was with you every time you have a cigarette. Also note how strongly you wanted to smoke (1 = just a little; 2 = some; 3 = a lot). You will probably need one copy for every day.

You will find that you light up a lot without thinking about it. And you may be tempted to skip writing down some of the cigarettes you smoke. But keeping this journal is very helpful if you do it right. You'll learn about your smoking triggers. And you'll learn which cigarettes are your favorites. These facts will help you prepare to fight your urge to smoke.

Know Your Triggers

Certain things trigger, or turn on, your need for a cigarette. They can be moods, feelings, places, or things you do. Think about what might tempt you to smoke.

- Feeling stressed
- Feeling down
- Talking on the phone
- Drinking liquor, like wine or beer

- Watching TV
- Driving your car
- Finishing a meal
- Playing cards
- Taking a work break
- Being with other smokers
- Drinking coffee
- Seeing someone else smoke
- Cooling off after a fight
- Feeling lonely
- After having sex

Knowing your triggers is very important. It can help you stay away from things that tempt you to smoke. It can prepare you to fight the urge when you are tempted.

- Stay away from places where smoking is allowed. Sit in the non-smoking section at restaurants.

- Keep your hands busy. Hold a pencil or paper clip. Doodle or write a letter. Carry a water bottle.

- Stay away from people who smoke. Spend time with nonsmoking friends.

- Put something else in your mouth. Chew sugar-free gum. Snack on a carrot or celery stick. Keep your mouth and hands busy with a toothpick, sugar-free lollipop, or straw.

- Drink less or stay away from alcohol. Drinking alcohol often makes people want to smoke. Drink juice, soda, or ice water instead.

Remember: The urge to smoke only lasts 3 to 5 minutes. Try to hold off until the urge passes.

Chapter 48

Preparations for Smoking Cessation

Set a Quit Date

Pick a date within the next two weeks to quit. That gives you enough time to get ready. But it's not so long that you will lose your drive to quit.

Think about choosing a special day:

- Your birthday or wedding anniversary
- New Year's Day
- Independence Day (July 4)
- World No Tobacco Day (May 31)
- The Great American Smokeout (the third Thursday of each November)

If you smoke at work, quit on the weekend or during a day off. That way you'll already be cigarette-free when you return.

Tell Your Family, Friends, and Co-Workers That You Plan to Quit

Quitting smoking is easier with the support of others. Tell your family, friends, and co-workers that you plan to quit. Tell them how they can help you.

Excerpted from "Clearing the Air: Quit Smoking Today," National Cancer Institute, NIH Pub. No. 03-1647, 2003; available online at: http://smokefree .gov/clearing_the_air.pdf.

Some people like to have friends ask how things are going. Others find it nosy. Tell the people you care about exactly how they can help. Here are some ideas:

- Ask everyone to understand your change in mood. Remind them that this won't last long. (The worst will be over within two weeks.) Tell them this: "The longer I go without cigarettes, the sooner I'll be my old self."

- Does someone close to you smoke? Ask them to quit with you, or at least not to smoke around you.

- Do you take any medicines? Tell your doctor and pharmacist you are quitting. Nicotine changes how some drugs work. You may need to change your prescriptions after you quit.

- Get support from other people. You can try talking with others one-on-one or in a group. You can also get support on the phone. You can even try an internet chat room. This kind of support helps smokers quit. The more support you get, the better. But even a little can help.

Anticipate and Plan for the Challenges You'll Face while Quitting

Expecting challenges is an important part of getting ready to quit.

Most people who go back to smoking do it within three months. Your first three months may be hard. You may be more tempted when you are stressed or feeling down. It's hard to be ready for these times before they happen. But it helps to know when you need a cigarette most.

Look over your craving journal. See when you may be tempted to smoke. Plan for how to deal with the urge before it hits.

You should also expect feelings of withdrawal. Withdrawal is the discomfort of giving up nicotine. It is your body's way of telling you it's learning to be smoke-free. These feelings will go away in time.

Remove Cigarettes and Other Tobacco from Your Home, Car, and Work

Getting rid of things that remind you of smoking will also help you get ready to quit. Try these ideas:

- Make things clean and fresh at work, in your car, and at home. Clean your drapes and clothes. Shampoo your car. Buy yourself flowers. You will enjoy their scent as your sense of smell re-turns.

- Throw away all your cigarettes and matches. Give or throw away your lighters and ashtrays. Remember the ashtray and lighter in your car.

- Have your dentist clean your teeth to get rid of smoking stains. See how great they look. Try to keep them that way.

- Some smokers save one pack of cigarettes. They do it "just in case." Or they want to prove they have the willpower not to smoke. Don't! Saving one pack just makes it easier to start smoking again.

Don't Use Other Forms of Tobacco Instead of Cigarettes

Light or low-tar cigarettes are just as harmful as regular cigarettes. Smokeless tobacco, cigars, pipes, and herbal cigarettes also harm your health. For example, bidi cigarettes are just as bad as regular ciga-rettes. Clove cigarettes are even worse. They have more tar, nicotine, and deadly gases. All tobacco products have harmful chemicals and poisons.

Talk to Your Doctor about Getting Help to Quit

Quitting "cold turkey" isn't your only choice. Talk to your doctor about other ways to quit. Most doctors can answer your questions and give advice. They can suggest medicine to help with withdrawal. You can buy some of these medicines on your own. For others, you need a prescription.

Your doctor, dentist, or pharmacist can also point you to places to find support or toll-free quit lines. If you cannot see your doctor, you can get some medicines without a prescription that can help you quit smoking. Go to your local pharmacy or grocery store for over the counter medicines like the nicotine patch, nicotine gum, or nicotine lozenge. Read the instructions to see if the medicine is right for you. If you're not sure, ask a pharmacist.

Medicines that Help with Withdrawal

When you quit smoking, you may feel strange at first. You may feel dull, tense, and not yourself. These are signs that your body is get-ting used to life without nicotine. It usually only lasts a few weeks.

311

Many people just can't handle how they feel after they quit. They start smoking again to feel better. Maybe this has happened to you. Most people slip up in the first week after quitting. This is when feelings of withdrawal are strongest.

There are medicines that can help with feelings of withdrawal:

- Bupropion SR pills
- Nicotine gum
- Nicotine inhaler
- Nicotine lozenge
- Nicotine nasal spray
- Nicotine patch

Using these medicines can *double* your chances of quitting for good. Ask your doctor for advice. But remember: Medicine alone can't do all the work. It can help with cravings and withdrawal, but quitting will still be hard at times.

Nicotine Gum, Patch, Inhaler, Spray, and Lozenge (NRT)

Nicotine gum, patches, inhalers, sprays, and lozenges are called nicotine replacement therapy (NRT). That's because they take the

Table 48.1. These are the names of some of the medications you can use to help you quit. Many large drug stores or pharmacies sell their own brands of nicotine gum and nicotine patch. The following is not intended to be a complete list of products nor does it constitute endorsement of any brand or product by the National Cancer Institute, National Institutes of Health, or the Department of Health and Human Services.

Bupropion SR pills	Zyban®, Wellbutrin®
Nicotine gum	drug store brands, Nicorette®, Nicotrol®
Nicotine inhaler	Nicotrol®
Nicotine lozenge	Commit™
Nicotine nasal spray	Nicotrol®
Nicotine patch	drug store brands, Nicoderm®

place of nicotine from cigarettes. NRT can help with withdrawal and lessen your urge to smoke.

You need a prescription to buy the inhaler and nasal spray. But you can buy nicotine gum, nicotine patches, and nicotine lozenges on your own.

Other Medicines

Bupropion SR is a medicine that has no nicotine. You need a prescription to get these pills. They seem to help with withdrawal and lessen the urge to smoke.

Some people have side effects when using bupropion SR pills. The side effects include dry mouth and not being able to sleep.

This medicine isn't right for:

- Pregnant women
- People who have seizures
- People with eating disorders
- Heavy drinkers

Ask your doctor, dentist, or pharmacist if this medicine is right for you. Make sure to use it the right way if your doctor prescribes it.

Join a Quit-Smoking Program

You may want to try a quit-smoking program or support group to help you quit. These programs can work great if you're willing to commit to them.

How do quit-smoking programs and support groups work? They help smokers spot and cope with problems they have when trying to quit. The programs teach problem-solving and other coping skills. A quit-smoking program can help you quit for good by:

- Helping you better understand why you smoke
- Teaching you how to handle withdrawal and stress
- Teaching you tips to help resist the urge to smoke

Where to Find Help

1. Your state may have a toll-free telephone quitline. Call the quitline to get one-on-one help.

2. Call the National Cancer Institute's Smoking Quitline at 877-44U-QUIT (877-448-7848). This number works anywhere in the U.S. You can get one-on-one help quitting. Or you can ask where to get help in your state.

3. Visit the National Cancer Institute's smokefree.gov website at http://www.smokefree.gov. This website offers science-driven tools, information, and support that has helped smokers quit. You will find state and national resources, free materials, and quitting advice from the National Cancer Institute and its partners.

4. More and more workplaces have help for workers who want to quit. Some offer quit-smoking clinics and support on the job. Others will pay for outside programs for their workers. Ask at work about the choices open to you.

5. Your doctor may know about a quit-smoking program or support group near you.

6. See Chapter 86—Smoking Cessation: Hotlines, Helplines, and Internet Resources.

Chapter 49

Smokeless Tobacco: Quitting

Quitting spit tobacco and staying quit can lower your risk of cancer.

Can you quit? Yes you can. It is hard because nicotine is addictive. The best thing to do is to not even start, but if you are addicted, the sooner you quit, the better it is for your health.

How can you quit? The first and most important step is deciding to quit. Once you decide, make sure you tell your friends, family, and others so they can support you in quitting.

Here are some ways to help you quit. You may want to use a combination of methods. You also may want to talk with your physician or dentist in order to get help in quitting. Your physician or dentist can:

- do an oral exam to identify lesions caused by spit tobacco

- give you advice

- help develop a quit plan

- discuss nicotine replacement therapy or other therapies

- provide encouragement

- provide information on how to learn skills to deal with quitting and staying off spit tobacco

"Smokeless Tobacco: Quitting," National Cancer Institute (NCI), 1999, and "Nicotine Patch Helps Smokeless Tobacco Users Quit, but Maintaining Abstinence May Require Additional Treatment," *NIDA Notes*, National Institute on Drug Abuse (NIDA), March 2001.

- provide information about quitting spit tobacco
- schedule follow-up contact to see how you're doing

Quit on your own. Once you decide to quit, you need to:

- pick a quit date—pick a date a least a week away so you can prepare to quit
- cut back on spit tobacco before you quit—keep lowering the amount of spit tobacco you use each day, and cut back on the number of times you use spit tobacco each day
- build support before you quit—talk to other people who have quit or who want you to quit and tell your friends you are quitting
- get ready to quit—get rid of the rest of your spit tobacco, get substitutes for spit tobacco like gum or sunflower seeds
- quit on your quit day—do something special for yourself and stay busy

Use nicotine replacement products. Nicotine replacement products, such as gum, patches, nasal spray, and nasal inhaler were approved by the Food and Drug Administration to help people quit smoking cigarettes. About twice as many people who have used these products were able to quit smoking cigarettes than those people who did not use the products. Nicotine replacement products help by allowing the gradual lowering of the amount of nicotine your body needs.

Even though we don't yet know how well these products work for spit tobacco users, they may be useful as an aid in helping you quit or at least help reduce your craving for spit tobacco. Nicotine replacement products are best used in combination with other help such as group sessions or counseling.

Both nicotine gum and patches can be bought without a prescription in drug stores. Make sure to follow the instructions and don't use any tobacco, including spit tobacco, when using nicotine gum or patches. You may want to talk with your physician, dentist, or pharmacist before using nicotine gum or patches.

Other nicotine replacement products are available, such as the nasal spray and nasal inhaler. They are prescription products and have not been evaluated in research studies for effectiveness with spit tobacco users. The inhaler may not be very useful for spit tobacco users since it is shaped like a cigarette filter tip to provide smokers the hand-to-mouth movements like in smoking.

Talk with your physician or dentist about using the non-nicotine prescription drug, bupropion. The Food and Drug Administration gave its approval in March 1998 for a prescription drug (brand name is Zyban) to be used by smokers to help them quit. The active ingredient in Zyban is bupropion, which helps stimulate the two brain chemicals that nicotine affects, dopamine and norepinephrine. These two brain chemicals give you energy and a sense of well being. Since Zyban is a prescription drug, you will need to talk with your physician or dentist about whether you should use it and how to use it. Bupropion is best used in combination with other help such as group sessions or counseling. At this time bupropion has not been formally evaluated for effectiveness with spit tobacco users.

Use non-nicotine products. Non-nicotine products have been developed as oral substitutes that contain no nicotine such as mint snuff and lozenges. They come in flavors such as mint, cinnamon, and licorice and may help reduce your craving for spit tobacco.

Program and written materials. Programs and materials are available to help you quit. Group sessions and counseling to deal with quitting have been found useful. There are also printed materials that give you information and can help you quit. You can call the National Cancer Institute's Cancer Information Service at 800-4-CANCER for ordering information.

If you can stay off spit tobacco for two weeks, your body is rid of the addicting nicotine.

Side effects of quitting—There are side effects to quitting and you need to know about them in order to deal with them.

- Craving spit tobacco—Since nicotine is addictive, you'll have cravings for spit tobacco. Try waiting it out. Each urge to use will usually last only three to five minutes. Deep breathing and exercise help you feel better right away.

- Feeling tense or edgy—You're going through nicotine withdrawal. Try some form of exercise; even walking can help.

- Feeling hungry—Yes, people can gain weight once they have stopped using tobacco products. If you get hungry, drink fruit juices or eat a low calorie snack. Drink a lot of water.

What if you start again? If you start using spit tobacco again, it does not mean you can't quit. You need to think about why you started again, so you can avoid the urge the next time. Learn from your quit attempt and try again. Each time it will be easier. Most people try three or four times before quitting for good.

Nicotine Patch Helps Smokeless Tobacco Users Quit, but Maintaining Abstinence May Require Additional Treatment

An estimated 9.6 million people in the United States used smokeless tobacco products—moist snuff and chewing tobacco—during 1998, according to the National Household Survey on Drug Abuse. More than 70 percent of these individuals had used smokeless tobacco during the month before they were surveyed.

People who are trying to quit using smokeless tobacco may benefit from a transdermal nicotine patch during the first critical months after stopping use, a NIDA-supported study suggests. Study participants treated with the nicotine patch experienced less severe withdrawal symptoms and lower levels of craving for nicotine and were significantly more likely to maintain short-term abstinence than users in a control group who were treated with an inactive patch. Treatment with nicotine-free mint snuff also reduced withdrawal symptoms and craving but had no effect on abstinence rates.

"These findings suggest that the nicotine patch can reduce the discomfort that people experience when quitting smokeless tobacco," says Dr. Dorothy Hatsukami of the University of Minnesota School of Medicine, who conducted the study. "Knowing that withdrawal symptoms can be minimized may encourage more people to try to quit," she says. While the study suggests that the nicotine patch may help patients achieve initial abstinence from smokeless tobacco, it remains unclear how the patch and other treatments should be used to sustain abstinence over the long term, she says.

Most tobacco-related research has focused on cigarette smoking with its more extensive range of harmful consequences, Dr. Hatsukami says. "However, we also need to study smokeless tobacco use because it is not an insignificant problem by any means," she says. Regular use of smokeless tobacco products may cause such problems as receding gums, tooth decay, mouth sores, precancerous lesions, and cancers of the mouth and throat. Smokeless tobacco users also may be at increased risk of heart disease and smoking cigarettes. Undesirable social consequences include bad breath, tobacco-stained teeth, and the need to spit tobacco juice.

Many individuals use smokeless tobacco despite its obvious drawbacks because they are hooked on nicotine, a highly addictive drug. As with cigarettes, smokeless tobacco products deliver substantial doses of nicotine along with powerful cancer-causing chemicals. Users of moist snuff—which consists of finely ground tobacco—place a pinch, or dip, of snuff between their cheek and gum and hold it there. Users of chewing tobacco—which comes in leaf and plug forms—place a wad, or chew, in their cheek pouch and chew it. Because nicotine from smokeless tobacco is absorbed through the mouth, the drug takes longer to produce its rewarding effect in the brain than it does when it is absorbed through the lungs during cigarette smoking. The amount of nicotine obtained from smokeless tobacco is comparable to that of cigarettes, and once smokeless tobacco users become addicted they find it just as difficult as cigarette smokers do to quit, Dr. Hatsukami says. She notes that more than 90 percent of the smokeless tobacco users in her study had tried unsuccessfully to quit on their own at least once. Nearly 25 percent of the study's participants had made more than six unsuccessful quit attempts, and nearly 10 percent had tried to quit more than ten times.

In her study, Dr. Hatsukami randomly assigned a total of 402 smokeless tobacco users to one of 4 treatments: active nicotine patch, inactive patch, a combination of active patch and a non-nicotine mint snuff, or a combination of inactive patch and mint snuff. All participants received initial counseling on smokeless tobacco cessation methods and a self-help manual to take home prior to beginning treatment. On their quit date, patients began using their assigned treatments and continued for 10 weeks. During treatment, participants met weekly with counselors for brief support sessions. Results were assessed 15, 25, 36, and 62 weeks after participants stopped using smokeless tobacco. The study found that both the active patch and mint snuff reduced craving and withdrawal symptoms, such as irritability, frustration, anger, anxiety, and depressed mood. Withdrawal symptoms generally peaked during the first week after use was stopped. Only the active patch improved rates of continuous abstinence at 10 and 15 weeks following cessation. By the 23rd week, the differences in abstinence rates among all treatments had become marginal, although active patch users were still slightly more likely to be abstinent. At 62 weeks following cessation, no significant differences in abstinence were observed for any of the treatment conditions.

Many individuals use smokeless tobacco despite its obvious drawbacks because they are hooked on nicotine, a highly addictive drug.

"A number of studies have shown that the nicotine patch is more effective than a placebo patch in sustaining long-term abstinence from cigarette smoking, but the patch appeared to be effective with smokeless tobacco users only during the period of actual patch use and shortly thereafter," notes Dr. Hatsukami. "We don't know if this means we need to use the patch for longer periods of time with smokeless tobacco users or if sensory or behavioral aspects of smokeless tobacco use, such as putting something in one's mouth, may be as important as the nicotine in sustaining use," she says. The fact that a nicotine-free mint snuff also reduced withdrawal symptoms illustrates the potential importance of the sensory aspects of smokeless tobacco in sustaining its use, she says. Previous research does suggest that intensive, multicomponent, behavioral treatment may help smokeless tobacco users to sustain abstinence over the longer term, she says.

"Many questions about smokeless tobacco use and its treatment remain unanswered," Dr. Hatsukami says. "We really need to learn more about all the dimensions of smokeless tobacco use to develop effective treatments that are better tailored to this underserved population," she says.

Sources

Hatsukami, D.K., et al. Treatment of spit tobacco users with transdermal nicotine system and mint snuff. *Journal of Consulting and Clinical Psychology* 68(2):241–249, 2000.

Hatsukami, D.K., and Severson, H. Oral spit tobacco: addiction, prevention and treatment. *Nicotine and Tobacco Research* 1(1):21–44, 1999.

Chapter 50

Today Is Your Quit Day

Today's the day you start your smoke-free life! Remind your family and friends that today is your quit date. Ask them to support you during the first few days and weeks. They can help you through the rough spots.

Here are more tips to help you get through this very important day.

Keep Busy

- Keep very busy today. Go to a movie. Exercise. Take long walks. Go bike riding.

- Spend as much free time as you can where smoking isn't allowed. Some good places are malls, libraries, museums, theaters, department stores, and places of worship.

- Do you miss having a cigarette in your hand? Hold something else. Try a pencil, a paper clip, a marble, or a water bottle.

- Do you miss having something in your mouth? Try toothpicks, cinnamon sticks, lollipops, hard candy, sugar-free gum, or carrot sticks.

- Drink a lot of water and fruit juice. Avoid drinks like wine and beer. They can trigger you to smoke.

Excerpted from "Clearing the Air: Quit Smoking Today," National Cancer Institute (NCI), NIH Pub. No. 03-1647, 2003; available online at http://smokefree.gov/pubs/clearing_the_air.pdf.

Keep in Mind

If you decided to use a support program, use it fully. Go to the sessions. Call your telephone quitline. Visit your internet site. The more support you get, the more likely you will quit for good.

Are you using medicine to help you quit? If so, follow the directions. If you don't, you're more likely to go back to smoking. Also, don't rush to stop using the medicine. Stick with it for at least 12 weeks. Or follow your doctor's advice.

Stay away from What Tempts You

- Instead of smoking after meals, get up from the table. Brush your teeth or go for a walk.

- If you always smoke while driving, try something new: Listen to a new radio station or your favorite music. Take a different route. Or take the train or bus for a while, if you can.

- Stay away from things that you connect with smoking. Do it today and for the next few weeks. These may include:
  - Watching your favorite TV show
  - Sitting in your favorite chair
  - Having a drink before dinner
  - Do things and go places where smoking is not allowed. Keep this up until you're sure that you can stay smoke-free.

- Remember, most people don't smoke. Try to be near nonsmokers if you must be somewhere you'll be tempted to smoke, for example at a party or in a bar.

Plan to Reward Yourself

- You will save money by becoming smoke-free. Is there something you'd like to buy for yourself or someone else? Make a list. Figure out what these things cost. Then start putting aside "cigarette money" to buy some of them.

- Buy yourself something special today to celebrate. See a movie. Buy a CD you've been wanting. Or buy some other treat. Be careful with food treats. You need less food when you don't smoke. This is true no matter how much you want to put something in your mouth.

When You Really Crave a Cigarette

Remember: The urge to smoke usually lasts only three to five minutes. Try to wait it out. Or, if you have previously written down steps to take at a time like this, try them. You can also try these tips:

- Keep other things around instead of cigarettes. Try carrots, pickles, sunflower seeds, apples, celery, raisins, or sugar-free gum.

- Wash your hands or the dishes when you want a cigarette very badly. Or take a shower.

- Learn to relax quickly by taking deep breaths. Take ten slow, deep breaths and hold the last one. Then breathe out slowly. Relax all of your muscles. Picture a soothing, pleasant scene. Just get away from it all for a moment. Think only about that peaceful image and nothing else.

- Light incense or a candle instead of a cigarette.

- Where you are and what is going on can make you crave a cigarette. A change of scene can really help. Go outside, or go to a different room. You can also try changing what you are doing.

- No matter what, don't think, "Just one won't hurt." It will hurt. It will undo your work so far.

- Remember: Trying something to beat the urge is always better than trying nothing.

Remember the Instant Rewards of Quitting

Your body begins to heal within 20 minutes after your last cigarette. The poison gas and nicotine start to leave your body. Your pulse rate goes back to normal. The oxygen in your blood rises to a normal level.

Within a few days you may notice other things:

- Your senses of taste and smell are better.

- You can breathe easier.

- Your "smoker's hack" starts to go away. (You may keep coughing for a while, though.)

The nicotine leaves your body within three days. Your body starts to repair itself. At first, you may feel worse instead of better. Withdrawal feelings can be hard. But they are a sign that your body is healing.

Find New Things to Do

Starting today you may want to create some new habits.
Here are some things you might try:

- Swimming, jogging, playing tennis, bike riding, or shooting baskets. It's hard to smoke and do these things at the same time. How about walking your dog?

- Keep your hands busy. Do crossword puzzles or needlework. Paint. Do woodworking, gardening, or household chores. You can also write a letter or paint your nails.

- Enjoy having a clean tasting mouth. Brush your teeth often and use mouthwash.

- Take a stretch when you're tempted to reach for a cigarette.

Set aside time for the activities that satisfy you and mean the most to you. There are natural breaks even during a busy day. After dinner, first thing in the morning, or just before bed are good examples. You'll also need plenty of rest while you get used to your smoke-free lifestyle.

Chapter 51

The First Few Days without Tobacco

Tips for the First Week

Nicotine is a powerful addiction. If you have tried to quit, you know how hard it can be. People who are trying to quit smoking go through both physical and psychological withdrawal. Here are some tips for the first few days after quitting.

Cravings

- Drink a lot of liquids, especially water. Try herbal teas or fruit juices. Limit coffee, soft drinks, or alcohol—they can increase your urge to smoke.

- Avoid sugar and fatty food. Try low-calorie foods for snacking— carrots and other vegetables, sugarless gum, air-popped popcorn, or low-fat cottage cheese. Don't skip meals.

From "Tips for the First Week. You Can Quit Smoking." March 2001. U.S. Public Health Service. http://www.surgeongeneral.gov/tobacco/1stweek.htm. "Physical Changes After Quitting" is from "The Health Consequences of Smoking: What It Means to You," prepared by the Centers for Disease Control and Prevention (CDC) based on U.S. Department of Health and Human Services. *The Health Consequences of Smoking: A Report of the Surgeon General*. U.S. Department of Health and Human Services, Centers for Disease Control and Prevention, National Center for Chronic Disease Prevention and Health Promotion, Office on Smoking and Health, 2004. "Stick with It" is excerpted from "Clearing the Air: Quit Smoking Today," National Cancer Institute (NCI), NIH Pub. No. 03-1647, 2003; available online at http://smokefree.gov/pubs/clearing_the_air.pdf.

- Exercise regularly and moderately. Regular exercise helps. Joining an exercise group provides a healthy activity and a new routine.

- Get more sleep. Try to go to sleep earlier and get more rest.

- Take deep breaths. Distract yourself. When cravings hit, do something else immediately, such as talking to someone, getting busy with a task, or taking deep breaths.

- Change your habits. Use a different route to work, eat breakfast in a different place, or get up from the table right away after eating.

- Do something to reduce your stress. Take a hot bath or shower, read a book, or exercise.

Psychological Needs

- Remind yourself every day why you are quitting.

- Avoid places you connect with smoking.

- Develop a plan for relieving stress.

- Listen to relaxing music.

- Watch a funny movie.

- Take your mind off a problem and come back to it later.

- Rely on your friends, family, and support group for help.

- Avoid alcohol. It lowers your chances for success.

Physical Changes after Quitting

Within 20 minutes after you smoke that last cigarette, your body begins a series of changes that continue for years.

- **20 minutes after quitting:** Your heart rate drops.

- **12 hours after quitting:** The carbon monoxide level in your blood drops to normal.

- **2 weeks to 3 months after quitting:** Your heart attack risk begins to drop, and your lung function begins to improve.

- **1 to 9 months after quitting:** Your coughing and shortness of breath decrease.

- **1 year after quitting:** Your added risk of coronary heart disease is half that of a smoker's.

- **5 years after quitting:** Your stroke risk is reduced to that of a non-smokers 5–15 years after quitting.

- **10 years after quitting:** Your lung cancer death rate is about half that of a smoker's. Your risk of cancers of the mouth, throat, esophagus, bladder, kidney, and pancreas decreases.

- **15 years after quitting:** Your risk of coronary heart disease is back to that of a non-smoker's.

Stick with It

Beating an addiction to nicotine takes a lot of will power and determination. You should feel great about yourself for making it so far. Now's the time to focus on sticking with it.

At first, you may not be able to do things as well as when you were smoking. Don't worry. This won't last long. Your mind and body just need to get used to being without nicotine.

After you've quit, the urge to smoke often hits at the same times. For many people, the hardest place to resist the urge is at home. And many urges hit when someone else is smoking nearby. Try to identify when you might be tempted. Then use the skills you've learned to get through your urges without smoking.

Stay Upbeat

As you go through the first days and weeks without smoking, keep a positive outlook. Don't blame or punish yourself if you do have a cigarette. Don't think of smoking as "all or none." Instead, take it one day at a time. Remember that quitting is a learning process.

If You Do Slip Up

Don't be discouraged if you slip up and smoke one or two cigarettes. It's not a lost cause. One cigarette is better than an entire pack. But that doesn't mean you can safely smoke every now and then...no matter how long ago you quit. One cigarette may seem harmless, but it can quickly lead back to one or two packs a day.

Many ex-smokers had to try stopping many times before they finally succeeded. When people slip up, it's usually within the first three months after quitting. Here's what you can do if this happens:

- Understand that you've had a slip. You've had a small setback. This doesn't make you a smoker again.

- Don't be too hard on yourself. One slip up doesn't make you a failure. It doesn't mean you can't quit for good.

- Don't be too easy on yourself either. If you slip up, don't say, "Well, I've blown it. I might as well smoke the rest of this pack." It's important to get back on the nonsmoking track right away. Remember, your goal is no cigarettes—not even one puff.

- Feel good about all the time you went without smoking. Try to learn how to make your coping skills better.

- Find the trigger. Exactly what was it that made you smoke? Be aware of that trigger. Decide now how you will cope with it when it comes up again.

- Learn from your experience. What has helped you the most to keep from smoking? Make sure to do that on your next try.

- Are you using a medicine to help you quit? Don't stop using your medicine after only one or two cigarettes. Stay with it. It will help you get back on track.

- START to stop again!

- See your doctor or another health professional. He or she can help motivate you to quit smoking.

Chapter 52

Coping with Urges to Smoke

What Are Urges?

Urges. Cravings. Desires. These are all words that smokers and ex-smokers use to describe how they feel when they want a cigarette. To some people, each word means something a little bit different. For example, some smokers say that a "craving" is much stronger than an "urge." However, to most people, the words mean pretty much the same thing. In this chapter, we will use all three words to mean the same thing.

Different Types of Urges

There are at least three kinds of cigarette urges that ex-smokers have:

1. Nicotine withdrawal urges

2. Habit urges

3. Memories of smoking

The information in this chapter is reprinted with permission from "Smoking Urges," part of the series, Forever *Free*™ A Guide to Remaining Smoke Free, produced by the Tobacco Research and Intervention Program at the H. Lee Moffitt Cancer Center & Research Institute, University of South Florida, Thomas H. Brandon, Ph.D., Director. © 2000 H. Lee Moffitt Cancer Center & Research Institute. For additional information, visit http://www.moffitt.usf.edu/trip/booklets.htm.

Nicotine Withdrawal Urges

Over your years of smoking, your body adjusted to the nicotine. Many of your organs made changes to get used to the effects of nicotine. These include your brain and your heart. These changes let you smoke without feeling all the effects of nicotine that you felt when you first started smoking. For example, after years of smoking you probably did not feel lightheaded after a cigarette. Your pulse no longer raced as fast.

But, when you quit smoking your body adjusted again. This time it had to adjust to not getting nicotine. Your brain, heart, and other organs now had to get used to you not smoking. This change can be unpleasant and is called nicotine withdrawal. The symptoms of nicotine withdrawal include:

- lightheadedness
- headache
- sleep problems
- nausea (sick to your stomach)
- decreased heart rate
- depression (feeling sad)
- craving for cigarettes
- irritability
- increased appetite
- anxiety (feeling tense)
- difficulty thinking
- constipation

Most people do not have all of these symptoms, but they do have some. Nicotine withdrawal begins about 20 minutes after your last cigarette. If you do not smoke, it lasts between one and two weeks. There are three ways to stop these unpleasant symptoms:

1. Wait for it to end on its own after one or two weeks.

2. Use nicotine replacement products such as nicotine gum or patch, or use Zyban™.

3. Smoke a cigarette.

The first two ways are, of course, how someone quits smoking. But it is very tempting to get relief the third way—by smoking a cigarette. This temptation is the "nicotine withdrawal urge." Smokers get this urge when the nicotine from their last cigarette clears their brain— about 20 minutes after smoking.

Why do most smokers say that their strongest craving for a cigarette is first thing in the morning?

It is because their body has been without nicotine for eight hours while they were sleeping.

How long do ex-smokers have nicotine withdrawal urges?

As long as nicotine withdrawal lasts. This is about one to two weeks after quitting smoking. Often a smoker tries to quit but does not completely quit smoking. He or she may have one or two cigarettes per day to deal with urges. This "cheating" just makes nicotine withdrawal longer. The "quick fix" actually causes more problems.

What does a nicotine withdrawal urge feel like?

If you are an ex-smoker, you may remember the feeling very well from your first week of quitting. Urges are hard to describe, but many ex-smokers say that this type of urge feels physical. This makes sense, since it occurs in response to physical changes in your body.

One ex-smoker told us that these urges felt like "a stone was in my chest." This is a good way to describe the feeling.

Habit Urges

Many ex-smokers have quit for long enough that they no longer have nicotine withdrawal urges.

Habit urges, on the other hand, may keep being a problem for them. Habit urges occur when an ex-smoker is in a situation that had been tied to smoking for that person. Here are some examples of habit urges:

- *Mary always smoked while talking on the telephone. Whenever the phone rang, she would reach for her pack and light a cigarette. Now she has quit smoking for three weeks. But whenever she hears that ring of the telephone she still wants to smoke.*

- *Scott was a bowler. Bowling and smoking used to go together like ham and eggs for him. While he was trying to quit smoking,*

Scott wisely avoided the bowling alley for three weeks. Now that he feels that he has cigarettes kicked, he has started bowling again. To his surprise, the first night of bowling caused cravings for cigarettes. And seeing all of his buddies smoking only seemed to make it worse.

- *Jestene and her sister started smoking together as teens. Although they now live 500 miles apart, whenever they get back together they tend to smoke cigarettes while catching up with one another. Jestene has grown to value the special times that she has with her sister once or twice a year. There is a strong sister bond between them at these times. Since their last visit, Jestene has quit smoking. She has not smoked for five months now, and she has had very little desire to smoke. However, when she and her sister sat down at the kitchen table and began to talk about their kids, Jestene's sister pulled out her pack and offered Jestene a cigarette. Jestene had a strong urge to smoke. Smoking seemed like the thing to do.*

- *Peter had been smoke-free for nearly a year, and he was proud of it. Last week, while driving his daughter to soccer practice, he was rear-ended by a drunk driver. He was not hurt, but his daughter broke both her legs. One person at the scene of the accident was smoking, and Peter felt that he too needed a cigarette to deal with the stress.*

These four stories were told to us by former smokers. In each case, something from the past set off the urge to smoke. For Mary, it was the telephone. For Scott it was bowling. For Jestene it was her sister. And for Peter it was stress. The things that set off these urges are called "triggers." The triggers can be people, places, things, and even moods. Here is a list of some common triggers for habit urges:

- talking on the phone
- driving a car
- seeing cigarettes or someone smoking
- being with an old smoking buddy
- having a fight with family
- feeling bored
- celebrating
- finishing a job

- eating

- drinking coffee

- feeling angry, sad or nervous

- feeling stressed

- feeling lonely

- trying to solve a problem

- drinking alcohol

As you can see, a lot of different things can cause habit urges. The good news is that you will not have habit urges forever. The longer you go without smoking, the fewer urges you will have. If you have a strong urge months after quitting, it may be because you are in a situation that you had not been in since quitting. After you get through that situation without smoking the urges will get easier, until they go away. This process is clear from the following story told by one of our clients:

Bill had his last cigarette over two months ago. He and his family were planning on eating out at Bill's favorite diner. The diner used to be a hang-out for Bill and his buddies. The diner just went "no smoking," and it was Bill's first time there since he had quit smoking. During the hour-long dinner, Bill had a strong craving for cigarettes. He told himself that he did not want to start smoking again. He made it through the meal without having a cigarette. It seemed like the longest hour of his life. However, on his next visit to the diner, Bill was very surprised to find that he was not bothered by smoking urges at all.

In Bill's case, being at his favorite diner was a trigger for him. The first time he visited there since quitting, he had strong urges. But because he did not give in to the urges, the next time he ate there he did not have any problem with urges. In most cases urges do not completely go away after only one time with a trigger situation. But after many times, the urges will go away.

The other type of trigger that can cause strong urges long after quitting is stress. Most smokers deal with stress by having a cigarette. So, after you quit smoking, it is common to want a cigarette when you're feeling stressed.

Pat had not smoked in eight months, and she rarely had any desire to smoke. However, today at work her supervisor told her that the company would be laying off 50% of its workers. Half the people in Pat's department would be getting pink slips next week. The supervisor did not know who would stay and who would be let go. Jobs were hard to find, and Pat was very concerned about losing her job. The first day after hearing the news, she had strong urges to smoke. She found herself thinking, "Who cares if I start smoking again? That's nothing like not having a job!" But, she did not smoke, and by the third day the urges were gone, even though she was still stressed.

Pat did get laid off. But even then, she did not start smoking again. Pat's story also shows how, in times of stress, people often feel that staying off cigarettes is not as important as the current problem. When a loved-one dies you might feel that you need a cigarette to cope, and you do not really care if you start smoking again. However, those people who start smoking because of stress may regret it once the stressful event passes.

Joe had been a fire fighter for 23 years. One day he had an accident on the job, and he was paralyzed below the waist. He could not keep doing his work, and he depended on others for nearly everything. He no longer cared if he got cancer or heart disease, and he started smoking again. Six months later, once the shock of his accident slowly faded, he was sorry he started smoking. "It was bad enough being a man in a wheelchair," he said, "but now I am a smoker in a wheelchair. That's two strikes against me. Besides, now I want to live!" He signed up for quit smoking classes and was able to quit again.

It is important to note that good moods can also trigger habit urges. You may have smoked cigarettes when you were feeling good or when something good happened. When this happens after you quit, you may have urges to smoke. We know people who started smoking again when they were having a good time, like at a wedding.

Remember, habit urges occur when you are in a situation that is tied to smoking for you. The urges will get easier if you get through the situation without smoking.

Memories of Smoking

You probably smoked for many, many years. You lived much of your life as a smoker. If you smoked a pack per day, you took about 70,000 puffs on cigarettes each year. There are few things that you have done as many times, besides breathing. Therefore, you will have memories of smoking. You may see someone smoking and recall that you used to do that. Other things may trigger memories of when you were a smoker—an old song, a certain food, old friends, etc. Each ex-smoker has memories about smoking. Sometimes they come on fast. Sometimes there is an urge when a smoking memory occurs. But the urge is so mild, that the smoker can deal with it. People who quit smoking many years ago sometimes say that they still have urges to smoke. They are mostly talking about memories they have from when they were smokers.

How to Deal with Urges to Smoke

There are three keys ways to deal with smoking urges without smoking. They are:

1. Think ahead

2. Prepare for the urge

3. Cope with the urge

Think Ahead

Most recent ex-smokers know the types of situations that are hard for Them. These are the kinds of situations previously listed. If you can plan ahead for these, you will be able to prepare for them. For example, before going to a wedding, you can tell yourself that the reception may cause urges to smoke. Or, if you have a stressful event coming up—a day in court, perhaps—you can tell yourself that you may crave a cigarette. If you used to smoke at baseball games, and the first game since you quit smoking is next week, you can think ahead that you might want to smoke.

Prepare for the Urge

Thinking ahead is only part of the solution. You also need to prepare for it. Think about what you will do if you do indeed have urges when the situation arrives. Will you be able to leave the situation? Can you have some candy to eat, or a carrot stick to chew until the urge passes? What can you tell yourself in the situation that will help you get through it? If you think of these things ahead of time, you will be more likely to use them when the time comes.

Cope with the Urge

This is the real key. Coping skills are the things that you do or tell yourself in order to get your mind off cigarettes. Research shows that people who use coping skills are much more likely to stay quit than people who do not. People who rely upon "willpower" tend to start smoking again. There are two types of coping skills that you can use: behavioral and mental.

Behavioral coping skills are things that you can do, actions that you take. Here is a list:

- Leave the situation.
- Call or talk to a friend who will listen.
- Exercise.
- Take deep breaths.
- Have a drink of water.
- Eat or chew on something (gum, candy, vegetables).
- Do a relaxation exercise.
- Keep your hands busy—play cards, sew, write.
- Take a shower.
- Do something with a nonsmoker.
- Do something else, like read, write, or listen to music.

Mental coping skills are things that you can tell yourself. Here is a list:

- Remind yourself of the reasons you wanted to quit.
- Think of how long you have been cigarette free. You do not want to start over again.
- Think of how you got through this situation in the past without smoking.
- Try to figure out what is making you want a cigarette now.
- Tell yourself that smoking will not solve any problem. It will only create new ones.
- Surf the urge. Imagine the urge is a wave that builds up, then breaks. Imagine you are a surfer riding the urge wave, rather than being "wiped out" by it.

- Think of how your health is improving because you quit smoking.

- Tell yourself that smoking is not an option.

That last mental coping skill is the all-time favorite of our smoking clients. They say that telling themselves, "Smoking is not an option," is simple and works well for them. Anything else may be an option, but not smoking.

You may like some of these coping skills better than others. That's ok. It really does not matter much which skills you use, as long as you do something when you have an urge to smoke. Some research shows that it is best to use both behavioral and mental coping skills when you have an urge.

There is one thing you want to avoid doing when you have an urge. You do not want to beat yourself up. Ex-smokers who tell themselves "I am so weak," or "I was so stupid to ever smoke," tend to start smoking again. Your coping skills should be positive, not negative.

When Will the Urges End?

Nicotine withdrawal urges usually last only one or two weeks if you don't smoke. Habit urges slowly go away as you have different situations without smoking. However, new situations or a lot of stress can still trigger urges. Most people who have quit for a year or more rarely have habit urges. You may always have memories of smoking. Some of these will be pleasant memories, but most ex-smokers do not feel strong urges to smoke while having these memories.

Chapter 53

Smoking Abstinence: Facing Common Challenges

Facing the Morning

What to Expect: When you wake up, begin thinking of your alternatives to smoking and the changes in your routine immediately. Expect that your morning coffee will not taste the same without a cigarette.

Begin each day with a preplanned activity that will keep you busy for an hour or more. If reducing, this will push that first cigarette to later in the day and if quitting cold-turkey, it will keep your mind and body busy so that you don't think about smoking for a while.

- Plan a different waking up routine.

- Be sure no cigarettes are available.

- Begin each day with deep breathing and one or more glasses of water.

This chapter includes text excerpted from "Facing the Morning," "Drinking Coffee or Tea," "Enjoying Meals," "Remembering the Good Times," "Facing Boredom," "Relaxing," "Handling Stress," "Irritability, Anger and Frustration," "Anxiety," "Depression," "Restlessness," "Talking on the Telephone," "Traveling by Car," "Watching TV," "Insomnia," "Difficulty Concentrating," "Rewarding Yourself," "Having a Drink," "Being around Smokers," reprinted with permission from the website of the Arizona Smoker's Helpline, www.ashline.org, funded by the Arizona Department of Health Services Tobacco Education and Prevention Program (TEPP), and hosted and maintained by the TEPP Internet Office, Mel and Enid Zuckerman Arizona College of Public Health. © 2004 State of Arizona. All rights reserved.

- Make a list of early morning triggers—and avoid them.

Nicotine and Your Body and Mind: After six to eight hours of sleep, your nicotine level drops and the body develops a need for a quick boost of nicotine when you wake up. Your mind must be ready to overcome this physical need. Before you go to sleep, make a list of things you need to avoid in the morning that will make you want to smoke.

Drinking Coffee or Tea

What to Expect: You do not have to give up coffee or tea to quit smoking. Expect to feel a strong urge to reach for a cigarette while drinking coffee or tea. You will have to note which coffee/tea drink gives you an urge, and you will have to find an alternative to keep you from reaching for a cigarette.

If you used to smoke while drinking coffee or tea, tell people you have quit, so they won't offer you a cigarette. Between sips of coffee or tea, take deep breaths to inhale the aroma. Breathe deeply and slowly, while you count to five, breathe out slowly, counting to five again.

- Try switching to decaffeinated coffee for a while.

- Nibble on toast, crackers, or other low calorie foods. Dip fat-free cookies in your coffee/tea to keep your hands busy.

- As you drink your coffee, get out a scratch pad, doodle, or make plans for the day.

- If the urge to smoke is very strong, drink your coffee or tea faster than usual and then change activities or rooms.

Nicotine and Your Body and Mind: Many studies have reported the euphoric, stimulating, and anti-anxiety effects of smoking may actually make you feel happier, more alert, etc. These feelings may reinforce tobacco use and you may have also associated these feelings with drinking coffee or tea. Drinking coffee or tea may spark all the positive feelings that you have associated with this activity in the past. When you quit, you may feel saddened at the loss of these feelings and drinking coffee or tea without smoking may make you feel even more saddened. Be prepared and think about the long term benefits of life as a nonsmoker.

Enjoying Meals

What to Expect: Expect to want to smoke after meals or with others at a restaurant. Expect the urge to smoke when you smell cigarette smoke at a restaurant. Smoking urges may be stronger at different meal times, sometimes breakfast, sometimes lunch, or sometimes dinner. Your smoking urges may be stronger with certain foods like spicy or sweet meals or snacks. Your desire to smoke after meals may depend on whether you are alone, with other smokers, or with nonsmokers.

- Know what kinds of foods increase your urge and stay away from them.

- If you are alone, call a friend as soon as you've finished eating.

- Brush your teeth or use mouthwash right after meals.

- If someone is at your home, have someone massage your shoulders.

- If you have coffee or a fruit drink, concentrate on the taste.

- Wash the dishes by hand after eating—you can't smoke with wet hands!

- Go for a brief walk after meals.

Nicotine and Your Body and Mind: Nicotine stops hunger pains in your stomach for as long as one hour and it also makes the blood sugar level go up. When you quit, this is reversed. Food may be used to get the same effect as cigarettes: stimulation, relaxation, pampering, time out, comfort, socialization etc. Smoking and eating are both ways to meet these needs, so when you quit smoking, you may eat more. Withdrawal from nicotine enhances the taste of sweeter foods— some foods may actually taste better—and you may want to eat more of them.

Memories May Trigger Desire to Smoke

What to Expect: A large number of ex-smokers feel like smoking when they think back to happy times that included cigarettes, such as a cup of coffee, sitting with friends, quiet times, driving, etc. These feelings will be strongest in the first two weeks after quitting. Figure out which memories make you want to smoke most and learn to manage them.

- Take up some new activities such as walking, reading, a hobby, playing a sport or attending community events.

- Repeat the following: "If I'd known then what I know now, I never would have started smoking."

- Focus on the thought that you will be able to enjoy your good memories longer, now that you've quit smoking.

Nicotine and Your Body and Mind: Something as simple as a smell, a sound, a color, or a voice can make you think of a cigarette. You may feel that you have lost a major source of happiness, but as an ex-smoker you will gain so much more.

Facing Boredom

What to Expect: About 41% of smokers say they sometimes smoke to overcome boredom. You will "take a break" from working and find that you now have nothing to do. You may feel very bored when waiting for something or someone (for example, a bus, your spouse, your kids).

- Plan more activities than you have time.
- For those empty minutes, make a list of things you like to do.
- Move! Do not stay in the same place too long.
- Carry a book or magazine for waiting times.
- Look at what is going on around you (for example, notice the shape of the buildings you pass, listen to the sounds of the city/outdoors)
- Carry something to keep your hands busy, like a Rubik's cube.
- Hum a tune or favorite song—maybe even listen to a portable radio.
- Go outdoors, if you can.

Nicotine and Your Body and Mind: For smokers, boredom often brings the urge to smoke—this urge may have a physical and chemical basis. Nicotine controls the way you feel by controlling the level of excitement in key parts of your brain and central nervous system. When you quit smoking, you may miss the increased excitement and good feeling that nicotine gave you. This may be true when you are feeling bored.

If You Feel Like You Need a Cigarette to Relax

What to Expect: Recent studies have found that 60–90% of quitters report feelings of increased (higher) anxiety within one week of quitting. If you feel anxious, it will usually begin within the first 24 hours after quitting, peak in the first 1–2 weeks, and disappear within a month.

- Repeat this to yourself: "I can learn to relax without having a cigarette."

- Engage in activities that use your hands, like sewing, carving, working puzzles, playing cards, etc.

- Make an extra effort to share your leisure time with a friend, a child, or even a pet.

- If the urge to smoke gets too strong, stop relaxing and start doing something physical until the urge passes.

- Deep breathing is a good way to deal with tension almost anywhere and at any time.

Nicotine and Your Body and Mind: When nicotine enters your brain, it acts just like some of the natural chemicals that control arousal, alertness, and mood. So, when you smoke, these chemical changes can make you feel happy, less anxious, and more relaxed. When you quit smoking, your brain activity slowly returns to normal. The natural chemicals in your body will still regulate arousal, alertness, and mood, but you may miss the instant kick that cigarettes provided.

Handling Stress

What to Expect: Almost 63% of smokers report smoking to handle stress. You may become more aware of stress during withdrawal. This may be largely because using cigarettes actually relieved some of this normal stress by releasing powerful chemicals in your brain. Nonsmokers have found many ways to break the stress cycle without lighting a cigarette.

- Know the cause of stress in your life (for example, your job, your children, money).

- Identify the stress signals (for example, headaches, nervousness, insomnia or trouble sleeping).

- Create peaceful times in your everyday schedule.

- Try new relaxation methods. Rehearse and visualize your relaxation plan. Change your plan as needed.

- Seek and learn relaxation techniques such as progressive relaxation.

Nicotine and Your Body and Mind: Mental or physical tensions, strains, or distress caused by worries, responsibilities, and hassles, which you encounter in normal everyday life, can all be a part of stress. Once nicotine enters your brain, it appears to stimulate production of a number of the brain's most powerful chemical messengers. These chemicals (epinephrine, norepinephrine, dopamine, arginine, vasopressin, beta-endorphin, acetylcholine) are involved in: alertness, pain reduction, learning, memory, pleasure, and the reduction of both anxiety and pain. When you smoke, the general effect is a temporary improvement in brain chemistry that you experience as enhanced pleasure, decreased anxiety, and a state of alert relaxation.

Handling Irritability, Anger, and Frustration

What to Expect: When you quit smoking, you may feel more "edgy" and short-tempered. You may want to give up on certain tasks more quickly than usual. You may be less tolerant of others' behavior. You may get into more arguments with others. If feelings of irritability, anger, and frustration occur, they will usually begin within the first 24 hours, peak (stay high) the first 1–2 weeks, and disappear within a month.

- Take a walk or exercise.

- Avoid caffeine.

- Soak in a hot bath.

- Read up on relaxation/meditation techniques and use one.

- Take one minute and, with your eyes closed, pay attention to your breathing pattern. Breathe in deeply through your nose and breathe out through your mouth.

Nicotine and Your Body and Mind: When your body does not get nicotine, feelings of irritability, anger, and frustration will often result. Quitting will temporarily change your brain chemistry. These temporary changes may result in your experiencing negative emotions.

Handling Anxiety

What to Expect: Recent studies have found that 60–90% of quitters report feelings of increased anxiety within one week of quitting.

If anxiety occurs, it will usually begin within the first 24 hours, peak in the first 1–2 weeks and disappear within a month. You may feel quite "tense" and agitated within 24 hours of quitting. You may feel a tightness in your muscles—especially around the neck and shoulders. These feelings will pass with time.

- Take a walk.

- Take a hot bath.

- Try a massage.

- Try to take a few minutes out of your day to meditate, or do stretching exercises.

- Set aside some "quiet time" every morning and evening—a time when you can be alone in a quiet environment.

Nicotine and Your Body and Mind: Anxiety is usually measured as an increase in muscle tension as well as an increased sensitivity to muscle tension. Laboratory research shows that the anxiety produced from quitting tobacco may be due to temporary changes in your brain chemistry. There is some evidence that tobacco use actually improves anxiety so it may be that part of the anxiety felt when you quit is what nonsmokers "normally" experience. Most of the anxiety felt immediately after you quit is due to temporary changes.

Coping with Depression

What to Expect: When you are feeling sad and blue and want to smoke, you know (deep down) that a cigarette is only a temporary answer. Having a cigarette will only make you feel worse in the long run-you may get even more depressed because you could not stick with your decision to quit.

Having a prior history of depression is associated with more severe withdrawal symptoms—including more severe depression. Some studies have found that 17–30% of people with a prior history of major depression will have a new major depressive episode after quitting. The incidence rate of major depression after quitting is low (2%) if you have no prior history of depression. If mild depression occurs, it will usually begin within the first 24 hours, continue in the first 1–2 weeks, and go away within a month.

- Identify your specific feelings at the time that you seem "depressed." Are you actually feeling tired, lonely, bored, or hungry? Focus on and address these specific needs.

- Add up how much money you have saved already by not purchasing cigarettes and imagine (in detail) how you will spend your savings in six months.

- Call a friend and plan to have lunch, go to a movie or to a concert.

- Make a list of things that are upsetting to you and write down solutions for them.

Nicotine and Your Body and Mind: Nicotine is a highly addictive drug. It acts as both a stimulant and a depressant, depending upon your mood and the time of day. It controls your mood by regulating the level of arousal of key parts of the brain and central nervous system.

Coping with Restlessness

What to Expect: Recent studies have found that 55–75% of quitters report increases in restlessness within one week of quitting. If restlessness occurs, it will usually begin within the first 24 hours, remain strong the first 1–2 weeks, and disappear within a month. You may feel unable to sit still for long periods of time. You may feel the need to do something with your hands. These thoughts and feelings will generally pass after a week or two. You may still feel bursts of restlessness for up to a month after quitting.

- Listen to your body. If you feel that you need to move around, you probably need a break…get up and stretch, go for a brief walk.

- Take regular ten minute mental and physical breaks from whatever work you are doing. Be active during those breaks…walk, stretch, run.

- You may want to try squeezing a rubber ball or one of many "stress relief" items to help keep your hands busy.

Nicotine and Your Body and Mind: Restlessness may be due to the lack of nicotine in the body's system. It may also be due to biochemical changes in your brain as well as more conditioned responses to various smoking situations. Now that you have quit smoking, you may not know what to do with yourself in situations that used to be associated with smoking.

Talking on the Telephone

What to Expect: Expect to be nervous because you want something in your hand while on the phone. You may want to smoke during every phone call, only during certain phone calls or only during calls made at specific times of the day. Be prepared; the urges will vary.

- Keep cigarettes, ashtrays, matches, and lighters away from your telephone.

- Pick up a pencil and have a large memo pad for doodling.

- Hold the phone with the hand you used for smoking.

- While you are on the phone, walk around as much as possible.

- Keep some gum by the phone; chew while you talk.

- Note down which calls make you want to smoke. Do specific types of calls or calls made at a certain time affect you more? Is calling a certain person (or certain people) more difficult?

- Each day, make a list of the difficult calls that you have to make and get them out of the way early.

Nicotine and Your Body and Mind: Having a telephone conversation may spark positive feelings that you have associated with smoking in the past. When you quit, you may feel the loss of these feelings and speaking on the phone without smoking may make you feel even more at a loss.

Traveling by Car

What to Expect: Like many smokers, you may like to light up when driving to and from work as a means to: relieve stress, stay alert, relax, or just pass the time. Your desire to smoke may be stronger and more frequent on longer trips. Expect to want to reach for a cigarette when driving a car or traveling as a passenger. Expect to want something to do, so turn your radio on or put on your favorite tape or CD and sing along. On longer trips, you may find yourself getting more sleepy than usual.

- Clean your car and make sure to use deodorizers to hide the tobacco smell.

- Tell yourself: "This urge will go away in a few minutes." "So, I'm not enjoying this car ride. Big Deal! It won't last forever!" "My car smells clean and fresh!" or "I'm a better driver now that I'm not smoking while driving."

- Things to do: Remove the ashtray, lighter, and cigarettes from your car.

- Ask friends not smoke in your car.

- If not driving, find something to do with your hands.

- Take an alternate route to work.

- Try carpooling.

- For a little while, avoid taking long car trips. If you do, take plenty of rest stops.

- Keep non-fattening snacks (such as licorice and gum) in your car.

- Take fresh fruit with you on long trips.

- Plan stops for water, fruit juice, sodas, etc.

Nicotine and Your Body and Mind: You may have become used to smoking while driving—to relax, stay alert, etc. There is some evidence that smoking actually does make you feel more awake and alert. In the past, you may have relied upon this during both short and long rides.

Watching TV

What to Expect: TV programs may provide you with many "triggers" to smoke (such as movies that show smoking, re-runs of old detective shows, etc.) The time of day that you watch TV may also be a smoking "trigger." For example, you may be used to smoking when watching a morning news program or a late night talk show. When smoking in the house, you may be used to smoking whenever you watch TV. You may also be more likely to smoke only while watching specific programs.

- Get rid of cigarettes, ashtrays, and lighters.

- Sit in a different place.

- Practice relaxation—take a minute and, with your eyes closed, pay attention to your breathing pattern. Breathe in deeply through your nose and breathe out through your mouth.

- If you fall asleep—enjoy it.

- Have low fat snacks handy.

- Change the channel when you see smoking.

- Try watching at different times of the day.

Nicotine and Your Body and Mind: When you quit smoking, you may feel deprived of the increased stimulation and positive mood that is brought on by tobacco use. Something as simple as a smell, a sound, a color, or a voice can remind you of cigarettes and of the feelings brought on by smoking—television provides many such "cues." You may have also come to associate both TV and smoking with relaxing.

Insomnia

What to Expect: Sleep disturbances may occur during the first 48 hours of quitting, but, your sleep will improve after the first week and disappear within a month. You may wake up a lot during the night. You may have trouble falling asleep. You may dream about smoking. While sleep may be disturbed, you may actually spend more time sleeping. Withdrawal from nicotine may further disrupt an already disrupted sleep pattern but, in the long run, being smoke-free will help you sleep better.

- Don't drink coffee, tea, or soda with caffeine after 6 P.M.

- Do drink herbal tea, decaffeinated coffee, fruit juices, and water.

- Read up on relaxation/meditation techniques and try one.

- Do not change your sleeping routine: always get up at the same time every morning.

- Prepare for sleep—before bed, allow for 15–30 minutes of "quiet time."

- If you can't sleep, it may help to get up. Make productive use of your time instead of tossing and turning—you will probably sleep better the next night.

Nicotine and Your Body and Mind: Nicotine is a stimulant and may delay sleep onset as well as decrease total sleep time. Nicotine has also been found to both increase and decrease the amount of time you spend dreaming—and thus negatively affect your waking performance.

Difficulty Concentrating

What to Expect: Recent studies have found that 55–75% of quitters report problems with concentration within one week of quitting. If difficulty concentrating occurs, it will usually begin within the first 24 hours, peak (stay high) for the first 1–2 weeks, and disappear within a month. You may feel unable to do one task for a long time. You may put off or avoid difficult or unwanted tasks. Cigarettes provided you with relaxation breaks. Now that you have quit, you still need to take a break. This may be quite difficult because cigarettes gave you a reason to stop working for 10–15 minutes and now you may have to manufacture a new reason.

- Take a break: gaze into a photo, look out a window, close your eyes and relax for ten minutes.

- Try to come up with other things that you can do on a ten minute break—maybe you can get some minor chores out of the way as a "break" from a repeated activity.

- Do different tasks instead of focusing on any one activity for too long.

- If you can, put off work when you feel unable to do it.

- Do important tasks during the times when you feel alert.

Nicotine and Your Body and Mind: Difficulty concentrating is one of the most commonly reported withdrawal symptoms. Results from a number of research studies indicate that quitting may "slow" the activity of a number of different brain chemicals and that this slowness may be reflected in drowsiness and poor concentration.

If You Feel Like Rewarding Yourself with a Cigarette

What to Expect: Finishing a hard job or celebrating a special occasion might lead you into wanting to treat yourself with a cigarette. Find out what it is about certain situations that make you feel that you have earned a cigarette. Be on your guard at these critical times. Feelings of wanting to treat yourself with a cigarette may happen along with regular cravings for cigarettes. Most of these cravings will begin 6–2 hours after you stop, stay strong for 1–3 days, and may last up to 3–4 weeks.

- Spoil yourself for a couple of months (for example, buy a little gift for yourself for every week you don't smoke, go out to dinner once a week or see a movie).

- Think of nonsmoking rewards; take time to read a book, listen to a favorite tape, or telephone a friend.

- Put the money you are saving by not smoking into a jar everyday. Keep a list of things you want to buy with the money and buy them.

- Remind yourself that your real reward will come later...in several extra years of health.

Nicotine and Your Body and Mind: Nicotine controls your mood by controlling the level of stimulation to key parts of the brain and central nervous system. When you quit smoking, you may miss the increased stimulation and positive mood that nicotine provided, but as a nonsmoker you will gain so much more.

Having an Alcoholic Beverage

What to Expect: As a smoker, you may feel a strong urge to smoke when drinking beer, wine, or mixed drinks. Know this up front if you are going to drink.

- Switch to non-alcoholic drinks during the first two weeks of withdrawal, especially fruit juices.

- Stay away from your usual haunts for awhile.

- Change drinks from "your usual."

- For the first few weeks after quitting, drink only with nonsmoking friends.

- Don't drink at home or by yourself.

Nicotine and Your Body and Mind: Studies have shown that if you are a drinker, you will tend to breathe deeper when you drink and smoke—making the negative effects of tobacco even worse. When you are drinking alcohol, your control over your behavior is limited. When you try to quit smoking, it is tough enough to take control of your behavior—drinking alcohol will make it even tougher to cope.

Being around Smokers

What to Expect: Expect some friends especially those who are smokers themselves, to end up trying to sabotage your efforts to cut down or quit. The changes you intend to make may disturb friends

351

and family members who are smokers. Friends may feel that your efforts to control your smoking will put a strain on your friendship. It will be tempting to join others for routine "smoke breaks." You will probably find that you don't always want to smoke when you see someone else doing it. It's something special about the circumstance that triggers you.

- Ask others not to smoke in your presence.

- Provide an outside area where smokers may go if they wish to smoke. Post a small "No Smoking" sign by your front door.

- If you are in a group and others light up, excuse yourself, and don't return until they have finished.

- Do not buy, carry, light, or hold cigarettes for others.

- Cut down with a buddy.

- Try not to get angry when family, friends, or coworkers hassle you for quitting.

Nicotine and Your Body and Mind: You must analyze situations in which watching others smoke triggers an urge in you. Find out what it is about that situation that really makes you want to smoke.

Chapter 54

You Can Control Your Weight as You Quit Smoking

The best action you can take to improve your health is to quit smoking.

Many people gain weight when they quit smoking. Even so, the best action you can take to improve your health is to quit smoking. Focus on stopping smoking first. Then you can continue to improve your health in other ways. These may include reaching and staying at a healthy weight for life.

Will I Gain Weight If I Stop Smoking?

Not everyone gains weight when they stop smoking. Among people who do, the average weight gain is between 6 and 8 pounds. Roughly 10 percent of people who stop smoking gain a large amount of weight—30 pounds or more.

What Causes Weight Gain after Quitting?

When smokers quit, they may gain weight for a number of reasons. These include:

- **Feeling hungry.** Quitting smoking may make a person feel hungrier than usual. This feeling usually goes away after several weeks.

"You Can Control Your Weight as You Quit Smoking," Weight-control Information Network, National Institute of Diabetes, and Digestive, and Kidney Diseases (NIDDK), May 2003.

- **Having more snacks and alcoholic drinks.** Some people eat more high-fat, high-sugar snacks and drink more alcoholic beverages after they quit smoking.

- **Burning calories at normal rate again.** Smoking cigarettes makes the body burn calories faster. After quitting smoking, the body's normal rate of burning calories returns. When calories are burned more slowly again, weight gain may take place.

Can I Avoid Weight Gain?

To help yourself gain only a small amount or no weight when you stop smoking, try to:

- Accept yourself
- Get regular moderate-intensity physical activity
- Limit snacking and alcohol
- Consider using medication to help you quit

Accept Yourself

Do not worry about gaining a few pounds. Instead, feel proud that you are helping your health by quitting smoking. Stopping smoking may make you feel better about yourself in many ways.

Stopping smoking may help you have:

- more energy
- whiter teeth
- fresher breath and fresher smelling clothes and hair
- fewer wrinkles and healthier-looking skin
- a clearer voice.

Get Regular Moderate-Intensity Physical Activity

Regular physical activity may help you avoid large weight gains when you quit smoking. It may help you look and feel good, and fit into your clothes better. You will likely find that you can breathe easier during physical activity after you quit smoking.

Try to get 30 minutes or more of moderate-intensity physical activity on most days of the week, preferably every day. The ideas below may help you to be active every day.

Ideas for being active every day:

- Take a walk after dinner.

- Sign-up for a class such as dance or yoga. Ask a friend to join you.

- Get off the bus one stop early if you are in an area safe for walking.

- Park the car farther away from entrances to stores, movie theatres, or your home.

- Take the stairs instead of the elevator. Make sure the stairs are well lit.

Limit Snacking and Alcohol

Having more high-fat, high-sugar snacks and alcoholic drinks may lead to large weight gains when you quit smoking. The ideas below may help you make healthy eating and drinking choices as you quit smoking.

Healthy eating and drinking choices as you quit smoking:

- Do not go too long without eating. Being very hungry can lead to less healthy food choices.

- Eat enough at meal times to satisfy you.

- Choose healthy snacks, such as fresh fruit or canned fruit packed in juice (not syrup), air-popped popcorn, or fat-free yogurt, when you are hungry between meals.

- Do not deny yourself an occasional "treat." If you crave ice cream, enjoy a small cone.

- Choose an herbal tea, hot cocoa made with nonfat milk, or sparkling water instead of an alcoholic beverage.

Consider Using Medication to Help You Quit

Talk to your health care provider about medications that may help you quit smoking. Some people gain less weight when they use a medication to help them stop smoking.

Medications that may help you quit smoking:

- Nicotine replacement therapy: patch, gum, nasal spray, or inhaler

- Antidepressant medication

The patch and gum are available without a prescription from your health care provider.

Will Weight Gain Hurt My Health?

A small—or even large—weight gain will not hurt your health as much as continuing to smoke will. The health risks of smoking are dramatic.

Health risks of smoking:

- Death—tobacco use is the leading cause of preventable death in the United States. It kills more than 400,000 people in the U.S. each year.

- Cancer—smoking greatly increases the risk for lung cancer, the leading cause of cancer death in the U.S. Smoking is also linked to cancer of the esophagus, larynx, kidney, pancreas, and cervix.

- Other health problems—smoking increases the risk for lung disease and heart disease. In pregnant women, smoking is linked to premature birth and low birth weight babies.

By quitting smoking, you are taking a big step to improve your health. Instead of worrying about weight gain, focus on quitting. Once you are tobacco-free, you can work toward having a healthy weight for life by becoming more physically active and choosing healthier foods.

For More Information

Weight-Control Information Network
1 Win Way
Bethesda, MD 20892-3665
Toll-Free: 877-946-4627
Phone: 202-828-1025
Fax: 202-828-1028
E-mail: win@info.niddk.nih.gov

The Weight-control Information Network (WIN) is a national service of the National Institute of Diabetes and Digestive and Kidney Diseases of the National Institutes of Health, which is the Federal Government's lead agency responsible for biomedical research on nutrition and obesity. Authorized by Congress (Public Law 103-43), WIN provides the general public, health professionals, the media, and Congress with up-to-date, science-based health information on weight control, obesity, physical activity, and related nutritional issues.

WIN answers inquiries, develops and distributes publications, and works closely with professional and patient organizations and government agencies to coordinate resources about weight control and related issues.

Publications produced by WIN are reviewed by both NIDDK scientists and outside experts. This chapter was also reviewed by Robert Eckel, M.D., Professor of Medicine, Physiology, and Biophysics, University of Colorado Health Sciences Center.

Chapter 55

Smoking, Stress, and Mood

What Causes Stress?

Stress is what we have when life gives us challenges. There are many ways that we may be challenged. Perhaps we have to change the way we live (like when we get a new job or have a baby). Perhaps we have to solve a problem (like finding ways to pay bills). Perhaps we have to get a task done in a short amount of time (like when the boss wants our report first thing in the morning). Perhaps we have to make a hard choice (for example, whether or not to have surgery). When we are challenged we may have stress. These challenges are called stressors.

Stressors come in all shapes and forms. Major events that happen to us are one type of stressor. The list below shows some types of major life events that most people would find stressful.

Some Major Life Events (Stressors)

- Death of a family member
- Jail sentence

The information in this chapter is reprinted with permission from "Smoking, Stress, & Mood," part of the series, Forever *Free*™ A Guide to Remaining Smoke Free, produced by the Tobacco Research and Intervention Program at the H. Lee Moffitt Cancer Center & Research Institute, University of South Florida, Thomas H. Brandon, Ph.D., Director. © 2000 H. Lee Moffitt Cancer Center & Research Institute. For additional information, visit http://www.moffitt.usf.edu/trip/booklets.htm.

- Partner is not faithful
- Bankruptcy
- Fired from job
- Miscarriage or stillbirth
- Divorce
- Unwanted pregnancy
- Serious illness
- Demotion
- Lawsuit

- Poor grades
- Fights with boss
- Move to a new place
- Menopause
- Retirement
- Child leaves home
- Birth of child
- Marriage
- Pregnancy

Note that "good" events, such as marriage, can also be stressful because people need to adjust to something new. But you do not have to have any of these major life events in order to have stress. Life is full of daily hassles that cause stress. Hassles are those things that happen on a regular basis. The list below shows a few examples of these.

Some Daily Hassles

- Minor money problems
- Car trouble
- Rude people
- Fights with partner
- Traffic jams

- Bad weather
- Home repairs
- Arranging childcare
- Housework
- Loud children

What Is Stress?

You probably know the answer to this question. What do you feel like when you are under stress? You may feel overwhelmed. You may feel tense. Perhaps you find that your heart beats faster and you sweat more. You may get an upset stomach or a headache. As you worry about the stressor, you may start to feel anxious or depressed. As the stressor keeps on going, you may want to find some way of getting away from it. Smokers may begin to have an urge for a cigarette.

People differ in how often they deal with stress, and how they react to it. Some people have more stress in their lives than others. Some people also react more to stress than others. And some people are better than others at dealing or coping with stress once it starts.

People who have trouble dealing with stress often have strong emotional reactions to stress. Their mood is easily affected by events in their lives. They may be more likely to feel sad and anxious in response to events. In some people, their moods are so serious that they suffer from depression and anxiety. (Not all depression and anxiety are caused by stressful events, but stress does cause or worsen a large part of such problems.)

How Is Stress Related to Smoking?

People who have a lot of stress tend to have a harder time quitting smoking. This is also true for people who are prone to negative moods, such as sadness and anxiety. We also know that when ex-smokers start smoking again, they often have their first cigarette in response to stress or moods. People who are depressed are twice as likely as others to be smokers. They also have a harder time quitting and staying quit.

Why is this? Think back to when you were a smoker. When you had stress or frustration, what did you do? When you were feeling down or bored, what did you do? When you were nervous, what did you do?

What Leads up to a Cigarette?

What leads ex-smokers to have their first cigarette? We followed a group of ex-smokers after they quit, and then asked them if and when they had a cigarette. Here is what the ex-smokers told us about what events led up to that cigarette.

- Unpleasant Mood: 70%
- Drinking Alcohol: 47%
- Happy Mood: 24%
- Eating: 12%
- Offered Cigarette: 2%

You can see that the most common event leading to smoking was being in a negative mood, such as feeling sad, tense, angry, or bored.

Why Do Smokers Deal with Stress by Smoking?

The answer to this question is not really known. However, we have some good ideas. Nicotine causes the brain to release chemicals, called neurotransmitters. Some of these chemicals, such as beta-endorphin and norepinephrine, can cause a person to feel better, but only for a short time. They can improve your mood for a while. So, smoking can serve as a quick "pick-me-up." Indeed, nicotine is a stimulant, which is why a smoker's pulse gets faster after a cigarette.

Aside from this chemical reason that smoking might seem to help someone who is under stress, there are also other reasons. Smokers often use the act of lighting and smoking a cigarette as a "time out" from thinking about or dealing with stress. Like any activity, smoking can distract a person from his or her troubles. Because smoking is often a social activity, some people find that lighting a cigarette brings to mind feelings of group support. This can comfort people in times of stress. Lastly, an addicted smoker will feel better after smoking because it relieves nicotine withdrawal symptoms.

So, Why Not Smoke when Stressed?

There are many problems with using cigarettes as a way to cope with stress or other unpleasant feelings:

- The relief only lasts a short time. Soon your stress will return and you will need to smoke another cigarette.

- Smoking does not solve your problem; it only hides it. The cause of your problem remains.

- Smoking is not a healthy way to deal with stress. The stress probably will not kill you, but the smoking may.

- Smoking actually causes more stress than it relieves. Studies show that stress levels go down after quitting.

- After you quit smoking, you may have trouble dealing with stress and bad moods. If smoking was your main way of coping with stress, you will need to find new, better ways after you quit.

Better Ways to Deal with Stress and Negative Moods

Most people, of course, are able to deal with stress and negative moods without smoking or using other drugs or alcohol. How do they do it?

Deal with the Problem

One good way to cope with life's challenges is to try to deal directly with the problem facing you. Look at the source of the problem. Think about ways to solve it, and then act.

Tiffany had quit smoking six months earlier. Today, on the way to work, her car ran into a guard rail. There was much damage to her *car's front end. That day, Tiffany felt very stressed and anxious. She was worried that she would not be able to afford to have the car fixed, and that she would have no way to get to work. She thought about having a cigarette, which was how she used to calm herself down. Instead, she decided to try to find solutions to her problems. First, she found a co-worker who would be able to give her a ride to work while her car was being fixed. One problem solved. Next, she called her insurance company and found out that they would cover the repairs, except for a $500 deductible. She didn't have $500 at hand, so she had to figure out how to get it. She decided to borrow some money from her parents, to hold a garage sale that she had been planning for years, and to delay buying some new clothes. This was not an ideal answer, but it did allow her to repair her car and get back to work. She solved the problem without smoking.*

Do Other Activities

There are other things besides smoking that can reduce stress. These include: reading, exercise, relaxation, deep breathing, prayer, meditation, or taking a walk. All of these can take your mind off of a stressful situation. They also can improve your mood.

Larry was one of those smokers who lit a cigarette when his mood was not good. When something the least bit stressful happened, he would reach right away for a cigarette. After he quit, he had urges to smoke when he felt stressed or down. He quickly found out that he needed to come up with something that helped him feel the way he did when he smoked. He came up with the idea of doing deep breathing exercises. The deep breathing was like smoking, and it also let his body relax. When he felt tense, this is what he would do. He would close his mouth, relax his shoulders, and inhale deeply while counting to eight. Then he would hold his breath for four seconds. Next he would exhale slowly while counting to eight. Larry found that if he repeated these steps five times he would feel relief of stress and tension. It worked, at least as well as smoking used to.

Talk to Someone

One of the best ways to deal with stress is to talk to someone. Most of us do this, by talking to friends, family, or co-workers.

Whenever Janice felt stressed, she would phone her best friend, Alice, and they would talk about her problem. Sometimes they were able to come up with good answers to the problem. But, even when they could not solve it, just talking about it helped Janice.

Other people like to join a support group. Often the people in a support group have the same types of problems, and they can help each other out.

When Bob was diagnosed with skin cancer, he felt overwhelmed. This was the worst thing that ever happened to him. He did not know if he was going to live or die. He did not know what the treatment was going to do to him. He was anxious, depressed, and afraid. His doctor suggested that he join a support group for cancer patients. At first he did not like the idea because he was never the kind of person who liked to talk about his problems and fears. Finally, he decided to give it a chance. At first, Bob was pretty quiet during the group meetings. But he felt that he was learning a lot about cancer and cancer treatment by listening to the other members talk. Later he became more active in the group himself. He found that he was not alone with his fears. He also found that he felt better after talking. Bob then began to help new members of the group.

Some people have very strong reactions to stress. They suffer from mood problems that get in the way of their lives. These people may benefit from seeing a health professional such as a psychologist, psychiatrist, or social worker.

Alex seemed to be living under a cloud. He could not remember the last time he was happy. The best he ever felt was neutral. Any kind of problem or stress seemed to make him feel sad or depressed. He had felt this way for quite some time, but it may have gotten worse since he quit smoking last year. He was having a hard time getting out of bed in the morning. There seemed to be nothing that he liked any more. At times he had thoughts about killing himself, but he did not really have the energy for that either. (Besides, he did not think that suicide would be fair to his family.) On the advice of his doctor he entered therapy with a psychologist. This has helped him to look at the causes of his depression. Together they are working on changing the way that Alex looks at the world, which should help relieve his depression.

Besides therapy, a doctor may prescribe medication as part of treatment for depression, anxiety, or other psychological problems.

Accept Temporary Stress

A certain amount of stress is a part of life. Success at quitting smoking may mean simply getting used to what stress feels like without smoking. You will learn that the feeling of stress will pass on its own even if you do not have a cigarette. Because smokers often have a cigarette when they feel stressed, they may forget that these feelings will get better on their own.

Look at Your Life

The methods just listed should help you deal with stress in your life. But another way is to change your lifestyle to reduce the number of stressors. Is your life more stressful than it has to be? Clearly, there are some stressors that people may have little control over. However, many types of stressors result from choices that we make about our lives. Ask yourself if there are ways to reduce the stress in your life. Ask yourself if there are ways to get more good things from life. Here is just one example from one of our clients:

> *After Steve quit smoking, he figured that it was a good time to take a look at the rest of his life. He was so proud of himself for quitting that he now felt that he could make other decisions that might improve his life. The main conclusion that he reached was that he was not spending the time with his family that he would like. He felt that he was missing much of his children's childhood years. Steve realized that he had become a "workaholic" in his effort to succeed. His job required long, stressful hours. During the little time he spent at home he was too tired to have fun with his family. But he decided to change. He looked for other jobs that would need less hours. After a couple of months he found a job that needed only 40 hours per week. He quit his current job to take the new one. This let him spend time after work and on weekends with his family. Steve found that he was much happier than before, and felt a lot less stressed.*

Of course, there are a lot of other ways to reduce stress in your life.

Chapter 56

Relapse: What If You Have a Cigarette?

Can't I Have Just One Cigarette?

The answer to this question is "No!" Sometimes ex-smokers try to tell themselves that they will be able to smoke only one cigarette without a problem. There are times when it can be very tempting to think of smoking "just one." For example: when you are under a lot of stress, when you are having a strong urge, when you are with smokers, or when you are in any high-risk situation.

The vast majority of ex-smokers can not have "just one." Research shows that if you have even one cigarette after quitting, there is a 90% chance that you will return to regular smoking. That's right—for every ten ex-smokers who have a cigarette after quitting, nine end up returning to regular smoking. It does not happen right away, but one cigarette can lead to another, and another. You may have heard that a recovering alcoholic should never drink alcohol. It is even more important for ex-smokers to avoid smoking than it is for alcoholics to avoid drinking alcohol. This is because nicotine is much more addicting than alcohol. Therefore, you must do everything you can to avoid having that first cigarette.

The information in this chapter is reprinted with permission from "What If You Have A Cigarette?" part of the series, Forever *Free*™ A Guide to Remaining Smoke Free, produced by the Tobacco Research and Intervention Program at the H. Lee Moffitt Cancer Center & Research Institute, University of South Florida, Thomas H. Brandon, Ph.D., Director. © 2000 H. Lee Moffitt Cancer Center & Research Institute. For additional information, visit http://www.moffitt.usf.edu/trip/booklets.htm.

Be Prepared for a Slip

Remember, if you do smoke the odds are against you. We added this part in order to give you a fighting chance against those odds. Some people are afraid to plan for a slip because they fear that they can then have a cigarette. Also, some smoking cessation programs never teach their clients what to do if they slip. They fear that talking about it will make it more likely to happen. We believe that it would be a mistake for us not to talk about slips.

Most people who try to quit smoking end up having a cigarette. As stated above, most of these people then return to regular smoking. We are not ready to write people off as failures if they have a cigarette after quitting. We think that it makes more sense to be prepared, just in case you have a cigarette.

Being prepared for a slip is **not** the same as telling yourself it is okay to smoke. It is important to think about what you should do in case you slip. You need to have your coping skills ready to help you put down that cigarette. You also need your coping skills to prevent you from lighting another one.

For example, compare preparing for a slip to preparing for a fire. If you have children, you may have taken the time to talk to them about what to do in case of fire. They should know ways to get out. They should roll on the ground if their clothes catch on fire. And so on. They should also know that a fire is very serious. Just because they know how to respond to a fire does not mean that it's okay for them to play with matches. They still need to prevent fires at all costs. The same is true for smoking. Having a cigarette after you have quit is like "playing with fire." Avoid smoking at all costs, but know what to do just in case you do have a cigarette.

Watch Out for the Effects of a Slip

Arlene quit smoking nearly three years ago. She was feeling very good about being a nonsmoker. She had been able to deal with the urges she felt soon after quitting. One evening when Arlene was dining out, she took her friend's offer of an after-dinner cigarette. She thought to herself, "What could it hurt. I know I have kicked my habit!" The next day Arlene felt very guilty. She figured that she had blown all her work to quit smoking. "What's the use? I'm a failure," she told herself. She felt that she may as well pick up a pack of cigarettes on her way home from work as a way to cheer herself up.

Arlene's story shows two things that tend to happen when people have a cigarette after quitting. First, they think that all is lost and that there is no point in trying any longer. This is like a dieter who has that first piece of pie and thinks, "I have blown my diet, so I may as well finish the whole pie." Thinking like that only gets you into deeper trouble. A whole pie is much worse than one slice, and a pack of cigarettes is much worse than one cigarette.

The second thing that happens after a cigarette is that smokers tend to feel guilty and bad. They tend to "beat themselves up." This makes them feel worse. And remember that one of the big risk factors for relapse is negative mood. Then, they get an even greater urge to smoke, which often leads to smoking again.

The common reaction to having a cigarette is to say "I blew it," and then give up and blame oneself. Because Arlene felt that all was lost, and that she was a failure, she then went on to smoke more. Within a few weeks she was back to smoking a pack per day. This is a very common response to having a slip. If you cannot avoid the slip, the next best thing is to know when it happens. Then, instead of going back to smoking, you can take action to get back on track.

The "I Blew It" Reaction

- Feeling that all is lost.
- Feeling guilty.
- Letting these feelings lead to more smoking.

Keep a Slip from Turning into a Full Relapse

Michael stopped smoking about six weeks ago. His physical withdrawal symptoms were gone, but he still felt a strong craving for cigarettes when he was out with friends. Michael decided to buy a pack one night when he was at a bar with some friends who smoked. The next day, he felt bad about his slip. Michael decided that he was not going to let it get him too down. He threw away the cigarettes he bought the night before. He thought to himself, "The cigarettes I smoked last night are the last ones I am going to smoke. I have made it this far, I'm not going to give up now!" He felt relieved right away that he had renewed his commitment to staying quit. Next time he went to a bar with friends, he was aware that he might be tempted to smoke. He prepared for it by bringing mints to chew on. He also told himself that if his smoking urges were too strong, he would leave.

369

Michael's story shows how a smoker can stop a slip from turning into a full relapse. Michael found that he was able to throw the cigarettes away to decrease his slip. He also used a mental coping strategy by telling himself that he was not going to smoke anymore. And instead of seeing himself as a failure, Michael learned to prepare for the next time.

You too will be a lot better off if you see your slip as a way to learn about yourself. Beating yourself up for slipping does not help.

Sometimes the danger of the first slip sneaks up on you.

Victor broke down and had a cigarette a couple of months after quitting. To his surprise, the cigarette didn't taste very good to him at all. He put it out and felt sure that he would not ever have another. But, two weeks later he was tempted again. He told himself, "I was able to control it last time without getting hooked. I'll be able to control it again." So he had one. This happened four or five times over the next month before Victor realized that he liked the cigarettes and the urges were coming more often.

This shows that a slip can be harmful even if you think you have handled it at the time. Each cigarette makes it easier to have just one more.

It Is Important to Commit to Quitting Again Right Away

Linda had her first slip on Thanksgiving, about a month after she had quit smoking. She had just totaled her car, and she bummed a cigarette from the tow-truck driver. She later felt guilty and believed she had failed. She also knew that she still wanted to be a nonsmoker. She decided that she would try to quit again after Christmas—two months away. She slowly increased her smoking until she was back at her old rate of a pack per day. On New Year's Day she quit smoking once again. But, because she waited so long she had withdrawal symptoms again.

Linda did what many people do after slipping. She put off quitting again. And, as each holiday went by, Linda became less and less like an ex-smoker. The longer she waited before stopping, the harder it became to quit again. That is because the smoking habit—and the nicotine addiction—gets stronger and stronger. It is far easier to quit again after smoking one cigarette than it is after smoking a pack. And it is easier to quit after smoking for one day than it is after smoking for one week or one month.

You should also try to learn from your slip. What do you think led up to your urge for the first cigarette? In other words, what was the high risk situation? How might you cope better with such an urge in the future? What coping skills should you use next time you have a strong urge to smoke?

Summary

The odds are stacked against you if you have a cigarette after quitting. So do what you can to avoid smoking. However, if you do have a cigarette:

1. Put it out and get rid of any cigarettes.

2. Think of that cigarette as a "slip," and not a "relapse." It does not have to mean that all is lost.

3. Even though you may be upset with yourself, do not "beat yourself up."

4. Use behavioral and mental coping strategies right away. Renew your commitment to quitting, leave the situation, call a friend.

5. Make that cigarette your last. Do not put off quitting again until tomorrow, next week, or next year. The sooner you commit yourself to quitting again, the easier it will be, because your body will not yet have readjusted itself to nicotine.

6. Learn from your slip. What led up to your smoking? You now know this is a high risk situation that will need better preparation the next time.

Chapter 57

Lifestyle Balance and Positive Addictions

Stress

Most people tend to remember the major events that occur in their lives. But the daily hassles, the little events of daily life, are often more important causes of stress. On a day-to-day basis your mental and physical health are affected by the minor problems of life. These problems include money concerns, problems with family and friends, hassles at work, and not enough time for rest and sleep, to name a few. Although these hassles seem minor, they add up each day.

"Shoulds" Versus "Wants"

One way to think about the causes of stress is to think about the "shoulds" in your daily life. Shoulds are the demands that you or other people place upon yourself. These are the things that you feel you should do: pay the bills, walk the dog, fix the car, clean the house, go to work, and so on. People will have different lists of shoulds.

In contrast to the shoulds in your life are the "wants. " These are things that you really want to do. These things give you pleasure. They

---

The information in this chapter is reprinted with permission from "Lifestyle Balance," part of the series, Forever *Free*™ A Guide to Remaining Smoke Free, produced by the Tobacco Research and Intervention Program at the H. Lee Moffitt Cancer Center & Research Institute, University of South Florida, Thomas H. Brandon, Ph.D., Director. © 2000 H. Lee Moffitt Cancer Center & Research Institute. For additional information, visit http://www .moffitt.usf.edu/trip/booklets.htm.

may be activities such as spending time with your children, reading, dancing, watching TV, and so on. Once again, each person will have his or her own list of wants. One person's should (such as walking) may be another person's want.

There is no way to avoid all the daily hassles or all the shoulds in your life. You could not survive. But a healthy lifestyle should be balanced. It is normal to have both shoulds and wants. We call this a balanced lifestyle. It is easy for a lifestyle to get out of balance over time. With life come responsibilities, and these responsibilities tend to increase with age. This is fine, as long as the unpleasant shoulds are balanced with pleasant wants.

However, many—if not most—people find that the shoulds slowly replace the wants in their lives. This may be especially true of smokers. Often, smokers use cigarettes as their want. That is, they begin to reward themselves by smoking rather than by doing other activities they enjoy. Over time, smokers use more cigarettes and do fewer other fun activities. It is easy to see how this happens. The nicotine in cigarettes can provide brief pleasure, energy, or even relaxation. Smoking is a quick and easy way to have a brief want. Of course, it is also a very poor way to get pleasure. It is not healthy and can harm you.

What happens after people quit smoking? If they have been using cigarettes to satisfy most of their wants, then they may not remember how to get pleasure. Instead, their life falls more out of balance. The hassles and shoulds are still there, but the wants are not.

Now would be a good time to get balance in your life.

- Make a list of the daily hassles in your life and then make a list of the shoulds in your life.

- Next, list the wants in your life. These should be the things that you really like to do and that you do on a regular basis.

- Now look over your lists. Your life is in balance if you have a want listed for every hassle and should that you listed. This is only a rough guide, because a big hassle may need more than one want to balance it out. In the same way, a strong want activity may balance out many smaller hassles or shoulds.

Is your lifestyle balanced? Do you have enough wants in your life? If not, go back to your wants list and try to add some things that give you pleasure. Add only those activities that you would be willing to do and can do regularly.

Are you having trouble coming up with wants for your list? If so, do not feel bad. Many people have an easier time listing shoulds than wants. But you are in luck. Table 57.1 is a list of pleasant events. Read this list to get some ideas.

Once you have created a list of wants that balances out your hassles and shoulds, then the trick is to do the wants. Keep these lists handy and try to add wants to your daily life. But do not put so much pressure on yourself that the wants turn into shoulds.

Positive Addictions

Smoking cigarettes was a negative addiction. That is, it was a habit that was bad for you and that you wanted to stop. There are also positive addictions. These are habits that are healthy. They can replace negative addictions, such as smoking, in your life.

Negative addictions often feel good at first, but they have negative effects in the long run. For example, smoking may seem to get rid of stress, but it is unhealthy. It can harm you. Positive addictions may feel bad at first but have positive effects in the long run. For example, at first running can be unpleasant, but with time, running can make you feel good. It is also healthy.

A positive addiction (habit) involves an activity that you choose to do and that you can spend about an hour per day doing. It is easy to do and does not take a lot of mental effort to do well. You feel it has some value (physical, mental, or spiritual) for you. And it is an activity that you can do without criticizing yourself. If you can not accept yourself during this time, the activity will not be addicting. And once again, you do not want to turn a positive addiction into a should in your life.

One way to change your life is to replace negative addictions (such as smoking) with positive addictions (habits). In other words, the goal is to change bad habits to good habits.

What Kind of Activities Can Become Positive Addictions?

- Exercise (but speak to your doctor before greatly increasing your normal exercise level)
- Relaxation
- Meditation
- Prayer
- Hobbies

Table 57.1. Pleasant Events List (continued on next page)

This list was developed by asking a lot of people what they do for fun. Read through this list and decide which activities that could be wants for you. Add those which you are able to do to your previous wants list. Then try to do them.[2]

- Being out in the country
- Talking about sports
- Meeting someone new
- Planning trips or vacations
- Buying things for yourself or someone you care about
- Going to the beach
- Doing art work (painting, sculpture, drawing, movie-making, etc.)
- Rock climbing
- Playing golf
- Decorating a room or house
- Going to a sports event
- Reading (fiction, non-fiction, religious material, magazines, newspapers, etc.)
- Going to lectures or hearing speakers
- Thinking up a song or music
- Boating (canoeing, motor-boating, sailing, etc.)
- Restoring antiques, refinishing furniture, etc.
- Watching TV
- Camping
- Working in politics or for social causes
- Working on machines (cars, bikes, motorcycles, tractors, etc.)
- Playing cards
- Completing a hard task
- Laughing
- Solving a puzzle, crossword, etc.
- Being at weddings, baptisms, confirmations, etc.
- Having lunch with friends
- Playing tennis
- Taking a shower
- Driving long distances
- Woodworking, carpentry
- Writing stories, novels, plays, or poetry
- Being with pets or other animals
- Riding in an airplane
- Hiking
- Going to a party
- Going to religious functions
- Speaking or learning foreign language
- Going to service, civic, or social club meetings
- Going to a business meeting or a convention
- Being in a sporty car
- Cooking
- Acting
- Taking a nap
- Solving a personal problem
- Taking a bath
- Singing
- Playing pool or billiards
- Playing chess or checkers
- Doing craft work (pottery, jewelry, leather, beads, weaving, etc.)
- Putting on makeup, fixing my hair, etc.
- Designing or drafting
- Visiting people who are sick or in trouble

Table 57.1. Pleasant Events List (continued on next page)

- Cheering
- Bowling
- Teaching someone or learning from someone
- Traveling
- Attending a concert, opera, ballet, play, or movie
- Looking at the stars or moon
- Coaching
- Watching wild animals
- Having a good idea
- Gardening
- Wearing new clothes, nice clothes, or clean clothes
- Dancing
- Sitting in the sun
- Riding a motorcycle
- Just sitting and thinking
- Seeing good things happen to my family or friends
- Going to a fair, circus, zoo, or park
- Talking about philosophy or religion
- Planning something
- Listening to the sounds of nature
- Dating, courting, etc.
- Racing in a car, motorcycle, boat, etc.
- Listening to the radio
- Introducing people I think would like each other
- Giving gifts
- Going to school or government meetings, court sessions, etc.
- Watching the sky, clouds, or a storm
- Going on outings (to the park, a picnic, a barbecue, etc.)
- Playing basketball
- Photography
- Giving a speech or lecture
- Gathering natural objects (wild foods or fruit, rocks, driftwood, shells, etc.)
- Working on finances
- Making a major purchase or investment (car, appliance, house, stocks, etc.)
- Helping someone
- Being in the mountains
- Hearing jokes
- Talking about children or grandchildren
- Talking about health
- Eating good meals
- Improving health (having teeth fixed, getting new glasses, changing diet, etc.)
- Going to the city
- Wrestling or boxing
- Hunting
- Playing in a musical group
- Going to a museum or exhibit
- Writing papers, essays, articles, reports, memos, etc.
- Doing a job well
- Fishing
- Loaning something
- Pleasing employers, teachers, etc.
- Going to a gym, health club, sauna bath, etc.
- Learning to do something new
- Praising someone
- Thinking about people I like
- Being with parents
- Horseback riding

Table 57.1. Pleasant Events List (continued on next page)

- Talking on the telephone
- Having daydreams
- Kicking leaves, sand, pebbles, etc.
- Playing lawn sports (badminton, croquet, shuffleboard, horse-shoes, etc.)
- Going to school reunions, alumni meetings, etc.
- Seeing famous people
- Being alone
- Outwitting a superior
- Doing odd jobs around the house
- Being at a family reunion or get together
- Going to a restaurant
- Seeing or smelling a flower or plant.
- Inviting someone out.
- Using cologne, perfume, or after shave
- Talking about old times
- Getting up early in the morning
- Having peace and quiet or spare time
- Doing experiments or other scientific work
- Visiting friends
- Writing in a diary
- Playing football
- Praying or meditating
- Giving or getting massages or back rubs
- Doing yoga
- Being relaxed
- Thinking about other people's problems
- Playing board games (Monopoly, Scrabble, etc.)

- Sleeping well at night
- Doing heavy outdoor work (cutting or chopping wood, clearing land, farm work, etc.)
- Being in a self-help or mutual-help group
- Dreaming at night
- Playing ping-pong
- Brushing my teeth
- Swimming
- Running, jogging, or doing gymnastics, fitness, or field exercises
- Walking barefoot
- Playing Frisbee or catch
- Doing housework or laundry; cleaning things
- Listening to music
- Knitting, crocheting, embroidery, or fancy needlework
- Going to a barber or beauty shop
- Having house guests
- Being with or thinking about a loved person
- Sleeping late
- Going to the library
- Bird watching
- Watching people
- Building or watching a fire
- Selling or trading something
- Finishing a project or task
- Confessing or apologizing
- Fixing things
- Working with others as a team
- Bicycling
- Being with happy people
- Playing party games
- Writing letters, cards, or notes

Table 57.1. Pleasant Events List (continued)

- Asking for help or advice
- Going to banquets, luncheons, potlucks, etc.
- Talking about my hobby or special interest
- Smiling at people
- Playing in sand, a stream, the grass, etc.
- Talking about other people
- Being with my husband, wife, or partner
- Going on field trips, nature walks, etc.
- Expressing my love to someone
- Caring for houseplants
- Having coffee, tea, a coke, etc., with friends
- Taking a walk
- Collecting things
- Playing handball, paddle ball, squash, etc.

- Sewing
- Remembering a departed friend or loved one, visiting the cemetery
- Doing things with children
- Eating snacks
- Staying up late
- Going to auctions, garage sales, etc.
- Thinking about an interesting question
- Doing volunteer work, working on community service projects
- Water skiing, surfing, scuba diving
- Hearing a good sermon
- Entering a competition
- Talking about my job or school
- Traveling with a group
- Seeing old friends

Note: This is list is excerpted from a longer list available online at http://www .smokefree.gov/pubs/FFree7.pdf.

There is not room in this chapter to describe each of these positive addictions in detail. But books can be found at the library and bookstores.

After Jenny quit smoking, she found that she did not seem to be enjoying life as much as she would like. She had slowly replaced most fun activities with smoking. Now that she had quit smoking, her life seemed empty. Jenny made lists of the shoulds and wants in her life. The shoulds included: taking care of her older parents, getting ahead in her job, keeping the house clean, paying her bills, and so on. She had trouble coming up with even one want for her list. After reading the Peasant Events List (see Table 57.1), she was able to think about the things she had liked to do when she was younger: going to the beach, eating out with friends, reading romance novels, and dancing. As she made time for putting these activities back into her life, she became more satisfied with her life. Jenny thought of cigarettes less and less often.

A common concern of people who try to increase the wants or positive addictions in their lives is that they simply do not have time for more activities. Work and chores seem to take up every waking moment.

How Can You Possibly Add Pleasant Events to Your Busy Life?

Almost everybody feels this way at first. The key is to start small, and set time for things you enjoy doing. If you do not set time aside for the wants at first, they tend to be crowded out by the shoulds. Perhaps you could begin by setting aside just one half hour per week for doing something fun. As you get more and more into the habit of doing that activity, you will find that it becomes easier and easier to find the time. Eventually that activity becomes a positive addiction, and you find the time to do it, just as you had found the time for smoking and for the shoulds in your life. Give it a try.

Summary

Most people find that they can reduce their level of stress by making minor changes in their lives. This often involves increasing the amount of pleasant activities (wants) in their lives, or by developing positive addictions. Both ways can help fill the gap that is often felt after quitting smoking.

By quitting smoking, you have improved your health and probably added years to your life. Now is the right time to make changes to increase your joy of living. Good luck.[1]

Sources

1. Many of the ideas in this chapter came from: Marlatt, G. A. (1985). Lifestyle modification. In G. A. Marlatt and J. R. Gordon (Eds.), *Relapse Prevention*. New York: Guilford.

2. MacPhillamy, D. J., and Lewinsohn, P. M. (1982). *Journal of Consulting and Clinical Psychology, 50*, 363–380.

Part Four

Tobacco-Related Research

Chapter 58

Nicotine's Multiple Effects on the Brain's Reward System Drive Addiction

National Institute on Drug Abuse (NIDA) researchers have added another piece to the puzzle of what makes nicotine so addictive. Dr. Daniel McGehee and colleagues at the University of Chicago have shown that along with directly stimulating the brain's reward system, nicotine also stimulates it indirectly by altering the balance of inputs from two types of neurons that help regulate its activity level. This additional stimulation intensifies the pleasure from smoking and makes it last longer.

Scientists have long known that nicotine, like other addictive drugs, attaches to the core neurons of the brain's reward system, where beneficial behaviors (such as drinking water when thirsty) are rewarded and reinforced. Situated in a region of the brain called the ventral tegmental area (VTA), these reward-system neurons, called dopaminergic neurons, trigger release of the neurotransmitter dopamine (DA) in a nearby brain region called the nucleus accumbens (NAc). When nicotine attaches to these neurons they increase their activity, flooding the NAc with dopamine, which produces pleasure and a disposition to repeat the behaviors that led to it. That pleasure and disposition drive the process of addiction.

"Nicotine's Multiple Effects on the Brain's Reward System Drive Addiction," by Patrick Zickler, *NIDA Notes*, Vol. 17, No. 6, National Institute on Drug Abuse (NIDA), March 2003. For more information about understanding addiction, visit www.nida.nih.gov.

Nicotine's Double Effect on Dopamine Release

Exposure to nicotine has direct and indirect effects on dopamine release in the brain's reward center, the nucleus accumbens.

In the new research, Dr. McGehee's team followed up on a clue that nicotine attachment to the DA neurons in the VTA accounts for only part of the drug's pleasure-producing and ultimately addictive effect: Nicotine attachment stimulates the DA neurons for only a few minutes at most, yet dopamine levels in the NAc remain elevated for much longer.

To explain this discrepancy, the researchers studied nicotine's impact on two other types of neurons that affect dopamine levels. These neurons produce neurotransmitters, called glutamate and GABA (γ-aminobutyric acid), that act as fundamental pacemakers throughout the brain. Once released by its producing neuron, glutamate attaches to other neurons, including the DA neurons in the VTA, and stimulates them to speed up their activities. GABA has the opposite effect: It slows neurons down.

The researchers hypothesized that nicotine might act on these pacemaker neurons so as to increase the ratio of glutamate to GABA in the VTA. If the amount of glutamate acting on DA cells were to increase while the amount of GABA remained the same or decreased, the result would favor high levels of dopamine in the NAc. If the glutamate-GABA imbalance were long-lasting, it would explain why dopamine levels in the NAc remain elevated even after nicotine stops directly affecting the dopamine-producing neurons.

To test their hypothesis, Dr. McGehee and his colleagues exposed rat VTA cells to nicotine for 10 minutes—roughly the time it takes a person to smoke a single cigarette. By measuring electrical properties of the brain tissue, they found that nicotine affected both pacemaker neurons. In glutamate-producing cells, the brief nicotine application induced a condition known as long-term potentiation, which promotes high-level activity for an extended time. When they evaluated the effect on GABA-producing cells, the researchers found that after an initial increase in GABA transmission lasting only a few minutes, GABA transmission decreased and did not recover fully for more than an hour after nicotine exposure ended. Overall, the result was what the researchers hypothesized: a sustained increase in the VTA's glutamate-to-GABA ratio.

The combination of effects—increasing dopamine release and decreasing the inhibitory (GABA) response—results in an amplification of the rewarding properties of nicotine.

"A brief application of nicotine can induce a lasting effect on excitatory (glutamate) signals to the brain's reward system," summarizes Dr. McGehee. "This suggests that in humans a relatively short nicotine exposure, even for someone who has never smoked before, can cause long-lasting changes in excitatory neurotransmission. It may be an important early step in the process that results in addiction.

"The combination of effects—increasing dopamine release and decreasing the inhibitory (GABA) response—results in an amplification of the rewarding properties of nicotine," explains Dr. McGehee. "It would be difficult to design a better drug to promote addiction."

"Understanding these mechanisms is an important step in explaining how a brief exposure to nicotine results in the long-term excitation of the brain's reward areas," says Dr. William Corrigall, director of NIDA's Nicotine and Tobacco Addiction Program. "It gives us a clearer picture of how smoking can lead so quickly to dependence and addiction, and it also suggests a possible new avenue of investigation for pharmacological treatment."

Sources

Mansvelder, H.D., and McGehee, D.S. Long-term potentiation of excitatory inputs to brain reward areas by nicotine. *Neuron* 27(2):349–357, 2000.

Mansvelder, H.D.; Keath, J.R.; and McGehee, D.S. Synaptic mechanisms underlie nicotine-induced excitability of brain reward areas. *Neuron* 33(6):905–919, 2002.

Chapter 59

Some Groups Are More Vulnerable Than Others to Becoming Nicotine Dependent

Rates of drug dependence—the percentage of users who experience symptoms that reinforce their drug use and have trouble quitting— are higher for nicotine than for marijuana, cocaine, or alcohol. Rates of dependence also vary among different groups of smokers, according to NIDA-supported research. A new study suggests that differences in sensitivity to nicotine make some smokers more likely than others to develop nicotine dependence. Age, sex, and race all appear to make a difference.

Dr. Denise Kandel and Dr. Kevin Chen of Columbia University in New York City analyzed data collected between 1991 and 1993 as part of the National Household Survey of Drug Abuse, which surveys a representative sample of the U.S. population 12 years and older. In examining data from 22,292 respondents who had smoked cigarettes during the preceding month, Dr. Kandel and her colleagues determined rates of nicotine dependence symptoms based on respondents' reports of tolerance (needing to smoke more to feel the effects), withdrawal symptoms, smoking more than intended, failed efforts to cut down, negative social and job-related consequences, and persistent health problems.

Data from the National Household Survey on Drug Abuse show that the rate of nicotine dependence is higher in people younger than

"Adolescents, Women, and Whites More Vulnerable Than others to Becoming Nicotine Dependent," by Patrick Zickler, *NIDA Notes*, National Institute on Drug Addiction (NIDA), May 2001.

25 than in other age groups and that the dependence develops with less exposure to nicotine.

The researchers found that among persons who smoke one-half pack of cigarettes each day, nicotine dependence rates are higher among females than males (31.6 percent compared with 27.4 percent) and higher among whites (31.3 percent) than among blacks (25 percent) and Hispanics (27.6 percent). Adolescents smoke fewer cigarettes than adults but experience significantly higher rates of dependence than adults at the same level of use. Dependence rates are lowest among adults older than 50. Overall, the researchers say, dependence rates increase sharply as consumption moves up to 10 cigarettes per day. The rates level off with higher consumption, although dependent smokers need to smoke more to feel the physical effects of nicotine.

"Understanding the differences among groups in their vulnerability to developing nicotine dependence will be valuable in developing targeted strategies for prevention," Dr. Kandel says. "The higher rates at which adolescent, women, and white smokers develop symptoms of nicotine dependence given the same quantity smoked daily seem to reflect differences in sensitivity to nicotine. Increased sensitivity may also account for the fact that adolescents develop symptoms of dependence at lower doses of nicotine than adults."

Adolescents appear to be particularly vulnerable to becoming nicotine dependent, especially at low levels of cigarette consumption and when they continue to smoke on a regular daily basis, according to the researchers. Adolescents' nicotine dependence rates were associated with the length of time that they had been daily smokers, in contrast with adults, in whom dependence rates were associated with the amount of tobacco smoked. "Once regular smoking has been established, quantity smoked may become a more important determinant of dependence than duration of daily smoking," Dr. Kandel says. "This possible connection suggests that with adolescents we should focus not only on preventing the uptake of smoking but on shortening smoking careers as soon as possible."

Source

Kandel, D.B., and Chen, K. Extent of smoking and nicotine dependence in the United States: 1991–1993. *Nicotine and Tobacco Research* 2(3):263–274, 2000.

Chapter 60

Genetic Variation May Increase Nicotine Craving and Smoking Relapse

Smokers who want to quit can get help with a variety of treatments, including counseling, nicotine replacement therapy (patches, gum, lozenges, or inhalers), and medications. Some smokers use these treatments and succeed; for many, however, the discomfort of withdrawal and craving for nicotine lead to relapse. Recent National Institute on Drug Abuse (NIDA)-funded research suggests that our genes may partly explain this variable success.

Genetically Determined Enzyme Activity Affects Treatment Response

In a study of 426 smokers in a 10-week smoking cessation program, those with a gene form that decreases activity of an enzyme that metabolizes nicotine reported greater craving and were less likely to achieve abstinence during treatment than were participants with the gene form that increases the enzyme's activity. Supplementing counseling with bupropion helped women with the less active enzyme nearly triple their abstinence rate to 54 percent—roughly equal that of women with the more active enzyme.

The research evaluated the effect of an enzyme, designated CYP2B6, on craving and relapse. This enzyme breaks down nicotine in the brain. Some people's genes produce a more active form of the enzyme, while

"Genetic Variation May Increase Nicotine Craving and Smoking Relapse," by Patrick Zickler, *NIDA Notes*, National Institute on Drug Abuse (NIDA), Vol. 18, No. 2, p. 1, 6, October 2003.

others have a less active form. Dr. Caryn Lerman at the NIDA- and NCI-supported Transdisciplinary Tobacco Use Research Center (TTURC) at the University of Pennsylvania found that among smokers enrolled in a smoking cessation program, those with the genetic variant that decreases activity of CYP2B6 reported greater craving than did those with the more active form of the enzyme. Moreover, those with the less active enzyme were 1.5 times more likely to resume smoking during treatment.

The same enzyme helps break down bupropion, an antidepressant medication that acts on the brain's dopamine system—where nicotine exerts much of its addictive influence—and helps some smokers quit. Dr. Lerman, along with colleagues at Georgetown University in Washington, D.C., the State University of New York at Buffalo, and Brown University in Providence, Rhode Island, also investigated the relationship of CYP2B6 activity with bupropion treatment. They found that bupropion nearly tripled the success rate for women with the less active enzyme.

"These findings provide initial evidence that smokers who have decreased CYP2B6 activity experience greater craving for nicotine than those with the more active form of this enzyme," Dr. Lerman says. "Perhaps of greater interest is the preliminary evidence that, among women, bupropion may overcome the effect this genetic predisposition has on relapse."

Genes, Treatment, and Abstinence

Most people—about 70 percent of the U.S. population—inherit two copies of the "C" variant of the gene that influences CYP2B6 activity. The rest of the population inherits from one or both parents the less common form of the gene—the "T" variant associated with decreased CYP2B6 activity. Among the 426 participants (232 men, 194 women) in the TTURC study, 128 (29.6 percent) had one or two copies of the T form of the gene. All participants received counseling to quit smoking; 229 received bupropion (300 mg/day) and 197 received placebo throughout the 10-week study. The participants provided weekly reports on craving and smoking rates. Abstinence (seven consecutive days without smoking) was verified with blood tests. At the end of treatment, participants who received counseling and bupropion had higher abstinence rates than those who received counseling and placebo. With one exception, participants with the less active enzyme had lower abstinence rates than those with the more active enzyme. Women with the less active enzyme who received bupropion showed the largest treatment effect, with 54 percent achieving abstinence, up from a 19-percent rate among women in the placebo group, notes Dr. Lerman.

This study suggests that properly selected treatment matched to a patient's characteristics can improve a smoker's chance of quitting.

Theories to Explain Outcomes

The higher abstinence rate with bupropion for women with the lower activity enzyme may be due, in part, to reduced susceptibility to low moods that accompany nicotine withdrawal; overall, women reported more negative feelings than did men when asked to rate their mood during withdrawal. "This rate may reflect better management of the negative moods and craving that abstinence can create. But more study is needed to clarify the mechanisms by which bupropion influences smokers' success in quitting," Dr. Lerman says.

Researchers theorize that the association between the less active enzyme and increased craving could be the result of nicotine's remaining longer in the brains of smokers with the less active enzyme. When nicotine lingers in the brains of these smokers, it may change their brain cells more profoundly than those of smokers with the more active enzyme. If so, the changes might produce more severe addiction marked by more intense craving during abstinence and increased risk of relapse.

"This study offers additional evidence of the important role genes play in smoking and treatment," says Dr. Joni Rutter of NIDA's Division of Neuroscience and Behavioral Research. "While illustrating the increased craving and vulnerability to relapse that may be associated with inherited traits, it also suggests that properly selected treatment matched to a patient's characteristics—in this case, bupropion for some women—can improve a smoker's chance of quitting."

Source

Lerman, C., et al. Pharmacogenetic investigation of smoking cessation treatment. *Pharmacogenetics* 12(8):627–634, 2002.

Chapter 61

Researchers Link Adolescent Cigarette Smoking with Anxiety Disorders

Scientists supported by the National Institute of Mental Health (NIMH) and the National Institute on Drug Abuse (NIDA) have documented that chronic cigarette smoking during adolescence may increase the likelihood that these teens will develop a variety of anxiety disorders in early adulthood. These disorders include generalized anxiety disorder, panic disorder, and agoraphobia, the fear of open spaces.

Researchers from Columbia University and the New York State Psychiatric Institute report their findings in the November 8, 2000 edition of the *Journal of the American Medical Association* (*JAMA*).

Scientists have known of strong connections between panic disorder and breathing problems in adults. Given this association, the research team hypothesized that smoking might also relate to risk for panic disorder in children and adolescents through an effect on respiration.

"Numerous studies have shown that smoking causes a number of diseases," says NIDA Director Dr. Alan I. Leshner. "This study is important because it highlights how cigarette smoking may rapidly and negatively affect a teen's emotional health-perhaps even before any of the widely known physical effects such as cancer may occur."

"These new data provide further evidence of commonalities between processes associated with anxiety in children and adults," says

"Researchers Link Adolescent Cigarette Smoking with Anxiety Disorders during Early Adulthood," National Institute of Mental Health (NIMH), National Institutes of Health (NIH) Press Release, November 7, 2000.

Dr. Daniel Pine, Chief of NIMH's Section on Developmental and Affective Neuroscience.

The researchers interviewed 688 youths and their mothers from 1985 to 1986 and from 1991 to 1993. They found that a startling 31 percent of those adolescents who smoked 20 or more cigarettes per day had anxiety disorders during early adulthood. Among those who smoked every day and had an anxiety disorder during adolescence, 42 percent began smoking prior to being diagnosed with an anxiety disorder and only 19 percent were diagnosed with anxiety disorders before they reported daily smoking.

The research team used a community-based sample that has served as the foundation of a longitudinal study that has been ongoing for the last 25 years. They were able to exclude a wide range of other factors that might determine whether or not a smoking adolescent or young adult develops anxiety disorders, including age, gender, childhood temperament, parental smoking, parental education, parental psychopathology, and the presence of alcohol and drug use, anxiety, and depression during adolescence.

The authors of the study were: Jeffrey G. Johnson, Ph.D; Patricia Cohen, Ph.D.; Daniel S. Pine, Ph.D.; Donald F. Klein, M.D.; Stephanie Kasen, Ph.D; and Judith S. Brook, Ed.D. Johnson, Cohen, Klein and Kasen are affiliated with Columbia University and the New York State Psychiatric Institute. Pine is associated with NIMH and Brook is with Mount Sinai School of Medicine.

Chapter 62

Studying the Link between Maternal Smoking and Child Behavior

Maternal Smoking during Pregnancy Associated with Negative Toddler Behavior and Early Smoking Experimentation

National Institute on Drug Abuse (NIDA)-funded researchers have added to the accumulating scientific evidence that women's smoking during pregnancy adversely affects their children's health and development. Two new studies have linked prenatal tobacco exposure to negative behavior in toddlers and smoking experimentation by pre-adolescents. In a study conducted by Dr. Judith Brook, Dr. David Brook, and Dr. Martin Whiteman of the Mount Sinai School of Medicine in New York City, mothers who smoked during pregnancy indicated that their toddlers exhibited more negative behaviors—impulsiveness, risk-taking, and rebelliousness—than mothers who did not smoke during pregnancy reported among their children.

A study conducted by NIDA-funded researchers Dr. Marie Cornelius and Dr. Nancy Day demonstrates that, even more than growing up in a home where the mother smokes, prenatal exposure to smoke may predispose children to early smoking experimentation.

Text in this chapter is from "Maternal Smoking during Pregnancy Associated with Negative Toddler Behavior and Early Smoking Experimentation," by Josephine Thomas, National Institute on Drug Abuse (NIDA), *NIDA Notes,* Vol. 16, no. 1, March 2001; and "Drug Abuse and Conduct Disorder Linked to Maternal Smoking during Pregnancy," by Raymond Varisco, *NIDA Notes,* Vol. 15, no. 5, October 2000.

Dr. Cornelius, Dr. Day, and their colleagues at the University of Pittsburgh School of Medicine found that not only does such exposure to maternal smoking predict early experimentation, it also appears linked to child anxiety, depression, and behaviors such as hitting and biting others.

Previous studies have supported a link between prenatal smoking exposure and behavioral problems in later childhood and adolescence (see "Drug Abuse and Conduct Disorder Linked to Maternal Smoking During Pregnancy" below). Combined with earlier results, the new studies suggest that prenatal smoking contributes to a train of developmental difficulties and health risks that begin at an early age.

Toddler Negativity

The Mount Sinai study included 99 mothers who smoked and their two-year-old children. The mothers are participants in a large community study that Dr. Judith Brook has been conducting with Dr. Patricia Cohen of Columbia University in New York City for the past 25 years. In the new study, the mothers answered a questionnaire that elicited information about their children's behaviors and their own smoking histories, alcohol and drug use, personalities and attitudes, styles of child-rearing, and socioeconomic characteristics.

Fifty-two of the women reported that they had smoked while pregnant, and 47 said they either stopped smoking during pregnancy or did not begin to smoke until after they had given birth. The mothers who smoked during pregnancy scored their children higher on the questions that measured toddler negativity. The mother's disciplinary style also was strongly linked to a toddler's negative behavior. However, when the researchers adjusted for this factor in the analysis, they determined that a mother's smoking during pregnancy independently increased the estimated risk of negativity at age two by fourfold.

"We found three major maternal risk factors related to toddler negativity," says Dr. Brook. "They are maternal smoking during pregnancy, conflicts between the mother and child, and the mother's use of power-assertive discipline, such as hitting the child. We can speculate that maternal smoking during pregnancy causes disturbances in the neurophysiological functioning of the fetus," says Dr. Brook. "This, in turn, could precipitate the toddler's negative behavior."

The potential implications of these findings reach beyond early childhood. Previous studies have demonstrated that toddlers who display negative behaviors are more likely to use drugs, exhibit delinquent behaviors, and achieve less as adolescents and to develop severe mental health problems later in life.

Early Experimentation with Tobacco

Although the effects of maternal smoking on childhood behaviors have been studied, few studies have investigated the connection between maternal smoking and childhood experimentation with tobacco. The connection is important because the earlier a person starts smoking, the more likely he or she is to become a regular smoker, become addicted, and suffer the long-term adverse health effects of smoking.

Dr. Cornelius and her colleagues interviewed 589 ten-year-olds. Six percent of the children said they had tried cigarettes, smokeless tobacco, or both. Most of the reported tobacco use was experimental; only a few children had used tobacco more than a few times.

In this prospective study, begun by Dr. Day in 1982, the children's mothers have been providing researchers with information about themselves, and they reported on their smoking at the time they were pregnant with the children who are now 10. Putting data from the children together with those reports, the researchers estimated that maternal smoking of at least a half-pack of cigarettes per day during pregnancy increased by fivefold the likelihood that a child would have tried tobacco by age ten. The only factor that produced a greater risk of early experimentation was exposure to smoking within the child's peer group.

It is not yet clear exactly why these factors are related to early experimentation. "Perhaps the nervous system damage caused by maternal smoking may later be expressed as impulsivity, inattention, aggression, depression, and/or anxiety and may create a vulnerability in the child that could contribute to poorer adjustment and an increased likelihood of early initiation of tobacco use," Dr. Cornelius says.

Dr. Cornelius notes that in her study, the ten-year-olds who were exposed prenatally to tobacco were more likely to have experimented than those whose mothers were current smokers. This finding reinforces the hypothesis that a physiological effect of prenatal exposure to smoking, rather than a genetic vulnerability affecting both mother and child, may be an important link between mothers' smoking during pregnancy and early childhood experimentation.

Sources

Brook, J.S.; Brook, D.W.; and Whiteman, M. The influence of maternal smoking during pregnancy on the toddler's negativity. *Archives of Pediatric and Adolescent Medicine* 154(4):381–385, 2000.

Cornelius, M.D.; Leech, S.L.; Goldschmidt, L.; and Day, N.L. Prenatal tobacco exposure: Is it a risk factor for early tobacco experimentation? *Nicotine and Tobacco Research* 2:45–52, 2000.

Drug Abuse and Conduct Disorder Linked to Maternal Smoking during Pregnancy

Researchers at Columbia University in New York City have found new evidence that children whose mothers smoke during pregnancy are at much greater risk than other children for drug abuse and conduct disorder. The findings reinforce those of other studies spanning more than 25 years that have shown similar problems associated with prenatal exposure to smoke in children ranging from toddlers through teens. The study also revealed marked gender differences, with girls at significantly increased risk for drug abuse and boys at significantly increased risk for conduct disorder.

The investigators interviewed 147 mother-child pairs three times over ten years, with the children ranging from ages 6 to 23 at the start of the study. Both mothers and children were interviewed on entry into the study, again two years after the initial interview, and, finally, about ten years after the initial interview. Because the researchers followed the children through either adolescence or young adulthood—something few studies have done before—they were able to collect data about whether and when the children began to abuse drugs, says Dr. Myrna Weissman, the study's principal investigator.

Data were gathered on psychiatric and substance abuse disorders of parents; family environmental factors, such as divorce and family discord; and maternal factors, such as alcohol and coffee consumption and postnatal smoking, to rule out other explanations for the presence of drug abuse and conduct disorder.

The researchers found that maternal smoking during pregnancy has long-term effects on children's behavior and health that cannot be explained by any other factor included in the study. Risk for adolescent drug abuse in girls was more than 5-fold higher if their mothers smoked more than ten cigarettes a day during pregnancy. Among boys whose mothers smoked more than ten cigarettes a day, risk for the onset of conduct disorder was greater than 4-fold that of boys whose mothers did not smoke, with the increase appearing in boys younger than 13. The drug most frequently abused by both boys and girls was marijuana, and the most frequent combination of drugs abused was marijuana and cocaine. Of the females who abused drugs, 70 percent abused more than one.

Why boys exposed to smoking before birth should be at risk for conduct disorder and girls at risk for drug abuse remains to be understood, Dr. Weissman says. She speculates that the differences may be related to sex differences in prenatal brain development.

Many of the findings of this study are consistent with those of related studies, she notes. Researchers at the University of Chicago also have found a link between maternal smoking during pregnancy and conduct disorder in boys, she says. Likewise, a 1994 study conducted by Dr. Weissman's co-investigator Dr. Denise Kandel found that maternal smoking during pregnancy increases risk for adolescent-onset smoking in girls. Studies also have found other behavioral problems in children exposed prenatally to smoke. For example, scientists at Massachusetts General Hospital found an association between prenatal exposure to smoke and attention deficit hyperactivity disorder. Similarly, a recent study by Dr. Judith Brook and her colleagues at Mount Sinai School of Medicine in New York City has found negative behavior in two-year-olds of mothers who smoked during pregnancy.

Sources

Brook, J.S.; Brook, D.W.; and Whiteman, M. The influence of maternal smoking during pregnancy on the toddler's negativity. *Archives of Pediatrics and Adolescent Medicine* 154:381–385, 2000.

Kandel, D.B.; Wu, P.; and Davies, M. Maternal smoking during pregnancy and smoking by adolescent daughters. *American Journal of Public Health* 84:1407–1413, 1994.

Wakschlag, L.S.; Lahey, B.B.; Loeber, R.; Green, S.M.; Gordon, R.A.; and Leventhal, B.L. Maternal smoking during pregnancy and the risk of conduct disorder in boys. *Archives of General Psychiatry* 54:670–676, 1997.

Weissman, M.M.; Warner, V.; Wickramaratne, P.J.; and Kandel, D.B. Maternal smoking during pregnancy and psychopathology in offspring followed to adulthood. *Journal of the American Academy of Child and Adolescent Psychiatry* 38:7, 1999.

Chapter 63

Are Health Risks Different for Menthol Cigarettes?

Introduction

Menthol is unique in that it is the only cigarette additive that is actively marketed to consumers. It is the only aspect of cigarette design that is explicitly marketed based on its physiological effects, as an anti-irritant and a cooling agent. It is the only cigarette additive about which consumers make conscious buying choices.

While the tobacco industry has actively investigated menthol as an additive, there have been relatively few studies in the public health literature about:

- the emergence of menthol cigarettes;
- the use of menthol cigarettes by some segments of the smoking population;
- the targeted marketing of menthol cigarettes to specific population groups;
- reported reasons for menthol cigarette use;

Text in this chapter is excerpted from "The First Conference on Menthol Cigarettes: Setting the Research Agenda, Executive Summary," U.S. Department of Health and Human Services, National Institutes of Health, National Cancer Institute, and Centers for Disease Control and Prevention, NIH Pub. No. 03-5439, September 2003. The complete text of this document, including references, is available online at http://dccps.nci.nih.gov/tcrb/MethnolExec SumRprt4_10-16.pdf.

- the addictive, physiological, and toxicological properties of menthol cigarettes, which are purportedly different from nonmentholated brands;

- the potential of menthol cigarettes to increase exposure to harmful smoke constituents;

- the propensity of menthol cigarettes to aid in the initiation of smoking among adolescents; and

- the impact of mentholated cigarettes on smoking-related disease, disability, and death.

Investigating the issues related to adding menthol to cigarettes will not only contribute to the knowledge about menthol's role in the initiation and progression of tobacco use, but will also aid in a better understanding of its effect on addiction to cigarettes and the rate of smoking-related diseases. New research also can lead to development of models to study the health impact of other cigarette additives and cigarette designs, including emerging potential reduced-exposure tobacco products.

The Emergence of Menthol Cigarettes

Menthol cigarettes were conceived as specialty products in the 1920s and 1930s. These cigarettes were initially marketed as a luxury product, through radio and magazine ads, and especially targeted to women smokers. Until the 1960s, the market share of menthol cigarettes never exceeded 5 percent. However, with the great migration of African Americans from the South to urban centers, peaking during and after World War II, the industry started targeting menthol cigarettes to African Americans. Launched in the early 1940s, the popular African American magazines (for example, *Ebony, Jet*) offered a unique opportunity for precision marketing. By the 1960s and 1970s, menthol brands had become the cigarettes of choice for the majority of African American smokers. Whereas only about 25 percent of White smokers use menthol cigarettes, more than 70 percent of African American smokers choose them; other population segments are now adopting menthol use, including young people, Asian and Pacific Islander Americans, and women. Today, menthol cigarettes represent about 26 percent of all cigarettes sold in the United States. Newport cigarettes are the leading menthol brand and are second only to Marlboro in overall market share.

Why It Is Important to Study Menthol Cigarettes

One urgent question that needs to be answered is whether menthol cigarettes contribute to the health disparities between White and African American smokers. Although African Americans tend to smoke fewer cigarettes per day than do White smokers, incidence and mortality rates of lung cancer and other smoking-related diseases are significantly higher among African Americans. For example, average age-adjusted annual incidence rates for lung cancer in the United States between 1992 and 1998 were 54.7/100,000 for Whites and 71.6/100,000 for African Americans; mortality rates, for the same period, were 48.8 for Whites and 59.1 for African Americans.

Historically, the age-adjusted smoking-related lung cancer death rates in the United States among African American males and White males were: in 1950, 15.7 and 21.9, respectively; in 1965, 47.8 and 47.3, respectively; and in 1990, 107.7 and 73.6, respectively. Whether these trends reflect the trends of use of menthol cigarettes by African Americans remains to be determined.

Menthol, a chemical compound extracted from the peppermint plant and classified as a mild local anesthetic, was commonly used in veterinary medicine. Colorless and with a mint scent, menthol was first added to cigarettes in the 1920s and 1930s to mask the harshness of tobacco smoke. Fifty-two percent of 174 African Americans interviewed in one study reported that mentholated cigarettes were less harsh on the throat, 48 percent stated that inhalation was easier, and 33 percent felt they could inhale more deeply.

Since the 1960s, menthol brands have been marketed by the industry as refreshing and cool. Menthol stimulates cold receptors, with the resulting sensation of coolness perceived not only in the mouth and pharynx, but also in the lungs. Stimulation of laryngeal cold receptors may reduce airway irritation. This sensation of coolness might result in deeper inhalation, but because of the difficulty in precisely measuring the inhalation phase of smoking, this issue has not been adequately studied. Menthol may increase salivary flow thereby enhancing the passage of harmful smoke constituents across mucus membranes.

Menthol has been shown to increase significantly involuntary breath holding. Breath holding at peak inspiration could contribute to increased uptake of inhaled tobacco smoke constituents, including nicotine and cancer-causing agents, from the alveoli of the lungs into the bloodstream.

There have been conflicting reports on the effect of menthol on smoking topography (for example, puff volume, puff frequency) that may be due to small samples and variations in study populations. The 1999 Massachusetts Benchmark Study of the 24 most popular U.S. filter cigarette brands and styles (six of them were menthol brands) provided some evidence that the chemical composition of the mainstream smoke of selected menthol cigarettes differs from that of their nonmenthol counterparts. The yields of tar, nicotine, carbon monoxide, and several carcinogenic compounds (for example, benzene, 1,3-butadiene, benzo[a]pyrene, NNK), obtained by the Massachusetts machine-smoking method, were 30–70 percent higher in the mainstream smoke of menthol cigarettes than in the smoke of the selected nonmentholated brands. There are many cigarette design characteristics (for example, tobacco blend, resistance to draw, paper porosity, amount of tobacco in the rod, cigarette length, and others) that may contribute to differences in yield that are independent of mentholation. For example, Newport, the most popular menthol brand in the United States, is a full flavor cigarette with no filter ventilation holes, while the most popular nonmentholated brand, full flavor Marlboro, averages 8 percent ventilation in the hard pack version and 11 percent ventilation in the soft pack.

Emerging Research on Behavior, Epidemiology, and Toxicology of Menthol Cigarettes

The tobacco industry and some members of the scientific community studied the effects of menthol on human tissue when menthol was first introduced into cigarettes. In 1944, Brown and Williamson commissioned a literature search on the toxic effects of menthol. Thus, the industry knew early on that menthol, when tested on animals, had distinct properties that had to be accounted for in the delivery of nicotine to cigarette smokers.

Although the industry had an early interest in the use and effects of menthol added to cigarettes, the public health community was not conducting extensive menthol-related research. Studies of the effects of smoking menthol cigarettes are now emerging. In 1989, the first epidemiological study of health effects of smoking menthol cigarettes was published, and there have since been several others. To date, epidemiological studies of the relationship between smoking menthol cigarettes and cancer risk have shown mixed results and have been limited by problems such as too few subjects exclusively smoking menthol cigarettes for too short a time. Little is known about the brand- and style-switching habits of smokers, so classifying subjects as exclusively menthol or nonmenthol smokers for a long enough time period is difficult. For instance, it is not known if the worried well may switch to menthol cigarettes because they perceive them to be less harmful or if subjects with a persistent cough may switch to a mentholated brand for its local anesthetic and cooling properties. Both aspects may cause a misclassification bias of unknown magnitude in epidemiological studies. Also, the increased dose delivered with menthol cigarettes may be no more than the equivalent of a few cigarettes a day among heavy smokers, or even a single extra cigarette among lighter smokers (which African American smokers generally are). Thus, parsing out the additional harm associated with smoking menthol cigarettes might require very large sample sizes or the exclusive use of menthol cigarettes for long periods. No studies have been reported on the effect of menthol cigarettes on noncancer health outcomes, such as nicotine addiction, cardiovascular disease, chronic obstructive pulmonary disease, and birth outcome.

The comparative studies of the uptake of smoke constituents, including nicotine and carcinogens, among smokers of menthol and nonmenthol cigarettes, as determined by measuring the levels of biological markers, are now emerging. One study reported that the levels of urinary 1-hydroxypyrene (a marker of polycyclic aromatic hydrocarbon [PAH] exposure) per cigarette smoked by male menthol smokers were about 2.7-fold higher than the levels measured among nonmenthol cigarette smokers based on equimolar benzo(a)pyrene dosage delivered in the mainstream smoke. The latter observation suggested that menthol may enhance the uptake of PAH from mainstream smoke and alter metabolism, or that racial differences in the metabolic activation of carcinogens are factors in uptake and metabolism of PAH. The absence of a crossover component, in which subjects are tested while smoking both menthol and nonmenthol styles, has been a significant limitation in the interpretation of some studies. Thus, it is not known if the results were attributable to interaction between individual differences in smoking (such as inhalation or breath-holding patterns), addiction and disease susceptibility, and the preference for menthol cigarettes, rather than menthol smoking per se. This is an important distinction given that cigarette smoking is a highly ritualistic activity developed, in part, to maintain a physiologically needed level of blood nicotine. Crossover designs will help separate individual idiosyncratic smoking patterns from those attributable to smoking menthol cigarettes. Direct measures of body burdens of carcinogens are required to better understand the relative harm of menthol and nonmenthol cigarettes. These studies are beginning to emerge.

Chapter 64

Can Cigarettes Be Manufactured in a Way that Reduces Burn-Related Fatalities?

Fact Sheet on Fire-Safe Cigarettes

Cigarettes are the leading cause of fatal home fires in the United States. At present, no regulation requires cigarettes to meet fire safety standards. American Burn Association (ABA)-supported legislation has been introduced in both the Senate (S. 2317) and in the House (H.R. 4607).

- Annually, between 900 and 1,000 people in the United States die from fires started by cigarettes and an additional 2,500 to 3,000 are injured.

- More than 100 victims who die every year are children and non-smokers.

- The cost of human life and property damage exceeds $6 billion every year.

- In 1997, there were more than 130,000 cigarette related fires.

This chapter includes excerpts from "ABA Fact Sheet on Fire Safe Cigarettes," reprinted with permission from the American Burn Association. © 2002. For additional information visit the American Burn Association website at http://www.ameriburn.org; and "Questions and Answers on NIST Reduced Ignition Propensity Cigarette Testing," National Institute of Standards and Technology - Building and Fire Research Laboratory, February 2001.

What Is a Fire-Safe Cigarette?

A fire-safe cigarette has significantly less propensity to ignite furniture or mattresses when carelessly discarded. Small design changes including use of less dense tobacco, less porous paper, a smaller diameter, filter tip, and no added citrates to the paper are key components of a fire safe cigarette. Although the technology to produce fire-safe cigarettes has been available for more than a decade, the tobacco industry refuses to manufacture and distribute them.

History of the Fire-Safe Cigarette

- 1929: First congressional research in fire-safe cigarettes is conducted by the National Bureau of Standards.

- 1974: Legislation mandating fire-safe cigarettes introduced in US Senate. Passes Senate and fails in House of Representatives.

- 1984: Federal Cigarette Safety Act of 1984 (Congressman Joseph Moakley, D-MA) mandated formation of a Technical Study Group to determine if it is technically and economically feasible to make a fire-safe cigarette.

- 1987: Technical Study Group reports to the U.S. Congress that is technically and economically feasible to produce cigarettes that are more fire safe.

- 1990: Federal Fire Safe Cigarette Act of 1990 (Joseph Moakley, D-MA) mandated the development of a fire safe test method for cigarettes.

- 1993: Technical Advisory Group reported to Congress that a fire safety test method had been developed in order to promulgate a fire safety standard for cigarettes.

- 1999: H.R. 1130, the Fire Safe Cigarette Act of 1999 (Joseph Moakley, D-MA) was introduced. This bill will require the establishment of a cigarette safety standard and direct the Consumer Product Safety Commission to implement this standard within 18 months of the date of enactment. After 18 months, only fire safe cigarettes can be sold or manufactured in the United States.

- 2000: New York state passes the first state law requiring fire-safe cigarettes.

- 2002: ABA supported legislation introduced in both the Senate and the House.

American Burn Association Position Statement Regarding Fire Safe Cigarettes

Cigarettes are the most common ignition source for fatal residential fires, accounting for approximately 29% of the nation's fire deaths. Every year, fires started by cigarettes are responsible for more than $6 billion in societal costs and direct property damage, about 2500 injuries and over 1000 deaths. More than a hundred fatal victims are innocent bystanders—children and nonsmokers.

Cigarettes are designed to continue burning when left unattended. The typical scenario is the delayed ignition of a sofa, chair or mattress from a lit cigarette that is forgotten or dropped by a smoker whose alertness may be impaired by alcohol or medication. Cigarettes vary in their potential to start fires, depending on cigarette design and content. The term 'fire safe' is defined as a cigarette with reduced propensity for starting a fire when dropped or left unattended. The technology needed to produce fire safe cigarettes has been available for over a decade.

The American Burn Association has been a strong advocate for the development of fire safe cigarettes for over 15 years, participating in two US Government studies that successfully demonstrated the technical and economic feasibility of commercial production of fire safe cigarettes.

The American Burn Association strongly and actively supports local, state and federal legislation mandating development and production of fire safe cigarettes. The American Burn Association supports the efforts of the Fire Safe Cigarette Coalition and the passage of S. 2317 and H.R. 4607.

American Burn Association
625 North Michigan Avenue, Suite 1530
Chicago, IL 60611
Toll Free: 800-548-2876
Phone: 312-642-9260
Fax: 312-642-9130
Website: www.ameriburn.org

Questions and Answers on Reduced Ignition Propensity Cigarette Testing

What is a reduced ignition propensity cigarette?

A reduced ignition propensity (more commonly, but incorrectly known as "fire-safe") cigarette is one that has been designed to be less likely than a conventional cigarette to ignite soft furnishings such as a couch or mattress.

The National Institute of Standards and Technology (NIST) has been involved in research concerning reduced ignition propensity cigarettes since the 1980s. In both 1984 and 1990, research studies were legislated by Congress as the responsibility of Technical Advisory Groups. These TAGs—led both times by NIST fire researcher Dr. Richard Gann—involved NIST, the Consumer Product Safety Commission, the U.S. Fire Administration, the Federal Trade Commission, the National Cancer Institute, representatives of the tobacco and furniture industries, fire safety professionals, and public health/safety advocates.

As mandated under the Cigarette Safety Act of 1984: The first TAG was assigned under the Cigarette Safety Act of 1984 to determine whether it was technically and commercially feasible to develop a cigarette that would have a significantly reduced propensity to ignite furniture and mattresses. The research showed that the manufacturing was within the capabilities of the tobacco industry at that time, and that such cigarettes may be commercially feasible as well.

The research also determined that thinner cigarettes with less tobacco and less porous paper, which cuts air circulation into the cigarette, could significantly reduce the chance of igniting soft furnishings.

As mandated by the Fire-Safe Cigarette Act of 1990: The second TAG was assigned under the Fire-Safe Cigarette Act of 1990 to develop a reliable test that would accurately and consistently reflect what happens when cigarettes are dropped on furnishings.

Two tests were developed, tested, and made available to the tobacco industry as the basis for a performance standard. Nine laboratories, including four in the cigarette industry, showed that both methods produced results that were repeatable and more reproducible than conventional fire tests at the time.

The 1990 act also directed NIST to compile performance data for commercial cigarettes using the test methods. NIST researchers found that, with one minor exception, the 14 best sellers at that time ignited the fabrics in all tests. The tobacco packing density, paper permeability, and circumference were similar among these brands. By contrast, tests of six other brands on the market at the time showed much lower ignition propensities. Both sets of cigarettes produced similar amounts of tar, nicotine, and carbon monoxide. This is an encouraging indicator that the toxicities of the smoke from the two sets of cigarettes were not likely to be greatly different.

Why did NIST get involved again with reduced ignition propensity cigarettes?

On May 15, 2000, the Federal Trade Commission requested that NIST conduct tests to determine whether and to what extent a new cigarette brand then being test marketed reduced the risk of ignition, if dropped or discarded. These data, the FTC said, would greatly assist the Commission in its responsibilities over tobacco products.

What was the nature of the NIST testing?

Two types of tests were conducted on both the modified cigarettes (purchased from a test market city) and locally purchased (in the Washington, D.C., area which was not a test market), non-modified Merit cigarettes. Both tests were developed by NIST under the Fire-Safe Cigarette Act of 1990 and are now under consideration as an industry standard by the American Society of Testing and Materials.

The first test, called the mockup ignition test, involves placing a lit cigarette on top of a flat surface "mocked" up to simulate a section from a piece of furniture. The model consists of a piece of fabric covering a layer of foam padding. The test reveals if the cigarette will ignite the mockup, and if so, how long it takes for that ignition to occur.

The second test, called the cigarette extinction test, involves placing a lit cigarette on several layers of filter paper. The filter paper is the same extremely pure and strictly standardized cellulose paper manufactured for the chemical industry. It is used to ensure repeatable test results. This test reveals if the cigarette self extinguishes or burns for its full length.

NIST measured the ignition propensity of the modified Merit cigarettes relative to the performance of the unmodified product. This

411

was not an absolute measure of ignition probability in real circumstances, but is a strong indicator as to whether a reduction in cigarette-initiated fires might be expected.

Analysis of the test data shows that the modified cigarette has a lower relative ignition propensity than the conventional cigarette.

Chapter 65

Researching
Tobacco-Related Cancers

Much is known and documented about the harmful effects of tobacco. Tobacco use is the leading preventable cause of illness and death in the United States. Cigarette smoking is the primary reason people die from lung cancer, coronary heart disease, chronic obstructive pulmonary disease, and stroke. Cancers of the lung, oral cavity, pharynx, larynx, esophagus, pancreas, urinary bladder, and renal pelvis all have been scientifically linked to tobacco use. More recent research connects tobacco use to still more cancers. A 2002 International Agency for Research on Cancer (IARC) monograph established a causal association between cigarette smoking and cancers of the nasal cavities and nasal sinuses, stomach, liver, kidney, and cervix, as well as myeloid leukemia. Why then do people choose to begin and continue smoking in spite of these health risks? This is the challenge for the National Cancer Institute (NCI) and other research organizations and institutions as we work to reduce tobacco's staggering burden on our nation's health.

Of the many obstacles that confront the research community in the fight against tobacco-related disease, two are particularly complex: (1) the addicting nature of tobacco products, and (2) the impact of tobacco advertising and marketing. These factors drive the continued use of tobacco products even when the users are fully aware of their

Excerpted from *The Nation's Investment in Cancer Research*, prepared by the Director, National Cancer Institute (NCI), NIH Pub. No. 03-5446, October 2003. The full text of this document is available online at http://www.annals.org/cgi/content/full/138/11/1-45.

increased risk of disease and premature death. Adolescents are particularly vulnerable; almost 90 percent of adult current smokers began smoking before the age of 18. At this age, individuals tend to be less than fully aware of the risks and their implications and less able to make an informed, educated decision independent of external influences. Therefore, research on preventing youth smoking must focus on increasing young people's awareness of the harmful consequences of tobacco use and addiction; deflecting the presence of tobacco industry advertising messages; and decreasing the acceptability of tobacco use in physical and social environments. Equally important is the role of genetics and its interaction with psychosocial and environmental factors in the development or onset of tobacco dependence.

Clearly, NCI cannot achieve its Challenge Goal to eliminate suffering and death due to cancer without dramatically reducing and treating tobacco use and tobacco-related cancers across all ages and populations. This requires an integrated, multidisciplinary approach to decipher the interplay of social, psychological, behavioral, environmental, and biological/genetic determinants of tobacco use and tobacco-related cancers. Because many tobacco-related cancers take years to develop, making investments consistent with the enormous burden of tobacco-related disease now will lead to substantial benefits in the future.

Progress in Pursuit of Our Goal

The intransigence of tobacco use and its disease consequences, along with its complex, multidimensional determinants, led the scientific community to recognize the need for new research models and paradigms that are integrated across disciplines. Transdisciplinary research, a process by which researchers work jointly, using a shared conceptual framework that draws together discipline-specific theories, concepts, and approaches to address common problems, was identified as the most promising approach to accelerate discovery. In 1999, NCI, the National Institute on Drug Abuse (NIDA), and the Robert Wood Johnson Foundation jointly funded Transdisciplinary Tobacco Use Research Centers (TTURCs) within seven academic institutions. As of 2003, over 100 researchers involved in nearly 100 major research projects, pilot projects, and cores (for example, training, biostatistics, administrative and transdisciplinary) are involved in research at these seven centers.

At one TTURC, investigators generated the first empirical evidence that the *CYP2B6* gene may influence the effectiveness of treatment with bupropion. This research team, composed of scientists who study behavior, neuroscience, pharmacology, and genetics, gained insight into specific neuronal and pharmacological mechanisms that may explain genetic effects on individual response to smoking cessation treatment. In clinical testing at another TTURC, researchers developed a single-photon emission computed tomography (SPECT) radiotracer for imaging certain nicotine acetylcholine receptors in the brain. This breakthrough will open new directions for cross-disciplinary research on receptor response during smoking and smoking cessation, while considering the effects of environmental, emotional, and behavioral factors. TTURC-supported research revealed links between attention deficit hyperactivity disorder (ADHD) and susceptibility to tobacco industry marketing among adolescents. Based on findings that nicotine increases dopamine levels in animal and preliminary clinical studies, one TTURC sponsored a study of selegiline (an MAO-B inhibitor that inhibits dopamine metabolism) as a treatment for tobacco addiction. In an early trial, selegiline was superior to placebo for smoking cessation.

Collaborative TTURC projects include:

- Development of a measure for nicotine dependence

- Joint studies related to genetic/cultural/environmental interactions in tobacco use

- Studies of the interrelationship of culture, mood, and smoking

- Adolescent studies investigating the influence of peer interaction, depression, and hostility on smoking initiation and maintenance

- Genetic studies of treatment response

Supporting Clinical and Population Studies on Smoking and Cancer

Longitudinal, screening, and cohort studies that involve genetic and biomarker components from tissue, blood, urine, sputum, and other bodily fluids are providing new information about the interplay among one's cancer risk and tobacco and other exposures such as alcohol, diet, occupation, and radon. For example, one of the largest molecular epidemiology studies of lung cancer in the world, a multicenter case-control study of lung cancer and tobacco use, is under way in Milan, Italy. This trial includes collection of extensive questionnaire and biospecimen data, and is unique in collecting information on many other factors, including tumor tissue obtained in surgery, demographics, tobacco use, alcohol use, occupational exposures, diet, and medical illness. Investigators will apply advanced technologies to explore protein and expression patterns and the genomic correlates of lung cancer and tobacco use.

The Prostate, Lung, Colorectal, and Ovarian Cancer Screening Trial (PLCO), the Alpha-Tocopherol Beta-Carotene Cancer Prevention Study (ATBC), and the Shanghai Women's Study are all large cohort studies that include biospecimens and questionnaire data with a focus on tobacco-related cancers. Two studies using high-throughput genotyping are planned within the PLCO to examine genes involved in "ever" and current smokers and explore the relationship of genes to emphysema and lung cancer. The Shanghai study includes occupational data and urine samples. Additional case-control studies of renal, pancreatic, bladder, and brain cancers, colon polyps, and second tumors are in progress in various national and international settings. The National Health and Nutrition Examination Survey (NHANES III) provides a population-based sample, with available serum and DNA that may prove useful in the future to conduct studies of the genetics of smoking and related traits. Results from these cohort studies will provide critical information that can be translated into effective prevention and treatment practices.

Supporting Epidemiological and Genetic Research

Lead investigators in the area of individual susceptibility to tobacco-related cancers have established a large database of epidemiologic, clinical, and laboratory data from over 3,000 study participants with and without lung cancer. Using advanced technologies, the researchers are assessing biomarkers to track the damaging effects of cigarette smoking. Investigators have recently reported an increased risk of lung cancer in people with genetic polymorphisms in the genes that eliminate carcinogens or repair DNA damage. Emerging technological advances will permit investigators to analyze the network of relationships among genetic, molecular, and environmental elements that control how tobacco damages individuals. For example, genetic differences that affect lung cancer risk may be used to identify highly susceptible subgroups and facilitate development of targeted intervention and prevention strategies.

The health of former smokers, who now comprise about half of those diagnosed with lung cancer, is a special concern to NCI. Through targeted initiatives released over the past several years, NCI is funding studies to identify newer, more potent agents to prevent cancers in former smokers. Preclinical studies focus on identifying and prioritizing agents that prevent cancers in tobacco-susceptible organ systems, and clinical researchers are evaluating the efficacy of chemopreventive agents in specific cohorts of former smokers.

Developing and Evaluating Innovative Interventions

NCI supports translation of knowledge unveiled by research findings into interventions to benefit all people affected by or at risk for tobacco use and/or tobacco-related cancers.

- NCI recently established the Tobacco Intervention Research Clinic to conduct innovative, state-of-the-science research on behavioral and pharmacological tobacco-use treatment interventions in clinical patient populations. The clinic's streamlined funding and review process allows high-priority topics in tobacco-use treatment to be addressed in a timely fashion.

- NCI and the National Institute on Drug Abuse (NIDA) have established the Working Group on Medication Development for Nicotine Addiction for exploring ways to advance progress in treatment for nicotine addiction.

- The National Conference on Tobacco and Health Disparities, held in December 2002, was the first scientific gathering to convene researchers and practitioners with the purpose of developing a research agenda to eliminate tobacco-related disparities.

- Women, Tobacco, and Cancer: An Agenda for the 21st Century, held in February 2003, provided a similar venue for a focus on current research on tobacco and tobacco-related cancers in women.

- NCI-supported researchers have developed an online guide to evidence-based measures for use in youth tobacco research interventions.

Delivering Evidence-Based Interventions

NCI's Smoking and Tobacco Control Monographs have provided timely information about emerging public health issues in smoking and tobacco control and accelerated its dissemination to the scientific and public policy communities. *Those Who Continue to Smoke: Is Achieving Abstinence Harder and Do We Need to Change Intervention?* was released in May 2003. The document is a result of a set of analyses funded jointly by NCI and the Tobacco Control Section of the California Department of Health Services. The *National Blueprint for Disseminating and Implementing Evidenced-Based Clinical and Community Strategies to Promote Tobacco-Use Cessation,* a document that resulted from the collaborative work of 10 public and private organizations, provides state-of-the-art research strategies for cessation interventions. Smoking-related NCI publications available to the public include *Clearing the Air,* a manual designed to help smokers quit; *Clear Horizons,* a quitting guide for those older than 50; and the recently published Spanish-language guide on smoking cessation, *Guia para Dejar de Fumar.* In addition, through NCI's Multimedia Technology Health Communications Grants to Small Business, NCI has supported the development of a number of interactive CD-ROMs and web-based applications designed to capture the attention of targeted population groups. Examples include *Rebels: The Battle for a Smoke-Free Future,* a CD-ROM game for high school students who smoke. The game includes a teacher's manual and student handouts. Two additional products are *Dig Deeper,* a CD-ROM for tobacco use prevention in 10- to 12-year-olds, and the *Appalachian Community Kit for Tobacco Prevention,* a second-hand smoke project. The community kit includes brochures, fact sheets, and videos designed for Appalachian women, who influence smoking cessation in their homes.

Additional Information about Smoking Cessation

NCI provides telephone-based assistance for smokers who want to quit through the Cancer Information Service (CIS) at 1-800-4-CANCER. Callers can speak with someone in English or Spanish in the United States, Puerto Rico, the U.S. Virgin Islands, and territories in Guam and Saipan. Smoking cessation service representatives:

- Assess the caller's individual smoking behavior.
- Provide brief educational messages.
- Help callers develop a personalized action plan for quitting.
- Reinforce the information with written materials.

Smokefree.gov (online at www.smokefree.gov), launched in Fall 2002, offers science-driven tools, information, and support to smokers who want to quit. Cosponsored by NCI and CDC, the website provides state and national resources, free materials, access to online cessation support, and a toll-free number (1-877-44U-QUIT) for telephone-based cessation support.

Additional Information about Cancer Research

The full text of *The Nation's Investment in Cancer Research*, the document from which this chapter has been excerpted, including links to key websites, is available online at http://plan.cancer.gov. You may also order this document:

- By e-mail: cisocc@pop.nci.nih.gov
- By internet: www.cancer.gov/publications
- By phone: 800-4-CANCER
- By fax: 301-330-7968

Additional information about tobacco and cancer is also available from the following sources:

- Cancer Research Portfolio: http://researchportfolio.cancer.gov
- International Cancer Research Portfolio: http://www.cancer portfolio.org
- Cancer News: http://newscenter.cancer.gov
- Cancer Science: http://newscenter.cancer.gov/sciencebehind
- By phone 800-4-CANCER (800-422-6237)
- For deaf and hard-of-hearing 800-332-8615
- Cancer Information Service website: http://cis.nci.nih.gov

Chapter 66

Associations between Smoking and Newly Identified Risk Factors for Cardiovascular Disease

What is the problem and what is known about it so far?

Heart disease and strokes (cardiovascular disease) are leading causes of death and disability in most western countries. Smoking, high-fat diets, high cholesterol, high blood pressure, diabetes, and kidney disease increase a person's risk for cardiovascular disease. Recently, researchers identified several additional risk factors for cardiovascular disease. These newer risk factors include proteins that are involved in blood clotting and are released in response to inflammation (fibrinogen and C-reactive protein). They also include an amino acid (homocysteine) that may be elevated when intake of vitamins, such as folic acid, is low. How the newer risk factors relate to older, more established risk factors, such as smoking, is not well studied.

Why did the researchers do this particular study?

To study the relationships between smoking and newer risk factors for cardiovascular disease.

Who was studied?

17,353 adults who had participated in a national survey.

How was the study done?

Researchers looked at data from a sample of the U.S. population that was collected from 1988 to 1994. Participants in the survey answered questions about cigarette smoking and medical history and had their blood pressure and weight measured. They also gave blood samples that were used to measure newer risk factors. The researchers then looked at whether people who smoked were more likely to have elevated levels of the newer risk factors, even after controlling for other traditional risk factors, such as diabetes and high blood pressure.

What did the researchers find?

Cigarette smoking was associated with elevated levels of fibrinogen, C-reactive protein, and homocysteine. Current smokers had higher levels of these risk factors than former smokers. Also, smoking more cigarettes daily was associated with higher levels of the risk factors.

What were the limitations of the study?

The study did not examine relationships over time. Whether smoking actually caused the elevated levels of the new risk factors could not be determined.

What are the implications of the study?

Smoking cigarettes is associated with elevated levels of several recently identified risk factors. These newer risk factors may be important mechanisms by which smoking promotes cardiovascular disease.

Author and Article Information

The full report is titled "Relationship Between Cigarette Smoking and Novel Risk Factors for Cardiovascular Disease in the United States." It is in the 3 June 2003 issue of *Annals of Internal Medicine* (volume 138, pages 891–897). The authors are L.A. Bazzano, J. He, P. Muntner, S. Vupputuri, and P.K. Whelton.

Summaries for Patients are a service provided by *Annals* to help patients better understand the complicated and often mystifying language of modern medicine.

Summaries for Patients are presented for informational purposes only. These summaries are not a substitute for advice from your own medical provider. If you have questions about this material, or need medical advice about your own health or situation, please contact your physician. The summaries may be reproduced for not-for-profit educational purposes only. Any other uses must be approved by the American College of Physicians.

Related Articles in Annals

Brief Communications: Relationship between Cigarette Smoking and Novel Risk Factors for Cardiovascular Disease in the United States; Lydia A. Bazzano, Jiang He, Paul Muntner, Suma Vupputuri, and Paul K. Whelton, *Annals* 2003 138: 891–897.

Chapter 67

Persistent Smokers Fail to Receive Full Benefits of Angioplasty

Persistent Smokers Skip Full Benefit of Angioplasty

People who continue to smoke after undergoing balloon angioplasty or other procedures to open obstructed heart arteries have a much worse health-related quality of life than nonsmokers and quitters, researchers report in today's *Circulation: Journal of the American Heart Association*.

The study at Boston's Beth Israel Deaconess Medical Center and Harvard Medical School monitored 1,432 angioplasty patients at intervals of six months and again at one year for eight factors influencing quality of life, including physical and social functioning, bodily pain, vitality, and mental health. People who continued to smoke scored significantly lower in all categories.

"While balloon angioplasty and other coronary interventions are life-saving in some cases, their main benefits are relief of angina (chest pain) and improved quality of life," says David J. Cohen, M.D., M. Sc., associate director of interventional cardiology at Beth Israel Deaconess Medical Center and assistant professor of medicine at Harvard University, Boston, Massachusetts.

"Our study shows that virtually every phase of quality of life suffers when patients keep smoking after these procedures, and that the quality-of-life benefits of angioplasty are greatly enhanced by quitting," Cohen says. "In addition to the other well-recognized risks of cigarette smoking, these data provide a further compelling reason for coronary disease patients not to smoke."

Among the patients studied, 301 continued to smoke following angioplasty, 141 had quit after the procedure, and 990 were nonsmokers. The participants completed questionnaires that were used to measure overall health. Improvements in quality-of-life scores were similar for nonsmokers and those who had quit smoking. Both outscored smokers by margins ranging from 5.5 points for mental health to 23.2 points for physical functioning. At both 6- and 12-month follow-ups, scores for quitters and nonsmokers averaged 4 to 7 points higher than those for smokers across the board.

Previous studies have shown that long-term risks of heart attack and death are higher for smokers than nonsmokers after both angioplasty and coronary bypass surgery. Other studies have demonstrated an association between smoking and reduced exercise capacity and impaired physical functioning after these procedures.

The new study points at the urgent need for more aggressive efforts by health care professionals to promote smoking cessation.

"Smoking is highly addictive, and quitting is very difficult," says Cohen. "A number of drugs, along with behavior modification therapy, have been shown to help patients quit, and we need to put more emphasis on these. Therefore, the first step has to be a sincere desire to quit on the part of the patient."

Cardiologists should redouble their efforts to help patients break the smoking habit, says Robert M. Califf, M.D., a researcher at Duke University Medical Center, Durham, North Carolina, and author of an accompanying editorial in *Circulation*.

"The effort will require a combination of consistent advice to patients and effective behavioral and pharmacological therapy aimed at a serious addiction that is the world's leading cause of self-inflicted disability and death," says Califf.

—Co-Authors: Deborah A. Taira, Sc.D.; Todd B. Seto, M.D., M.P.H.; Kalon K.L. Ho, M.D., M.Sc.; Harlan M. Krumholz, M.D., M.P.H.; Donald E. Cutlip, M.D.; Ronna Berezin, M.P.H.; and Richard E. Kuntz, M.D., M.Sc.

Chapter 68

Vitamin C, Fish, and Gout Drug May Reduce Artery Damage from Smoking

Researchers found that vitamin C and taurine, an amino acid in fish, reversed abnormal blood vessel response associated with cigarette smoking—a discovery that may provide insight into how smoking contributes to "hardening of the arteries," according to an Irish study in today's [January 7, 2003] rapid access issue of *Circulation: Journal of the American Heart Association.*

In a second study, researchers from Iowa demonstrated that a drug used to treat gout—allopurinol—rapidly reversed the abnormal blood vessel constriction caused by smoking.

"When blood vessels are exposed to cigarette smoke it causes the vessels to behave like a rigid pipe rather than a flexible tube, thus the vessels can't dilate in response to increased blood flow," says David J. Bouchier-Hayes, M.D., senior author of the taurine study and professor of surgery at the Royal College of Surgeons in Ireland, Beaumont Hospital, Dublin. This is a condition called endothelial dysfunction.

Endothelial dysfunction is one of the earliest signs of the atherosclerosis, which is a major cause of heart attacks and stroke. "We're not trying to find a therapeutic treatment for smoking, because we believe that the best therapy for smokers is to stop smoking," says Bouchier-Hayes. "Nonetheless, smokers provide a good clinical model for treatment of endothelial dysfunction."

Bouchier-Hayes and colleagues recruited 15 healthy smokers aged 20 to 37 and 15 healthy nonsmoking volunteers. The smokers were given either two grams per day of vitamin C for five days or 1.5 grams per day of taurine. Smokers then waited for a two-week "wash-out" period and switched therapies for five more days.

Researchers assessed blood vessel functioning by flow mediated dilation (FMD), which takes ultrasound images of blood vessel diameter in the arm after a tourniquet is placed on the forearm. Greater diameter after FMD assessment indicates good endothelial function. They assessed FMD at baseline and after taurine and vitamin C supplementation.

The researchers report that taurine restored normal vessel function according to FMD measurements. At baseline, nonsmokers' blood vessel diameter was 3.39 mm and smokers' diameter was 3.33. Before treatment, FMD increased dilation in nonsmokers to 3.7 mm, while smokers' vessels were virtually unchanged at 3.36 mm after FMD. When they took vitamin C, smokers' vessel diameter increased to 3.45 mm after FMD. When they were given taurine, the smokers' vessel response was the same as the nonsmokers' at 3.7 mm after FMD.

Taurine is found in many foods but is most abundant in fish, says Bouchier-Hayes, who adds that taurine is present even in mild, white fish not just fatty fish. The taurine supplement used in the study is equivalent to that found in one serving of fish.

William G. Haynes, M.D., senior author of the allopurinol study and associate professor of internal medicine, University of Iowa College of Medicine, Iowa City, agrees that treatments that are effective in smokers are likely to be applicable to nonsmokers who have similar endothelial dysfunction.

Haynes studied 14 heavy smokers aged 18 to 85 and 14 age- and sex-matched nonsmoking volunteers. The subjects underwent tests to assess blood vessel functioning at baseline and after treatment. The subjects were randomized to receive either a single 600 mg oral dose of allopurinol or no drug on the day of the study.

At baseline smokers had impaired blood vessel function as measured by blood vessel dilation in response to the stimulant acetylcholine. A greater change in vessel dilation after acetylcholine indicates better endothelial function. The change in dilation produced by acetylcholine was significantly less in smokers (254 percent) than in nonsmokers (390 percent). After taking allopurinol, smokers' response to acetylcholine improved to 463 percent, while nonsmokers' response remained about the same (401 percent).

Allopurinol inhibits an enzyme called xanthine oxidase, which increases oxidative stress in the blood vessels. "This is the first study to show that a single oral dose of allopurinol can have rapid and substantial endothelial effects in smokers," says Haynes.

"These studies provide further evidence of the damaging effect cigarette smoking has on blood vessels," says Sidney Smith, M.D., past president of the American Heart Association. "They may also provide insight into the mechanism by which smoking causes injury to blood vessels. This and other evidence further emphasizes the importance of not smoking if one is to avoid the risk of heart attack or stroke."

—Bouchier-Hayes co-authors were Fiona M. Fennessy, Ph.D.; D. S. Moneley, M.B.; J.H. Wang, M.D., Ph.D.; and C.J. Kelly, M.B.

—Haynes co-authors were Sashi Guthikonda, M.D., M.P.H.; Christine Sinkey, R.N.; and Therese Barenz, R.N.

Dr. Haynes' research was partly funded by the National Institutes of Health and by the Iowa Affiliate of the American Heart Association.

Chapter 69

Long-Term Effects
from Vitamin Supplements
in Smokers

Alpha-Tocopherol, Beta-Carotene (ATBC) Cancer Prevention Trial

In order to determine the long-term effects from vitamin supplements in smokers, ATBC researchers followed the participants for an additional eight years after the trial ended. The findings from this follow-up study, published in the July 23, 2003 issue of the *Journal of the American Medical Association,* as well as the initial trial results, are summarized in this chapter.

What was the purpose and design of the Alpha-Tocopherol, Beta-Carotene Cancer Prevention (ATBC) Trial?

The Alpha-Tocopherol, Beta-Carotene Cancer Prevention (ATBC) Trial was a cancer prevention trial conducted by the U.S. National Cancer Institute (NCI) and the National Public Health Institute of Finland from 1985 to 1993. The purpose of the study was to determine whether certain vitamin supplements would prevent lung cancer and other cancers in a group of 29,133 male smokers in Finland. The 50- to 69-year-old participants took a pill daily for five to eight years that contained one of the following: 50 milligrams (mg) alpha-tocopherol (a form of vitamin E), 20 mg of beta-carotene (a precursor of vitamin A), both, or a placebo (inactive pill that looked like the vitamin).

"Alpha-Tocopherol, Beta-Carotene Cancer Prevention (ATBC) Trial," July 22, 2003, Cancer.gov. Available online at http://www.cancer.gov.

What were the principal findings?

ATBC researchers reported that men who took beta-carotene had an 18 percent increased incidence of lung cancers and an 8 percent increased overall mortality. Vitamin E had no effect on lung cancer incidence or overall mortality. The men taking both supplements had outcomes similar to those taking beta-carotene alone (*New England Journal of Medicine* 1994;330:1029).

The adverse effects of beta-carotene appeared stronger in men with a relatively modest alcohol intake (more than 11 grams per day; 15 grams of alcohol is equivalent to one drink) and in those smoking at least 20 cigarettes daily (*Journal of the National Cancer Institute* 1996;88:1560).

Participants taking vitamin E had 32 percent fewer cases of prostate cancer and 41 percent fewer deaths from prostate cancer. Death from hemorrhagic stroke (a deficit of blood to the brain due to the rupture of a blood vessel) was also increased by 50 percent in men taking alpha-tocopherol supplements; the increase occurred primarily among men with hypertension. (*Journal of the National Cancer Institute* 1998;90:440 and *Arterioscler Thromb Vasc Biol* 2000;20:230).

What were the principal findings of the post-trial follow-up?

The participants stopped taking the vitamin supplements in April 1993. However, in order to evaluate the long-term effects of the vitamins on cancer incidence, and overall and cause-specific mortality, they were followed after the trial ended using data from the national registries in Finland. The researchers acquired additional data for cancer incidence and mortality related to specific causes through April 1999 (six years beyond the end of the trial), and for total mortality through April 2001 (eight years beyond the end of the trial). Following are the principal findings from the post-trial follow-up (*Journal of American Medical Association* 2003;290:476).

- In the eight-year follow-up period, the participants taking beta-carotene experienced 7 percent higher overall mortality than men on the placebo. However, this elevation was largely limited to the first four to six years of follow-up; during the last two years, the overall mortality rates were comparable to participants who did not receive beta-carotene.

- In the beta-carotene group, the higher mortality during the trial was due to cardiovascular disease and lung cancer. In contrast, the higher mortality during the post-intervention period was due to cardiovascular disease alone.

- The increased risks for lung cancer that occurred in participants supplemented with beta-carotene began to fall soon after the men stopped taking the vitamin, and were similar to the placebo group within four years.

- The lower prostate cancer incidence rates in participants taking alpha-tocopherol supplements during the trial returned toward normal soon after the trial ended, but remained below the placebo group rates throughout the six-year post-intervention period.

What were the conclusions and recommendations from the post-trial follow-up?

- The adverse effects from beta-carotene and the beneficial effects from supplementation with alpha-tocopherol (vitamin E) largely disappeared during the post-trial follow-up period.

- The findings indicate a symmetry in the time course during and after the trial. That is, the time it took for the elevated lung cancer rates and lower prostate cancer rates to occur was similar to the time for these adverse and beneficial effects to disappear.

- There were no additional beneficial late effects on cancer or mortality observed after the trial ended.

- The results of both the trial and post-trial follow-up of the ATBC Study, in conjunction with results from the CARET Study (beta-Carotene and Retinol Efficacy Trial) completed in 1996, continue to support the recommendation that beta-carotene supplementation should be avoided by smokers. The possible preventive effects of alpha-tocopherol on prostate cancer require confirmation in other ongoing trials.

- Continued follow-up of the participants will provide unique and valuable information on the duration of trial effects and potential late effects of intervention with these antioxidant vitamins. Further follow-up will also contribute to our understanding of the biological mechanisms through which such chemoprevention agents affect carcinogenesis and human cancer risk.

Why were vitamin E and beta-carotene chosen for this trial?

Vitamin E and beta-carotene were chosen because epidemiologic studies have linked high dietary intake and high serum levels of these micronutrients to a reduced risk of cancer, particularly lung cancer. Both are antioxidants, compounds that may prevent carcinogens from damaging DNA and other cellular systems.

Why was the ATBC Study conducted in Finland in men only?

The study was conducted in Finland because of the high lung cancer rates in men in that country, which were due primarily to cigarette smoking. Furthermore, Finland had a clinic system for the screening and treatment of lung diseases (mainly tuberculosis) through which the recruited population of smokers could participate in the study. Finland also has a national cancer registry, which keeps track of all the cancer cases identified in that country, a vital measurement for the large trial.

Finnish women were not included in the study because their rate of lung cancer was substantially lower than the rate for Finnish men. In 1985, the annual age-adjusted lung cancer rate for Finnish men was 67 cases per 100,000 men and for women was eight cases per 100,000 women.

How much did the study cost?

NCI allocated about $20 million over 10 years for the trial, with a similar sum contributed by the government and research institutions in Finland. In addition, F. Hoffmann-LaRoche Ltd., a pharmaceutical company based in Basel, Switzerland, supplied the 60 million pills the men took during the trial, without charge, at a cost to the company of about $3 million. The cost for the eight-year follow-up was about $3 million.

What are the results from other large-scale prevention studies?

The Beta-Carotene and Retinol Efficacy Trial (CARET) compared the effects of beta-carotene plus vitamin A (retinyl palmitate) to placebo in 18,314 men and women ages 45 to 74 who were either smokers, former smokers, and/or had been exposed to asbestos. A 28 percent higher lung cancer incidence and 17 percent higher overall mortality occurred in the group taking the vitamin supplementation.

The Physician's Health Study showed that beta-carotene supplementation had no effect on lung cancer or overall mortality among the 22,071 men ages 40 to 84 followed for an average of 12 years. However, this population was at lower risk for lung cancer compared to the participants in the ATBC or CARET trials.

What other large-scale dietary intervention studies are underway?

The Selenium and Vitamin E Cancer Prevention Trial (SELECT), sponsored by NCI, began in July 2001, and will determine if these two dietary supplements can protect against prostate cancer. The 32,400 participants will be randomized to receive daily supplements of either: selenium and vitamin E (alpha-tocopherol); selenium and placebo; vitamin E and placebo; two placebos. The trial is expected to end in 2013.

The Women's Health Study, headed by researchers at Boston's Brigham and Women's Hospital, is evaluating the benefits and risks of low-dose aspirin and vitamin E on cardiovascular disease and cancer among 40,000 female health professionals. When the trial began in 1992, there was a beta-carotene arm, which was dropped when the results from the other beta-carotene trials were announced. The trial is expected to end in August 2004.

The Physicians' Health Study II, headed by investigators at Harvard Medical School in Boston, is evaluating vitamin E, vitamin C, beta-carotene and a multivitamin for the prevention of cardiovascular disease, total cancer, and prostate cancer among 15,000 male physicians age 50 or older. The trial began in 1997 and is expected to end in December 2007.

Chapter 70

Studying How Cigarette Smoke Affects Peripheral Organs

It is well known that smoking cigarettes can directly and often fatally damage the lungs. But new research—with support from the National Institute for Biomedical Imaging and Bioengineering and the National Institute on Drug Abuse (NIDA), National Institutes of Health (NIH), and the Department of Energy—shows that cigarette smoke also decreases levels of a critical enzyme called monoamine oxidase B (MAO B) in the kidneys, heart, lungs, and spleen. Too much or too little of this crucial enzyme can have an effect on a person's mental or physical health.

MAO B is important because it breaks down the chemicals that allow nerve cells to communicate and regulate blood pressure.

PET, or positron emission tomography, employs computer technology and radioactive compounds to produce images of biochemical processes within living systems.

"Smoking is a major public health problem that results in approximately 440,000 deaths per year in the United States alone," says NIH Director Dr. Elias Zerhouni. "This new finding highlights the fact that the act of smoking cigarettes can affect biochemical systems within multiple organs other than the lungs and upper airways."

"When we think about smoking and the harmful effects of smoke, we usually think of the lungs and of nicotine," says NIDA Director Dr. Nora D. Volkow, one of the authors of the study. "But here we see

"PET Scans Show Cigarette Smoke Affects Peripheral Organs," from National Institutes of Health (NIH), *NIH News,* September 8, 2003; available online at http://www.nih.gov/news/pr/sep2003/nida-08.htm.

a marked effect on a major body enzyme in sites far removed from the lungs that we know is due to a substance other than nicotine. This alerts us to the fact that smoking, which is highly addictive, exposes the whole body to the thousands of compounds in tobacco smoke."

Dr. Joanna Fowler, together with Dr. Volkow and others at Brookhaven National Laboratory and the State University of New York at Stony Brook, conducted the study.

Dr. Fowler and the research team compared PET scans showing MAO B activity in 12 smokers with scans from 8 nonsmokers. The researchers observed that MAO B activity in the peripheral organs was reduced by one-third to almost one-half in smokers compared with nonsmokers.

The scientists caution that the effects of this finding remain unknown at present. "The consequences of reduced levels of this important enzyme need to be examined in greater detail," explains Dr. Fowler. "Though we do not know the physiological effects of such a reduction in MAO B in peripheral organs, we do know we need the enzyme to break down blood pressure-elevating chemical compounds in certain foods, as well as those that are released by nicotine. Thus, it is possible that lower levels of this enzyme in peripheral organs could have medical consequences."

Previous research by these scientists has shown that the level of MAO B is lower in the brains of smokers.

The study also was funded by the Office of National Drug Control Policy.

To view the PET scan, go to http://www.drugabuse.gov/Newsroom/03/NR9-08.html.

Chapter 71

ASSIST:
Americans Stop Smoking
Intervention Study

Questions and Answers about the Americans Stop Smoking Intervention Study

What is ASSIST?

At the time of the study (1991–1999), the American Stop Smoking Intervention Study (ASSIST) was the largest government-funded demonstration project to help states develop effective strategies to reduce smoking. In 1991, the National Cancer Institute (NCI), part of the National Institutes of Health, funded 17 state health departments and formed a partnership with the American Cancer Society to undertake the study. Focusing on policy change, the goal of ASSIST was to alter states' social, cultural, economic, and environmental factors that promote smoking.

What was the design of the study?

ASSIST was a large-scale experiment in which the observational unit was the state (its entire population and environment), and the goal was to change social, cultural, economic, and environmental factors

---

This chapter includes excerpts from "Questions and Answers: ASSIST Evaluation," National Cancer Institute (NCI), November 2003, and "Study Shows Strong Tobacco Control Programs and Policies Can Lower Smoking Rates," NCI, November 2003. For more information from the National Cancer Institute visit www.cancer.gov.

in the state that promote smoking behavior. This goal was accomplished primarily through interventions in four policy areas: 1) promoting smoke-free environments, 2) countering tobacco advertising and promotion, 3) limiting youths' tobacco access and availability, and 4) increasing tobacco prices by raising excise taxes. The statewide tobacco control plans were carried out in the 17 ASSIST states by a network of state and local coalitions charged with developing and implementing interventions.

The ASSIST states implemented the project in two phases: a two-year planning phase (October 1991 through October 1993) and a six-year implementation phase (November 1993 through September 1999).

The ASSIST evaluation compared changes in tobacco control policies, state per capita cigarette consumption, and adult smoking prevalence in the 17 ASSIST states with those in the 33 non-ASSIST states and the District of Columbia. The authors also analyzed the effect of program components and tobacco control policies on smoking prevalence and per capita cigarette consumption.

How were the intervention and outcomes measured?

The ASSIST evaluation compared changes in tobacco control policies, state per capita cigarette consumption, and adult smoking prevalence in ASSIST vs. non-ASSIST states and the District of Columbia. Smoking prevalence, or the number of people who smoke, was obtained from adults interviewed in the NCI-sponsored Tobacco Use Supplement to the U.S. Census Bureau's Current Population Survey in 1992-1993 and 1998-1999. Per capita cigarette consumption was calculated every two months for each state from sales data for the total number of cigarette packs moved from wholesale warehouses, divided by the state's adult population.

The focus of the ASSIST project was on policy change, which was assessed with a measure called Initial Outcomes Index (IOI). IOI was developed to serve as an indication of the intensity of states' tobacco control policies. It includes the percentage of smokers covered by 100 percent smoke-free work sites, total cigarette price, and legislative ratings. The authors also developed Strength of Tobacco Control Index (SOTC) to evaluate the ASSIST program. SOTC summarizes the multiple components of tobacco control efforts and provides information on which components of ASSIST or ASSIST-like programs might be related to lower smoking prevalence or cigarette consumption. SOTC is a multi-element measure that assesses the effects of three variables in each state: tobacco control resources (funding), capacity and infrastructure, and program efforts focused on policy and environmental change. Both IOI and SOTC are promising measures that can be used for future research in tobacco control and evaluation.

What were the key findings of the ASSIST evaluation?

The authors found that ASSIST states had a greater decrease in adult smoking prevalence than non-ASSIST states. The ASSIST evaluation also showed that states that experienced greater improvement in tobacco control policies had larger decreases in per capita cigarette consumption. States (not including the District of Columbia) with higher policy scores also had lower smoking prevalence. In addition, the authors found that states with greater "capacity," or ability to implement tobacco control activities—such as states with tobacco control infrastructure in the health department, staff experience, and strong interagency and statewide relationships—had lower per capita cigarette consumption. Lastly, there was evidence that policy interventions may be more effective at reducing women's smoking.

What do these results tell us?

The results from ASSIST are the latest evidence that investing in state tobacco control programs that focus on strong tobacco regulations and policies is an effective strategy for reducing tobacco use. The small but statistically significant differences in the reduction of adult smoking prevalence in ASSIST states, when applied on a population basis, could be expected to have a large impact on the public. If all 50 states and the District of Columbia had implemented ASSIST, there would be approximately 278,700 fewer smokers nationally.

The finding that states with a greater change in their tobacco control policies during ASSIST had larger decreases in per capita cigarette consumption suggests that interventions which result in tobacco control policy change can have a strong and sustained effect on the amount of cigarettes smoked. This conclusion adds to the body of similar research and expert reports that document the importance of a comprehensive approach to tobacco control. Although policy efforts take time, they can bring about major changes in social norms, including smoking behavior.

The finding that states with stronger infrastructure or capacity (ability to implement tobacco control activities) had lower per capita cigarette consumption is more evidence that when tobacco control programs are strong and well-supported, a decrease in the amount of smoking can be achieved. This is the first study to provide a method to quantify states' capacity to implement tobacco control programs.

What states participated in the study?

The 17 ASSIST states were: Colorado, Indiana, Maine, Massachusetts, Michigan, Minnesota, Missouri, New Jersey, New Mexico, New York, North Carolina, Rhode Island, South Carolina, Virginia, West Virginia, Washington, and Wisconsin. However, the evaluation encompassed all states and the District of Columbia and includes comparisons between the 17 ASSIST states and the 33 non-ASSIST states and D.C.

The ASSIST states had a combined population of 91 million people, more than a third of the population of the United States. The ASSIST population included more than 10 million African Americans and 7 million people of Hispanic origin or other racial or ethnic minority groups.

How were the 17 ASSIST states chosen?

All 50 states and the District of Columbia were eligible to compete for the NCI ASSIST contracts; 35 states applied for the contracts and 23 of those 35 states were deemed eligible for funding based on published selection criteria. Only 17 states were awarded contracts due to budgetary constraints.

ASSIST was a demonstration project and not a randomized experiment. Therefore, the states chosen for ASSIST funding represented a wide range in terms of their ability and experience in developing and implementing tobacco control programs.

Did the evaluation include youth smokers, as well?

No. This study measured cigarette consumption and smoking prevalence in adults, defined as persons at least 18 years old.

How much or how often must a person smoke to be considered a smoker in this evaluation?

A smoker was defined as a person who used cigarettes on a current, everyday, or some-day basis and had smoked at least 100 cigarettes in his or her lifetime.

How much did the study cost?

NCI provided an average of $1.14 million per state per year during the six-year implementation phase (1993–1999), for a total of $128 million over the eight years of the program. Other additional funding and resources were available to the states through voluntary organizations and other non-federal sources.

What were the limitations of the study?

An evaluation of states restricts the number of observations to 51 (50 states plus the District of Columbia) and reduces the ability to detect small but statistically important changes, particularly for per capita cigarette consumption. Despite this lower ability to detect changes, the authors did find some statistically significant differences.

Complicating the ASSIST evaluation was the diffusion of materials and interventions from ASSIST states to non-ASSIST states, with no restriction on the free flow of knowledge and technical assistance. ASSIST served as an impetus for change, as by 1994, the Centers for Disease Control and Prevention supported tobacco control programs in all non-ASSIST states, and the Robert Wood Johnson Foundation's SmokeLess States program was implemented in many ASSIST and non-ASSIST states. In addition, during the 1990s, tobacco control activities and issues received more media attention than ever before in most states. These factors possibly decreased the relative difference in outcomes between ASSIST and non-ASSIST states.

Although the ASSIST researchers attempted to identify and address as many factors as possible that affect smoking behavior, some political, social, and economic factors outside the control of the ASSIST intervention could have caused the delivery of the intervention strategies to differ between states. For example, some ASSIST states might have been better able than others to build their infrastructure and focus on policy change as outlined in the ASSIST program plans.

In addition, during the period of the ASSIST project, the tobacco industry spent approximately $47 billion nationwide to market tobacco products (Federal Trade Commission, 1992–1999 spending) and previously confidential tobacco industry documents demonstrate that the tobacco industry acted to counter the ASSIST project and to oppose the policy measures it sought to implement at the state level. However, the authors of the ASSIST evaluation were not able to develop a quantitative measure of the tobacco industry's countervailing efforts and are unable to determine the degree to which the tobacco industry affected the success of the ASSIST project.

Conclusion

"Our research emphasizes the importance of strong tobacco control programs and effective policies," said Frances A. Stillman, Ph.D., of the Johns Hopkins Bloomberg School of Public Health in Baltimore, Md., first author of the study and director of the ASSIST evaluation. "States can reduce smoking prevalence and the enormous health and economic burden of smoking if they put in place proven programs and policies." According to the Centers for Disease Control and Prevention (CDC), cigarette smoking is responsible for more than 440,000 deaths in the United States each year.

Source: Stillman FA, Hartman AM, Graubard BI, Gilpin EA, Murray DM, Gibson JT. Evaluation of the American Stop Smoking Intervention Study (ASSIST): A report of outcomes. *Journal of the National Cancer Institute* 2003 Nov. 19;95 (22):1681–91.

Part Five

Tobacco Control and Use Prevention

Chapter 72

Preventing Tobacco Use

The Reality

- Tobacco use is the single most preventable cause of death and disease, causing more than 440,000 premature deaths annually in the United States during 1995–1999.

- Smoking can cause chronic lung disease, coronary heart disease, and stroke, as well as cancer of the lungs, larynx, esophagus, mouth, and bladder. In addition, smoking contributes to cancer of the cervix, pancreas, and kidneys.

- Nearly 70% of the more than 46.5 million American adults who smoke cigarettes want to quit, but few are able to quit permanently without help.

- Approximately 80% of adult smokers started smoking before the age of 18. Every day, nearly 5,000 young people under age 18 try their first cigarette.

- If current smoking patterns in the United States persist, an estimated 6.4 million of today's children will die prematurely of tobacco-related diseases.

National Center for Chronic Disease Prevention and Health Promotion, 2003; available online at http://www.cdc.gov/nccdphp/pe_factsheets/pe-tobacco.htm.

The Cost of Tobacco Use

• Direct medical expenditures attributed to smoking total more than $75 billion per year. In addition, smoking costs an estimated $80 billion per year in lost productivity.

• About 14% of all Medicaid expenditures are for smoking-related illnesses.

• Each of the approximately 22 billion packs of cigarettes sold in the United States in 1999 cost the nation an estimated $7.18 in medical care costs and lost productivity.

Table 72.1. Average Annual Number of U.S. Deaths Attributable to Cigarette Smoking, 1995–1999 (Total average number: 442,398)

Lung Cancer	124,813
Other Cancers	30,948
Chronic Lung Disease	82,431
Coronary Heart Disease	81,976
Stroke	17,445
Other Diagnoses	104,785

Source: CDC. Annual smoking-attributable mortality, years of potential life lost, and economic costs in the United States, 1995–1999. *MMWR* 2002;51(14):300–3.

How Tobacco Control Saves Lives

A *New England Journal of Medicine* report concluded that the California Tobacco Control Program was associated with 33,000 fewer deaths from heart disease from 1989 to 1997.

Rates of lung cancer among men have declined more rapidly in California than in other parts of the country, and rates of lung cancer among women in California are declining while they continue to increase elsewhere.

Following the establishment of the Massachusetts Tobacco Control Program, state rates of smoking during pregnancy dropped sharply, from 25% in 1990 to 13% in 1996. Eliminating smoking during pregnancy could reduce the percentage of infants with low birth weight by 17%–26%.

How Tobacco Control Saves Money

The State of California estimates that their program has resulted in an overall cost savings of $8.4 billion. For every $1 spent on the program between 1990 and 1998, an estimated $3.62 in direct medical costs were avoided.

Smokers who successfully quit smoking reduce the anticipated medical costs associated with heart attack and stroke by an estimated $47 in the first year and $853 during the following seven years.

Recent studies have concluded that reducing smoking prevalence among pregnant women by one percentage point over seven years would prevent 57,200 low-birthweight births and save $572 million and that every $1 invested an effective school-based tobacco prevention program saves $19.90 in associated medical costs.

An economic assessment found that a health care plan's annual cost of covering treatment to help people quit smoking ranged from $0.89 to $4.92 per smoker, whereas the annual cost of treating smoking-related illness ranged from $6.00 to $33.00 per smoker.

Effective Strategies

CDC's *Best Practices for Comprehensive Tobacco Control Programs,* based on data from states that have comprehensive programs, provides evidence-based guidelines for establishing a tobacco control program that has the following nine components: community programs to reduce tobacco use, chronic disease programs to reduce the burden of tobacco-related diseases, school programs, enforcement, statewide programs, counter-marketing, cessation programs, surveillance and evaluation, and administration and management.

These guidelines are further supported by the independent Task Force on Community Preventive Services, which strongly recommends increasing the price of tobacco products, conducting mass media campaigns, developing multicomponent cessation programs, and instituting smoking bans and restrictions to reduce exposure to environmental tobacco smoke.

Funding comprehensive local programs—as Arizona, California, Florida, Massachusetts, and Oregon have done—produces measurable progress toward meeting statewide tobacco control objectives, including declines in per capita cigarette consumption, in rates of exposure to secondhand smoke, and in the percentage of successful attempts by young people to buy cigarettes.

Hope for the Future

If these effective tobacco control strategies are fully implemented, we will achieve the *Healthy People 2010* objectives of reducing the percentage of the U.S. population who smoke cigarettes to 12% of adults and 16% of adolescents. Meeting this goal will prevent more than 4 million deaths that would otherwise occur due to tobacco-related diseases.

Table 72.2. Percentage of High School Students Who Reported Current Cigarette Smoking,* United States, 1991–2001

Year	Percent
1991	27.5
1993	30.5
1995	34.8
1997	36.4
1999	34.8
2001	28.5
Healthy People 2010 Goal	16.0

* Smoking one or more cigarettes during the previous 30 days.
Source: CDC, Youth Risk Behavior Surveillance System.

State Programs in Action: Arizona

In 1994, Arizona passed the Tobacco Tax and Healthcare Act, which increased the tax on cigarettes from 18 cents to 58 cents and allocated 23% of the resulting revenues to tobacco-control activities. Since 1995, Arizona has used these tobacco-control funds (approximately $30 million per year) to support the Tobacco Education and Prevention Program (TEPP), a comprehensive program to prevent and reduce tobacco use. TEPP, which also receives CDC support, currently funds approximately 22 local community organizations or agencies, including those among American Indian tribes. The program also administers the statewide quit-smoking help line in both English and Spanish. TEPP has worked with other groups in the state to develop a checklist for schools to assess their progress toward meeting the new tobacco-free schools guidelines and to help schools adopt their own tobacco-use policies.

TEPP has already had a dramatic effect on tobacco use in Arizona. According to the 1999 Arizona Adult Tobacco Survey Report, the percentage of smokers 18–24 years old declined 24% from 1996 to 1999, and the percentage of all adults who reported smoking decreased by 21%. The prevalence of tobacco use decreased among women, men, whites, and Hispanics throughout the state. Two of the sharpest decreases were among those with incomes less than $10,000 and those with less than an eighth-grade education, a finding that offers promise for eliminating tobacco-related disparities. These declines in tobacco use are a striking example of what a comprehensive tobacco control program can accomplish when it is supported by adequate resources.

Chapter 73

Comprehensive Tobacco Control Programs

Facts about Comprehensive Tobacco Control Programs

Rationale for Comprehensive Interventions

- Statewide programs have emerged as the new laboratory for developing and evaluating comprehensive plans to reduce tobacco use.

- Initial results from statewide tobacco control programs are encouraging, particularly in per capita declines of tobacco consumption.

This chapter includes "Comprehensive Programs: Fact Sheet," National Center for Chronic Disease Prevention and Health Promotion (NCCDPHP), Centers for Disease Control and Prevention (CDC), April 2001; excerpts from "Best Practices for Comprehensive Tobacco Control Programs, August 1999: Executive Summary," NCCDPHP, CDC, reviewed September 2003 with supplemental information from the full report: Centers for Disease Control and Prevention. *Best Practices for Comprehensive Tobacco Control Programs—August 1999*. Atlanta GA: U.S. Department of Health and Human Services, Centers for Disease Control and Prevention, National Center for Chronic Disease Prevention and Health Promotion, Office on Smoking and Health, August 1999. Reprinted, with corrections, and available online at www.cdc.gov/tobacco/ research_data/stat_nat_data/bestprac.pdf; "Comprehensive School Programs Boost Smoking Prevention Success among Oregon Eighth Graders," Press Release, NCCDPHP, CDC, August 10, 2001, with supplemental information from "School-Based Tobacco Use Prevention Programs," NCCDPHP, CDC, August 10, 2001; and "Teens Report Being More Susceptible to Smoking after Minnesota Ends Anti-Tobacco Campaign," Office of Communication, CDC, April 15, 2004.

- State findings also suggest that youth behaviors regarding tobacco use are more difficult to change than adult ones.

- People do not make behavior choices in isolation, but rather in a larger, complex context that includes the family, community, and culture; the economy and physical environment; formal and informal government policy; and the prevailing legal atmosphere. Programs to reduce tobacco use will be most effective if they address all the components that may influence the individual's behavior choices.

- There are several advantages to shifting from an approach that targets the individual to a population approach that uses social, policy, and environmental strategies.

- First, by recognizing that many environmental determinants of health behavior are not under the direct control of the individual, the population approach avoids blaming persons who fail to change their behavior.

- Second, many individual efforts may fail to reach those in greatest need. Because many of these strategies are most effective with better-educated, wealthier persons, the disparities in health between population groups may widen.

- Third, making regulatory and policy changes can be more cost-effective than conducting numerous interventions to modify individual behavior.

CDC's National Tobacco Control Program

In May 1999, the Centers for Disease Control and Prevention (CDC) launched the National Tobacco Control Program (NTCP), bringing the various federal initiative activities into one national program. In fiscal year 2000, the NTCP distributed $59 million for comprehensive tobacco control efforts in all states, the District of Columbia, seven U.S. territories, and Native American tribal organizations. CDC recommends four program goals in its comprehensive framework for statewide programs:

- Prevent initiation of tobacco use among young people.

- Promote quitting among adults and young people.

- Eliminate exposure to environmental tobacco smoke (ETS).

- Identify and eliminate health disparities among population groups.

Each program goal would be fully addressed by implementing four program components:

- community interventions, which include diverse entities such as schools, health agencies, city and county governments, and civic, social, and recreational organizations;

- counter-marketing, which includes using media advocacy, paid media, pro-health promotions, and other media strategies to change social norms related to tobacco use;

- program policy and regulation, which addresses such issues as minors' access, tobacco pricing, advertising and promotion, clean indoor air, product regulation, and tobacco use treatment; and

- surveillance and evaluation, which includes monitoring the tobacco industry's promotional campaigns, evaluating the economic impact of ETS laws and policies, conducting surveys of public opinion on program interventions, and making ongoing refinements that lead to more effective prevention strategies.

The elimination of health disparities among population groups remains a challenge due to the lack of culturally appropriate programs of proven efficacy. However, in recent years, a number of people and organizations with more diverse backgrounds have assumed a greater role in efforts to reduce tobacco use. Particularly in view of the tobacco industry's targeted marketing to women, young people, and racial/ethnic populations, such heightened activity is critically important for ensuring that non-smoking becomes the norm within diverse communities.

To be effective, comprehensive programs should include campaigns that:

- target young people and adults with complementary messages;

- highlight nonsmoking as the majority behavior;

- communicate the dangers of tobacco while providing constructive alternatives;

- use multiple non-preachy voices in a complementary, reinforcing mix of media and outdoor advertising;

- include grassroots promotions, local media advocacy, event sponsorships, and other community tie-ins; and

- encourage youth empowerment and involvement.

Best Practices for Comprehensive Tobacco Control Programs

CDC recommends that states establish tobacco control programs that are comprehensive, sustainable, and accountable. The information in this section document draws upon "best practices" determined by evidence-based analyses of comprehensive state tobacco control programs. Evidence supporting the programmatic recommendations are of two types. Recommendations for chronic disease programs to reduce the burden of tobacco-related diseases, school programs, cessation programs, enforcement, and counter-marketing program elements are based primarily upon published evidence-based practices. Other program categories rely mainly upon the evidence of the efficacy of the large-scale and sustained efforts of two states (California and Massachusetts) that have been funding comprehensive tobacco prevention and control programs using state tobacco excise taxes.

The funding required for implementing programs will vary depending on state characteristics, such as demographic factors, tobacco use prevalence, and other factors. Although the type of supporting evidence for each of the recommended nine program components differs, evidence supports the implementation of some level of activity in each program area. Approximate annual costs to implement all of the recommended program components have been estimated to range from $7 to $20 per capita in smaller States (population under 3 million), $6 to $17 per capita in medium-sized States (population 3 to 7 million), and $5 to $16 per capita in larger States (population over 7 million).

The best practices address nine components of comprehensive tobacco control programs.

1. Community Programs to Reduce Tobacco Use

Local community programs cover a wide range of prevention activities including engaging youth in developing and implementing tobacco control interventions; developing partnerships with local organizations; conducting educational programs for young people, parents, enforcement officials, community and business leaders, health care providers, school personnel, and others; and promoting governmental and voluntary policies to promote clean indoor air, restrict access to tobacco products, provide coverage for treatment, and achieve other policy objectives.

Community programs should focus on four goals: 1) prevention of the initiation of tobacco use among young people, 2) cessation for current users of tobacco, 3) protection from environmental tobacco smoke, and 4) elimination of disparities in tobacco use among populations. These goals can best be achieved by programs that 1) increase the number of organizations and individuals involved in planning and conducting community-level education and training programs; 2) use state and local counter-marketing campaigns to place pro-health messages that inform, educate, and support local tobacco control initiatives and policies; 3) promote the adoption of public and private tobacco control policies; and 4) measure outcomes using surveillance and evaluation techniques.

To achieve the individual behavior change that supports the non-use of tobacco, communities must change the way tobacco is promoted, sold, and used while changing the knowledge, attitudes, and practices of young people, tobacco users, and nonusers. Effective community programs involve people in their homes, work sites, schools, places of worship and entertainment, civic organizations, and other public places. To achieve lasting changes, programs in local governments, voluntary and civic organizations, and community-based organizations require funds to hire staff, cover operating expenses, purchase resource and educational materials, provide education and training programs, support communication campaigns, organize the community to debate the issues, establish local plans of action, and draw other leaders into tobacco control activities.

2. Chronic Disease Programs to Reduce the Burden of Tobacco-Related Diseases

Even if current tobacco use stopped, the residual burden of disease among past users would cause disease for decades to come. As part of a comprehensive tobacco control program, communities can focus attention directly on tobacco-related diseases both to prevent them and to detect them early. The following are examples of such disease programs:

- Cardiovascular disease prevention
- Asthma prevention
- Oral health programs
- Cancer registries

3. School Programs

Because most people who start smoking are younger than age 18, programs that prevent the onset of smoking during the school year are a crucial part of a comprehensive tobacco prevention program. Several studies have shown that school-based tobacco prevention programs that identify the social influences that promote tobacco use among youth and that teach skills to resist such influences can significantly reduce or delay adolescent smoking. Programs that vary in format, scope, delivery methods, and community setting have produced differences in smoking prevalence between intervention and nonintervention groups ranging from 25% to 60% and persisting for one to five years after completion of the programs. Although long-term follow-ups of programs have indicated that the effect may dissipate over time, other studies have shown that the effectiveness of school-based tobacco prevention programs is strengthened by booster sessions and community-wide programs involving parents and community organizations and including school policies, mass media, and restrictions on youth access. Because many students begin using tobacco before high school and impressions about tobacco use are formed even earlier, tobacco use prevention education must be provided in elementary school and continued through middle and high school grades.

School program activities include implementing CDC's *Guidelines for School Health Programs to Prevent Tobacco Use and Addiction*, which call for tobacco-free policies, evidence-based curricula, teacher training, parental involvement, and cessation services; implementing evidence-based curricula identified through CDC's Research to Classroom Project; and linking school-based efforts with local community coalitions and statewide media and educational campaigns.

4. Enforcement

Enforcement of tobacco control policies enhances their efficacy by deterring violators and by sending a message to the public that community leaders believe that these policies are important. The two primary policy areas that require enforcement activity are restrictions on minors' access to tobacco and on smoking in public places.

Examples of enforcement activities related to minors' access to tobacco include:

- Conducting frequent retailer compliance checks to identify retailers who sell tobacco to minors.

- Imposing a graduated series of civil penalties on the retailer, including license revocation if possible.

- Eliminating tobacco vending machines and self-service displays in stores accessible to young people.

In addition, providing comprehensive merchant education, including information on health effects, can deter retailer violators.

Examples of enforcement activities related to smoking in public places include:

- Establishing and publicizing telephone hotlines for reporting violations of clean indoor air ordinances and laws and investigating reports received.

- Reporting violations noted by state officials performing health, environmental, and other routine inspections.

5. Statewide Programs

Statewide projects can increase the capacity of local programs by providing technical assistance on evaluating programs, promoting media advocacy, implementing smoke-free policies, and reducing minors' access to tobacco. Supporting organizations that have statewide access to racial, ethnic, and diverse communities can help eliminate the disparities in tobacco use among the state's various population groups. Statewide and regional grants to organizations representing cities, business and professional groups, law enforcement, and youth groups inform their membership about tobacco control issues and encourage their participation in local efforts.

6. Counter-Marketing

Counter-marketing activities can promote smoking cessation and decrease the likelihood of initiation. In addition, counter-marketing messages can have a powerful influence on public support for tobacco control intervention and set a supportive climate for school and community efforts. Counter-marketing attempts to counter pro-tobacco influences and increase pro-health messages and influences throughout a State, region, or community. Counter-marketing consists of a wide range of efforts, including paid television, radio, billboard, and print counter-advertising at the state and local level; media advocacy and other public relations techniques using such tactics as press releases, local events, and health promotion activities;

and efforts to reduce or replace tobacco industry sponsorship and pro-motions.

Tobacco advertising and promotion activities appear both to stimu-late adult consumption and to increase the risk of youth initiation. Children buy the most heavily advertised brands and are three times more affected by advertising than are adults. One study estimated that 34% of all youth experimentation with smoking in California between 1993 and 1996 can be attributed to tobacco promotional ac-tivities. Today's average 14-year-old already has been exposed to more than $20 billion in imagery advertising and promotions since age six, creating a "friendly familiarity" with tobacco products and an environ-ment in which smoking is seen as glamorous, social, and normal.

In light of these ubiquitous and sustained pro-tobacco messages, counter-marketing efforts of comparable intensity are needed to alter the environmental context of tobacco use. Although the relative effectiveness of specific message concepts and strategies is widely debated, research from all available sources shows that counter-marketing must have sufficient reach, frequency, and duration to be successful. Effective counter-marketing efforts should:

- Combine messages on prevention, cessation, and protection from secondhand smoke; target both young people and adults; and address both individual behaviors and public policies.

- Include grassroots promotions, local media advocacy, event sponsorships, and other community tie-ins to support and rein-force the statewide campaign.

- Maximize the number, variety, and novelty of messages and produc-tion styles rather than communicate a few messages repeatedly.

- Use nonauthoritarian appeals that avoid direct exhortations not to smoke and do not highlight a single theme, tagline, identifier, or sponsor.

Counter-marketing campaigns are a primary activity in all states with comprehensive tobacco control programs.

7. Cessation Programs

Programs that successfully assist young and adult smokers in quit-ting can produce a quicker and probably larger short-term public health benefit than any other component of a comprehensive tobacco control program. Smokers who quit smoking before age 50 cut in half their risk of dying in the next 15 years. In addition, the cost savings from reduced tobacco use resulting from the implementation of moderately-priced, effective smoking cessation interventions would more than pay for these interventions within three to four years. One smoker successfully quitting reduces the anticipated medical costs associated with acute myocardial infarction and stroke by an estimated $47 in the first year and $853 during the next seven years. Smoking cessation is more cost-effective than other commonly provided clinical preventive services, including mammography, colon cancer screening, PAP tests, treatment of mild to moderate hypertension, and treatment of high cholesterol.

State action on tobacco-use treatment should include the following elements:

- Establishing population-based counseling and treatment programs, such as cessation helplines.

- Fully implementing the Agency for Health Care Policy and Research smoking cessation guidelines.

- Covering treatment for tobacco use under both public and private insurance.

- Eliminating cost barriers to treatment for underserved populations, particularly the uninsured.

8. Surveillance and Evaluation

A surveillance and evaluation system monitors program accountability for state policymakers and others responsible for fiscal oversight. Surveillance is the monitoring of tobacco-related behaviors, attitudes, and health outcomes at regular intervals of time. Program evaluation efforts build upon surveillance systems by linking statewide and local program efforts to progress in achieving intermediate and primary outcome objectives.

Administration and Management

An effective tobacco control program requires a strong management structure to facilitate coordination of program components, involvement of multiple state agencies (for example, health, education, and law enforcement) and levels of local government, and partnership with statewide voluntary health organizations and community groups. In addition, administration and management systems are required to prepare and implement contracts and provide fiscal and program monitoring.

Comprehensive School Programs Boost Smoking Prevention Success among Oregon Eighth Graders

A new study from the state of Oregon and the Centers for Disease Control and Prevention (CDC) shows that students in school districts funded to implement CDC's school tobacco use prevention guidelines were about 20 percent less likely to smoke than students in non-funded schools.

The Oregon Health Division found that between spring 1999 and spring 2000, smoking rates among eighth graders declined significantly more in a self-selected sample of funded schools (from 16.6 to 13 percent) than in a comparison group of non-funded schools (from 17 to 15.7 percent).

In addition, among the funded schools, the study found a strong dose-response effect between how fully schools implemented CDC's guidelines and how much smoking rates declined. Between 1999 and 2000 rates declined from 14.2 to 8.2 percent in schools with the highest implementation scores, from 17.8 to 13.9 percent in schools with middle scores, and from 17.1 to 15.6 percent in schools with the lowest scores. Smoking declines in the lowest-scoring schools were almost equal to the declines observed in non-funded schools.

"This study shows that comprehensive school programs really do work to prevent teen smoking and can be an effective part of a state's effort to prevent and reduce tobacco use," said CDC Director, Dr. Jeffrey Koplan. "Along with good, tested curricula, we need strong policies that keep our schools tobacco-free, and the involvement of parents and the whole community are an important part of the package."

The Oregon study adds to a large body of evidence documented in the 2000 Surgeon General's Report, *Reducing Tobacco Use*, that school-based programs, combined with community and media-based activities, can effectively prevent or postpone smoking onset in 20 to 40 percent of U.S. adolescents.

"Unfortunately, very few schools nationwide are implementing the major components of our tobacco use prevention guidelines," said Lawrence W. Green Dr.P.H, acting director of CDC's Office on Smoking and Health. "We hope this latest study will motivate more schools to adopt effective comprehensive programs and implement them fully, as they were designed to be."

CDC's school guidelines call for tobacco-free school policies, family involvement, community involvement, tobacco prevention curriculum instruction, teacher and staff training, and student tobacco use cessation support.

CDC's *Guidelines for School Health Programs to Prevent Tobacco Use and Addiction*, recommends schools should:

- Develop and enforce a school policy on tobacco use.

- Provide instruction about the short- and long-term effects of tobacco use, social influences on tobacco use, peer norms regarding tobacco use, and refusal skills.

- Provide tobacco-use prevention education in kindergarten through 12th grade, with especially intensive instruction in junior high or middle school.

- Provide program-specific training for teachers.

- Involve parents and families in support of school-based programs to prevent tobacco use.

- Support cessation efforts among students and school staff who use tobacco.

- Assess the tobacco-use prevention program at regular intervals.

Programs with the most educational contacts during the critical years for smoking adoption (age 11 to 15 years) are more likely to be effective, as are programs that address a broad range of educational needs. Educational curricula that address social influences that encourage tobacco use among youth (friends, family, and media), have shown consistently more effectiveness than programs based on other models.

For More Information

The Oregon study appears in the August 10, 2001 issue of CDC's *Morbidity and Mortality Weekly Report*. More information about CDC's school health program activities can be found at CDC's Division of Adolescent and School Health website, http://www.cdc.gov/nccdphp/dash.

Teens Report Being More Susceptible to Smoking after Minnesota Ends Anti-Tobacco Campaign

The halt to an aggressive tobacco prevention campaign in Minnesota led to a rapid and significant increase in the proportion of that state's teens who reported being susceptible to cigarette smoking— an important predictor of youth tobacco use. After the program ended, youth self-reported susceptibility to cigarette smoking increased nearly 10 percentage points—from 43.3 percent in July–August 2003 to 52.9 percent in November–December 2003.

The study—published in the April 16, 2004 issue of the Centers for Disease Control and Prevention (CDC) journal, *Morbidity and Mortality Weekly Report*—provides early evidence of the possible detrimental public health impact of state cutbacks in paid anti-tobacco campaigns. Information collected from telephone surveys of Minnesota youths aged 12 to 17 found that teens reported being more susceptible to cigarette smoking in less than six months following the elimination of the state's Target Market youth prevention campaign. Susceptibility to cigarette smoking was defined as a response other than "strongly disagree" to the statement, "You will smoke a cigarette in the next year."

"It's simply unacceptable that youth in our country continue to smoke," said CDC Director Dr. Julie Gerberding. "Young people are our future and we must continue to provide them with the knowledge, support, and self-esteem necessary for them to make healthy choices like not smoking."

The phone surveys also found that the percentage of young people aware of the anti-tobacco campaign fell by a third—from 84.5 percent in July–August 2003 to 56.5 percent in November–December 2003. The Target Market campaign began in Minnesota in 2000. Two previous surveys, the first conducted in July–September 2002 and the second in March–April 2003 found both an increase in confirmed campaign awareness and no increase in susceptibility to smoking. Confirmed campaign awareness was defined as awareness of the Target Market brand logo (the capital letters "TM" inside a circle).

In Minnesota, annual funding for the tobacco prevention and control program was reduced more than 80 percent—from \$23.7 million in 2000 to \$4.6 million in July 2003, ending the youth-focused Target Market campaign. The new survey findings are consistent with evaluation data from Massachusetts, where a 92 percent cut in that state's tobacco control program was followed by a large increase in illegal tobacco sales to minors.

"We are seeing the early signs of the reversal of the last five years of progress in preventing young people from starting smoking. It would be unconscionable to have tools as effective as these media campaigns at our disposal and not fully support them to reduce the epidemic of teen smoking," said Dr. James Marks, director, CDC's National Center for Chronic Disease Prevention and Health Promotion.

The Minnesota surveys were conducted by a team from the University of Miami School of Medicine in collaboration with the Minnesota Department of Health.

Chapter 74

Issues in Reducing Tobacco Use

Overview

Tobacco use, particularly smoking, remains the number one cause of preventable disease and death in the United States. This report of the Surgeon General on smoking and health is the first to offer a composite review of the various methods used to reduce and prevent tobacco use. It evaluates each of five major approaches to reducing tobacco use: educational, clinical, regulatory, economic, and comprehensive. Further, the report attempts to place the approaches in the larger context of tobacco control, providing a vision for the future of tobacco use prevention and control based on these available tools. The report is clear in its overriding conclusion: Although our knowledge about tobacco control remains imperfect, we know more than enough to act now.

This chapter includes excerpts from: "Reducing Tobacco Use: A Report of the Surgeon General—At a Glance," Centers for Disease Control and Prevention, National Center for Chronic Disease Prevention and Health Promotion, Office on Smoking and Health, reviewed September 2003; *Reducing Tobacco Use: A Report of the Surgeon General—Executive Summary*. Atlanta, Georgia: U.S. Department of Health and Human Services, Centers for Disease Control and Prevention, National Center for Chronic Disease Prevention and Health Promotion, Office on Smoking and Health, 2000; and *Reducing Tobacco Use: A Report of the Surgeon General* (Full Report). Atlanta, Georgia: U.S. Department of Health and Human Services, Centers for Disease Control and Prevention, National Center for Chronic Disease Prevention and Health Promotion, Office on Smoking and Health, 2000.

Major Conclusions of the Surgeon General's Report

- Efforts to prevent the onset or continuance of tobacco use face the pervasive, countervailing influence of tobacco promotion by the tobacco industry, a promotion that takes place despite overwhelming evidence of adverse health effects from tobacco use.

- The available approaches to reducing tobacco use—educational, clinical, regulatory, economic, and comprehensive—differ substantially in their techniques and in the metric by which success can be measured. A hierarchy of effectiveness is difficult to construct.

- Approaches with the largest span of impact (economic, regulatory, and comprehensive) are likely to have the greatest long-term, population impact. Those with a smaller span of impact (educational and clinical) are of greater importance in helping individuals resist or abandon the use of tobacco.

- Each of the modalities reviewed provides evidence of effectiveness.

- Educational strategies, conducted in conjunction with community- and media-based activities, can postpone or prevent smoking onset in 20 to 40 percent of adolescents.

- Pharmacologic treatment of nicotine addiction, combined with behavioral support, will enable 20 to 25 percent of users to remain abstinent at one year post treatment. Even less intense measures, such as physicians advising their patients to quit smoking, can produce cessation proportions of 5 to 10 percent.

- Regulation of advertising and promotion, particularly that directed at young people, is very likely to reduce both prevalence and uptake of tobacco use.

- Clean air regulations and restriction of minors' access to tobacco products contribute to a changing social norm with regard to smoking and may influence prevalence directly.

- An optimal level of excise taxation on tobacco products will reduce the prevalence of smoking, the consumption of tobacco, and the long-term health consequences of tobacco use.

- The impact of these various efforts, as measured with a variety of techniques, is likely to be underestimated because of the synergistic effect of these modalities. The potential for combined effects underscores the need for comprehensive approaches.

- State tobacco control programs, funded by excise taxes on tobacco products and settlements with the tobacco industry, have produced early, encouraging evidence of the efficacy of the comprehensive approach to reducing tobacco use.

The Attraction of Cigarettes

Throughout its boom period, from the 1920s until the mid-1960s, cigarette smoking was generally regarded as a consumer activity rather than as a medical problem. In its commercial essence, the cigarette is simply a "package," as a Philip Morris Companies Inc. memorandum has suggested, for a "product." In fact, the cigarette is by far the most commercially successful package for the product—tobacco, itself a delivery device for nicotine—yet devised. Such thinking fits well with the notion that consumption is an act of imagination—that is, that one buys not the product but rather the attributes for which the product is merely the vehicle.

Each vehicle for nicotine delivery has different social propensities. The unique qualities of the cigarette as a tobacco form were critical in its role as the agent through which tobacco use was made both available and acceptable to all social classes. Put simply, cigarettes not only made tobacco cheaper (through automated production) but also easier to use. This utility stemmed from several distinctive features that separated cigarettes from other modes of tobacco use and fueled the spread of the smoking habit.

The first distinctive feature of the cigarette is its mildness. This attribute, along with its inexpensive unit cost, made the cigarette especially appealing to boys. Before the cigarette became popular, adolescent males were likely to first try smoking by using cigars, a practice that required a degree of skill to draw in but not inhale the strong smoke. The unpleasant side effects resulting from failing this tobacco rite of passage were largely avoided when new smokers tried cigarettes, which used a milder form of tobacco that was meant to be inhaled. Many of the legislative efforts during the 1890s and after were directed not at tobacco use generally but at cigarettes exclusively because they were so accessible to boys and young men and because they were inhaled.

The inhalability of the milder tobaccos used in cigarettes is the source of a second important distinction between cigarettes and other forms of tobacco. Because the smoke of pipes, cigars, and dark tobacco is relatively alkaline, its nicotine dose is absorbed through the linings of the mouth and nose. Flue-cured "blond" or light-colored tobacco, from which American cigarettes are normally blended, produces slightly acidic tobacco smoke; the nicotine dose thus must be inhaled to be absorbed. Drawn into the lungs through cigarette smoking, nicotine is absorbed into the systemic circulation more quickly than in other forms of smoking—hence the greater potential for nicotine addiction.

A third distinctive feature of the cigarette is its relative convenience and disposability. Facility of use was further augmented by the introduction of the safety match just before World War I. Cigarettes fit more easily than other forms of tobacco into brief moments of relaxation, they were more readily used while working, and they were more easily managed without the use of one's hands. Cigarettes helped combat the tedium of industrial work. Changing attitudes about hygiene also stimulated this predilection for convenience and disposability. From a strictly hygienic perspective, the cigarette appeared to give a cleaner smoke than the cigar.

One final distinctive feature of the cigarette is its cultural connotation as a minor moral transgression. Smoking cigarettes is—and has always been—considered slightly illicit. The pleasure it offers is culturally mediated—that is, part of the pleasure of smoking is the guilt connected with it. None of the marketing efforts of the tobacco giants ever fully legitimized the image of smoking—and there is some suspicion that they never meant to.

Issues in Reducing Tobacco Use

Two themes have permeated the history of tobacco use in the United States. First, tobacco is an extraordinary economic fuel, and its powerful economic impact comes into direct conflict with its vast social costs. Second, anti-tobacco activity has a continuous history characterized by waxing and waning and by a changing mix of motivations and strategies. These two themes are inextricably linked, and their interaction provides a backdrop for current efforts to reduce tobacco use.

Such efforts take place in a complicated context. Chronic diseases largely replaced infectious processes as the leading causes of death during the 20th century (but this replacement occurred during a period of remarkable gains in life expectancy), and the single most important risk associated with the leading chronic diseases is cigarette smoking. The evidence for that statement fills volumes of Surgeon General's reports on smoking and health, and these volumes are merely summaries of a massive literature. Since the first of these reports in 1964, the prevalence of smoking has declined by nearly half, and it is clear that the declining use of tobacco has contributed to the observed decline in mortality. But the decline has been a slower decline than would be warranted by awareness of the well-publicized public health threat that smoking poses. The forces that have tried to accelerate the decline may be thought of collectively as "interventions," although the term, in a more narrow sense, is often reserved for circumscribed, planned, and measurable activities. Many of the maneuvers described in this report do not meet the narrower definition, but all share the common characteristic of being directed toward a reduction in tobacco use.

The result is a considerable challenge for evaluation. In an environment in which multiple interventions are in play, the ability to attribute an individual positive outcome (for example, smoking cessation, prevention of smoking uptake) to one of them is virtually impossible. Although the epidemiologic methods exist to evaluate attribution in the aggregate, data are rarely available to make such judgments. The challenge of evaluating these separate efforts and strategies results from their disparate nature and the type of metric that may be appropriate to their evaluation.

Historical Review

The forces that have shaped the movement to reduce tobacco use over the past 100 years are complex and intertwined. In the early years (1880–1920), anti-tobacco activity—some of it quite successful—was motivated by moral and hygienic principles. After important medical and epidemiologic observations of the mid-century linked smoking to lung cancer and other diseases, and after the subsequent appearance of the 1964 report of the advisory committee to the Surgeon General on smoking and health (U.S. Department of Health, Education, and Welfare 1964), the movement to reduce tobacco use was fueled by knowledge of the health risks that tobacco use poses and by reaction against the continued promotion of tobacco in the face of such known risks. Despite overwhelming evidence of adverse health consequences of smoking, the stubborn norm of smoking in the United States has receded slowly, in part because of such continued promotion that works synergistically with tobacco addiction. Although strategies have varied, health advocates have focused in recent years on the prevention of harm to nonsmokers and on the concept of smoking as a pediatric disease, with the consequent need for protecting young persons from forces influencing them to smoke.

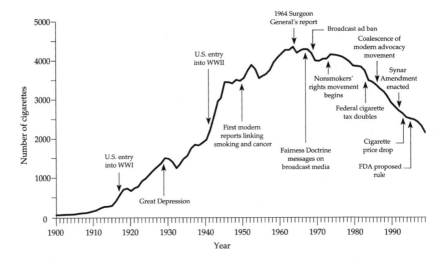

Figure 74.1. *Adult per capita cigarette consumption and major smoking and health events, United States, 1900–1999. The 1999 data are preliminary. Sources: Adapted from Warner 1985; U.S. Department of Health and Human Services 1989; Creek et al. 1994; U.S. Department of Agriculture 2000.*

Educational Strategies

The design of educational programs for tobacco use prevention and the methods used to evaluate them have become increasingly refined over the past two decades. Early studies tended to be confined to the school context, to have short duration, and to be of low intensity. Studies tended to focus on a single modality and to ignore the larger context in which prevention takes place. The reported size, scope, and duration of program effects have become larger in recent reports. In particular, several large programs have attempted a multifaceted approach that incorporates other than school-based modalities. Improvements in evaluation designs have increased confidence in the validity of these reports. The pattern of consistency across this group of large studies also provides assurance that these effects can be achieved in a variety of circumstances when programs include the critical multiple elements that have been defined by this research literature.

To summarize the major findings, school-based social influences programs have significant and substantial short-term impacts on smoking behavior. Those programs with more frequent educational contacts during the critical years for smoking adoption are more likely to be effective, as are programs that address a broad range of educational needs. These effects have been demonstrated in a range of implementation models and student populations. The smoking prevention effects of strong school programs can be extended through the end of high school or longer when combined with relatively intensive efforts directed through other powerful channels, such as strategies that vigorously engage the influences of parents, the mass media, and other community resources. These conclusions have been codified in national guidelines for school programs to prevent tobacco use.

Thus, an extensive body of research findings document the most effective educational programs for preventing tobacco use. This research has produced a wide array of curricula, protocols, and recommendations that have been codified into national guidelines for schools. Implementing guidelines could postpone or prevent smoking onset in 20 to 40 percent of U.S. adolescents. Unfortunately, existing data suggest that evidence-based curricula and national guidelines have not been widely adopted.

Schools, however, should not bear the sole responsibility for implementing educational strategies to prevent tobacco use. Research findings indicate that school-based programs are more effective when combined with mass media programs and with community-based efforts involving parents and other community resources.

Management of Nicotine Addiction

The management of nicotine addiction is a complex field that continues to broaden its understanding of the determinants of smoking cessation. Current literature suggests that several modalities are effective in helping smokers quit. Although the overall effect of such intervention is modest if measured by each attempt to quit, the process of overcoming addiction is a cyclic one, and many who wish to quit are eventually able to do so. The available approaches to management of addiction differ in their results.

Self-Help Manuals and Minimal Clinical Interventions: Although self-help manuals have had only modest and inconsistent success at helping smokers quit, manuals can be easily distributed to the vast population of smokers who try to quit on their own each year.

Adjuvant behavioral interventions, particularly proactive telephone counseling, may significantly increase the effect of self-help materials.

Substantial evidence suggests that minimal clinical interventions (for example, a health care provider's repeated advice to quit) foster smoking cessation and that the more multifactorial or intensive interventions produce the best outcomes. These findings highlight the importance of cessation assistance from clinicians, who have access to more than 70 percent of smokers each year.

Intensive Clinical Interventions: Intensive programs—more formally, systematic services to help people quit smoking—serve an important function in the nation's efforts to reduce smoking, despite the resources the programs demand and the relatively small population of smokers who use them. Such programs may be particularly useful in treating those smokers who find it most difficult to quit. Because intensive smoking cessation programs differ in structure and content, evaluation is often hampered by variation in methodology and by a lack of research addressing specific treatment techniques. Because few studies have chosen to isolate single treatments, assessment of the effectiveness of specific approaches is difficult. Nonetheless, skills training, rapid smoking, and both intratreatment and extratreatment social support have all been associated with successful smoking cessation. When such treatments are shown to be effective, they are usually part of a multifactorial intervention.

Pharmacologic Interventions: Abundant evidence confirms that nicotine gum and the nicotine patch are effective aids to smoking cessation. The efficacy of nicotine gum may depend on the amount of behavioral counseling with which it is paired. The 4-mg dose (rather than the 2-mg dose) may be the better pharmacologic treatment for heavy smokers or for those highly dependent on nicotine. The nicotine patch appears to exert an effect independent of behavioral support, but absolute abstinence rates increase as more counseling is added to patch therapy. Nicotine inhalers and nicotine nasal spray are effective aids for smoking cessation, although their mechanisms of action are not entirely clear.

Bupropion was the first non-nicotine pharmacotherapy for smoking cessation to be studied in large-scale clinical trials, and results suggest that bupropion is an effective aid to smoking cessation. Evidence has also suggested that clonidine is capable of improving smoking cessation rates and that antidepressants and anxiolytics are potentially useful agents for smoking cessation.

In summary, research on methods to treat nicotine addiction has documented the efficacy of a wide array of strategies. The broad implementation of these effective treatment methods could produce a more rapid and probably larger short-term impact on tobacco-related health statistics than any other component of a comprehensive tobacco control effort. It has been estimated that smoking cessation is more cost effective than other commonly provided clinical preventive services, including Pap tests, mammography, colon cancer screening, treatment of mild to moderate hypertension, and treatment of high levels of serum cholesterol.

Regulatory Efforts

Advertising and Promotion: Attempts to regulate advertising and promotion of tobacco products were initiated in the United States almost immediately after the appearance of the 1964 report to the Surgeon General on the health consequences of smoking. Underlying these attempts is the hypothesis that advertising and promotion recruit new smokers and retain current ones, thereby perpetuating a great risk to public health.

The initial regulatory action, promulgated in 1965, provided for a general health warning on cigarette packages but effectively preempted any further federal, state, or local requirements for health messages. In 1969, a successful court action invoked the Fairness Doctrine (not previously applied to advertising) to require broadcast media to air anti-tobacco advertising to counter the paid tobacco advertising then running on television and radio. Indirect evidence suggests that such counter-advertising had considerable impact on the public's perception of smoking. Not surprisingly, the tobacco industry supported new legislation (adopted in 1971) prohibiting the advertising of tobacco products on broadcast media, because such legislation also removed the no-cost broadcasting of anti-tobacco advertising. A decade later, a Federal Trade Commission (FTC) staff report asserted that the dominant themes of remaining (non-broadcast) cigarette advertising associated smoking with "youthful vigor, good health, good looks and personal, social and professional acceptance and success." A nonpublic version of the report detailed some of the alleged marketing strategy employed by the industry; the industry denied the allegation that the source material for the report represented industry policy. Nonetheless, some of these concerns led to the enactment of the Comprehensive Smoking Education Act of 1984 (Public Law 98-474), which required a set of four rotating warnings on cigarette packages.

The law did not, however, adopt other FTC recommendations that product packages should bear information about associated risks of addiction and miscarriage, as well as information on toxic components of cigarettes. In fact, many FTC-recommended requirements for packaging information that have been enacted in other industrialized nations have not been enacted in the United States.

Product Regulation: Current tobacco product regulation requires that cigarette advertising disclose levels of "tar" (an all-purpose term for particulate-phase constituents of tobacco smoke, many of which are carcinogenic or otherwise toxic) and nicotine (the psychoactive drug in tobacco products that causes addiction) in the smoke of manufactured cigarettes and that warning labels appear on packages and on some (but not all) advertising for manufactured cigarettes and smokeless tobacco. The current federal laws preempt, in part, states and localities from imposing other labeling regulations on cigarettes and smokeless tobacco. Federal law (the Comprehensive Smokeless Tobacco Health Education Act of 1986 and the Comprehensive Smoking Education Act of 1984) requires cigarette and smokeless tobacco product manufacturers to submit a list of additives to the Secretary of Health and Human Services; attorneys for the manufacturers released such lists in 1994 to the general public. Smokeless tobacco manufacturers are required to report the total nicotine content of their products, but these data may not be released to the public. Tobacco products are explicitly protected from regulation in various federal consumer safety laws. No federal public health laws or regulations apply to cigars, pipe tobaccos, or fine-cut cigarette tobaccos (for "roll-your-own" cigarettes).

Clean Indoor Air Regulation: Unlike the regulation of tobacco products per se and of their advertising and promotion, regulation of exposure to environmental tobacco smoke (ETS) has encountered less resistance. This course is probably the result of (1) long-standing grassroots efforts to diminish exposure to ambient tobacco smoke and (2) consistent epidemiologic evidence of adverse health effects of ETS. Since 1971, a series of rules, regulations, and laws have created smoke-free environments in an increasing number of settings: government offices, public places, eating establishments, worksites, military establishments, and domestic airline flights.

The effectiveness of clean indoor air restrictions is under intensive study. Most studies have concluded that even among smokers, support for smoking restrictions and smoke-free environments is high.

Research has also verified that the institution of smoke-free workplaces effectively reduces nonsmokers' exposure to ETS. Although smoke-free environments have not reduced smoking prevalence in most studies, such environments have been shown to decrease daily tobacco consumption among smokers and to increase smoking cessation.

Minors' Access to Tobacco: There is widespread approval for restricting the access of minors to tobacco products. Recent research, however, has demonstrated that a substantial proportion of teenagers who smoke purchase their own tobacco, and the proportion varies with age, social class, amount smoked, and factors related to local availability. In addition, research has shown that most minors can easily purchase tobacco from a variety of retail outlets. It has been suggested that a reduction in commercial availability may result in a reduced prevalence of tobacco use among minors.

Litigation Approaches: Private litigation shifts enforcement of public health remedies from the enterprise or the government to the private individual—typically, victims or their surrogates. Private litigation against tobacco has occurred in several distinct waves. The first wave was launched in 1954 and typically used one or both of two legal theories: negligence and implied warranty. Courts proved unreceptive to both these arguments, and this approach had receded by the mid-1970s. A second wave began in 1983 and ended in 1992. In these cases, the legal theory shifted from warranty to strict liability. The tobacco industry based its defense on smokers' awareness of risks and so-called freedom of choice.

In the third wave, still ongoing, diverse legal arguments have been invoked. This third wave of litigation differs from its predecessors by enlarging the field of plaintiffs, focusing on a range of legal issues, using the class action device, and making greater attempts to use private law for public policy purposes. These new claims have been based on theories of intentional misrepresentation, concealment, and failure to disclose, and such arguments have been joined to a new emphasis on addiction.

Economic Approaches

The argument for using economic policy for reducing tobacco use requires considerable technical and analytic understanding of economic theory and data. Because experiments and controlled trials—in the usual sense—are not available to the economist, judgment and forecasting depend on the results of complex analysis of administrative and survey data. Such analyses have led to a number of conclusions regarding the importance of the tobacco industry in the U.S. economy and regarding the role of policies that might affect the supply of tobacco, affect the demand for tobacco, and use different forms of taxation as a possible mechanism for reducing tobacco use.

Supply: The tobacco support program has successfully limited the supply of tobacco and raised the price of tobacco and tobacco products. However, the principal beneficiaries of this program are not only the farmers whose income is supported but also the owners of the tobacco allotments. If policies were initiated to ameliorate some short-run effects, the tobacco support program could be removed without imposing substantial losses for many tobacco farmers. Eliminating the tobacco support program would lead to a small reduction in the prices of cigarettes and other tobacco products, which would lead to slight increases in the use of these products. However, because the support program has created a strong political constituency that has successfully impeded stronger legislation to reduce tobacco use, removing the support program could make it easier to enact stronger policies that would more than offset the impact that the resulting small reductions in price would have on demand.

Industry Importance: Although employment in the tobacco industry is substantial, the industry greatly overstates the importance of tobacco to the U.S. economy. Indeed, most regions would likely benefit—for example, through redistribution of spending and changes in types of job—from the elimination of revenues derived from tobacco products. Moreover, as the economies of tobacco-growing regions have become more diversified, the economic importance of tobacco in these areas has fallen. Higher tobacco taxes and stronger prevention policies could be joined to other efforts to further ease the transition from tobacco in major tobacco-producing regions. Finally, trading lives for jobs is an ill-considered strategy, particularly with the availability of stronger policies for reducing tobacco use.

Demand: Increases in the price of cigarettes will lead to reductions in both smoking prevalence and cigarette consumption among smokers; relatively large reductions are likely to occur among adolescents and young adults. Limited research indicates that increases in smokeless tobacco prices will similarly reduce the use of these products. More research is needed to clarify the impact of cigarette and other tobacco prices on the use of these products in specific sociodemographic groups, particularly adolescents and young adults. Additional research also is needed to address the potential substitution among cigarettes and other tobacco products as their relative prices change.

Taxation: After the effects of inflation are accounted for, federal and average state excise taxes on cigarettes are well below their past levels. Similarly, average cigarette excise taxes in the United States are well below those imposed in most other industrialized countries. Moreover, U.S. taxes on smokeless tobacco products are well below cigarette taxes. Studies of the economic costs of smoking report a wide range of estimates for the optimal tax on cigarettes. However, when recent estimates of the costs of ETS (including the long-term costs of fetal and perinatal exposure to ETS) are considered, and when the premature death of smokers is not considered an economic benefit, a tax that would generate sufficient revenues to cover the external costs of smoking is almost certainly well above current cigarette taxes. The health benefits of higher cigarette taxes are substantial. By reducing smoking, particularly among youth and young adults, past tax increases have significantly reduced smoking-related morbidity and mortality. Further increases in taxes, indexed to account for the effects of inflation, would lead to substantial long-run improvements in health.

Comprehensive Programs

The large-scale interventions conducted in community trials have not demonstrated a conclusive impact on preventing and reducing tobacco use. Statewide programs have emerged as the new laboratory for developing and evaluating comprehensive plans to reduce tobacco use. Initial results from the statewide tobacco control programs are favorable, especially regarding declines in per capita consumption of tobacco products. Results of statewide tobacco control programs suggest that youth behaviors regarding tobacco use are more difficult to change than adult ones, but initial results of these programs are generally favorable.

Reducing Tobacco Use in the 21st Century

Continuing to Build the Scientific Base

Tobacco control policy in this nation has been built on a foundation of scientific knowledge. In the process of applying our current state of knowledge about preventing and controlling tobacco use, accountability and evaluation of the public health effort will be critical. However, because of the wide array of educational, clinical, regulatory, economic, and social influences that have and will need to be brought to bear on the tobacco use problem, the direct impact of a specific maneuver on a specific outcome becomes less meaningful as the combined effects become more substantial. Investigators tend to work on small, manageable aspects of the tobacco use problem, but the synergistic influence of multiple factors over time will likely extend far beyond the outcomes predicted from these smaller research undertakings. For example, the most efficacious educational programs are those that take place in a larger community context, one that engenders and supports an environment of nonsmoking. Similarly, although clinical interventions to manage tobacco addiction clearly have some specific power to help smokers quit, primarily through pharmacologic means, the social environment remains a major determinant of whether these new former smokers maintain their abstinence from nicotine addiction. Regulatory efforts, on the other hand, raise a host of social and economic issues and can produce broad societal changes—issues and changes, however, that are difficult to isolate, document, and evaluate. Economic strategies also have a great potential, but being fundamentally political in nature, they require public consensus and changes in social norms before they can be attempted. Finally, the public health advocacy involved in social program modalities is virtually impossible to assess in a prospective or controlled research design.

The research and evaluation tools of public health must expand to meet these complex issues. Comprehensive, multifactorial approaches to tobacco control appear to offer the most promise. However, the penalty for comprehensive approaches is a loss of statistical power to attribute outcomes to specific activities. Within each of the modalities, appropriate evaluation methodologies are being used. However, many of these methodologies involve retrospective case study, time trend, econometric, and surveillance approaches to evaluate the "natural experiment" as it evolves in the changing social environment. Thus, the traditional biomedical and epidemiologic research methods that have worked so well in defining the health consequences of tobacco use are not well suited to evaluate the potentially most efficacious methods to reduce tobacco use.

The Changing Tobacco Industry

This country's efforts to prevent the onset or continuance of tobacco use have faced the pervasive, countervailing influences of tobacco

478

promotion by the tobacco industry. Despite the overwhelming and continually growing body of evidence of adverse health consequences of tobacco use, the norm of social acceptance of tobacco use in this nation has receded more slowly than might be expected, in part because of such continued promotion.

Litigation and legal settlements have produced notable changes in the tobacco industry's public positions on health risks, nicotine addiction, and advertising and promotion limits. Additionally, individual manufacturing companies have become more directly involved in efforts to limit the access of underage persons to tobacco products and to prevent young people from initiating tobacco use. In this rapidly changing social and legal environment, it is difficult to project the nature and scope of future changes by the industry or their impact on the national effort to reduce tobacco use. Nevertheless, any analysis of changes in patterns of tobacco use must consider the influence of these industry changes.

The Need for Comprehensive Approaches

Public health success in reducing tobacco use requires activity using multiple modalities. A comprehensive approach—one that optimizes synergy from applying a mix of educational, clinical, regulatory, economic, and social strategies—has emerged as the guiding principle for future efforts to reduce tobacco use. The public health goals of such comprehensive programs are to reduce disease, disability, and death related to tobacco use through prevention and cessation, as well as through protection of the nonsmoker from ETS.

The emerging body of data on statewide tobacco control efforts is coming from programs broadly focused on prevention, cessation, and protection of the nonsmoker from ETS. Preventing initiation among young people is a primary goal of any tobacco control effort. However, young people will perceive contradictory or inconsistent messages in prevention efforts if programs do not also address the smoking behavior of millions of parents and other adult role models and the public health risks of ETS.

CDC released *Best Practices for Comprehensive Tobacco Control Programs* (CDC 1999), which recommends that states establish tobacco control programs that are comprehensive, sustainable, and accountable. This document draws on "best practices" determined by evidence-based conclusions from research and evaluation of such comprehensive programs at the state level. In the review of evidence from these states, it was evident that reducing the broad cultural acceptability of tobacco use necessitates changing many facets of the social environment. Nine specific elements of a comprehensive program are defined in the guidance document. Although, the importance of each of the elements is highlighted, the document stresses that these individual components must work together to produce the synergistic effects of a comprehensive program.

Best Practices thus provides effective guidance for state-level efforts; a comprehensive national tobacco control effort, however, requires strategies that go beyond this guidance to states. Moreover, a comprehensive national effort should involve the application of a mix of educational, clinical, regulatory, economic, and social strategies. In each of these modalities, some of the program and policy changes that are needed can be addressed most effectively at the national level.

Identifying and Eliminating Disparities

Cultural, ethnic, religious, and social differences are clearly important in understanding patterns of tobacco use, but little research has been completed on the relative effectiveness of interventions for prevention and treatment in some of the population groups or communities. Reaching the national goal of eliminating health disparities related to tobacco use will necessitate improved collection and use of standardized data to correctly identify disparities in both health outcomes and efficacy of prevention programs among various population groups. Broader historical, societal, and community characteristics can have a significant influence on the manner in which prevention and control strategies that work overall for the population as a whole may impact diverse groups. Many of these broader variables do not lend themselves to traditional measurement methods nor are they easily assessed at the individual level through using traditional epidemiologic methods.

Improving the Dissemination of State-of-the-Art Interventions

One of the greatest challenges in tobacco control and public health in general continues to be overcoming the difficulty in getting advances in prevention and treatment strategies effectively disseminated, adopted, and implemented in their appropriate delivery systems. Simply stated, our recent lack of progress in tobacco control is attributable more to the failure to implement proven strategies than it is to a lack of knowledge about what to do. The result is that each year in this nation, more than 1 million young people continue to become regular smokers, and more than 400,000 adults continue to die prematurely from tobacco-related diseases.

Within each of the modalities reviewed in this report, some specific research advances in tobacco prevention and control strategies have not been fully implemented. Studies are urgently needed to identify the social, institutional, and political barriers to the more rapid dissemination of these research advances. Understanding these barriers and determining how they could be overcome would benefit not only tobacco control but public health efforts more broadly.

For More Information

To obtain a copy of *Reducing Tobacco Use: A Report of the Surgeon General*, full report, executive summary, or At-A-Glance, please call CDC's Office on Smoking and Health at (770) 488-5705 and press 3 to speak with an information specialist. Please note that the report, along with supporting documents, is also available online at the Office on Smoking and Health website at www.cdc.gov/tobacco.

Chapter 75

Environmental Tobacco Smoke (Secondhand Smoke)

Environmental Tobacco Smoke

Environmental tobacco smoke (ETS), also called secondhand smoke, is the combination of two forms of smoke from burning tobacco products:

- Sidestream smoke, or smoke that is emitted between the puffs of a burning cigarette, pipe, or cigar, and

- Mainstream smoke, or the smoke that is exhaled by the smoker.

When a cigarette is smoked, about half of the smoke generated is sidestream smoke, which contains essentially the same compounds as those identified in the mainstream smoke inhaled by the smoker. Some of the chemicals in ETS include substances that irritate the lining of the lung and other tissues, carcinogens (cancer-causing compounds), mutagens (substances that promote genetic changes in the

This chapter includes: "Environmental Tobacco Smoke," Cancer Facts, National Cancer Institute (NCI), February 2000; "Secondhand Smoke in Your Home," National Center for Chronic Disease Prevention and Health Promotion (NCCDPHP), Centers for Disease Control and Prevention (CDC), reviewed April 2003; "Study Shows Effects of Prenatal Exposure to Second-hand Smoke Greater for Socioeconomically Disadvantaged Children," *NIH News*, National Institutes of Health (NIH), March 25, 2004; and "Exposure to Environmental Tobacco Smoke and Cotinine Levels—Fact Sheet" NCCDPHP, CDC, reviewed October 2002.

cell), and developmental toxicants (substances that interfere with normal cell development). Tobacco smoke is known to contain at least 60 carcinogens, including formaldehyde and benzo[a]pyrene, and six developmental toxicants, including nicotine and carbon monoxide.

Nonsmokers who are exposed to ETS absorb nicotine and other compounds just as smokers do. As the exposure to ETS increases, the levels of these harmful substances in the body increase as well. Although the smoke to which a nonsmoker is exposed is less concentrated than that inhaled by smokers, research has demonstrated significant health risks associated with ETS.

Health Effects Associated with ETS Exposure

In 1986, two landmark reports were published on the association between ETS exposure and the adverse health effects in nonsmokers: one by the U.S. Surgeon General and the other by the Expert Committee on Passive Smoking, National Academy of Sciences' National Research Council (NAS/NRC). Both of these reports concluded that:

- ETS can cause lung cancer in healthy adult nonsmokers;

- Children of parents who smoke have more respiratory symptoms and acute lower respiratory tract infections, as well as evidence of reduced lung function, than do children of nonsmoking parents; and

- Separating smokers and nonsmokers within the same air space may reduce but does not eliminate a nonsmoker's exposure to ETS.

In 1992, the U.S. Environmental Protection Agency (EPA) confirmed the previously stated findings in its study on the respiratory health effects of ETS. In addition, the EPA classified ETS as a group A carcinogen—a category reserved only for the most dangerous cancer-causing agents in humans. The EPA report, a compilation of 30 epidemiological studies that focused on the health risks of nonsmokers with smoking spouses, concluded that there is a strong association between ETS exposure and lung cancer. Scientists estimate that ETS is responsible for approximately 3,000 lung cancer deaths per year among nonsmokers in the United States. Recent studies and the EPA's report point to a 20-percent increased risk of lung cancer in nonsmokers due to ETS.

In response to evidence that ETS causes diseases beyond lung cancer and respiratory problems in children, the California Environmental Protection Agency (Cal/EPA) conducted a comprehensive assessment of the range of health effects connected with ETS exposure. In 1999, the National Cancer Institute (NCI) published the Cal/EPA's results as part of its *Smoking and Tobacco Control* monograph series in *Health Effects of Exposure to Environmental Tobacco Smoke*. Table 75.1 outlines the health effects that were found to have a significant association with ETS exposure.

Other health effects that were found to be possibly associated with ETS were as follows:

- spontaneous abortion (miscarriage)
- adverse impact on cognition and behavior during child development
- exacerbation of cystic fibrosis (a disease marked by overproduction of mucus in the lungs)
- decreased lung function
- cervical cancer

However, further research is needed to confirm the link between the these health risks and ETS.

Table 75.1. Health Effects Associated with ETS Exposure

Developmental Effects	low birth weight or small for gestational age; sudden infant death syndrome (SIDS)
Respiratory Effects	acute lower respiratory tract infections in children; asthma induction and exacerbation in children; chronic respiratory symptoms in children; eye and nasal irritation in adults; middle ear infections in children
Carcinogenic Effects	lung cancer; nasal sinus cancer
Cardiovascular Effects	heart disease mortality; acute and chronic coronary heart disease

Carcinogenic Effects of ETS

More than 3,000 chemicals are present in tobacco smoke, including at least 60 known carcinogens such as nitrosamines and polycyclic aromatic hydrocarbons. Some of these compounds become carcinogenic only after they are activated by specific enzymes (proteins that control chemical reactions) found in many tissues in the body. These activated compounds can then become part of deoxyribonucleic acid (DNA) molecules and possibly interfere with the normal growth of cells. Tobacco also contains nicotine, a chemical that causes physical addiction to smoking and makes it difficult for people to stop smoking.

Although much of the research into the carcinogenicity of ETS has focused on lung cancer, ETS has also been linked with other cancers, including those in the nasal sinus cavity, cervix, breast, and bladder. The role of ETS in the development of nasal sinus cancer has been investigated in three recent studies; all three showed a significant positive association between ETS exposure and the development of nasal sinus cancer in nonsmoking adults. Several studies that focused on ETS as a risk factor for cervical cancer have shown a possible association between ETS and cancer of the cervix, although no specific conclusions could be made. Similarly, studies of the relationship between ETS exposure and breast cancer suggested an association between the two, but the evidence was weak. Although active smoking has been identified as a cause of bladder cancer, the results of studies focusing on ETS and bladder cancer have not been conclusive. More research is needed into the impact of ETS on nonsmokers' risk for cancers of the cervix, breast, and bladder.

Public Policies Restricting Smoking

Studies dating from the early 1970s have consistently shown that children and infants exposed to ETS in the home have significantly elevated rates of respiratory symptoms and respiratory tract infections. These findings prompted recommendations that ETS be eliminated from the environment of small children.

In adults, ETS can worsen existing pulmonary symptoms for people with asthma and chronic bronchitis, as well as for people with allergic conditions. Even individuals who are not allergic can suffer eye irritation, sore throat, nausea, and hoarseness. Contact lens wearers can find tobacco smoke very irritating.

Following the release of the 1986 reports by the Surgeon General and the NAS, many new laws, regulations, and ordinances were enacted that severely restrict or ban public smoking. Many more such laws can be expected:

- On the federal level, the General Services Administration issued regulations restricting smoking to designated areas only in federal office buildings. Many agencies within the Public Health Service, which includes the National Institutes of Health, have banned smoking completely.

- By law, smoking on all airline flights of 6 hours or less within the United States is banned; however, in practice, all U.S. airlines have banned smoking on all domestic flights. All interstate bus travel is smoke free.

- ETS meets the criteria of the Occupational Safety and Health Administration (OSHA) for classification as a potential occupational carcinogen. (OSHA is the federal agency responsible for health and safety regulations in the workplace.)

- The National Institute for Occupational Safety and Health (NIOSH) is another federal agency that is concerned with ETS exposure in the workplace. NIOSH conducts ETS-related research, evaluates work sites for possible health hazards, and makes safety recommendations. NIOSH recommends that ETS be regarded as a potential occupational carcinogen, in conformance with the OSHA carcinogen policy, and that exposures to ETS be reduced to the lowest possible levels.

- Currently, nearly every state has some form of legislation to protect nonsmokers; some states require private employers to enact policies that protect employees who do not smoke. Information about state-level tobacco regulations can be accessed through the Centers for Disease Control and Prevention (CDC)'s State Tobacco Activities Tracking and Evaluating (STATE) System website, which can be found at http://www2.cdc.gov/nccdphp/osh/state. In addition to state legislation, a number of local jurisdictions have enacted ordinances addressing nonsmokers' rights, and most are more restrictive than their state counterparts.

Additional Resources about the Effects of ETS

The 1999 NCI monograph *Health Effects of Exposure to Environmental Tobacco Smoke* can be ordered from the Cancer Information

Service. U.S. residents can order the monograph online at http://cissecure.nci.nih.gov/ncipubs.

Additional information on the health effects of tobacco is available from the CDC's Tobacco Information and Prevention Source at http://www.cdc.gov/tobacco on the internet. This program collects and distributes reports and news about tobacco, lists services available for people trying to quit using tobacco products, and produces publications about tobacco and the dangers of its use.

Secondhand Smoke in Your Home

We spend more time in our homes than anywhere else. So, the thought of cancer-causing chemicals circulating throughout our houses and apartments can be quite unsettling. Yet, according to the Environmental Protection Agency (EPA), that is exactly what happens when someone lights a cigarette in your home.

Those most affected by secondhand smoke are children. Because their bodies are still developing, exposure to the poisons in secondhand smoke puts children in danger of severe respiratory diseases and can hinder the growth of their lungs. On top of that, the effects can last a lifetime.

Ventilation systems in homes cannot filter and circulate air well enough to eliminate secondhand smoke. Blowing smoke away from children, going into another room to smoke, or opening a window may help reduce children's exposure but will not protect them from the dangers of secondhand smoke.

Benefits of a Smoke-Free Home

The greatest benefit, of course, is that you will remove all the health risks associated with secondhand tobacco smoke. Plus:

- When your home is smoke-free, it will smell much better.

- Your food will taste better.

- You'll spend less time, energy, and money cleaning your curtains, walls, windows, and mirrors.

- Your insurance rates may be lower—check with your insurance company.

- Even your pets will be happier. For example, secondhand smoke increases the risk of lung cancer in dogs.

How to Make (and Keep) Your Home Smoke-Free

It may feel awkward at first to tell people not to smoke in your home—no one wants to make guests uncomfortable—but if you simply explain the facts about secondhand smoke, they should understand completely. Tell them that for the sake of your family's health, you simply cannot allow smoking in your home. Have gum or mints available as an alternative to lighting up. If visitors absolutely must smoke, tell them they can do so outside.

If someone in your household smokes, be sympathetic and understanding—but encourage him or her to quit. Let that person know that cigarette smoke affects everyone, not just the smoker. Let them know you care and you want to help. Again, if someone absolutely must smoke, ask that person to do so outside.

Don't Forget Schools and Day Care

Make sure your child's school and day care programs are smoke-free. And insist that babysitters not smoke around your children.

Prenatal Exposure to Second-Hand Smoke Greater for Socioeconomically Disadvantaged Children

The effects of prenatal exposure to second-hand smoke on mental development are exacerbated in children who experience socioeconomic hardships, such as substandard housing and inadequate food and clothing, during the first two years of life, according to a new study funded by the National Institute of Environmental Health Sciences, one of the National Institutes of Health, the U.S. Environmental Protection Agency, and other private foundations.

While the study results indicate that prenatal exposure to second-hand smoke can be harmful to the unborn child regardless of socioeconomic conditions, the data also suggest that lower-income children may be less able to compensate for these effects over the next few years of life. The study appeared in the March 2004 issue of the journal *Neurotoxicology and Teratology*.

The study, conducted by researchers at the Columbia Center for Children's Environmental Health (CCCEH), part of the Mailman School of Public Health at Columbia University, found that children whose mothers are exposed during pregnancy to second-hand smoke have reduced scores on tests of cognitive development at age two, when compared to children from smoke-free homes.

The reduction amounts to almost five developmental quotient points out of an average score of 100. In addition, the children exposed to second-hand smoke during pregnancy are approximately twice as likely to have developmental scores below 80, which is indicative of developmental delay.

These differences are magnified for children whose mothers lived in inadequate housing or had insufficient food or clothing during pregnancy. The combined effect results in a developmental deficit of about seven points in tests of cognitive performance.

While the influence of material hardship on the association between second-hand smoke and cognitive development was measured during the postnatal period, the test results show that the subjects' postnatal exposure to second-hand smoke does not confer any additional risk for developmental deficit over and above that contributed by prenatal exposure alone.

"These findings reveal the dangers for pregnant women and their unborn children of multiple 'toxic' exposures—both chemical and socioeconomic," said Dr. Virginia Rauh, a Deputy Director of the Center and Associate Professor at the Mailman School of Public Health and principal author of the study. "They show, for the first time, that urban children exposed to both conditions experience a kind of double jeopardy with consequences persisting into early childhood and possibly beyond."

The study is part of a broader, multi-year research project, "The Mothers & Children Study In New York City," started in 1998, which examines the health effects of exposure of pregnant women and babies to air pollutants from vehicle exhaust, the commercial burning of fuels, and tobacco smoking, as well as from residential use of pesticides, and cockroach and mouse allergens.

The research involved a sample of 226 infants of non-smoking African American and Dominican women in Washington Heights, Central Harlem and the South Bronx. Each of the women was interviewed during the third trimester of pregnancy, for approximately 45 minutes, by a specially trained bilingual interviewer.

From those interviews, data were obtained on their exposure to second-hand smoke, also known as Environmental Tobacco Smoke (ETS), and on their socioeconomic status and living conditions. The ETS exposure was further validated using a short-term biomarker of exposure: the level of cotinine in the umbilical cord blood at the time of delivery.

"This finding reinforces the need to prevent serious developmental problems in children by addressing harmful prenatal exposures," said Dr. Frederica P. Perera, Director of the Center and the study team leader. "From a health policy standpoint, it is important both to limit exposure to second-hand smoke and to better the living conditions of pregnant women and their children."

—Other co-authors of this study include Drs. Robin Whyatt, Robin Garfinkel, Howard Andrews, Lori Hoepner, Andria Reyes, and Diurka Diaz of CCCEH and David Camann from Southwest Research Institute.

Exposure to Environmental Tobacco Smoke and Cotinine Levels

Cotinine is a major metabolite of nicotine. Exposure to nicotine can be measured by analyzing the cotinine levels in the blood, saliva, or urine. Since nicotine is highly specific for tobacco smoke, serum cotinine levels track exposure to tobacco smoke and its toxic constituents.

In 1991, data showed that nearly 90 percent of the U.S. population had measurable levels of serum cotinine in their blood. The Centers for Disease Control and Prevention's *National Report on Human Exposure to Environmental Chemicals* found more than a 75 percent decrease in median cotinine (metabolized nicotine) levels for nonsmokers in the United States since 1991.

Children and teenagers, 3–19 years old, had higher levels of cotinine than did adults, 20 years old and above.

Involuntary exposure to ETS remains a common, serious public health hazard that is entirely preventable by adopting and enforcing appropriate regulatory policies. Smoke-free environments are the most effective method for reducing ETS exposure. *Healthy People 2010* objectives address this issue and seek optimal protection of nonsmokers through policies, regulations, and laws requiring smoke-free environments in all schools, work sites, and public places.

Only California meets the nation's *Healthy People 2010* objective to eliminate exposure to ETS by either banning indoor smoking or limiting it to separately ventilated areas. Because of a comprehensive statewide tobacco control program, virtually all indoor workplaces in California are now smoke free, including restaurants, bars, and gaming clubs.

The dramatic declines in serum cotinine levels among nonsmokers are a good indication that efforts to ensure clean indoor air through smoking restrictions in workplaces, restaurants and other public places are working. However, there are still too many people, especially young people, who continue to be exposed to environmental tobacco smoke (ETS).

Chapter 76

Clean Indoor Air Regulations

Reasons for Concern

As reported in 1992 by the U.S. Environmental Protection Agency (EPA), exposure to tobacco smoke in the environment can cause lung cancer in adult nonsmokers. Environmental tobacco smoke (ETS) also has been linked to an increased risk of heart disease among nonsmokers. ETS causes about 3,000 lung cancer deaths annually among adult nonsmokers.

In 1997, the California EPA concluded that ETS causes coronary heart disease and death in nonsmokers. Scientific studies have estimated that ETS accounts for as many as 62,000 deaths from coronary heart disease annually in the United States.

The 1992 EPA report also concluded that ETS causes serious respiratory problems in children, such as greater number and severity of asthma attacks and lower respiratory tract infections. ETS exposure increases children's risk for sudden infant death syndrome (SIDS) and middle ear infections as well.

Each year ETS causes 150,000–300,000 lower respiratory tract infections, such as pneumonia and bronchitis, in children.

In a large U.S. study, maternal exposure during pregnancy and postnatal exposure of the newborn to ETS increased the risk for SIDS.

National Center for Chronic Disease Prevention and Health Promotion, Centers for Disease Control and Prevention (CDC), reviewed April 2001.

Comparative risk studies performed by the EPA have consistently found ETS to be a risk to public health. ETS is classified as a group A carcinogen (known to cause cancer in humans) under the EPA's carcinogen assessment guidelines.

Several studies have documented the widespread exposure of ETS among nonsmoking adults and children in the United States. Testing nonsmokers' blood for the presence of cotinine, a chemical produced when the body metabolizes nicotine, shows that nearly nine out of ten nonsmoking Americans (88%) are exposed to ETS.

A 1988 *National Health Interview Survey* reported that an estimated 37% of the 79.2 million nonsmoking U.S. workers were employed in places that permitted smoking in designated areas, and that 59% of these workers experienced moderate or great discomfort from ETS exposure in the workplace.

ETS Regulations

- Under common law (laws based on court decisions rather than government laws and regulations), employers must provide a work environment that is reasonably free of recognized hazards. Courts have ruled that common-law duty requires employers to provide nonsmoking employees protection from the proven health hazards of ETS exposure.

- The Occupational Safety and Health Administration (OSHA) is considering regulations that would either prohibit smoking in all workplaces or limit it to separately ventilated areas.

- The federal government has instituted increasingly stringent regulations on smoking in its own facilities. On August 9, 1997, President Clinton signed an *Executive Order* declaring that Executive Branch federal work sites be smoke-free, thereby protecting nonsmoking federal employees and thousands of citizens who visit federal facilities from the dangers of ETS.

- *The Pro-Children's Act of 1994* (Public Law 103–227, sections 1041–1044) prohibits smoking in facilities where federally funded children's services are provided on a regular or routine basis.

- As of December 31, 1999, at least some degree of smoke-free indoor air laws were present in 45 states and the District of Columbia. These laws vary widely, from limited smoking restrictions on public transportation to comprehensive restrictions in work sites and public places.

- Twenty states and the District of Columbia limit smoking in private work sites. Of these states, only one (California) meets the nation's *Healthy People 2010* objective to eliminate exposure to ETS by either banning indoor smoking or limiting it to separately ventilated areas.

- Forty-one states and the District of Columbia have laws restricting smoking in state government work sites, but only 13 of these states meet the nation's *Healthy People 2010* objective.

- Thirty-one states have laws that regulate smoking in restaurants; of these, only Utah and Vermont completely prohibit smoking in restaurants. California requires either a no smoking area or separate ventilation for smoking areas.

Additional Benefits

An additional benefit of clean indoor air regulations may contribute to a reduction in smoking prevalence among workers and the general public. Studies have found that moderate or extensive laws for clean indoor air are associated with a lower smoking prevalence and higher quit rates.

The majority of smokers support smoke-free hospitals. Smokers and nonsmokers were in favor of smoke-free workplace six months after a smoke-free policy was implemented.

Employers are likely to save money by implementing policies for smoke-free workplaces. Savings include costs associated with such things as fire risk, damage to property and furnishings, cleaning, workers' compensation, disability, retirement, injuries, and life insurance. Cost savings were estimated at $1,000 per smoking employee based on 1988 dollars.

The EPA estimates a nationwide, comprehensive policy on clean indoor air would save $4 billion to $8 billion per year in building operations and maintenance costs.

Establishing Public Policy

Involuntary exposure to ETS remains a common public health hazard that is entirely preventable by adopting appropriate regulatory policies.

To fight the establishment of such policies, the tobacco industry tries to shift the focus from the science-based evidence on the health hazards of ETS to the controversial social issue of personal freedom.

The industry has lobbied extensively against legislation to restrict smoking, and has supported the passage of state laws that preempt stronger local ordinances. (Preemptive legislation is defined as legislation that prevents a local jurisdiction from enacting laws more stringent than, or at a variance with, the state law.)

A case study conducted in six states found that the existence of an organized smoking prevention coalition among local citizens was a key determinant in successfully enacting clean indoor air legislation.

Smoke-free environments are the most effective method for reducing ETS exposure. *Healthy People 2010* objectives address this issue and seek optimal protection of nonsmokers through policies, regulations, and laws requiring smoke-free environments in all schools, work sites, and public places.

Chapter 77

Healthy People 2010: Goals for Reducing Tobacco Use

Overview

Scientific knowledge about the health effects of tobacco use has increased greatly since the first Surgeon General's report on tobacco was released in 1964. Cigarette smoking causes heart disease, several kinds of cancer (lung, larynx, esophagus, pharynx, mouth, and bladder), and chronic lung disease. Cigarette smoking also contributes to cancer of the pancreas, kidney, and cervix. Smoking during pregnancy causes spontaneous abortions, low birth weight, and sudden infant death syndrome.

Other forms of tobacco are not safe alternatives to smoking cigarettes. Use of spit tobacco causes a number of serious oral health problems, including cancer of the mouth and gum, periodontitis, and tooth loss. Cigar use causes cancer of the larynx, mouth, esophagus, and lung. In recent years, reports have shown an increase in the popularity of bidis. Bidis are small brown cigarettes, often flavored, consisting of tobacco hand-rolled in tendu or temburni leaf and secured with a string at one end. Research shows that bidis are a significant health hazard to users, increasing the risk of coronary heart disease and cancer of the mouth, pharynx and larynx, lung, esophagus, stomach, and liver.

Excerpted from "27: Tobacco Use," *Healthy People 2010: Understanding and Improving Health. 2nd ed.* U.S. Department of Health and Human Services, Washington, DC: U.S. Government Printing Office, November 2000. The full text of this document, including references, is available online at http://www.healthypeople.gov/document/html/volume2/27tobacco.htm.

Issues and Trends

Tobacco use is responsible for more than 430,000 deaths per year among adults in the United States, representing more than 5 million years of potential life lost. If current tobacco use patterns persist in the United States, an estimated 5 million persons under age 18 years will die prematurely from a smoking-related disease. Direct medical costs related to smoking total at least $50 billion per year; direct medical costs related to smoking during pregnancy are approximately $1.4 billion per year.

Evidence is accumulating that shows maternal tobacco use is associated with mental retardation and birth defects such as oral clefts. Exposure to secondhand smoke also has serious health effects. Researchers have identified more than 4,000 chemicals in tobacco smoke; of these, at least 43 cause cancer in humans and animals. Each year, because of exposure to secondhand smoke, an estimated 3,000 non-smokers die of lung cancer, and 150,000 to 300,000 infants and children under age 18 months experience lower respiratory tract infections. Asthma and other respiratory conditions often are triggered or worsened by tobacco smoke.

Studies also have found that secondhand smoke exposure causes heart disease among adults. Data reported from a study of the U.S. population aged four years and older indicated that among non-tobacco users, 88 percent had detectable levels of serum cotinine, a biological marker for exposure to secondhand smoke. Both home and workplace environments have contributed to the widespread exposure to secondhand smoke. Data from a 1996 study indicated that 22 percent of U.S. children and adolescents under age 18 years (approximately 15 million children and adolescents) were exposed to secondhand smoke in their homes.

Smoking among adults declined steadily from the mid-1960s through the 1980s. However, smoking among adults appears to have leveled off in the 1990s. The rate of smoking among adults in 1997 was 25 percent.

Tobacco use and addiction usually begin in adolescence. Furthermore, tobacco use may increase the probability that an adolescent will use other drugs. Among adults in the United States who have ever smoked daily, 82 percent tried their first cigarette before age 18 years, and 53 percent became daily smokers before age 18 years. Preventing tobacco use among youth has emerged as a major focus of tobacco control efforts.

Tobacco use among adolescents increased in the 1990s after decreasing in the 1970s and 1980s. Data from the 1999 Monitoring the

Future Study indicated that past-month smoking among 8th, 10th, and 12th graders was 18, 26, and 35 percent, respectively. These rates represent increases of 20 to 33 percent since 1991. Data from the Youth Risk Behavior Survey revealed that past-month smoking among 9th to 12th graders rose from 28 percent in 1991 to 36 percent in 1997. Past-month spit tobacco use among 9th to 12th graders was 9 percent in 1997 (2 percent among females and 16 percent among males). In 1997, past-month cigar use among 9th to 12th graders was 22 percent (11 percent of females and 31 percent of males).

Youth are put at increased risk of initiating tobacco use by sociodemographic, environmental, and personal factors. Sociodemographic risk factors include coming from a family with low socioeconomic status. Environmental risk factors include accessibility and availability of tobacco products, cigarette advertising and promotion practices, the price of tobacco products, perceptions that tobacco use is normal, peers' and siblings' use and approval, and lack of parental involvement. Personal risk factors include low self-image and low self-esteem, the belief that tobacco use provides a benefit, and the lack of ability to refuse offers to use tobacco.

Overwhelming evidence indicates that nicotine found in tobacco is addictive and that addiction occurs in most smokers during adolescence. Among students who were high school seniors during 1976–86, 44 percent of daily smokers believed that in five years they would not be smoking. Followup studies, however, indicated that five to six years later 73 percent of these persons remained daily smokers. In 1995, 68 percent of current smokers wanted to quit smoking completely, and 46 percent of the current daily smokers had stopped smoking for at least one day during the preceding 12 months.

Disparities

Men are more likely to smoke than women (26 percent compared to 22 percent). Disparities in tobacco use exist among certain racial and ethnic populations. American Indians or Alaska Natives (35 percent) are more likely to smoke than other racial and ethnic groups, with considerable variations in percentages by Tribe. Hispanics (18 percent) and Asians or Pacific Islanders (13 percent) are less likely to smoke than other groups. Regional and local data, however, reveal much higher smoking levels among specific population groups of Hispanics and Asians or Pacific Islanders. Smoking levels among Vietnamese and Korean Asian Americans are higher than previously reported, according to a 1997 multilingual survey.

Studies have found higher levels of cigarette use among gay men and lesbians than among heterosexuals. Gay men and lesbians with higher education levels are less likely to use cigarettes as frequently as those with lower levels of education.

Persons with 9 to 11 years of education (38 percent) have significantly higher levels of smoking than individuals with eight years or less of education or 12 years or more. Individuals with 16 or more years of education have the lowest smoking rates (11 percent). Individuals who are poor are significantly more likely to smoke than individuals of middle or high income (34 percent compared to 21 percent).

Data reveal high levels of tobacco use among college students. In 1995, 29 percent of college students smoked in the previous month (28 percent of females and 30 percent of males). Five percent of college students used spit tobacco in the previous month (0.3 percent of females and 12 percent of males).

Among adolescents, smoking rates differ between whites and African Americans. By the late 1980s, smoking rates among white teens were more than triple those of African American teens. In recent years, smoking has started to increase among African American male teens, but African American female teens continue to have lower smoking rates. In 1997, 40 percent of white high school females were smokers, compared to 17 percent of African American high school females.

Spit tobacco use among adolescents also differs significantly by students' gender, race, and ethnicity. In 1997, 15.8 percent of male high school students currently used spit tobacco, compared to only 1.5 percent of female high school students. Current spit tobacco use was 12.2 percent for non-Hispanic whites, 2.2 percent for non-Hispanic African Americans, and 5.1 percent for Hispanics.

Opportunities

Efforts to reduce tobacco use in the United States have shifted from focusing primarily on smoking cessation for individuals to more population-based interventions. Such interventions emphasize prevention of initiation, reduction of exposure to environmental tobacco smoke, and policy changes in health care systems to promote smoking cessation. Federal, state, and local government agencies and numerous health organizations have joined together to develop and implement population-based approaches.

Community research studies and evidence from California, Florida, Massachusetts, and Oregon have shown that comprehensive programs can be effective in reducing average cigarette consumption per person.

Both California and Massachusetts increased cigarette excise taxes and designated a portion of the revenues for comprehensive tobacco control programs. Data from these states indicate that (1) increasing excise taxes on cigarettes is one of the most cost-effective short-term strategies to reduce tobacco consumption among adults and to prevent initiation among youth and (2) the ability to sustain lower consumption increases when the tax increase is combined with an anti-smoking campaign. In addition, recent data from Florida indicate that past-month smoking decreased significantly among public middle school students (19 percent to 15 percent) and high school students (27 percent to 25 percent) from 1998 to 1999 following implementation of a comprehensive program to prevent and reduce tobacco use among youth in that state.

As education programs for school-aged youth are developed and proven effective in preventing initiation and in cessation, these programs should be included in quality health education curricula at the grade level. Education should aim to prevent initiation among youth, provide knowledge about effective cessation methods, and increase understanding of the health effects of tobacco use.

The goals of comprehensive tobacco prevention and reduction efforts include preventing people from starting to use tobacco, helping people quit using tobacco, reducing exposure to secondhand smoke, and identifying and eliminating disparities in tobacco use among population groups. To address these goals, community programs, media interventions, policy and regulatory activities, and surveillance and evaluation programs are being implemented. Specifically, the following elements are used to build capacity to implement and support tobacco use prevention and control interventions: a focus on change in social norms and environments that support tobacco use, policy and regulatory strategies, community participation, establishment of public and private partnerships, strategic use of media, development of local programs, coordination of statewide and local activities, linkage of school-based activities to community activities, and use of data collection and evaluation techniques to monitor program impact.

The importance of these various strategic elements has been demonstrated in a number of states, such as Arizona, California, Florida, Massachusetts, and Oregon. In these and other states, tobacco control programs are supported through funding from the federal government, private foundations, state tobacco taxes, state lawsuit settlements, and other sources. These programs address issues such as reducing exposure to secondhand smoke, restricting minors' access to tobacco, treating nicotine addiction, limiting the impact of tobacco

501

advertising, increasing the price of tobacco products, and directly regulating the product (for example, requiring product ingredient reporting). Tobacco control programs and materials should be culturally and linguistically appropriate.

Interim Progress Toward Year 2000 Objectives

Of the 26 tobacco-related objectives, three have been met: reducing the rate of lung cancer deaths, reducing the rate of oral cancer deaths, and increasing the number of states that have tobacco control plans.

Sixteen additional objectives are showing progress. These include reducing cigarette smoking among adults, which declined in the early part of the 1990s and then leveled off, and reducing children's exposure to secondhand smoke, which also declined. Some objectives, though showing progress, are far from their targets. For example, although 13 states have laws limiting smoking in public places and worksites, few ban smoking or limit it to separately ventilated areas in private workplaces or restaurants. As of December 31, 1998, only one state had met the objective for private worksites, and three had met it for restaurants. All 50 states and the District of Columbia have laws prohibiting the sale of tobacco to minors. However, the objective on enforcement of minors' access laws to achieve illegal buy rates of no more than 20 percent is far from being met: in fiscal year 1998, only 12 states had met this target. Although *Healthy People 2000* data indicate that smoking among adolescents is declining somewhat, other surveys indicate that smoking among youth increased through 1997 and remained unchanged or declined somewhat in 1998 and 1999. Two additional objectives that include the use of and perception of harm from using drugs, alcohol, and cigarettes by high school seniors show mixed progress; for cigarettes there is slight progress.

Three objectives (perception of social disapproval of cigarette smoking among adolescents, states with preemptive clean indoor air laws, and smoking cessation during pregnancy) are moving away from the targets.

Data beyond baseline were not available for two objectives (tobacco product advertising and promotion to youth, and health plans offering treatment for nicotine addiction).

Note: Unless otherwise noted, data are from the Centers for Disease Control and Prevention, National Center for Health Statistics, *Healthy People 2000 Review*, 1998–99.

Healthy People 2010—Objectives

Tobacco Use Goals in Population Groups

Adults

- Reduce tobacco use by adults (baseline 1998 [age-adjusted to the year 2000 standard population]; target 2010)
  - Cigarette smoking: from 24 percent to 12 percent
  - Spit tobacco: from 2.6 percent to 0.4 percent
  - Cigars: from 2.5 percent to 1.2 percent

Adolescents

- Reduce tobacco use by adolescents (baseline 1999; target 2010)
  - Tobacco product use (past month): from 40 percent to 21 percent
  - Cigarette use (past month): from 35 percent to 16 percent
  - Spit tobacco use (past month): from 8 percent to 1 percent
  - Cigar use (past month): from 18 percent to 8 percent

- Reduce the initiation of tobacco use among children and adolescents (developmental). Because the majority of initiation of tobacco use occurs in adolescence, direct measures of tobacco use in adolescence are important health indicators.

- Increase the average age of first use of tobacco products by adolescents and young adults (baseline 1997; target 2010)
  - Increase in average age of first tobacco use among adolescents aged 12 to 17 years from 12 years to 14 years; and among young adults aged 18 to 25 years from 15 years to 17 years

Cessation and Treatment

- Increase smoking cessation attempts by adult smokers.
  - Baseline: 41 percent of adult smokers aged 18 years and older stopped smoking for one day or longer because they were trying to quit in 1998 (age adjusted to the year 2000 standard population).
  - Target: 75 percent.

- Increase smoking cessation during pregnancy.
  - Baseline: 14 percent of females aged 18 to 49 years stopped smoking during the first trimester of their pregnancy in 1998.
  - Target: 30 percent.

- Increase tobacco use cessation attempts by adolescent smokers.
  - Baseline: 76 percent of ever-daily smokers in grades 9 through 12 had tried to quit smoking in 1999.
  - Target: 84 percent.

- Increase insurance coverage of evidence-based treatment for nicotine dependency.
  - Increase coverage by managed care organizations from 75 percent (baseline 1997–98) to 100 percent (target 2010)
  - Increase coverage by Medicaid programs in States and the District of Columbia from 24 percent (baseline 1998) to 51 percent (target 2010)
  - Increase coverage by all insurance (developmental).

Exposure to Secondhand Smoke

- Reduce the proportion of children who are regularly exposed to tobacco smoke at home.
  - Baseline: 27 percent of children aged six years and under lived in a household where someone smoked inside the house at least four days per week in 1994.
  - Target: 10 percent.

- Reduce the proportion of nonsmokers exposed to environmental tobacco smoke.
  - Baseline: 65 percent of nonsmokers aged four years and older had a serum cotinine level above 0.10 ng/mL in 1988–94 (age adjusted to the year 2000 standard population).
  - Target: 45 percent.

- Increase smoke-free and tobacco-free environments in schools, including all school facilities, property, vehicles, and school events.

- Baseline: 37 percent of middle, junior high, and senior high schools were smoke-free and tobacco-free in 1994.
- Target: 100 percent.

- Increase the proportion of worksites with formal smoking policies that prohibit smoking or limit it to separately ventilated areas.
  - Baseline: 79 percent of worksites with 50 or more employees had formal smoking policies that prohibited or limited smoking to separately ventilated areas in 1998–99.
  - Target: 100 percent.

- Establish laws on smoke-free indoor air that prohibit smoking or limit it to separately ventilated areas in public places and worksites. Number of jurisdictions (states and the District of Columbia) with laws on smoke-free air 1998 baseline; 2010 target:
  - Private workplaces: from 1 to 51
  - Public workplaces: from 13 to 51
  - Restaurants: from 3 to 51
  - Public transportation: from 16 to 51
  - Day care centers: from 22 to 51
  - Retail stores: from 4 to 51

- Tribes and territories with laws on smoke-free air (developmental).

Social and Environmental Changes

- Reduce the illegal sales rate to minors through enforcement of laws prohibiting the sale of tobacco products to minors. Jurisdictions with a 5 percent or less illegal sales rate to minors (baseline 1998; target 2010):
  - States and the District of Columbia: from 0 to 51
  - Territories: from 0 to All

- Increase the number of states and the District of Columbia that suspend or revoke state retail licenses for violations of laws prohibiting the sale of tobacco to minors.

- Baseline: 34 States with some form of retail licensure could suspend or revoke the license for violation of minors' access laws in 1998.
- Target: All States and the District of Columbia.

- Eliminate tobacco advertising and promotions that influence adolescents and young adults (developmental).

- Increase adolescents' disapproval of smoking (baseline 1998; target 2010)
  - 8th grade: from 80 percent to 95 percent
  - 10th grade: from 75 percent to 95 percent
  - 12th grade: from 69 percent to 95

- Increase the number of Tribes, Territories, and States and the District of Columbia with comprehensive, evidence-based tobacco control programs (developmental).

- Eliminate laws that preempt stronger tobacco control laws. Preemptive state laws limit the ability of State and local programs to address major areas of tobacco control, in particular smoke-free indoor air and minors' access policies. A preemptive state tobacco control law prevents local jurisdictions from enacting restrictions that are more restrictive than or vary from state law.
  - Baseline: 30 states had preemptive tobacco control laws in the areas of clean indoor air, minors' access laws, or marketing in 1998.
  - Target: Zero states.

- Reduce the toxicity of tobacco products by establishing a regulatory structure to monitor toxicity (developmental).

- Increase the average federal and state tax on tobacco products (baseline 1998; target 2010):
  - Cigarettes: from $0.63 (24 cent federal tax; 38.9 cent average state tax) to $2
  - Spit tobacco (developmental; 2.7 cent federal tax in 1999; 7 states and the District of Columbia did not tax smokeless tobacco products in 1999.)

Chapter 78

Tobacco Use Prevention: Identifying Strategies that Work

A Call for Action

"If the recommendations in this report were fully implemented, the Healthy People 2010 objectives related to tobacco use could be met, including cutting in half the rates of tobacco use among young people and adults."

—David Satcher, MD, PhD, U.S. Surgeon General

Tobacco use, particularly cigarette smoking, is the leading cause of preventable illness and death in the United States. Each year, more than 400,000 Americans die too young because of smoking-related diseases. Today, nearly one in four U.S. adults and one in three teenagers smoke. Tragically, if current trends continue, an estimated 25 million people (including 5 million of today's children) will die prematurely of a smoking-related disease. A major challenge to our

This chapter includes "A Call for Action: Surgeon General's Report—Reducing Tobacco Use," National Center for Chronic Disease Prevention and Health Promotion, Centers for Disease Control and Prevention, reviewed April 2003; and "Tobacco Use Prevention and Control," "Effectiveness of Smoking Bans and Restrictions to Reduce Exposure to Environmental Tobacco Smoke (ETS)," "Increasing the Unit Price for Tobacco Products is Effective in Reducing Initiation of Tobacco Use and In Increasing Cessation," and "Effectiveness of Mass Media Campaigns to Reduce Initiation of Tobacco Use and Increase Cessation," *The Guide to Community Preventive Services*, Task Force on Community Preventive Services, updated January 2003.

nation's public health leaders and policy makers in the new millennium is to provide the support and resources necessary to carry out tobacco control programs that work.

Educational Intervention

Increase the number of schools that fully implement the Centers for Disease Control and Prevention (CDC)'s *Guidelines for School Health Programs to Prevent Tobacco Use and Addiction*. Less than 5% of schools nationwide currently use these guidelines, even though full implementation could help 20% to 40% of U.S. adolescents postpone or never start smoking.

Establish a smoke-free and tobacco-free environment in schools, including all school facilities, property, vehicles, and school events, as called for in Healthy People 2010. In 1994 only 37% of middle, junior high, and senior high schools were free of smoke and tobacco. Fully implementing the Pro-Children's Act of 1994, which prohibits smoking in facilities that receive any federal funding for children's services, will bring us closer to the Healthy People 2010 target of 100% smoke-free schools.

Clinical Interventions

Begin providing universal insurance coverage of evidence-based treatment for nicotine dependency as called for in *Healthy People 2010*. It is estimated that smoking cessation programs are more cost-effective than other commonly provided clinical preventive services, including screening for cervical, breast, and colon cancer; treatment of mild to moderate high blood pressure; and treatment of high cholesterol.

Encourage more physicians to advise their patients to quit smoking. This simple intervention could produce quit rates of 5% to 10% per year.

Combine behavioral counseling with pharmacologic treatments such as nicotine gum or nicotine patches. A combination of counseling and treatment can produce 20% to 25% quit rates after one year.

Regulatory Interventions

Increase smoking bans to reduce people's exposure to environmental tobacco smoke (ETS). ETS contains more than 4,000 chemicals; of these, at least 43 are known carcinogens. ETS is still a common public health hazard that can be easily eliminated, and smoking bans are the most effective method for reducing ETS exposure. *Healthy People 2010* calls for an increase in laws that prohibit smoking or limit it to separately ventilated areas in public places and worksites.

Strengthen warning labels on tobacco products sold in the United States. Current U.S. labels are weaker and less conspicuous than those in other countries.

Better regulate the advertising, promotion, and sale of tobacco products in the United States. Tobacco marketing here is considerably less restricted than in several other countries, notably Canada and New Zealand. U.S. youth have easy access to tobacco—a high proportion of underage smokers across the country continue to be able to purchase their own tobacco. *Healthy People 2010* calls for more states to suspend or revoke retail licenses for violating laws that prohibit the sale of tobacco to minors. Stricter regulation of selling and promoting tobacco products is needed to keep young people from starting to smoke.

To protect young people around the world, make exported tobacco products subject to the same laws as domestic tobacco products. Federal laws and regulations concerning the packaging and advertising of domestic cigarettes do not apply to tobacco products exported from the United States.

Economic Interventions

Raise tobacco prices to *Healthy People 2010* target levels by increasing the average federal and state tax on tobacco products to $2.00 for both cigarettes and spit tobacco products. Research shows that increasing the price of tobacco products would decrease the prevalence of tobacco use, particularly among minors and young adults. However, both the average price of cigarettes and the average cigarette excise tax in this country are well below those in most other industrialized countries, and the taxes on smokeless tobacco products are well below those on cigarettes.

Comprehensive Interventions

Allocate more Master Settlement Agreement funds to tobacco control. The National Conference of State Legislatures reported that less than 10% of tobacco settlement funds appropriated by state legislatures in fiscal year 2000 were allocated for tobacco prevention and control programs.

Reduce the cultural acceptability of tobacco use. By carrying out a comprehensive program that includes educational, clinical, regulatory, and economic interventions, we can change the social environment that makes tobacco use acceptable.

Finally, while putting all these activities into motion, we must focus on making the elimination of tobacco-related health disparities a priority. Cultural, ethnic, religious, and socioeconomic differences clearly are important in understanding patterns of tobacco use. For example, the average smoking rate among American adults is 24%, but among Native American adults is 34%. People with 16 or more years of education smoke much less than people with 9 to 11 years of education—11% and 36%, respectively. Achieving the goal of eliminating tobacco-related health disparities will require stronger research efforts to find new and more effective interventions for our nation's diverse population groups.

Tobacco Use and Prevention Control: What Works?

What works to make tobacco use prevention and control successful at the population or community level? *The Guide to Community Preventive Services* addresses the effectiveness of community-based interventions within three strategic areas of tobacco use prevention and control: 1) prevent tobacco product use initiation, 2) increase cessation and 3) reduce exposure to environmental tobacco smoke (ETS). The findings strengthen and complement existing guidelines on tobacco prevention and control.

Summary of Findings

The independent Task Force on Community Preventive Services issues findings for interventions within strategic areas. Recommendations are based on the strength of the evidence of effectiveness found through a systematic review of published evidence conducted by a team of experts on behalf of the Task Force. A determination that there is "insufficient evidence to determine effectiveness" does not mean that the intervention does not work, but rather indicates that additional research is needed to determine whether or not the intervention is effective. Decision makers should consider these evidence-based recommendations in light of local needs, goals, and constraints when choosing interventions to implement. Interventions and recommendations are summarized in Table 78.1.

Table 78.1. Tobacco Control Strategies.

Intervention	Recommendation
Strategies to Reduce Exposure to Environmental Tobacco Smoke (ETS)	
Smoking bans and restrictions	Recommended (Strong Evidence)
Community education to reduce ETS exposure in the home environment	Insufficient Evidence to determine effectiveness
Strategies to Reduce Tobacco Use Initiation by Children, Adolescents, and Young Adults	
Increasing the unit price for tobacco products	Recommended (Strong Evidence)
Mass media education (campaigns) when combined with other interventions	Recommended (Strong Evidence)
Strategies to Increase Tobacco Cessation	
Increasing the unit price for tobacco products	Recommended (Strong Evidence)
Mass media education	
Campaigns when combined with other interventions	Recommended (Strong Evidence)
Smoking cessation series	Insufficient Evidence to determine effectiveness
Smoking cessation contests	Insufficient Evidence to determine effectiveness
Interventions appropriate for health care systems	
Provider reminder systems (alone)	Recommended (Sufficient evidence)
Provider education programs (alone)	Insufficient Evidence to determine effectiveness
Provider reminder + Provider education (with or without patient education)	Recommended (Strong Evidence)
Provider feedback system	Insufficient Evidence to determine effectiveness
Reducing patient out-of-pocket costs for effective treatments for tobacco use and dependence	Recommended (Sufficient evidence)
Patient telephone support (quit lines) when combined with other interventions	Recommended (Strong Evidence)

511

Effectiveness of Smoking Bans and Restrictions

Policies to reduce smoking indoors reduce exposure to ETS; they can also result in both a reduction in the number of cigarettes smoked each day and an increase in the number of smokers who quit. The question is: what strategies are most effective in reducing exposure to environmental tobacco smoke (ETS)?

A systematic review of published studies, conducted on behalf of the Task Force on Community Preventive Services by a team of experts, found that smoking bans and restrictions are effective in reducing exposure to ETS. Based on this review, the Task Force recommends that this strategy be implemented on the basis of strong evidence of effectiveness.

Background on Smoking Bans and Restrictions

- Smoking bans and restrictions are policies, regulations, and laws that limit smoking in workplaces and other public areas.

- Smoking bans prohibit smoking entirely; smoking restrictions limit smoking to designated areas.

Findings from the Systematic Review

- Studies that evaluated the effect of smoking bans in workplaces observed an average reduction in exposure to components of ETS (for example, nicotine vapor) of 72%.

- Smoking bans were more effective in reducing ETS exposures than were smoking restrictions.

- Smoking bans were effective in a wide variety of public and private workplaces and healthcare settings. Their effectiveness should extend to most indoor workplaces in the United States.

- Studies evaluating smoking bans also observed reductions in the amount smoked.

Increasing the Unit Price for Tobacco Products

Smoking prevalence among adolescents—the age at which most smokers take up the habit—rose dramatically in the early 1990s. Yet 70% of adolescents who smoke want to quit completely. The question is: what strategies are most effective in reducing the number of people who start using tobacco and increasing the number who stop?

A systematic review of published studies, conducted on behalf of the Task Force on Community Preventive Services by a team of experts, found that interventions to increase the unit price for tobacco products are effective both in reducing the number of people who start using tobacco and in increasing the number who quit. Based on this review, the Task Force recommends that this strategy be implemented on the basis of strong evidence of effectiveness.

Background on Increasing the Unit Price for Tobacco Products

- The unit price for tobacco products can be increased by raising the product excise tax, through legislation at the state or national level.

- In several states, excise tax increases have provided revenue for comprehensive tobacco use prevention and control programs.

Findings from the Systematic Review

- In seven of eight studies reviewed, increases in the price of tobacco products resulted in decreases in both the number of people who use tobacco and the quantity they consume.

- The median estimates from the reviewed studies suggest that a 10% increase in the price of tobacco products will result in a 3.7% decrease in the number of adolescents who use tobacco and 4.1% decrease in the amount of tobacco used by the general population.

- Price increases reviewed were effective among a variety of adolescents and young adults in the United States. Increases in the price of tobacco products also reduce tobacco use in older adults.

Mass Media Campaigns

A systematic review of published studies, conducted on behalf of the Task Force on Community Preventive Services by a team of experts, found that mass media campaigns are effective in reducing initiation of tobacco use when combined with other actions (for example, increasing the excise tax). Mass media campaigns may also decrease consumption of tobacco products and increase tobacco use cessation. Based on this review, the Task Force recommends that this strategy be implemented on the basis of *strong* evidence of effectiveness.

Background on the Effectiveness of Mass Media Campaigns

- Messages are developed through formative research, and use broadcast messages on television and radio, although other formats, such as billboards, print media, and movies, have been used.

- Campaigns are conducted over long periods of time and employ brief, recurring messages to inform and motivate individuals to quit or remain tobacco-free.

Findings from the Systematic Review

- Campaigns that are combined with other activities to reduce tobacco use are effective in (1) reducing consumption of tobacco products, and (2) increasing cessation among tobacco users.

- Seven studies, which lasted two years or longer, evaluated campaigns to reduce tobacco use initiation. They observed a median decrease in tobacco initiation of 8.0 percentage points compared with groups not exposed to the campaign.

- Studies evaluating the effectiveness of mass media campaigns in reducing tobacco consumption in statewide populations (as measured by statewide sales of cigarettes) found a median decrease of 15 packs per capita per year.

- The results of mass media campaigns should be applicable in most settings and populations. Studies reviewed worked with a variety of populations across geographic regions within the United States.

Additional Information

The Guide to Community Preventive Services (Community Guide) provides recommendations on population-based interventions to promote health and to prevent disease, injury, disability, and premature death, appropriate for use by communities and healthcare systems. For more information about the Community Guide (including links to publications and a variety of resources) see www.thecommunityguide.org and for more information about tobacco interventions see www.thecommunityguide.org/tobacco.

Chapter 79

What Is Needed to Reduce Smoking among Women

Efforts to Reduce Tobacco Use among Women and Girls

Smoking Cessation

- Studies show no major or consistent differences between women's and men's motivation to quit, readiness to quit, general awareness of the harmful health effects of smoking, or the effectiveness of intervention programs for tobacco use.

- The probability of attempting to quit smoking and to succeed has been equally high among women and men since late 1970s or early 1980s.

Minimal Clinical Interventions

- The likelihood of having been counseled to stop smoking was slightly higher for women (39%) than for men (35%); women report more physician visits than men, which allows more opportunity for counseling.

This chapter includes excerpts from "Efforts to Reduce Tobacco Use Among Women and Girls," and "What Is Needed to Reduce Smoking Among Women," fact sheets developed by the National Center for Chronic Disease Prevention and Health Promotion, Centers for Disease Control and Prevention (CDC), reviewed September 2003.

Intensive Clinical Interventions

- Women are somewhat more likely than men to use intensive treatment programs. Similarly, women have a stronger interest than men in smoking cessation groups that offer mutual support through a buddy system and in treatment meetings over a long period.

Pharmacologic Interventions

- Pharmacologic approaches to smoking cessation raise a number of issues specific to women. Nevertheless, nicotine replacement has been shown to be more effective than placebo among women smokers and, thus, remains recommended for use.

- More research is needed to determine the effects of nicotine replacement therapy on pregnant women and their offspring.

Smoking Cessation Issues Unique to Women

- Studies have identified numerous gender-related factors that should be studied as predictors for smoking cessation as well as factors for continued smoking or relapse after quitting. These factors include hormonal influences, pregnancy, fear of weight gain, lack of social support, and depression.

- Women stop smoking more often during pregnancy—both spontaneously and with assistance—than at any other time in their lives. However, most women return to smoking after pregnancy: up to 67% are smoking again by 12 months after delivery.

- Pregnancy-specific programs benefit both maternal and infant health and are cost-effective. If the national prevalence of smoking before or during the first trimester of pregnancy were reduced by one percentage point annually, it would prevent 1,300 babies from being born at low birth weight and save $21 million (in 1995 dollars) in direct medical costs in the first year alone. Prenatal smoking cessation interventions can be of economic benefit to healthcare insurers.

- More women than men fear weight gain if they quit smoking; however, few studies have found a relationship between weight gain concerns and smoking cessation among either women or men. Further, actual weight gain during cessation efforts does not predict relapse to smoking.

- Smoking cessation treatment and social support derived from family and friends improve cessation rates. Whether there are gender differences in the role of social support on long-term smoking cessation is inconclusive.

Smoking Cessation among Women of Low Socioeconomic Status

- Women of low socioeconomic status (SES) have lower rates of smoking cessation than do women of higher SES. Studies that analyze the effects of mass media campaigns suggest that smokers of low SES, especially women, are more likely than smokers of high SES to watch and obtain cessation information from television.

- Women of low SES enrolled in intensive cessation intervention programs (stress management, self-esteem enhancement, group support, and other activities that improve quality of life) have 20%–25% successful cessation rates. Unfortunately, only a small proportion of women of low SES appear to take advantage of these programs.

Smoking Cessation among Women from Racial and Ethnic Populations

- In general, African-American, Hispanic, and American-Indian or Alaska-Native women want to stop smoking at rates similar to those of white women, but there is little research on smoking cessation among women in racial/ethnic minority populations.

Reducing Smoking among Women

- **Increase awareness of the devastating impact of smoking on women's health:** Smoking is the leading known cause of preventable death and disease among women. In 1987, lung cancer became the leading cause of cancer death among women, and by 2000, about 27,000 more women in the United States died of lung cancer (about 68,000) than of breast cancer (about 41,000).

- **Expose and counter the tobacco industry's deliberate targeting of women and decry its efforts to link smoking, which is so harmful to women's health, with women's rights and progress in society:** In 1999 tobacco companies spent more than $8.24 billion (more than $22.6 million a day) to advertise and promote cigarettes. To sell its products, the tobacco industry exploits themes of success and independence, particularly in its advertising in women's magazines.

- **Encourage a more vocal constituency on issues related to women and smoking:** Taking a lesson from the success of advocacy to reduce breast cancer, we must make concerted efforts to call public attention to the toll of lung cancer and other smoking-related diseases on women's health. Women affected by tobacco-related diseases and their families and friends can partner with women's and girls' organizations, women's magazines, female celebrities, and others—not only in an effort to raise awareness of tobacco-related disease as a women's issue, but also to call for policies and programs that deglamorize and discourage tobacco use.

- **Recognize that nonsmoking is by far the norm among women:** Publicize that most women are nonsmokers. Nearly four-fifths of U.S. women are nonsmokers, and in some subgroup populations, smoking is relatively rare (for example, only 11.2 % of women who have completed college are current smokers, and only 5.4 % of black high school seniors girls are daily smokers). It important to recognize that among adult women those who are most empowered, as measured by educational attainment, are the least likely to be smokers. Moreover, most women who smoke want to quit.

- **Conduct further studies of the relationship between smoking and certain outcomes of importance to women's health:** Additional research is needed to explore these issues:

  - The link between exposure to environmental tobacco smoke and the risk of breast cancer.

  - Cigarette brand variations in toxicity and whether any of these possible variations may be related to changes in lung cancer histology during the past decade.

- Changes in tobacco products and whether increased exposure to tobacco-specific nitrosamines may be related to the increased incidence rates of adenocarcinoma (malignant glandular tumor) of the lung.

- Health effects of smoking among women in the developing world.

- **Encourage the reporting of gender-specific results from studies of influences on smoking behavior, smoking prevention and cessation interventions, and the health effects of tobacco use, including use of new tobacco products:** Research is needed to better understand and to reduce current disparities in smoking prevalence among women of different groups as defined by socioeconomic status, race, ethnicity, and sexual orientation. Women with only 9 to 11 years of education are about three times as likely to be smokers as are women with a college education. American Indian or Alaska Native women are much more likely to smoke than are Hispanic women and Asian or Pacific Islander women. Among teenage girls, white girls are much more likely to smoke than are African American girls.

- **Determine why, during most of the 1990s, smoking prevalence declined so little among women and increased so markedly among teenage girls:** This lack of progress is a major concern and threatens to prolong the epidemic of smoking-related diseases among women. More research is needed to determine the influences that encourage many women and girls to smoke even in the face that all that is known of the dire health consequence of smoking. If, for example, smoking in movies by female celebrities promotes smoking, then discouraging such practices as well as engaging well-known actresses to be spokespersons on the issue of women and smoking should be a high priority.

- **Develop a research and evaluation agenda related to women and smoking:** Research agendas should focus on these issues:

  - Determining whether gender-tailored interventions increase the effectiveness of various smoking prevention and cessation methods.

519

- Documenting whether there are gender differences in the effectiveness of pharmacologic treatments for tobacco cessation.

- Determining which tobacco prevention and cessation interventions are most effective for specific subgroups of girls and women.

- Designing interventions to reduce disparities in smoking prevalence across all subgroups of girls and women.

- **Support efforts, at both individual and societal levels, to reduce smoking and exposure to environmental tobacco smoke among women:** Tobacco-use treatments are among the most cost-effective of preventive health interventions at the individual level, and they should be part of all women's health care programs. Health insurance plans should cover such services. Societal strategies to reduce tobacco use and exposure to environmental tobacco smoke include counter-advertising, increasing tobacco taxes, enacting laws to reduce minors' access to tobacco products, and banning smoking in work sites and in public places.

- **Enact comprehensive statewide tobacco control programs proven to be effective in reducing and preventing tobacco use:** Results from states such as Arizona, California, Florida, Maine, Massachusetts, and Oregon show that science-based tobacco control programs have successfully reduced smoking rates among women and girls. California established a comprehensive statewide tobacco control program more than ten years ago, and is now starting to observe the benefits of its sustained efforts. Between 1988 and 1997, the incidence rate of lung cancer among women declined by 4.8% in California but increased by 13.2% in other regions of the United States.

- **Increase efforts to stop the emerging epidemic of smoking among women in developing countries:** Strongly encourage and support multinational policies that discourage the spread of smoking and tobacco-related diseases among women in countries where smoking prevalence has traditionally been low. It is urgent that what is already known about effective means of tobacco control at the societal level be disseminated throughout the world.

Chapter 80

Talking to Your Child about Tobacco

Talking to Your Child about Smoking and Smokeless Tobacco

Advertisers spend billions of dollars each year trying to get children to smoke. Talking to your kids honestly, clearly, and convincingly about the dangers of tobacco and nicotine addiction is an essential part of good parenting. To be blunt: your words can save their lives. Read this text to find out how.

Why Do I Need to Talk to My Child about Tobacco?

According to the U.S. Surgeon General, smoking is the chief cause of preventable deaths in the United States. At the same time, however, the U.S. Centers for Disease Control and Prevention reports that each day more than 3,000 kids become regular smokers and that about one third of these children will eventually die a "smoker's death" from cancer, heart disease, or lung disease.

And the danger isn't just smoking cigarettes. Smokeless tobacco (chewing or spit tobacco) can also lead to nicotine addiction, oral cancer, gum disease, and an increased risk of cardiovascular disease,

This information was provided by KidsHealth, one of the largest resources online for medically reviewed health information written for parents, kids, and teens. For more articles like this one, visit www.KidsHealth.org, or www.TeensHealth.org. © 2000 The Nemours Center for Children's Health Media, a division of The Nemours Foundation.

521

including heart attacks. Despite these dangers, about 16% of U.S. high school boys in grades 9 to 12 use smokeless tobacco, with rates rising as high as 35% in some western states.

Nicotine affects mood as well as the heart, lungs, stomach, and nervous system. Short-term effects of smoking include coughing and throat irritation. Over time, more serious conditions may develop, including increases in heart rate and blood pressure. Smoking also leads to bronchitis and emphysema and increases the risk of heart attacks.

Finally, numerous studies indicate that young smokers are more likely to experiment with marijuana, cocaine, heroin, or other illicit drugs.

About 90% of today's adult smokers started as children, so it's important that you take the opportunity to talk to your kid about smoking before she starts. Older children who haven't started to smoke are less likely to begin smoking.

"The most important way you can prepare to deal with smoking is by establishing good communication. The more you talk with your child, the better chance you have of staying close when things get tough," says Neil Izenberg, M.D., pediatrician and author of *How to Raise Non-Smoking Kids*.

Did You Know? Nearly 90% of all adult smokers start when they are teens—and never intend to get hooked.

What Should I Say?

When talking to your child about smoking, Dr. Izenberg recommends that parents stick to the facts. "There's no need to invent—the truth is bad enough," he says. Resist lecturing or turning your advice into a sermon; the point is to communicate values such as honesty, self-reliance, and responsibility to your children—and how good values make good decisions easier to make.

How can you translate these standards to your child? To start with, even the youngest child can understand that smoking is bad for your body. Young children also imitate their parents, so if you smoke, quit. Kids want to be like their parents, so setting an example is vitally important. You can also establish firm rules that exclude smoking and smokeless tobacco from your house and explain why: smokers smell bad, look bad, and feel bad.

Teach children from an early age about the differences between images used by advertisers of tobacco products and reality. One anti-smoking group suggests letting kids compare an ad for a toy on television with what the toy really does, and then using this example to compare images of people smoking in ads and what smoking is truly like. Teaching media literacy (helping your kids become critical consumers) is an important parenting task.

As children grow older, steer them toward positive role models in entertainment or sports who don't smoke, and continue to compare images in movies or television of heroes who smoke with what smoking does to real people. "Make it part of your daily routine to sit and talk with your kid," Dr. Izenberg says. "Don't avoid subjects because you might find them uncomfortable or you're afraid you don't know just the right words."

By sharing time with your 8- to 11-year-old and valuing her opinions and ideas, you help build her self-confidence and self-worth—qualities that will help her to combat subtle advertising messages that promote rebellion and being cool above all. Kids who believe in themselves and have support at home may be better able to reject these messages.

The need to be socially accepted often increases as kids approach their teens. But if you've equipped your child with the facts about tobacco's dangers and helped your child to develop healthy self-esteem, she won't want to smoke or use smokeless tobacco. What she probably will want is simply to be accepted by her peers.

"Saying 'no' to people your child wants desperately to please can seem far worse than smoking a few cigarettes," Dr. Izenberg says.

To help your teen, talk to her about how to respond to those who encourage her to light up. Responses may range from simply saying "no" to excuses about smoking being a waste of money. When discussing these issues with your teen, be a patient listener. "Don't expect teens to be consistent, logical, articulate, or even conscious of the reasons why they do things. It will take time to develop a defensible position against smoking," Dr. Izenberg warns. If your child seems overly angry or depressed, however, you may want to consult your child's doctor.

Risk Factors

Kids may be drawn to smoking for any number of reasons—to look cool, act older, lose weight, win cool merchandise, seem tough, or feel independent.

To combat these images, you can explain that virtually all the adults who smoke started when they were teens and continue to smoke because they are addicted. Give your child the facts: nine out of ten new teen smokers say they plan to quit within a year; few actually do.

Talk about what true independence means and how much of your teen's daily routine would be governed by cigarettes if she began to smoke. How would this affect her friendships? How will she afford the habit? Discuss what being an adult really means. And while you're talking about independence and adulthood, encourage your teen to take on some constructive and healthy responsibilities that come with being older, such as having a part-time job or volunteering.

If your child is using cigarettes to be cool or rebel, you can try a couple of things. Remind your child of the difference between image and substance: what cigarettes do to your looks or your health vs. the so-called glamorous image. Talk about how what your kid may see as rebellion is actually the result of being the dupe of clever marketing—hardly the sign of a rebel.

Remember that a kid may also be using smoking as a way to test your limits, so maintain your rules. If your child is smoking to test her own limitations to see if she can smoke and quit, steer her toward some other, less deadly forms of risk taking. Hiking, swimming, and climbing are a few activities that can put your child on the edge.

Did You Know? Wondering what kills more people each year than AIDS, fires, car accidents, murders, suicides, alcohol, and other drugs combined? You've got it—smoking.

Tips for Parents

Below are some tips for improving communication about tobacco products:

- Be a good listener. Make sure your child feels comfortable bringing problems or questions to you. Note what your child is not saying. If she doesn't tell you about her friends, for example, take the initiative and ask questions.

- Be available to discuss sensitive subjects. Children need to know they can rely on their parents for accurate information.

- Emphasize what your child does right rather than wrong. Self-confidence is your child's best protection against peer pressure.

- Give clear, specific messages when talking about tobacco and tobacco products so your child will know exactly what is expected.

- Help your kid to get involved in activities that preclude smoking, such as sports activities. Many coaches actively discourage smoking. Among other things, it negatively affects performance.

- Encourage your child to walk away from friends who don't recognize or respect her reasons for not smoking.

- Read, watch television, and go to the movies with your child. Compare media images to reality. For example, watch a heavy smoking hero run from "bad" guys. Does he end up wheezing or coughing when he finally escapes? Also talk about what you don't see or hear. When the camera moves in on two smokers whispering to one another, do you hear a wheeze or see wrinkles? Why not?

- Be aware of who your kid hangs out with. If she has at least one close friend who smokes, the chances that she'll pick up a cigarette are much greater. If that's the case, don't wait until you know your child has started to smoke. Instead, Dr. Izenberg suggests you might want to try asking something like "Your friend, Steve, smokes, doesn't he? Do you feel tempted to smoke when you're with him?"

Chapter 81

Facts about Tobacco Advertising and Promotion

- Despite the overwhelming evidence of the adverse health effects from tobacco use, efforts to prevent the onset or continuance of tobacco use face the pervasive challenge of promotion activity by the tobacco industry.[1]

- Regulating advertising and promotion, particularly that directed at young people, is very likely to reduce both the prevalence and initiation of smoking.[1]

- The tobacco industry uses a variety of marketing tools and strategies to influence consumer preference, thereby increasing market share and attracting new consumers.[1]

- Among all U.S. manufacturers, the tobacco industry is one of the most intense in marketing its products. Only the automobile industry markets its products more heavily.[1]

- In 1998 tobacco companies spent nearly $7 billion—or more than $18 million a day—to advertise and promote cigarettes. In recent years, these marketing dollars pay for activities that may have special appeal to young people.[2]

- Children and teenagers constitute the majority of all new smokers, and the industry's advertising and promotion campaigns often have special appeal to these young people.[1]

"Tobacco Advertising and Promotion," a fact sheet produced by the National Center for Chronic Disease Prevention and Health Promotion, Centers for Disease Control and Promotion (CDC), April 2001.

- One tobacco company, the Liggett Group, Inc., has admitted that the entire tobacco industry conspired to market cigarettes to children.[1]

- Tobacco documents recently obtained in litigation indicate that tobacco companies have purposefully marketed to children as young as 14 years of age.[1,4]

- About 85% of adolescent smokers who buy their own cigarettes buy either Marlboro, Newport, or Camel—the three most heavily advertised brands of cigarettes in the United States.[3]

- The effect of tobacco advertising on young people is best epitomized by R.J. Reynolds Company's introduction of the Joe Camel campaign. From the introduction of the Old Joe cartoon character in 1988, Camel's share of the adolescent cigarette market increased dramatically—from less than 1% before 1988, to 8% in 1989, to more than 13% in 1993.[1,4]

- In 1997 the Federal Trade Commission (FTC) filed a complaint against R.J. Reynolds alleging that "the purpose of the Joe Camel campaign was to reposition the Camel brand to make it attractive to young smokers." The FTC ultimately dismissed its complaint after the November 23, 1998, Master Settlement Agreement (MSA), which calls for the ban of all cartoon characters, including Joe Camel, in the advertising, promotion, packaging, and labeling of any tobacco product.[1]

- The MSA prohibits a number of promotional activities such as banning brand name sponsorship of events with a significant youth audience; the use of tobacco brand names in stadiums and arenas; payments to promote tobacco products in movies, television shows, theater productions or live performances, videos and video games; all transit and outdoor advertising; and specialty items bearing product names and logos.

- The greatest growth of tobacco advertising aimed at women followed the introduction of Virginia Slims in 1968 with its slogan "You've Come a Long Way, Baby!" Since then, there has been an increasing number of cigarette brands and advertising campaigns targeted toward women.[5]

- In 1997 Woman Thing Music, a new record company owned by Philip Morris Tobacco Company, offered unsigned female music artists lucrative recording contracts and an opportunity to be featured on a new CD. This CD, targeted toward young women, was available only with the purchase of two packs of Virginia Slims cigarettes. Outraged by this promotion, the celebrity artists organized a counter-music campaign, Virginia SLAM.[6]

- In December 1999 Philip Morris launched a new $40 million campaign targeting women, particularly minority women, with the slogan "Find Your Own Voice." The ads have been featured in a variety of publications such as *Glamour, Ladies' Home Journal, People,* and *Essence.* In response to this ad campaign, several women's groups, led by the American Medical Women's Association and the National Coalition For Women Against Tobacco, joined together on a campaign to counter the tobacco industry's targeting of women.[7,8]

- Many public health and smoking prevention groups are concerned about the tobacco industry's practice of targeting cultural and ethnic minorities through product development, packaging, pricing, advertising, and promotional activities.[1]

- A one-year study found that three major African American publications—*Ebony, Jet,* and *Essence*—received proportionately higher profits from cigarette advertisements than did other magazines.[8]

- Tobacco products are advertised and promoted disproportionately in racial/ethnic minority communities. Examples of targeted promotions include the introduction of cigarette products with the brand names "Rio" and "Dorado" that were advertised and marketed at different times to the Hispanic community.[8]

- Studies have found a higher density of tobacco billboards in racial/ethnic minority communities. For example, a 1993 study in San Diego, California, found that the highest proportion of tobacco billboards were posted in Asian American communities and the lowest proportion were in white communities.[8]

- The tobacco industry commonly uses cultural symbols and designs to target racial/ethnic populations. American Spirit cigarettes were promoted as natural cigarettes; the package featured an American Indian smoking a pipe. In addition, certain tobacco product advertisements have used visual images, such as American Indian warriors, to target their products.[8]

References

1. U.S. Department of Health and Human Services. *Reducing To-bacco Use: A Report of the Surgeon General.* Atlanta: U.S. Department of Health and Human Services, Centers for Disease Control and Prevention, 2000.

2. Federal Trade Commission Report to Congress for 1998, Pursuant to the Federal Cigarette Labeling and Advertising Act. Issued: 2000.

3. The University of Michigan. Cigarette Brands Smoked By American Teens: One Brand Predominates; Three Account for Nearly All Teen Smoking (press release). April 14, 1999.

4. Centers for Disease Control and Prevention. Trends in smoking initiation among adolescents and young adults—United States, 1980–1989. *MMWR* 1995; 44:521–25.

5. O'Keefe AM, Pollay RW. Deadly targeting of women in promoting cigarettes. *JAMWA* 1996; No. 1 and 2:67–69.

6. Centers for Disease Control and Prevention. "SLAM" (educational video). Issued 2000.

7. Pollack J. Virginia Slims translates theme for many cultures: cigarette brand's $40 mil effort may be historic; uses multipage magazine. *Advertising Age* 1999 September 13;70:3,73.

8. American Medical Women's Association (press release) National Coalition for Women against Tobacco Launches Defense Against the Tobacco Industry. October 12, 1999.

9. U.S. Department of Health and Human Services. Tobacco Use among U.S. Racial/Ethnic Minority Groups—African Americans, American Indians and Alaska Natives, Asian Americans and Pacific Islanders, and Hispanics: A Report of the Surgeon General. Atlanta: U.S. Department of Health and Human Services, Centers for Disease Control and Prevention, 1998.

Chapter 82

Federal Cigarette Labeling and Advertising Act

What is FCLAA?

FCLAA is the acronym for the Federal Cigarette Labeling and Advertising Act, Public Law 89-92. This statute was designed to "establish a comprehensive federal program to deal with cigarette labeling and advertising with respect to any relationship between smoking and health." There have been two amendments to FCLAA, one in 1984 by the Comprehensive Smoking Education Act (P.L. 98-474, October 12, 1984; 15 U.S.C. Section 1331 and following), and the other in 1986 by the Comprehensive Smokeless Tobacco Health Education Act (P.L. 99-252, February 27, 1986; 15 U.S.C. Section 4401 and following). These amendments serve to make the American public "more aware of any adverse health effects" resulting from the compounds, design and use of cigarette and smokeless tobacco products. This is achieved in part by HHS' laboratories reviewing and analyzing the list of ingredients used in the manufacture of tobacco products.

What products are covered by FCLAA?

As amended, FCLAA requires ingredient reports to be filed with the Secretary of Health and Human Services for all cigarettes and

This chapter includes excerpts from "Tobacco Ingredient Reporting—Frequently Asked Questions" and "Warning Label," both produced by the National Center for Chronic Disease Prevention and Health Promotion, Centers for Disease Control and Prevention (CDC), reviewed 2003.

smokeless tobacco (SLT) products. The Comprehensive Smoking Education Act defines cigarettes as "any roll of tobacco wrapped in paper or in any substance not containing tobacco, and any roll of tobacco wrapped in any substance containing tobacco which, because of its appearance, the type of tobacco used in the filler, or its packaging and labeling, is likely to be offered to, or purchased by consumers as a cigarette," 15 U.S.C. Section 1332(1)(A)-(B). This definition includes bidis, kreteks and little cigars. The Comprehensive Smokeless Tobacco Health Education Act defines SLT products as "any finely cut, ground, powdered or leaf tobacco that is intended to be placed in the oral cavity," 15 U.S.C. Section 4408. This definition includes hookah products.

What tobacco products are not covered by FCLAA?

FCLAA does not apply to cigar companies or manufacturers of cut rag tobacco unless the cut rag tobacco is packaged as a final product for consumption.

To whom does FCLAA apply?

Manufacturers, packagers, and importers of tobacco products.

Does the ingredient report contain the same information for cigarettes and smokeless tobacco products?

No. Both the Comprehensive Smoking Education Act and the Comprehensive Smokeless Health Education Act require companies to submit an ingredient report; however, the SLT ingredient report must also contain the nicotine data report (nicotine, pH and unionized pH contents).

What are CAS numbers?

CAS is the acronym for Chemical Abstract Service Registry number. The American Chemical Society (ACS) assigns a CAS number to all chemical compounds for purposes of identification. ACS has a comprehensive database of CAS assignments accessible through their web page (http://www.cas.org). The Food and Drug Administration (FDA) also has an extensive list of CAS assignments.

Why must CAS numbers be included with the report?

To properly identify and reduce ambiguity among ingredients used in tobacco products. This is particularly important as an ingredient may have a common name but different chemical names and thus, different CAS assignments. An example of this is sugar, whose chemical names can be fructose, glucose, or sucrose.

Is it necessary to report trade secret or confidential information?

Yes. The U.S. Congress gave full weight and consideration to the sensitive nature of tobacco ingredients in drafting the federal statutes. Tobacco ingredients are trade secret and confidential information and therefore, cannot be disclosed by OSH with few exceptions as outlined in the federal statute. In the event that an exception exists and OSH is required to disclose the list of ingredients, OSH will notify the company or its representative of action taken.

Must representatives disclose the identity of their clients when submitting the ingredient report?

Under federal law, manufacturers, importers, and packagers have the option of submitting their ingredient report directly to OSH or through a representative. The identity of the manufacturer, importer, or packager must be disclosed but can be done in such a manner that does not reveal the association between the manufacturer and the ingredient list. It is necessary for OSH to know the identify of the person submitting the ingredient list to ensure that our office issues timely and accurate compliance letters.

Must an ingredient report be submitted if it contains no additives?

Yes. Even if the packager or importer does not add ingredients the manufacturer may and that must be reported to OSH. However, if the brand is made with no additives and none are added at a later date, then a statement of such would suffice for cigarette ingredient reports. One must still submit the nicotine data report for SLT products.

Are there other federal agencies responsible for collecting information under FCLAA?

Yes. The Federal Trade Commission's (FTC) Division of Advertising Practices is responsible for reviewing and approving health warning label plans for all tobacco products, whether manufactured domestically or abroad, that enter the U.S. stream of commerce. The U.S. Department of Treasury houses two agencies with whom manufacturers, packagers, and importers may have to interact: U.S. Customs (Customs) and the Alcohol and Tobacco Tax and Trade Bureau (TTB). Customs and TTB implement and enforce the Contraband Cigarette Trafficking Act, Jenkins Act, and the Import Cigarette Compliance Act.

Are there any penalties for failing to comply with FCLAA?

Yes. Failure to comply or making false representations regarding materials submitted under FCLAA is a criminal offense. "Any person who violates the provisions of this chapter shall be guilty of a misdemeanor and shall on conviction thereof be subject to a fine of not more than $10,000." 15 U.S.C. Section 1338.

Does FCLAA preempt state and local initiatives?

Yes. The Comprehensive Smoking Education Act, 15 U.S.C. Section 1334(a)–(b), reads:

> "(a) Additional statements: No statement relating to smoking and health, other than the statement required by section 1333 of this title, shall be required on any cigarette package.

> (b) State regulations: No requirement or prohibition based on smoking and health shall be imposed under state law with respect to the advertising or promotion of any cigarettes the packages of which are labeled in conformity with the provisions of this chapter."

And, the Comprehensive Smokeless Tobacco Health Education Act, 15. U.S.C. Section 4406(a)–(c), states:

> "(a) Federal action: No statement relating to the use of smokeless tobacco products and health, other than the statements required by section 4402 of this title, shall be required by any federal agency to appear on any package or in any advertisement (unless the advertisement is an outdoor billboard advertisement) of a smokeless tobacco product.

> (b) State and local action: No statement relating to the use of smokeless tobacco products and health, other than the statements required by section 4402 of this title, shall be required by any state or local statute or regulation to be included on any package or in any advertisement (unless the advertisement is

an outdoor billboard advertisement) of a smokeless tobacco product.

(c) Effect on liability law: Nothing in this chapter shall relieve any person from liability at common law or under state statutory law to any other."

Warning Label

Since the release of the first Surgeon General's report on smoking and health in the United States in 1964, about 10 million people have died from smoking-related diseases in the United States—heart disease, lung cancer, emphysema, and other respiratory diseases.[1]

If current smoking patterns continue, an estimated 25 million Americans will die prematurely from a smoking-related illness, including an estimated 5 million people who are now children and adolescents under the age of 18 years.[1]

The Federal Cigarette Labeling and Advertising Act of 1965 (Public Law 89-92) required that the warning "Caution: Cigarette Smoking May Be Hazardous to Your Health" be placed in small print on one of the side panels of each cigarette package. The act prohibited additional labeling requirements at the federal, state, or local levels.[2]

In June 1967 the Federal Trade Commission (FTC) issued its first report to Congress recommending that the warning label be changed to "Warning: Cigarette Smoking Is Dangerous to Health and May Cause Death from Cancer and Other Diseases."[2]

In 1969 Congress passed the Public Health Cigarette Smoking Act (Public Law 91-222), which prohibited cigarette advertising on television and radio and required that each cigarette package contain the label "Warning: The Surgeon General Has Determined That Cigarette Smoking Is Dangerous to Your Health."[2]

In 1981 the FTC issued a report to Congress that concluded health warning labels had little effect on public knowledge and attitudes about smoking. As a result of this report, Congress enacted the Comprehensive Smoking Education Act of 1984 (Public Law 98-474), which required four specific health warnings on all cigarette packages and advertisements:

- SURGEON GENERAL'S WARNING: Smoking Causes Lung Cancer, Heart Disease, Emphysema, and May Complicate Pregnancy.

- SURGEON GENERAL'S WARNING: Quitting Smoking Now Greatly Reduces Serious Risks to Your Health.

- SURGEON GENERAL'S WARNING: Smoking by Pregnant Women May Result in Fetal Injury, Premature Birth, and Low Birth Weight.

- SURGEON GENERAL'S WARNING: Cigarette Smoke Contains Carbon Monoxide.[2]

Smokeless Tobacco

By the mid-1980s scientific evidence revealed that smokeless tobacco use causes oral cancer, nicotine addiction, and other health problems. The Comprehensive Smokeless Tobacco Health Education Act of 1986 (Public Law 99-252) required three rotating warning labels on smokeless tobacco packaging and advertisements:

- WARNING: This product may cause mouth cancer.

- WARNING: This product may cause gum disease and tooth loss.

- WARNING: This product is not a safe alternative to cigarettes.[2,4]

Warning labels that appear on smokeless tobacco products in the United States are weaker, less informative, and less obvious labels used on the products than they are in some countries. The FTC is reviewing public comments on the effectiveness of the existing warning labels.[3]

Cigar Label Requirements

There is clear scientific evidence that cigar smoking represents a significant health risk and is not a safe alternative to cigarette smoking. Cigar use has been linked to oral, esophageal, laryngeal, and lung cancer. Regular cigar smokers who inhale, particularly those who smoke several cigars per day, have an increased risk for coronary heart disease and chronic obstructive pulmonary disease.[5]

On June 26, 2000, the FTC announced a settlement with seven of the largest U.S. cigar companies requiring health warnings on cigar products. Health warnings must appear on the principal display panel to ensure warnings are easily seen. Each of the five required warnings must be displayed an equal number of times. The agreement also calls for warnings to be placed on various types of advertising, such as magazines and other periodicals, point-of-purchase displays, and catalogues.

Every cigar package and advertisement will require the following warnings on a rotating basis:

- SURGEON GENERAL'S WARNING: Cigar Smoking Can Cause Cancers of the Mouth and Throat, Even If You Do Not Inhale.

- SURGEON GENERAL'S WARNING: Cigar Smoking Can Cause Lung Cancer and Heart Disease.

- SURGEON GENERAL'S WARNING: Tobacco Use Increases the Risk of Infertility, Stillbirth and Low Birth Weight.

- SURGEON GENERAL'S WARNING: Cigars Are Not a Safe Alternative to Cigarettes.

- SURGEON GENERAL'S WARNING: Tobacco Smoke Increases the Risk of Lung Cancer and Heart Disease, Even in Nonsmokers.[6]

References

1. Centers for Disease Control and Prevention. Smoking-Attributable Mortality and Years of Potential Life Lost—United States, 1984. *MMWR* 1997 46:444–51.

2. U.S. Department of Health and Human Services. *Reducing Tobacco Use: A Report of the Surgeon General.* Atlanta: U.S. Department of Health and Human Services, Centers for Disease Control and Prevention, 2000.

3. Centers for Disease Control and Prevention. Federal Trade Commission Request for Comments Concerning Regulations Implementing the Comprehensive Smokeless Tobacco Health Education Act of 1986. Accessed [March 7, 2000].

4. Health Canada New Cigarette Labeling Measures, January 19, 2000 (http://www.tobaccolaw.org).

5. National Cancer Institute. *Cigars Health Effects and Trends. Smoking and Tobacco Control Monograph No. 9.* Bethesda (MD): U.S. Department of Health and Human Services, Public Health Service, National Institutes of Health, National Cancer Institute. NIH Publication No. 98-4302, 1998.

6. Federal Trade Commission. FTC Announces Settlements Requiring Disclosure of Cigar Health Risks: Landmark Agreements Require Strong Warnings on Both Packaging and Advertisements. (press release). June 26, 2000.

Chapter 83

Tobacco Taxation

Taxation of Tobacco Products

In the United States, tobacco is taxed in various ways by the federal, state, and local governments. The most important of these are the excise, or per unit, taxes imposed on cigarettes and the general sales tax (an ad valorem tax) applied to cigarettes and other tobacco products in most states. Ad valorem taxes are a fixed percentage of the price and thereby increase or decrease as price changes. Excise taxes, on the other hand, do not change over time with prices.

Tobacco taxes have relatively low administrative costs and can generate substantial revenues. In recent years, increased taxation of tobacco products has been used as a strategy to reduce tobacco consumption and thereby to improve public health. Anticipated large reductions in youth smoking were, in part, the rationale for tax increases of up to $2.00 per pack proposed as part of most proposals for national tobacco legislation and the average $2.00 state and federal tax set as a goal for 2010 by the *Healthy People 2010* initiative. The health benefits of higher taxes were also the focus of the large

---

This chapter includes "Taxation of Tobacco Products," excerpted from *Reducing Tobacco Use: A Report of the Surgeon General*. Atlanta, Georgia: U.S. Department of Health and Human Services, Centers for Disease Control and Prevention (CDC), National Center for Chronic Disease Prevention and Health Promotion, Office on Smoking and Health, 2000; and "Tobacco Taxation Fact Sheet," National Center for Chronic Disease Prevention and Health Promotion, CDC, reviewed April 11, 2001.

voter-initiated tax increases in Arizona, California, Massachusetts, Michigan, and Oregon, as well as the large legislated tax increases in Alaska, Maine, and elsewhere.

Table 83.1. Federal Excise Taxes, Selected Dates.

Date	Cigarettes[1]	Chewing tobacco[2]	Snuff[2]	Pipe tobacco[2]
1991	20.0	10.0	30.0	56.25
1993	24.0	12.0	36.0	67.5
2000	34.0	17.0	51.0	95.67
2002	39.0	19.5	58.5	109.69

[1] tax in cents per pack of 20 cigarettes
[2] tax in cents per pound

Rationales for Tobacco Taxation

Alternative approaches have been used to determine the appropriate level of cigarette and other tobacco taxes. One such approach is the historical or comparative standard, which looks at the relative value of these taxes over time or cross-sectionally. A second approach is to use an efficiency standard based on the external costs of smoking; this approach implies that tobacco taxes can be thought of as "user fees" sufficient to cover the external costs of tobacco use. This approach, however, raises questions concerning the fairness of such taxes. A further argument has been made for substantial increases in tobacco taxes, because these tax hikes would lead to substantial reductions in the morbidity and mortality associated with cigarette smoking. Finally, because taxes on cigarettes and other tobacco products are a relatively simple way to generate revenues, it has been suggested that these taxes can be set at levels that maximize their returns.

Tobacco Taxation Facts

- Substantial scientific evidence shows that higher cigarette prices result in lower overall cigarette consumption. Most studies indicate that a 10% increase in price will reduce overall cigarette consumption by 3% to 5%.

- Youth, minorities, and low-income smokers are two to three times more likely to quit or smoke less than other smokers in response to price increases.

- Increases in cigarette excise taxes are an effective policy tool in deterring smoking initiation among youth, prompting smoking cessation among adults, and reducing the average cigarette consumption among continuing smokers.

- Despite the proven effects of increasing both the price of cigarettes and tobacco excise taxes, the average price and excise tax on cigarettes in the United States is well below those of most other industrialized nations.

- Higher cigarette prices will not simply reduce average cigarette consumption but also will reduce overall smoking prevalence. Higher prices will result in more smokers deciding to quit and fewer young people opting to begin smoking.

- Studies of smokeless tobacco products suggest that increasing their prices would reduce the prevalence of smokeless tobacco use as well.

- Taxes on smokeless tobacco products are much lower than taxes on cigarettes, particularly at the federal level. Research suggests that increases in cigarette excise taxes, while reducing cigarette smoking, may have contributed to greater use of smokeless tobacco products. Some public health advocates and others have therefore called for the equalization of taxes on tobacco.

- *Healthy People 2010* calls for state and federal taxes to increase to an average of $2 for both cigarettes and smokeless tobacco products by the year 2010.

- The importance of tobacco to the U.S. economy has been overstated. Judicious policies combined with higher tobacco taxes and stronger prevention policies can help foster economic diversification in tobacco-producing areas.

Part Six

Additional Help and Information

Chapter 84

Glossary of Terms Related to Tobacco Use and Smoking Cessation

addiction: A chronic, relapsing disease, characterized by compulsive drug-seeking and use and by neurochemical and molecular changes in the brain.

adenocarcinoma: Cancer that begins in cells that line certain internal organs and that have glandular (secretory) properties.

adrenal glands: Glands located above each kidney that secrete hormones, for example, adrenaline.

aerosol: A solution of a drug that is made into a fine mist for inhalation.

airway obstruction: A narrowing, clogging, or blocking of the passages that carry air to the lungs.

alpha-1-protease inhibitor: A substance in blood transported to the lungs that inhibits the digestive activity of trypsin and other proteases which digest proteins. Deficiency of this substance is associated with emphysema.

alveoli: Tiny sac-like air spaces in the lungs where transfer of carbon dioxide from blood into the lungs and oxygen from air into blood takes place.

This glossary contains terms excerpted from glossaries produced by the National Cancer Institute (www.cancer.gov), National Heart, Lung, and Blood Institute (www.nhlbi.nih.gov), and National Institute on Drug Abuse (www.nida.nih.gov); accessed November 2003.

anterior mediastinotomy: A procedure in which a tube is inserted into the chest to view the tissues and organs in the area between the lungs and between the breastbone and heart. The tube is inserted through an incision next to the breastbone. This procedure is usually used to get a tissue sample from the lymph nodes on the left side of the chest. Also called the Chamberlain procedure.

asbestos: A natural material that is made of tiny fibers. Asbestos can cause several serious diseases, including cancer.

aspiration: Removal of fluid or tissue through a needle. Also, the accidental breathing in of food or fluid into the lungs.

benign: Not cancerous. Benign tumors do not spread to tissues around them or to other parts of the body.

biopsy: The removal of cells or tissues for examination under a microscope. When only a sample of tissue is removed, the procedure is called an incisional biopsy or core biopsy. When an entire lump or suspicious area is removed, the procedure is called an excisional biopsy. When a sample of tissue or fluid is removed with a needle, the procedure is called a needle biopsy or fine-needle aspiration.

bone scan: A technique to create images of bones on a computer screen or on film. A small amount of radioactive material is injected into a blood vessel and travels through the bloodstream; it collects in the bones and is detected by a scanner.

bronchi: Larger air passages of the lungs.

bronchiole: Air passages of the lungs; finer than bronchi.

bronchitis: Inflammation (swelling and reddening) of the bronchi.

broncho-constriction: Tightening of the muscles surrounding bronchi, the tubes that branch from the windpipe.

bronchodilator: A drug that relaxes the smooth muscles and opens the constricted airway.

bronchoscope: A thin, lighted tube used to examine the inside of the trachea and bronchi, the air passages that lead to the lungs.

bronchoscopy: A procedure in which a thin, lighted tube is inserted through the nose or mouth. This allows examination of the inside of the trachea and bronchi (air passages that lead to the lung), as well as the lung. Bronchoscopy may be used to detect cancer or to perform some treatment procedures.

buccal mucosa: The inner lining of the cheeks and lips.

cancer: A term for diseases in which abnormal cells divide without control. Cancer cells can invade nearby tissues and can spread through the bloodstream and lymphatic system to other parts of the body. There are several main types of cancer. Carcinoma is cancer that begins in the skin or in tissues that line or cover internal organs. Sarcoma is cancer that begins in bone, cartilage, fat, muscle, blood vessels, or other connective or supportive tissue. Leukemia is cancer that starts in blood-forming tissue such as the bone marrow, and causes large numbers of abnormal blood cells to be produced and enter the bloodstream. Lymphoma is cancer that begins in the cells of the immune system.

capillaries: The smallest blood vessels in the body through which most of the oxygen, carbon dioxide, and nutrient exchanges take place.

carcinogen: Any substance that causes cancer.

chemotherapy: Treatment with anticancer drugs.

continuous positive airway: A mechanical ventilation technique used to deliver continuous positive airway pressure (CPAP) pressure.

cor pulmonale: Heart disease due to lung problems.

corticosteroids: A group of hormones produced by adrenal glands.

craving: A powerful, often uncontrollable desire for drugs.

CT scan: Computed tomography scan. A series of detailed pictures of areas inside the body taken from different angles; the pictures are created by a computer linked to an x-ray machine. Also called computerized tomography and computerized axial tomography (CAT) scan.

cyanosis: Bluish color of the skin associated with insufficient oxygen.

dopamine: A neurotransmitter present in regions of the brain that regulate movement, emotion, motivation, and the feeling of pleasure.

dyspnea: Shortness of breath; difficult or labored breathing.

elastase inhibitors: Substances in the blood transported to the lungs and other organs which prevent the digestive action of elastases.

elastin: An elastic substance in the lungs (and some other body organs) that support their structural framework.

elastin degrading enzymes (elastases): Substances in the blood transported to the lungs and other organs which digest or breakdown elastin.

emphysema: A lung disease in which tissue deterioration results in increased air retention and reduced exchange of gases. The result is difficult breathing and shortness of breath. It is often caused by smoking.

erythroplakia: A reddened patch with a velvety surface found in the mouth.

gas exchange: A primary function of the lungs involving transfer of oxygen from inhaled air into blood and of carbon dioxide from blood into lungs.

hypoventilation: A state in which there is an insufficient amount of air entering and leaving the lungs to bring oxygen into tissues and eliminate carbon dioxide.

hypoxemia: Deficient oxygenation of the blood.

hypoxia: A state in which there is oxygen deficiency.

intermittent positive pressure breathing (IPPB) machine: A device that assists intermittent positive pressure inhalation of therapeutic aerosols without hand coordination required in the use of hand nebulizers or metered dose inhalers.

laser: A device that concentrates light into an intense, narrow beam used to cut or destroy tissue. It is used in microsurgery, photodynamic therapy, and for a variety of diagnostic purposes.

leukoplakia: A white patch that may develop on mucous membranes such as the cheek, gums, or tongue and may become cancerous.

lobe: A portion of an organ, such as the liver, lung, breast, thyroid, or brain.

lobectomy: The removal of a lobe.

lymphatic system: The tissues and organs that produce, store, and carry white blood cells that fight infections and other diseases. This system includes the bone marrow, spleen, thymus, lymph nodes, and lymphatic vessels (a network of thin tubes that carry lymph and white blood cells). Lymphatic vessels branch, like blood vessels, into all the tissues of the body.

malignant: Cancerous. Malignant tumors can invade and destroy nearby tissue and spread to other parts of the body.

mediastinoscopy: A procedure in which a tube is inserted into the chest to view the organs in the area between the lungs and nearby lymph nodes. The tube is inserted through an incision above the breastbone. This procedure is usually performed to get a tissue sample from the lymph nodes on the right side of the chest.

mediastinum: The area between the lungs. The organs in this area include the heart and its large blood vessels, the trachea, the esophagus, the bronchi, and lymph nodes.

metastasis: The spread of cancer from one part of the body to another. A tumor formed from cells that have spread is called a secondary tumor, a metastatic tumor, or a metastasis. The secondary tumor contains cells that are like those in the original (primary) tumor. The plural form of metastasis is metastases.

MRI: Magnetic resonance imaging; a procedure in which radio waves and a powerful magnet linked to a computer are used to create detailed pictures of areas inside the body. These pictures can show the difference between normal and diseased tissue. MRI makes better images of organs and soft tissue than other scanning techniques, such as CT or x-ray. MRI is especially useful for imaging the brain, spine, the soft tissue of joints, and the inside of bones. Also called nuclear magnetic resonance imaging.

neonatal: Period up to the first four weeks after birth.

nicotine: An alkaloid derived from the tobacco plant that is responsible for smoking's psychoactive and addictive effects; is toxic at high doses but can be safe and effective as medicine at lower doses.

non-small cell lung cancer: A group of lung cancers that includes squamous cell carcinoma, adenocarcinoma, and large cell carcinoma.

oat cell cancer: A type of lung cancer in which the cells look like oats when viewed under a microscope. Also called small cell lung cancer.

oropharynx: The middle part of the throat that includes the soft palate, the base of the tongue, and the tonsils.

palate: The roof of the mouth. The front portion is bony (hard palate), and the back portion is muscular (soft palate).

pathologist: A doctor who identifies diseases by studying cells and tissues under a microscope.

physical dependence: An adaptive physiological state that occurs with regular drug use and results in a withdrawal syndrome when drug use is stopped; usually occurs with tolerance.

pneumonectomy: An operation to remove an entire lung.

pneumonia: An inflammatory infection that occurs in the lung.

postural bronchial drainage: Draining of liquids from the lungs by placing the patient in postures (for example, head below chest) which facilitate liquid flow.

precancerous: A term used to describe a condition that may (or is likely to) become cancer. Also called premalignant.

prognosis: The likely outcome or course of a disease; the chance of recovery or recurrence.

radiation therapy: The use of high-energy radiation from x-rays, gamma rays, neutrons, and other sources to kill cancer cells and shrink tumors. Radiation may come from a machine outside the body (external-beam radiation therapy), or from materials called radioisotopes. Radioisotopes produce radiation and can be placed in or near the tumor or in the area near cancer cells. This type of radiation treatment is called internal radiation therapy, implant radiation, interstitial radiation, or brachytherapy. Systemic radiation therapy uses a radioactive substance, such as a radiolabeled monoclonal antibody, that circulates throughout the body. Also called radiotherapy, irradiation, and x-ray therapy.

radionuclide scanning: A test that produces pictures (scans) of internal parts of the body. The person is given an injection or swallows a small amount of radioactive material; a machine called a scanner then measures the radioactivity in certain organs.

radon: A radioactive gas that is released by uranium, a substance found in soil and rock. Breathing in too much radon can damage lung cells and lead to lung cancer.

resection: Removal of tissue or part or all of an organ by surgery.

respiratory system: The organs that are involved in breathing. These include the nose, throat, larynx, trachea, bronchi, and lungs. Also known as the respiratory tract.

rush: A surge of pleasure that rapidly follows administration of some drugs.

small cell lung cancer: A type of lung cancer in which the cells appear small and round when viewed under the microscope. Also called oat cell lung cancer.

sputum: Mucus and other matter that is brought up from the lungs by coughing.

thoracentesis: Removal of fluid from the pleural cavity through a needle inserted between the ribs.

thoracotomy: An operation to open the chest.

tissue: A group or layer of cells that are alike and that work together to perform a specific function.

tobacco: A plant widely cultivated for its leaves, which are used primarily for smoking; the tabacum species is the major source of tobacco products.

tolerance: A condition in which higher doses of a drug are required to produce the same effect as during initial use; often leads to physical dependence.

tumor: An abnormal mass of tissue that results from excessive cell division. Tumors perform no useful body function. They may be benign (not cancerous) or malignant (cancerous).

ventilation: The process of exchange of air between the lungs and the atmosphere leading to exchange of gases in the blood.

withdrawal: A variety of symptoms that occur after use of an addictive drug is reduced or stopped.

Chapter 85

Tobacco Information and Control Resources

Action on Smoking and Health
2013 H Street, NW
Washington, DC 20006
Phone: 202-659-4310
Website: http://ash.org
E-mail: webmaster@ash.org

Produces materials on a variety of smoking and health topics for the public with emphasis on legal action to protect nonsmokers' health.

Advocacy Institute
1629 K St., NW
Suite 200
Washington, DC 20006-1629
Phone: 202-777-7575
Fax: 202-777-7577
Website: http://www.advocacy.org/tobacco.htm
E-mail: info@advocacy.org

This chapter includes excerpts from "Government Agencies," and "Nongovernment Agencies," produced by the National Center for Chronic Disease Prevention and Health Promotion, and other documents produced by the Centers for Disease Control and Prevention, the National Heart, Lung, and Blood Institute, and the National Cancer Institute. All contact information was updated and verified in May 2004.

Works on efforts to counter the influence of the tobacco industry and provides strategic consulting and advocacy support on policy issues related to tobacco control.

Agency for Healthcare Research and Quality (AHRQ)
AHRQ Publications Clearinghouse
P.O. Box 8547
Silver Spring, MD 20907-8547
Toll-Free: 800-358-9295
Phone: 703-437-2078
TDD: 888-586-6340
Fax: 301-594-2800
Website: http://www.ahcpr.gov
E-mail: ahrqpubs@ahrq.gov

Provides materials on smoking cessation for health professionals and consumers.

American Cancer Society
1599 Clifton Road, NE
Atlanta, GA 30329
Toll-Free: 800-ACS-2345
Website: http://www.cancer.org

Provides smoking education, prevention, and cessation programs and distributes pamphlets, posters, and exhibits on smoking. Refer to your phone book for the ACS chapter in your area or contact the national office for further information.

American College of Obstetricians and Gynecologists
409 12th Street, SW
Washington, DC 20090-6920
Toll-Free: 800-762-2264
Phone: 202-638-5577
Website: http://www.acog.org
E-mail: publication@acog.org

Provides tobacco-related health information for pregnant women.

American Council on Science and Health
1995 Broadway, 2nd Floor
New York, NY 10023-5860

Phone: 212-362-7044
Fax: 212-362-4919
Website: http://www.acsh.org

Provides scientific evaluations on tobacco-related topics.

American Heart Association National Center
7272 Greenville Avenue
Dallas, TX 75231
Toll-Free: 800-AHA-USA1
Website: http://www.americanheart.org

Promotes smoking intervention programs at schools, workplaces, and health care sites. Refer to your phone book for the AHA chapter in your area or contact the national office for further information.

American Legacy Foundation
2030 M Street, NW, Sixth Floor
Washington, DC 20036
Phone: 202-454-5555
Fax: 202-454-5599
Website: http://www.americanlegacy.org
E-mail: info@americanlegacy.org

Collaborates with national, state, and local organizations through grant awards, research initiatives, marketing efforts, and training programs in an effort to reduce youth tobacco use, decrease exposure to second-hand smoke, increase successful quit rates, and reduce disparities in access to prevention and cessation services and in exposure to secondhand smoke.

American Lung Association (ALA)
61 Broadway, Sixth Floor
New York, NY 10006
Toll-Free: 800-LUNG-USA
Phone: 212-315-8700
Website: http://www.lungusa.org

Conducts programs addressing smoking cessation, prevention, and the protection of nonsmokers' health and provides a variety of educational materials for the public and health professionals. Refer to your phone book for the ALA chapter in your area or contact the national office for further information.

American Medical Association (AMA)
515 North State Street
Chicago, IL 60610
Toll-Free: 800-621-8335
Phone: 312-464-5000
Fax: 312-464-5600
Website: http://www.ama-assn.org

Provides smoking intervention guides for physicians and health care providers.

Americans for Nonsmokers' Rights (ANR)
2530 San Pablo Avenue, Suite J
Berkeley, CA 94702
Phone: 510-841-3032
Fax: 510-841-3071
Website: http://www.no-smoke.org
E-mail: anr@no-smoke.org

Provides information to organizations and individuals to assist in passing ordinances, implementing workplace regulations, and developing smoking policies in the workplace.

Association of State and Territorial Health Officials (ASTHO)
1275 K street, NW, Suite 800
Washington, DC 20005-4006
Phone: 202-371-9090
Fax: 202-371-9797
Website: http://www.astho.org

Provides information about state health department activities related to tobacco and other health issues.

Bureau of Alcohol, Tobacco and Firearms (BATF)
United States Department of Treasury
650 Massachusetts Avenue, N.W., Room 8290
Washington, DC 20226
Toll-Free: 888-283-2662
Phone: 202-927-7760
Website: http://www.atf.treas.gov
E-mail: ATFMail@atf.gov

Provides general information about current tax rates and tax revenues pertaining to tobacco.

Cancer Research Foundation of America (CRFA)
1600 Duke Street, Suite 500
Alexandria, VA 22314
Toll-Free: 800-227-2732
Phone: 703-836-4412
Fax: 703-836-4413
Website: http://www.preventcancer.org
E-mail: info@preventcancer.org

Focuses on cancer prevention through research and education.

Center for Substance Abuse Prevention
National Clearinghouse for Alcohol and Drug Information
P.O. Box 2345
Rockville, MD 20847-2345
Toll-Free: 800-729-6686
Phone: 301-468-2600
Website: http://www.health.org

Provides information about the health risks of using addictive drugs, including tobacco. Information is available in various forms, including videos, fact sheets, posters, and pamphlets.

Center for Tobacco Research and Intervention (CTRI)
University of Wisconsin Medical School
1930 Monroe St.
Madison, WI 53711
Phone: 608-262-8673
Fax: 608-265-3102
Website: http://www.ctri.wisc.edu

An academic center working to help smokers overcome nicotine addiction and improve their health; conducts research and produces educational material.

Centers for Disease Control and Prevention (CDC)
Office on Smoking and Health
Mail Stop K-50
4770 Buford Highway, NE
Atlanta, GA 30341-3724

Toll-Free: 800-311-3435
Phone: 770-488-5705
Fax: 888-232-3299
Website: http://www.cdc.gov
E-mail: tobaccoinfo@cdc.gov

The CDC's Office on Smoking and Health (OSH) is the government's lead agency on smoking control. OHS funds booklets on smoking topics, such as relapse, helping a friend or family member quit smoking, the health hazards of smoking, and the effects of parental smoking on teenagers.

Doctors Ought to Care (DOC)
5615 Kirby Drive, Suite 440
Houston, TX 77005
Phone: 713-528-1487
Fax: 713-528-2146
Website: http://www.bcm.tmc.edu/doc

Provides school curricula, smoking intervention information, and tobacco counter advertisements for use in clinics, classrooms, and communities.

Environmental Protection Agency (EPA)
Indoor Air Quality Information Clearinghouse
P.O. Box 37133
Washington, DC 20013-7133
Toll-Free: 800-438-4318
Phone: 202-343-9370
Fax: 202-343-2394
Website: http://www.epa.gov/iaq
E-mail: iaqinfo@aol.com

Serves as the U.S. government's lead agency on environmental issues. The EPA offers publications and information on the adverse effects of environmental tobacco smoke and indoor air pollution.

Federal Trade Commission (FTC)
Public Reference Branch
600 Pennsylvania Avenue, N.W.
Washington, DC 20580
Toll-Free: 877-382-4357
Phone: 202-326-2222 (publications)

Phone: 202-326-3090 (tobacco-related questions)
TDD/TTY: 866-653-4261
Website: http://www.ftc.gov

Serves as the U.S. government's main authority on trade issues. The FTC provides publications and information related to trade policies and tobacco advertising, including health warning labels, and produces a report that contains data on the tar, nicotine, and carbon monoxide of domestic cigarettes.

Food and Drug Administration (FDA)
Office of Consumer Affairs
5600 Fishers Lane
HFE-50
Rockville, MD 20857
Toll-Free: 888-463-6332
Phone: 301-827-4420
Fax: 301-443-9767
Website: http://www.fda.gov

Responds to consumer requests for information and publications and provides information regarding the regulations restricting the sale and distribution of cigarettes and smokeless tobacco to protect children and adolescents.

Group Against Smokers' Pollution (GASP)
P.O. Box 5165
Pittsburgh, PA 15206
Phone: 412-441-6650
Website: http://www.gasp-pgh.org
E-mail: gasp@gasp-pgh.org

Provides educational and information and referral services concerning the health hazards of secondhand smoke and the establishment of nonsmoking laws and policies.

Robert Wood Johnson Foundation (RWJF)
PO Box 2316
College Road East and Route 1
Princeton, NJ 08543-2316
Toll-Free: 888-631-9989
Website: http://www.rwjf.org

Seeks to help all Americans improve their health, including avoiding harm caused by tobacco use.

March of Dimes Birth Defects Foundation
1275 Mamaroneck Avenue
White Plains, NY 10605
Toll-Free: 800-996-2724
Phone: 914-997-4629
Fax: 914-997-4537
Website: http://www.modimes.org

Distributes health education materials to the public, including materials about the effects of smoking during pregnancy.

National Cancer Institute (NCI)
Office of Cancer Communications
31 Center Drive
MSC-2580
Building 31, Room 10A24
Bethesda, MD 20892-2580
Toll-Free: 800-4-CANCER
TTY: 800-332-8615
Smoking Quitline: 877-44U-QUIT
Website: http://www.cancer.gov

Develops and implements smoking intervention programs and produces publications on smoking. NCI also provides telephone counseling services for smoking cessation. Programs and materials are available to health professionals and the public.

National Center for Chronic Disease Prevention and Health Promotion
Centers for Disease Control and Prevention
Mail Stop K-50
4770 Buford Highway, NE
Atlanta, GA 30341-3717
Toll-Free: 800-CDC-1311
Website: http://www.cdc.gov/nccdphp
Website for Tobacco Information: http://www.cdc.gov/tobacco

Stands at the forefront of the nation's efforts to prevent and control chronic diseases, including those associated with tobacco use.

National Center for Tobacco-Free Kids
1400 Eye Street
Suite 1200
Washington DC 20005
Phone: 202-296-5469
Website: http://www.tobaccofreekids.org

Works to protect children from exposure and addiction to tobacco by raising awareness; changing public policies to limit the marketing and sales of tobacco to children; altering the environment in which tobacco use and policy decisions are made; and actively countering the tobacco industry and its special interests. The Campaign for Tobacco Free Kids also encourages youth advocacy to support policy change, to hold tobacco control activities and to help educate peers on the dangers of tobacco.

National Families in Action (NFIA)
2957 Clairmont Road, NE
Suite 150
Atlanta, Georgia 30329
Phone: 404-248-9676
Fax: 404-248-1312
Website: http://www.nationalfamilies.org
E-mail: nfia@nationalfamilies.org

National Families in Action has formed a partnership with other national organizations to rebuild the parent drug prevention movement it helped create and lead in the 1970s. Their goal is to ensure that the parent movement of the 1990s includes all parents and families.

National Federation of State High School Associations
P.O. Box 690
Indianapolis, IN 46206
Phone: 317-972-6900
Fax: 317-822-5700
Website: http://www.nfhs.org

Provides healthy lifestyle education/prevention information primarily for high school athletic/activity associations and secondary school personnel. Catalog available.

National Governors' Association
444 North Capital Street
Suite 267
Washington, DC 20001-1512
Phone: 202-624-5300
Website: http://www.nga.org

Offers the latest information about how the states are spending funds obtained through the tobacco settlement agreement with the industry.

National Health Information Center
P.O. Box 1133
Washington, DC 20013-1133
Toll-Free: 800-336-4797
Phone: 301-565-4167
Fax: 301-984-4256
Website: http://www.health.gov/nhic
E-mail: info@nhic.org

Helps the public and health professionals locate information on tobacco and other topics through identification of resources, an information and referral system, and publications. Uses a database containing descriptions of health-related organizations to refer inquirers to the most appropriate resources. Prepares and distributes publications and directories on health promotion and disease prevention topics.

National Heart, Lung, and Blood Institute (NHLBI)
Information Center
P.O. Box 30105
Bethesda, MD 20824-0105
Phone: 301-592-8573
TTY: 240-629-3255
Fax: 301-592-8563
Website: http://www.nhlbi.nih.gov
E-mail: nhlbiinfo@nhlbi.nih.gov

A component of the National Institutes of Health, NHLBI offers information about the impact of tobacco on cardiovascular health and respiratory functioning.

National Institute for Dental and Craniofacial Research (NIDCR)
Information and Liaison Branch
45 Center Drive, MSC 6400
Bethesda, MD 20892-6400
Phone: 301-496-4261
Website: http://www.nidcr.nih.gov
E-mail: nidcrinfo@mail.nih.gov

A component of the National Institutes of Health, NIDCR provides information about the oral health implications of tobacco use.

National Institute on Drug Abuse (NIDA)
National Institutes of Health
6001 Executive Blvd., Room 5213
Bethesda, MD 20892-9561
Phone: 301-443-1124
Website: http://www.nida.nih.gov
E-mail: information@lists.nida.nih.gov

A component of the National Institutes of Health, NIDA offers information about the addictive properties of nicotine.

National Latino Council on Alcohol and Tobacco Prevention (LCAT)
1616 P Street, NW
Suite 430
Washington, DC 20036
Phone: 202-265-8054
Fax: 202-265-8056
Website: http://www.nlcatp.org
E-mail: lcat@nlcatp.org

Provides community education, training, and information dissemination and conducts research and policy analysis to reduce the harm caused by alcohol and tobacco use in the Latino community.

National Spit Tobacco Education Program
Oral Health America, Suite 352
410 North Michigan Avenue
Chicago, IL 60611
Phone: 312-836-9900
Website: http://www.nstep.org

Works to prevent people, especially young people, from starting to use tobacco, and to help users to quit. NSTEP offers information and materials on spit tobacco use, prevention, and cessation.

Office of the Surgeon General
5600 Fishers Lane, Room 18-66
Rockville, MD 20857
Phone: 301-443-4000
Website: http://www.surgeongeneral.gov

The nation's leading spokesman on matters of public health, including the effects of tobacco use; the Surgeon General is appointed by the U.S. president.

SmokeFree.net
2100 R Street, NW
Washington, DC 20008
Phone: 212-NO-SMOKE
Fax: 630-214-4917
Website: www.smokefree.net

Provides smoking and health educational materials for schools and workplaces in the form of booklets, posters, videos, and stickers.

Substance Abuse and Mental Health Services Administration (SAMHSA)
5600 Fishers Lane
Room 12-105 Parklawn Bldg.
Rockville, MD 20857
Phone: 301-443-8956
Fax: 301-443-9050
Website: http://www.samhsa.gov

Responsible for improving the quality and availability of prevention, treatment, and rehabilitative services in order to reduce illness, death, disability, and cost to society resulting from substance abuse, including tobacco, and mental illnesses, including addiction disorders.

Tobacco Technical Assistance Consortium (TTAC)
Rollins School of Public Health, Emory University
1518 Clifton Road, GCR 808
Atlanta, GA 30322

Phone: 404-712-8474
Website: http://www.ttac.org/home.html
E-mail: ttac@sph.emory.edu

TTAC builds capacity to achieve effective tobacco prevention and control programs and policies.

United States Department of Agriculture (USDA)
Tobacco and Peanut Division
Stop 0514
1400 Independence Avenue, SW
Washington, DC 20250-0514
Phone: 202-720-4319
Website: http://www.usda.gov

Provides information related to tobacco price support programs and other agricultural issues pertaining to tobacco.

Chapter 86

Smoking Cessation: Hotlines, Helplines, and Internet Resources

Nationwide Smoking Cessation Hotlines and Helplines

American Cancer Society (ACS)
Toll-Free: 800-ACS-2345 (800-227-2345)
Toll-Free: 877-YES-QUIT (877-937-7848)
TDD/TTY: 866-228-4327

American Legacy Foundation's Great Start
Toll-Free: 866-66-START (A quitline for pregnant smokers)

American Lung Association
Toll-Free: 800-LUNG-USA

National Cancer Institute's Smoking Quitline
Toll-Free: 877-44U-QUIT
TDD/TTY: 800-332-8615

State-by-State Help for Smoking Cessation

If your state is not listed, please contact one of the national resources listed above.

The resources listed in this chapter were compiled from various sources considered reliable. All contact information was updated and verified in May 2004.

Alaska
Toll-Free: 888-842-QUIT (888-842-7848)

Arizona
Toll-Free: 800-556-6222
Website: http://www.ashline.org

Arkansas
Toll-Free: 866-NOW-QUIT (866-669-7848)

California
Toll-Free: 800-NO-BUTTS (800-662-8887)
Spanish: 800-45-NO-FUME (800-456-6386)
Vietnamese: 800-778-8440
Mandarin and Cantonese: 800-838-8917
Korean: 800-556-5564
TDD/TTY: 800-933-4TDD (800-933-4833)
Smokeless Tobacco: 800-844-CHEW (800-844-2439)
Website: http://www.californiasmokershelpline.org

Colorado
Toll-Free: 800-639-QUIT (800-639-7848)
TDD/TTY: 866-228-4327
Website: http://www.co.quitnet.com

Connecticut
Toll-Free: 866-END-HABIT (866-363-4224)
Website: http://www.ctquitline.org

Delaware
Toll-Free: 866-409-1858

Florida
Toll-Free: 877-U-CAN-NOW (877-822-6669)
TDD/TTY: 866-228-4327

Georgia
Toll-Free: 877-270-STOP (877-270-7867; in-state calls only)
Spanish: 877-2NO-FUME (1-877-266-3863)
TDD/TTY: 877-777-6534
Website: http://www.unitegeorgia.com

Illinois
Toll-Free: 800-QUIT-YES (800-784-8937)

Iowa
Toll-Free: 866-U-CAN-TRY (866-822-6879)
TDD/TTY: 866-822-2857
Website: http://www.public-health.uiowa.edu/itrc/quitline

Maine
Toll-Free: 800-207-1230
TDD/TTY: 800-457-1220

Maryland
Toll-Free: 800-492-1056 ext. 353
Website: http://www.smokefreemd.org

Massachusetts
Toll-Free: 800-9-GET-A-TIP (800-943-8284)
Spanish and Portuguese: 800-8DEJALO (800-833-5256)
TDD/TTY: 800-TDD-1477
Website: http://www.trytostop.org

Michigan
Toll-Free: 800-537-5666
Website: www.hpclearinghouse.org

Mississippi
Toll-Free: 877-4US-2ACT (877-487-2228)
Toll-Free: 800-244-9100

Montana
Toll-Free: 877-612-1585

Nebraska
Toll-Free: 866-NEB-QUIT (866-632-7848)

Nevada
Toll-Free: 888-86-NONIC (888-866-6642)
Phone: 702-877-0684 (Las Vegas)
Website: http://www.livingtobaccofree.com

New Jersey
Toll-Free: 866-NJSTOPS (866-657-8677)
TDD/TTY: 866-257-2971
Website: www.nj.quitnet.com

New Mexico
Website: http://www.theStink.org

New York
Toll-Free: 866-NYQUITS (866-697-8487)
TDD/TTY: 800-280-1213
Website: http://www.nysmokefree.com

Ohio
Toll-Free: 800-934-4840

Oklahoma
Toll-Free: 866-PITCH-EM (866-748-2436)
TDD/TTY: 866-228-4327

Oregon
Toll-Free: 877-270-7867; Spanish: 877-266-3863
TTY: 877-777-6534
Website: http://www.oregonquitline.org

Pennsylvania
Toll-Free: 877-724-1090
TDD/TTY: 866-228-4327

Rhode Island
Toll-Free: 800-TRYTOSTOP; Spanish: 800-833-5256
TDD/TTY: 800-TDD-1477
Website: http://www.trytostop.org/iwant/quitline.asp

South Dakota
Toll-Free: 866-SD-QUITS (866-737-8487)
TDD/TTY: 866-228-4327

Utah
Toll-Free: 888-567-TRUTH; Spanish: 877-2NO-FUME
General Information: 877-220-3466; TDD/TTY: 877-777-6534
Website: http://www.tobaccofreeutah.org

Virginia
Toll-Free: 877-856-5177 (Printed materials only)
Website: http://www.smokefreevirginia.org

Washington
Toll-Free: 877-270-STOP; Spanish: 877-2NO-FUME
TDD/TTY: 877-877-6534
Website: http://www.quitline.com

West Virginia
Toll-Free: 877-Y-NOT-QUIT (877-966-8784)
Website: http://www.ynotquit.com

Wisconsin
Toll-Free: 877-270-STOP (877-270-7867; in-state calls only)
Spanish: 877-2NO-FUME (877-266-3863)
TDD/TTY: 877-777-6534

Additional Online Resources

Clear Horizons
University of Rochester
http://www.myclearhorizons.com

Clinical Guidelines for Prescribing Pharmacotherapy for Smoking Cessation
http://www.ahrq.gov/clinic/tobacco/prescrib.htm

Committed Quitters
http://www.quit.com

Don't Let Another Year Go Up in Smoke
http://www.cdc.gov/tobacco/quit/quittip.htm

Guía para Dejar de Fumar
http://dccps.cancer.gov/tcrb/No_FumarC.pdf

Kick Butts Day
http://kickbuttsday.org

National Lung Health Education Program
http://www.nlhep.org

Nicotine Anonymous
http://www.nicotine-anonymous.org

Pathways to Freedom
http://www.smokefree.gov/docs/pathways_final.pdf

QuitNet
http://www.quitnet.com

Smokefree.gov
http://www.smokefree.gov

Smoking: It's Never Too Late to Stop
http://www.niapublications.org/engagepages/smoking.asp

Tackling Tobacco
http://tacklingtobacco.tamushsc.edu

Tobacco Cessation Guideline
http://www.surgeongeneral.gov/tobacco

You Can Quit Smoking: Consumer Guide
http://www.cdc.gov/tobacco/quit/canquit.htm

Index

Index

575

Health Reference Series
COMPLETE CATALOG

Adolescent Health Sourcebook

Basic Consumer Health Information about Common Medical, Mental, and Emotional Concerns in Adolescents, Including Facts about Acne, Body Piercing, Mononucleosis, Nutrition, Eating Disorders, Stress, Depression, Behavior Problems, Peer Pressure, Violence, Gangs, Drug Use, Puberty, Sexuality, Pregnancy, Learning Disabilities, and More

Along with a Glossary of Terms and Other Resources for Further Help and Information

Edited by Chad T. Kimball. 658 pages. 2002. 0-7808-0248-9. $78.

"It is written in clear, nontechnical language aimed at general readers. . . . Recommended for public libraries, community colleges, and other agencies serving health care consumers."
— *American Reference Books Annual, 2003*

"Recommended for school and public libraries. Parents and professionals dealing with teens will appreciate the easy-to-follow format and the clearly written text. This could become a 'must have' for every high school teacher." — *E-Streams, Jan '03*

"A good starting point for information related to common medical, mental, and emotional concerns of adolescents." — *School Library Journal, Nov '02*

"This book provides accurate information in an easy to access format. It addresses topics that parents and caregivers might not be aware of and provides practical, useable information." — *Doody's Health Sciences Book Review Journal, Sep-Oct '02*

"Recommended reference source."
— *Booklist, American Library Association, Sep '02*

■

AIDS Sourcebook, 3rd Edition

Basic Consumer Health Information about Acquired Immune Deficiency Syndrome (AIDS) and Human Immunodeficiency Virus (HIV) Infection, Including Facts about Transmission, Prevention, Diagnosis, Treatment, Opportunistic Infections, and Other Complications, with a Section for Women and Children, Including Details about Associated Gynecological Concerns, Pregnancy, and Pediatric Care

Along with Updated Statistical Information, Reports on Current Research Initiatives, a Glossary, and Directories of Internet, Hotline, and Other Resources

Edited by Dawn D. Matthews. 664 pages. 2003. 0-7808-0631-X. $78.

ALSO AVAILABLE: *AIDS Sourcebook, 1st Edition.* Edited by Karen Bellenir and Peter D. Dresser. 831 pages. 1995. 0-7808-0031-1. $78.

AIDS Sourcebook, 2nd Edition. Edited by Karen Bellenir. 751 pages. 1999. 0-7808-0225-X. $78.

"The 3rd edition of the *AIDS Sourcebook*, part of Omnigraphics' *Health Reference Series*, is a welcome update. . . . This resource is highly recommended for academic and public libraries."
— *American Reference Books Annual, 2004*

"Excellent sourcebook. This continues to be a highly recommended book. There is no other book that provides as much information as this book provides."
— *AIDS Book Review Journal, Dec-Jan 2000*

"Recommended reference source."
— *Booklist, American Library Association, Dec '99*

"A solid text for college-level health libraries."
— *The Bookwatch, Aug '99*

Cited in *Reference Sources for Small and Medium-Sized Libraries, American Library Association, 1999*

■

Alcoholism Sourcebook

Basic Consumer Health Information about the Physical and Mental Consequences of Alcohol Abuse, Including Liver Disease, Pancreatitis, Wernicke-Korsakoff Syndrome (Alcoholic Dementia), Fetal Alcohol Syndrome, Heart Disease, Kidney Disorders, Gastrointestinal Problems, and Immune System Compromise and Featuring Facts about Addiction, Detoxification, Alcohol Withdrawal, Recovery, and the Maintenance of Sobriety

Along with a Glossary and Directories of Resources for Further Help and Information

Edited by Karen Bellenir. 613 pages. 2000. 0-7808-0325-6. $78.

"This title is one of the few reference works on alcoholism for general readers. For some readers this will be a welcome complement to the many self-help books on the market. Recommended for collections serving general readers and consumer health collections."
— *E-Streams, Mar '01*

"This book is an excellent choice for public and academic libraries."
— *American Reference Books Annual, 2001*

"Recommended reference source."
— *Booklist, American Library Association, Dec '00*

"Presents a wealth of information on alcohol use and abuse and its effects on the body and mind, treatment, and prevention." — *SciTech Book News, Dec '00*

"Important new health guide which packs in the latest consumer information about the problems of alcoholism." — *Reviewer's Bookwatch, Nov '00*

SEE ALSO *Drug Abuse Sourcebook, Substance Abuse Sourcebook*

Allergies Sourcebook, 2nd Edition

Basic Consumer Health Information about Allergic Disorders, Triggers, Reactions, and Related Symptoms, Including Anaphylaxis, Rhinitis, Sinusitis, Asthma, Dermatitis, Conjunctivitis, and Multiple Chemical Sensitivity

Along with Tips on Diagnosis, Prevention, and Treatment, Statistical Data, a Glossary, and a Directory of Sources for Further Help and Information

Edited by Annemarie S. Muth. 598 pages. 2002. 0-7808-0376-0. $78.

ALSO AVAILABLE: *Allergies Sourcebook, 1st Edition.* Edited by Allan R. Cook. 611 pages. 1997. 0-7808-0036-2. $78.

"This book brings a great deal of useful material together. . . . This is an excellent addition to public and consumer health library collections."
— *American Reference Books Annual, 2003*

"This second edition would be useful to laypersons with little or advanced knowledge of the subject matter. This book would also serve as a resource for nursing and other health care professions students. It would be useful in public, academic, and hospital libraries with consumer health collections." — *E-Streams, Jul '02*

Alternative Medicine Sourcebook, 2nd Edition

Basic Consumer Health Information about Alternative and Complementary Medical Practices, Including Acupuncture, Chiropractic, Herbal Medicine, Homeopathy, Naturopathic Medicine, Mind-Body Interventions, Ayurveda, and Other Non-Western Medical Traditions

Along with Facts about such Specific Therapies as Massage Therapy, Aromatherapy, Qigong, Hypnosis, Prayer, Dance, and Art Therapies, a Glossary, and Resources for Further Information

Edited by Dawn D. Matthews. 618 pages. 2002. 0-7808-0605-0. $78.

ALSO AVAILABLE: *Alternative Medicine Sourcebook, 1st Edition.* Edited by Allan R. Cook. 737 pages. 1999. 0-7808-0200-4. $78.

"Recommended for public, high school, and academic libraries that have consumer health collections. Hospital libraries that also serve the public will find this to be a useful resource." — *E-Streams, Feb '03*

"Recommended reference source."
—*Booklist, American Library Association, Jan '03*

"An important alternate health reference."
— *MBR Bookwatch, Oct '02*

"A great addition to the reference collection of every type of library." — *American Reference Books Annual, 2000*

Alzheimer's Disease Sourcebook, 3rd Edition

Basic Consumer Health Information about Alzheimer's Disease, Other Dementias, and Related Disorders, Including Multi-Infarct Dementia, AIDS Dementia Complex, Dementia with Lewy Bodies, Huntington's Disease, Wernicke-Korsakoff Syndrome (Alcohol-Reated Dementia), Delirium, and Confusional States

Along with Information for People Newly Diagnosed with Alzheimer's Disease and Caregivers, Reports Detailing Current Research Efforts in Prevention, Diagnosis, and Treatment, Facts about Long-Term Care Issues, and Listings of Sources for Additional Information

Edited by Karen Bellenir. 645 pages. 2003. 0-7808-0666-2. $78.

ALSO AVAILABLE: *Alzheimer's, Stroke & 29 Other Neurological Disorders Sourcebook, 1st Edition.* Edited by Frank E. Bair. 579 pages. 1993. 1-55888-748-2. $78.

ALSO AVAILABLE: *Alzheimer's Disease Sourcebook, 2nd Edition.* Edited by Karen Bellenir. 524 pages. 1999. 0-7808-0223-3. $78.

"This very informative and valuable tool will be a great addition to any library serving consumers, students and health care workers."
—*American Reference Books Annual, 2004*

"This is a valuable resource for people affected by dementias such as Alzheimer's. It is easy to navigate and includes important information and resources."
— *Doody's Review Service, Feb. 2004*

"Recommended reference source."
— *Booklist, American Library Association, Oct '99*

SEE ALSO *Brain Disorders Sourcebook*

Arthritis Sourcebook, 2nd Edition

Basic Consumer Health Information about Osteoarthritis, Rheumatoid Arthritis, Other Rheumatic Disorders, Infectious Forms of Arthritis, and Diseases with Symptoms Linked to Arthritis, Featuring Facts about Diagnosis, Pain Management, and Surgical Therapies

Along with Coping Strategies, Research Updates, a Glossary, and Resources for Additional Help and Information

Edited by Amy L. Sutton. 593 pages. 2004. 0-7808-0667-0. $78.

ALSO AVAILABLE: *Arthritis Sourcebook, 1st Edition.* Edited by Allan R. Cook. 550 pages. 1998. 0-7808-0201-2. $78.

". . . accessible to the layperson."
—*Reference and Research Book News, Feb '99*

Asthma Sourcebook

Basic Consumer Health Information about Asthma, Including Symptoms, Traditional and Nontraditional Remedies, Treatment Advances, Quality-of-Life Aids, Medical Research Updates, and the Role of Allergies, Exercise, Age, the Environment, and Genetics in the Development of Asthma

Along with Statistical Data, a Glossary, and Directories of Support Groups, and Other Resources for Further Information

Edited by Annemarie S. Muth. 628 pages. 2000. 0-7808-0381-7. $78.

"A worthwhile reference acquisition for public libraries and academic medical libraries whose readers desire a quick introduction to the wide range of asthma information." — Choice, Association of College & Research Libraries, Jun '01

"Recommended reference source."
— Booklist, American Library Association, Feb '01

"Highly recommended." — The Bookwatch, Jan '01

"There is much good information for patients and their families who deal with asthma daily."
— American Medical Writers Association Journal, Winter '01

"This informative text is recommended for consumer health collections in public, secondary school, and community college libraries and the libraries of universities with a large undergraduate population."
— American Reference Books Annual, 2001

Attention Deficit Disorder Sourcebook

Basic Consumer Health Information about Attention Deficit/Hyperactivity Disorder in Children and Adults, Including Facts about Causes, Symptoms, Diagnostic Criteria, and Treatment Options Such as Medications, Behavior Therapy, Coaching, and Homeopathy

Along with Reports on Current Research Initiatives, Legal Issues, and Government Regulations, and Featuring a Glossary of Related Terms, Internet Resources, and a List of Additional Reading Material

Edited by Dawn D. Matthews. 470 pages. 2002. 0-7808-0624-7. $78.

"Recommended reference source."
— Booklist, American Library Association, Jan '03

"This book is recommended for all school libraries and the reference or consumer health sections of public libraries." — American Reference Books Annual, 2003

Back & Neck Sourcebook, 2nd Edition

Basic Consumer Health Information about Spinal Pain, Spinal Cord Injuries, and Related Disorders, Such as Degenerative Disk Disease, Osteoarthritis, Scoliosis,

Sciatica, Spina Bifida, and Spinal Stenosis, and Featuring Facts about Maintaining Spinal Health, Self-Care, Pain Management, Rehabilitative Care, Chiropractic Care, Spinal Surgeries, and Complementary Therapies

Along with Suggestions for Preventing Back and Neck Pain, a Glossary of Related Terms, and a Directory of Resources

Edited by Amy L. Sutton. 600 pages. 2004. 0-7808-0738-3 $78.

ALSO AVAILABLE: Back & Neck Disorders Sourcebook, 1st Edition. Edited by Karen Bellenir. 548 pages. 1997. 0-7808-0202-0. $78.

"The strength of this work is its basic, easy-to-read format. Recommended."
— Reference and User Services Quarterly, American Library Association, Winter '97

Blood & Circulatory Disorders Sourcebook

Basic Information about Blood and Its Components, Anemias, Leukemias, Bleeding Disorders, and Circulatory Disorders, Including Aplastic Anemia, Thalassemia, Sickle-Cell Disease, Hemochromatosis, Hemophilia, Von Willebrand Disease, and Vascular Diseases

Along with a Special Section on Blood Transfusions and Blood Supply Safety, a Glossary, and Source Listings for Further Help and Information

Edited by Karen Bellenir and Linda M. Shin. 554 pages. 1998. 0-7808-0203-9. $78.

"Recommended reference source."
— Booklist, American Library Association, Feb '99

"An important reference sourcebook written in simple language for everyday, non-technical users. "
— Reviewer's Bookwatch, Jan '99

Brain Disorders Sourcebook

Basic Consumer Health Information about Strokes, Epilepsy, Amyotrophic Lateral Sclerosis (ALS/Lou Gehrig's Disease), Parkinson's Disease, Brain Tumors, Cerebral Palsy, Headache, Tourette Syndrome, and More

Along with Statistical Data, Treatment and Rehabilitation Options, Coping Strategies, Reports on Current Research Initiatives, a Glossary, and Resource Listings for Additional Help and Information

Edited by Karen Bellenir. 481 pages. 1999. 0-7808-0229-2. $78.

"Belongs on the shelves of any library with a consumer health collection." — E-Streams, Mar '00

"Recommended reference source."
— Booklist, American Library Association, Oct '99

SEE ALSO Alzheimer's Disease Sourcebook

Breast Cancer Sourcebook, 2nd Edition

Basic Consumer Health Information about Breast Cancer, Including Facts about Risk Factors, Prevention, Screening and Diagnostic Methods, Treatment Options, Complementary and Alternative Therapies, Post-Treatment Concerns, Clinical Trials, Special Risk Populations, and New Developments in Breast Cancer Research

Along with Breast Cancer Statistics, a Glossary of Related Terms, and a Directory of Resources for Additional Help and Information

Edited by Sandra J. Judd. 595 pages. 2004. 0-7808-0668-9. $78.

ALSO AVAILABLE: Breast Cancer Sourcebook, 1st Edition. Edited by Edward J. Prucha and Karen Bellenir. 580 pages. 2001. 0-7808-0244-6. $78.

"It would be a useful reference book in a library or on loan to women in a support group."
— Cancer Forum, Mar '03

"Recommended reference source."
— Booklist, American Library Association, Jan '02

"This reference source is highly recommended. It is quite informative, comprehensive and detailed in nature, and yet it offers practical advice in easy-to-read language. It could be thought of as the 'bible' of breast cancer for the consumer." — E-Streams, Jan '02

"The broad range of topics covered in lay language make the Breast Cancer Sourcebook an excellent addition to public and consumer health library collections."
— American Reference Books Annual 2002

"From the pros and cons of different screening methods and results to treatment options, Breast Cancer Sourcebook provides the latest information on the subject."
— Library Bookwatch, Dec '01

"This thoroughgoing, very readable reference covers all aspects of breast health and cancer. . . . Readers will find much to consider here. Recommended for all public and patient health collections."
— Library Journal, Sep '01

SEE ALSO Cancer Sourcebook for Women, Women's Health Concerns Sourcebook

Breastfeeding Sourcebook

Basic Consumer Health Information about the Benefits of Breastmilk, Preparing to Breastfeed, Breastfeeding as a Baby Grows, Nutrition, and More, Including Information on Special Situations and Concerns Such as Mastitis, Illness, Medications, Allergies, Multiple Births, Prematurity, Special Needs, and Adoption

Along with a Glossary and Resources for Additional Help and Information

Edited by Jenni Lynn Colson. 388 pages. 2002. 0-7808-0332-9. $78.

SEE ALSO Pregnancy & Birth Sourcebook

"Particularly useful is the information about professional lactation services and chapters on breastfeeding

when returning to work. . . . Breastfeeding Sourcebook will be useful for public libraries, consumer health libraries, and technical schools offering nurse assistant training, especially in areas where Internet access is problematic."
— American Reference Books Annual, 2003

Burns Sourcebook

Basic Consumer Health Information about Various Types of Burns and Scalds, Including Flame, Heat, Cold, Electrical, Chemical, and Sun Burns

Along with Information on Short-Term and Long-Term Treatments, Tissue Reconstruction, Plastic Surgery, Prevention Suggestions, and First Aid

Edited by Allan R. Cook. 604 pages. 1999. 0-7808-0204-7. $78.

"This is an exceptional addition to the series and is highly recommended for all consumer health collections, hospital libraries, and academic medical centers."
— E-Streams, Mar '00

"This key reference guide is an invaluable addition to all health care and public libraries in confronting this ongoing health issue."
— American Reference Books Annual, 2000

"Recommended reference source."
— Booklist, American Library Association, Dec '99

SEE ALSO Skin Disorders Sourcebook

Cancer Sourcebook, 4th Edition

Basic Consumer Health Information about Major Forms and Stages of Cancer, Featuring Facts about Head and Neck Cancers, Lung Cancers, Gastrointestinal Cancers, Genitourinary Cancers, Lymphomas, Blood Cell Cancers, Endocrine Cancers, Skin Cancers, Bone Cancers, Sarcomas, and Others, and Including Information about Cancer Treatments and Therapies, Identifying and Reducing Cancer Risks, and Strategies for Coping with Cancer and the Side Effects of Treatment

Along with a Cancer Glossary, Statistical and Demographic Data, and a Directory of Sources for Additional Help and Information

Edited by Karen Bellenir. 1,119 pages. 2003. 0-7808-0633-6. $78.

ALSO AVAILABLE: Cancer Sourcebook, 1st Edition. Edited by Frank E. Bair. 932 pages. 1990. 1-55888-888-8. $78.

New Cancer Sourcebook, 2nd Edition. Edited by Allan R. Cook. 1,313 pages. 1996. 0-7808-0041-9. $78.

Cancer Sourcebook, 3rd Edition. Edited by Edward J. Prucha. 1,069 pages. 2000. 0-7808-0227-6. $78.

"With cancer being the second leading cause of death for Americans, a prodigious work such as this one, which locates centrally so much cancer-related information, is clearly an asset to this nation's citizens and others." — Journal of the National Medical Association, 2004

"This title is recommended for health sciences and public libraries with consumer health collections."
— *E-Streams, Feb '01*

". . . can be effectively used by cancer patients and their families who are looking for answers in a language they can understand. Public and hospital libraries should have it on their shelves."
— *American Reference Books Annual, 2001*

"Recommended reference source."
— *Booklist, American Library Association, Dec '00*

Cited in *Reference Sources for Small and Medium-Sized Libraries*, American Library Association, 1999

"The amount of factual and useful information is extensive. The writing is very clear, geared to general readers. Recommended for all levels." — *Choice, Association of College & Research Libraries, Jan '97*

SEE ALSO Breast Cancer Sourcebook, Cancer Sourcebook for Women, Pediatric Cancer Sourcebook, Prostate Cancer Sourcebook

■

Cancer Sourcebook for Women, 2nd Edition

Basic Consumer Health Information about Gynecologic Cancers and Related Concerns, Including Cervical Cancer, Endometrial Cancer, Gestational Trophoblastic Tumor, Ovarian Cancer, Uterine Cancer, Vaginal Cancer, Vulvar Cancer, Breast Cancer, and Common Non-Cancerous Uterine Conditions, with Facts about Cancer Risk Factors, Screening and Prevention, Treatment Options, and Reports on Current Research Initiatives

Along with a Glossary of Cancer Terms and a Directory of Resources for Additional Help and Information

Edited by Karen Bellenir. 604 pages. 2002. 0-7808-0226-8. $78.

ALSO AVAILABLE: Cancer Sourcebook for Women, 1st Edition. Edited by Allan R. Cook and Peter D. Dresser. 524 pages. 1996. 0-7808-0076-1. $78.

"An excellent addition to collections in public, consumer health, and women's health libraries."
— *American Reference Books Annual, 2003*

"Overall, the information is excellent, and complex topics are clearly explained. As a reference book for the consumer it is a valuable resource to assist them to make informed decisions about cancer and its treatments." — *Cancer Forum, Nov '02*

"Highly recommended for academic and medical reference collections." — *Library Bookwatch, Sep '02*

"This is a highly recommended book for any public or consumer library, being reader friendly and containing accurate and helpful information."
— *E-Streams, Aug '02*

"Recommended reference source."
— *Booklist, American Library Association, Jul '02*

SEE ALSO Breast Cancer Sourcebook, Women's Health Concerns Sourcebook

Cardiovascular Diseases & Disorders Sourcebook, 1st Edition

SEE Heart Diseases & Disorders Sourcebook, 2nd Edition

■

Caregiving Sourcebook

Basic Consumer Health Information for Caregivers, Including a Profile of Caregivers, Caregiving Responsibilities and Concerns, Tips for Specific Conditions, Care Environments, and the Effects of Caregiving

Along with Facts about Legal Issues, Financial Information, and Future Planning, a Glossary, and a Listing of Additional Resources

Edited by Joyce Brennfleck Shannon. 600 pages. 2001. 0-7808-0331-0. $78.

"Essential for most collections."
— *Library Journal, Apr 1, 2002*

"An ideal addition to the reference collection of any public library. Health sciences information professionals may also want to acquire the *Caregiving Sourcebook* for their hospital or academic library for use as a ready reference tool by health care workers interested in aging and caregiving." — *E-Streams, Jan '02*

"Recommended reference source."
— *Booklist, American Library Association, Oct '01*

■

Child Abuse Sourcebook

Basic Consumer Health Information about the Physical, Sexual, and Emotional Abuse of Children, with Additional Facts about Neglect, Munchausen Syndrome by Proxy (MSBP), Shaken Baby Syndrome, and Controversial Issues Related to Child Abuse, Such as Withholding Medical Care, Corporal Punishment, and Child Maltreatment in Youth Sports, and Featuring Facts about Child Protective Services, Foster Care, Adoption, Parenting Challenges, and Other Abuse Prevention Efforts

Along with a Glossary of Related Terms and Resources for Additional Help and Information

Edited by Dawn D. Matthews. 620 pages. 2004. 0-7808-0705-7. $78.

■

Childhood Diseases & Disorders Sourcebook

Basic Consumer Health Information about Medical Problems Often Encountered in Pre-Adolescent Children, Including Respiratory Tract Ailments, Ear Infections, Sore Throats, Disorders of the Skin and Scalp, Digestive and Genitourinary Diseases, Infectious Diseases, Inflammatory Disorders, Chronic Physical and Developmental Disorders, Allergies, and More

Along with Information about Diagnostic Tests, Common Childhood Surgeries, and Frequently Used Medications, with a Glossary of Important Terms and Resource Directory

Edited by Chad T. Kimball. 662 pages. 2003. 0-7808-0458-9. $78.

"This is an excellent book for new parents and should be included in all health care and public libraries."
— *American Reference Books Annual, 2004*

Colds, Flu & Other Common Ailments Sourcebook

Basic Consumer Health Information about Common Ailments and Injuries, Including Colds, Coughs, the Flu, Sinus Problems, Headaches, Fever, Nausea and Vomiting, Menstrual Cramps, Diarrhea, Constipation, Hemorrhoids, Back Pain, Dandruff, Dry and Itchy Skin, Cuts, Scrapes, Sprains, Bruises, and More

Along with Information about Prevention, Self-Care, Choosing a Doctor, Over-the-Counter Medications, Folk Remedies, and Alternative Therapies, and Including a Glossary of Important Terms and a Directory of Resources for Further Help and Information

Edited by Chad T. Kimball. 638 pages. 2001. 0-7808-0435-X. $78.

"A good starting point for research on common illnesses. It will be a useful addition to public and consumer health library collections."
— *American Reference Books Annual 2002*

"Will prove valuable to any library seeking to maintain a current, comprehensive reference collection of health resources. . . . Excellent reference."
— *The Bookwatch, Aug '01*

"Recommended reference source."
— *Booklist, American Library Association, July '01*

Communication Disorders Sourcebook

Basic Information about Deafness and Hearing Loss, Speech and Language Disorders, Voice Disorders, Balance and Vestibular Disorders, and Disorders of Smell, Taste, and Touch

Edited by Linda M. Ross. 533 pages. 1996. 0-7808-0077-X. $78.

"This is skillfully edited and is a welcome resource for the layperson. It should be found in every public and medical library." — *Booklist Health Sciences Supplement, American Library Association, Oct '97*

Congenital Disorders Sourcebook

Basic Information about Disorders Acquired during Gestation, Including Spina Bifida, Hydrocephalus, Cerebral Palsy, Heart Defects, Craniofacial Abnormalities, Fetal Alcohol Syndrome, and More

Along with Current Treatment Options and Statistical Data

Edited by Karen Bellenir. 607 pages. 1997. 0-7808-0205-5. $78.

"Recommended reference source."
— *Booklist, American Library Association, Oct '97*

SEE ALSO Pregnancy & Birth Sourcebook

Consumer Issues in Health Care Sourcebook

Basic Information about Health Care Fundamentals and Related Consumer Issues, Including Exams and Screening Tests, Physician Specialties, Choosing a Doctor, Using Prescription and Over-the-Counter Medications Safely, Avoiding Health Scams, Managing Common Health Risks in the Home, Care Options for Chronically or Terminally Ill Patients, and a List of Resources for Obtaining Help and Further Information

Edited by Karen Bellenir. 618 pages. 1998. 0-7808-0221-7. $78.

"Both public and academic libraries will want to have a copy in their collection for readers who are interested in self-education on health issues."
— *American Reference Books Annual, 2000*

"The editor has researched the literature from government agencies and others, saving readers the time and effort of having to do the research themselves. Recommended for public libraries."
— *Reference and User Services Quarterly, American Library Association, Spring '99*

"Recommended reference source."
— *Booklist, American Library Association, Dec '98*

Contagious Diseases Sourcebook

Basic Consumer Health Information about Infectious Diseases Spread by Person-to-Person Contact through Direct Touch, Airborne Transmission, Sexual Contact, or Contact with Blood or Other Body Fluids, Including Hepatitis, Herpes, Influenza, Lice, Measles, Mumps, Pinworm, Ringworm, Severe Acute Respiratory Syndrome (SARS), Streptococcal Infections, Tuberculosis, and Others

Along with Facts about Disease Transmission, Antimicrobial Resistance, and Vaccines, with a Glossary and Directories of Resources for More Information

Edited by Karen Bellenir. 643 pages. 2004. 0-7808-0736-7. $78.

Contagious & Non-Contagious Infectious Diseases Sourcebook

Basic Information about Contagious Diseases like Measles, Polio, Hepatitis B, and Infectious Mononucleosis, and Non-Contagious Infectious Diseases like Tetanus and Toxic Shock Syndrome, and Diseases Occurring as Secondary Infections Such as Shingles and Reye Syndrome

Along with Vaccination, Prevention, and Treatment Information, and a Section Describing Emerging Infectious Disease Threats

Edited by Karen Bellenir and Peter D. Dresser. 566 pages. 1996. 0-7808-0075-3. $78.

Death & Dying Sourcebook

Basic Consumer Health Information for the Layperson about End-of-Life Care and Related Ethical and Legal Issues, Including Chief Causes of Death, Autopsies, Pain Management for the Terminally Ill, Life Support Systems, Insurance, Euthanasia, Assisted Suicide, Hospice Programs, Living Wills, Funeral Planning, Counseling, Mourning, Organ Donation, and Physician Training

Along with Statistical Data, a Glossary, and Listings of Sources for Further Help and Information

Edited by Annemarie S. Muth. 641 pages. 1999. 0-7808-0230-6. $78.

"Public libraries, medical libraries, and academic libraries will all find this sourcebook a useful addition to their collections."
— American Reference Books Annual, 2001

"An extremely useful resource for those concerned with death and dying in the United States."
— Respiratory Care, Nov '00

"Recommended reference source."
— Booklist, American Library Association, Aug '00

"This book is a definite must for all those involved in end-of-life care." — Doody's Review Service, 2000

■

Dental Care & Oral Health Sourcebook, 2nd Edition

Basic Consumer Health Information about Dental Care, Including Oral Hygiene, Dental Visits, Pain Management, Cavities, Crowns, Bridges, Dental Implants, and Fillings, and Other Oral Health Concerns, Such as Gum Disease, Bad Breath, Dry Mouth, Genetic and Developmental Abnormalities, Oral Cancers, Orthodontics, and Temporomandibular Disorders

Along with Updates on Current Research in Oral Health, a Glossary, a Directory of Dental and Oral Health Organizations, and Resources for People with Dental and Oral Health Disorders

Edited by Amy L. Sutton. 609 pages. 2003. 0-7808-0634-4. $78.

ALSO AVAILABLE: Oral Health Sourcebook, 1st Edition. Edited by Allan R. Cook. 558 pages. 1997. 0-7808-0082-6. $78.

"This book could serve as a turning point in the battle to educate consumers in issues concerning oral health."
— American Reference Books Annual, 2004

"Unique source which will fill a gap in dental sources for patients and the lay public. A valuable reference tool even in a library with thousands of books on dentistry. Comprehensive, clear, inexpensive, and easy to read and use. It fills an enormous gap in the health care literature." — Reference and User Services Quarterly, American Library Association, Summer '98

"Recommended reference source."
— Booklist, American Library Association, Dec '97

Depression Sourcebook

Basic Consumer Health Information about Unipolar Depression, Bipolar Disorder, Postpartum Depression, Seasonal Affective Disorder, and Other Types of Depression in Children, Adolescents, Women, Men, the Elderly, and Other Selected Populations

Along with Facts about Causes, Risk Factors, Diagnostic Criteria, Treatment Options, Coping Strategies, Suicide Prevention, a Glossary, and a Directory of Sources for Additional Help and Information

Edited by Karen Belleni. 602 pages. 2002. 0-7808-0611-5. $78.

"Depression Sourcebook is of a very high standard. Its purpose, which is to serve as a reference source to the lay reader, is very well served."
— Journal of the National Medical Association, 2004

"Invaluable reference for public and school library collections alike." — Library Bookwatch, Apr '03

"Recommended for purchase."
— American Reference Books Annual, 2003

■

Diabetes Sourcebook, 3rd Edition

Basic Consumer Health Information about Type 1 Diabetes (Insulin-Dependent or Juvenile-Onset Diabetes), Type 2 Diabetes (Noninsulin-Dependent or Adult-Onset Diabetes), Gestational Diabetes, Impaired Glucose Tolerance (IGT), and Related Complications, Such as Amputation, Eye Disease, Gum Disease, Nerve Damage, and End-Stage Renal Disease, Including Facts about Insulin, Oral Diabetes Medications, Blood Sugar Testing, and the Role of Exercise and Nutrition in the Control of Diabetes

Along with a Glossary and Resources for Further Help and Information

Edited by Dawn D. Matthews. 622 pages. 2003. 0-7808-0629-8. $78.

ALSO AVAILABLE: Diabetes Sourcebook, 1st Edition. Edited by Karen Bellenir and Peter D. Dresser. 827 pages. 1994. 1-55888-751-2. $78.

Diabetes Sourcebook, 2nd Edition. Edited by Karen Bellenir. 688 pages. 1998. 0-7808-0224-1. $78.

"This edition is even more helpful than earlier versions. . . . It is a truly valuable tool for anyone seeking readable and authoritative information on diabetes."
— American Reference Books Annual, 2004

"An invaluable reference." — Library Journal, May '00

Selected as one of the 250 "Best Health Sciences Books of 1999." — Doody's Rating Service, Mar-Apr 2000

"Provides useful information for the general public."
— Healthlines, University of Michigan Health Management Research Center, Sep/Oct '99

". . . provides reliable mainstream medical information . . . belongs on the shelves of any library with a consumer health collection." — E-Streams, Sep '99

"Recommended reference source."
— Booklist, American Library Association, Feb '99

Diet & Nutrition Sourcebook, 2nd Edition

Basic Consumer Health Information about Dietary Guidelines, Recommended Daily Intake Values, Vitamins, Minerals, Fiber, Fat, Weight Control, Dietary Supplements, and Food Additives

Along with Special Sections on Nutrition Needs throughout Life and Nutrition for People with Such Specific Medical Concerns as Allergies, High Blood Cholesterol, Hypertension, Diabetes, Celiac Disease, Seizure Disorders, Phenylketonuria (PKU), Cancer, and Eating Disorders, and Including Reports on Current Nutrition Research and Source Listings for Additional Help and Information

Edited by Karen Bellenir. 650 pages. 1999. 0-7808-0228-4. $78.

ALSO AVAILABLE: Diet & Nutrition Sourcebook, 1st Edition. Edited by Dan R. Harris. 662 pages. 1996. 0-7808-0084-2. $78.

"This book is an excellent source of basic diet and nutrition information." — Booklist Health Sciences Supplement, American Library Association, Dec '00

"This reference document should be in any public library, but it would be a very good guide for beginning students in the health sciences. If the other books in this publisher's series are as good as this, they should all be in the health sciences collections."
—American Reference Books Annual, 2000

"This book is an excellent general nutrition reference for consumers who desire to take an active role in their health care for prevention. Consumers of all ages who select this book can feel confident they are receiving current and accurate information." — Journal of Nutrition for the Elderly, Vol. 19, No. 4, '00

"Recommended reference source."
—Booklist, American Library Association, Dec '99

SEE ALSO Digestive Diseases & Disorders Sourcebook, Eating Disorders Sourcebook, Gastrointestinal Diseases & Disorders Sourcebook, Vegetarian Sourcebook

■

Digestive Diseases & Disorders Sourcebook

Basic Consumer Health Information about Diseases and Disorders that Impact the Upper and Lower Digestive System, Including Celiac Disease, Constipation, Crohn's Disease, Cyclic Vomiting Syndrome, Diarrhea, Diverticulosis and Diverticulitis, Gallstones, Heartburn, Hemorrhoids, Hernias, Indigestion (Dyspepsia), Irritable Bowel Syndrome, Lactose Intolerance, Ulcers, and More

Along with Information about Medications and Other Treatments, Tips for Maintaining a Healthy Digestive Tract, a Glossary, and Directory of Digestive Diseases Organizations

Edited by Karen Bellenir. 335 pages. 2000. 0-7808-0327-2. $78.

"This title would be an excellent addition to all public or patient-research libraries."
—American Reference Books Annual, 2001

"This title is recommended for public, hospital, and health sciences libraries with consumer health collections." — E-Streams, Jul-Aug '00

"Recommended reference source."
—Booklist, American Library Association, May '00

SEE ALSO Diet & Nutrition Sourcebook, Eating Disorders Sourcebook, Gastrointestinal Diseases & Disorders Sourcebook

■

Disabilities Sourcebook

Basic Consumer Health Information about Physical and Psychiatric Disabilities, Including Descriptions of Major Causes of Disability, Assistive and Adaptive Aids, Workplace Issues, and Accessibility Concerns

Along with Information about the Americans with Disabilities Act, a Glossary, and Resources for Additional Help and Information

Edited by Dawn D. Matthews. 616 pages. 2000. 0-7808-0389-2. $78.

"It is a must for libraries with a consumer health section." — American Reference Books Annual 2002

"A much needed addition to the Omnigraphics Health Reference Series. A current reference work to provide people with disabilities, their families, caregivers or those who work with them, a broad range of information in one volume, has not been available until now. . . . It is recommended for all public and academic library reference collections." — E-Streams, May '01

"An excellent source book in easy-to-read format covering many current topics; highly recommended for all libraries." — Choice, Association of College and Research Libraries, Jan '01

"Recommended reference source."
—Booklist, American Library Association, Jul '00

■

Domestic Violence Sourcebook, 2nd Edition

Basic Consumer Health Information about the Causes and Consequences of Abusive Relationships, Including Physical Violence, Sexual Assault, Battery, Stalking, and Emotional Abuse, and Facts about the Effects of Violence on Women, Men, Young Adults, and the Elderly, with Reports about Domestic Violence in Selected Populations, and Featuring Facts about Medical Care, Victim Assistance and Protection, Prevention Strategies, Mental Health Services, and Legal Issues

Along with a Glossary of Related Terms and Resources for Additional Help and Information

Edited by Dawn D. Matthews. 628 pages. 2004. 0-7808-0669-7. $78.

ALSO AVAILABLE: Domestic Violence & Child Abuse Sourcebook, 1st Edition. Edited by Helene Henderson. 1,064 pages. 2001. 0-7808-0235-7. $78.

"Interested lay persons should find the book extremely beneficial. . . . A copy of *Domestic Violence and Child Abuse Sourcebook* should be in every public library in the United States."

— *Social Science & Medicine, No. 56, 2003*

"This is important information. The Web has many resources but this sourcebook fills an important societal need. I am not aware of any other resources of this type." — *Doody's Review Service, Sep '01*

"Recommended for all libraries, scholars, and practitioners." — *Choice, Association of College & Research Libraries, Jul '01*

"Recommended reference source." — *Booklist, American Library Association, Apr '01*

"Important pick for college-level health reference libraries." — *The Bookwatch, Mar '01*

"Because this problem is so widespread and because this book includes a lot of issues within one volume, this work is recommended for all public libraries." — *American Reference Books Annual, 2001*

∎

Drug Abuse Sourcebook, 2nd Edition

Basic Consumer Health Information about Illicit Substances of Abuse and the Misuse of Prescription and Over-the-Counter Medications, Including Depressants, Hallucinogens, Inhalants, Marijuana, Stimulants, and Anabolic Steroids

Along with Facts about Related Health Risks, Treatment Programs, Prevention Programs, a Glossary of Abuse and Addiction Terms, a Glossary of Drug-Related Street Terms, and a Directory Resources for More Information

Edited by Catherine Ginther. 600 pages. 2004. 0-7808-0740-5. $78.

ALSO AVAILABLE: Drug Abuse Sourcebook, 1st Edition. Edited by Karen Bellenir. 629 pages. 2000. 0-7808-0242-X. $78.

"Containing a wealth of information . . . . This resource belongs in libraries that serve a lower-division undergraduate or community college clientele as well as the general public." — *Choice, Association of College and Research Libraries, Jun '01*

"Recommended reference source." — *Booklist, American Library Association, Feb '01*

"Highly recommended." — *The Bookwatch, Jan '01*

"Even though there is a plethora of books on drug abuse, this volume is recommended for school, public, and college libraries." — *American Reference Books Annual, 2001*

SEE ALSO *Alcoholism Sourcebook, Substance Abuse Sourcebook*

Ear, Nose & Throat Disorders Sourcebook

Basic Information about Disorders of the Ears, Nose, Sinus Cavities, Pharynx, and Larynx, Including Ear Infections, Tinnitus, Vestibular Disorders, Allergic and Non-Allergic Rhinitis, Sore Throats, Tonsillitis, and Cancers That Affect the Ears, Nose, Sinuses, and Throat

Along with Reports on Current Research Initiatives, a Glossary of Related Medical Terms, and a Directory of Sources for Further Help and Information

Edited by Karen Bellenir and Linda M. Shin. 576 pages. 1998. 0-7808-0206-3. $78.

"Overall, this sourcebook is helpful for the consumer seeking information on ENT issues. It is recommended for public libraries." — *American Reference Books Annual, 1999*

"Recommended reference source." — *Booklist, American Library Association, Dec '98*

∎

Eating Disorders Sourcebook

Basic Consumer Health Information about Eating Disorders, Including Information about Anorexia Nervosa, Bulimia Nervosa, Binge Eating, Body Dysmorphic Disorder, Pica, Laxative Abuse, and Night Eating Syndrome

Along with Information about Causes, Adverse Effects, and Treatment and Prevention Issues, and Featuring a Section on Concerns Specific to Children and Adolescents, a Glossary, and Resources for Further Help and Information

Edited by Dawn D. Matthews. 322 pages. 2001. 0-7808-0335-3. $78.

"Recommended for health science libraries that are open to the public, as well as hospital libraries. This book is a good resource for the consumer who is concerned about eating disorders." — *E-Streams, Mar '02*

"This volume is another convenient collection of excerpted articles. Recommended for school and public library patrons; lower-division undergraduates; and two-year technical program students." — *Choice, Association of College & Research Libraries, Jan '02*

"Recommended reference source." — *Booklist, American Library Association, Oct '01*

SEE ALSO *Diet & Nutrition Sourcebook, Digestive Diseases & Disorders Sourcebook, Gastrointestinal Diseases & Disorders Sourcebook*

∎

Emergency Medical Services Sourcebook

Basic Consumer Health Information about Preventing, Preparing for, and Managing Emergency Situations, When and Who to Call for Help, What to Expect in the Emergency Room, the Emergency Medical Team, Patient Issues, and Current Topics in Emergency Medicine

Along with Statistical Data, a Glossary, and Sources of Additional Help and Information

Edited by Jenni Lynn Colson. 494 pages. 2002. 0-7808-0420-1. $78.

"Handy and convenient for home, public, school, and college libraries. Recommended."
— *Choice, Association of College and Research Libraries, Apr '03*

"This reference can provide the consumer with answers to most questions about emergency care in the United States, or it will direct them to a resource where the answer can be found."
— *American Reference Books Annual, 2003*

"Recommended reference source."
— *Booklist, American Library Association, Feb '03*

■

Endocrine & Metabolic Disorders Sourcebook

Basic Information for the Layperson about Pancreatic and Insulin-Related Disorders Such as Pancreatitis, Diabetes, and Hypoglycemia; Adrenal Gland Disorders Such as Cushing's Syndrome, Addison's Disease, and Congenital Adrenal Hyperplasia; Pituitary Gland Disorders Such as Growth Hormone Deficiency, Acromegaly, and Pituitary Tumors; Thyroid Disorders Such as Hypothyroidism, Graves' Disease, Hashimoto's Disease, and Goiter; Hyperparathyroidism; and Other Diseases and Syndromes of Hormone Imbalance or Metabolic Dysfunction

Along with Reports on Current Research Initiatives

Edited by Linda M. Shin. 574 pages. 1998. 0-7808-0207-1. $78.

"Omnigraphics has produced another needed resource for health information consumers."
— *American Reference Books Annual, 2000*

"Recommended reference source."
— *Booklist, American Library Association, Dec '98*

■

Environmental Health Sourcebook, 2nd Edition

Basic Consumer Health Information about the Environment and Its Effect on Human Health, Including the Effects of Air Pollution, Water Pollution, Hazardous Chemicals, Food Hazards, Radiation Hazards, Biological Agents, Household Hazards, Such as Radon, Asbestos, Carbon Monoxide, and Mold, and Information about Associated Diseases and Disorders, Including Cancer, Allergies, Respiratory Problems, and Skin Disorders

Along with Information about Environmental Concerns for Specific Populations, a Glossary of Related Terms, and Resources for Further Help and Information

Edited by Dawn D. Matthews. 673 pages. 2003. 0-7808-0632-8. $78.

ALSO AVAILABLE: Environmentally Induced Disorders Sourcebook, 1st Edition. Edited by Allan R. Cook. 620 pages. 1997. 0-7808-0083-4. $78.

"This recently updated edition continues the level of quality and the reputation of the numerous other volumes in Omnigraphics' *Health Reference Series*."
— *American Reference Books Annual, 2004*

"Recommended reference source."
— *Booklist, American Library Association, Sep '98*

"This book will be a useful addition to anyone's library."
— *Choice Health Sciences Supplement, Association of College and Research Libraries, May '98*

". . . a good survey of numerous environmentally induced physical disorders . . . a useful addition to anyone's library."
— *Doody's Health Sciences Book Reviews, Jan '98*

". . . provide[s] introductory information from the best authorities around. Since this volume covers topics that potentially affect everyone, it will surely be one of the most frequently consulted volumes in the *Health Reference Series*."
— *Rettig on Reference, Nov '97*

■

Environmentally Induced Disorders Sourcebook, 1st Edition

SEE *Environmental Health Sourcebook, 2nd Edition*

■

Ethnic Diseases Sourcebook

Basic Consumer Health Information for Ethnic and Racial Minority Groups in the United States, Including General Health Indicators and Behaviors, Ethnic Diseases, Genetic Testing, the Impact of Chronic Diseases, Women's Health, Mental Health Issues, and Preventive Health Care Services

Along with a Glossary and a Listing of Additional Resources

Edited by Joyce Brennfleck Shannon. 664 pages. 2001. 0-7808-0336-1. $78.

"Recommended for health sciences libraries where public health programs are a priority."
— *E-Streams, Jan '02*

"Not many books have been written on this topic to date, and the *Ethnic Diseases Sourcebook* is a strong addition to the list. It will be an important introductory resource for health consumers, students, health care personnel, and social scientists. It is recommended for public, academic, and large hospital libraries."
— *American Reference Books Annual 2002*

"Recommended reference source."
— *Booklist, American Library Association, Oct '01*

"Will prove valuable to any library seeking to maintain a current, comprehensive reference collection of health resources. . . . An excellent source of health information about genetic disorders which affect particular ethnic and racial minorities in the U.S."
— *The Bookwatch, Aug '01*

Eye Care Sourcebook, 2nd Edition

Basic Consumer Health Information about Eye Care and Eye Disorders, Including Facts about the Diagnosis, Prevention, and Treatment of Common Refractive Problems Such as Myopia, Hyperopia, Astigmatism, and Presbyopia, and Eye Diseases, Including Glaucoma, Cataract, Age-Related Macular Degeneration, and Diabetic Retinopathy

Along with a Section on Vision Correction and Refractive Surgeries, Including LASIK and LASEK, a Glossary, and Directories of Resources for Additional Help and Information

Edited by Amy L. Sutton. 543 pages. 2003. 0-7808-0635-2. $78.

ALSO AVAILABLE: Ophthalmic Disorders Sourcebook, 1st Edition. Edited by Linda M. Ross. 631 pages. 1996. 0-7808-0081-8. $78.

". . . a solid reference tool for eye care and a valuable addition to a collection."
— *American Reference Books Annual, 2004*

■

Family Planning Sourcebook

Basic Consumer Health Information about Planning for Pregnancy and Contraception, Including Traditional Methods, Barrier Methods, Hormonal Methods, Permanent Methods, Future Methods, Emergency Contraception, and Birth Control Choices for Women at Each Stage of Life

Along with Statistics, a Glossary, and Sources of Additional Information

Edited by Amy Marcaccio Keyzer. 520 pages. 2001. 0-7808-0379-5. $78.

"Recommended for public, health, and undergraduate libraries as part of the circulating collection."
— *E-Streams, Mar '02*

"Information is presented in an unbiased, readable manner, and the sourcebook will certainly be a necessary addition to those public and high school libraries where Internet access is restricted or otherwise problematic." — *American Reference Books Annual 2002*

"Recommended reference source."
— *Booklist, American Library Association, Oct '01*

"Will prove valuable to any library seeking to maintain a current, comprehensive reference collection of health resources. . . . Excellent reference."
— *The Bookwatch, Aug '01*

SEE ALSO Pregnancy & Birth Sourcebook

■

Fitness & Exercise Sourcebook, 2nd Edition

Basic Consumer Health Information about the Fundamentals of Fitness and Exercise, Including How to Begin and Maintain a Fitness Program, Fitness as a Lifestyle, the Link between Fitness and Diet, Advice for Specific Groups of People, Exercise as It Relates to Specific Medical Conditions, and Recent Research in Fitness and Exercise

Along with a Glossary of Important Terms and Resources for Additional Help and Information

Edited by Kristen M. Gledhill. 646 pages. 2001. 0-7808-0334-5. $78.

ALSO AVAILABLE: Fitness & Exercise Sourcebook, 1st Edition. Edited by Dan R. Harris. 663 pages. 1996. 0-7808-0186-5. $78.

"This work is recommended for all general reference collections."
— *American Reference Books Annual 2002*

"Highly recommended for public, consumer, and school grades fourth through college."
— *E-Streams, Nov '01*

"Recommended reference source." — *Booklist, American Library Association, Oct '01*

"The information appears quite comprehensive and is considered reliable. . . . This second edition is a welcomed addition to the series."
— *Doody's Review Service, Sep '01*

"This reference is a valuable choice for those who desire a broad source of information on exercise, fitness, and chronic-disease prevention through a healthy lifestyle." — *American Medical Writers Association Journal, Fall '01*

"Will prove valuable to any library seeking to maintain a current, comprehensive reference collection of health resources. . . . Excellent reference."
— *The Bookwatch, Aug '01*

■

Food & Animal Borne Diseases Sourcebook

Basic Information about Diseases That Can Be Spread to Humans through the Ingestion of Contaminated Food or Water or by Contact with Infected Animals and Insects, Such as Botulism, E. Coli, Hepatitis A, Trichinosis, Lyme Disease, and Rabies

Along with Information Regarding Prevention and Treatment Methods, and Including a Special Section for International Travelers Describing Diseases Such as Cholera, Malaria, Travelers' Diarrhea, and Yellow Fever, and Offering Recommendations for Avoiding Illness

Edited by Karen Bellenir and Peter D. Dresser. 535 pages. 1995. 0-7808-0033-8. $78.

"Targeting general readers and providing them with a single, comprehensive source of information on selected topics, this book continues, with the excellent caliber of its predecessors, to catalog topical information on health matters of general interest. Readable and thorough, this valuable resource is highly recommended for all libraries."
— *Academic Library Book Review, Summer '96*

"A comprehensive collection of authoritative information." — *Emergency Medical Services, Oct '95*

Food Safety Sourcebook

Basic Consumer Health Information about the Safe Handling of Meat, Poultry, Seafood, Eggs, Fruit Juices, and Other Food Items, and Facts about Pesticides, Drinking Water, Food Safety Overseas, and the Onset, Duration, and Symptoms of Foodborne Illnesses, Including Types of Pathogenic Bacteria, Parasitic Protozoa, Worms, Viruses, and Natural Toxins

Along with the Role of the Consumer, the Food Handler, and the Government in Food Safety; a Glossary, and Resources for Additional Help and Information

Edited by Dawn D. Matthews. 339 pages. 1999. 0-7808-0326-4. $78.

"This book is recommended for public libraries and universities with home economic and food science programs." — *E-Streams, Nov '00*

"Recommended reference source." —*Booklist, American Library Association, May '00*

"This book takes the complex issues of food safety and foodborne pathogens and presents them in an easily understood manner. [It does] an excellent job of covering a large and often confusing topic." —*American Reference Books Annual, 2000*

Forensic Medicine Sourcebook

Basic Consumer Information for the Layperson about Forensic Medicine, Including Crime Scene Investigation, Evidence Collection and Analysis, Expert Testimony, Computer-Aided Criminal Identification, Digital Imaging in the Courtroom, DNA Profiling, Accident Reconstruction, Autopsies, Ballistics, Drugs and Explosives Detection, Latent Fingerprints, Product Tampering, and Questioned Document Examination

Along with Statistical Data, a Glossary of Forensics Terminology, and Listings of Sources for Further Help and Information

Edited by Annemarie S. Muth. 574 pages. 1999. 0-7808-0232-2. $78.

"Given the expected widespread interest in its content and its easy to read style, this book is recommended for most public and all college and university libraries." — *E-Streams, Feb '01*

"Recommended for public libraries." —*Reference & User Services Quarterly, American Library Association, Spring 2000*

"Recommended reference source." —*Booklist, American Library Association, Feb '00*

"A wealth of information, useful statistics, references are up-to-date and extremely complete. This wonderful collection of data will help students who are interested in a career in any type of forensic field. It is a great resource for attorneys who need information about types of expert witnesses needed in a particular case. It also offers useful information for fiction and nonfiction writers whose work involves a crime. A fascinating compilation. All levels." — *Choice, Association of College and Research Libraries, Jan 2000*

"There are several items that make this book attractive to consumers who are seeking certain forensic data. . . . This is a useful current source for those seeking general forensic medical answers." —*American Reference Books Annual, 2000*

Gastrointestinal Diseases & Disorders Sourcebook

Basic Information about Gastroesophageal Reflux Disease (Heartburn), Ulcers, Diverticulosis, Irritable Bowel Syndrome, Crohn's Disease, Ulcerative Colitis, Diarrhea, Constipation, Lactose Intolerance, Hemorrhoids, Hepatitis, Cirrhosis, and Other Digestive Problems, Featuring Statistics, Descriptions of Symptoms, and Current Treatment Methods of Interest for Persons Living with Upper and Lower Gastrointestinal Maladies

Edited by Linda M. Ross. 413 pages. 1996. 0-7808-0078-8. $78.

". . . very readable form. The successful editorial work that brought this material together into a useful and understandable reference makes accessible to all readers information that can help them more effectively understand and obtain help for digestive tract problems." — *Choice, Association of College & Research Libraries, Feb '97*

SEE ALSO *Diet & Nutrition Sourcebook, Digestive Diseases & Disorders, Eating Disorders Sourcebook*

Genetic Disorders Sourcebook, 3rd Edition

Basic Consumer Health Information about Hereditary Diseases and Disorders, Including Facts about the Human Genome, Genetic Inheritance Patterns, Disorders Associated with Specific Genes, such as Sickle Cell Disease, Hemophilia, and Cystic Fibrosis, Chromosome Disorders, such as Down Syndrome, Fragile X Syndrome, and Turner Syndrome, and Complex Diseases and Disorders Resulting from the Interaction of Environmental and Genetic Factors, such as Allergies, Cancer, and Obesity

Along with Facts about Genetic Testing, Suggestions for Parents of Children with Special Needs, Reports on Current Research Initiatives, a Glossary of Genetic Terminology, and Resources for Additional Help and Information

Edited by Karen Bellenir. 777 pages. 2004. 0-7808-0742-1. $78.

ALSO AVAILABLE: *Genetic Disorders Sourcebook, 1st Edition.* Edited by Karen Bellenir. 642 pages. 1996. 0-7808-0034-6. $78.

Genetic Disorders Sourcebook, 2nd Edition. Edited by Kathy Massimini. 768 pages. 2001. 0-7808-0241-1. $78.

"Recommended for public libraries and medical and hospital libraries with consumer health collections." —*E-Streams, May '01*

Head Trauma Sourcebook

Basic Information for the Layperson about Open-Head and Closed-Head Injuries, Treatment Advances, Recovery, and Rehabilitation

Along with Reports on Current Research Initiatives

Edited by Karen Bellenir. 414 pages. 1997. 0-7808-0208-X. $78.

Headache Sourcebook

Basic Consumer Health Information about Migraine, Tension, Cluster, Rebound and Other Types of Headaches, with Facts about the Cause and Prevention of Headaches, the Effects of Stress and the Environment, Headaches during Pregnancy and Menopause, and Childhood Headaches

Along with a Glossary and Other Resources for Additional Help and Information

Edited by Dawn D. Matthews. 362 pages. 2002. 0-7808-0337-X. $78.

Health Insurance Sourcebook

Basic Information about Managed Care Organizations, Traditional Fee-for-Service Insurance, Insurance Portability and Pre-Existing Conditions Clauses, Medicare, Medicaid, Social Security, and Military Health Care

Along with Information about Insurance Fraud

Edited by Wendy Wilcox. 530 pages. 1997. 0-7808-0222-5. $78.

Health Reference Series Cumulative Index 1999

A Comprehensive Index to the Individual Volumes of the Health Reference Series, Including a Subject Index, Name Index, Organization Index, and Publication Index

Along with a Master List of Acronyms and Abbreviations

Edited by Edward J. Prucha, Anne Holmes, and Robert Rudnick. 990 pages. 2000. 0-7808-0382-5. $78.

Healthy Aging Sourcebook

Basic Consumer Health Information about Maintaining Health through the Aging Process, Including Advice on Nutrition, Exercise, and Sleep, Help in Making Decisions about Midlife Issues and Retirement, and Guidance Concerning Practical and Informed Choices in Health Consumerism

Along with Data Concerning the Theories of Aging, Different Experiences in Aging by Minority Groups, and Facts about Aging Now and Aging in the Future; and Featuring a Glossary, a Guide to Consumer Help, Additional Suggested Reading, and Practical Resource Directory

Edited by Jenifer Swanson. 536 pages. 1999. 0-7808-0390-6. $78.

SEE ALSO *Physical & Mental Issues in Aging Sourcebook*

Healthy Children Sourcebook

Basic Consumer Health Information about the Physical and Mental Development of Children between the Ages of 3 and 12, Including Routine Health Care, Preventative Health Services, Safety and First Aid, Healthy Sleep, Dental Care, Nutrition, and Fitness, and Featuring Parenting Tips on Such Topics as Bedwetting, Choosing Day Care, Monitoring TV and Other Media, and Establishing a Foundation for Substance Abuse Prevention

Along with a Glossary of Commonly Used Pediatric Terms and Resources for Additional Help and Information.

Edited by Chad T. Kimball. 647 pages. 2003. 0-7808-0247-0. $78.

of timely information on health promotion and disease prevention for children aged 3 to 12."
— *American Reference Books Annual, 2004*

"The strengths of this book are many. It is clearly written, presented and structured."
— *Journal of the National Medical Association, 2004*

Healthy Heart Sourcebook for Women

Basic Consumer Health Information about Cardiac Issues Specific to Women, Including Facts about Major Risk Factors and Prevention, Treatment and Control Strategies, and Important Dietary Issues

Along with a Special Section Regarding the Pros and Cons of Hormone Replacement Therapy and Its Impact on Heart Health, and Additional Help, Including Recipes, a Glossary, and a Directory of Resources

Edited by Dawn D. Matthews. 336 pages. 2000. 0-7808-0329-9. $78.

"A good reference source and recommended for all public, academic, medical, and hospital libraries."
— *Medical Reference Services Quarterly, Summer '01*

"Because of the lack of information specific to women on this topic, this book is recommended for public libraries and consumer libraries."
— *American Reference Books Annual, 2001*

"Contains very important information about coronary artery disease that all women should know. The information is current and presented in an easy-to-read format. The book will make a good addition to any library."
— *American Medical Writers Association Journal, Summer '00*

"Important, basic reference."
— *Reviewer's Bookwatch, Jul '00*

SEE ALSO *Heart Diseases & Disorders Sourcebook, Women's Health Concerns Sourcebook*

Heart Diseases & Disorders Sourcebook, 2nd Edition

Basic Consumer Health Information about Heart Attacks, Angina, Rhythm Disorders, Heart Failure, Valve Disease, Congenital Heart Disorders, and More, Including Descriptions of Surgical Procedures and Other Interventions, Medications, Cardiac Rehabilitation, Risk Identification, and Prevention Tips

Along with Statistical Data, Reports on Current Research Initiatives, a Glossary of Cardiovascular Terms, and Resource Directory

Edited by Karen Bellenir. 612 pages. 2000. 0-7808-0238-1. $78.

ALSO AVAILABLE: *Cardiovascular Diseases & Disorders Sourcebook, 1st Edition.* Edited by Karen Bellenir and Peter D. Dresser. 683 pages. 1995. 0-7808-0032-X. $78.

"This work stands out as an imminently accessible resource for the general public. It is recommended for the reference and circulating shelves of school, public, and academic libraries."
— *American Reference Books Annual, 2001*

"Recommended reference source."
— *Booklist, American Library Association, Dec '00*

"Provides comprehensive coverage of matters related to the heart. This title is recommended for health sciences and public libraries with consumer health collections."
— *E-Streams, Oct '00*

SEE ALSO *Healthy Heart Sourcebook for Women*

Household Safety Sourcebook

Basic Consumer Health Information about Household Safety, Including Information about Poisons, Chemicals, Fire, and Water Hazards in the Home

Along with Advice about the Safe Use of Home Maintenance Equipment, Choosing Toys and Nursery Furniture, Holiday and Recreation Safety, a Glossary, and Resources for Further Help and Information

Edited by Dawn D. Matthews. 606 pages. 2002. 0-7808-0338-8. $78.

"This work will be useful in public libraries with large consumer health and wellness departments."
— *American Reference Books Annual, 2003*

"As a sourcebook on household safety this book meets its mark. It is encyclopedic in scope and covers a wide range of safety issues that are commonly seen in the home."
— *E-Streams, Jul '02*

Hypertension Sourcebook

Basic Consumer Health Information about the Causes, Diagnosis, and Treatment of High Blood Pressure, with Facts about Consequences, Complications, and Co-Occurring Disorders, Such as Coronary Heart Disease, Diabetes, Stroke, Kidney Disease, and Hypertensive Retinopathy, and Issues in Blood Pressure Control, Including Dietary Choices, Stress Management, and Medications

Along with Reports on Current Research Initiatives and Clinical Trials, a Glossary, and Resources for Additional Help and Information

Edited by Dawn D. Matthews and Karen Bellenir. 613 pages. 2004. 0-7808-0674-3. $78.

Immune System Disorders Sourcebook

Basic Information about Lupus, Multiple Sclerosis, Guillain-Barré Syndrome, Chronic Granulomatous Disease, and More

Along with Statistical and Demographic Data and Reports on Current Research Initiatives

Edited by Allan R. Cook. 608 pages. 1997. 0-7808-0209-8. $78.

Infant & Toddler Health Sourcebook

Basic Consumer Health Information about the Physical and Mental Development of Newborns, Infants, and Toddlers, Including Neonatal Concerns, Nutrition Recommendations, Immunization Schedules, Common Pediatric Disorders, Assessments and Milestones, Safety Tips, and Advice for Parents and Other Caregivers

Along with a Glossary of Terms and Resource Listings for Additional Help

Edited by Jenifer Swanson. 585 pages. 2000. 0-7808-0246-2. $78.

"As a reference for the general public, this would be useful in any library." —E-Streams, May '01

"Recommended reference source."
—Booklist, American Library Association, Feb '01

"This is a good source for general use."
—American Reference Books Annual, 2001

■

Infectious Diseases Sourcebook

Basic Consumer Health Information about Non-Contagious Bacterial, Viral, Prion, Fungal, and Parasitic Diseases Spread by Food and Water, Insects and Animals, or Environmental Contact, Including Botulism, E. Coli, Encephalitis, Legionnaires' Disease, Lyme Disease, Malaria, Plague, Rabies, Salmonella, Tetanus, and Others, and Facts about Newly Emerging Diseases, Such as Hantavirus, Mad Cow Disease, Monkeypox, and West Nile Virus

Along with Information about Preventing Disease Transmission, the Threat of Bioterrorism, and Current Research Initiatives, with a Glossary and Directory of Resources for More Information

Edited by Karen Bellenir. 634 pages. 2004. 0-7808-0675-1. $78.

■

Injury & Trauma Sourcebook

Basic Consumer Health Information about the Impact of Injury, the Diagnosis and Treatment of Common and Traumatic Injuries, Emergency Care, and Specific Injuries Related to Home, Community, Workplace, Transportation, and Recreation

Along with Guidelines for Injury Prevention, a Glossary, and a Directory of Additional Resources

Edited by Joyce Brennfleck Shannon. 696 pages. 2002. 0-7808-0421-X. $78.

"This publication is the most comprehensive work of its kind about injury and trauma."
—American Reference Books Annual, 2003

"This sourcebook provides concise, easily readable, basic health information about injuries. . . . This book is well organized and an easy to use reference resource suitable for hospital, health sciences and public libraries with consumer health collections."
—E-Streams, Nov '02

"Practitioners should be aware of guides such as this in order to facilitate their use by patients and their families."
—Doody's Health Sciences Book Review Journal, Sep-Oct '02

"Recommended reference source."
—Booklist, American Library Association, Sep '02

"Highly recommended for academic and medical reference collections." —Library Bookwatch, Sep '02

■

Kidney & Urinary Tract Diseases & Disorders Sourcebook

Basic Information about Kidney Stones, Urinary Incontinence, Bladder Disease, End Stage Renal Disease, Dialysis, and More

Along with Statistical and Demographic Data and Reports on Current Research Initiatives

Edited by Linda M. Ross. 602 pages. 1997. 0-7808-0079-6. $78.

■

Learning Disabilities Sourcebook, 2nd Edition

Basic Consumer Health Information about Learning Disabilities, Including Dyslexia, Developmental Speech and Language Disabilities, Non-Verbal Learning Disorders, Developmental Arithmetic Disorder, Developmental Writing Disorder, and Other Conditions That Impede Learning Such as Attention Deficit/ Hyperactivity Disorder, Brain Injury, Hearing Impairment, Klinefelter Syndrome, Dyspraxia, and Tourette Syndrome

Along with Facts about Educational Issues and Assistive Technology, Coping Strategies, a Glossary of Related Terms, and Resources for Further Help and Information

Edited by Dawn D. Matthews. 621 pages. 2003. 0-7808-0626-3. $78.

ALSO AVAILABLE: Learning Disabilities Sourcebook, 1st Edition. Edited by Linda M. Shin. 579 pages. 1998. 0-7808-0210-1. $78.

"The second edition of Learning Disabilities Sourcebook far surpasses the earlier edition in that it is more focused on information that will be useful as a consumer health resource."
—American Reference Books Annual, 2004

"Teachers as well as consumers will find this an essential guide to understanding various syndromes and their latest treatments. [An] invaluable reference for public and school library collections alike."
—Library Bookwatch, Apr '03

Named "Outstanding Reference Book of 1999."
—New York Public Library, Feb 2000

"An excellent candidate for inclusion in a public library reference section. It's a great source of information. Teachers will also find the book useful. Definitely worth reading."
—Journal of Adolescent & Adult Literacy, Feb 2000

"Readable . . . provides a solid base of information regarding successful techniques used with individuals who have learning disabilities, as well as practical suggestions for educators and family members. Clear language, concise descriptions, and pertinent information for contacting multiple resources add to the strength of this book as a useful tool." —*Choice, Association of College and Research Libraries, Feb '99*

"Recommended reference source."
—*Booklist, American Library Association, Sep '98*

"A useful resource for libraries and for those who don't have the time to identify and locate the individual publications." —*Disability Resources Monthly, Sep '98*

∎

Leukemia Sourcebook

Basic Consumer Health Information about Adult and Childhood Leukemias, Including Acute Lymphocytic Leukemia (ALL), Chronic Lymphocytic Leukemia (CLL), Acute Myelogenous Leukemia (AML), Chronic Myelogenous Leukemia (CML), and Hairy Cell Leukemia, and Treatments Such as Chemotherapy, Radiation Therapy, Peripheral Blood Stem Cell and Marrow Transplantation, and Immunotherapy

Along with Tips for Life During and After Treatment, a Glossary, and Directories of Additional Resources

Edited by Joyce Brennfleck Shannon. 587 pages. 2003. 0-7808-0627-1. $78.

"Unlike other medical books for the layperson, . . . the language does not talk down to the reader. . . . This volume is highly recommended for all libraries."
—*American Reference Books Annual, 2004*

∎

Liver Disorders Sourcebook

Basic Consumer Health Information about the Liver and How It Works; Liver Diseases, Including Cancer, Cirrhosis, Hepatitis, and Toxic and Drug Related Diseases; Tips for Maintaining a Healthy Liver; Laboratory Tests, Radiology Tests, and Facts about Liver Transplantation

Along with a Section on Support Groups, a Glossary, and Resource Listings

Edited by Joyce Brennfleck Shannon. 591 pages. 2000. 0-7808-0383-3. $78.

"A valuable resource."
—*American Reference Books Annual, 2001*

"This title is recommended for health sciences and public libraries with consumer health collections."
—*E-Streams, Oct '00*

"Recommended reference source."
—*Booklist, American Library Association, Jun '00*

∎

Lung Disorders Sourcebook

Basic Consumer Health Information about Emphysema, Pneumonia, Tuberculosis, Asthma, Cystic Fibrosis, and Other Lung Disorders, Including Facts about

Diagnostic Procedures, Treatment Strategies, Disease Prevention Efforts, and Such Risk Factors as Smoking, Air Pollution, and Exposure to Asbestos, Radon, and Other Agents

Along with a Glossary and Resources for Additional Help and Information

Edited by Dawn D. Matthews. 678 pages. 2002. 0-7808-0339-6. $78.

"This title is a great addition for public and school libraries because it provides concise health information on the lungs."
—*American Reference Books Annual, 2003*

"Highly recommended for academic and medical reference collections." —*Library Bookwatch, Sep '02*

∎

Medical Tests Sourcebook, 2nd Edition

Basic Consumer Health Information about Medical Tests, Including Age-Specific Health Tests, Important Health Screenings and Exams, Home-Use Tests, Blood and Specimen Tests, Electrical Tests, Scope Tests, Genetic Testing, and Imaging Tests, Such as X-Rays, Ultrasound, Computed Tomography, Magnetic Resonance Imaging, Angiography, and Nuclear Medicine

Along with a Glossary and Directory of Additional Resources

Edited by Joyce Brennfleck Shannon. 654 pages. 2004. 0-7808-0670-0. $78.

ALSO AVAILABLE: Medical Tests, 1st Edition. Edited by Joyce Brennfleck Shannon. 691 pages. 1999. 0-7808-0243-8. $78.

"Recommended for hospital and health sciences libraries with consumer health collections."
—*E-Streams, Mar '00*

"This is an overall excellent reference with a wealth of general knowledge that may aid those who are reluctant to get vital tests performed."
—*Today's Librarian, Jan 2000*

"A valuable reference guide."
—*American Reference Books Annual, 2000*

∎

Men's Health Concerns Sourcebook, 2nd Edition

Basic Consumer Health Information about the Medical and Mental Concerns of Men, Including Theories about the Shorter Male Lifespan, the Leading Causes of Death and Disability, Physical Concerns of Special Significance to Men, Reproductive and Sexual Concerns, Sexually Transmitted Diseases, Men's Mental and Emotional Health, and Lifestyle Choices That Affect Wellness, Such as Nutrition, Fitness, and Substance Use

Along with a Glossary of Related Terms and a Directory of Organizational Resources in Men's Health

Edited by Robert Aquinas McNally. 644 pages. 2004. 0-7808-0671-9. $78.

Mental Health Disorders Sourcebook, 2nd Edition

Basic Consumer Health Information about Anxiety Disorders, Depression and Other Mood Disorders, Eating Disorders, Personality Disorders, Schizophrenia, and More, Including Disease Descriptions, Treatment Options, and Reports on Current Research Initiatives

Along with Statistical Data, Tips for Maintaining Mental Health, a Glossary, and Directory of Sources for Additional Help and Information

Edited by Karen Bellenir. 605 pages. 2000. 0-7808-0240-3. $78.

Mental Retardation Sourcebook

Basic Consumer Health Information about Mental Retardation and Its Causes, Including Down Syndrome, Fetal Alcohol Syndrome, Fragile X Syndrome, Genetic Conditions, Injury, and Environmental Sources

Along with Preventive Strategies, Parenting Issues, Educational Implications, Health Care Needs, Employment and Economic Matters, Legal Issues, a Glossary, and a Resource Listing for Additional Help and Information

Edited by Joyce Brennfleck Shannon. 642 pages. 2000. 0-7808-0377-9. $78.

Movement Disorders Sourcebook

Basic Consumer Health Information about Neurological Movement Disorders, Including Essential Tremor, Parkinson's Disease, Dystonia, Cerebral Palsy, Huntington's Disease, Myasthenia Gravis, Multiple Sclerosis, and Other Early-Onset and Adult-Onset Movement Disorders, Their Symptoms and Causes, Diagnostic Tests, and Treatments

Along with Mobility and Assistive Technology Information, a Glossary, and a Directory of Additional Resources

Edited by Joyce Brennfleck Shannon. 655 pages. 2003. 0-7808-0628-X. $78.

Muscular Dystrophy Sourcebook

Basic Consumer Health Information about Congenital, Childhood-Onset, and Adult-Onset Forms of Muscular Dystrophy, Such as Duchenne, Becker, Emery-Dreifuss, Distal, Limb-Girdle, Facioscapulohumeral (FSHD), Myotonic, and Ophthalmoplegic Muscular Dystrophies, Including Facts about Diagnostic Tests, Medical and Physical Therapies, Management of Co-Occurring Conditions, and Parenting Guidelines

Along with Practical Tips for Home Care, a Glossary, and Directories of Additional Resources

Edited by Joyce Brennfleck Shannon. 577 pages. 2004. 0-7808-0676-X. $78.

Obesity Sourcebook

Basic Consumer Health Information about Diseases and Other Problems Associated with Obesity, and Including Facts about Risk Factors, Prevention Issues, and Management Approaches

Along with Statistical and Demographic Data, Information about Special Populations, Research Updates, a Glossary, and Source Listings for Further Help and Information

Edited by Wilma Caldwell and Chad T. Kimball. 376 pages. 2001. 0-7808-0333-7. $78.

Ophthalmic Disorders Sourcebook, 1st Edition

SEE Eye Care Sourcebook, 2nd Edition

Oral Health Sourcebook

SEE Dental Care & Oral Health Sourcebook, 2nd Ed.

Osteoporosis Sourcebook

Basic Consumer Health Information about Primary and Secondary Osteoporosis and Juvenile Osteoporosis and Related Conditions, Including Fibrous Dysplasia, Gaucher Disease, Hyperthyroidism, Hypophosphatasia, Myeloma, Osteopetrosis, Osteogenesis Imperfecta, and Paget's Disease

Along with Information about Risk Factors, Treatments, Traditional and Non-Traditional Pain Management, a Glossary of Related Terms, and a Directory of Resources

Edited by Allan R. Cook. 584 pages. 2001. 0-7808-0239-X. $78.

"This would be a book to be kept in a staff or patient library. The targeted audience is the layperson, but the therapist who needs a quick bit of information on a particular topic will also find the book useful."
— Physical Therapy, Jan '02

"This resource is recommended as a great reference source for public, health, and academic libraries, and is another triumph for the editors of Omnigraphics."
— American Reference Books Annual 2002

"Recommended for all public libraries and general health collections, especially those supporting patient education or consumer health programs."
— E-Streams, Nov '01

"Will prove valuable to any library seeking to maintain a current, comprehensive reference collection of health resources. . . . From prevention to treatment and associated conditions, this provides an excellent survey."
— The Bookwatch, Aug '01

"Recommended reference source."
— Booklist, American Library Association, July '01

SEE ALSO Women's Health Concerns Sourcebook

Pain Sourcebook, 2nd Edition

Basic Consumer Health Information about Specific Forms of Acute and Chronic Pain, Including Muscle and Skeletal Pain, Nerve Pain, Cancer Pain, and Disorders Characterized by Pain, Such as Fibromyalgia, Shingles, Angina, Arthritis, and Headaches

Along with Information about Pain Medications and Management Techniques, Complementary and Alternative Pain Relief Options, Tips for People Living with Chronic Pain, a Glossary, and a Directory of Sources for Further Information

Edited by Karen Bellenir. 670 pages. 2002. 0-7808-0612-3. $78.

ALSO AVAILABLE: Pain Sourcebook, 1st Edition. Edited by Allan R. Cook. 667 pages. 1997. 0-7808-0213-6. $78.

"A source of valuable information. . . . This book offers help to nonmedical people who need information about pain and pain management. It is also an excellent reference for those who participate in patient education."
— Doody's Review Service, Sep '02

"The text is readable, easily understood, and well indexed. This excellent volume belongs in all patient education libraries, consumer health sections of public libraries, and many personal collections."
— American Reference Books Annual, 1999

"A beneficial reference." — Booklist Health Sciences Supplement, American Library Association, Oct '98

"The information is basic in terms of scholarship and is appropriate for general readers. Written in journalistic style . . . intended for non-professionals. Quite thorough in its coverage of different pain conditions and summarizes the latest clinical information regarding pain treatment." — Choice, Association of College and Research Libraries, Jun '98

"Recommended reference source."
— Booklist, American Library Association, Mar '98

Pediatric Cancer Sourcebook

Basic Consumer Health Information about Leukemias, Brain Tumors, Sarcomas, Lymphomas, and Other Cancers in Infants, Children, and Adolescents, Including Descriptions of Cancers, Treatments, and Coping Strategies

Along with Suggestions for Parents, Caregivers, and Concerned Relatives, a Glossary of Cancer Terms, and Resource Listings

Edited by Edward J. Prucha. 587 pages. 1999. 0-7808-0245-4. $78.

"An excellent source of information. Recommended for public, hospital, and health science libraries with consumer health collections." — E-Streams, Jun '00

"Recommended reference source."
— Booklist, American Library Association, Feb '00

"A valuable addition to all libraries specializing in health services and many public libraries."
— American Reference Books Annual, 2000

Physical & Mental Issues in Aging Sourcebook

Basic Consumer Health Information on Physical and Mental Disorders Associated with the Aging Process, Including Concerns about Cardiovascular Disease, Pulmonary Disease, Oral Health, Digestive Disorders, Musculoskeletal and Skin Disorders, Metabolic Changes, Sexual and Reproductive Issues, and Changes in Vision, Hearing, and Other Senses

Along with Data about Longevity and Causes of Death, Information on Acute and Chronic Pain, Descriptions of Mental Concerns, a Glossary of Terms, and Resource Listings for Additional Help

Edited by Jenifer Swanson. 660 pages. 1999. 0-7808-0233-0. $78.

"This is a treasure of health information for the layperson." — *Choice Health Sciences Supplement, Association of College & Research Libraries, May 2000*

"Recommended for public libraries." —*American Reference Books Annual, 2000*

"Recommended reference source." —*Booklist, American Library Association, Oct '99*

SEE ALSO Healthy Aging Sourcebook

■

Podiatry Sourcebook

Basic Consumer Health Information about Foot Conditions, Diseases, and Injuries, Including Bunions, Corns, Calluses, Athlete's Foot, Plantar Warts, Hammertoes and Clawtoes, Clubfoot, Heel Pain, Gout, and More

Along with Facts about Foot Care, Disease Prevention, Foot Safety, Choosing a Foot Care Specialist, a Glossary of Terms, and Resource Listings for Additional Information

Edited by M. Lisa Weatherford. 380 pages. 2001. 0-7808-0215-2. $78.

"Recommended reference source." —*Booklist, American Library Association, Feb '02*

"There is a lot of information presented here on a topic that is usually only covered sparingly in most larger comprehensive medical encyclopedias." —*American Reference Books Annual 2002*

■

Pregnancy & Birth Sourcebook, 2nd Edition

Basic Consumer Health Information about Conception and Pregnancy, Including Facts about Fertility, Infertility, Pregnancy Symptoms and Complications, Fetal Growth and Development, Labor, Delivery, and the Postpartum Period, as Well as Information about Maintaining Health and Wellness during Pregnancy and Caring for a Newborn

Along with Information about Public Health Assistance for Low-Income Pregnant Women, a Glossary, and Directories of Agencies and Organizations Providing Help and Support

Edited by Amy L. Sutton. 626 pages. 2004. 0-7808-0672-7. $78.

ALSO AVAILABLE: Pregnancy & Birth Sourcebook, 1st Edition. Edited by Heather E. Aldred. 737 pages. 1997. 0-7808-0216-0. $78.

"A well-organized handbook. Recommended." —*Choice, Association of College and Research Libraries, Apr '98*

"Recommended reference source." —*Booklist, American Library Association, Mar '98*

"Recommended for public libraries." —*American Reference Books Annual, 1998*

SEE ALSO Congenital Disorders Sourcebook, Family Planning Sourcebook

■

Prostate Cancer Sourcebook

Basic Consumer Health Information about Prostate Cancer, Including Information about the Associated Risk Factors, Detection, Diagnosis, and Treatment of Prostate Cancer

Along with Information on Non-Malignant Prostate Conditions, and Featuring a Section Listing Support and Treatment Centers and a Glossary of Related Terms

Edited by Dawn D. Matthews. 358 pages. 2001. 0-7808-0324-8. $78.

"Recommended reference source." —*Booklist, American Library Association, Jan '02*

"A valuable resource for health care consumers seeking information on the subject. . . .All text is written in a clear, easy-to-understand language that avoids technical jargon. Any library that collects consumer health resources would strengthen their collection with the addition of the *Prostate Cancer Sourcebook.*" —*American Reference Books Annual 2002*

■

Public Health Sourcebook

Basic Information about Government Health Agencies, Including National Health Statistics and Trends, Healthy People 2000 Program Goals and Objectives, the Centers for Disease Control and Prevention, the Food and Drug Administration, and the National Institutes of Health

Along with Full Contact Information for Each Agency

Edited by Wendy Wilcox. 698 pages. 1998. 0-7808-0220-9. $78.

"Recommended reference source." —*Booklist, American Library Association, Sep '98*

"This consumer guide provides welcome assistance in navigating the maze of federal health agencies and their data on public health concerns." —*SciTech Book News, Sep '98*

■

Reconstructive & Cosmetic Surgery Sourcebook

Basic Consumer Health Information on Cosmetic and Reconstructive Plastic Surgery, Including Statistical Information about Different Surgical Procedures, Things to Consider Prior to Surgery, Plastic Surgery Techniques and Tools, Emotional and Psychological Considerations, and Procedure-Specific Information

Along with a Glossary of Terms and a Listing of Resources for Additional Help and Information

Edited by M. Lisa Weatherford. 374 pages. 2001. 0-7808-0214-4. $78.

"An excellent reference that addresses cosmetic and medically necessary reconstructive surgeries. . . . The

style of the prose is calm and reassuring, discussing the many positive outcomes now available due to advances in surgical techniques."
— *American Reference Books Annual 2002*

"Recommended for health science libraries that are open to the public, as well as hospital libraries that are open to the patients. This book is a good resource for the consumer interested in plastic surgery."
— *E-Streams, Dec '01*

"Recommended reference source."
— *Booklist, American Library Association, July '01*

Rehabilitation Sourcebook

Basic Consumer Health Information about Rehabilitation for People Recovering from Heart Surgery, Spinal Cord Injury, Stroke, Orthopedic Impairments, Amputation, Pulmonary Impairments, Traumatic Injury, and More, Including Physical Therapy, Occupational Therapy, Speech/ Language Therapy, Massage Therapy, Dance Therapy, Art Therapy, and Recreational Therapy

Along with Information on Assistive and Adaptive Devices, a Glossary, and Resources for Additional Help and Information

Edited by Dawn D. Matthews. 531 pages. 1999. 0-7808-0236-5. $78.

"This is an excellent resource for public library reference and health collections."
— *American Reference Books Annual, 2001*

"Recommended reference source."
— *Booklist, American Library Association, May '00*

Respiratory Diseases & Disorders Sourcebook

Basic Information about Respiratory Diseases and Disorders, Including Asthma, Cystic Fibrosis, Pneumonia, the Common Cold, Influenza, and Others, Featuring Facts about the Respiratory System, Statistical and Demographic Data, Treatments, Self-Help Management Suggestions, and Current Research Initiatives

Edited by Allan R. Cook and Peter D. Dresser. 771 pages. 1995. 0-7808-0037-0. $78.

"Designed for the layperson and for patients and their families coping with respiratory illness. . . . an extensive array of information on diagnosis, treatment, management, and prevention of respiratory illnesses for the general reader."
— *Choice, Association of College and Research Libraries, Jun '96*

"A highly recommended text for all collections. It is a comforting reminder of the power of knowledge that good books carry between their covers."
— *Academic Library Book Review, Spring '96*

"A comprehensive collection of authoritative information presented in a nontechnical, humanitarian style for patients, families, and caregivers."
— *Association of Operating Room Nurses, Sep/Oct '95*

SEE ALSO Lung Disorders Sourcebook

Sexually Transmitted Diseases Sourcebook, 2nd Edition

Basic Consumer Health Information about Sexually Transmitted Diseases, Including Information on the Diagnosis and Treatment of Chlamydia, Gonorrhea, Hepatitis, Herpes, HIV, Mononucleosis, Syphilis, and Others

Along with Information on Prevention, Such as Condom Use, Vaccines, and STD Education; And Featuring a Section on Issues Related to Youth and Adolescents, a Glossary, and Resources for Additional Help and Information

Edited by Dawn D. Matthews. 538 pages. 2001. 0-7808-0249-7. $78.

ALSO AVAILABLE: Sexually Transmitted Diseases Sourcebook, 1st Edition. Edited by Linda M. Ross. 550 pages. 1997. 0-7808-0217-9. $78.

"Recommended for consumer health collections in public libraries, and secondary school and community college libraries."
— *American Reference Books Annual 2002*

"Every school and public library should have a copy of this comprehensive and user-friendly reference book."
— *Choice, Association of College & Research Libraries, Sep '01*

"This is a highly recommended book. This is an especially important book for all school and public libraries."
— *AIDS Book Review Journal, Jul-Aug '01*

"Recommended reference source."
— *Booklist, American Library Association, Apr '01*

"Recommended pick both for specialty health library collections and any general consumer health reference collection."
— *The Bookwatch, Apr '01*

Skin Disorders Sourcebook

Basic Information about Common Skin and Scalp Conditions Caused by Aging, Allergies, Immune Reactions, Sun Exposure, Infectious Organisms, Parasites, Cosmetics, and Skin Traumas, Including Abrasions, Cuts, and Pressure Sores

Along with Information on Prevention and Treatment

Edited by Allan R. Cook. 647 pages. 1997. 0-7808-0080-X. $78.

". . . comprehensive, easily read reference book."
— *Doody's Health Sciences Book Reviews, Oct '97*

SEE ALSO Burns Sourcebook

Sleep Disorders Sourcebook

Basic Consumer Health Information about Sleep and Its Disorders, Including Insomnia, Sleepwalking, Sleep Apnea, Restless Leg Syndrome, and Narcolepsy

Along with Data about Shiftwork and Its Effects, Information on the Societal Costs of Sleep Deprivation, Descriptions of Treatment Options, a Glossary of Terms, and Resource Listings for Additional Help

Edited by Jenifer Swanson. 439 pages. 1998. 0-7808-0234-9. $78.

"This text will complement any home or medical library. It is user-friendly and ideal for the adult reader."
—American Reference Books Annual, 2000

"A useful resource that provides accurate, relevant, and accessible information on sleep to the general public. Health care providers who deal with sleep disorders patients may also find it helpful in being prepared to answer some of the questions patients ask."
— Respiratory Care, Jul '99

"Recommended reference source."
— Booklist, American Library Association, Feb '99

■

Smoking Concerns Sourcebook

Basic Consumer Health Information about Nicotine Addiction and Smoking Cessation, Featuring Facts about the Health Effects of Tobacco Use, Including Lung and Other Cancers, Heart Disease, Stroke, and Respiratory Disorders, Such as Emphysema and Chronic Bronchitis

Along with Information about Smoking Prevention Programs, Suggestions for Achieving and Maintaining a Smoke-Free Lifestyle, Statistics about Tobacco Use, Reports on Current Research Initiatives, a Glossary of Related Terms, and Directories of Resources for Additional Help and Information

Edited by Karen Bellenir. 621 pages. 2004. 0-7808-0323-X. $78.

■

Sports Injuries Sourcebook, 2nd Edition

Basic Consumer Health Information about the Diagnosis, Treatment, and Rehabilitation of Common Sports-Related Injuries in Children and Adults

Along with Suggestions for Conditioning and Training, Information and Prevention Tips for Injuries Frequently Associated with Specific Sports and Special Populations, a Glossary, and a Directory of Additional Resources

Edited by Joyce Brennfleck Shannon. 614 pages. 2002. 0-7808-0604-2. $78.

ALSO AVAILABLE: Sports Injuries Sourcebook, 1st Edition. Edited by Heather E. Aldred. 624 pages. 1999. 0-7808-0218-7. $78.

"This is an excellent reference for consumers and it is recommended for public, community college, and undergraduate libraries."
— American Reference Books Annual, 2003

"Recommended reference source."
— Booklist, American Library Association, Feb '03

Stress-Related Disorders Sourcebook

Basic Consumer Health Information about Stress and Stress-Related Disorders, Including Stress Origins and Signals, Environmental Stress at Work and Home, Mental and Emotional Stress Associated with Depression, Post-Traumatic Stress Disorder, Panic Disorder, Suicide, and the Physical Effects of Stress on the Cardiovascular, Immune, and Nervous Systems

Along with Stress Management Techniques, a Glossary, and a Listing of Additional Resources

Edited by Joyce Brennfleck Shannon. 610 pages. 2002. 0-7808-0560-7. $78.

"Well written for a general readership, the Stress-Related Disorders Sourcebook is a useful addition to the health reference literature."
— American Reference Books Annual, 2003

"I am impressed by the amount of information. It offers a thorough overview of the causes and consequences of stress for the layperson. . . . A well-done and thorough reference guide for professionals and nonprofessionals alike." — Doody's Review Service, Dec '02

■

Stroke Sourcebook

Basic Consumer Health Information about Stroke, Including Ischemic, Hemorrhagic, Transient Ischemic Attack (TIA), and Pediatric Stroke, Stroke Triggers and Risks, Diagnostic Tests, Treatments, and Rehabilitation Information

Along with Stroke Prevention Guidelines, Legal and Financial Information, a Glossary, and a Directory of Additional Resources

Edited by Joyce Brennfleck Shannon. 606 pages. 2003. 0-7808-0630-1. $78.

"This volume is highly recommended and should be in every medical, hospital, and public library."
— American Reference Books Annual, 2004

■

Substance Abuse Sourcebook

Basic Health-Related Information about the Abuse of Legal and Illegal Substances Such as Alcohol, Tobacco, Prescription Drugs, Marijuana, Cocaine, and Heroin; and Including Facts about Substance Abuse Prevention Strategies, Intervention Methods, Treatment and Recovery Programs, and a Section Addressing the Special Problems Related to Substance Abuse during Pregnancy

Edited by Karen Bellenir. 573 pages. 1996. 0-7808-0038-9. $78.

"A valuable addition to any health reference section. Highly recommended."
— The Book Report, Mar/Apr '97

". . . a comprehensive collection of substance abuse information that's both highly readable and compact. Families and caregivers of substance abusers will find

the information enlightening and helpful, while teachers, social workers and journalists should benefit from the concise format. Recommended."
— *Drug Abuse Update, Winter '96/'97*

SEE ALSO *Alcoholism Sourcebook, Drug Abuse Sourcebook*

Surgery Sourcebook

Basic Consumer Health Information about Inpatient and Outpatient Surgeries, Including Cardiac, Vascular, Orthopedic, Ocular, Reconstructive, Cosmetic, Gynecologic, and Ear, Nose, and Throat Procedures and More

Along with Information about Operating Room Policies and Instruments, Laser Surgery Techniques, Hospital Errors, Statistical Data, a Glossary, and Listings of Sources for Further Help and Information

Edited by Annemarie S. Muth and Karen Bellenir. 596 pages. 2002. 0-7808-0380-9. $78.

"Large public libraries and medical libraries would benefit from this material in their reference collections."
— *American Reference Books Annual, 2004*

"Invaluable reference for public and school library collections alike." — *Library Bookwatch, Apr '03*

Transplantation Sourcebook

Basic Consumer Health Information about Organ and Tissue Transplantation, Including Physical and Financial Preparations, Procedures and Issues Relating to Specific Solid Organ and Tissue Transplants, Rehabilitation, Pediatric Transplant Information, the Future of Transplantation, and Organ and Tissue Donation

Along with a Glossary and Listings of Additional Resources

Edited by Joyce Brennfleck Shannon. 628 pages. 2002. 0-7808-0322-1. $78.

"Along with these advances [in transplantation technology] have come a number of daunting questions for potential transplant patients, their families, and their health care providers. This reference text is the best single tool to address many of these questions. . . . It will be a much-needed addition to the reference collections in health care, academic, and large public libraries."
— *American Reference Books Annual, 2003*

"Recommended for libraries with an interest in offering consumer health information." — *E-Streams, Jul '02*

"This is a unique and valuable resource for patients facing transplantation and their families."
— *Doody's Review Service, Jun '02*

Traveler's Health Sourcebook

Basic Consumer Health Information for Travelers, Including Physical and Medical Preparations, Transportation Health and Safety, Essential Information about Food and Water, Sun Exposure, Insect and Snake Bites, Camping and Wilderness Medicine, and Travel with Physical or Medical Disabilities

Along with International Travel Tips, Vaccination Recommendations, Geographical Health Issues, Disease Risks, a Glossary, and a Listing of Additional Resources

Edited by Joyce Brennfleck Shannon. 613 pages. 2000. 0-7808-0384-1. $78.

"Recommended reference source."
— *Booklist, American Library Association, Feb '01*

"This book is recommended for any public library, any travel collection, and especially any collection for the physically disabled."
— *American Reference Books Annual, 2001*

Vegetarian Sourcebook

Basic Consumer Health Information about Vegetarian Diets, Lifestyle, and Philosophy, Including Definitions of Vegetarianism and Veganism, Tips about Adopting Vegetarianism, Creating a Vegetarian Pantry, and Meeting Nutritional Needs of Vegetarians, with Facts Regarding Vegetarianism's Effect on Pregnant and Lactating Women, Children, Athletes, and Senior Citizens

Along with a Glossary of Commonly Used Vegetarian Terms and Resources for Additional Help and Information

Edited by Chad T. Kimball. 360 pages. 2002. 0-7808-0439-2. $78.

"Organizes into one concise volume the answers to the most common questions concerning vegetarian diets and lifestyles. This title is recommended for public and secondary school libraries." — *E-Streams, Apr '03*

"Invaluable reference for public and school library collections alike." — *Library Bookwatch, Apr '03*

"The articles in this volume are easy to read and come from authoritative sources. The book does not necessarily support the vegetarian diet but instead provides the pros and cons of this important decision. The *Vegetarian Sourcebook* is recommended for public libraries and consumer health libraries."
— *American Reference Books Annual, 2003*

Women's Health Concerns Sourcebook, 2nd Edition

Basic Consumer Health Information about the Medical and Mental Concerns of Women, Including Maintaining Health and Wellness, Gynecological Concerns, Breast Health, Sexuality and Reproductive Issues, Menopause, Cancer in Women, the Leading Causes of Death and Disability among Women, Physical Concerns of Special Significance to Women, and Women's Mental and Emotional Health

Along with a Glossary of Related Terms and Directories of Resources for Additional Help and Information

Edited by Amy L. Sutton. 748 pages. 2004. 0-7808-0673-5. $78.

ALSO AVAILABLE: *Women's Health Concerns Sourcebook, 1st Edition.* Edited by Heather E. Aldred. 567 pages. 1997. 0-7808-0219-5. $78.

618

"Handy compilation. There is an impressive range of diseases, devices, disorders, procedures, and other physical and emotional issues covered . . . well organized, illustrated, and indexed." —*Choice, Association of College and Research Libraries, Jan '98*

SEE ALSO *Breast Cancer Sourcebook, Cancer Sourcebook for Women, Healthy Heart Sourcebook for Women, Osteoporosis Sourcebook*

Workplace Health & Safety Sourcebook

Basic Consumer Health Information about Workplace Health and Safety, Including the Effect of Workplace Hazards on the Lungs, Skin, Heart, Ears, Eyes, Brain, Reproductive Organs, Musculoskeletal System, and Other Organs and Body Parts

Along with Information about Occupational Cancer, Personal Protective Equipment, Toxic and Hazardous Chemicals, Child Labor, Stress, and Workplace Violence

Edited by Chad T. Kimball. 626 pages. 2000. 0-7808-0231-4. $78.

"As a reference for the general public, this would be useful in any library." —*E-Streams, Jun '01*

"Provides helpful information for primary care physicians and other caregivers interested in occupational medicine. . . . General readers; professionals." — *Choice, Association of College & Research Libraries, May '01*

"Recommended reference source." —*Booklist, American Library Association, Feb '01*

"Highly recommended." —*The Bookwatch, Jan '01*

Worldwide Health Sourcebook

Basic Information about Global Health Issues, Including Malnutrition, Reproductive Health, Disease Dispersion and Prevention, Emerging Diseases, Risky Health Behaviors, and the Leading Causes of Death

Along with Global Health Concerns for Children, Women, and the Elderly, Mental Health Issues, Research and Technology Advancements, and Economic, Environmental, and Political Health Implications, a Glossary, and a Resource Listing for Additional Help and Information

Edited by Joyce Brennfleck Shannon. 614 pages. 2001. 0-7808-0330-2. $78.

"Named an Outstanding Academic Title." —*Choice, Association of College & Research Libraries, Jan '02*

"Yet another handy but also unique compilation in the extensive Health Reference Series, this is a useful work because many of the international publications reprinted or excerpted are not readily available. Highly recommended." —*Choice, Association of College & Research Libraries, Nov '01*

"Recommended reference source." —*Booklist, American Library Association, Oct '01*

619

Teen Health Series
Helping Young Adults Understand, Manage, and Avoid Serious Illness

Cancer Information for Teens

Health Tips about Cancer Awareness, Prevention, Diagnosis, and Treatment

Including Facts about Frequently Occurring Cancers, Cancer Risk Factors, and Coping Strategies for Teens Fighting Cancer or Dealing with Cancer in Friends or Family Members

Edited by Wilma R. Caldwell. 428 pages. 2004. 0-7808-0678-6. $58.

▪

Diet Information for Teens

Health Tips about Diet and Nutrition

Including Facts about Nutrients, Dietary Guidelines, Breakfasts, School Lunches, Snacks, Party Food, Weight Control, Eating Disorders, and More

Edited by Karen Bellenir. 399 pages. 2001. 0-7808-0441-4. $58.

"Full of helpful insights and facts throughout the book. ... An excellent resource to be placed in public libraries or even in personal collections."
—*American Reference Books Annual 2002*

"Recommended for middle and high school libraries and media centers as well as academic libraries that educate future teachers of teenagers. It is also a suitable addition to health science libraries that serve patrons who are interested in teen health promotion and education." —*E-Streams, Oct '01*

"This comprehensive book would be beneficial to collections that need information about nutrition, dietary guidelines, meal planning, and weight control. ... This reference is so easy to use that its purchase is recommended." —*The Book Report, Sep-Oct '01*

"This book is written in an easy to understand format describing issues that many teens face every day, and then provides thoughtful explanations so that teens can make informed decisions. This is an interesting book that provides important facts and information for today's teens." —*Doody's Health Sciences Book Review Journal, Jul-Aug '01*

"A comprehensive compendium of diet and nutrition. The information is presented in a straightforward, plain-spoken manner. This title will be useful to those working on reports on a variety of topics, as well as to general readers concerned about their dietary health." —*School Library Journal, Jun '01*

Drug Information for Teens

Health Tips about the Physical and Mental Effects of Substance Abuse

Including Facts about Alcohol, Anabolic Steroids, Club Drugs, Cocaine, Depressants, Hallucinogens, Herbal Products, Inhalants, Marijuana, Narcotics, Stimulants, Tobacco, and More

Edited by Karen Bellenir. 452 pages. 2002. 0-7808-0444-9. $58.

"A clearly written resource for general readers and researchers alike." —*School Library Journal*

"The chapters are quick to make a connection to their teenage reading audience. The prose is straightforward and the book lends itself to spot reading. It should be useful both for practical information and for research, and it is suitable for public and school libraries." —*American Reference Books Annual, 2003*

"Recommended reference source." —*Booklist, American Library Association, Feb '03*

"This is an excellent resource for teens and their parents. Education about drugs and substances is key to discouraging teen drug abuse and this book provides this much needed information in a way that is interesting and factual." —*Doody's Review Service, Dec '02*

▪

Fitness Information for Teens

Health Tips about Exercise, Physical Well-Being, and Health Maintenance

Including Facts about Aerobic and Anaerobic Conditioning, Stretching, Body Shape and Body Image, Sports Training, Nutrition, and Activities for Non-Athletes

Edited by Karen Bellenir. 425 pages. 2004. 0-7808-0679-4. $58.

▪

Mental Health Information for Teens

Health Tips about Mental Health and Mental Illness

Including Facts about Anxiety, Depression, Suicide, Eating Disorders, Obsessive-Compulsive Disorders, Panic Attacks, Phobias, Schizophrenia, and More

Edited by Karen Bellenir. 406 pages. 2001. 0-7808-0442-2. $58.

"In both language and approach, this user-friendly entry in the *Teen Health Series* is on target for teens needing information on mental health concerns." —*Booklist, American Library Association, Jan '02*

"Readers will find the material accessible and informative, with the shaded notes, facts, and embedded glossary insets adding appropriately to the already interesting and succinct presentation."
— *School Library Journal, Jan '02*

"This title is highly recommended for any library that serves adolescents and parents/caregivers of adolescents."
— *E-Streams, Jan '02*

"Recommended for high school libraries and young adult collections in public libraries. Both health professionals and teenagers will find this book useful."
— *American Reference Books Annual 2002*

"This is a nice book written to enlighten the society, primarily teenagers, about common teen mental health issues. It is highly recommended to teachers and parents as well as adolescents."
— *Doody's Review Service, Dec '01*

■

Sexual Health Information for Teens

Health Tips about Sexual Development, Human Reproduction, and Sexually Transmitted Diseases

Including Facts about Puberty, Reproductive Health, Chlamydia, Human Papillomavirus, Pelvic Inflammatory Disease, Herpes, AIDS, Contraception, Pregnancy, and More

Edited by Deborah A. Stanley. 391 pages. 2003. 0-7808-0445-7. $58.

"This work should be included in all high school libraries and many larger public libraries.... highly recommended."
— *American Reference Books Annual 2004*

"Sexual Health approaches its subject with appropriate seriousness and offers easily accessible advice and information."
— *School Library Journal, Feb. 2004*

■

Skin Health Information For Teens

Health Tips about Dermatological Concerns and Skin Cancer Risks

Including Facts about Acne, Warts, Hives, and Other Conditions and Lifestyle Choices, Such as Tanning, Tattooing, and Piercing, That Affect the Skin, Nails, Scalp, and Hair

Edited by Robert Aquinas McNally. 430 pages. 2003. 0-7808-0446-5. $58.

"This volume, as with others in the series, will be a useful addition to school and public library collections."
— *American Reference Books Annual 2004*

"This volume serves as a one-stop source and should be a necessity for any health collection."
— *Library Media Connection*

Sports Injuries Information For Teens

Health Tips about Sports Injuries and Injury Protection

Including Facts about Specific Injuries, Emergency Treatment, Rehabilitation, Sports Safety, Competition Stress, Fitness, Sports Nutrition, Steroid Risks, and More

Edited by Joyce Brennfleck Shannon. 425 pages. 2003. 0-7808-0447-3. $58.

"This work will be useful in the young adult collections of public libraries as well as high school libraries."
— *American Reference Books Annual 2004*

Suicide Information for Teens

Health Tips about Suicide Causes and Prevention

Including Facts about Depression, Risk Factors, Getting Help, Survivor Support, and More

Edited by Joyce Brennfleck Shannon. 400 pages. 2004. 0-7808-0737-5. $58.